S0-BEH-581

Fourth Edition

Public Personnel Management

Contexts and Strategies

Donald E. Klingner
Florida International University

John Nalbandian
University of Kansas

Prentice Hall
Upper Saddle River, New Jersey 07458

Library of Congress Cataloging-in-Publication Data

KLINGNER, DONALD E.
Public personnel management: contexts and strategies / DONALD E. KLINGNER, JOHN NALBANDIAN.—4th ed.
p. cm.
Includes bibliographical references and index.
ISBN 0-13-624818-7
1. Civil service—Personnel management. 2. Personnel management. 3. Public administration. I. Nalbandian, John, [date].
JF1601.K56 1998
352.6—dc21 97-9746

Editorial director: Charlyce Jones Owen
Editor-in-chief: Nancy Roberts
Acquisitions editor: Michael Bickerstaff
Assistant editor: Nicole Signoretti
Production editor: Edie Riker
Cover design: Karen Salzbach
Buyer: Bob Anderson
Marketing manager: Christopher DeJohn

This book was set in 10/12 Baskerville by East End Publishing Services and was printed and bound by Courier Companies, Inc. The cover was printed by Phoenix Color Corp.

Printed in the United States of America

10 9 8 7 6 5

ISBN 0-13-624818-7

Prentice-Hall International (UK) Limited, *London*
Prentice-Hall of Australia Pty. Limited, *Sydney*
Prentice-Hall of Canada, Inc., *Toronto*
Prentice-Hall Hispanoamericana, S. A., *Mexico*
Prentice-Hall of India Private Limited, *New Delhi*
Prentice-Hall of Japan, Inc., *Tokyo*
Prentice-Hall Asia Pte. Ltd., *Singapore*
Editora Prentice-Hall do Brasil, Ltda., *Rio de Janeiro*

Contents

PART III ACQUISITION

PART IV DEVELOPMENT

Preface

Writing the fourth edition was much like writing the first—everything seemed new. Other events in our lives prevented us from preparing the fourth edition earlier, and in a way we were lucky. Instead of an incremental change, we see the fourth edition as a major departure from earlier editions.

Two major changes have affected public personnel management since we wrote the third edition. First, modern organizational life is changing. Work is becoming more specialized, teams are becoming more prevalent, change rather than stability is the watchword, and diversity no longer is unique. Second, societal values and economic practicalities have de-emphasized government, increased focus on the marketplace as a model for service delivery, and brought more attention to individual accountability.

These changes are challenging civil service systems left and right. They have brought about privatization and contracting out as well as the use of a contingent workforce—increasing use of temporary and part-time workers. The formalism and quasi-legal nature of civil service systems, designed to protect individual rights and employees from inappropriate partisan political influence, is under attack by the need for flexibility that has accompanied continual change in politics and technology.

The increasing need for specialized knowledge brought about by increasingly complex public problems requires more emphasis on coordination and linking of workers through teams. This, in turn, challenges the fundamental notion of civil service systems that individual jobs and positions form the core of public personnel management.

In addition, with part-time and temporary workers comes an increasing distinction between those who have good jobs and those who do not. The apparent distinction, brought about by fiscal conservatism and downsizing, has caused workers to rethink the relationship they have with their employers. No longer is loyalty rewarded with job security. The best workers may find themselves the victims of downsizing. Individual workers become individual entrepreneurs, each one managing his or her own career at the same time that modern management trends are calling for more cooperation, management by consensus, and empowerment of technical workers.

The times are changing, and public personnel management is changing with them. In a nutshell, the job of the public personnel manager has become more political and more technical. It is more political in that there is increasing disagreement over the values and assumptions that underlie the field. And it is more technical in that personnel managers must understand the concepts and techniques relevant to alternative personnel systems, as well as those that have long been associated with civil service, collective bargaining, and affirmative action. Finally, these increasingly technical demands in an unstable and complex environment mean that the personnel manager's job now requires even more skills as a mediator and human resource management expert. The fourth edition tries to capture these changes, focusing both on volatility and changes in the political, social, economic, and technological environment of modern society and on the consequences for how public employers carry out the planning, acquisition, development, and sanction functions of public personnel management.

So, welcome to the new edition. It has stimulated much excitement, thought, and communication between us during its preparation, and we hope faculty and students who use it have the same good fortune. Frankly, we cannot wait to use it in our own classes. Please let us know how it works for you. We have included electronic references at the end of several chapters, and we are including our e-mail addresses here in hopes that you will communicate with us. We would like to share other exercises and thoughts on how you might use the book, and we would enjoy hearing about what you like and what you take issue with.

Donald E. Klingner (KLINGNER@servax.fiu.edu)
John Nalbandian (nalband@falcon.cc.ukans.edu)

To my students at Florida International University, whose questions and comments have greatly improved this edition; to my fellow personnel managers, whose need to understand and function under new conditions and systems was the reason we wrote the fourth edition; to my colleagues throughout the country who have used this book for the past fifteen years; to my sponsors as a Fulbright Senior Scholar under the Central American Republics program, who helped me to understand public personnel management from the perspective of developing democracies; and to my wife, Janette, for demonstrating that two-career families can work, given love and constant attention to problem solving.

Donald E. Klingner
Miami, Florida

Since we wrote the third edition, twice I have successfully run for a seat on the city council, including two terms as mayor, in Lawrence. You will find some of my experiences in this book, along with those of the elected officials I have met along the way. These recent years have given me an entirely new perspective on public life and public administration, and we have tried to reflect that learning where appropriate.

I would especially like to thank my wife, Carol, whose love and companionship I treasure. In addition, she prepared the initial drafts of Chapters 8 and 9, and her insights into organizational life have helped fashion mine.

John Nalbandian
Lawrence, Kansas

1

The World of Public Personnel Management

INTRODUCTION

Public **personnel management** has been studied extensively, from at least four perspectives. First, it is the *functions* needed to manage human resources in public agencies. Second, it is the *process* by which public jobs are allocated. Third, it is the interaction among fundamental societal *values* that often conflict over who gets public jobs and how they are allocated. Finally, public personnel management is personnel *systems*—the laws, rules, organizations, and procedures used to express these abstract values in fulfilling personnel functions.

In the United States, public personnel management is widely recognized as a critical element of democratic society and effective public administration. The development of public personnel management in the United States is complex because there are multiple levels of government and thousands of governments, each with its own personnel system. Nonetheless, there is general agreement among scholars that the development of public personnel management in the United States has proceeded according to a pattern that reflects competition among four traditional values, and three emergent ones. Underlying the four traditional values is an implicit endorsement of collective action though government. Underlying the three emergent values is the disappointment and mistrust of government that periodically characterize our political climate. Today, public personnel management in the United States may be described as a dynamic equilibrium among these competing values, each championed by a particular personnel system, for allocating scarce public jobs in a complex and changing environment. As one might expect, this conflict exhibits a commingling of technical decisions (*how* to do a personnel function) with political ones (*what* value to favor or *what* system to use).

Internationally, the end of the twentieth century has been characterized by dramatic political changes, notably the demise of international Communism and the emergence of democratic institutions in much of Latin America, in the former Soviet Union, and in parts of Africa. The global nature of these changes, and the similarity of the transitional process from authoritarian to democratic regimes, raises the intriguing possibility that there is a general pattern for the relationship between public personnel management and democratization in developing countries.

By the end of this chapter, you will be able to:

1. Define the functions needed to manage human resources in public agencies (planning, acquisition, development, and sanction—PADS).
2. Explain why public jobs are scarce resources, and how scarcity causes competition over who gets government jobs, and how they are allocated.
3. Describe the four pro-government values that have traditionally underlain the conflict over public jobs in the United States (responsiveness, efficiency, individual rights, and social equity).
4. Discuss the contemporary shift toward three emergent anti-government values (individual accountability, limited and decentralized government, and community responsibility).
5. Define a personnel system as the set of laws, policies, and practices used to fulfill the four public personnel functions (PADS), and give examples of the four traditional personnel systems now operating in the United States (political appointments, civil service, collective bargaining, and affirmative action).
6. Discuss two contemporary alternatives (alternative organizations or mechanisms for providing public services, and flexible employment relationships); how and why they have emerged; and what has been their impact on traditional values and systems.
7. Discuss conflict and compromise among alternative personnel systems.
8. Describe the history of public personnel management in the United States as a conflict among competing personnel systems and values.
9. Propose a general model for the relationship between public personnel management and democratization in developing countries.

PUBLIC PERSONNEL MANAGEMENT FUNCTIONS

Public personnel management consists of four fundamental functions needed to manage human resources in public organizations. These functions, designated by the acronym PADS, are planning, acquisition, development, and sanction. They are shown in Table 1-1, along with the activities that comprise them.

PUBLIC JOBS AS SCARCE RESOURCES

Basic decisions about public personnel management are important because jobs are the most visible way we measure economic and social status for individuals and groups in the United States. Public jobs are scarce resources because they are limited by tax revenues, and their allocation is of enormous significance for the course of public policy making generally. Because public jobs are scarce and

TABLE 1-1 Public Personnel Management Functions

Function	*Purpose*
Planning	Budget preparation and human resource planning; dividing tasks among employees (job analysis, classification, and evaluation); deciding how much jobs are worth (pay and benefits)
Acquisition	Recruitment and selection of employees
Development	Orienting, training, motivating, and evaluating employees to increase their knowledge, skills, and abilities
Sanction	Establishing and maintaining expectations and obligations that employees and the employer have toward one another; discipline, grievances, health and safety, and employee rights

important, there is intense competition for them among individuals and more broadly among advocates of competing public personnel values and systems. Each system is supported by specific values and beliefs that have played important roles in the history of public personnel management in the United States. These systems often compete and interact within public agencies to influence the process by which individual employees are hired, paid, developed, and controlled. The allocation of public jobs, both in broad public policy terms and in specific cases involving a single individual, is the issue that shapes the way the four functions are carried out and focuses conflict among competing values.

THE FOUR TRADITIONAL VALUES: RESPONSIVENESS, EFFICIENCY, INDIVIDUAL RIGHTS, AND SOCIAL EQUITY

Public personnel management may be seen as the continuous interaction among four fundamental societal values that often conflict. The goal of much public policy making is to develop compromises among two or more of the values. The goal of those who must actually carry out the policies is to translate these compromises into specific rules, regulations, procedures, and practices that will effectively fulfill the four functions (PADS). And they must do this without violating the spirit of the political compromises that authorize their action.

Traditionally, conflict within public personnel management in the United States centered around four values: political responsiveness, organizational efficiency and effectiveness, individual rights, and social equity.

Political **responsiveness** is the belief that government answers to the will of the people expressed through elected officials. Political and personal loyalty to elected officials are best ensured through an appointment process that considers political loyalty, along with education and experience, as indicators of merit. Often, in order to promote responsive government, the filling of a number of public jobs is made the prerogative of authorized elected officials.

Organizational **efficiency** (and effectiveness) reflect the desire to maximize the ratio of inputs to outputs in any management process. This value is captured in the phrase "the biggest bang for the buck." In the personnel world, efficiency means that decisions about who to hire, reassign, or promote should be based on the **knowledge, skills, and abilities (KSAs)** of applicants and employees. Merit is defined traditionally in terms of KSAs and performance rather than political loyalty.

Individual rights emphasizes that individual citizens will be protected from unfair actions of government officials. These rights are protected by the Bill of Rights as well as the Fourteenth Amendment to the Constitution. In addition to these legal protections, public employees' rights are maintained through job security and due process (civil service), and through **merit system** rules and regulations that protect public employees from inappropriate partisan political pressure (such as requiring them to campaign for elected officials or contribute a portion of their salary toward election campaigns, or run the risk of losing their jobs if they refuse), and provide job security and due process. In a parallel fashion, public employees who are union members will have recourse to work rules, contained in collective bargaining agreements, that protect them from arbitrary management decisions.

Social equity is the belief that individuals should be accorded preference in selection and promotion in public positions based on previous sacrifices (veterans) or discrimination (minorities and women) that prevent them from competing fairly for jobs. Like individual rights, social equity is concerned with fairness. But unlike individual rights, it is the *social* aspect of equity that provides its group orientation. Social equity emphasizes fairness to groups like women, racial minorities, the disabled, and veterans, that would otherwise be disadvantaged by a market economy that accepts the legitimacy of discrimination in hiring and in pay.

EMERGENT ANTI-GOVERNMENT VALUES: INDIVIDUAL ACCOUNTABILITY, LIMITED AND DECENTRALIZED GOVERNMENT, AND COMMUNITY RESPONSIBILITY FOR SOCIAL SERVICES

In the traditional view of public personnel management, it was possible to evaluate techniques based on their contribution to the maximization of one or more of these four competing values. Thus, for example, affirmative evaluation programs could be evaluated favorably based on their contribution to social equity, or unfavorably based on their denial of individual rights for non-minorities. The state of the field at any one time could be evaluated in terms of the balance among the four competing values, with public personnel managers and others functioning to resolve conflict arising from the simultaneous implementation of competing values and systems. Thus, the traditional model reinforced all four conflicting values, and the role of personnel managers and others in mediating value conflicts.

In recent years, we have seen contemporary political, social, and economic forces influence the values that underlie public personnel management, and indeed all of government, in a unique way. The contemporary context of public personnel management is shaped by three emerging *anti-government* values: *personal accountability, limited and decentralized government,* and *community responsibility for social services.*

These values are not new in the history of the United States, but they are newly emphasized and for some younger Americans, they are new. Together, these values reflect disappointment, lack of faith and credibility in government. Underlying the four traditional values is an implicit endorsement of collective action through government. In return for a willingness and obligation to subordinate private interests and judgments for collective or majority rule, citizens are promised representation of those interests (responsiveness), due process (individual rights to protect them from capricious and arbitrary actions of the majority), and equal protection (guarantees against second-class citizenship).[1] This is the *quid pro quo* of the social contract that permits citizens to give up some of their individual freedom to the majority of citizens.

The emergent values of individual accountability, limited and decentralized government, and community responsibility for social services contrast sharply with that contract. In effect, they represent anti-government sentiment; and theoretically, a return to the libertarian values of individualism, small government, and community (not government) responsibility for those who have been left aside in society's competition for jobs. Let's look at these emerging values and then at their consequences for the traditional values and personnel systems.

First, proponents of **individual accountability** expect that people will make individual choices consistent with their own goals, and accept responsibility for the consequences of these choices, rather than passing responsibility for their actions onto the rest of society. Collectively, we are responsible for providing each other with equal opportunity to develop our individual knowledge, skills, and abilities; but fundamentally, the responsibility for that development (or lack of it) falls on the individual.

Second, proponents of **limited and decentralized government** believe, fundamentally, that government is to be feared for its power to arbitrarily or capriciously deprive individuals of their rights. It is this libertarian belief that gave rise to the Constitution's Bill of Rights, which basically sought to limit the national government's power to infringe on individuals' freedoms of speech, press, association, and privacy. Proponents of this value also believe that it is easier to connect public policy, service delivery, and revenue generation in a smaller unit of government than in a way that is not possible with a larger one, in that decision makers are known, revenues are predictable, and services are directly visible. And for some, the reduction in size and scope of government is justified by the perceived ineffectiveness of government; by the high value accorded to individual freedom, responsibility, and accountability; and, finally, by a reluctance to devote a greater share of personal income to taxes.

It is argued that at the local level, decision makers are known, revenues are predictable with the amounts understandable (millions versus trillions of dollars), and services are directly visible. **Decentralization of government** to the local level raises issues of equity in service delivery and regulation, but its proponents argue that these issues are generally best addressed not by uniform national policies or standards, but by increasingly representative legislative bodies and increasingly powerful ethnic group representation. The fact that this diversity and representativeness is likely to result in political gridlock at a national level is a primary reason for limiting and decentralizing government, as well as for avoiding attempts to "level the playing field" through income redistributive policies and programs.

Third, limited and decentralized government and individual accountability are supplemented with a third value—**community responsibility** for social services. Even civil libertarians and free enterprise capitalists recognize that some individuals will be unable to compete economically and politically because they lack the necessary knowledge, skills, abilities, or emotional makeup to do so, regardless of the incentives they are offered. The answer to this distributional problem is not government "handouts," but the maintenance of a safety net through the combined efforts of government social service agencies and non-governmental social institutions. A key development here is the emergence of not-for-profit non-governmental organizations responsible for social services, recreation, and community development activities. These may be churches, groups of civic activists, community centers, condominium associations, neighborhood associations, and other community-based organizations that President Bush praised in his "Thousand Points of Light" speech in 1992. The most significant consequence of emergence of this value, at least as far as public personnel management is concerned, has been the creation of organizations that provide an alternative to the traditional notion that government has to fund *and* deliver social services. The trend toward downsizing and decentralizing government would be incomplete without the thousands of nonprofit organizations that routinely provide local government social services funded by taxes, user fees, and charitable contributions.

PERSONNEL SYSTEMS

In public policy making generally, **values** are ultimately reflected in laws and policies. This is the way that values become more than philosophical or ideological statements. Similarly, values in public personnel management are not articulated directly, but rather through personnel systems. These systems are the laws, policies, rules, regulations, and practices through which personnel functions (PADS) are fulfilled. In short, these systems can trace their origins and sustaining energy to a value base.

Traditional Systems: Political Appointments, Civil Service, Collective Bargaining, and Affirmative Action

There are four basic public personnel systems within the traditional model of public personnel management: political systems, civil service, collective bargaining, and affirmative action. These systems not only consist of laws, rules, and policies but also are accompanied by organizational cultures.[2] Civil service is the predominant traditional system, and the only complete system (because it includes all four functions and can incorporate all four competing values). It is the dominant organizational culture underlying the practice of public management as well.

Political systems are those in which personnel functions and decisions are carried out with political motives and objectives uppermost. They are characterized by **political patronage** (legislative or executive approval of individual hiring decisions, particularly for policy-making positions). In federal and state governments, for example, cabinet members and other directors of administrative agencies are political appointees. Political appointees serve at the discretion of those who appoint them; they may be fired at any time, particularly if successful job performance depends on political philosophy or loyalty. The most qualified candidates in political systems are those whose political loyalty is unquestioned.

Civil service systems are designed with two objectives: the enhancement of administrative efficiency and the maintenance of employee rights. Proponents of civil service systems think that staffing public agencies rationally (based on jobs needed to carry out specific programs and the KSAs needed to accomplish these goals), and treating employees fairly are the best ways to maintain an efficient and professional public service. This means giving them good pensions and health benefits; giving them equal pay for work of comparable worth; hiring and promoting them on the basis of KSAs; treating them impartially once on the job; and protecting them from partisan political influences.

Overall policy objectives of civil service systems are controlled by elected officials, who often appoint agency heads responsible for managing the bureaucracy. The legislature (Congress, a state legislature, or a local governing body) maintains control over resources by limiting the total number of employees an agency can hire, staffing levels in particular agencies or programs, and the personnel budget (money allocated for wages, salaries, and benefits). These tools help ensure political responsiveness.

Civil service systems are supported by citizens and groups who want to keep "politics" out of public personnel decisions and "run government like a business." They are also favored by employees holding civil service jobs, by job applicants seeking fair consideration for public jobs, and by federal court decisions that uphold the job security rights of civil service employees. But because advocates of privatization and "cutting the fat out of big government" also believe in "running government like a business," there are some conflicts among proponents of this objective. Together, these outcomes are considered desirable by those who support the notion of a professional public service as the best way to achieve the values of efficiency and individual rights and a bureaucracy responsive to political direction. The most qualified candidates in civil service systems are those with superior knowledge, skills, and abilities.

Collective bargaining systems exist within civil service systems. Under collective bargaining, employees negotiate with management over such items as wages, benefits, and conditions of employment. In all cases, contracts negotiated between an agency's managers and leaders of the union representing its employees are subject to the approval of the appropriate legislative body (Congress, a state legislature, a county or city commission, or a school board), because these political bodies are the only ones who can legally make a policy decision. Contracts may also provide for additional protections for individual employees against disciplinary action or discharge, an obvious indication of the intermingling of civil service and collective bargaining systems. Because some overlap exists in the grievance procedures available under civil service and collective bargaining systems, employees are usually required to select one procedure but not both.

Collective bargaining systems are supported by employee organizations (unions or professional associations). They reflect the values of individual rights (of union members). Even though collective bargaining is commonly associated with negotiation over wages, the primary motive is to ensure equitable treatment by management. The most qualified candidates for promotions and job openings in collective bargaining systems are those with the most seniority.

Affirmative action systems are specialized personnel systems that usually exist within civil service systems. For the affirmative action system to operate, the governmental jurisdiction must have acknowledged an imbalance in the percentage of minorities in its workforce and those qualified minorities in a relevant labor force. Alternatively, members of a group protected against discrimination may have sued the public employer, resulting in a judicial ruling requiring the agency to give special consideration to members of the "protected class" in various personnel decisions, especially hiring and promotion.

Affirmative action is supported by female, minority, and disabled job applicants and employees, and by the interest groups supporting them. It is also supported by social equity advocates who contend that the effectiveness of representative democracy depends upon the existence of a **representative bureaucracy**. The most qualified candidates in affirmative action systems are those from underrepresented classes.

CONTEMPORARY SYSTEMS: ALTERNATIVE ORGANIZATIONS AND FLEXIBLE EMPLOYMENT RELATIONSHIPS

The four traditional personnel systems have been heavily affected by the contemporary political environment. Just as the historical dominance of public personnel management by the four traditional values led to the creation of accompanying personnel systems, so the rise of anti-government values has led to the emergence of their own personnel systems (or "anti-systems"). Even though they might not qualify by formal definition as "personnel systems," these contemporary public personnel practices have had a fundamental impact on the way public services are delivered. Two trends have become apparent: (1) reducing the role of government and the number of public employees by **using alternative organizations or mechanisms for providing public services** and (2) **increasing the flexibility of employment relationships** for the public employees that remain. The existence of these alternative instrumentalities is not new. But a review of recent examples indicates how commonplace they have become, and how much they have supplanted traditional service delivery by civil service employees hired through appropriated funding of public agencies. If the emergent anti-government values of individual accountability, limited and decentralized government, and community responsibility for social services become more popular, these trends will become more prevalent.

Alternative Organizations or Mechanisms for Providing Public Services

The current conservative political climate has the objective of reducing the role of government and the number of public employees. The primary ways of doing this are providing services formerly provided by government agencies by alternative organizations or mechanisms: purchase-of-service agreements with other public or non-governmental organizations; privatization; franchise agreements; subsidy arrangements; vouchers; volunteers; self-help; and regulatory and tax incentives.[3]

Purchase-of-service agreements with other governmental agencies and **non-governmental organizations (NGOs)** have become commonplace.[4] For example, Metropolitan Dade County now provides fire and rescue services to almost every small- and medium-sized municipality in Dade County (the exceptions are the cities of Hialeah, Miami Beach, and Miami). These arrangements were negotiated because they offer persuasive advantages for Dade County and the municipalities. For Dade County, there is the opportunity to expand services within a given geographic area, utilizing economies of scale. For the municipalities, the arrangement offers the opportunity to reduce capital costs, personnel costs, and legal liability risks. In addition, because firefighters are heavily unionized, it offers the opportunity to avoid the immediate political and economic costs associated with collective bargaining.

As another example, many local governments contract with individual consultants or private businesses to conduct personnel services such as employee development and training. The use of outside consultants and businesses (hired under fee-for-service arrangements on an "as needed" basis) increases available expertise *and* managerial flexibility by reducing the range of qualified technical and professional employees that the agency must otherwise hire to provide training. The costs of service purchase agreements may actually be lower than the same function performed by in-house personnel, in that the government agency pays no personnel costs or associated employment taxes, and reduces its own legal liability risks.

Privatization, as the term is commonly used in the United States, is the performance of a formerly public function by a private contractor. It differs from service purchase agreements primarily in philosophy and scope. While service purchase agreements contract for delivery of a particular service to a public agency, privatization means abolition of the entire public agency, replacing the infrastructure with an outside contractor who then provides all services formerly provided by the public agency. Privatization has become popular over the past fifteen years because it offers all the advantages of service purchase agreements, but on a larger scale. Privatization has become popular in areas such as solid waste disposal, where there is an easily identifiable "benchmark" (standard cost and service comparison with the private sector), and where public agency costs tend to be higher because of higher pay and benefits. But privatization is spreading rapidly in other areas that have previously been almost entirely the prerogative of the public sector: schools and prisons.[5] In both instances, privatization is one option for increasing government performance while attempting to hold down labor and construction costs.

Franchise agreements often allow private businesses to monopolize a previously public function within a geographic area, charge competitive rates for it, and then pay the appropriate government a fee for the privilege. Examples are private shuttle bus companies which are developing in many major cities in competition with public transit. The vans frequently duplicate public transportation services by "skimming" riders off of popular bus routes; but municipalities often encourage the procedure because it reduces their own costs, provides some revenue in return, and results in a continuation of a desirable public service.

Subsidy arrangements enable private businesses to perform public services, funded by either user fees to clients or cost reimbursement from public agencies. Examples would be airport security operations (provided by private contractors and paid for by both passengers and airlines), some types of hospital care (e.g., emergency medical services provided by private hospitals and reimbursed by public health systems), and some higher education programs. For example, a state may choose to subsidize a private university by paying it to operate a specialized program, rather than to assign responsibility and resources for it to a public institution. Because of subsidy arrangements, the University of Miami, a private institution with a prestigious (and expensive) medical center, receives more appropriated funds from the state of Florida than does Florida International University, the state university in Miami. Or local housing authorities may choose to subsidize rent in public housing projects based on tenant income to encourage occupancy by low-income residents.

Vouchers enable individual recipients of public goods or services to purchase them from competing providers on the open market. Recent public opinion has focused on educational vouchers as a possible alternative to public school monopolies. Under this system, parents would receive a voucher that could be applied to the cost of education for their child at a number of competing institutions—public schools, private schools, and so on. Another variant is housing vouchers as a substitute for publicly constructed and managed housing. These vouchers would allow public housing recipients to purchase the best possible housing on a competitive basis from available private landlords.

Volunteers are widely used by a range of public agencies to provide services that might otherwise be performed by paid employees. These include community crime watch programs, which work in cooperation with local police departments. Volunteer teachers' aides provide tutoring and individual assistance in many public schools, thereby bolstering classroom resources and counteracting (to a certain extent) the negative impact of overcrowded classrooms on teaching and learning.

Self-help is common in community development programs and correctional facilities. Community development programs frequently use residents on a volunteer basis to provide recreation, counseling, and other support services for a community. Frequently, such contributions are required to "leverage" a federal or state grant of appropriated funds. Contrary to the popular image of prisons as vacation resorts, prison inmates are usually responsible for laundry, food service, and facilities maintenance.

Regulatory and **tax incentives** are typically used to encourage the private sector to perform functions that might otherwise be performed by public agencies with appropriated funds. For example, the Comprehensive Employment and Training Act (CETA) was a federally funded program that passed money through to state and local governments for assessment, training, and job placement activities. Its successor, the Job Training Partnership Act (JTPA), offered income tax deductions for corporations that hired, trained and retained disadvantaged employees. The intended effect—human resource development and employment—was the same as with CETA, only the mechanism was different (tax incentives rather than public employees).

Regulatory incentives include the zoning variances granted to condominium associations. Frequently, construction requires variances for roads, parking, and waste collection and disposal. In return for these variances, the condominium association agrees to provide many services normally performed by local government. These include security (if the condominium has a gated entrance), waste disposal, public works (maintenance of common areas), and the like. This arrangement may seem unfair to residents, who pay both maintenance fees to the condominium association and local property taxes for the same services (which are not provided by the municipality). But it does explain the increasing popularity of condominiums among builders and elected officials—their lower unit cost often makes them the only available low- or moderate-cost housing available; and they would not be approved by local planning councils or zoning boards unless the contractor agreed in advance to require the condominium association to be responsible for services that otherwise would be the municipality's responsibility.

Increasing the Flexibility of Public Employment Relationships

Even in those cases where public services continue to be provided by public employees working in public agencies funded by appropriations, massive changes have occurred in employment practices. Chief among these are increased use of temporary, part-time, and seasonal employment; and increased hiring of exempt employees (those outside the classified civil service) through employment contracts. These two devices, along with the increased use of outside contractors, have markedly changed the face of the public workforce.[6]

Increasingly, employers reduce costs and enhance flexibility by meeting minimal staffing requirements through career employees, and by hiring temporary, part-time or seasonal workers to meet peak workload demands. These positions usually offer lower salaries and benefits than career positions. And employees can be hired and fired "at will" (without reference to due process entitlements of civil service employees, or collective bargaining agreements). Skill requirement of these jobs are reduced by job redesign or work simplification.

Where commitment *and* high skills are required on a temporary basis, employers may seek to save money or maintain flexibility by using contract or leased employees to positions exempt from civil service protection. **Exempt positions** are classified, in that positions must be created and funded before they can be filled. But they are not classified within civil services systems, so their incumbents are not "permanent" (at least, not in the sense of having a property interest in their positions). Instead, the terms and conditions of these positions are specified through performance contracts specifying pay and benefits, and limiting the term of employment. While contracts may be routinely renewed with the approval of the employee and the employer, employees may also be discharged at will in the event of a personality conflict, a change in managerial objectives, or a budget shortfall. Frequently, once employees become exempt, they lose their "bumping rights" back into a classified position in the event of a reduction in force (RIF). Increasingly, managerial and technical employees are hired into these types of contracts. They usually receive higher salaries and benefits than can be offered to even highly qualified civil service employees, and they enhance managerial flexibility to trim personnel costs quickly should this be necessary, without having to resort to the bureaucratic chaos precipitated by the exercise of bumping rights during a RIF situation.

The impact of these two devices is accelerated by retirement "buyouts," which offer employees close to retirement age an incentive to retire early within a limited period of eligibility ("window"). In a typical example, employees with seventeen to twenty years of service (in a jurisdiction with a twenty year eligibility requirement for retirement) may be offered, for a limited time period of two months, the opportunity to resign and receive retirement benefits equal to those they would have received with three additional years service. And the employer may even "sweeten the pot" by offering to pay its share of the cost of employee and family health benefits during the early retirement period (before the employee is eligible for Medicare). If the plan is designed properly so that enough employees retire to save substantially, but enough stay to provide for organizational continuity and skills, both employer and employee benefit. The employee gets an option to retire early at close to current salary; and the employer gets to fill the vacant position with an entry-level employee at a much lower salary. The major financial drawback for the municipality is unexpectedly large lump-sum payments for accrued annual leave or sick leave. For example, the city of Miami needed to find an estimated $10 million to compensate 339 employees who elected early retirement. The highest payout was $87,000; the average was $20,000.[7]

Impact of Emergent Systems on Traditional Values

These two emergent public personnel systems—using alternative organizations or mechanisms for providing public services, and increasing the flexibility of employment relationships for those public employees that remain—have implications for each of the four values that underlie the traditional model of public personnel management.

Impact on Employee Rights. Traditional merit systems are built on the principles that government employers should attempt to select those employees with the best knowledge, skills, and abilities, and then protect them from partisan politics primarily through guarantees of job security unless performance falters. In return for this job security, public employees implicitly pledge their political neutrality in the implementation of public policy.

Employee rights are diminished by the new systems. It is more likely that employees will hired "at will," will be hired into **temporary** and **part-time positions**, will receive lower pay and benefits, and will be unprotected by civil service regulations or collective bargaining agreements.[8] The absence of job security signals to employees, "You are on your own, now— look out for yourself!" **Downsizing** of government agencies or programs is usually done without regard to the performance of individual employees. Thus, the message, "If you work hard and are loyal, you will be rewarded with job security," is undermined. Whether or not the political neutrality of public employees suffers in this environment is unknown presently, but it seems logical to assume that as the criteria for success become more arbitrary or capricious, civil service employees—particularly those in mid-management positions—will begin to behave more like the political appointees whose jobs depend on political or personal loyalty to elected officials.

Impact on Social Equity. Social equity is also diminished by the new model. Comparisons of pay equity between the public and private sectors over the past twenty years have concluded rather uniformly that minorities and women in public agencies are closer to equal pay for equal work than are their counterparts in the private sector. Managerial consultants are overwhelmingly white and male. Many part-time and temporary positions are exempt from protection under the Americans with Disabilities Act (1990) and the Family and Medical Leave Act (1992). And retrenchment in federal agencies responsible for enforcing affirmative action compliance means that their activities will be less visible and effective, in addition to the removal of many positions from their purview.

Impact on Efficiency. The impact of the emergent systems on public agency efficiency has been both positive and negative. On the positive side, some of its characteristics clearly increase public agency productivity and lower costs, particularly for civil service employees in appropriated positions. In many cases, the threat of privatization and/or layoffs has forced unions to agree to pay cuts, reduced employer-funded benefits, and changes in work rules.[9] A common example is that municipal trash collectors now are more likely to work a full shift by the clock, rather than being allowed to leave work when their route is completed.

But the personnel techniques that have become more common under the new paradigm may actually *increase* some personnel costs, particularly those connected with employment of independent contractors, reemployed annuitants, and temporary employees. Downsizing may eventually lead to higher recruitment, orientation and training costs. Maintaining minimum staffing levels also results in increased payment of overtime, and higher rates of employee accidents and injuries. As the civil service workforce shrinks, it is also aging. This means unforeseen increases in several critical areas: pension payouts, disability retirements, workers' compensation claims, and health-care costs.

The impact of these two new **public personnel systems** on public program effectiveness is also debatable. While the intention may be to create a government that "works better and costs less," it may have several unintended consequences for agency effectiveness.[10] First, downsizing causes a flow of human capital from the agency. While this may have no short term costs, in the long run it reduces organizational memory, hampers the development of clear and efficient procedures, and increases the orientation and training burden on the employees and supervisors that remain.

Second, the new paradigm tends to increase workforce tension and fear. For the past fifteen years, public employees have been told that they are part of the **problem** rather than part of the **solution**. Most managerial analysts would conclude that this does not enhance employees' professionalism, self-respect, or performance. In addition, career employees may be afraid of losing their jobs, afraid of training temporary workers who may become their replacements, and afraid of taking risks. Temporary workers are unhappy about working side-by-side with career employees who have higher pay, benefits, and job security.

Third, increased outsourcing makes contract compliance the primary control mechanism over the quality of service, rather than traditional supervisory practices. This creates a real possibility of fraud and abuse.[11] Contracts that are poorly drafted, or inadequately enforced, can cost agencies much more than if the same service were provided by public agencies and employees. For example, a state audit in Florida recently revealed that taxicab companies hired by Palm Beach County to provide transportation services to indigent public health patients had submitted exorbitant bills for reimbursement. In one flagrant case, auditors calculated that one cab would have had to have been driven 24 hours per day at 40 miles per hour to have accumulated the miles for which the county was being billed! And in another, U.S. Immigration and Naturalization Service officials canceled a contract with a private prison management company after releasing a scathing report detailing an atmosphere of abuse and penny-pinching in the jail for illegal immigrants and asylum seekers.[12]

Fourth, downsizing "squeezes" all programs, effective and ineffective alike. Continual budget cuts result in agencies that are budget driven rather than mission driven. That is, agencies tend to focus on achievement of short-term performance indicators that will result in maintenance of appropriated funding levels. This means that long-range planning, or indeed any planning beyond the current budget cycle, is likely to become less important. This means that agencies will not be able to do effective capital budgeting, to maintain capital assets (human or infrastructure) with any degree of adequacy, or to request incremental resources for long-range projects. And budget-driven agencies that address public problems with short-term solutions designed to meet short-term legislative objectives are not likely to be effective.

Impact on Political Responsiveness. Political responsiveness is the ultimate value. This is because stakeholders (voters and special interests) support elected officials because the actions they support are perceived as being beneficial to these groups, or to their conception of what constitutes the public interest. Political responsiveness by elected and appointed officials means favoring the value that has the most, or the most vocal, public support.

It is with respect to political responsiveness that the emergent public personnel values and systems have had the greatest impact on public administration in general, and public personnel management in particular. The traditional values and systems assumed that government, particularly a powerful central national government, was the major societal institution concerned with setting national objectives and reallocating the resources to pay for program implementation. The emergent values and systems place much less importance on the role of national government, particularly with respect to domestic issues (those not connected with defense or international affairs). That is because the first value (individual accountability) generally reduces the role of government in society. If public problems are viewed as the results of personal choices by individuals, then the responsibility for dealing with the consequences of these problems is individual rather than societal. Second, emphasis on downsizing and **decentralization** reduces the comparative importance of government in society, and refocuses governmental activity from a national to a state and local level.[13] Third, the maintenance of a "safety net" of social responsibility (comprising state and local government agencies, and other not-for-profit NGOs) de-emphasizes the role of the national government in making social welfare policies and redistributing income, a role that has been central to the concept of national government since 1933, and reemphasizes the obligations of citizens and employees as opposed to their rights.

CONFLICT AND COMPROMISE AMONG ALTERNATIVE PERSONNEL SYSTEMS

We have seen that public personnel management consists of the four human resource management functions carried out within public agencies. These functions are carried out differently in different personnel systems. In theory, each system would shape some personnel activities in a different way. Each system proposes alternative processes for deciding who gets public jobs, and is supported by at least one of four competing values of the traditional model, or the three combined values of the emergent model.

While civil service systems predominate, several other systems (political appointments, collective bargaining, affirmative action, alternative mechanisms, or at will employment) might be present in any public organization. When the governing body consists primarily of advocates of one personnel system and the values it enhances, personnel systems tend to have a clear and recognizable influence on the entire range of personnel functions. For example, a governing body dominated by union supporters would be expected to protect union jobs and resist privatization, **contracting out**, and political appointments. A governing body dominated by partisan political interests could be expected to attempt to fill public jobs or award contracts for political gain. A governing body influenced by racially or ethnically dominated neighborhood groups might advocate political influence over hiring practices and affirmative action. A municipal governing body elected to achieve "good government" would probably favor civil service systems for the city. Finally, a government dominated by those who advocate less government and more personal responsibility could be expected to reject all previous systems in favor of alternative mechanisms or flexible employment relationships.

When the governing body consists of advocates of each of these alternative personnel systems and values, the actual practice of personnel management in government agencies may be weak, unstable, or poorly articulated—that is, different systems may have a differential impact on different personnel functions. Disagreements over individual selection and promotion decisions reflect more basic disagreements over the criteria (decision rules) by which scarce public jobs should be allocated. Or personnel policies and practices may operate at two levels—an ideal level of desirable law, rules, and practice; and actual practices that may not be supported by law and regulations, but are widely used by personnel specialists and line managers to "get the job done." For example, an agency may maintain an elaborate affirmative action system to give the appearance of complying with affirmative action law, but its actual selections may reflect the biases of managers who make the hiring decisions. Or an agency may engage in collective bargaining but do so in bad faith because it is really more interested in undercutting the union by privatizing the service (and laying off the employees who are union members). In these circumstances, public personnel management becomes highly politicized.

Conflict among values and public personnel systems is limited and regulated by the dynamic realities of the competition itself. Because jobs and resources are finite, jobs allocated through one system cannot be allocated through others. This means that the ultimate conflict among values and systems may require resolution at a micro level with each specific selection decision.

Each value, carried to its extreme, creates distortions that limit the effectiveness of human resource management because other values are artificially suppressed. This means that attempts by each system or value to dominate lead inevitably to stabilizing reactions and value compromises. For example, responsiveness carried to extremes results in the hiring of employees solely on the basis of patronage, without regard for other qualifications; or in the awarding of contracts based solely on political considerations (graft and corruption). Efficiency, carried to extremes, results in overrationalized personnel procedures—for example, going to decimal points on test scores to make selection or promotion decisions, or making the selection process rigid in the belief that systematic procedures will produce the "best" candidate. Individual rights, carried to extremes, results in overemphasis on seniority or overemphasis on due process and rigid disciplinary procedures (as opposed to the rights of the public, managers, and other employees to have employees who are competent, diligent, and not liability risks). And social equity, carried to extremes, results in personnel decisions being made solely on the basis of group membership, disregarding individual merit or the need for efficient and responsive government.

We can use this view of public personnel management as conflict and symbiosis among alternative values to predict the probable outcome of the conflict between pro- and anti-government values with some degree of certainty. It might be expected that anti-government values, if carried to extreme, would eventually result in the emergence of a society exhibiting the characteristics of unbridled **free enterprise capitalism**, civil libertarianism, and Dickensian philanthropy. Indeed, critics of the emergent anti-government values have already pointed out the weaknesses of a market model for providing public services to those who can pay for them; a "race to the bottom" as different states and communities cut social services so as to encourage emigration of actual or potential social service recipients; and reduced effectiveness of community agencies that are unable to cope with increased demands for services as their revenues diminish. These conditions might in turn lead to the resurgence of pro-government values, as occurred during the Great Depression of the 1930s when anti-government values came under attack by proponents of well-financed national government with an active role in public policy making.

Under ideal circumstances, public personnel management might reflect one dominant value and, hence, one dominant system. But in reality, it is often hard to draw a clear distinction between political appointments and those resulting from civil service or affirmative action systems. For example, is a civil service employee who buys a ticket to a political fund raising dinner making a voluntary contribution reflecting a constitutional right to political expression and association, or a coerced decision reflecting the belief that the cost of the ticket is less than the risk of negative job consequences? And what about appeals by United Way local board members—who also happen to be chief executive officers (CEOs) of major public and private employers—for pledges by employees, with considerable pressure from supervisors to have all the employees in a work unit contribute? Are these pledges voluntary, or are they implicitly coerced by prominent administrators who have been invited to become board members—and to enjoy the social status and recognition this brings—in return for their ability to generate support from their agencies' employees?

The boundary between political appointments and affirmative action is equally difficult to draw in some cases. For example, in a city characterized by ethnic or racial tensions, the choice of a black or Hispanic police chief may be widely perceived as affecting not only the political strength of various groups, but also the policies of the police department with respect to patrol techniques, citizen complaints, and so on.

Nor is the boundary between politics and efficient administration easy to determine. Political appointees may be highly qualified on the basis of merit; and, in addition, have similar values and policy preferences as the official who appoints them. But if a county commissioner hires an ex-wife to a political position in order to reduce her demands for alimony and/or child support, is this an example of greater efficiency or merely political corruption and the substitution of private interest for the public good?

Legal guidelines do not necessarily provide clear answers to these questions. The Supreme Court has clearly decided that individual employees in state or local government administrative agencies may not be removed from positions for patronage reasons, with the exception of positions where political affiliation can make a difference in job performance. But it has also refused to review state court decisions upholding the exclusion of many employees from administrative agency designation. For example, county sheriff's deputies in Broward County, Florida (Fort Lauderdale), are hired and fired at will because they are considered judicial employees. Their Dade County (Miami) counterparts, fifteen miles to the south, are given civil service protection because they are classified as administrative employees within a unified city-county (charter) form of government. Civil service employees have no legal basis (under civil service laws or collective bargaining agreements) to protest job privatization or contracting out through the courts. Though these decisions result in job loss for groups of employees in the affected areas, this job loss is related to overall issues of funding and government structure, not to individual disciplinary action for cause.

Over time, personnel systems will reflect the dominant values in a particular jurisdiction. The more stable the values, the more permanent the personnel system and practices will become. Although several alternative systems can be present in an agency simultaneously, in reality one or two systems are dominant within society—and the culture of the organization—at any one time.

SYSTEMS IN COLLISION: A HISTORICAL ANALYSIS OF PUBLIC PERSONNEL MANAGEMENT IN THE UNITED STATES

The development of public personnel management in the United States is complex because there are multiple levels of government and thousands of governments, each with its own personnel system. Nonetheless, there is general agreement that the development of public personnel management in the United States has proceeded according to a pattern.[14]

Political Systems

First, public jobs were allocated primarily among elites ("government by gentlemen"). Then President Andrew Jackson articulated a philosophy of patronage following his election in 1828. It was his view that public jobs in the federal sector were quite simple to master, and that they belonged to the common people. Jackson's election roughly coincided with the development of political parties, and signaled the birth of the **spoils system**, which rewarded party members and campaign workers with jobs once their candidate was elected.

The spoils system expanded as the functions of government and the number of government employees grew after the Civil War (1861-1865). Political "machines" developed in big cities, supported by newly arrived immigrants. These systems were designed from the street level up, with precinct workers, district committees, assembly districts, and county committees arranged in a sort of political hierarchy whose mission was to nominate candidates and win elections. With electoral victory of candidates who had been nominated in conventions of loyalist delegates came the opportunity and obligation to dispense patronage or public jobs to those who had worked hardest for the party. Party loyalty would be verified, a political clearance might be issued, and in return the new jobholder would pay (often monthly) a "voluntary" assessment to the party. This went to pay the party officials who had provided the job and to finance future election campaigns.

The political patronage system had many virtues. While it did not result in the selection of highly qualified employees or efficient government services, it did help millions of immigrants make the transition from rural areas of countries like Germany, Italy, Poland, and Ireland to cities like New York, Boston, Philadelphia, and Chicago. Effective party machines, partisan political leaders (often serving as role models because they were of the same culture and language as the immigrants they represented), and local precinct workers brought government to these people. In some cases, "government" was the help they needed to survive—baskets of food when they had none, buckets of coal in the winter, help in paying for weddings and funerals, help filling out immigration and voter registration forms, and sometimes a job with the city gas company or street repair department when one became available. The patron also showed more recent immigrants that assimilation into the alien American culture was the key to economic, social, and political power. In return, the party asked only for each person's vote, for loyalty, and for a small percentage (say 2 percent) of salary from patronage jobs.

Reaction against political patronage systems focused at the federal level in 1883 when the assassination of newly elected President Garfield by a disappointed job seeker caused an outpouring of criticism against the inefficiencies of the spoils system. But patronage remained a powerful force at the state and local levels.[15] In 1888, when New York City comprised only Manhattan and a slice of the Bronx, the Tweed Ring (a political machine) controlled some 12,000 jobs and a $6 million payroll. During the 1960s, many county sheriff's deputies throughout the East and Midwest were political appointees. The county sheriff is an elected position. Newly elected sheriffs routinely discharged the patronage employees appointed by their predecessors and replaced them with their own appointees, who received their jobs on the basis of having supported the sheriff's candidacy—and sometimes because of an informal commitment to "voluntarily" return a percentage of their salaries to the sheriff as a direct political contribution, or as a disguised contribution through the purchase of tickets to political dinners or other fund raising events. The same system prevailed for appointments in many state agencies, such as transportation, public works, or corrections. Although elected officials and other supporters of patronage systems defended the contributions as voluntary, in reality employees who quit making contributions risked losing their jobs, because local party leaders declined to give them the political clearance they needed to certify their loyalty for the patronage position.[16]

There are several good reasons why political patronage systems have been popular throughout most of our nation's history. First, both elected officials and scholars have defended the need for elected officials to achieve partisan political objectives by placing loyal supporters in key confidential and policy-making positions within administrative agencies. Otherwise, there is no way that these agencies or their actions will be responsive to the mandates of the electorate. Second, elected officials have always viewed public jobs as one of the rewards they have available to encourage financial contributions and other forms of political support. And there is often no clear distinction between legitimate and illegitimate rewards. For example, if the director of a state human service agency calls a subordinate and brings to his attention the job application of the wife of a contributor to the governor's upcoming campaign, is this unacceptable political meddling, or a harmless effort to maintain political responsiveness by ensuring that a qualified yet politically connected applicant receives an opportunity to be considered for the job? Or if a county commissioner calls the director of the county planning department to ask that favorable consideration be given to an upcoming request for a zoning variance by a developer who is also a major campaign contributor, is this corruption, or a sign of accessible government decisions? Or is it something in between, something Plunkett of Tammany Hall would have called "honest graft"?

Elected officials get elected—and reelected—by providing voters with access to bureaucrats who often seem not to understand that rules must sometimes be bent, or broken, for voters to feel that justice has been done. Elected officials have always defended patronage jobs as necessary to the survival of a strong political party system: Without jobs to distribute as rewards, how can parties earn the loyalty and financial support they need to run campaigns and win elections? Unless they get many smaller contributions from grateful patronage employees, candidates are forced to rely on larger contributions from fewer interest groups, making them more indebted to lobbyists or interest groups with narrow objectives.

Civil Service Systems

Next, civil service reformers and other political progressives forced a gradual transition from political patronage to merit systems that emphasized efficiency by defining personnel management as a neutral administrative function. Civil service, or merit, systems arose out of public outrage at the waste and inefficiency of political patronage systems. By the 1880s, the federal government had grown larger and more complex as additional cabinet-level departments were added to acknowledge the importance of agriculture, interstate commerce, and protection of natural resources (Interior). Along with this increased size and complexity of federal activities came a growing public recognition that public jobs were not simply the spoils of office. Rather, they were technically or professionally demanding positions of public trust. They should therefore be allocated and rewarded on the basis of the knowledge, skills, and abilities of jobholders and applicants, rather than on the basis of political loyalty or party affiliation. Civil service systems were initiated in major eastern states such as New York and Pennsylvania during the 1880s, but the event that galvanized public attention was President Garfield's assassination in 1883 by a disgruntled unsuccessful office seeker, which led to the immediate passage of the **Pendleton Act** by Congress.

A civil service system consists of a body of impersonal rules that grow out of the principles listed in Table 1-2.

The period between 1883 and 1937 is important in the development of public personnel administration based on merit principles. These principles of merit

TABLE 1-2 Civil Service System Principles[17]

1. Recruitment should be from qualified individuals from appropriate sources in an endeavor to achieve a workforce from all segments of society, and selection and advancement should be determined solely on the basis of relative ability, knowledge, and skills, after fair and open competition which assures that all receive equal opportunity.
2. All employees and applicants for employment should receive fair and equitable treatment in all aspects of personnel management without regard to political affiliation, race, color, religion, national origin, sex, marital status, age, or handicapping condition, and with proper regard for their privacy and constitutional rights.
3. Equal pay should be provided for work of equal value with appropriate consideration of both national and local rates paid by employers in the private sector, and appropriate incentives and recognition should be provided for excellence in performance.
4. All employees should maintain high standards of integrity, conduct, and concern for the public interest.
5. The workforce should be used efficiently and effectively.
6. Employees should be retained on the basis of the adequacy of their performance, inadequate performance should be corrected, and employees should be separated who cannot or will not improve their performance to meet required standards.
7. Employees should be provided effective education and training in cases in which such education and training would result in better organizational and individual performance.
8. Employees should be:
   a. protected against arbitrary action, personal favoritism, or coercion for partisan political purposes.
   b. prohibited from using their official authority or influence for the purpose of interfering with or affecting the result on an election or a nomination for election.
9. Employees should be protected against reprisal for the lawful disclosure of information which the employees reasonably believe evidences:
   a. a violation of any law, rule, or regulation,
   b. mismanagement, a gross waste of funds, an abuse of authority, or a substantial and specific danger to public health or safety.

and political neutrality reflect what Hugh Heclo has identified as the civil service ideal—the principle that a competent, committed workforce of career civil servants is essential to the professional conduct of the public's business.[18] While the Pendleton Act of 1883 espoused efficiency as well as the elimination of politics from personnel decisions, efficient methods of recruiting, selecting, and paying employees were not available then. The application of science to administration in the twentieth century began to provide the tools, for example, in the areas of selection and position classification. The U.S. Army's experience with selecting officer candidates during World War I gave birth to the field of personnel measurements and testing. Because of the need to select candidates with the necessary abilities to become officers, and to not waste training resources (or to allow those lacking these critical skills and abilities to make risky battlefield decisions), psychologists developed aptitude, ability, and performance tests that were carried over into the private industrial sector during the 1920s.

Position classification is often cited as the cornerstone of public personnel management, not only because of its centrality among personnel functions but also because it epitomizes the connection between efficiency and the elimination of politics from administration. It suggests that public personnel management can be conducted in a routine and politically neutral fashion. This provides merit systems with their philosophical attraction, even if the precept is less than accurate in practice.

Position classification offers management a uniform basis for grouping jobs by occupational type and skill level, an equitable and logical pay plan based on the KSAs (knowledge, skills, and abilities) needed to perform the job, and translates labor costs (for pay and benefits) into impersonal grades that can be added, subtracted, averaged, and moved about to create organizational charts; it clarifies career ladders, and it aids in the recruitment, selection, training, and assessment processes through its specification of duties and qualifications for each position.

At the same time, it can be used to minimize political or administrative abuse and protection of individual rights with regard to personnel functions. Pay rates are tied to positions, so individual favorites cannot be paid more than others. The work to be performed is specified in a job description. Thus, hiring people at a high salary and asking them to assume few if any responsibilities—which occurs frequently in political patronage positions—is minimized. Budgets are allocated in terms of positions, so ceilings can be established to preclude hiring. Units may be assigned an average allowable position grade, thus ensuring that they will not become top heavy.

The relationship between political patronage systems and civil service systems is intermittently marked by intense conflict, for both systems represent powerful and equally legitimate values—responsiveness and efficiency. Further, the relationship between politics and administration centers around the enduring question of how governments can bring expertise to bear on the development of public policy while retaining the supremacy of political values. For example, the tremendous economic, military, and social problems confronting the United States during the New Deal and World War II (1933-1945) brought about the emergence of **administrative effectiveness,** which combines the scientific principle of efficiency with the political principle of accomplishing objectives demanded by events. This combination of efficiency and effectiveness required that most positions be covered by the civil service system, but that sensitive or policy-making positions be filled by political appointees who were either personally or politically responsive to the elected officials who appointed them. This represented a new kind of patronage, one made to foster program goals in addition to maintenance of party strength executive/legislative relationships. It resulted in programs consistent with elected officials' philosophy and vision of government, and with administrators' ability to make operational plans and manage resources efficiently (including human resources).

Inevitably, the predominance of administrative effectiveness as a hybrid of politics and efficiency created strains in the civil service reform model of public personnel management, which had been based on the fundamental distinction between politics and administration. The civil service model viewed personnel management as a neutral administrative function; the effectiveness model viewed it as a management-oriented function under the direction of the executive branch. Administrators saw the need for effectiveness but were loathe to return to the politics of the patronage system as the only alternative to civil service systems.[19]

Given the obvious need for politically responsive agency management, one might wonder why civil service systems pay so much attention to protection from political influence. The reason is that incidents which occur frequently indicate that elected officials consider political loyalty the most important criterion for selection to administrative positions, regardless of the applicants' qualifications. For example, the National Endowment for the Arts came under heavy attack in 1990 from conservative Republican Senator Jesse Helms because of its sponsorship of art exhibitions containing works some observers considered pornographic or supportive of homosexuality. The director of the NEA found himself under fire from conservatives (who objected to public support of "unacceptable" art), and from artists (who considered this to be censorship). Under these circumstances, the director's qualifications were less important than his ability to walk a political tightrope between the two positions.

Much of the history of public personnel management can be viewed as efforts to reconcile civil service and patronage systems at an operational level. The Pendleton Act (1883) created the civil service system at the federal level, leading eventually to the development and implementation of civil service systems for a majority of professional and technical positions. The **Civil Service Reform Act** (CSRA) of 1978, passed almost a century later, was designed to maintain bureaucratic responsiveness but still protect the career civil service from political interference. It created a **Senior Executive Service (SES)** of high-level administrators who voluntarily elected to leave their civil service positions in return for multi-year performance contracts, in exchange for the possibility of higher salaries and greater career challenge and flexibility. As might have been expected, the results of the CSRA are mixed. Some administrators successfully made the transition to SES appointments and received performance bonuses. Other administrators, and impartial observers, felt that the system was flawed from the beginning because of inadequate rewards, unclear performance standards, political pressure on career civil servants to join the SES, and inadequate training for new SES members to teach them how to function in an environment where productivity and control over expenses were more important than they had been in traditional civil service positions. The CSRA did establish that public personnel management agencies had at least two contradictory objectives—protecting employee rights and making agencies politically responsive—which required that the old federal Civil Service Commission be split into two agencies, the **Merit Systems Protection Board (MSPB)** and the **Office of Personnel Management (OPM).** The MSPB is responsible for hearing appeals from employees alleging that their rights under civil service system laws and rules have been violated; the OPM is responsible for developing and implementing personnel policies within federal agencies.

Collective Bargaining Systems

During the 1960s and 1970s a third personnel system came to the fore in the public sector—collective bargaining. It emerged to represent collective employee rights (the equitable treatment of members by management through negotiated work rules over wages, benefits, and working conditions). While all public employees covered by collective bargaining agreements are also covered by civil service systems, under collective bargaining the terms and conditions of employment are set by direct contract negotiations between agency management and unions (or employee organizations). This is in contrast to the patronage system, where they are set and operationally influenced by elected officials, or the civil service system, where they are set by law and regulations issued by management and administered by management or an outside authority (such as a civil service board).

Collective bargaining in the public sector has many of the same procedures as its private-sector counterpart, such as contract negotiations and grievance procedures. But fundamental differences in law and power outweigh these similarities. Public-sector unions never have the right to negotiate binding contracts with respect to wages, benefits, or other economic issues. The right to approve (or disapprove) negotiated contracts is reserved to the appropriate legislative body (such as the city council, school board, or state legislature) because only legislatures are policy-making bodies with the authority to appropriate money to fund contracts. This means that both labor and management realize that ratification of negotiated contracts is more critical than negotiation of them, and set their political strategies accordingly. Second, the closed shop, where employees have to join a union to be eligible for employment, is common in private-sector trade and craft unions throughout the United States. But federal and state laws have uniformly considered this an illegal abridgement of an employee's constitutionally guaranteed "freedom of association"—the right to join, or not join, an organization as a condition of employment. So, many public employees are "free riders"—they are covered by the terms of a collective bargaining agreement, but they are not dues-paying union members.

Collective bargaining systems emphasize the protection of individual employee rights through emphasis on seniority as the sole criterion governing layoffs, eligibility for overtime, eligibility for training or apprenticeship programs, and even promotions. Naturally, collective bargaining systems in their extreme manifestations are opposed by both patronage and civil service proponents because collective bargaining poses an alternative model for the allocation and retention of jobs.

Affirmative Action Systems

Affirmative action emerged to represent social equity through voluntary or court-mandated recruitment and selection practices to correct the underrepresentation of veterans, minorities, and women in the workplace. Affirmative action systems arose in the public sector as a direct result of the civil rights movement of the 1960s and the women's rights movement of the 1970s. They were based on the observation that public- and private-sector personnel systems frequently discriminated against minorities and women (sometimes deliberately and at other times inadvertently). They were supported by the fundamental beliefs that a representative bureaucracy was essential for our government to function as a democracy; and that other personnel systems had not been effective at ensuring proportional representation.[20] In fact, all these systems had worked (albeit for different reasons) to perpetuate the dominance of white males. Because patronage systems are based on personal and political loyalty, and since most elected officials are white males, appointments of white males to patronage jobs are the rule. Civil service systems favor education and experience, which traditionally have been a strength of white males who have access to higher education and managerial positions. And the seniority systems favored by collective bargaining tend to perpetuate the racist or sexist bias toward the selection of white males that was so frequent until the civil rights movement of the 1960s.

Affirmative action systems are controlled by state and federal administrative agencies, which are responsible for monitoring compliance with affirmative action laws by public agencies or contractors. This system takes effect when a gross disparity exists between the percentage of minority or female employees in an agency and their percentage in a relevant labor pool (such as the community served by that agency, or the percentage of applicants qualified for the position), and when the agency has resisted the voluntary adoption of techniques (such as recruitment, selection, training, or promotion) that would reduce this disparity. In such a case, members of the affected class may sue the agency to force it to take affirmative action in the selection or retention of women or minority group members. If successful, these court efforts may result in considerable judicial control of the agency's personnel system. The court can require an agency to hire or promote specific numbers or percentages of underutilized groups (qualified females or minority group members) until their representation in the agency workforce is more proportionate with their representation in the community. Thus, state and federal courts are also responsible for implementation and enforcement of affirmative action laws.

Speaking realistically, there are some legal and political limits to this control. Given the current composition of the Supreme Court, and fact that most Justices consider quotas to be a violation of the individual rights of applicants who are not members of a protected class, the federal court system is not likely to compel federal or state agencies to observe hiring quotas. The Court cannot compel affirmative action compliance for legislative or judicial positions. It cannot require an agency to hire minority or female employees if agency managers elect not to fill any vacancies, or to retain minority and women employees in civil service positions if funds are not available to do so. But because courts have the ultimate authority to adjudicate conflicts within our political system, they can effectively influence the manner in which the other three public personnel systems operate. They can discourage avoidance of affirmative action compliance by requiring agencies to justify the transfer of positions to political patronage systems; they can order the abandonment of civil service rules or techniques that have a disparate effect on women and minorities; and they can abrogate collective bargaining agreements that use seniority rules to perpetuate previous patterns of racism or sexism.

Alternative Organizations and Mechanisms, and Flexible Employment Relationships

Over the past two centuries, the evolution of public personnel management has been driven by the gradual and sequential emergence of alternative competing values. As each emergent value has gained political strength, its increased importance has been reflected in the forming of the corresponding public personnel system and its related techniques. And most significantly, this evolutionary process gave implicit recognition to the importance of public administration (and to public personnel management as a subset of this discipline) because it assigned to public administration and public administrators the authority to (1) incorporate diverse values and perspectives and (2) resolve conflicts over the implementation of these values in particular administrative situations.[21]

Because evolutionary change is by nature slow, it is difficult to pinpoint the precise point at which this consensus began to be altered. But if pressed, one could do worse than pick the 1976 presidential campaign, won by Jimmy Carter, who ran against the national government as a Washington "outsider." Following the election, he proposed the 1978 CSRA on grounds which included poor performance in the public service and difficulty in controlling and directing bureaucrats. Beginning in 1980, the Reagan administration, though starting from fundamentally different values and policy objectives, continued to cast government as part of the problem, and to campaign against the infrastructure of public agencies and public administrators.

The anti-government assumptions behind this shift were paralleled by a related transition from political to economic perspectives on public policy.[22] This shift in perspectives emphasized the role of market forces on individuals and the economy, rather than program implementation by government agencies and employees, as the most efficacious tools of public policy. While public administration retained its role as the "great compromiser" among competing values, economic perspectives and the value of administrative efficiency clearly reflected these intense political and economic pressures on the public sector to "do more with less," a mandate that has "come with the territory" of public management since 1981. The first pressure—to do more—caused government to become more accountable through such techniques as program budgeting, management by objectives, program evaluation, and management information systems. The second pressure—to do more *with less*—caused governments to lower expenditures through such methods as tax ceilings, expenditure ceilings, deficit reduction, deferred expenditures, accelerated tax collection, service fees, user charges, and a range of legislative and judicial efforts to shift program responsibilities and costs away from each affected government.

Since from 50 percent to 75 percent of public expenditures go toward employee salaries and benefits, efforts to increase accountability and reduce expenditures have focused on those managerial functions subsumed by public personnel management. The shift focused on philosophies and techniques used to enhance accountability in previous eras (such as the 1930s and the 1960s) by emphasizing program outputs and by rationally tying program inputs to outputs. Examples of these trends were program budgeting, human resource forecasting, job evaluation, management by objectives, objective performance appraisal, training needs assessment, cost-benefit analysis, and gain-sharing (productivity bargaining). As the information systems revolution expanded access to information formerly used by management for coordination and control, this pressure has also been reflected in organizational restructuring and "downsizing" middle managerial positions.

The presidential election of 1992 offered a fascinating perspective on civil service reform, for it pitted proponents of sweeping, major change against proponents of even greater change. Less than a year after taking office, Vice-President Gore issued the National Performance Review, aimed at creating a government that "works better and costs less." The changes initiated by this report have been hotly debated in the public management literature since then, with an emergent consensus on several broad conclusions. Basically, increased government effectiveness required (1) fundamental changes in organizational structure and accountability epitomized by the term *reinventing government,* (2) a decentralization of most public personnel functions to operating agencies and a corresponding reduction in the functions and authority of the U.S. Office of Personnel Management, and (3) a 10 percent reduction in federal civilian employment, largely in staff positions (personnel, budget, auditing, procurement, and middle management).

The Republican Party swept into control of Congress in 1994 for the first time in over forty years. The emphasis of the "Contract with America" was that government, especially the federal government, should be doing less and with fewer resources. This gradual shift in emphasis from pro-government to anti-government values leaves fundamental issues unresolved, at least for now. What *is* the appropriate role of government? To what extent are individuals responsible for their choices, and the consequences of these choices? Who owns the vast public infrastructure now up for privatization—current taxpayers or future ones? To what extent are elected and appointed officials who preside over the dismantling of social and public infrastructure for the sake of short-term political gain abdicating their responsibility to the public welfare? Are states, local governments, not-for-profits, and community-based organizations capable of maintaining a social safety net once the national government abandons its hegemonic role in social welfare policy? Or are we are essentially abandoning the political and social ideal of government as a provider of public goods and services in favor of the economic ideal of government as protector of private wealth and privilege? Does the emergent paradigm indeed reflect alternative values, or are these "alternative values" simply the rationalization of covert self-interest by political and economic elites? Are they in fact an emergent model of government, or fundamentally rhetorical "sound bites" and political slogans designed for emotional and symbolic appeal rather than rational clarification and compromise among competing values?

These troubling issues are exemplified by cuts in local and state government services now occurring in California. This state's Proposition 13, passed in 1976, was the initial grassroots effort to limit government growth by capping property taxes for current residents. With Washington cutting back, the state facing perpetual deficits, and county governments in danger of bankruptcy, facing the impact of twenty years of budget cuts may now be unavoidable. Perhaps the greatest question to answer in evaluating the impact of budget cuts on political responsiveness is this: How much decline in quality of public life will people accept as the price of lower taxes? And there can be no doubt that the quality of public life has declined. Thirty years ago, for example, California had the fifth highest rate of spending per pupil in the country, and an envied educational system. Today it ranks forty-second in spending; it has one of the highest dropout rates in the country (only two states are worse); and last year its fourth graders tied for last place in an educational assessment test that was given in thirty nine states.[23]

The contrast between pro-government and anti-government values and systems is best highlighted by the contrasting responses of their adherents to these events. Adherents of pro-government values see the declining quality of public life as equivalent to a declining quality of life; adherents to the emergent anti-government values view it as an enhanced opportunity for individuals to make personal choices about their own spending priorities, including community responsibilities. Adherents to the emergent model see their values as liberating, in the sense that they emphasize individual choice and community responsibility. Adherents to the traditional model see the emergent values as a hypocritical overlay atop greed and self-interest. So both the way the debate is framed in the minds of partisans on both sides and the outcome of the conflict are still the subject of political and social controversy.

But whatever the eventual outcome of this controversy, one thing is certain. Historically, it was taken for granted that public program innovations would be accomplished by a staff of career civil service employees, working within the structure of centralized public agencies budgeted with appropriated funds. Today, none of these are true—public programs are more than likely performed by alternative market mechanisms rather than directly by public agencies; and when public agencies are used, they are more likely to be staffed by temporary employees hired through flexible employment mechanisms rather than permanent employees protected by civil service regulations and collective bargaining agreements.

A Developmental Model

Today, public personnel management in the United States may be described as a dynamic equilibrium among these competing values, each championed by a particular personnel system, for allocating scarce public jobs in a complex and changing environment. As one might expect, this conflict exhibits a commingling of technical decisions *(how* to do a personnel function) with political ones (*what* value to favor or *what* system to use).[24]

These stages are shown in Figure 1-1.

FIGURE 1–1 Evolution of Public Personnel Management in the United States

Stage	*Dominant Value*	*Dominant Personnel System*	*Pressures for Change*
One (1789–1883)	Responsiveness	Patronage	Modernization Democratization
Two (1883–1933)	Efficiency Individual rights	Civil service	Responsiveness and effective government
Three (1933–1964)	Responsiveness Efficiency Individual rights	Patronage Civil service	Individual rights Social equity
Four (1964–1992)	Responsviness Efficiency Individual rights Social equity	Patronage Civil service Collective bargaining Affirmative action	Dynamic equilibrium among four competing values and systems
Five (1992–present)	Individual accountability Decentralized government Community responsibility	Alternative organizations and mechanisms Flexible employment relationships	Emergence of anti-government values

TOWARD A GENERAL MODEL: PUBLIC PERSONNEL MANAGEMENT, DEVELOPMENT AND DEMOCRATIZATION[25]

Thus far, our analysis has focused on the development of public personnel management in the United States. But the demise of international Communism and the resurgence of democratic institution-building throughout Eastern Europe and Latin America, make it important for us to consider the development of personnel management and **democratization** from an international perspective.[26] Because this developmental process differs among regions, Central American republics will be used as an illustrative example.

In the United States, public personnel management is widely regarded as a critical element of democratic society[27] and of effective public administration.[28] Although U.S. interest and aid for Central America has faded with the Sandinista threat, this region remains important. And public personnel management plays a critical role in four of the ten U.S. foreign policy objectives specified for the Central American democratization process during the 1990s:[29]

> (1) improving the administration of justice by increasing the independence, professionalism and effectiveness of the judiciary and police by upgrading judicial personnel through promotion of higher selection standards and effective training programs; (2) strengthening the ability of legislatures to conduct appropriate legal, economic, and technical analyses of proposed legislation by trained professional staff; (3) strengthening local and municipal governments' effectiveness by enhanc-

ing their control over financial and human resources; and (4) promoting honesty and efficiency in government through transparency of decision-making processes and heightened accountability of civil service structures.

Yet despite this consensus on the importance of public personnel management to the development of democratic government and society, there has been little comparative research on the development of public personnel management in Central America or of its relationship to democratization there. Comparative administration texts do discuss civil service reform, though they do not focus specifically on this topic or region.[30] Consequently, critical questions remain unanswered:

1. How does the development of public personnel management in Central America compare with its development in other Latin American countries or in other developing countries?
2. How does the process by which public personnel management has developed in the United States compare with the developmental process in other developed countries?
3. To what extent are findings about the relationship between democratization and public personnel management in Central America generalizable to the study of democratization in other developing countries?

Comparative analysis allows us to establish some key points about the development of public personnel management, and about its relationship to the democratization process in Central America.[31]

First, each country evidences background characteristics that are similar to and yet different than the others. Among the similarities are a common language, history as parts of the Spanish colonial empire, and structure of government. Yet each also differs from the others in historical, social, political, and economic characteristics. And understanding these similarities and differences is the key to understanding their laws, government structure, and personnel processes.

Second, the history of each country shows that the development of each country is influenced by complex and interactive pressures toward democratization and modernization. For example, there are internal pressures to allow greater political freedom (characterized by the development of political institutions), economic development (characterized by external investment and the creation of adequate private sector employment), and improved socioeconomic well-being of the population (as measured by levels of income, health, and education); and external pressures for enhanced governmental performance and stability, the growth of a stable and adequate economy, and the protection of human rights. While the conceptual and operational relationships between democratization and other variables are debated,[32] an examination of national characteristics demonstrates that a close relationship exists between the effectiveness of a government and the effectiveness of its public personnel system.[33]

Third, public personnel systems within these three Central American republics have developed through a relatively uniform process similar to, yet not identical with, the evolution of the field in the United States. In the beginning there is a patronage system, then a transition toward merit marked by three milestones (passage of a civil service law; creation of a civil service agency with adequate location, staffing, and funding; and implementation of effective personnel procedures). This proposed model is shown in Figure 1-2.

In Central America, patronage-based personnel systems constitute the first stage as political leaders seek to maximize political responsiveness.[34] As pressures for efficiency (modernization) and employee rights (democratization) increase, the second stage is a transition to merit systems marked by three milestones: passage of a civil service law, creation of an effective civil service agency, and elaboration of effective policies and procedures. Third, if and when this occurs, policy makers must strive to maintain an appropriate balance among the desirable but contradictory objectives that characterize public personnel management in developed countries: (1) Establish an optimum level of public employment, (2) protect public employees' rights yet achieve administrative efficiency, (3) achieve both uniformity and flexibility of personnel policies and procedures, and (4) balance conflicting values and personnel systems.

Although this transition from patronage to merit is due to a number of external pressures, it is also spurred by internal consensus (among a coalition of administrators, academicians, political leaders, and other "change agents") on the general disadvantages of patronage systems:[35] (1) Excessive political appointments are tied to government corruption; (2) the wholesale employee turnover that accompanies elections promotes inefficiency and wastes human resources; and (3) the resultant instability, corruption, and poor government performance discourage international investors and engender cynicism or apathy among the people.[36] The advantages of a merit system are also widely accepted by this reform coalition: (1) It allows gov-

FIGURE 1–2 Development of Public Personnel Management in Central America

Stage	*Dominant Value*	*Dominant Personnel System*	*Pressures for Change*	*Transitional Milestones*
One	Responsiveness	Patronage	Modernization Democratization	
Two	Efficiency Individual rights	Civil service	Modernization Democratization	Civil service law passed and civil service agency formed; effective personnel policies and procedures
Three	Responsiveness Efficiency Individual rights	Patronage Civil service Collective bargaining	Dynamic balance among three competing values and systems (self-correcting)	Public employment at an appropriate level. Balance between rights and efficiency; central ization v. decentral ization; flexibiliy v. uniformiformity in policy; three competing values

ernments to predict personnel expenses, and to control them within a prescribed budget; (2) adoption of a merit system allows each agency to manage its own human resources most effectively;[37] and (3) it permits public employees in professional and technical positions to develop as individuals, and as a national resource.[38]

While the general developmental process in these three Central American republics appears similar to that found historically in the United States, there are three major differences. First, because in Central America unions are a potent political force against patronage, they emerge prior to (rather than after) the transition from patronage to civil service. Second, because public employment rights for minorities and women are not yet a critical public policy issue in Central America (except in relatively developed countries such as Costa Rica), social equity as a value does not yet have significant impact on personnel systems. So stage three in Central American republics is at present a dynamic equilibrium among three (rather than four) traditional values and their respective public personnel systems. Third, while there exist considerable pressures toward privatization as part of the overall economic policy of international lending organizations to reduce public expenditures and external debt, there is widespread realization in Central America that the development of a strong civil service is essential to democratization and development. Thus, the alternative values and systems that comprise the emergent Contract with America do not at present have a Central American counterpart. So again, stage three in Central American republics is at present a dynamic equilibrium among three values and their respective public personnel systems, with considerable outside pressure toward privatization.

Although there has been little research into the process by which administrative innovations are developed or transferred from one country to another,[39] this developmental uniformity appears to be based on three factors: (1) Conditions in developing countries, including pressures for modernization and democratization, may parallel (though lag behind) those in the United States; (2) personnel innovations tend to be exotic (introduced into developing countries by consultants from developed countries) rather than indigenous ("home grown"); and (3) international lenders often mandate administrative reform as a condition of continued credit.

Two additional characteristics of this developmental model of public personnel management may be mentioned in closing. First, it allows policy makers and researchers to describe the level of a country's development at a point in time; to predict the transition from one stage to the other by examining changes in political, economic, and social conditions; and possibly even to encourage transition from one stage to the other by specific public policies. Second, the evolutionary process is neither uniform or unidirectional. The speed of a country's transition from patronage to merit systems (and the capability with which it confronts stage three dilemmas) can be slowed or reversed by a deterioration in political, economic, or social conditions, which in turn impedes democratization and modernization. For example, in the case of Panama it might be said that the transition from a spoils system to a merit system was hindered by the breakdown of democratic government during the dictatorships and the U.S. invasion that marked the 1970s and 1980s. And in the case of Honduras it could be said that the same transition was slowed because of the weakness of the state, the diversion of scarce resources from health and education to the armed forces, and U.S. intervention in the country's internal politics. And it also might be argued that the recent and rapid movement of both countries toward a merit system is a result of internal and external pressures for democratization and modernization.

SUMMARY

Public personnel management can be viewed from several perspectives. First, it is the *functions* (planning, acquisition, development, and sanction) needed to manage human resources in public agencies. Second, it is the *process* by which a scarce resource (public jobs) is allocated. Third, it reflects the influence of seven symbiotic and competing *values* (political responsiveness, efficiency, individual rights, and social equity under the traditional pro-government model; and individual accountability, downsizing and decentralization, and community responsibility under the emergent anti-government model) over how public jobs should be allocated. Fourth, it is the laws, rules, and regulations used to express these abstract values—personnel *systems* (political appointments, civil service, collective bargaining, and affirmative action under the traditional model; and alternative mechanisms for providing public services, and flexible employment relationships under the emergent anti-government model). The history of public personnel management in the United States can be understood conceptually as the conflict among competing personnel systems and values.

The history of public personnel management in Central American republics may be seen as a similar evolutionary conflict among competing systems and values, though there are three critical differences with the evolutionary process that has occurred in the United States. The similarity of evolutionary models leads to the intriguing possibility that further research may validate a general model for the relationship between modernization, democratization, and the evolution of public personnel management in developing countries.[40]

KEY TERMS

acquisition (personnel function)
administrative effectiveness
affirmative action system
Civil Service Reform Act (1978)
civil service (merit) system
collective bargaining system
community responsibility
contracting out
decentralized government
democratization
downsizing
efficiency
exempt positions
franchise agreements
free enterprise capitalism
individual accountability
individual rights
knowledge, skills and abilities (KSAs)
limited government
merit system
Merit Systems Protection Board (MSPB)
non-governmental organizations (NGOs)
not-for-profit organizations
Office of Personnel Management (OPM)
part-time positions
Pendleton Act (1883)
personnel management
planning, acquisition, development, sanction (PADS)
political patronage

political systems
position management
privatization
public personnel system
purchase-of-service agreements
regulatory incentives
representative bureaucracy
responsiveness
self-help
Senior Executive Service (SES)
social equity
spoils system
subsidy arrangements
tax incentives
temporary positions
values
volunteers
vouchers

DISCUSSION QUESTIONS

1. Identify and describe the four public personnel management functions (PADS).
2. Why are public jobs scarce resources? What is the significance of this observation?
3. What are the four competing values that have traditionally affected the allocation of public jobs? What are the three more recently emergent "anti-government" values that conflict with them?
4. What is a personnel system?
5. Identify and describe the four traditional competing public personnel systems. What are the two emergent anti-government personnel systems that have recently been added to them?
6. Why is it possible to trace the development of public personnel management as conflict and symbiosis among alternative personnel systems?
7. What values and systems have dominated public personnel management in the United States over the past two centuries?
8. In what respects is the evolution of public personnel management in developing countries similar to, and different from, its evolution in the United States?
9. What is the relationship between modernization, democratization, and the development of public personnel management in developing countries? Is it possible to develop and defend a general model for this relationship?

CASE STUDY VALUES AND FUNCTIONS IN PUBLIC PERSONNEL MANAGEMENT

Identify the appropriate value(s), systems, and functions in the following examples. Explain your choices.

1. A state is going to fill a vacancy in its community development agency. The state representative who controls the appropriations committee for all legislation involving the agency has suggested the position be filled by an applicant from her district. A major contributor to the governor's reelection campaign contends that the job ought to be filled by a prominent real estate developer. Neither candidate has the education or experience specified as desirable in the job description.
2. A federal agency is considering a layoff. It anticipates a budget shortfall that is going to require cutbacks in personnel. The agency director has suggested that a layoff score be computed for each employee, based primarily on the person's perfor-

mance appraisal. The Federation of Federal Employees, which is the recognized bargaining agent for the agency's employees, strongly objects and proposes that the layoffs be based on seniority.

3. A county anticipates a request by surrounding cities to provide water services for all county residents. This will require upgrading the skills of a substantial number of county employees and will provide those employees with opportunities for advancement. The union insists that the training slots be allocated to current employees on a seniority basis. The affirmative action officer, seeing this as an opportunity to increase the number of minorities in higher paying positions, proposes that several of the openings be set aside for current minority employees.
4. A city government is looking for ways to reduce costs. The city commission amends its charter to remove the sanitation department from the civil service system. This in effect nullifies the collective bargaining agreement between the city and its unionized sanitation employees. The city lays off all these employees, and contracts instead for solid waste services provided by an outside private contractor.
5. A state government closes many of its public parks and recreation areas because prison construction has taken an increasing share of state revenues, and caused corresponding budget cuts in many other state agencies. It has increased user fees at others, in an effort to generate revenues sufficient to keep the parks open. The three results from this are all predictable: The number of visitors at state parks and recreation areas declines, as many people are excluded by higher user fees; those visitors that do come to the parks complain increasingly about inadequate facilities and maintenance; and attendance and profits at private recreation theme parks within the state (Disney World, Busch Gardens, etc.) increases dramatically.

NOTES

[1] Tussman, J. (1960). *Obligation and the body politic.* New York: Oxford University Press.

[2] Freyss, S. F. (Fall 1995). Municipal government personnel systems. *Review of Public Personnel Management,* 16, 69-93.

[3] International City Management Association (1989). *Service delivery in the 90s: Alternative approaches for local governments.* Washington, DC: ICMA.

[4] Mahtesian, C. (April 1994). Taking chicago private. *Governing,* pp. 26-31.

[5] Applebome, P. (April 9, 1995). Private enterprise enters the public schools. *The New York Times,* p. Y-10.

[6] United States Merit Systems Protection Board (1994). T*emporary federal employment: In search of flexibility and fairness.* Washington, DC: U.S. Merit Systems Protection Board.

[7] Cavanaugh, J. (August 27, 1995). Where (unused) time is money. *The Miami Herald,* p. A-1.

[8] Kilborn, P. T. (April 15, 1995). Take this job: Up from welfare: It's harder and harder. *The New York Times,* pp. 4-1, 4.

[9] Cohen, S., and W. Eimicke (1994). The overregulated civil service. *Review of Public Personnel Administration, 15,* 11-27.

[10] Peters, B. G., and D. J. Savoie (1994). Civil service reform: Misdiagnosing the patient. *Public Administration Review, 54,* 418-425.

[11] Moe, R. C. (1987). Exploring the limits of privatization. *Public Administration Review, 47,* 453-460.

[12] Sullivan, J., and M. Purdy (July 23, 1995). In corrections business, shrewdness pays. *The New York Times,* pp. A-1, 13.

[13] Pear, R. (October 29, 1995). Altered states: Shifting where the buck stops. *The New York Times,* p. 4-1.

[14] Heclo, H. (1977). *A government of strangers.* Washington, DC: The Brookings Institution; Sayre, W. (1948). The triumph of techniques over purpose. *Public Administration Review,* 8, 134-137; and Fischer, J. (October 1945). Let's go back to the spoils system. *Harper's, 191,* 362-368.

[15] Riordan, W. L. (1963). *Plunkett of Tammany Hall.* New York: Dutton.

[16] Klingner, D. (1980). *Public personnel management: Contexts and strategies.* Englewood Cliffs, NJ: Prentice Hall, Ch. 1.

[17] Civil Service Reform Act of 1978. P.L. 95-454, October 13, 1978.

[18] Heclo. *A government of strangers.* p. 20.

[19] Sayre. *The triumph of techniques,* pp. 134-137; Fisher. Let's go back, pp. 362-368.

[20] Mosher, F. (1982). *Democracy and the Public Service* (2nd ed.). New York: Oxford University Press.

[21] Meier, K. J. (October 1994). Public administrative theory or breathes there a man with soul so dead who never to himself hath said, this is my own, my paradigm. *SPAR* (Newsletter of the Section on Public Administration Research), American Society for Public Administration, 5, 1-2, 4-5.

[22] Lan, Z., and D. H. Rosenbloom (1992). Public administration in transition? *Public Administration Review,* 52, 535-538.

[23] Sterngold, J. (July 30, 1995). The budget knife boomerangs home. *The New York Times,* p. E-3.

[24] Freedman, A. (1994). Commentary on patronage. *Public Administration Review,* 54, 313; and Nalbandian, J. (1981). From compliance to consultation: The role of the public personnel manager. *Review of Public Personnel Administration,* 1, 37-51.

[25] Klingner, D. E. (1996). Public personnel management and democratization: A view from three Central American republics. *Public Administration Review,* 56, 390-399.

[26] Geddes, B. (1994). *Politician's dilemma: Building state capacity in Latin America.* Berkeley, CA: University of California Press; Graham, L. (1990). *The state and policy outcomes in Latin America.* New York: Praeger and the Hoover Institution Press; Lijphart, A. (1992). The Southern European examples of democratization: Six lessons for Latin America. *Government and Opposition, 25,* 68-84; Mainwaring, S., G. O'Donnell, and S. Valenzuela (Eds.). (1992). *Issues in democratic consolidation.* Notre Dame: University of Notre Dame Press; Sloan, J. (1989). The policy capabilities of democratic regimes in Latin America. *Latin American Research Review, 24,* 113-127; and Wynia, G. (1990). *The politics of Latin American development.* Cambridge: Cambridge University Press.

[27] Mosher. *Democracy and the public service.*

[28] Hays, S., and R. Kearney (1990). *Public personnel management: Problems and prospects* (2nd ed.). Englewood Cliffs: Prentice Hall; and Shafritz, J., N. Riccucci, A. Hyde, and D. Rosenbloom (1992). *Personnel management in government: Politics and process* (4th ed.). New York: Marcel Dekker.

[29] United States Agency for International Development (January 1991). *Economic assistance strategy for Central America: 1991-2000.* Washington, DC: U.S. Agency for International Development.

[30] Heady, F. (1991). *Public administration: A comparative perspective* (4th ed.). New York: Marcel Dekker.

[31] The author wishes to thank colleagues for their helpful suggestions on previous drafts of this analysis: Charles Frankenhoff, James D. Carroll, David H. Rosenbloom, Patricia Ingraham, and Jean-Claude Garcia-Zamor.

[32] Olson, M. (1993). Dictatorship, democracy and development. *American Political Science Review, 87,* 567-576; Honey, J. (1968). *Toward strategies for public administration development in Latin America.* Ithaca, NY: Syracuse University Press; and Thurber, C., and L. Graham (Eds.). (1973) *Development administration in Latin America.* Chapel Hill, NC: Duke University Press.

[33] Wiarda, H. (1995). *Latin American politics.* Belmont, CA: Wadsworth, pp. 160-161.

[34] Kearney, R. (1986). Spoils in the Caribbean: The struggle for merit-based civil service in the Dominican Republic. *Public Administration Review, 46,* 144-151; and Ruffing-Hilliard, K. (1991). Merit reform in Latin America: A comparative perspective. In A. Farazmand (Ed.). *Handbook of comparative and development public administration.* New York: Marcel Dekker.

[35] Vargas Alfáro, G. (October 6, 1993). *Exposición sobre la naturaleza y efectos de un sistema de servicio civil frente a los del botín político.* Panama: Asamblea Legislativa, Segundo Seminario Sobre Carrera Administrativa, USAID and FIU.

[36] PNUD (May 1991). Coloquio Nacional Sobre "Perfeccionamiento democrático y readecuación constitucional del estado." *Informe de Resultados.* Tegucigalpa, Honduras: Programa de Las Naciones Unidas Para el Desarrollo (PNUD) y Presidencia, Oficina del Programa de Mejoramiento de la Gestión del Estado, Proyecto Hon/90/501.

[37] COREC (1990). *Reforma del estado en Costa Rica.* San José, Costa Rica: Comisión de Reforma del Estado Costarricense (COREC), EDICOSTA, S.A.

[38] Román de Ríos, G. (July 19, 1993). La eliminación del nepotismo en el estado. *La Estrella de Panamá,* p. B-1.

[39] Sabet, M., and D. Klingner (1993). Exploring the impact of professionalism on administrative innovation. *Journal of Public Administration Research and Theory,* 3, 252-266; and Sierra, E. (July/December 1985). Los recursos humanos y las innovaciones técnicas administrativas. *Revista Centroamericana de Administración Pública,* 9, 81-92.

[40] While this issue is at the heart of a comparative analysis of the characteristics and development of public personnel systems worldwide, they are beyond the scope of this textbook. Readers wishing to pursue this topic might begin with the references cited in notes 25, 30, 32, and 34 of this chapter.

2

The Public Personnel Manager's Job

INTRODUCTION

Not long ago, a municipal government conference was held in Chile to discuss strategies for professionalizing and decentralizing local government there following seventeen years of dictatorship. But these inquiries led to a discussion of more general themes, among them the globalization of public management contexts and strategies. Our conclusion: We are not only the first generation of public management professionals in history to routinely confront the reality of global change on an international level, but we also confront local variants of global issues, utilizing common perspectives and solutions, and reflecting similar values and objectives.

Public personnel management is one part of this big picture. It is an international profession dedicated to the management of human resources in public agencies toward public objectives. Public personnel management is functions, underlying values, systems, and techniques. It is also "what public personnel managers do" and what human resource management is about.

But two factors complicate the situation. First, personnel management functions are shared among elected officials (who authorize systems), appointed officials (who design systems), personnel managers (who develop policies and procedures), and managers and supervisors (who implement these systems in the day-to-day process of working with employees). Second, because the context of public personnel management influences the way in which personnel managers and personnel departments perform their roles, we must examine how personnel systems and values influence the way public personnel managers do their jobs.

By the end of this chapter, you will be able to:

1. Discuss the size and scope of public employment in the United States.
2. Explain how the responsibility for performing the functions of personnel management are shared among elected and appointed officials, managers and supervisors, and the personnel department.

3. Describe the job of the public personnel manager under different public personnel systems, both traditional and emergent.
4. Describe the role of the public personnel manager as technician, professional, mediator, human resource management specialist, and mediator.
5. Discuss the knowledge, skills, and abilities that public personnel managers are likely to need in the future, as compared to the past or present.
6. Discuss career patterns of public personnel managers, particularly their preservice education and how they enter the field.
7. Tell what public personnel managers can do as individuals to enhance their own career development through the services offered by professional associations, conferences and training seminars, research libraries, and the information superhighway.

THE SIZE AND SCOPE OF PUBLIC EMPLOYMENT IN THE UNITED STATES

Public employment is complex in the United States because it is decentralized and there are multiple levels of government. While in the public's view federal employees often symbolize government bureaucracy, in reality they constitute only about 17 percent of all public employees. Federal government employment peaked at 3.4 million during World War II, receded to 2.0 million in 1947, and rose again to 2.5 million in 1951. After fifteen years of minor fluctuations, federal employment gradually rose again to 3.1 million in 1987. It began to decline again in 1990, reaching a current level of 3.0 million in 1992, about the same level as in 1985.

State and local government employment both grew steadily after World War II from a total of 3.6 million in 1946 to over 13.3 million in 1980. While the rate of growth has slowed since 1977, total state and local government employment has increased to 15.7 million in 1992. Of the 11.1 million local government employees (1992), 2.3 million are employed by counties, 2.7 million by cities and towns, 5.1 million by school districts, and .6 million by other special districts (such as airports).

Table 2-1 shows these historical trends. Statistics are for full-time equivalent employment using hours worked by part-time employees. Nearly 3.7 million of the state and local government workers were employed on a part-time basis in 1992.

TABLE 2-1 Government Civilian Employment, 1940-1992[1]

	EMPLOYEES (IN MILLIONS)			
Year	*Total*	*Federal*	*State*	*Local*
1940	4.4	1.1	3.3	(includes local)
1950	6.4	2.1	1.1	3.2
1960	8.8	2.4	1.5	4.9
1970	13.1	2.9	2.8	7.4
1980	16.3	2.9	3.8	9.6
1988	17.5	3.1	4.2	10.2
1992	18.7	3.0	4.6	11.1

TABLE 2-2 Government Employment by Function and Level of Government, 1992[2]

EMPLOYEES (IN THOUSANDS, AND PERCENT)						
Function	*Total*	*%*	*Federal*	*%*	*State and Local*	*%*
Total	18,745	100.0	3,047	100.0	15,698	100.0
Education	8,238	43.9	14	.5	8,225	49.4
Health & hospital	1,577	9.8	310	10.2	1,544	9.8
National defense	984	5.2	1,043	32.3		
Police	858	4.6	88	2.9	770	4.9
Postal service	774	4.1	774	25.4		
Corrections	567	3.0	24	.8	543	3.5
Highways	565	3.0	4	.1	561	3.6
Welfare	507	2.7	10	.3	496	3.2
Financial administration	493	2.6	138	4.5	355	2.3
Utilities	459	2.4			459	2.9
Natural resources	436	2.3	232	7.6	204	1.3
Parks and recreation	345	1.8	27	.9	318	2.0
Fire protection	344	1.8			344	2.2
Judicial	274	2.0	51	1.7	323	2.1
Housing/ community development	137	0.7	28	.9	109	0.7
Sewerage	128	0.7			128	0.8
Solid waste	116	0.6			116	0.7
All other	1,943	10.3	304	10	1,203	7.7

In 1992, these 18.7 million public employees were employed in a variety of functions, as shown in Table 2-2. The primary federal functions were national defense, postal service, and financial management; the primary state and local functions were education, police protection, highways, corrections, welfare, and utilities—with the emphasis on education.

SHARED RESPONSIBILITY FOR PUBLIC PERSONNEL MANAGEMENT

Responsibility for the design and implementation of public personnel systems is shared among three general groups: political leaders, personnel directors and specialists, and line managers and supervisors. Political leaders (legislators, executives, and their political appointees) are responsible for authorizing personnel systems, and for establishing their objectives and constraints. Agencies must be created, program priorities established, and funds allocated to meet program objectives before jobs can be designed or positions filled. In addition, the personnel system itself must be designed and authorized. This is true regardless of which system (political appointment, civil service, collective bargaining, or affirmative action) dominates the way personnel functions are performed.

Personnel directors and **specialists** are responsible for designing and implementing personnel systems, or for supervising and helping those who do so. In civil service systems, they usually work within a personnel department that functions as a staff support service for **line managers** and supervisors. Personnel directors and specialists both help line managers use human resources effectively and constrain their personnel actions within the limits imposed by political leaders, laws, and regulations.

Most public personnel management functions (PADS) are performed by the managers and supervisors who operate personnel systems, rather than by the personnel departments that design them. Supervisors are responsible for the day-to-day activities that, in the end, determine the nature of the relationship between employees and the organization, which is the most important factor in personnel management. Supervisors tell employees what is expected of them, train employees, provide feedback to let them know how they are doing, and recommend pay increases and promotion (or disciplinary action and dismissal) based on their assessment of the employee's job performance. Line managers and supervisors are responsible for "street-level" implementation of personnel systems. Their behavior is critical because the relationship between individual employees and supervisors is the most important factor influencing the effectiveness with which employees are developed and utilized. In short, supervisors set the tone of the relationship between employee and employer.

Table 2-3 illustrates how responsibility is shared among these three groups.

TABLE 2-3 Shared Responsibility for Personnel Functions

FUNCTION	LEVEL		
	Elected and Appointed Officials	*Managers and Supervisors*	*Personnel Directors and Specialists*
Planning	Estimate revenues; set program priorities	Manage to mission within a budget	Develop job descriptions, implement pay and benefit plans
Acquisition	Influence values that guide the selection process	Hire and fire employees	Develop hiring rules and procedures
Development	Define agency and program goals and priorities	Make sure employees have clear goals, skills, feedback, and rewards	Develop training and evaluation systems
Sanction	Determine appropriate personnel systems	Counsel and discipline employees and policies	Develop policies and programs for drug testing, discipline

THE PUBLIC PERSONNEL MANAGER'S JOB UNDER DIFFERENT PERSONNEL SYSTEMS

The previous chapter discussed the four personnel systems (political appointment, civil service, collective bargaining, and affirmative action) that arise out of the four traditional pro-government values (political responsiveness, organizational efficiency, individual rights, and social equity) that compete as criteria for allocating public jobs. The existence and legitimacy of civil service systems and their three competitors do much to complicate the role of the public personnel manager, and the ways in which the personnel department performs its functions. This section first describes the role of the public personnel manager in each of the traditional systems and clarifies ways in which the personnel manager's job differs among them by showing how patterns of law and historical practice have led alternative systems to emphasize different functions and to perform them differently.

But the emergence of strong anti-government sentiments since the 1970s has introduced three new anti-government values: individual responsibility, limited and decentralized government, and community responsibility for social programs. And from our discussion in the previous chapter, it should be clear that this model also proposes a different array of **public personnel management** systems (chiefly using alternative mechanisms or organizations to deliver public services, and increasing the use of flexible at-will employment relationships for those public employees that remain), in place of either civil service, collective bargaining, or affirmative action systems. So this section next describes the role of the public personnel manager in each of the emergent systems and emphasizes how the public personnel manager's job is likely to differ from the traditional model.

The Traditional Job of the Public Personnel Manager

Civil Service. In a civil service system, the personnel director usually directs a personnel department or office that functions as an administrative support service to the city manager, school superintendent, hospital administrator, or other agency administrator. The personnel department develops policies and procedures for managing the agency's human resources.

In the area of planning (classification and compensation), the personnel department is responsible for managing the civil service system. This means maintaining the system of positions that have been categorized into a plan according to criteria like degree of difficulty or type of work. The pay system is usually tied to the classification system, with jobs involving similar degrees of difficulty being compensated equally. Periodic checks are conducted to compare the actual work a person is doing with the duties outlined in a job description for the position. Yearly updates of the pay plan are also performed in anticipation of collective bargaining and budget planning within a civil service system.

The personnel department is also responsible for developing and updating the agency's retirement and benefits programs, and for negotiating with benefit providers. It maintains records like eligibility and use of sick leave and vacation time, enrollment and maintenance in various health insurance programs, and life insurance or savings bond purchases. It also handles eligibility and processing of personnel action requests (retirements and other related changes in job status), including calculation of authorized retirement benefits, disability retirement determinations, and monitoring of workers' compensation claims for job-related injuries and illnesses.

In the area of acquisition (recruitment, testing, and selection), the personnel department might be responsible for scheduling tests for jobs that are frequently available, like secretary, clerk, and maintenance worker. It advertises vacant or new positions, conducts an initial review of job applications, and administers written tests. It might arrange interviews with applicants, conduct them, and evaluate test results. The personnel department compiles a list of those eligible for employment, maintains the list to ensure it is up to date as job applicants secure other employment, and provides a list of eligible applicants to managers in units where vacancies actually exist. The manager conducts interviews and selects one applicant. The personnel department then processes the paperwork required to employ and pay the person.

With respect to development, the personnel department might be responsible for orienting new employees to the organization, its work rules, and the benefits it provides. It might also keep track of and distribute notices of training or transfer opportunities. It might conduct training to familiarize supervisors with the technical aspects of a newly developed performance appraisal system.

The personnel department must also keep track of and process all personnel actions—promotions, transfers, and dismissals. It also has a section that establishes and staffs an employee grievance and appeals procedure. People who work in this section are responsible for advising supervisors throughout the organization of appropriate codes of conduct for employees, the procedures and paperwork necessary to discipline an employee for violations of these rules, and the procedures to follow in the event the employee appeals this disciplinary action or files a grievance.

Political Appointment. In a political appointment system, the personnel director functions primarily as a staffing specialist and political adviser. His or her title is usually not even that of personnel director. But regardless of the title, it is this person's responsibility to identify individuals who deserve or require a top-level political position working for an elected official, and to make recommendations to that official as to who should be hired in which position. The official then makes the appointment (or nominates the individual, if legislative confirmation is required) based upon the candidate's objective KSAs, political or personal loyalty, financial or campaign support for the elected official, or support by an influential interest group seeking access to the policy-making process.

Once hired, political appointees are subject to the whims of the elected official. Few rules govern their job duties, pay, or rights, and they are usually fired at will. Nor is development a priority. Employees are hired for their current positions, not for a career.

Collective Bargaining. If any employees in the agency are covered by a collective bargaining agreement, the personnel department is usually responsible for negotiating the agreement (or hiring an outside negotiator who performs this function), bringing pay and benefit provisions into accord with contract provisions, orienting supervisors on how to comply with the contract, and representing the agency in internal grievance resolution or outside arbitration procedures. Because collective bargaining is a partial personnel system, civil service systems continue to provide most of the rules and procedures relating to acquisition and development.

Affirmative Action. The affirmative action department is responsible primarily for implementing human resource acquisition decision rules emphasizing social equity for protected classes (minorities, women, and persons with disabilities). Thus, it most heavily affects recruitment, selection, and promotion policies and procedures. The affirmative action director shares responsibility with the personnel director in this area. Once members of protected classes are hired, other personnel systems (civil service or collective bargaining) influence the way in which planning, development, and sanction functions are performed.

Similarities and Differences under the Traditional Model. The primary conclusion to be drawn from this discussion is that while public personnel directors perform some or all of the same functions regardless of the system in which they operate, the system has profound effects on the relative importance of these functions, their organizational location, and their method of implementation. The authority of personnel managers varies widely. Those working in predominantly political systems have little authority beyond that given to them by political leaders and are concerned mainly with acquisition. Those working in civil service systems are more constrained by laws and have responsibilities for a wider range of functions. Those working with collective bargaining systems are responsible for negotiating and administering collective bargaining agreements with unionized employees, who are also members of civil service systems. Those working in affirmative action systems are usually affirmative action officers, with predominant responsibilities for acquisition.

But it is overly simplistic to say that public personnel directors work within one system or another. It is much more likely that an individual director will be in charge of all personnel functions in an agency that includes several personnel systems. Thus, while someone might be in charge of labor relations, that person might report to the personnel director; the same would be true for the affirmative action officer in many public agencies. The role of the personnel director involves significant elements of role conflict because the director is responsible not only for supervising all the personnel functions but also for resolving conflicts in how they are performed, based on alternative values and decision rules. This leads directly to the issues of professionalism and ethics.

In addition, organizational size makes a difference. In large units, the personnel function may be staffed by hundreds of employees or divided into divisions. In a small local government, the functions may be carried out as part of the responsibilities of the chief administrative officer or an assistant. And there are many possible variants within this range.

The New Job of the Public Personnel Manager

The emergence of alternative anti-government personnel systems has meant changes in relative importance of personnel functions (planning, acquisition, development, and sanction), and how they are performed. They have also complicated the public personnel manager's job by deepening conflicts with the traditional pro-government values and systems.

Providing Public Services through Alternative Organizations or Mechanisms. The use of non-governmental organizations reduces the absolute number of public employees, thereby diminishing the human resource functions of the personnel department—especially those related to acquisition, development, and sanction of public employees. However, it does increase the importance of planning and oversight, which is necessary to estimate the type and number of contract employees needed to provide a desired level of service; share in developing contract proposals for outside organizations; and evaluate responses to proposals by comparing costs and services, and overseeing contract administration.

The use of volunteers and self-help means that personnel directors and other departmental staff work increasingly with citizen volunteers and community-based organizations, much as personnel directors for not-for-profit organizations (community recreation programs, hospitals, and schools) have traditionally used volunteers to supplement paid staff. In these cases, public managers need to become more skilled in recruitment, selection, training, and motivation of volunteer workers.

Increased Use of Flexible Public Employment Relationships. Flexibility in employment relationships is achieved primarily by the increased use of temporary, part-time, and seasonal employment; and by increased hiring of exempt employees (those outside the classified civil service) through employment contracts. Use of contingent employment relationships generally means less emphasis on planning and employee development, at least for these employees. The organization is typically staffed for minimum workload levels, and additional employees are added temporarily as needed based on fluctuations in workload.

Development of employees (through training, performance evaluation, or motivation) is largely irrelevant. Contingent workers are hired with the skills needed to perform the job immediately. Performance evaluation is unnecessary—if they do their jobs adequately, they get paid; if not, they are simply released at the end of their contract and not called back when workload once again increases. Their motivation is financial, perhaps augmented by the chance of being hired into a civil service position if vacancies become available.

July 5, 1996

TO: John Nalbandian and Donald Klingner

FR: Tom Lewinsohn, Former Personnel Director, Kansas City, Missouri, and Past President International Personnel Management Association

RE: The Staffing Function

I was taught and believed that the public service was a career that truly practiced equal employment opportunity for entry into the service and for subsequent promotional opportunities. I started my career as a intern with the state of Kansas, and retired as Director of Personnel for Kansas City, Missouri. I am an advocate of merit principles as defined by the Office of Personnel Management.

In the last few years, the personnel function relabeled itself as the human resources function. In my opinion, the purpose was for personnel to become more "management" oriented and to add "value" to the organization. It sounds terrific, and I am sure that there are human resources departments that accomplish those goals. I am also seeing the basic function of recruitment and selection contracted out to the private sector which can result in preselection and circumventing of equal employment opportunity. On the one hand, this practice concerns me because it goes around the "open" process, but on the other hand, I can understand that the operating departments welcome this kind of outsourcing since they no longer have to interview the "unknown" masses from the eligible register. After all, hiring temporaries, which is occuring in an ever-increasing variety of positions, has become a common practice at all levels of government. It's simple and quick, and all we have to do is call the agency and say, "Send another one." The private sector thrives on this practice. What is good for business should be good for government, shouldn't it? It is expedient preselection without accountability. It is *not* a merit system that affords equal employment opportunity.

In a recent exposé of city workers goofing off and sleeping on the job, the operating department responded by stating that the workers caught on the cameras were "temporaries" and that the city will not pay the agency for hours not worked!

What are the consequences of this accelerated privatization? I think it impacts negatively on the very foundation that attracted persons to the public service. With the "temporaries" there is no job security and in turn no loyalty to the public service. The supervisors of these temporaries have complete discretion as to who comes back or not, and who will be rewarded for permanent appointments. It is employment "at will" with considerably less legal consequences to complaints by these non-employees.

Over the past few years, many vital personnel functions, especially those that have fiscal ramifications like insurance programs, have been contracted out to the private sector for the appearance of business-like practices as opposed to "politics." Recruitment and selection, based on a current grade classification system with a competitive wage and benefits program, is the core of the human resources function. When this function is contracted out for administration and enforcement of EEO principles, we abate the management function of personnel.

Questions

1. How would you summarize Lewinsohn's message?
2. Do you agree that privatization of personnel functions diminishes merit principles?
3. Is the core of merit-based human resources management recruitment and classification based on a current grade classification system with a competitive wage and benefit program?
4. Do you think that EEO principles are more likely to be followed by a government personnel department as opposed to a private employment agency?

Nor is the sanction function particularly important for public personnel managers with respect to these workers. Of course, employers are required to maintain a safe and healthy workplace; but compliance with the Americans with Disabilities Act, the Family and Medical Leave Act, and the Fair Labor Standards Act are not required for temporary, part-time, or seasonal workers. Nor is it at all difficult, from the employer's perspective, to maintain the terms of the employment relationship—at-will employment means just that. Like political appointments, but unlike their civil service counterparts, at-will employees have no right to retain their jobs. They can be discharged for any reason, or for no reason, without management having to give a reason or to support it.

The Changing Role of the Public Personnel Manager: From Compliance to Consultation to Contract Compliance. The evolution of public personnel management values and systems has meant corresponding changes in the role of the public personnel manager. During the development of public personnel management as part of the transition from patronage to merit systems (Stage Two in the developmental model presented in Figure 1-1 on p. 29), public personnel management functioned as the champion of merit system principles. The growth of public personnel management regulations and procedures occurred within the context of civil service systems whose development was characterized by a bipolar dynamic of competition between political patronage appointments (the "spoils system") and civil service appointments (the "merit system"). In this context, the public personnel manager was viewed as a moral guardian responsible for protecting employees, applicants and the public from the evils of the spoils system. This required knowledge of civil service policies and procedures, and a willingness to apply them in the face of political pressure.

During Stage Three (1933-1964), public personnel managers sought to maintain efficiency and accountability, and legislators and chief executives sought to maintain bureaucratic compliance through budgetary controls and **position management**. Through such devices as personnel ceilings and average grade-level restrictions, it became the role of public personnel management to control the behavior of public managers and to help assure compliance with legislative authority. In effect, it was the responsibility of public personnel managers to synthesize two distinct values (bureaucratic compliance as the operational definition of organizational efficiency, and civil service protection as the embodiment of employee rights). There was tension between them because they were both symbiotic and conflicting. Taken to extremes, either would diminish the other; in moderation, both supported the concept of a qualified and effective public service that was at the heart of bureaucratic theory and scientific management. And together with the value of bureaucratic neutrality, they supported the concept of political responsiveness.

During Stage Four (1964-1992), due to a variety of political and economic pressures, the focus of public personnel management shifted to **work management** as managers and public personnel specialists continued to demand flexibility and equitable reward allocation through such alterations to classification and pay systems as rank-in-person personnel systems, broad pay banding, and group performance evaluation and reward systems. This trend coincided with *employee* needs for utilization, development, and recognition.[3] In addition, because this period was characterized by a dynamic and self-correcting equilibrium among four competing values, the role of the public personnel manager involved professional and political (mediating and conflict resolution) skills in addition to technical knowledge. During this period, public personnel managers functioned as interpreters and mediators of the four conflicting values. This was difficult, yet it gave value to the profession.

Even though skepticism of government is an American tradition, because the current period (Stage Five) has emerged so intensely of late, the ways in which it is changing the role of the public personnel manager are not yet entirely clear. But it is possible to predict their probable impact.

Public personnel managers will still be required to be good managers under Stage Five, but the definition of "good management" is narrow by previous standards. First, public personnel managers are required, more than ever, to manage government employees and programs in compliance with legislative and public mandates for cost control. Given the common public and legislative presumption that the public bureaucracy is an enemy to be controlled rather than a tool to be used to accomplish public policy objectives, public personnel managers in the future may have less opportunity to exercise professional responsibilities in balancing conflicting values. The scope of their authority may be diminished by legislative micromanagement, or the value of cost control may be so dominant as to preclude other considerations—even concern for employee rights, organizational efficiency, or social equity.

Second, good management may in time comprise skills that are more directed to minimizing maximum loss (such as risk management and contract compliance) than to maximizing human development and organizational performance for permanent employees. "People skills" will continue to be important. For example, public personnel managers will increasingly be responsible for developing and managing a range of public employment systems for contract, temporary, and at-will employees. They may be required to work increasingly with volunteers and community-based not-for-profit organizations that increasingly constitute the social safety net by which the value of **community responsibility** is carried out. Civil service and collective bargaining continue to be important, for many public employees (particularly school teachers and administrators, police and firefighters) are still covered by union contracts and collective bargaining agreements. But risk management, cost control, and management of other types of employment contracts will become more important than ever. In this sense, substituting a calculating perspective for an optimistic view of the joint possibilities for organizational productivity and individual growth represents a narrowing of the public personnel manager's perspective.

Third, and somewhat paradoxically, even as this minimalist view of personnel management emerges, there are countervailing pressures to develop an employment relationship characterized by commitment, teamwork, and innovation. Productivity is prized, risk taking is espoused, and variable pay systems that reward individual and group performance are touted. Perhaps the key to the paradox is the emerging distinction between "core" employees (those regarded as essential assets) and contingent workers (those regarded as replaceable costs). For personnel managers, success in the coming millennium will mean the ability to develop two divergent personnel systems, one for each type of worker within a dual labor market system, and to maintain both at the same time despite their conflicting objectives and assumptions.

In considering the impact of environmental factors on the role of the public personnel manager, it may be interesting to note that the search and screen process for the personnel director of a mid size Florida city resulted in the highest ranking being given to a person with no previous civil service personnel experience. Instead, this person was a labor attorney with extensive private-sector experience in negotiating and administering employment contracts with outside vendors and contractors. In brief, KSAs related to alternative personnel systems were considered more desirable than those related to traditional civil service and collective bargaining.

The impact of changing values and public personnel systems on the role of the public personnel manager can be seen in Table 2-4 (p. 50). The dominant values and systems represented by Stage One through Stage Four repeat the information given in Figure 1-1; the left-hand column summarizes the above analysis of the public personnel manager's role in each stage.

THE JOB OF THE PUBLIC PERSONNEL MANAGER: TECHNICIAN, PROFESSIONAL, HUMAN RESOURCE MANAGEMENT SPECIALIST AND MEDIATOR

In the end, like at other points in time during the past century, we can only speculate on the emergent role of the public personnel manager as the field continues to evolve. But if the past is any indication, it is likely to include four key roles: technician, professional, human resource management specialist, and mediator.

Technician

Entry-level public personnel managers are usually technical specialists or generalists. In a large personnel department, **technicians** are expected to know how to perform specialized functions within civil service systems.

Staffing specialists administer examinations, establish lists of eligible applicants, and refer eligible applicants to line managers for interviews and selection. This job requires knowledge of personnel law and recruitment and selection procedures, and experience in employment interviewing, and affirmative action.

TABLE 2-4 The Role of the Public Personnel Manager in the United States

Stage	*Dominant Value*	*Dominant System*	*Public Personnel Manager's Role*
One (1789-1883)	Responsiveness	Patronage	Recruitment and political clearance
Two (1883-1933)	Efficiency Individual rights	Civil service	Watchdog against the spoils system
Three (1933-1964)	Responsiveness Efficiency Individual right	Patronage Civil service	Adherence to legislative mandates Watchdog against the spoils system
Four (1964-1992)	Responsiveness Efficiency Individual rights Social equity	Patronage Civil service Collective bargaining Affirmative action	Consultation Balance among competing values and and objectives
Five (1992- present)	Individual accountability Limited and decentralized government Community responsibility	Alternative organizations and mechanisms Flexible employment relationships	Adherence to legislative limits Contract compliance

Job analysts or **position classifiers** analyze jobs to determine the appropriate KSAs and minimum qualifications, respond to managers' requests for reclassification (to determine if duties, KSAs, and minimum qualifications have changed over time), recommend the appropriate salary for a position (based on job worth factors or market conditions), and determine whether employees can perform the essential functions of a position under ADA (the Americans with Disabilities Act). This job requires task analysis, knowledge of job classification and evaluation procedures, and survey research.

Testing specialists developing valid and reliable selection criteria for positions, and defend the reliability and validity of current tests. This job requires knowledge of testing, measurement, test validation procedures.

Pay and benefits specialists administer the payroll system, enroll new employees in benefit programs, advise employees of changes in benefit programs, and ensure compliance with federal pay and benefit laws (such as FLSA and COBRA). This job requires knowledge of pay and benefit systems; employment contracts; pensions; federal laws with respect to wages, hours, and benefits; and health, life, and disability insurance.

Affirmative action compliance officers are responsible for compliance with equal employment opportunity and affirmative action laws and regulations (U.S.

Equal Employment Opportunity Commission), the Americans with Disabilities Act (ADA), gender equity with respect to pay and benefits (U.S. Department of Labor), and the Age Discrimination in Employment Act. They are the persons most concerned with recruitment, selection, and promotion activities within civil service and affirmative action systems. This job requires knowledge of state and federal AA/EEO laws and compliance agencies, and of related personnel functions (primarily staffing and pay and benefits).

Training and development specialists determine training needs, develop and conduct training programs, and evaluate their effectiveness. Trainers must have training or experience as adult educators.

Employee assistance program directors coordinate employee assistance programs offered by the organization or by contract providers, as a response to personal employee problems that become workplace issues: alcohol and drug abuse, financial counseling, domestic and workplace violence, life-threatening diseases, legal assistance, and psychological counseling. They should know federal laws protecting the rights of employees with physical or mental disabilities (such as the Americans with Disabilities Act and the Family and Medical Leave Act); be able to conduct informal counseling with supervisors and employees; and be able to advise employees of the health and insurance benefit programs offered by the employer.

Risk managers are responsible for developing or enforcing personnel policies designed to limit the organization's exposure to legal or financial liability due to violations of employee rights, unsafe or unhealthy working conditions, or poor management practice. In particular, personnel managers who function as risk managers are responsible for reducing employer liability for workers' compensation, disability retirement, and negligent hiring, retention, or referral claims. This function may also be shared with the organization's attorney and budget officer. Risk managers must know personnel law, Occupational Safety and Health (OSHA), workers' compensation systems and procedures, and the Family Medical Leave Act.

Contract specialists' responsibilities vary depending upon the personnel system. Under collective bargaining systems, they are responsible for developing background information to support management's positions during contract negotiations; or for administering collective bargaining by ensuring that labor and management comply with negotiated agreements. Under alternative systems, they are responsible for developing and negotiating fee for service contracts with outside vendors, or individual employment contracts with employees or independent contractors. Contract specialists have experience with business law, policy analysis, contract negotiation, or contract compliance.

Professional

The issue of whether public personnel managers are **professionals** has been debated for years. In many practical ways, the issue seems to boil down to the extent to which personnel managers can engage in the conflicts among public personnel systems and values, and yet keep from being captured by any one of them. Conceptually, the issue seems to focus on the extent to which there is an identifiable body of KSAs that define the occupation of the human resource manager, an accepted process of education and training for acquiring these KSAs, and a standard of ethics that guides their application. For academics who develop theory in the field, the issue of professionalism seems to focus on the extent to which there is an underlying body of theory that forms the basis for developing and implementing alternative approaches to the personnel functions; setting these approaches theoretically within the governmental context; and then describing the extent to which role strain or role conflict among the conflicting expectations of alternative personnel systems are an aberration or "come with the territory."

If the previous discussion of competing values and systems has demonstrated anything, it is that public personnel managers will continue to be responsible for making the difficult decisions required to implement not only competing pro-government values but also their opposing anti-government values. More than ever, good job performance will require that they recognize the inherent conflicts in their role, and yet continue to make sound professional decisions in a climate of political and economic uncertainty.

Human Resource Management Specialist

Pay and benefits constitute about two thirds of the operating costs of the typical organization. **Human resource management specialis**ts are—or should be—experts consulted by other managers who wish to improve their ability to manage people. So in addition to professional and technical capabilities, personnel directors are responsible for experimentation, technology transfer, and education within the organization. Each of these roles merits discussion. Experimentation means the testing of personnel policies or procedures to determine their impact on a desired value (such as the effect of a new benefit, or a new performance evaluation method, on employee productivity or turnover). But personnel directors rarely initiate personnel management innovations. Usually, these are developed in one setting and transferred to others where variables and objectives are similar. From this perspective, innovations such as **privatization** or use of independent contractors are administrative innovations which have been introduced initially in one government as experiments, and then adapted and adopted in other settings as a technology transfer process. Lastly, human resource management specialists function as educators for employees and other managers concerning public personnel systems—the laws, policies, and procedures used to manage employees in organization. This educational function is performed formally, through training and development, and informally, through organizational interactions, as they perform the four personnel functions.

Mediator

Initially, civil service reformers sought to establish the credibility of personnel management by emphasizing its political neutrality and focusing on administrative **efficiency**. This emphasis served to establish public personnel management as a technical field with a body of techniques used to perform human resource management functions, and it separated public personnel administration from politics. Ironically, however, this emphasis on political neutrality and insistence on discovering the "one best way" to manage human resources had an opposite effect on the field as well. It isolated public personnel managers from the value conflicts that characterized the world of other professionals (such as law and medicine) and minimized the ethical dilemmas that constantly confronted them—dilemmas that grew out of the political context in which all public employees operate. This created the illusion among public officials (and among personnel directors and specialists themselves) that the field was value-free. It focused personnel management on administrative techniques instead of broad human resource policy questions. This devalued the status of the profession and downgraded the importance accorded the study of personnel systems and values.

Traditional public personnel managers are usually impatient or complacent with ethical choices. In their view of public personnel administration, ethical dilemmas are easily resolved because this system is based entirely upon the civil service system as a moral ideal, with the political patronage system as its arch-enemy and moral opposite (or at best something to be continually wary of). The competing claims of alternative systems (politics, collective bargaining, and affirmative action) are considered challenges to the morally superior civil service system.[4] Public personnel managers operating under these beliefs function either as "true believers" or as pragmatists. They are inclined to consider **ethics** unnecessary, because it is easier to think of administrative actions as purely technical and rational and infused with moral superiority, or impractical because competing claims require pragmatic compromise.

Today, the extent to which the three emergent anti-government values will diminish the impact of the traditional four is uncertain. But if the past is any indication, it is likely that the inherent weaknesses of the new values will be self-limiting and that there will be a swing back toward the pro-government alternatives. Therefore, it is reasonable to predict that public personnel managers will continue to play their traditional role as **mediators** among conflicting values, albeit on a smaller scale because of the diminished role of government in society.

Therefore, contemporary public personnel managers are more likely to find that ethical dilemmas are challenging and inevitable because they arise directly out of the role conflicts implicit in the public personnel manager's job. They "come with the territory." To succeed, public personnel managers must not only do things right, they must do the right things.[5] It is the fate of the public personnel manager to wrestle with choices imposed by external conflicts among competing systems, and to derive from these choices the existential satisfaction of each day coming closer to unattainable objectives under conditions of ethical uncertainty.

The inevitability of political and ethical dilemmas for the modern public personnel administrator is a dominant theme of this book, in that these dilemmas are based upon conflict among personnel systems, values, and power centers for the right to allocate scarce public jobs. Not only does resource scarcity prohibit maximum achievement of all values simultaneously, but each of them can often be maximized only at the expense of the others. In addition, the use of management information for evaluative purposes presupposes some purpose for evaluation. The evaluator collects and interprets information for the purpose of changing organizational behavior. Just as value-free administration is impossible, so value-free evaluation is a contradiction in terms.

The problem of ethical administration, then, is neither illusory nor easily resolved. It arises inevitably out of legitimate but conflicting role expectations. How can ethical dilemmas be resolved? Six steps are worthy of discussion.

1. Assume that administrative acts have ethical content.
2. Determine in advance whom they affect.
3. Visualize the effect of alternative actions on the people or groups involved.
4. Make a choice consistent with your own moral standards, drawing on other guidelines such as applicable laws, the advice of friends, or the expectations of co-workers.
5. Understand that you may have to explain this choice later to outsiders unfamiliar with your job, and prepare yourself to do so.
6. Forget this choice—put it behind you so you can face the next one clearly.

Yesterday and Today: Multiple Roles in Testing and Selection

It is evident that the practice of public personnel management may require managers to resolve ethical dilemmas in seeking compromise among competing personnel systems, and among the values and interest groups these systems represent. Effective job performance requires that they not only be adept at using a range of techniques but also sensitive to the competing values and systems that influence technical choices. To the extent that they operate as mediators among these competing systems and values, public personnel managers function as professionals, and academicians see them as such. To the extent that they act as if they function in an environment devoid of value conflicts, public personnel managers are likely to function as technical specialists and to be viewed as such by academicians.

A look at the history of testing and selection will emphasize the consequences of these multiple expectations for the role of the public personnel manager. Beginning in the 1920s, public personnel directors began to develop testing and selection techniques that emphasized selection of the best candidate through the use of objective hiring standards. But necessary as these techniques were to move past the previous focus on political responsiveness and a spoils system which dictated appointments to technical and professional jobs, it distracted the focus of personnel professionals from the value conflicts inherent in the acquisition function.

In the "real world" of contemporary public personnel management, political leaders often disagree about which personnel system should predominate in determining how personnel functions are performed. In those instances where competing systems have developed and implemented contradictory rules for performing a function, it is usually the public personnel director who responds to, mediates among, or initiates conflict among competing systems. For example, the creation of a vacant position by the retirement or transfer of the incumbent will require the personnel manager to respond, propose, or attempt to mediate among competing decision rules for filling the position:

1. *Civil service.* Fill the position with one of the applicants who placed highest on the civil service test for the position.
2. *Civil service/political appointment.* Revise the minimum qualifications for the position to include the candidate with the most political support, and then pick that candidate from among the most qualified applicants for the position.
3. *Civil service/affirmative action appointment.* Conduct targeted recruitment efforts, making sure the applicant pool has a sufficient representation of women and minorities who also meet the minimum qualifications for the position. Then pick either the most qualified applicant or the most qualified minority applicant, depending on the extent of pressure and legal authority to appoint a minority group member.
4. *Civil service/collective bargaining appointment.* See if the position can be filled from within through a bidding process that emphasizes seniority, as specified by the collective bargaining agreement.
5. *Civil service/"at will" appointment.* Offer civil service employees the opportunity to compete for a promotional vacancy. The vacancy is an exempt position outside the civil service; filled through an annual employment contract. The employee has a significantly higher salary and an attractive benefit package, but no longer qualifies for civil service protection or "bumping rights" back into a classified position in the event of a layoff.
6. *Civil service/independent contractor appointment.* Technical specialist positions (engineering, management analyst, etc.) that have been filled as permanent, full-time positions through civil service are abolished. In their place, independent contractors are hired on a temporary, part-time, as needed basis to perform these functions. The hourly pay rate increases considerably, but it does not include employee benefits (such as vacations, sick leave, or health benefits) or employer payroll taxes (worker's compensation or Social Security) because these are the contractor's responsibility. Frequently, highly qualified civil servants will retire from their classified positions and be rehired as independent contractors or consultants to perform essentially the same duties as before, but through a distinctly different type of employment relationship.

Some Conclusions

What conclusions can be drawn from this variety of activities? First, historical traditions emphasize the technical side of personnel management, with less emphasis on policy-related analytical work, relationships with outside organizations, and conflicting values. In addition, both employees and line management are seen as clients and are perceived as being served through the merit system. The traditional department's work includes record keeping and the processing of personnel transactions, especially in smaller government agencies or units.

A more contemporary view emphasizes different activities and relationships. While the traditional functions continue to be important, they are relatively less important than the "brokering" or mediating of conflicts among competing personnel systems. For example, the modern personnel director might be called upon to prepare cost-benefit analyses of alternative pay and benefit proposals related to collective bargaining with employees in the solid waste department. At the same time, he or she might also be asked to evaluate the comparative feasibility, productivity, and cost of privatizing or contracting out this entire function (thus making the collective bargaining analysis irrelevant). Or since the majority of employees in department are minorities, the director might be asked to assess the impact of contracting out on the city's overall level of affirmative action compliance. Modern personnel directors do not work in isolation; rather, they work closely with other officials within their own agency (budget directors, attorneys, collective bargaining negotiators, affirmative action compliance officers, and supervisors) and outside it (legislative staff, union officials, affirmative action agencies, civil service boards, health and life insurance benefit representatives, pension boards, ethics commissions, and employee assistance programs dealing with substance abuse and other personal problems).

Most public personnel departments have moved cautiously into the modern era because of their traditional reluctance to be identified with or become involved in "politics." Yet, as their function is increasingly viewed as the development and management of human resource systems involving the reconciliation of value conflicts, they are overcoming this reluctance and working outside the confining environment of the civil service system. And they are finding that this expanded role brings benefits as well as risks. They are able to bring their expertise to bear on a range of critical human resource issues in a variety of contexts—issues traditional personnel managers might define as falling outside their area of responsibility. For example, they can work with legislators on privatization and benefits issues, with labor negotiators on alternative pay and grievance procedures, and with affirmative action compliance agencies on affirmative action proposals or minority business contracting procedures. By continuing to assert their central role in the most critical issues of agency management, they are developing not only their own professional status but also the status of their profession.[6]

WHAT KNOWLEDGE, SKILLS, AND ABILITIES DO PUBLIC PERSONNEL MANAGERS NEED?

Traditional public personnel management requires that personnel directors know the laws and regulations that control practices within a particular system, as well as the techniques used to perform personnel functions within that system. For example, traditional civil-service-oriented personnel management requires knowledge of civil service rules and regulations (such as competitive examination procedures, or how to select from a list of eligible applicants), as well as how to develop and administer examinations, write job descriptions, administer pay and benefit programs, and process personnel actions.

Contemporary public personnel management requires these skills and more. It requires a knowledge of public personnel management techniques, an understanding of historical developments in the field, and the ability to resolve ethical dilemmas among competing values under conditions of change and uncertainty. Personnel rules and procedures are not value-neutral; rather, they are the implicit or explicit implementation of a particular public personnel system (or compromises among several such systems). This means that each selection or promotion decision must be viewed not merely as a technical exercise, but as a case that reflects and exemplifies this historical conflict over alternative values, power, and public personnel systems.

Public personnel directors must be sensitive to the need for administrative systems to be responsive to legitimate political values and public participation in governance, especially in local government. These kinds of changes inevitably challenge the shield that the rhetoric of merit has provided the traditional manager. Now there is no escaping the political pressure personnel managers must face. They work under consent decrees and with unions that traditionally have set barriers to hiring women and minorities. At the same time, they are expected to respond to their political leaders while maintaining the integrity of the civil service system they oversee. Yet they have no guidance from within the traditional civil service system for how to integrate these increasingly insistent and conflicting demands.

Modern public personnel managers tend to view their world as a conflict- and change-oriented environment, rather than as a stable one. First, theirs is a world in which trends such as privatization and contracting out have blurred distinctions between public and private. Second, their world is controlled by a myriad of complex and conflicting laws involving affirmative action, labor relations, personal/professional liability, employee privacy, due process, and pay equity. Third, their world is characterized by constant technological innovations in areas such as data security, teleconferencing, computerized data bases and report generation,[7] and applications of interactive video to training and orientation.[8] Fourth, their world is characterized by changes in workforce composition (demographics). For example, robotics and automation have led to the creation and absorption of many middle management and clerical positions; the workforce is aging, and the number of women and minorities is increasing by 1980, over half the workforce employed outside the home in the United States was female. And the number of blacks and Hispanics is increasing as well (they will constitute 50 percent of the births in the United States by 2076).[9] Fifth, this leads to changes in organization such as real-time problem solving, decentralization, and networking.[10]

These changes in the context of public administration have led public personnel managers to adopt a changing definition of the field. In general, there is increased awareness of the impact of environmental factors—among them technology, economics, politics, and social conditions. There is also continued awareness of the importance of human resources to organizational productivity. Within the field of human resource management, this means increased responsibilities in the general area of environmental mediation and adaptation, including interpretation and compliance with government regulations, predicting the effects of changes in technology and workforce composition on jobs,[11] and developing programs and systems to help line managers increase productivity. Examples are job humanization, flexible work schedules and benefits, training and education, and performance-oriented evaluation systems.

Potentially, the power of public personnel managers in public organizations is increasing. This is a *potential* consequence resulting from their successful ability to move from a traditional view of the field (involving primarily technical skills) to a modern view (involving primarily professional skills as an interpreter of conflicting interests and mediator among them). At the same time, they will be called upon to protect the integrity of merit systems.

The modern public personnel manager needs several general types of KSAs to perform well in this enhanced role. Public personnel managers must exhibit continued concern for productivity and effectiveness. They must become and remain competent in law, technology, and quantitative/analytic skills. They must have a humanistic orientation toward employees, a positive orientation to managerial objectives, and close working relationships with other personnel professionals inside and outside the organization. No one manager can possess expertise in all these areas, but no complex personnel department can overlook them in their complement of KSAs.

HOW DO PUBLIC PERSONNEL MANAGERS GET INTO THE FIELD?

Previous discussion indicated that public personnel management is a set of functions (planning, acquisition, development and sanction) performed by personnel specialists, managers, and elected and appointed officials. Personnel specialists, in particular, function as technicians, professionals, human resource management experts, and mediators. They perform these multiple roles in a central personnel office or in a public agency. Usually, at least in entry-level positions, they specialize in some aspect of the field, such as staffing, test development, job analysis and evaluation, affirmative action compliance, contract negotiation or administration, training and development, or pay and benefits. In smaller jurisdictions or agencies, the personnel function may be part of another job, and this provides basic exposure and experience.

While the personnel specialist's work involves primarily civil service systems and the employees working in them, it includes other systems as well—collective bargaining, affirmative action, political appointments, alternative mechanisms for providing public services (such as outsourcing), and **flexible employment relationships** (such as exempt positions, temporary, and part-time employment).

While all students of public personnel management need to know something about the job of the personnel manager as part of learning about the field, some students have a more specific interest—they want a job. Thus, their interest in what public personnel managers do is followed by two other questions: As a student, what courses should I be taking to qualify myself for a job as a public personnel manager? As a first-time job applicant, how do I get a job?

While public personnel management is a profession, it is also a profession of generalists in that people become public personnel managers through a variety of career paths. Most have some formal academic training, undergraduate and/or graduate, in public management or business administration. This may include course work in personnel management from a private-sector perspective; or in public personnel management from the perspective of civil service and collective bargaining systems. There are specialized graduate curricula in personnel management taught by a number of programs; information on public administration programs can be obtained from the **National Association for Schools of Public Affairs and Administration (NASPAA)**; information on business administration programs can be obtained through the **American Association for Schools and Colleges of Business (AACSB).**

In addition to required courses in human resource management, many graduate programs also include a specialization area in human resource management. While the content of programs differs among institutions, common topics in a specialization are included, either as separate courses or as elements in a curriculum.

1. *Administrative law:* impact of rules and regulations on public administration, including personnel management.
2. *Collective bargaining:* impact of unions on public personnel management, legal and political antecedents, contract negotiation and administration procedures.
3. *Test development:* development and validation of devices for selection, promotion, and placement (sometimes taught by psychology).
4. *Pay and benefits:* job analysis, classification, and evaluation; setting wages and salaries through job evaluation and/or market surveys; statutorily required employee benefits (workers' compensation, Social Security), and optional ones (health insurance, pensions, etc.).
5. *Training and employee development:* design, implementation and evaluation of orientation, training, and career development programs.
6. *Affirmative action compliance:* work force diversity, equal employment opportunity, affirmative action, and employment equity without respect to gender, race, national origin, age, religion, or disability.
7. *Organizational development and change:* assessing organizational performance, and changing structure and culture to make it more effective.
8. *Role of women and minorities:* changing organizational culture to make it more equitable for women and minorities.
9. *Personnel policies and procedures:* "topics" courses specializing current policy issues (such as workforce diversification, workplace violence, alcohol and drug abuse, and life-threatening diseases).
10. *Productivity improvement:* How to make organizations more efficient and effective through the application of policy-analytic techniques.
11. *Comparative or development administration:* offered through public administration, business administration, economics, or international relations programs.
12. Alternatives to civil service: use of alternative organizations or mechanisms for providing public services, or of flexible employment relationships for public employees.

University training (a BPA, a Master's degree, or even a graduate professional certificate program in public personnel management) will give personnel specialists added knowledge that can enhance their performance as specialist, professional, mediator, or human resource management expert, thereby enhancing their career options. And because public personnel functions also involve other besides personnel specialists (such as managers, supervisors, and appointed officials) many human resource managment courses have more general usefulness for anyone considering a career in public policy or management.

Those without significant personnel management experience may have a harder time breaking into the field. Worldwide changes in labor markets, plus the changing political conditions under which public administrators work today, mean that there is more competition for professional jobs in many fields, including public personnel management. Often, recent college graduates without significant public personnel management experience are competing against experienced professionals who are on the job market because they have been laid off (or, if you prefer current terminology, "outplaced" or "reengineered" out of their jobs). Under pressure to "do more with less," employers will seek to hire employees who will not incur start-up costs. They may prefer to hire the experienced professional over the recent graduate. How do you "get your foot in the door" under these conditions?

The first suggestion is to take courses as part of your university education that provide you with knowledge and abilities needed by public personnel managers, particularly the entry-level positions discussed above. Take enough courses (usually semester credit hours) and the right courses so that you can apply for a major, a minor, or a certificate in human resource management or personnel management.

Second, include an internship as part of your university curriculum. Make sure it is with an organization that is looking for employees—one that uses internship programs as a recruitment mechanism rather than just a source of temporary, free labor. Your best gauge of this is by asking your university's internship placement coordinator, your professors, or current employees who started work there as interns.

While a formal internship option may not be feasible for the mid-career student, expressing interest and aptitude on-the-job may help with a lateral transfer into personnel work. With some creative thinking and job design it may be possible to share some time in the personnel office or to gain experience by seeking out personnel-related tasks in your own office.

Third, tailor your résumé so it highlights the education, experience, skills, and knowledge needed for a job in personnel management. Identify related courses in management, computer sciences, statistics, psychology, law, or other fields.

Fourth, practice applying for jobs and taking interviews so you know how to respond to questions interviewers ask. Why do you want this job? What work experience have you had that shows your aptitude or ability for personnel work? If you lack related experience, what skills and abilities do you have that would make it easy to learn? Why are you the best candidate for the position? Good luck!

TAKING CHARGE OF YOUR OWN CAREER DEVELOPMENT AS A PROFESSIONAL PUBLIC PERSONNEL MANAGER

Any preprofessional training begins to become obsolete the moment the course is over. Clearly, it is incumbent upon personnel professionals to take charge of their own self-development through continued self-study and career development. Some suggested sources public personnel managers can use as individuals to enhance their own skills and abilities are professional associations, research libraries, and the Internet.

Professional Associations

Professional associations offer the opportunity to network with other professionals locally, to attend national and regional conferences, and to receive free member services such as newsletters or professional journals. All of these offer continued education and career advancement options for working professionals.[12]

Universities, professional associations, and private professional development institutes provide training courses and seminars for public personnel practitioners. Check the continuing studies or university outreach programs of local universities, or the calendars of local chapters of professional associations.

Research Libraries

Research libraries are indispensable for students or practitioners seeking to keep their knowledge of law and practice up to date. People tend to think of libraries as places where books are kept, but in reality, the past ten years has witnessed their transformation into sources of information, much of it stored or transmitted electronically rather than on paper. A generation ago, students researched papers by checking books out of the library, or by photocopying journal articles. They took the materials home, wrote a draft of the paper, and typed the final copy. Books are a good source of historical data, but they are rarely useful for researching current topics because the long lead time between writing and publication (usually a minimum of two years). Books are cataloged by subject area, usually according to the Library of Congress cataloging system.

Research is totally different today. It's possible to research excellent papers without using books at all, by utilizing alternative information sources: **reference books,**[13] looseleaf services, indexes, professional journals, and government documents. **Looseleaf services** are serial publications issued on a regular basis to provide researchers, lawyers, and practitioners with current information on specified areas of personnel practice and procedure.[14] **Indexes** are bound books or CD-ROM disks that provide bibliographic sources on human resource management topics from a range of professional journals and other periodicals. Data are arranged so that references may be located by author, publication, key word, and so on. They are published monthly, quarterly, or annually.[15] Many professional associations publish **professional journals** to keep members informed about current law, practice, innovations, and issues in the field. These are sent to members or are available through research libraries. Generally, periodicals in the human resource management area are found in the HF5549.5 area (Library of Congress cataloging system).[16] The federal government, and many state and local governments, routinely send publications to so-called repository libraries throughout the country. These **government documents** are sometimes hard to locate because they are not indexed by Library of Congress codes (as are books and professional journals). But reference librarians can help you if you can't locate what you need through the indexes of public documents.[17] Or you may contact these agencies directly to request specific documents—most are free or low-cost.[18]

It's also possible to research a popular current topic through newspapers and magazines. While the quality of news magazines and newspapers is uneven, some periodicals (such as *The New York Times* and *The Wall Street Journal*) are noted for their thoughtful, well-researched coverage. Frequently, this is the only source you can use for current topics, as the lead time to publication in professional journals is often over a year. Some periodicals (including the two mentioned above) have their own indexes. If your library subscribes to a comprehensive index of periodicals (such as **LEXIS/NEXIS**), you will be able to search the whole universe for material on a specific topic. Some popular magazines are also indexed in the indexes mentioned previously.

Doing Research through the Information Superhighway

While it is of course possible to do research by visiting the library and browsing through these information sources there, all this information—and a lot more—is available on the information superhighway (**Interne**t). This is the global information network that connects the researcher with a wealth of electronic information. All you need is an office or home computer, a phone line with a modem, and communications software (which may even be provided free by your university or your employer. Using these tools, it's possible to use four major applications of the Internet: e-mail, listservs, gophers, and web sites (home pages).[19]

E-mail (short for **electronic mail**) is fundamental to Internet connections, since it provides the computer address from which and to which electronic messages are sent. Electronic messages are sent from one computer to another through each computer's **modem**, using phone lines as the transmission method across distances. E-mail has several critical advantages over conventional communication by memo, fax, or voice communication by telephone. First, it is paperless, meaning less waste and less transmission time. Second, messages are received and stored automatically for the recipient, who can "pick up the mail" and read it from any software-compatible computer using the individual's e-mail address and a confidential access code. This avoids playing "phone tag," because the complete message or question is stored, waiting to be accessed by the recipient. It also avoids long-distance phone charges since information is transferred instantaneously from computer to computer. Messages can be sent to lists of recipients simultaneously, creating the opportunity for a true communications net among people with common interests.

Listservs are tools which organize and expand the usefulness of e-mail by providing an easy way for persons with common interests to share information. Once people join a listserv, they are automatically sent every message sent on the Internet to every other member of that listserv; and a message they send to that listserv is automatically referred to all other members as well.

The positive implications of the Internet are enormous and obvious. It enables students and scholars to communicate easily and directly around the world. The problems are equally obvious: organization and quality control. With all this data floating around in cyberspace, how do users know where to look for it, and how do they evaluate the correctness or quality of the data out there? **Gophers** are automated retrieval services used to locate materials on a particular subject, using branching logic trees and key-word addresses in a fashion similar to CD-ROM indexes used by reference libraries. Many government agencies, the Library of Congress, and universities engaged in public management research maintain gophers to help scholars find their way around the web.[20] Individuals, organizations, or agencies may create their own **home page,** a web site identified with their particular e-mail address and used to transmit information to users through gophers. For example, readers who wish to ask questions, suggest changes, or communicate information to other readers may do so by contacting either author's e-mail address (klingner@servax.fiu.edu, or nalband@falcon.cc.ukans.edu).

SUMMARY

There are about 18.6 million public employees in the United States. While it is widely believed that most work for the national government in social welfare programs, in fact 15.7 million, including 3.5 million part-time employees, work for state and local governments, primarily in education.

Public personnel management consists of the functions needed to manage human resources in public agencies. These functions are shared among political leaders, line managers and supervisors, and the personnel department. Civil service systems are the predominant public personnel system because they have articulated rules and procedures for performing the whole range of personnel functions. Other systems, though incomplete, are nonetheless legitimate and effective influences over one or more personnel functions. While personnel functions remain the same across different systems, their organizational location and method of performance differ depending upon the system and on the values that underlie it.

Public personnel managers may be viewed as technicians, professionals, mediators, and human resource management specialists. Traditional personnel managers (those who operate within a consensus on one system and its underlying values) tend to define themselves, and to be defined by others, as technical specialists working within a staff agency. Contemporary personnel managers (those who operate as human resource management experts or as mediators among competing systems and values) tend to define themselves, and to be defined by others, as professionals whose role involves a blend of technical skills and ethical decision making.

Public personnel managers normally receive specialized undergraduate or graduate training. But it may take a combination of specialized experience and education to advance into the profession. And rapid changes in the field require lifelong learning and career development through such mechanisms as professional associations, research libraries, and the Internet.

KEY TERMS

affirmative action compliance officer
American Association of Colleges and Schools of Business (AACSB)
American Society for Public Administration (ASPA)
contract specialist
electronic mail (e-mail)
employee assistance program director
ethics
flexible employment relationships
gophers
government documents
home page
human resource management specialist
indexes
International Personnel Management Association (IPMA)
Internet
job analyst
LEXIS/NEXIS
line manager
listservs
looseleaf services
mediator
modem
National Association for Schools of Public Affairs and Administration (NASPAA)
pay and benefits specialist
personnel director
personnel specialist
position classifier
professional association
professional journal
public personnel management
reference books
research library
risk manager
staffing specialist
technician
testing specialist
training and development specialist
work management

DISCUSSION QUESTIONS

1. How many public employees are there? Which functional areas predominate for each level of government?
2. What are the shared roles of political officials, managers, and personnel directors for fulfilling public personnel functions?
3. Describe similarities and differences in the way personnel managers perform their functions in different systems (both the four traditional ones and the two emergent ones).
4. What are the five stages in the development of the role of the public personnel manager? What have been the key components of their role in each stage?
5. Why have public personnel managers continued to perform multiple roles as technicians, professionals, human resource management specialists, and mediators?
6. What knowledge, skills, and abilities does the public personnel manager need?
7. How adequate is the education and training now available to public personnel managers? How would you suggest it be improved?
8. What suggestions would you offer public personnel managers who want to develop professionally? How might they use professional associations, university courses, libraries, and the Internet as part of their professional development plan?

CASE STUDY CHOOSING A MUNICIPAL PERSONNEL DIRECTOR

A south Florida city needed a new personnel director. It published the following advertisement in the local newspaper, and in the *Recruiter* section of the *IPMA Newsletter:*

DIRECTOR OF HUMAN RESOURCES

CITY OF SUNNY SKIES

The city of Sunny Skies is a city of 60,000 with 650 employees. It has a mayor-council form of government. It is primarily residential, with population shifting from older Anglo retirees to a broader mix of working-class families from a range of racial and ethnic groups. The city police department's officers are covered by a collective bargaining agreement with the PBA; a three-year contract was negotiated last year. The city's civil service system covers 400 employees. Others, including all managers, are in exempt positions filled through performance contracts.

The city seeks a human resource director with the proven ability to manage a personnel department responsible for testing, selection, affirmative action, job analysis, salary and benefits, performance evaluation, and collective bargaining. Excellent benefits, including an employer-funded 457 pension program. Salary range $45,000 to $62,000, dependent upon qualifications. Proof of citizenship required. We are a drug-free workplace and an AA/EEO employer.

Two hundred applications were received from all over the United States. Initial screening was conducted by an outside consultant firm, looking for the following minimum qualifications:

1. *Experience:* Ten to fifteen years of progressively responsible personnel experience, including at least three years as a personnel director. Public-sector and municipal experience preferred.
2. *Education:* BA/BS degree in human resource management or a related field (public administration, business administration, organizational psychology). MA/MS in public administration, human resource administration, or related field preferred.

An interview panel was formed, headed by the assistant city manager and included the assistant director of the public works department, a police department major, two personnel managers from other nearby cities, and an outside expert. The panel was representative of the city's employees and labor market, with respect to gender, ethnicity, and race.

After the outside consultant firm had selected the twelve most qualified applicants, the interview panel scheduled appointments with eight of them. Four were interviewed in their local communities through videotape. The interview panel and the videotape operator asked the following questions of each applicant:

PANEL INTERVIEW QUESTIONS

First, tell us something about your career:

1. What is your most innovative accomplishment in your present position? Why is it so significant?
2. Describe the most difficult personnel problem you have encountered in recent years. How did it arise? How did you resolve it? How did you communicate your decision to employees and/or other managers? How did they respond? If you encountered the problem now, how would you handle it differently?
3. What has been your greatest professional disappointment or setback? How did you respond to it? What did you learn from the experience?
4. Where do you see yourself working in five years?

Next, please tell us something about your human resource management style:

5. What kind of supervisor do you like, and why?
6. When evaluating the performance of your subordinates, what factors are most important to you?
7. What methods do you use to keep informed of personnel issues or problems coming up in your organization? How have these methods worked for you?
8. What do you perceive affirmative action to be? What general policies do you establish to achieve it?

Briefly describe your work experience with each of these specific personnel issues:

9. collective bargaining contract negotiations
10. workers' compensation issues or claims
11. termination of civil service employees
12. sexual harassment issues and policies
13. disciplinary action and grievances

If you were personnel director, how would you deal with each of these issues the city now faces?

14. What is your understanding of the drug and alcohol testing and related requirements of the Omnibus Transportation Employee Testing Act of 1991?
15. What is the best balance between flexibility and uniformity of personnel policies and procedures? If you had to, how would you increase uniformity and structure? How would you "sell" these changes to the city manager, the department directors, and employees?
16. The city hires contract attorneys to handle some personnel-related legal issues and handles others in-house through the city attorney. In your view, which issues should be handled which way? If it is determined that the city's reliance on contract attorneys' services is excessive, what would you do to reduce this reliance? What in-house resources (financial and personnel) would you need to do this? How long would it take?
17. As a representative of the city in contract negotiations, you may be required to conduct collective bargaining negotiations when you do not have authorization to offer a COLA increase or any other increase in benefits to the union. Have you ever been in such a situation? How would you conduct the negotiation?

18. The city manager has asked you to evaluate the city's classification and pay plan. It appears that the shrinking tax base could result in civil service layoffs due to possible budget shortfalls. If cuts could not be met through attrition or by not filling vacant positions, what alternatives to layoffs are there? If layoffs are unavoidable, how would you do them?
19. Bringing employees on the job after their interviews sometimes takes several months. What timetable is reasonable? What possible methods would you consider to expedite the hiring process?
20. A promotional exam was administered, and an eligibility list established and published, for a contractually covered position. A person on that list approaches you and claims that the employee at the top of the list is believed to have been given answers to the questions by the department head of the unit in which the promotional position exists. What would you do?
21. A female employee tells you in confidence that she feels she is being sexually harassed by a male co-worker. The harassment involves unwanted and unsolicited sexual remarks, and some nonsexual touching. She has not mentioned this problem to anyone else. She insists that she wants no action taken against the offending employee and that she can handle the situation on her own. What do you do?
22. Same as above, except now the offending party is her immediate supervisor. Would you handle the issue any differently?
23. The city has several different types of employees (civil service, contract, no benefits, etc.). Performance evaluation and reward systems differ for each group, which causes frustration for employees and equity issues for the personnel department. What would you do about this, if anything?

In closing:

24. What knowledge, skills and abilities make you the most qualified candidate for this position?
25. If you were offered the job today, when would you be able to start?
26. What questions, if any, do you want to ask us about the job or the city?

After reading this case study, answer the following questions:

1. Why did the City receive 200 applicants for the position? How qualified are the top applicants likely to be?
2. What are the primary job duties? What do you think the human resource director will spend most of his or her time doing?
3. What specific knowledge, skills, or abilities is the city looking for?
4. Which of these knowledge, skills, or abilities are likely to be gained through formal education and degrees? Which through experience?
5. What knowledge, skills, or abilities do *you* think are most important for this position? Why?

EXERCISE: A SELF-DEVELOPMENT PLAN FOR A PUBLIC PERSONNEL MANAGER

Assume you are a personnel specialist now employed by the city of Sunny Skies. You earned a BPA (Bachelor of Public Administration) degree four years ago. After looking for work for six months, you landed a job as a half-time intern in the personnel department. Six months later, a full-time vacancy was announced and you got the job on a probationary basis. Thus far, you have been working as a personnel technician with responsibilities for civil service recruitment and testing, job reclassification requests, and payroll and benefits administration. All of your work has been under the general supervision of personnel specialists in staffing, job analysis, and payroll.

Now you want to increase your professional capabilities by adding skills and abilities that are in demand, either in Sunny Skies or another public personnel department. Using the previous case study as a guide, answer the following questions:

1. What knowledge, skills, or abilities do you consider most important to add, given your own education and experience?
2. How would you go about adding them, given your present circumstances?
3. Once you had them, what jobs would you consider yourself eligible to apply for?
4. How would you hunt for a job in the field of public personnel management if you had to do so today?

NOTES

[1] U.S. Bureau of the Census (1994). *Public employment: 1992.* Series GE-92-1. Washington, DC: U.S. Government Printing Office, pp. v-vi.

[2] *Ibid.*, p. ix.

[3] National Performance Review (1993). *Reinventing human resource management.* Washington, DC: Office of the Vice President.

[4] Mosher, F. (1982). *Democracy and the public service* (2nd ed.). New York: Oxford University Press.

[5] Bennis, W., and B. Nanus (1985). *Leaders: The strategies for taking charge.* New York: Harper & Row.

[6] Klingner, D. (September 1979). The changing role of public personnel management in the 1980s. *The Personnel Administrator,* 24, 41-48; and Nalbandian, J. (Spring 1981). From compliance to consultation: The role of the public personnel manager. *Review of Public Personnel Administration,* 1, 37-51.

[7] Dertouzos, M., and J. Moses (Eds.). (1980). *The computer age: A twenty-year view.* Cambridge, MA: MIT Press.

[8] U.S. Congress, House Committee on Science, Space and Technology (1992). *The power of video teleconferencing: Changing the way we do business.* Hearings of November 6, 1991. Washington, DC: U.S. Government Printing Office.

[9] Downs, A. (1982). 2076—A look at the third century. Conference Presentation, University of Chicago Policy Studies Symposium. Washington, DC: The Brookings Institution.

[10] Ferguson, M. (1980). *The aquarian conspiracy.* Los Angeles, CA: J.P. Tarcher; and Naisbitt, J. (1980). Megatrends (2nd ed.). New York: Warner.

[11] Goldberg, A. (Ed.). (1988). *A history of personal workstations.* Reading, MA: Addison-Wesley.

[12] Chief among these are the International Personnel Management Association (IPMA), 1617 Duke Street, Alexandria, Virginia 22314, (703) 549-7100; the American Society for Public Administration (ASPA), Section on Personnel Administration and Labor Relations (SPALR), 1120 G Street, NW, Suite 700, Washington, DC 20005, (202) 393-7878; and the National Academy of Public Administration, 1120 G Street, NW, Suite 850, Washington, DC 20005-3801, (202) 347-3190.

[13] Good public personnel management reference books are:

American Salaries and Wages Survey HD4973.A67
The Compensation Handbook HF5549.5C67H36 1991
Consultants and Consulting Organizations Directory HD69.C6R4C647
Employee Benefits Dictionary HD4928.N6B75 1992
Inter-City Cost of Living Index HD6977.C63
Job Analysis Handbook for Business, Industry and Government HF5549.5.J6J63 1988
Occupational Outlook Handbook HD8051.A62
Occupational Outlook Quarterly DOC PER L2.70/4
Occupational Safety and Health HD7654.P43 1985
Training and Development Organizations Directory HD30.42.U5T72

[14] Looseleaf services. Current employment law on personnel policy and practice areas; published by West, Bureau of National Affairs (BNA), Prentice Hall (PH), and Commerce Clearing House (CCH). Examples:
Americans with Disabilities BNA Vol. 1-present BUS KF3469.A5A45
Collective Bargaining Negotiation & Contracts BNA BUS HD6500.B8
EEOC Compliance Manual CCH BUS KF3464.A6C6
EEOC Decisions CCH BUS KF3464.A56E65
Employment Practices Decisions CCH Vol. I-present BUS KF3464.A6E46
Employment Practices Guide CCH BUS KF3464.A5C65
Fair Employment Practice Cases BNA Vol. 1-present 3 BUS KF3464.A6E46
Human Resources Management CCH HF5549.H865
Individual Employment Rights Cases BNA Vol. 1-present BUS HD6971.8.I5
Individual Retirement Plans CCH BUS KF3510.A6I5
Labor Arbitration Reports BNA Vol. 56-present
Labor Relations Reference Manual BNA Vol. 61-present BUS HD5503.A7224
Labor Relations Reporter BNA BUS KF3385.L3
Occupational Safety & Health Cases BNA Vol. 1-present BUS KF3568.A2B87
Occupational Safety & Health Reporter BNA 1973-present BUS KF3570.Z9B9
Payroll Management Guide CCH BUS KF6436.A6C6
Pension Plan Guide CCH BUS HD7106.U5C6
Wage and Hour Cases BNA Vol. 19-present BUS HD4974.W3

[15] Indexes: bound books or CD-ROM disks. Examples: *ABI/Inform; Business Periodicals Index* (HF5001.B845); *Personnel Management Abstracts* (HF5549.P452); *PAIS (Public Affairs Information Service)* (H1.B8); *Psychological Abstracts* (BF1.P652); *Social Sciences Index* (H1.S63); and *Sociological Abstracts* (HM1.S67).

[16] Professional journals: *Review of Public Personnel Administration; Public Personnel Management; American Review of Public Administration, Personnel Journal, Compensation and Benefits Review, Training and Development Journal; Public Productivity Review,* the *IPMA Newsletter,* and *Public Administration Review.*

[17] Indexes to government documents: *Government Publications Index, Government Periodical Index, Congressional Masterfile, and Statistical Masterfile.*

[18] Suggested agencies are:

The U.S. Office of Personnel Management (OPM)
Office of Systems Innovation and Simplification
1900 E Street, NW
Washington, DC 20415-0001
(202) 653-2511

U.S. Merit Systems Protection Board (MSPB)
Office of Policy and Evaluation
1120 Vermont Avenue, NW
Washington, DC 20419
(202) 653-7208

U.S. Equal Employment Opportunity Commission (EEOC)
Office of Communications and Legislative Affairs
1801 L Street, NW
Washington, DC 20507
(800) 669-EEOC

[19] Krol, E. (1994). *The whole internet user's guide & catalog.* Sebastopol, CA: O'Reilly & Associates; Maxwell, B. (1997). *How to access the government's electronic bulletin boards: Washington online.* Washington, DC: Congressional Quarterly.

[20] Examples of public management-oriented gophers are "gopher.unomaha.edu" (University of Nebraska at Omaha), and "marvel.loc.gov" (Library of Congress).

3

Budgeting, Planning, and Productivity

Through the budget process, political differences are debated and transformed into new, expanded, reduced, or eliminated government programs. The budget preparation and approval process brings human resource management into a larger political context. Because pay and benefits can constitute some 70 percent of an agency's budget, the most vital budgetary items often are the number of personnel and the costs associated with their employment. **Human resource planning** is that aspect of public personnel management that mediates between the external political environment and core activities such as job analysis, job classification, job evaluation, and compensation. In brief, human resource planning matches "wish lists" proposed by agency managers with political realities generated by projected revenues and political philosophies and goals. The process begins with a request to line managers from the budget office: "What kind and how many positions do you need in order to meet program objectives?" It ends with legislative authorization of programs and funds connected to these requests and others initiated at the legislative level.

Refusals to allocate requested funds focus attention on doing more with less or simply the desire to reduce the size and scope of government. At best this stimulates productivity with innovations in service delivery, technology, and personnel practices; but in many cases it also has resulted in decreased quality and quantity of public services.

By the end of this chapter, you will be able to:

1. Explain why budgeting and financial management are of critical importance to public personnel management.
2. Describe the role of the public personnel manager in the budget preparation, approval, and management process.
3. Describe various methods of forecasting future human resource needs.
4. Evaluate the pressures for downsizing and impact of uncertainty on the human resource planning process; and assess its impact on underlying values.

5. Define productivity as efficiency, effectiveness, and responsiveness.
6. Discuss the pros and cons of contracting with private firms for public services.
7. Identify ways of expanding the personnel manager's role in productivity programs.

THE CRITICAL LINK: WHY BUDGETING AND FINANCIAL MANAGEMENT ARE ESSENTIAL TO PUBLIC PERSONNEL MANAGEMENT

A **budget** is a document that attempts to reconcile program priorities with projected revenues. It combines a statement of organizational activities or objectives for a given time period with information about the funds required to engage in these activities or reach these objectives. A budget has many purposes: information, control, planning, evaluation.[1]

Purposes of a Budget

Historically, the most important purpose of a public-sector budget has been external control—that is, limiting the total resources available to an agency and preventing expenditure for activities or items not allowed by law. This control has applied to both money and jobs. The type of budget used for control purposes is called a *ceiling budget*: It controls an agency directly by specifying limits to expenditures through appropriations legislation or indirectly by limiting agency revenues.

Other types of budgets have been developed for different purposes. A line-item budget, which classifies expenditures by type, is useful for controlling types of expenditures as well as their total amount. Performance and program budgets are useful for specifying the activities or programs on which funds are spent, and thereby assist in their evaluation. By separating expenditures by function (such as health or public safety) or by type of expenditure (such as personnel and equipment) or by source of revenue (such as property tax or user fees), administrators and legislators can keep accurate records of an agency's financial transactions for the maintenance of efficiency and control.

Budgeting is like a game in that its participants, rules, and time limits usually are known in advance by all players.[2] The primary participants are interest groups (including employees), public agency administrators, the chief executive, and legislatures and their committees.

Shared Roles: Preparation Approval, Management and Audit

Although each participant's game plan will differ with circumstances, each has a generally accepted role to play. Interest groups exert pressure on administrators and legislators to propose or expand favorable programs. Department administrators use these pressures and their own sense of their department's goals and capabilities to develop proposals and specify the resources (money, time, and people) needed to accomplish them. Chief executives coordinate and balance the requests of various departments. After all, resources are limited and departmental objectives should be congruent with the overall objectives of the city, state, or national government. In many cases, the chief executive has a staff agency responsible for informing departments or agencies of planning limitations, objectives, and resource limits. The chief executive presents the combined budget request of all departments within the executive branch to a legislature or board (city council, county commission, state legislature, or Congress).

Legislative action on appropriations requests varies, depending on the legislature's size and the staff's capabilities. At the national and state levels, committees consider funding requests from various agencies. These committees examine funding requests in the light of prior expenditures, testimony from department heads and lobbyists, and the committee members' own feelings about the comparative importance of the agency's programs and objectives. Appropriations requests are approved (reported out of committee) when the committee agrees on which programs should be funded, and on the overall level of funding.

The entire legislature usually approves committee proposals, unless the funding relates to programs that affect the interests of groups that have not expressed their opinions adequately during committee hearings. Legislation authorizing new programs is usually considered separately from bills that appropriate funds for those programs.

In an elementary view, after new programs are authorized, funded, and signed into law, the executive branch is responsible for executing them. The chief executive is responsible for administering the expenditure of funds to accomplish the objectives intended by the legislature; department administrators are responsible for managing their budgets and programs accordingly. **Financial management** is the process of developing and using systems to ensure that funds are spent for the purposes for which they have been appropriated. Through an accounting system, each agency keeps records of financial transactions and compares budgets with actual expenditures. Agency managers engage in financial management when they take steps to limit expenditures, when they transfer funds from one budget category to another to meet program priorities, or when they borrow or invest idle funds.

Audit, the last step in the budget cycle, is the process of ensuring that funds were actually spent for the intended purpose and in the prescribed manner. Controller's offices inside the organization, and auditors outside, review expenditures for compliance with legislative mandates and prescribed procedures. In the case of waste, fraud, and abuse, agencies may be required to return funds; and responsible officials may be subject to organizational reprimand and criminal prosecution by state authorities.

The process of budget preparation, approval, and management is shown in Figure 3-1. This process is a recurrent ritual whose frequency depends on the length of the appropriations cycle. Most governments budget annually, although the problems associated with continually developing and evaluating programs have led many state legislatures to develop biennial budgets (every two years). In

FIGURE 3-1 The Budget Process (*Source*: Donald E. Klingner, *Public Administration: A Management Approach* © 1983 by Houghton Mifflin, Boston, Mass. All rights reserved)

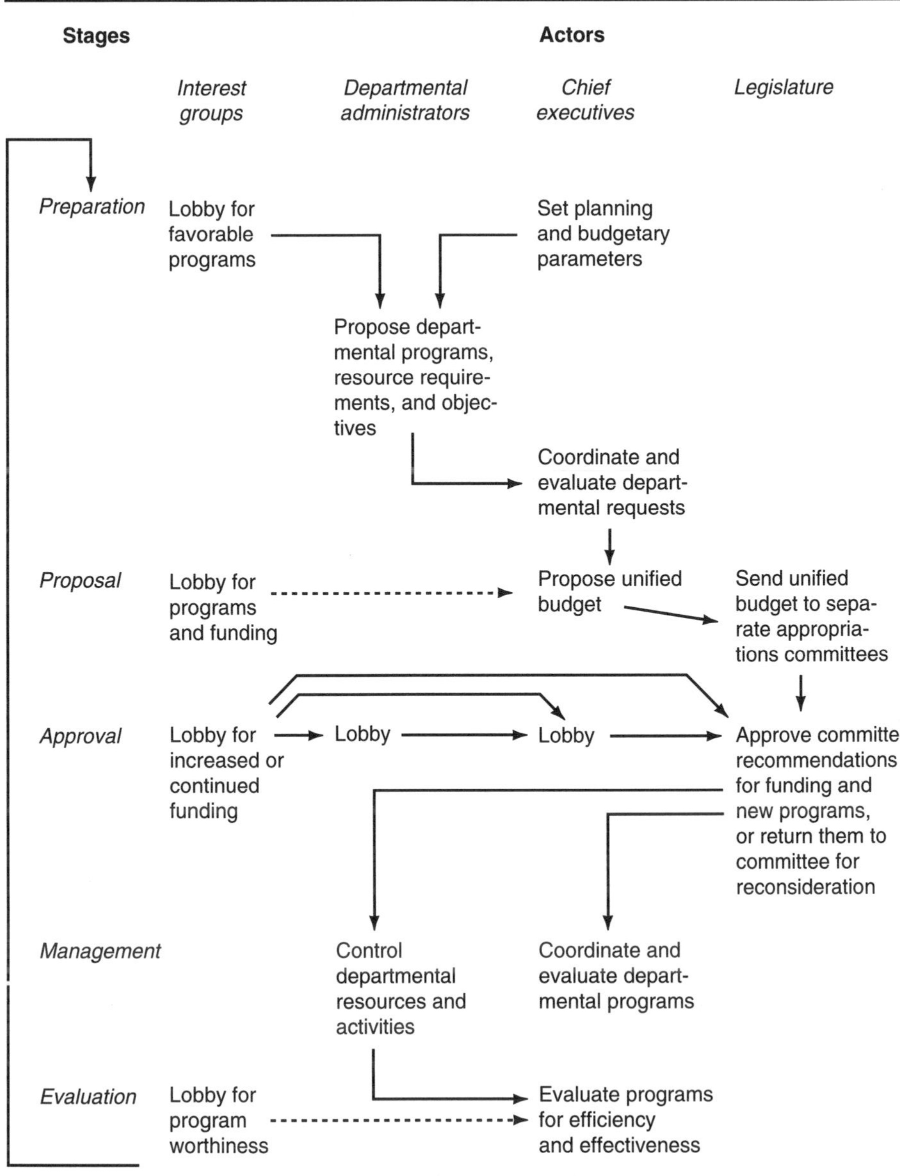

the typical annual budget cycle, an agency or a department normally is developing the next year's budget a year in advance of the period for which it is requesting funds. At the same time, it is also evaluating programs from the prior year. Figure 3-2 represents the time frame within which annual budgets occur. Although most governments follow an annual cycle, their budget years begin and end on different dates. Most state governments use a fiscal year beginning July 1 and ending June 30, while the federal government's fiscal year begins October 1 and ends September 30. Other governments use a calendar year, January 1 to December 31.

Budgeting, then, is the process by which general policy objectives are translated into specific programs, with funds allocated for their accomplishment. Financial management and auditing are the means by which expenditures are limited to those purposes. These practices are therefore at the heart of the resource allocation process, and they constitute a key relationship between politics and public administration. The budget preparation and approval process is complex. It can be viewed politically as a contest among opposing agencies for scarce resources; organizationally as the formal set of policies and procedures that govern the approval process; or informally as a ritualized interaction among the conflicting expectations of program managers, political executives, legislators, and lobbyists.

The less revenue available, the more contentious the budgeting process with access to legislators and legislative committees a scarce resource. Furthermore, where anti-government emotion infuses legislative sessions, the stakes are high for agency administrators who see their agency's programs threatened with reduction, elimination, or transfer to the private/nonprofit sectors. Budgeting is likely to become much more "political" in this context, with decisions made more on philosophical inclination or particularized interests than on rational and analytic planning that administrators are more comfortable with.

FIGURE 3-2 The Budget Cycle (*Source*: Donald E. Klingner,. *Public Administration: A Management Approach*. Copyright © 1983 by Houghton Mifflin Company. Used with permission.)

	Prior year (*Jan. Apr. Jul. Oct.*)	*Current year* (*Jan. Apr. Jul. Oct.*)	*Proposed year* (*Jan. Apr. Jul. Oct.*)
Prior year's budget	Management	Evaluation	
Current year's budget	Preparation / Proposal / Approval	Management	Management
Proposed year's budget		Preparation / Proposal / Approval	Management

THE ROLE OF THE PERSONNEL DIRECTOR IN BUDGET PREPARATION, APPROVAL, AND MANAGEMENT

The role public personnel managers play in the budget preparation and approval process combines their staff responsibility of assisting other department heads, and their line responsibility of directing their own departments. Their staff responsibility is to work with department heads so that budget requests will conform to personnel policy and practices and will reflect the hiring or downsizing needs of agencies. For example, a city police chief may have received a mandate from the city council to "put a hold on crime." Translated into budget terms, this may mean that the council is willing to allocate additional money to hire more police officers. Working with the chief executive officer and the personnel and budget departments, the police department will analyze staffing, examine the classification scheme to determine the salary associated with each new position, and determine total costs including wages, benefits, uniform allowances, recruitment, training, and equipment. Then the department will develop a request reflecting the combined analysis and possibly the political realities of the budget process in order to anticipate the city council's reaction. The police chief will submit the request to the city manager (or mayor), who then reviews it against other council priorities and revenue projections, and forwards it to the council, or appropriate council committee, as part of a total proposed budget.

The second major budget preparation function of a personnel director is to develop and defend the budget needed to provide support services to other departments: human resource planning, recruitment and selection, job analysis and classification, operation of the payroll and benefits system, training and orientation, performance evaluation, grievances and disciplinary action, and collective bargaining. For example, in a metropolitan area comprised of many local governments, personnel managers will commonly conduct an annual or semiannual wage and salary survey to determine the pay scales for certain positions common to all jurisdictions. These data will then be used to make recommendations to the city manager concerning whether or not pay rates should be changed, or to support the government's position in salary negotiations with a union. Or the city may need to develop new job descriptions or testing procedures as a result of affirmative action pressure. The cost of these activities, including their rationale, is presented by the personnel director to the city manager. In this respect, the personnel director functions as a line manager.

Because pay and benefits constitute such a large proportion of an agency's budget, human resource managers as well as budget officers are heavily involved in budget management throughout the year. In this instance, agency managers and supervisors play the primary role because they are responsible for controlling and reallocating human resources to meet program priorities within budget constraints. Agency personnel managers respond to the priorities set by managers by filling positions, paying employees, and otherwise implementing their decisions. However, they also monitor accident rates that affect worker compensation premiums and use of health-care benefits for their impact on future insurance premiums.

In a cutback situation, agency personnel managers may have to help prepare plans to reduce personnel expenditures. These plans commonly include freezes on hiring and promotions and cutbacks on hours worked, proposed reductions in benefits, and contracting out for services previously provided by government and the replacement of permanent workers with part-time or temporary employees.

An example of the linkages between budgeting, productivity, and a human resource information system might focus on whether cost reductions can beneficially occur through an early retirement program. The pension costs, lump-sum payouts, payouts for sick leave, and loss of valued knowledge, skills, and abilities have to be weighed against the lower salaries and benefits of younger workers who might need to be added. Recruitment, selection, and training costs of newer workers have to be calculated as well, along with the newer knowledge that they might bring to the workplace.

VARIOUS TECHNIQUES FOR FORECASTING HUMAN RESOURCE NEEDS

The budget preparation and approval process is, in effect, the "engine" that forces legislative and executive decisions on programs and expenditures. While the budget is a central policy-making and control mechanism, human resource planning would be incomplete if it did not include a concern for the interaction among goals, budget, position allocations, workforce skills and competencies, and final products or services.[3]

Given the extent to which public agency expenditures are comprised of pay and benefits, and the use of personnel ceilings to control agency activity, human resource planning is the means by which public officials use the budget to allocate resources among competing priorities and programs.

In addition, human resource planning relates to two other important allocation and planning activities: job analysis and classification, and compensation and benefits. By establishing the duties and qualifications for positions, job analysis allows positions to be classified by type of occupation and level of difficulty. This in turn enables uniform and equitable pay and benefit programs to be established for each position. Without these two additional steps, it would not be possible for human resource planners to use forecasts to estimate human resource costs.

Because of the uncertainty surrounding the planning function, most human resource planning is done incrementally. But in some cases, the need for planning is so great that analytical methods must be employed even if the past is not a good predictor of the future because the contemporary economic, political, social, and technological environment is changing so rapidly. Large metropolitan police departments or the U.S. military, for example, simply cannot do human resource planning incrementally without inviting chaos in training, equipment budgets, supervisory capacity, career ladders, or racial tensions.

The primary goal of human resource planning is to match the demand for employees with the supply. In budgetary crises this requires cutbacks; in times of growth or changes in priorities, obviously, a government must plan for new employees. The larger the government unit, the more important it is to anticipate not only personnel needs but also the available supply of labor. Will the knowledge, skills, and abilities be available in the market when the public employer needs them? Again, in larger government units the public personnel manager could work with department heads and the budget office to forecast future human resource needs and then use these combined estimates to develop a coordinated staffing program for the agency or government.

Incrementalism (or **decrementalism**) is a forecasting method that projects straight-line changes in personnel needs based on various factors that influence the quality and quantity of service delivery. The defining characteristic of incrementalism in **human resource**s **forecasting** and planning is its assumption that goals and purposes remain the same or will change only marginally. For example, an incremental human resource plan might call for a 5 percent increase in the number of positions allocated to each organizational unit for each 5 percent increase in population served. Similarly, a 5 percent increase in revenues might trigger requests for more personnel incrementally. A decremental plan might call for a 5 percent reduction in personnel for a 5 percent reduction in population served or revenue shortfall. Neither one is very effective as a comprehensively rational forecasting technique because both assume no changes in policy goals and purposes, and therefore project no changes in the kinds of people that may need to be hired or laid off.[4] The simplest version of incrementalism, and often the most frustrating to agency staff, is when the chief administrative officer asks the governing body what they want to see in the next budget, and the governing body members respond based on a few vocal citizen complaints rather than on a more deliberative process weighing alternatives and opportunity costs.

The most widely used forecasting technique is **collective opinion**. It involves first gathering information from a variety of sources inside and outside the agency and then reaching a group consensus about the interpretation of these data. Some information sources are shown in Table 3-1.

This information could relate to such external factors as enabling legislation, budgetary and personnel ceilings, changes in agency structure or objectives, affirmative action goals, collective bargaining, or pressures for political responsiveness.

TABLE 3-1 Sources of Information

Location of source	*Relationship*	*Sources of Information*
Outside agency	Personal	Clients, legislators, lobbyists, other agency administrators
	Impersonal	Newspapers, budget hearings, professionl conferences, polls
Inside agency	Personal	Subordinates, supervisors, co-workers
	Impersonal	Meetings, conferences

Source: Reprinted from Donald E. Klingner, *Public Administration: A Management Approach* 1983 by Houghton Mifflin, Boston, MA.

Internal factors might include current human resource utilization, projected staffing needs, or shifts in program priorities. For example, a group of agency personnel directors might conclude that a new state law requiring the issuance of environmental impact permits for beach-front developers, and the funding of the program for a certain dollar figure, would require a 20 percent increase in employees for the state environmental management agency over the next three years.

Usually, the incremental and collective opinion approaches to human resource planning process are more political than analytical/rational.[5] That is, new positions are created and abolished as a reaction to legislative funding priorities influenced by agency plans, interest group pressures, political trade-offs, and anticipated revenue, rather than to meet a systematic and multiyear analysis of agency needs and labor market supply.

More rational approaches to human resource planning are available as well. Macro-level **forecasting** techniques such as categorical forecasting and cluster forecasting may be used. *Categorical forecasting* estimates further needs for separate occupational groups, such as doctors, lawyers, and personnel managers. *Cluster forecasting* groups those occupations with common skill requirements and those that are required for other positions to function. These techniques are most often used by larger organizations. Regression analysis is a general statistical tool used with a number of forecasting techniques to estimate the relationships between two or more variables based on past experience. For example, through a regression analysis a personnel manager might estimate that he or she needs to add one job analyst to the personnel department for every 1,000 new employees in the organization, because this is the ratio of analysts to employees needed to handle routine requests for reclassification.

Modeling, or *simulation* forecasting techniques usually require the use of mathematics and computers.[6] The simulation process requires developing a model that duplicates reality with respect to the crucial environmental, organizational, or interpersonal factors affecting a particular agency goal. A model specifies the conditions that affect the relative feasibility of procuring alternative personnel levels and skills. It requires that guidelines be established, current programs identified, and outputs determined. Next, it requires that possible alternative combinations of human resources be substituted to determine their effect on outputs.

For example, a personnel director seeking to estimate future personnel costs for a department might review the turnover rate for secretarial positions. If the rate were 20 percent annually, he or she would conclude that if the number of positions in the agency were to remain constant, one fifth of the secretarial positions would need to be filled annually. Anticipated costs for this activity could then be projected by computing the cost of recruitment, selection, orientation, and training for new employees, minus any salary dollars saved for the time positions were vacant.

Which forecasting technique should be used? Although most organizations will continue to use nonrational, incremental approaches largely geared to revenue forecasts and political interests, rational techniques may be adopted fairly easily by many agencies, particularly those that have adequate and competent staff, sufficient data on current programs and resource requirements, receptive management, and access to sophisticated software.[7] The administrator's skill and commitment to seeking the best solution determines the technique used and its effectiveness in forecasting. While in some cases rational planning is impractical or optional, in others it is a necessity. For example, rational planning is essential in determining staffing and skill requirements in the military where doctrine and force levels are changing, and it is not unusual at the federal level where research is done on overall demographic trends and the implications for the federal civil service.[8]

Having used a variety of techniques to forecast the *demand* for human resources within the agency, managers may use similar techniques to forecast the *supply* of qualified applicants—the potential labor market from which the agency can recruit. This is influenced by a number of factors inside and outside the agency: among them the state of the economy; the level of technology; the educational system; competing employers; the nature of the labor market; the agency's compensation system; the number of vacancies; availability of knowledge, skills, and abilities; training and retraining opportunities; the agency's recruitment practices; affirmative action considerations; and any collective bargaining working rules regarding staffing procedures.

In theory, by subtracting the aggregate *supply* of human resources from the aggregate *demand* for these resources within the organization, human resource planners can compute the *need*. This figure is then used to set up programs and financial mechanisms for acquiring, developing, and utilizing human resources, and this is not as theoretical as it might seem.

For example, even in a municipality of some 100,000, governing board members often find it easier and more comfortable to fund a plan rather than incremental requests. After a while of hearing administrators talk about "using overtime for police foot patrols downtown and losing officers through attrition," the governing body is likely to be receptive to a plan that sets out population growth, police department goals and objectives, and average annual need for new officers. The same is true for a number of departments, like fire and emergency medical services, utilities, and parks and recreation. Some kind of human resource planning will occur by necessity where reductions in revenue are projected, but it is just as important in growth communities so that citizens and governing body members as well as staff can feel like the ship is sailing on a course rather than wherever the wind wants to take it.

On the other hand, in a highly politicized environment where plans are utilized only when they support a partisan majority's interests, it may be rational to establish minimum staffing levels for permanent civil service positions and then respond to shifting political priorities with lower cost, temporary employees. Thus, instead of hiring new police officers, utilizing auxiliary officers might be an option for traffic control.

Human Resource Planning and Other Personnel Activities

Human resource planning provides external legislative control over resources and program priorities through activities like job analysis, classification, and evaluation. But managers must also relate forecasts to other personnel activities—recruitment, performance evaluation, training, selection and promotion, affirmative action, compensation, labor-management relations, and career development.[9]

If governmental goals and community needs are to be anticipated effectively, recruitment must occur far enough in advance to be completed by the time a program must be operational. Given the nature of the labor market for the particular position, this may require that recruiters be given substantial lead time, something not very practical in a changing technological environment and global economy.

If the labor market is a difficult one to recruit in, test-validation specialists may need to assist in developing selection or promotion criteria that screen out unqualified applicants or employees but do not screen out qualified ones as well. If anticipated needs are to be met from within the agency, the personnel department must help develop and encourage a performance evaluation or assessment system to identify qualified employees, and possibly training programs to qualify people for them.

If career development is important, the personnel department can assist employees by identifying model career patterns that they can use to plan their future in the organization. Having identified these patterns, it is then up to the agency to follow through by utilizing its performance evaluation, training, and affirmative action programs to see that employees have a substantial and equitable opportunity to achieve their objectives.

The level of compensation for a position determines the size and quality of the applicant pool. A position characterized by both low salary and benefits in relation to market conditions will be hard to fill with qualified employees, or it will show high turnover as employees become sufficiently qualified to compete for jobs in the private-sector market. The personnel manager can often justify higher salaries by showing that the cost of replacing and training new employees is greater than the cost of a boost in pay and benefits. Compensation and benefits have to be adjusted to meet conditions in the external labor market or the terms of a negotiated collective bargaining agreement. This is particularly true if the employer bargains collectively with multiple employee associations, or if the union representing a group of employees also represents similar employees in nearby competing organizations.

If certain groups are underutilized and this is reflected in the affirmative action objectives of the agency, human resource supply forecasts will have to consider not only the aggregate supply of employees in a particular type of job but also the similarities and differences between this general labor market and the specific market for female or minority group employees and applicants.

UNCERTAINTY IN HUMAN RESOURCE PLANNING AND DOWNSIZING

The cartoons that decorate office cubicles are often clear indicators of the differences between public management theory and practice. As one cartoon states, "It is the objective of all good managers to carefully plan their activities and to effectively allocate available resources based on program priorities—but when you're up to your ass in alligators, it's difficult to remember that your initial objective was to drain the swamp!!"

The contemporary environment in which public managers operate is filled with "alligators"—political and economic constraints that impede their ability to make rational and reflective choices. Here are several examples of how the contemporary environment negatively influences human resource planning.

The first involves the hiring of new police officers. Shortages of police officers and concerns about public safety have led to a political climate conducive to the hiring of new officers. In large municipalities, implementing this public policy initiative highlights the importance and difficulty of good planning. Mahtesian reports that "Too often, a rush to put police officers on the street has significantly diluted the quality of individual police departments."[10] He cites the cases of Washington, DC, and Miami, where political pressure to put new officers on the streets resulted in haphazard background checks and inadequate training to meet goals and timetables. Further, once on the street, supervision and oversight were lacking due to an overload of new officers in relation to the number of supervisors.

According to Mahtesian, in Houston the process has gone more smoothly but not without problems. While Houston has managed the training challenge, it has not been able to do as well integrating the racially diverse group of newcomers into a largely Anglo force. "While HPD [Houston Police Force] is looking for a few good men and women, it wants most of them to be brown or black."[11] Apparently, the faster HPD has moved to diversify in order to reflect the racial composition of the citizenry, the more racially divided the police force has become.

In Los Angeles the problem is attrition. *The Los Angeles Times* reports that Mayor Riordan pledged to expand LAPD by 3,000 officers in four years.[12] Frustrating the emphasis on hiring, LAPD is losing nearly 500 officers annually. Disputes over causes of the attrition have pitted the mayor and his aides against LAPD officials. The union has joined as a strained ally of the police chief. The mayor's aides intimate that the problem is with LAPD leadership; LAPD and union officials counter that the problem is with wages and benefits. One consequence of the attrition is that LAPD is financing the training of new officers only to lose many of them to higher-paying suburban police departments.

As a last example of the political forces that affect human resource planning, Los Angeles County's new director of health services finds himself embroiled in turmoil surrounding the composition of health-care agencies in south central Los Angeles.[13] After race riots in the 1960s, King Hospital and Drew Medical Center were established in the riot-torn area of south central Los Angeles. For years a source of community pride, the health facility represented a substantial employer in an African-American-dominated area of the city. Health facilities employees were and still are predominantly African-American. But the area's population has been changing with an influx of Latin American immigrants, and now Latinos are underrepresented by the county's public health-care agencies, and political pressure to diversify the workforce is bubbling hot. This has meant that personnel directors must anticipate not only the mix of skills needed when hiring new employees but also the racial and ethnic makeup of the available applicant pool.

Some commentators emphasize the importance of the "three Rs"—reading, writing, and 'rithmetic—to a high-quality elementary school education. Most public managers have been introduced, usually unwillingly and with much pain, to a different "three Rs" during the past fifteen years—re-engineer, reduce, and re-invent.

With cuts in federal spending, demands on state and local governments escalate. At the same time, taxpayers may resist increases in state and local taxes to pay for services. The problem is worsened by the regressive nature of sales and property taxes, which disproportionately affect the poor but are revenue staples for state and local governments.

Reductions in revenue often mean that public agencies are required to practice **cutback management**. This means that agencies will hire fewer permanent employees, freeze wages, or downsize by eliminating current employees, because such a large portion of a government's budget goes for salaries and benefits, especially in school districts and local governments.

A recent *Wall Street Journal* article reported that in Indianapolis, outsourcing work has reduced public employment 40 percent in three years; similarly, in Sunnyvale, California, 25 percent of the workforce is temporary.[14] Savings in wages and benefits are significant and often result in no reductions in service. But problems can occur when more attention is paid to the revenue side of things rather than service delivery. For example, cuts in the school district's budget results in fewer teachers and larger classes and less variety in course offerings; cuts in the public works department can mean haphazard pothole repair, postponed street maintenance, and less frequent trash pickup; cuts in the police department mean slower responses to calls for service, including 911 calls, less attention to minor crimes, and more time in police cars than in mixing with the community face to face; cuts at the state department of environment will mean reduced enforcement of environmental regulations; and reduction in force at the department of motor vehicles means longer lines.

These reductions in service are unnoticed by citizens until the service is needed, and then the typical response often is a complaint about response time or service quality rather than acknowledgment that lower service levels are a function of lower budgets.

Potentially, one of the benefits of the devolution of government to the local level is the relative ease with which citizens can see the connection between revenue and service. For example, reasonable citizens can understand that expecting a school district to reduce transportation costs while maintaining equity in school boundaries is probably expecting the impossible. The average citizen simply cannot make these kinds of connections with federal revenue and services or programs, making it easier to call for cuts in taxes.

As teachers of government and public servants, we tend to look at calls for layoffs as driven by emotion and faulty common sense. But in part, the **downsizing** movement reflects more fundamental conclusions that citizens have drawn about government. Public issues that they see on television, and read and talk about seem unsolvable, and yet the traditional strategies for dealing with them continues to be funding government programs.

Fundamentally, government must be able to accomplish objectives that individuals are unable to do own their own: build roads, wastewater and water treatment plants; provide public safety and education and so on. When it takes ten years to build a road because of court battles and multi-jurisdictional and agency conflict, when we cannot educate our children to our satisfaction, and when citizens do not feel safe walking public street, the basic reasons for government are questioned. In this context, downsizing seems logical even if all the consequences are not well thought out, and political leadership often follows and leads this sentiment.

At the agency level, the cutback process is felt in several ways. First, it is difficult to cut an agency's programs equitably. Both the contributions of each program to agency goals and the comparative effects of alternative cuts on public services are difficult to measure without resolving the problems related to productivity measurement and program evaluation. Furthermore, many larger agencies are likely to have multiple missions and goals, and it is impossible to assess the contribution of specific programs and divisions to the agency's mission. A second problem, one closely related to the responsibilities of the public personnel manager, is that the easiest methods of reducing agency expenditures are seldom the most appropriate from a productivity or effectiveness standpoint. A **reduction-in-force** could involve across-the-board cuts, hiring freezes, a layoff, or **attrition.** Across-the-board cuts, like the incremental or decremental methods discussed earlier in the chapter, are practical but non-analytic methods of reducing expenditures in the absence of more definitive program evaluation information or non-conflictual politics. And layoffs often result in organizational paralysis, particularly if based on seniority: "Bumping rights" cause productive junior employees to be replaced by disgruntled managers who may lack current technical or professional expertise.

In addition to the convulsive effects of large-scale cutbacks, these allocational decisions spotlight value conflicts. Advocates of fiscal responsiveness and administrative efficiency often advocate downsizing, with consequences sharply felt not only in reduced service levels generally but also by proponents of social equity and individual rights. If the agency has been hiring a high percentage of minorities and/or women to redress previous patterns of discrimination, reductions in force will mean that they are the first to be dismissed, because on the whole they have less seniority than their white male counterparts. As the seniority of the average employee increases, this has consequences for compensation and retirement benefits. Since most employees laid off are at the bottom of the organization, the average grade level of employees also tends to rise

The National Academy of Public Administration recently identified several lessons learned from downsizing experiences.[15] They are:

- "Restructure the organization to reflect the changed mission, staffing levels, and performance expectations before you determine staff reductions—simply cutting staff will only leave fewer employees to do the same amount of work;
- "Target separation incentives to organizations and occupations that will be downsized to minimize loss of skills in key mission areas that will carry on after the downsizing;
- "Tap employee and union knowledge and involvement when planning and undertaking downsizing;

- "Communicating honestly to everyone about the downsizing is critical—in effect, poor communications can turn downsizing into a disaster for morale;
- "Giving as much advanced notice as possible about when, who, how, and why better prepares people for taking action;
- "Use involuntary separations (reductions in force) as necessary due to mission needs or timeframes, but they should be the last resort; and
- "Address the needs of the affected employees including the survivors so that mission objectives and organizational performance are achieved."

The turmoil that results from downsizing and the threat of downsizing, including rumors of downsizing and what unit will be next, affects the psychological nature of the expectations and obligations the employee has of the employer. When it appears to employees that layoffs are scheduled and implemented simply as a means of reducing expenditures without connection to the demand for their services, their individual productivity, or seniority, employees lose any sense of control over their own fate. Normally, you would expect an employee to work harder to keep a threatened job. But where cutbacks are made without reference to individual productivity or some other formula or set of criteria publicly acknowledged, employees are left in a psychological netherworld where their traditional sense that working hard brings rewards is undermined.

Given the problems brought about by any "solution" to cutback management, public personnel managers will find appropriate answers elusive. However, they should recognize their mediating role in arranging compromises among the competing values in this situation. If cuts are inevitable, their impact can be minimized by examining the organizational mission and limiting activities to those programs required by law; or by using the results of rational mechanisms such as cost-benefit analysis or program evaluation. Often, however, cutbacks occur in programs that serve a deserved but politically isolated or unpopular clientele or where outsourcing, privatization, or the hiring of part-timers or temporary employees is feasible.

Maintaining communication with users, clients, and employees is vital to the success of cutback management. At some point those who must bear the consequences of the cutback should be informed fully and frequently about anticipated actions. When clients and employees discover cutback plans on their own, the poor communication or secrecy produces distrust of virtually all elected and administrative officials.

WHAT IS PRODUCTIVITY?

The governmental response to revenue shortfalls has focused attention on the productivity of public employees. For example, the Civil Service Reform Act of 1978 included a pay-for-performance provision designed to motivate and reward superior performance. In addition, experiments with alternative work schedules, assistance programs for employees with drug and alcohol problems, and the innovative design of work to capture the motivation of employees all represent the impact of the efficiency value on public employment.

Alternative Definitions: Efficiency, Effectiveness, and Responsiveness

Various terms like output, performance, efficiency, effectiveness, and "bang for the buck" are commonly associated with **productivity.** Technically, productivity concerns two specific assessments of performance. First, **efficiency** is measured as a ratio of outputs to inputs. In other words, measuring efficiency requires identification of a performance outcome, such as the number of school lunches served in the cafeteria or the number of arrests made by a police officer or police department, and identification of the resources used to produce the outcome, such as employee hours worked or funds allocated to meal service or wages in the police department. The efficiency ratio then becomes:

$$\frac{\text{number of meals served}}{\text{number of cafeteria employee hours worked}}$$

The resultant ratio measures number of meals served per hour worked. Efficiency will increase in either of two ways: by increasing the number of meals served with the same number of employees, or by serving the same number of meals with fewer employees.

In the private sector and in many public-sector cases, efficiency and productivity are synonymous. But what if, in our example, efficiency were increased by serving more meals and making more arrests—yet the meals were unappetizing and not fully consumed and the arrests failed to lead to convictions and instead crowded the courts? Could we say that productivity had improved? Probably not.

Second, productivity implies **effectiveness,** a concern with the quality of the output measured against some standard. Thus, a more valid productivity measure would be:

$$\frac{\text{number of meals consumed}}{\text{number of cafeteria hours worked}}$$

where consumption is distinguished from meal preparation. Similarly,

$$\frac{\text{number of arrests leading to convictions}}{\text{salary and wages of police officers}}$$

attempts to incorporate a quality measure for the original output, number of arrests.

Concerns for efficiency focus attention on input-output ratios and answer the question "Are we getting the most for our money?" Implied in this question is another, "Are we accomplishing the goal we set out to accomplish?" On top of this pyramid of questions is a third, "Is the goal we set out to accomplish worthwhile in light of the other goals we might have chosen?" Question 1 looks at efficiency, question 2 at effectiveness, and question 3 at **responsiveness.**

Thus, in the cafeteria example, the responsiveness question might have been, "Do we want to invest public money in school lunches or library books?" Once this question is answered, the school district can attend to the effectiveness and efficiency questions. Because the responsiveness question requires explicit value judgments resulting in allocational winners and losers, governments frequently focus on efficiency questions—saving money. It is a lot easier and more popular to ask why the superintendent of schools is making $80,000 a year than it is to determine whether the school district should be hiring more teachers or buying more computers. Critical responsiveness questions are often avoided until losses in service become so obvious that explicit discussions of political priorities cannot be avoided.

Examples of Productivity Improvement

Productivity programs seem to cluster into three areas. The first set of projects and innovations involve changes in organizational structure, processes, and operating procedures:

1 Privatization
2. Contracting out
3. Substituting temporary and part-time employees for career employees
4. Reduction-in-force
5. Flexibility in civil service procedures
6. Pooling fiscal accounts to increase interest revenue
7. Selective decentralization or reorganization into homogeneous units
8. Increased use of performance measures and work standards to monitor productivity
9. Consolidation of services
10. Use of economic-rational decision models for scheduling and other problems

A second area includes increased use of technology:

1. Labor-saving capital equipment—shifting from three- and two-person sanitation crews to a one-person side-loaded truck
2. More sophisticated software in areas like record keeping, payroll, and billing
3. Electronic tools for scheduling, tracking of projects, and early warning of problems

The third area includes personnel-related activities:

1. Job simplification
2. Incentive awards
3. Increased sophistication in training
4. Job-related performance appraisal methods
5. Specification of work standards
6. Increased office communication, team building, and organizational development
7. Total quality management
8. Alternative work schedules

These represent the kinds of activities undertaken to increase productivity in the public sector. One popular focus for productivity involves contracting with private firms to provide public services.[16]

PRODUCTIVITY AND PRIVATIZATION: WHAT'S A PERSONNEL MANAGER TO DO?

Why should a city government collect trash when a private vendor could do the same? Why should the government manage lodging and concessions in public parks when private businesses could do the same?

These examples highlight the most popular form of privatization—contracting with private business to deliver services governments have been providing. Governments have contracted with private business for services like street construction and repair, tree trimming and planting, ambulance service, vehicle towing and storage, building and grounds maintenance, data processing, legal services, and tax bill processing.[17]

Human resource directors are not the primary decision makers when privatization is discussed. The discussion is led by elected officials, appointed city managers, and department directors. But personnel directors are often asked to assess the pros and cons of privatization. How should they respond to such requests?

Chandler and Feuille identify four characteristics of the services most frequently contracted for by local governments.[18] First, there is no compelling reason that government deliver the service. Second, there are usually a number of private-sector firms that could supply the service. Third, the service usually requires low levels of skilled labor. Fourth, outputs are usually easy to monitor.

Sharp's literature review shows that contracting out frequently saves public dollars.[19] Advocates claim that firms competing in the marketplace are likely to provide services more efficiently than government monopolies. They also highlight the savings that can be achieved through economies of scale. For example, while one city may be unable to purchase an expensive piece of equipment to repave streets, a private company with contracts to several cities could. Advocates also point out that private companies have more flexible personnel practices, allowing them to hire and lay off employees easily and save money with less generous wages and benefit packages and with more temporary and part-time employees.

According to Sharp, critics assert that privatization may result in cutting corners to maximize profits, provide incentives to deal only with clients who are easy to serve, increase the risk of graft and corruption, and reduce the capacity to deliver the service if privatization does not work. Another concern is that the flexibility which accompanies privatization may release the private firm from obligations to follow open meetings laws and open records acts. Further, privatization confuses questions of accountability. Whom do citizens hold accountable when they are dissatisfied with a service provided by a private firm but contracted for by the government?

Goodman and Loveman claim that the issue of public versus private gets caught up in symbolic and philosophical arguments when the real issue is "under what conditions will managers [whether public or private] be more likely to act in the public's interest. Managerial accountability to the public's interest is what counts most, not the form of ownership."[20] They continue: "Takeover artists like Carl Icahn saw the same excesses in corporations that many people see in governmental entities: high wages, excess staffing, poor quality, and an agenda at odds with the goals of shareholders. Monitoring of managerial performance needs to occur in both public and private enterprises, and the failure to do so can cause problems whether the employer is public or private."[21]

Also, they observe that competition is likely to reduce costs. There is no more reason to believe that the public will benefit from a private monopoly driven by a profit motive than by a public monopoly oriented toward public service. According to Goodman and Loveman, the issue is competition versus monopoly not private versus public.

Contracting out for public services is often a rational way to increase government productivity. It holds the promise of saving tax dollars and providing a reasonable level of service. But in many circles it remains a controversial avenue to productivity enhancement because it involves the reallocation of jobs. Reallocation of jobs from the public to the private sector brings values and personnel systems into conflict and points out the inherently political underpinnings of public personnel policy and administration. For example, those responsible for finances may favor contracting out as a way of averting a costly union contract and work rules. But the loss of public jobs invites the political displeasure of employee unions. Even though many public employees would be hired by the private contractor, unions object strenuously to contracting out because their members will usually find themselves with lower wages and benefits even if they do not lose their jobs.[22]

Social equity may suffer as women and minorities who benefit from gains in government employment find themselves at a disadvantage with employers who might show less commitment to affirmative action and merit. On the other hand, as the Supreme Court has closed the door on opportunities for patronage in government jobs, contracting out provides an opportunity for rewarding political supporters. In large urban areas this may work to the advantage of minority contractors who are politically favored by an administration in power.[23]

While those who advocate contracting out point to "inflexibility" and "red tape" in government personnel systems, merit system protections for the individual rights of public employees suffer with private personnel systems, where grievance procedures are less developed. And, of course, private employers are under no obligation to provide constitutional protections to their employees or to the clients they serve.[24]

While the beginnings of an initiative to contract out a public service may simply reflect a concern to save public dollars, it is worthwhile to remember that jobs are scarce resources in our society. Any attempt to publicly manage their allocation is likely to invite strong reactions from those invested in the current distribution. As we will see throughout this book, those investments reflect fundamental differences in the values that shape public personnel management.

EXPANDING THE PERSONNEL DIRECTOR'S ROLE IN PRODUCTIVITY PROGRAMS

The enthusiasm for productivity improvement in government opens opportunities for an expanded role for the personnel manager. Activities aimed at productivity improvement affect core personnel functions but do not necessarily fall within the formal responsibilities of the personnel department. In the productivity area, line managers connected to technological developments in their field and budget analysts concerned with financial matters consistently play a larger role than personnel specialists. In a way, this role assignment is understandable, since line managers are most familiar with daily operations and because in reality the primary motive of productivity enhancement in the public sector is saving money. In addition, the line manager and the budget analyst are familiar with numbers and ratios and tracking production figures and budgetary accounts throughout the year. Thus, it is very easy for the personnel department to be shut out of the productivity action.

The price for entering this field is expertise that those initially involved in productivity projects will value and subsequently search out. The personnel department has an opportunity to contribute in at least three areas. First, many projects involve some kind of management by objectives and the writing of job standards that specify minimally acceptable work performance. When performance appraisal systems measure what employees actually do rather than the kinds of people they are (dependable, reliable, trustworthy, and so on), there is probably no one more competent to advise on the writing of these performance objectives or standards than the personnel department. The use of the results-oriented job descriptions described in Chapter 4 clearly shows this kind of connection between the formal aspects of personnel administration and productivity improvement. Along similar lines, the personnel department is in a unique position to compare and suggest adjustments in performance standards from different departments within a government jurisdiction. Nothing lowers morale more than an employee's perception that two people who are doing the same kind of work and who are paid the same wages are operating under different job standards.

The second area focuses on productivity improvements directly relating to the motivation of employees. In grouping productivity projects, one cluster centers around issues like work incentives, job design, job-related performance assessments, realistic training goals and workable designs, and alternative work schedules. These kinds of projects are aimed directly at enhancing both the employee's motivation and his or her ability to work. To develop programs in these areas and to anticipate their consequences requires sophisticated understanding of employee motivation, the factors contributing to job satisfaction, equity theory, how people learn, and how organizations and work units change as well as how they resist change. In the vast majority of organizations, public and private, this knowledge does not exist in a way that is readily accessible to the line managers and planners who might need it. Academically, this knowledge is found in other disciplines: psychology, sociology, anthropology, social psychology, communication studies, and political science. The application of social science knowledge to real-life problems is often referred to as **applied behavioral science (ABS).** In the federal government, the extensive research by the Office of Personnel Management and the Merit Systems Protection Board into federal employee attitudes and the effectiveness of pay for performance fall into this category of expertise. Furthermore, the psychological drama of downsizing often places those with sophisticated knowledge of human behavior in the important position of anticipating and ameliorating the effects of job loss as well as the guilt that comes from employees who watch their friends and colleagues being laid off and struggling.

The third area of expertise extends the personnel administrator's knowledge into the areas of financial and risk management. Most prominent is an understanding of health insurance and health benefits, and workers' compensation and disability insurance. In addition, successful programs designed to boost the motivation of employees must develop out of expert knowledge of motivation, and expertise in the fiscal assessment of program results. Thus, anyone who can develop models that include the fiscal implications of projects that apply behavioral science knowledge will be valued. For example, knowing the cost of hiring and training a new employee and the time it takes before that employee is performing satisfactorily can lead to dollar savings. The sooner that employee leaves the organization, the less time the organization has to recover its costs. Given that the greatest turnover occurs among employees with a short time on the job, knowledge of how to retain good employees, for example, through realistic job interviews,[25] can translate into cost savings. As another example, it is commonly known that dissatisfied employees are more likely to quit.[26] Once one can establish the cost of turnover, it is statistically possible through regression analysis to determine the fiscal implications of variations in the morale of a workforce. The design of such an evaluation is complex, but the point here is that knowledge of the applied behavioral sciences allows one to develop models that assess the costs of productivity projects which will affect employees.

SUMMARY

There is a close relationship between budgeting, planning, and productivity in human resource administration, which involves both political and technical decisions. Often, the human resource manager is centrally involved in both. Because government budgets are largely personnel budgets, personnel managers unfamiliar with budgeting, human resource planning, and productivity enhancement are likely to influence only peripherally critical organizational and governmental issues.

A budget represents compromises over political and technical issues concerning governmental programs and objectives. In part, these decisions are influenced by the demand and supply of labor connected to the achievement of government objectives. Productivity concerns focus on how to implement government programs and services with as few resources as possible. Frequently, the focus is on how to scale back on programs and service levels without damaging the quality of public services unacceptably.

One area that continues to attract advocates of administrative efficiency is the privatization of public services. But the hope that the private sector can deliver public services at lower cost is tempered by concerns that employee and client rights will be eroded, that social equity claims will receive less attention, and that accountability mechanisms like open meeting laws and open records requirements will be diminished.

KEY TERMS

applied behavioral sciences (ABS)
attrition
budget
collective opinion
cutback management
downsizing
effectiveness
efficiency
financial management
human resource forecasting
human resource planning
incremental/decremental planning
productivity
reduction-in-force
responsiveness

DISCUSSION QUESTIONS

1. How does budgeting epitomize the impact of the value of political responsiveness on public personnel management?
2. How are human resource planning and forecasting in public agencies related to the budgetary process?
3. Describe the relationship between human resource planning and other personnel management activities.
4. What are the effects of cutback management on a workforce, and how should the human resource manager respond to them?
5. Define each term and then describe the relationship among three alternative definitions of productivity (efficiency, effectiveness, and responsiveness).
6. What are the pros and cons of contracting out?
7. Describe the public personnel manager's expanded role in seeking productivity improvements.

CASE STUDY 1 A DAY IN THE LIFE OF A CITY MANAGER

One year ago, in April, Cityville (population 80,000), a suburban city, hired you, Arlene Mayberry, as the new city manager. You brought a reputation for sound financial management and were chosen unanimously by the council. Cityville has experienced revenue shortfalls in the past two years due to a revenue decline in sales tax. The shortfall resulted in modest increases in the mill levy during these two years. The school board's mill levy increased substantially a year ago due to a cutback in state aid to school districts. The county's levy is scheduled to rise modestly for the next three years due to commitments previous commissions have made to a significant capital improvements program.

In April, Save Our City, a group dedicated to holding the line on taxes, surprised everyone, including you, by electing two of its slate of three candidates to the city council. The council now consists of these two members, Robert Pipes and Caroline Nixon, both elected to four-year terms; Jane Scott, a very politically astute middle-of-the-road council member who has two years remaining of her term; Max Laney, an ex-police officer supported by the Fraternal Order of Police, with two years remaining on the council; and Ron Reaume, who ran on a platform expressing concern for rebuilding a sense of community and respect for diversity and was elected to a two-year term. Reaume has already said he will not run for reelection. Scott and Laney have not indicated their plans.

You view this group as very diverse politically and potentially difficult to work with. You expect that a number of issues will be decided on split votes. In the summer following the election, after considerable debate and political maneuvering, the new council accepted the budget you had proposed on one of those 3-2 votes. The fiscal year runs from January 1 to December 31. None of the council members wanted to raise taxes, and the two mill increase you reluctantly proposed was reduced to one mill with the two Save Our City council members voting against adoption; they favored no tax increase under anything other than financial exigency.

After adoption, Pipes and Nixon jointly issued a press release calling for tightening the belt, increased productivity, and sacrifices just like those made by private-sector small businesses and ordinary citizens. The newspaper carried a front-page story without editorial comment, even though the publisher is known to be sympathetic to their cause.

After the budget was adopted, during the fall and winter it became obvious that police-community relations were showing signs of strain. A self-appointed task force representing a coalition of culturally diverse groups met and held a number of forums to gather information about how citizens felt they were being treated by the police. Every opinion imaginable was expressed during these forums, which were not well attended. It was clear that individual members of minority populations in Cityville felt they had been treated inequitably by the police. For example, one African-American youth said he was walking home from a late-night job carrying a bag of groceries when he was stopped by the police and told to empty the contents of the bag.

In the spring, responding to a 911 family disturbance call, the police shot and killed an Asian wielding a knife. The police claimed self-defense; the family, speaking little English, was distraught and suggested that the police had acted too quickly and more out of concern for their own safety than for the victim or family.

The event heightened tension in the community, even though the vast majority of Cityville supported the police. The council was aware of this majority, but Reaume in particular believed something ought to be done and urged city staff to make some suggestions. He became an occasional visitor to the meetings of the task force on police-community relations and pledged to introduce their anticipated report to the council. Laney defended the police at the next council meeting, noting that police work had become more dangerous in Cityville, and that these events, tragic as they are, happen in today's violent world.

The next week, Pipes and Nixon declared that it might be worthwhile to look into a possible contract with the sheriff's department for law enforcement. They contended that the sheriff's department was larger, had better training, and could provide law enforcement more cheaply than Cityville could on its own. Laney went through the roof. The leadership of the police union quickly set up appointments with each of the council members. Reaume backtracked a bit, suggesting that rebuilding the sense of community in Cityville practically required maintaining an independent police force.

As this political maneuvering was going on, the budget process was beginning. The police chief, Jack "Buck" Fischbach, requested a meeting with you. Buck is a no-nonsense cop, professionally trained and tolerant of city managers at best. He had been one of the original founders of the Fraternal Order of Police in Cityville when he was just a corporal, years ago. He reminded the city manager that ten years ago the city had passed a half cent sales tax to hire new police officers. You knew this. The chief added that since that time, in order to show fiscal restraint, the city had not hired a single officer, despite the addition of some 10,000 citizens. This was news to you, and you kicked yourself for not knowing it already. Further, the chief claimed that the police had become exasperated and very angry because lack of staffing had required them to cut back on the very community-oriented activities they were now being criticized for not having performed. He said he was going to develop and present to you a budget proposal designed to augment staff over a five-year period. You knew that the only way to hire more police would be to raise the mill levy.

After the chief leaves, you get a call from the newspaper publisher wanting to know how things are going.

Questions

1. What are you going to tell the publisher?
2. How are you going to approach the budget?
3. How are you going to deal with the chief of police?
4. How are you going to deal with the council?
5. Why did you want to become a city manager in the first place?

CASE STUDY 2 PRIVATIZATION

A majority of the governing body has pledged to the voters that it would explore all avenues available to privatize city services. It has directed the chief administrative officer to present council with some options. After discussion with department heads, the CAO has suggested the following: The city can save some $500,000 annually if it privatizes its sanitation service. This savings could translate into a reduction in the property tax of some 5 percent.

Council member Rodriguez asks how this savings can be achieved and whether the present sanitation workers will lose their jobs. The CAO responds that in conversations with various private contractors it appears that the contractor could be expected to hire all of the displaced employees who apply. "However," she adds, "a large amount of the savings probably would be achieved by reducing employee benefits, including health-care coverage. There will be no pension benefit."

Council member Johnston indicates that 70 percent of the employees who will have to change jobs are racial minorities. He noted that the skill level of the sanitation workers is such that they will not have any choice but to accept the reduced standard of living.

Council member Reyes acknowledges Johnston's concern but indicates that the savings will be reflected in a property tax reduction that should benefit the poorest landowners the most—those on fixed incomes in modest homes.

Council member Richardson suggests that the city's economic development strategy is aimed at developing good paying-jobs. He asks if the privatization of sanitation services will advance that goal, for minorities as well as other citizens and taxpayers.

Prior to the evening that the city council will discuss this item, the council members report that a number of taxpayers have called urging privatization and following through on campaign pledges. It appears to the council members that the majority of voters would favor the privatization.

At the evening the item is on the council's agenda, the room is packed. On one side are members of a taxpayer's group in favor of the privatization. On the other side are about half the city's sanitation employees, and a group of black and Hispanic clergy and community activists who are opposed to privatization.

Questions

1. What makes this case so difficult?
2. What expressions of different values can you find?
3. Who should make the decision whether or not to privatize?

NOTES

[1] Axelrod, D. (1988). *Budgeting for modern government.* New York: St. Martin's Press.

[2] Rubin, I. (1993). *The politics of public budgeting* (2nd ed.). Chatham, NJ: Chatham House; Wildavsky, A. (1988). *The new politics of the budgetary process.* Glenview, IL: Scott, Foresman.

[3] McGregor, E. B., Jr. (1988). The public sector human resource puzzle: Strategic management of a strategic resource. *Public Administration Review, 48,* 945.

[4] Duane, M. J. (1996). *Customized human resource planning.* Westport, CT: Quorum.

[5] Lengnick-Hall, C. A., and M. L. Lengnick-Hall (1988). Strategic human resources management: A review of literature and a proposed typology. *Academy of Management Review, 13,* 457.

[6] Duane, *Customized human resource planning.*

[7] Ibid.

[8] Kawecki, C., K. Cameron, and J. Jorgenson (1993). *Revisiting civil service 2000: New policy direction needed.* Washington, DC: U.S. Office of Personnel Management.

[9] McGregor, E. B., Jr. (1991). *Strategic management of human knowledge, skills and abilities.* San Francisco: Jossey-Bass.

[10] Mahtesian, C. (January 1996). The big blue hiring spree. *Governing, 9,* 29.

[11] Ibid., 30.

[12] Newton, J. (January 21, 1996). LAPD attrition may pit mayor against chief. *Los Angeles Times,* pp. A-1, 20.

[13] Rabin, J. L., and J. Meyer (February 18, 1996). Health director confronts racial disparity. *Los Angeles Times,* pp. B-1, 5.

[14] Zachary, G. P. (August 6, 1996). Some public workers lose well-paying jobs as agencies outsource. *The Wall Street Journal,* p. A-6.

[15] National Academy of Public Administration (1995). *Effective downsizing: A compendium of lessons learned for government operations.* Washington, DC: National Academy of Public Administration.

[16] The Reason Foundation (1996). *Privatization 1996: Tenth annual report on privatization.* Los Angeles: The Reason Foundation; Wass, G. (Ed.). (1996). *From privatization to innovation: A study of 16 cities.* Chicago: The Civic Federation.

[17] Sharp, E. B. (1990). *Urban politics and administration.* New York: Longman; and Halachmie, A., and M. Holzer. (1993). Towards a competitive public administration. *International Review of Administrative Sciences, 59,* 29-45.

[18] Chandler, T., and P. Feuille (1991). Municipal unions and privatization. *Public Administration Review, 51,* 15-22.

[19] Sharp. *Urban politics and administration.*

[20] Goodman, J. B., and G. W. Loveman (1991). Does privatization serve the public interest? *Harvard Business Review, 69,* 28.

[21] Ibid., 35.

[22] Chandler and Feuille. Municipal unions and privatization; Walters, J. (November 1995). The Whitman squeeze. *Governing Magazine, 8,* 22.

[23] Chandler and Feuille. Municipal unions and privatization.

[24] Kettl, D. F. (1991). Privatization: Implications for the public work force. In C. Ban and N. Riccucci (Eds.). *Public personnel management: Current concerns—future challenges.* New York: Longman.

[25] Wanous, J. P. (1982). *Organizational entry: Recruitment, selection and socialization of newcomers.* Reading, MA: Addison-Wesley.

[26] Mobley, W. H. (1982). *Employee turnover: Causes, consequences, and control.* Reading, MA: Addison-Wesley.

4

Analysis, Classification, and Evaluation

INTRODUCTION

Scholars and personnel practitioners have long insisted that job analysis, job classification, and job evaluation are the heart of personnel management. In the past, whether you got hired as a fledgling personnel specialist might have been based on your answer to a single interview question: "Can you write a good job description?" This was because the technical ability to accurately specify a job's duties and the minimum qualifications ("quals") needed to perform them satisfactorily (specified in terms of the type, level, and length of education and/or experience) was considered an essential prerequisite to perform most other personnel functions. For example, establishing job duties was considered essential for recruitment, selection, training, and performance evaluation. And setting minimum quals was essential to establishing an equitable pay range for the position, and to encourage career development by creating career "ladders" (vertically linked positions within the same occupational field) by which employees could advance to positions of increasing responsibility as they met the "qual standard" for the next higher position on the ladder.

Job analysis, classification, and evaluation were also considered essential to the control of political patronage appointments and the development of civil service systems. First, by requiring that positions had to be defined and classified before people could be hired into them, these personnel activities limited the ability of elected and appointed officials to indefinitely expand the public payroll by creating patronage jobs for their political supporters. Anyone who takes for granted the ability of modern industrialized nations with sophisticated personnel systems to accurately determine how many employees are on the public payroll and what they are actually paid, has simply not had enough experience with the difficulties faced by developing countries that wish to make their budget development, program management, and policy evaluation processes more rational. Without effective systems of job analysis, classification, and evaluation, it is exceedingly difficult to predict public expenditures, to limit them within tax revenues, or to focus them on desired public policy objectives.

Second, by defining job duties and qualifications objectively, these personnel activities helped to ensure that employees were hired and promoted based on ability and performance, and that jobs of equivalent difficulty were paid the same salaries. Without job classification or evaluation systems, it is simply not possible to hire or pay employees so as to support the values of individual rights or administrative efficiency. Again, anyone who assumes that objective and fair pay systems are inevitable, or that they are easy to achieve, has only to look at the chronic and interrelated economic, political and social problems that plague governments in developing countries—corruption, incompetence, and "brain drain." Consider how difficult economic development must be in a country where elected officials feel obligated to create jobs for unqualified employees in response to chronic unemployment and pressures for political patronage, where the public treasury is routinely drained by customs inspectors who accept bribes as an alternative to payment of import duties because their salaries are eroded by inflation, where capital needed for domestic economic development is instead funneled into overseas bank accounts or spent on luxury goods imported for upper-class consumers, and where the brightest and most qualified public employees leave public service for better opportunities in the private sector or overseas. And consider that these problems have a circular and interactive effect on the level of confidence in a government's ability to collect taxes and spend revenues wisely and fairly, on the part of both the country's citizens and the international banking community on which the country depends for development capital.

Taken together, then, the importance of job evaluation, classification, and evaluation to the processes of modernization and democratization cannot be overemphasized. They enable the transition from patronage to civil service systems by limiting the number of patronage positions and by promoting administrative efficiency and pay equity within the civil service as it develops. And finally, because personnel management simply does not develop unless the country values efficiency and equity in managing people as human resources, these functions are critical to the emergence of personnel management as an administrative career and as a profession.

But the nature of personnel management has changed dramatically over time. So it is not surprising that the focus of these activities has also changed significantly. As Chapter 1 indicated, organizations will continue to perform the same personnel management functions (PADS), regardless of the dominant system or the underlying values it seeks to articulate. But the purpose of the functions, and the way in which they are performed, can change significantly as political, social, and economic conditions impel changes in systems and values. And this has certainly been true of analysis, classification, and evaluation. Because both the objectives of public personnel management and the nature of work have changed over time, the focus of analysis and classification is shifting from management of *positions* to management of *work* or of *human resources*. This chapter will explore why the turbulent history of personnel management has led us to this transition, and how it is affecting the way work is defined, classified, and evaluated in public agencies today.

By the end of this chapter, you will be able to:

1. Relate the historical development of analysis and classification to the differing objectives of position management, work management, and human resource management.
2. Describe how traditional job descriptions (those oriented toward position management) are unsuitable for supporting public personnel management as its focus has changed to work management and employee management.
3. Understand why job descriptions are important for jobs filled through traditional civil service, collective bargaining, and affirmative action systems; and for implementing the alternative mechanisms and flexible employment relationships that characterize the emergent anti-government personnel systems.
4. Analyze work using a results-oriented description (ROD), which incorporates the objectives and philosophy of work management and employee management into the traditional process of job analysis.
5. Define *classification*; and show how its objectives and techniques have been influenced by its changing historical focus within alternative personnel systems.
6. Define *job evaluation,* and describe the point-factor method.
7. Be able to critique point-factor evaluation based on its focus on jobs rather than on work or employees; and discuss three alternatives to it: rank-in-person systems, market models, and grade banding.
8. Discuss how the relationship between evaluation and pay equity illustrates the conflict between *efficiency* and *individual rights.*
9. Discuss the relationship between evaluation and other personnel activities.

FROM POSITION MANAGEMENT TO MANAGEMENT OF WORK AND OF HUMAN RESOURCES

The history of public personnel management is, among other things, the history of conflict among values and personnel systems. While the functions required to manage human resources remain the same, the way in which organizations perform these functions is heavily influenced by the impact of political, economic, and social conditions.

The history of public personnel management is also the history of conflict among values and systems over the allocation of public jobs. Therefore, enumerating and describing the number of public employees, and the kinds of work they do, is important to job allocation.

Initially, under political patronage systems, jobs were not analyzed or classified at all. Employees simply received a salary because they had been political supporters of a successful candidate for elected office. The primary purpose of public jobs was their function as "spoils," not the completion of work necessary for public welfare. While some minimally acceptable level of performance might be required to avoid political embarrassment for the elected official who was the employee's "angel," in some cases the employees did not even have to show up for work to get paid. Indeed, many advocates of the spoils system felt that any individual could perform any public job, without the necessity of setting minimum qualifications. Not only were minimum qualifications considered unnecessary, they also tended to interfere with elected officials' freedom to allocate jobs to their supporters.

The Transition from Patronage to Merit

Developing countries have made the transition from patronage to civil service as a result of internal and external pressures for reform. Historically, government reformers have emphasized the ways in which the country would benefit from using public resources more wisely and rationally. Among other things, they have emphasized being able to control the level of public expenditure by limiting the number of public employees, and being able to direct the objectives of public policy making by controlling how many employees, and what kinds, are hired by various agencies.

Once the advantages of rational human resource management are recognized by political and social leaders to the point where a civil service system is created and an administrative agency established to administer it, public agencies will begin to develop several key public personnel functions necessary to a successful transition from patronage to merit. The most important of these systems are a position management information system and a job analysis and classification system.

First, policy makers must accurately determine how many employees work for each agency, by job type, geographic location, and salary. This enables personnel specialists to develop a **staffing table** (a roster of all authorized positions in an agency). Hopefully, as personnel actions result in employees being hired, transferred, or discharged, the position management information system will keep this information current.

While the need to develop an adequate position management information system may seem self-evident, and the steps involved in doing so may seem childishly simple to complete, the political culture of patronage politics can make it difficult to achieve basic administrative reforms.

This is why, under patronage systems, it is actually quite difficult to determine the correct answer to the fundamental question of how many employees actually work for an agency. That is because there are three possible different answers: the total number of (1) the individuals listed on the payroll and therefore receiving paychecks, (2) the individuals listed on the payroll who actually show up for work, and (3) the authorized positions in an agency, whether or not they are filled and whether or not those individuals actually show up for work.

Each of these answers is the result of different pressures on patronage systems. The first option, a payroll "padded" with persons who get paid but never show up for work, results from allowing elected officials to place non-employees on the public payroll as a reward for political or personal loyalty (and perhaps to pocket a percentage of salary as a "kickback" from the non-working "employee"). The second option, a valid payroll matching the number of actual employees, is the objective of civil service reformers. The third option, a payroll inflated by showing as filled positions those that are actually vacant, allows senior managers to pocket the salaries of "ghost" employees as a reward for their own political loyalty. To get an idea of how this system works, consider that the size of the Honduran army is variously estimated at 16,000 to 25,000 soldiers. The higher figure is the authorized strength of units, the staffing level for which budgets are developed. The lower figure is the actual number of soldiers, once vacant positions and ghost employees are subtracted.

It is widely accepted that the first and third options are corrupt and wasteful. But given that the primary function of public employment under a patronage system is to buy political support, this waste and corruption are irrelevant, or a least less important than maintaining a leader or party in power. This tension between patronage and merit systems is by no means limited to the past or to underdeveloped countries. Frequently, local governments in the United States will cut civil service positions to save money at the same time they are adding political employees to the payroll. These may be legitimate excepted appointments (outside the merit system), or they may simply be positions created because a powerful elected official wants a friend to have a job and happens to control the budget of the agency in which the new job is to be created.

Position Management under a Civil Service System

Once this transition from patronage to civil service is under way, legislators and top administrators have sought to restrict patronage by **position management**—limiting the number of employees an agency can hire. This also enables rational budgeting by limiting the total amount that can be spent on salaries and benefits. And it fosters rational policy making and implementation by making the staffing of agencies consistent with the intent of the law and the objectives of public programs.

The underlying assumption of position management is that bureaucratic agencies tend to resist policy direction from elected officials. The way for these officials to control agencies is by limiting the amount of money they can spend, through a budget, and limiting the number and type of personnel they can employ, through position management. Frequently, position and budgetary controls are combined through the imposition of average grade-level restrictions, which limit the number of positions that can be created and filled at each level of the agency hierarchy. A low average grade-level means that most positions are low-level positions.

Theoretically, at least, these position management techniques are analogous to the line-item budgeting discussed in Chapter 3, in that they focus on *inputs* to the governmental process (number and type of employees). Together, line-item budgeting and position management have historically been successful at forcing compliance and accountability because the first controls the budget and policies of the executive branch; and the second controls the allocation of personnel and money to implement programs in executive agencies.

Work Management

As might be expected, however, the control over program inputs that is accomplished by line-item budgets and position management becomes comparatively less important as the objectives of public personnel systems shift away from legislative control and toward managerial effectiveness. This is because budgets and personnel ceilings function well to control the size and direction of inputs to an agency; they are quite ineffective at making the agencies more productive, as measured by program outputs. Public managers have policy objectives to accomplish and limited resources with which to do so. For the work to get done with the most efficient use of human resources, the agency must hire the right number of people, with the right qualifications, for the right jobs, in the right locations. It must pay people enough money to be competitive with other employers, but not more. This is true regardless of which type of public personnel system predominates, but especially for agencies that focus on mission and consider themselves bound to definite performance standards and clear paths of political accountability. Under these conditions, managers need to be rewarded for flexible and responsible stewardship of personnel and financial resources. They are likely to resent legislative "micromanagement" because it restricts their flexibility and autonomy. Or, alternatively, they may be unable or unwilling to function as managers because they have for too long been accustomed to citing legislative controls as the reason for not managing resources creatively or effectively.

Job analysis and position classification arose from a heritage of civil service reform which reflected growing support for the application of scientific principles to administration (scientific management), and growing acceptance of the need for insulating public agencies from political pressure in order to promote efficiency and protect employee rights (politics-administration dichotomy).

Personnel management, as a branch of administrative science, is based on the bureaucratic model described by the German sociologist Max Weber. According to this model, bureaucratic organizations are the most efficient form of organization. They are characterized by a division of labor, a hierarchy of authority, reliance on rational rules as the basis for decision making, and selection and promotion on the basis of merit. Organizational applications of the bureaucratic model were developed during the early 1900s by "scientific managers" such as Frederick W. Taylor and his adherents. Taylor was an industrial engineer who believed there was "one best way" to do a job or run an organization. Given this rational, engineering-oriented approach to management, it followed that the manager's primary function was to plan and organize work in the most technically efficient manner.

With respect to jobs, this involves the first principle of any science— organizing and classifying phenomena. In the case of work, jobs are classified into distinct groups on the basis of characteristics and level of responsibility. This was first embodied in the Classification Act of 1923, which provided for job analysis and classification for some federal positions. It is important to realize that classification developed and thrived in personnel administration because it was based on a scientific principle augmented by morality. That is, classification was considered beneficial not only because it carried the principle of description over from the natural sciences, but also because it supported the twin values of agency efficiency and individual equity. On the one hand, classification helps the line manager and the personnel manager to divide labor more efficiently. On the other, it provides for the equitable compensation of employees according to the true worth of their jobs. Last, it decreased the opportunity for political favoritism by providing that pay be based on a realistic assessment of duties and qualifications, rather than as a reward for political responsiveness.

We have seen that the history of public personnel management represents a continual tension among conflicting values that is to a certain extent self-regulated, in that any value, carried to extremes, loses effectiveness in comparison with other values. And this is true with job analysis and classification systems. Under the best of circumstances, classification systems help managers do a better job: They enable managers to match employees skills with work needs, to reward employees fairly and equitably based on their contributions to a work unit, and to establish clear, consistent standards for reassignment or promotion.

But over time, they can become increasingly elaborate, as job classification specialists make more and more distinctions among types of work and levels of responsibility. While this specialization of tasks begins with the intention of making work more efficient, it ends with a system that is so complex and rigid that it inhibits managers' ability to move people easily from one job to another as work needs change, or of employees to move easily from one position to another as their skills, abilities, and interests change. For example, in 1991 a group of seventeen federal agencies asked the National Academy of Public Administration to recommend changes in the federal government's classification system for civilian employees. The problem was this: Since the system had been developed in the 1920s, the number of separate **job classifications** had gradually increased to about 2,500, each with its own title, code number, and job description (tasks and qualifications for the position). And the pay system had also become more elaborate, with a total of eighteen separate pay grades, each with ten "steps" to allow for annual seniority-based pay raises for employees, even though they were not being promoted from one position to another.

Needless to say, managers found this classification system to be overly rigid and irrational, and therefore extremely difficult to work with. Employees in one classification could not be reassigned to another unless the qualifications were identical, or they were fully qualified in both positions. And employees often found the system a barrier to career advancement, since the difficulty of accomplishing lateral transfers (from one job type to another) often meant that employees could move up only as far as the classification system allowed in their job series; thereafter, they were limited to step increases based on seniority. For example, a senior personnel clerk could only advance to grade 6 based on prior experience as a lower-grade personnel clerk. Higher-level positions, such as personnel staffing specialist, went all the way from grade 5 through grade 13 but required a college degree. Even if the personnel clerk (now at grade 6, plus step 5 or 10) could get a college degree at night, it made no economic sense to accept an entry-level personnel specialist position (grade 5, step 1): The advancement potential was greater, but the initial salary was much lower.

Therefore, those managers interested in maximizing flexibility and efficiency came to view job descriptions and job classification systems as "administrivia," needed to justify budget requests and to keep the folks in personnel happy, but not related to agency mission or day-to-day supervision. As these systems became increasingly arcane, managers and personnel specialists became adept at working "the system" so as to make it more flexible and user-friendly. They learned how to transfer employees by taking advantage of loopholes in personnel regulations, to promote valuable employees ahead of schedule to give them additional rewards, or to justify hiring employees at higher-than-normal salaries by demonstrating market necessity. But on the whole, the negatives outweighed the positives, in that the system worked in spite of itself, and it gave personnel managers a bad reputation besides. After all, they were the ones always telling managers and employees that what they wanted to do, could not be done within the system.

Employee Management

Employees have a different perspective than either managers or elected and appointed officials. They want to be treated as individuals, through a continual process of supervision, feedback, and reward. They want to know what their job duties are and how performance will be measured. They want to be paid fairly, based on their contributions to productivity and compared with the salaries of other employees. They want their individual skills and abilities to be fully utilized in ways that contribute to a productive agency and to their own personal career development.

Today, the current emphasis on flexible employment relationships makes us forget that civil service classification systems were originally created to prevent elected and appointed officials from hiring and firing public employees at will. This stability was designed to make government more efficient and to increase public confidence in the quality of public service. And today, the widely accepted notion that civil service systems provide a safe haven for lazy and incompetent employees makes us forget that civil service classification systems were originally created to protect employee rights by establishing clear criteria and procedures for selection, reassignment, promotion, or discharge. Taken in context, this can be seen as one more example of a system that, when carried to extremes, subverts the values (efficiency and individual rights) it was originally designed to protect.

The chapters on productivity and performance management represent a combination of work focus and employee focus for analysis and classification. This is based on the assumption that people work most productively when they have adequate skills, clear objectives, adequate resources and organizational conditions to do their jobs, and clear feedback and consequences. They work not only as individuals but also as members of groups that collectively shape the culture of the agency and the ways in which employees work together to meet objectives.

These three different perspectives on job analysis, classification, and evaluation frequently come in conflict. Employees emphasize human resources management; managers emphasize work management; and legislators and chief executives have traditionally emphasized position management. Much of the trend toward professional (rather than technical) personnel management can be seen as the transition of public personnel managers from a policing role (control over employees and managers through position management) to an enabling role (facilitation of employee productivity and satisfaction, or of managerial autonomy and responsibility) through more enlightened job analysis, classification, and evaluation techniques. And this change in roles affects the way all personnel functions are performed, including job analysis and classification.

THE TWO PROBLEMS WITH TRADITIONAL JOB ANALYSIS AND JOB DESCRIPTIONS

Job analysis is the process of recording information about each employee's job. It is done by watching the employee work, talking with the employee about the job, and corroborating this information by checking it with other employees and the supervisor. It results in a **job description**—a written statement of the employee's responsibilities, duties, and qualifications. It may also include a **qualifications standard ("qual standard")** which specifies the minimum KSAs and qualifications (education, experience, or others) an employee needs to perform the position's duties at a satisfactory level.

Traditionally, job descriptions have been used as the "building blocks" of position management. By requiring that a legislatively authorized position be identified before an employee could be hired or promoted into it, job descriptions controlled the size of the bureaucracy and its occupational diversity. They have functioned well in this capacity because they specify the job title, occupation classification, level of responsibility, salary, and location of the job in the organizational hierarchy. Similar jobs (positions) can be classified into an occupational series, along with other jobs involving similar job duties. Jobs in different occupations, but of comparable difficulty (requiring similar skill, effort, or responsibility, and performed under similar working conditions) can be classified into a common **grade level.** Each position can be identified by an occupational and grade level code, much as a point on a graph can be identified by measuring its distance from the vertical and horizontal axes.

Because each job (position) can be classified into a common occupational series as one of a number of identical positions in the agency, its grade level served to fix salary and relationship to other positions above and below it in the agency's bureaucratic hierarchy. This has had the additional benefit of identifying, in a manner similar to military rank, the power of the individual in the organization. To emphasize the power of classification systems, consider that federal government employees in Washington, DC, have long been accustomed to identifying themselves, and evaluating others, based on classification system shorthand. A federal employee might say, in describing another federal employee to a co-worker, "She's an 11 at Agriculture, a program analyst." Both of them would immediately understand that the employee in question was a GM-305-11: that is, a classified civil service employee, pay grade 11, in the occupational specialty of program analyst.

While not all classification systems are as complex as that used by the federal government, all traditional job descriptions contain common elements, as shown in Figure 4-1 below: an occupational code and/or title, a pay grade, an organizational locator, a position in the hierarchy, job duties, and required minimum qualifications (education, experience and other factors).

The traditional job description is designed to limit patronage appointments by classifying all positions by job type, skill level, and agency; and to promote efficiency and employee rights by ensuring that employees are qualified to perform their jobs and paid equitably based on their qualifications. But once a country has made the transition to a civil service system, it begins to confront the dilemmas that characterize personnel systems at the third stage of development specified in Chapter 1. That is, it must attempt to reconcile the opposing objectives of political responsiveness and administrative efficiency in order to produce effective government; it must balance both these values with individual rights and social equity. Traditional job descriptions begin to lose effectiveness at this point because they are simply not designed to achieve position management, work management, and employee management all at the same time.

First, traditional job descriptions are ill-suited to work management because they eventually impede the rational allocation of employees to work, or the flexible assignment of employees to jobs as the mission of the agency changes. To discover why, we need only to look at the self-defeating limitations of rationality itself. As job analysis becomes more detailed, classification and pay systems become more complex to keep pace. After a while, this results in the creation of so many occupational categories and skill levels that people become frozen into a job. Career "ladders"

FIGURE 4-1 Traditional Job Description

Job Title: Secretary
Position No: 827301-2
Pay Grade: GS-322-4

Responsibilities	Works under the direction of the Supervisor, Operations Support Division
Duties	Performs a variety of clerical functions in support of the Supervisor and the mission of the Division: types correspondence and reports compiles reports maintains inventory of supplies arranges meetings and conferences answers the phone handles routine correspondence performs other duties as assigned
Qualifications	High school degree or equivalent Typing speed of 40 wpm At least six months experience as a Secretary at grade GS-322-3, or equivalent

require prior experience at a lower grade level before being eligible for promotion to the next one, regardless of whether an applicant can demonstrate the knowledge and abilities needed for successful job performance at a higher level. And supervisors are frequently impeded from moving employees from one type of work to another, in that their tasks are "frozen" by their original job description.

Thus, traditional job descriptions promote an artificially static view of work and organizations. Jobs change over time as an organization's goals shift; and if the goal of the personnel system is to promote rational management of work or employees, it does not make sense to "freeze" a job or an organization at one point in time. Nor does it make sense to unduly restrict the ability of the organization to move people from one job to another as work needs change. From a manager's perspective, traditional job descriptions are deficient because they do not spell out the performance expected of the employee, nor do they specify the linking or enabling relationship among KSAs, performance standards, and minimum qualifications which in reality both supervisors and employees need for employees to work productively in an organization.

The traditional job description promotes a hierarchical and control-oriented relationship between the organization and its employees which works against employee involvement and "ownership" of the organization or its mission. The job description in Figure 4-1 lists the general duties performed by any number of secretaries. Because it applies to a range of positions, it is necessarily vague concerning the nature of the tasks (job elements) involved. The employee may be working in a foundry, a personnel office, or a chemical supply house. In each case, specific duties will differ. The entry "other duties as assigned" leaves the job description open to any additions the supervisor may assign but does not leave room for changes in the work caused by the employee's particular skills or abilities. Thus, this traditional job description is flexible, but only unilaterally, and in a way that assumes hierarchical and downward control over work performance by the agency.

Employees and supervisors both know that a general statement of job duties must at some point be augmented by more specific information about the conditions under which the job is performed. For example, is the work done individually or in a team setting? That fact, in combination with the skills and motivation of a range of applicants, will make a real difference in how work is performed, and it calls into question the relevance of the concept of individual productivity. Is the filing system a database or a manual system using paper documents? What types of correspondence are considered "routine"? Do all duties occur continuously, or do some require more work at certain times? Are all duties equally important, or are some more important than others? What written guidelines or supervisory instructions are available to aid the employee? What conditions make task performance easier or harder?

Thus, the traditional job description does not contain enough useful information to orient applicants or employees. So the supervisor must use orientation or an initial on-the-job adjustment period to teach employees how the work they do *really* fits into the organization's mission.

More critically, there are no **standards** for minimally acceptable employee performance of job duties. This omission causes basic problems for the supervisor, who is the person responsible for arranging the conditions of work so as to make the employee productive. How can this be done if the quantity, quality, or timeliness of service required is not specified? Moreover, it is hard to establish or evaluate performance standards unless these take into account fluctuating conditions. For example, it is easier for a salesperson to increase sales 10 percent annually in an industry growing by 20 percent annually than to achieve the same rate of increase in a declining market.

Moreover, traditional job descriptions specify a general set of minimum qualifications for each position. If jobs have been classified according to the type of skill required, these minimum qualifications may also be based on the KSAs needed to perform duties. In general, however, traditional methods blur the following logical sequence of relationships among **tasks**, standards, KSAs, and minimum qualifications:

1. Each task must be performed at a certain minimum standard for the organization to function well.
2. Certain KSAs are required to perform each task up to standard.
3. Certain minimum qualifications ensure that the employee will have the requisite KSAs.

Thus, even though position descriptions are traditionally seen as the cornerstone of personnel management, it is evident that in their traditional form they are most effective at position management, rather than management of work or employees. The use of standardized job descriptions for a range of positions, with each one identified by a different position number and organizational location, is useful for reducing paperwork and providing position management (external control over the total number of positions and their salary level). But these advantages work against their usefulness as a work management or employee management tool. For these purposes, individual jobs should each have a separate job description, in recognition of the variability of tasks, conditions, standards, and KSAs they require. They should help the manager and the employee by serving as links among personnel functions such as selection, orientation, training, and performance appraisal. These two problems—the lack of evident relationship among tasks, standards, KSAs, and qualifications; and the lack of clear information about the nature of the job—reduce the usefulness of job descriptions for executives, managers, and employees.

Executives are handicapped because such traditional job descriptions describe only the personnel inputs into a job and not the resultant outputs in terms of organizational productivity. That is, they do not specify how many employees would be needed to produce outputs at a given level of quantity, quality, or timeliness. Because traditional job descriptions do not lend themselves to output analysis, they are not a useful part of the human resource planning, management, or evaluation process.

Managers are handicapped because they cannot readily use such job descriptions for recruitment, orientation, goal setting, or performance evaluation. If new employees are recruited on the basis of the brief description of duties and qualifications given in the traditional job description, extensive interviewing by managers may be needed to select the applicants most qualified for a particular job. Orientation will require clarification of the job description to fit the particular organizational context, and it may be incomplete because of other demands on the manager's time. If the organization uses MBO goal setting and evaluation procedures, these will be unrelated to the job descriptions used by the personnel department for position management and recruitment.

Employees are generally unable to use traditional job descriptions for orientation, performance improvement, or career development. Because job descriptions give only a brief outline of duties, employees must wait to find out about working conditions and performance standards until after they have been hired. Yet this may be too late; unclear or inequitable psychological contracts are a cause of much unrest between employees and organizations. Evaluating employees without giving them clear performance standards is a sure way to increase anxiety and frustration.

Moreover, employees cannot use traditional job descriptions for career development because they do not specify how increases in minimum qualifications are related to increases in skills required for satisfactory task performance. It is easiest for employees to accept the qualifications for a position and to strive to meet them through upward mobility programs if these linkages are more apparent.

But personnel managers, and the personnel management function itself, are most seriously affected by the focus of traditional job descriptions on managing positions rather than work. Because traditional job descriptions are not very suitable to work management, they are regarded as irrelevant by executives, managers, and employees. Inevitably, job descriptions tend to be regarded in the same light as inventories of office equipment or the updating of workplace safety regulations—something that must be done, yet adds no value. If personnel managers consider job descriptions to be one of the most important personnel tools, and if job descriptions are perceived by managers and employees as useless for their purposes, then the impression may be created that other personnel activities are equally unimportant. This logic is frequently used to belittle performance evaluation, job analysis, training needs surveys, and other items from the personnel manager's stock in trade.

Consequently, the primary result of the traditional job description's focus on position management is to make it more difficult for personnel managers to focus on management of work and employees. This traditional view of job descriptions has in large part been responsible for the traditional view of personnel management as a series of low-level operational techniques used mainly for external control or system maintenance purposes.

THE IMPORTANCE OF JOB DESCRIPTIONS UNDER OTHER PUBLIC PERSONNEL SYSTEMS

Because all personnel systems involve similar functions, job descriptions are important under affirmative action, collective bargaining, and the two emergent "anti-government" systems (alternative organizations and mechanisms for delivering public services, and flexible employment relationships for the public employees that remain).

Affirmative Action

By specifying the minimum qualifications for a position, and by logically relating minimum quals to job tasks, job descriptions are the most critical element of equitable personnel practice. That is, they act affirmatively to ensure that applicants and employees are not discriminated against on the basis of non-merit factors. Moreover, they reduce the impact of the "good old boy" system that implicitly favors white males, by requiring that vacancies be identified and posted, that all qualified applicants have the opportunity to apply, and that applicants not hired be informed as to the reason for their non-selection. Of course, there are widespread abuses in recruitment and selection procedures, and the folklore of public personnel management is filled with fables confirming every suspicion: highly qualified white male applicants who were not hired because they were the "wrong gender" or the "wrong color," highly qualified minority or female applicants who were included in the interview pool only to demonstrate a "good faith effort" at recruiting a diverse workforce, yet who never had a real chance of being fairly considered for the position. But job analysis is at the heart of test validation, affirmative action compliance, and reasonable accommodation of persons with handicaps under the Americans with Disabilities Act.

Collective Bargaining

Job analysis and classification are also central to collective bargaining. First, collective bargaining starts with the identification of an appropriate bargaining unit, either occupation based or agency based. In either case, the number and identity of positions eligible for inclusion in the bargaining unit presumes that all positions, those included as well as those excluded, have been analyzed and classified in advance.

Once a union has been selected as a bargaining agent, it begins to negotiate with management. Frequently, contract negotiators justify requested pay and benefits by comparing pay and benefit levels with similar jobs in other jurisdictions. Contracts stipulate pay, benefits, and working conditions applicable to covered employees, or to employees in specified occupations. Contracts may prohibit management from assigning employees work outside their classification or above their grade level. They will certainly specify that discipline can only be taken against employees who do not perform their jobs satisfactorily, for tasks assigned in their job descriptions, as measured against previously defined performance standards.

Alternative Organizations and Mechanisms

In one sense, job descriptions hinder productivity because they tie up resources without adding value. That is, they require work to write and review, without directly contributing to the outputs by which the effectiveness of the organization is measured. But in another sense, they create value by specifying the nature of the work to be done, and the rewards the organization is prepared to pay to have it done. It takes but a moment's reflection to realize that clarity with respect to performance expectations and rewards is at the heart of most alternative organizations and mechanisms for delivering public services without using government agencies, employees, or appropriated funds.

Outsourcing and privatization cannot be compared with in-house performance using civil service employees unless the nature of the work to be done, the performance standards, and the pay and benefits attached to the positions are clearly specified. For example, a city considering contracting out security services at public housing or transit facilities will have to define what level of service, and what level of employee qualifications, will be needed to do the job—whether it is eventually done in-house or contracted out.

Flexible Employment Relationships

Flexible employment relationships make it easier for management to hire, fire, and reassign workers. And they also tend to remove agencies somewhat from legislative controls based on position management. But job descriptions are more important than ever under these alternative and flexible employment systems because their objective is work management and their function is to define jobs. Consider that management needs some criteria to separate "core" and "contingent" positions. These criteria can include occupation, level of difficulty, or geographic location. But whatever criteria are used, jobs need to be defined and classified based on the nature of the work. And consider employment of workers on short-term performance contracts. These need to clearly specify the terms and conditions of employment, lest the rewards offered are not proportionate to the skills and responsibilities.

HOW TO IMPROVE TRADITIONAL JOB DESCRIPTIONS

Job descriptions continue to be useful under a range of personnel systems, but their reputation has been tarnished. This is because, in their present form, they are more effective at position management than management of work or employees. What changes would make them more relevant to managers' and employees' needs?

Job descriptions would be more useful if they clarified the organization's expectations of employees and the links among tasks, standards, KSAs, and minimum qualifications. These improved job descriptions would contain the following information:

1. *Tasks.* What work duties are important to the job?
2. *Conditions.* What things make the job easy (such as close supervision or written guidelines explaining how to do the work) or hard (such as angry clients or difficult physical conditions)?
3. *Standards.* What objective performance levels (related to organizational objectives) can reasonably be set for each task, measured in terms of objectives such as quantity, quality, or timeliness of service?
4. *KSAs.* What knowledge, skills, and abilities are required to perform each task at the minimum standard under the above conditions?

5. *Qualifications.* What education, experience, and other qualifications are needed to ensure that employees have the necessary KSAs?

These changes are all related because they clarify the enabling relationship among tasks, conditions, standards, KSAs, and qualifications. In other words, they specify the qualifications needed to demonstrate that an employee has the KSAs required to perform essential job functions at acceptable performance standards under a given set of conditions. Taken together, these refinements emphasize the relationship of jobs to management of work and employees, rather than of positions. They do so by focusing on outputs (what is actually produced by a job) rather than inputs (which positions are allocated to the agency).Two examples of **results-oriented descriptions** (RODs) are shown in Figure 4-2a, b.

These examples show why results-oriented job descriptions are superior for management of work and employees. They provide clearer organizational expectations to employees. They encourage supervisors and employees to recognize that both standards and KSAs can be contingent upon conditions. For example, a secretary can type neater copy more quickly with a word processor than with a manual typewriter, and different skills are required. In the second example, an increase in each probation officer's caseload from 60 to 100 clients would inevitably affect the quantity, quality, or timeliness of visits with probationers. A probation officer preparing PSIs for a new judge might be expected to have a lower level of accepted recommendations.

Thus, job descriptions can do more than just establish a link between tasks, conditions, and standards that is useful to employees and supervisors. This link is the logical connection between duties and qualifications required for content validation of qualifications standards under affirmative action programs or civil service systems; and for employee productivity under personal service contracts and other alternative/flexible employment relationships.

THE HISTORY OF CLASSIFICATION

The history of personnel management can be seen as the history of classification. Initially, the dual objectives of external political control and mechanistic internal management practices derived from the application of administrative science and hierarchical control meant that *positions* were what was classified, and the name of the field was position classification. Viewed in this context, position classification is the process of categorizing positions according to **occupation** or **level of responsibility**. That is, all positions are grouped within a matrix, or classified, based on the type of work performed and the level of responsibility required.

Position classification follows logically from job analysis, for it assumes that each position can be logically placed both vertically and horizontally within a lattice (the **organization chart** or **table of organization**). Traditional position classification simplifies job analysis and position management, for it means that a standardized description can be written for an entire group of positions (those requiring the same qualifications because they comprise the same tasks, conditions, and standards).

FIGURE 4–2a Results-Oriented Descriptions (RODs)

Word Processor/Receptionist
Operations Support Division
Position No.: 827301-2
Pay Grade: GS-322-4

Responsibilities: Works under the direction of the Supervisor, Operations Support Division

TASKS	CONDITIONS	STANDARDS
Type letters	Use IBM PC, Word Perfect, and agency style manual	Letter completed in 2 hours, error-free
Greet visitors	Use appointment log provided by Supervisor	No complaints from scheduled visitors about waiting, provided Supervisor is on time
Maintain files	Use DBM software and instructions provided by Supervisor	Update files weekly, with accuracy and completeness

KNOWLEDGE, SKILLS, AND ABILITIES REQUIRED

Able to type 40 wpm
Courtesy
Word Perfect, Lotus 1-2-3

MINIMUM QUALIFICATIONS

High school degree or equivalent
Two years word processing, especially Word Perfect
One year database management, especially Lotus 1-2-3

Position classification simplifies external control of agencies because it is possible for legislators or elected officials to control the personnel inputs to an agency by specifying (and limiting) the number, occupational type, and grade levels of all positions in the agency. It is useful to managers because it limits and specifies the ways in which employees can be moved from position to position. Two types of position classification are commonly used: types of work and level of responsibility.

On the other hand, those who emphasize the relation of analysis to **work management** or **employee management** generally consider position classification irrelevant or counterproductive. That is, the focus of traditional classification is on inputs: How many positions, at what grade level, and in which occupations, are allocated to a particular work unit? This focus is largely irrelevant to output or to employee needs, which tend to direct attention to an entirely different set of questions. For the manager who wishes to focus on work performance, the classification system is an impediment that prevents flexible reassignment of people based on their relative skills and abilities and the work needs of the agency. For employees, the classification system is an artificial and infuriating barrier that prohibits advancement and fails to recognize the impact of the individual on the job.

FIGURE 4–2b Results-Oriented Descriptions (RODs)

Juvenile Probation Officer
State Department of Corrections

TASKS	CONDITIONS	STANDARDS
Meet clients to record their behavior	Caseload of not more than 60; supervisor will help with hard cases; use departmental rules...regulation	See each probationer weekly keep accurate and complete records per DOC rules & regulations
Report criminal activity to supervisor		
Prepare presentence investigation reports	Average of 5 per week; per court instructions; supervisor will review	Reports complete & accurate per Judge; Judge will accept recomendations in 75% of cases

KNOWLEDGE, SKILLS, AND ABILITIES REQUIRED

Knowledge of the factors contributing to criminal behavior
Ability to counsel probationers
Ability to write clear and concise probation reports
Knowledge of different judges' sentencing preferences for particular types of offenders and offenses
Knowledge of law and DOC regulations concerning presentencing investigations and probation

MINIMUM QUALIFICATIONS

High school degree or equivalent plus four years of experience working with juvenile offenders, or a BS degree in criminal justice, psychology, or counseling
Possess a valid driver's license

The incompatibility of traditional position classification with the ascendant objectives of work management and employee management has given rise to a number of "nether world" personnel practices. These activities are carried on by personnel directors and supervisors to achieve agency objectives and manage employees within the confines of an inflexible and unresponsive position classification system. They include gaining approval for individual changes in classification based on the impact of the person on the job; and escaping from the confines of a classification system by making positions exempt (unclassified political appointments). Two examples will illustrate.

A major reorganization of the federal government's classification system occurred with the passage of the Civil Service Reform Act of 1978. One of the provisions of this reform was the reclassification of senior administrative positions (grades GS-16 through GS-18) into a Senior Executive Service (SES). Employees in these positions were offered the option of continuing in civil service positions or transferring into **exempt positions** where individual performance contracts provided more opportunity for merit pay for productive performance, and greater flexibility for supervisors to use top-notch executives regardless of their specific occupational skills.

As a second example, a major county government recently centralized fire and rescue service by consolidating all municipal fire departments into one central county agency. One of the major obstacles to this reorganization was the differences in duties and pay of various fire and rescue personnel in different municipal governments.

POINT-FACTOR JOB EVALUATION

The data used in analyzing a job for purposes of developing a job description also form the basis for **job evaluation**. The purpose of job evaluation is to determine the worth of the job or position (rather than the value of the work or quality of the person's performance). Although several methods of job evaluation have been used, the most prominent today is the **point-factor method**. It compares jobs on an absolute scale of difficulty, using several predetermined **job worth factors** which are quantified to make numerical comparisons easier. This is how it is done:

1. Analyze all jobs in the organization.
2. Select factors that measure job worth across all positions. Common factors include supervisory responsibility, difficulty of duties, working conditions, and budgetary discretion. It may be necessary to break jobs into broad occupational classes first, and to develop separate compensable factors for each class.
3. Weight job factors so that the maximum possible value is 100. (For example, there could be five factors worth 20 points each, or two worth 20 each and one worth 60.)
4. Develop and define **quality levels** for each job worth factor, and apportion points within that factor to each quality level. For example, if "working conditions" is selected as a job worth factor with a total value of 20 points out of 100, then the following quality levels might be established for this job worth factor:
   a. 0 points: office work
   b. 10 points: occasional outside work, some walking or standing required
   c. 20 points: constant outside work in bad weather; heavy lifting required.
5. Evaluate each job along each job worth factor, and compute the point total.
6. Establish realistic pay ranges for benchmark positions based on market comparisons with similar jobs elsewhere.
7. Pay benchmark jobs the market rate, and pay other jobs in proportion to their comparative point totals.

Table 4-1 shows a simplified example of the point-factor method. It compares the worth of five jobs, based on three job worth factors, each defined by three quality levels.

It can immediately be seen that this initial attempt to create an equitable pay system has resulted in some apparent inequities: Police lieutenants would make more than the police chief, and police officers would make more than the sergeants who supervise them. Note, however, that this is entirely due to the choice of job worth factors and quality levels, and their relative weights. Each of these four choices is based on the professional judgment of the job analyst. When

TABLE 4–1 Example of Point-Factor Job Evaluation

JOB WORTH FACTORS skill (30 points), working conditions (30 points), and responsibility (40 points) = 100 points total

QUALITY LEVELS

Skill:	30—professional knowledge and independent judgment
	20—technical knowledge under supervision
	10—some technical skill under close supervision
Working conditions:	30—constantly unpleasant and dangerous
	20—occasionally unpleasant or dangerous
	0—office work
Responsibility:	40—makes decisions affecting a major program area
	25—makes decisions affecting a department
	10—makes decisions affecting a service to individual clients

		COMPENSABLE FACTORS			
Position	*Skill*	*Conditions*	*Responsibility*	*Total*	*Salary*
Mayor	30	0	40	70	$35,000
Police chief	30	0	25	55	27,500
Lieutenant	30	10	25	65	32,500
Sergeant	20	10	10	40	20,000
Policeofficer	10	30	10	50	25,000

the results appear to defy reality or common sense, the job analyst will usually alter the choice or relative weight of the job worth factors, or the definition and relative weight of the quality levels for each factor.

These changes would probably result in alterations of the method to the example shown in Table 4-2 (p. 116). In this case, the relative value of the five jobs has been altered by changing the value of the job worth factor "responsibility" from 40 to 60 points, and by reducing the value of the other two factors to 20 points each. And the quality factors' point values have been readjusted based on the change in point allocation to the three job worth factors.

Once ratings have been established by the job analyst, they should be reviewed for objectivity and "reality testing" by a committee representing the major divisions of the agency. The committee should be chaired by an objective facilitator who will get the group to reach consensus on adjustments to the point values and relative salaries for the various positions.

A CRITIQUE OF JOB EVALUATION, AND ALTERNATIVES TO IT

Point-factor methods of job evaluation are extremely popular because of their objectivity, stability, and reliability for pay-setting purposes.[1] Despite their complexity and high development costs, they have largely supplanted other evaluation methods because of their perceived internal validity (within the agency) and the ease with which objective factors can be used to validate the system in the face of attacks by employees, unions, and affirmative action compliance agencies.[2]

TABLE 4-2 Revised Example of Point-Factor Job Evaluation

JOB WORTH FACTORS skill (20 points), working conditions (20 points), and responsibility (60 points) = 100 points total

QUALITY LEVELS

Skill:	20—exercises professional judgment independently
	14—exercises judgment with some supervision
	7—exercises technical skill under supervision
Working conditions:	20—constant danger and discomfort
	10—occasional danger or discomfort
	0—office work
Responsibility:	60—in charge of a large organization
	45—in charge of a major department
	30—supervises more than ten employees
	15—supervises fewer than ten employees
	0—no supervisory responsibilities

POINT-FACTOR EVALUATION

Position	*Skill*	*Conditions*	*Responsibility*	*Total*	*Salary*
Mayor	20	0	60	80	$60,000
Police chief	20	0	45	65	48,750
Lieutenant	20	10	30	60	45,000
Sergeant	14	20	15	49	36,750
Police officer	7	20	0	27	20,250

But all job evaluation methods have a fundamental weakness—they focus on the relative worth of jobs or positions, rather than the relative importance of the work to the mission of the agency or the relative quality of employee's performance. Thus, in an era where the focus of human resource management is shifting from inputs to outputs, and where work is allocated flexibly rather than hierarchically, job evaluation has increasingly come under attack as outmoded and off target.[3] Critics charge that it reinforces bureaucratic hierarchy and lack of initiative and discourages innovation, development of internal and external relationships, and mission orientation among employees. Employees tend to focus on internal competition for upward classification and pay increases rather than on customers and mission. And classification and evaluation systems tend to stifle organizational change by tying any alteration in work duties or relationships to potential changes in internal status and pay. Creative managers soon learn that jobs can be "upgraded" by rewriting job descriptions to gain more job evaluation points. Thus, job evaluation creates incentives to create additional supervisory positions and waste resources, because supervisors can gain higher grades based on the number of resources they use and the number of employees they supervise.

There are at least three alternatives to traditional job evaluation: rank-in-person systems, market models, and "grade banding."

Rank-in-Person Systems

Rank-in-person systems are traditionally found in the military, in paramilitary organizations such as police and fire departments and the U.S. Public Health service, in the U.S. Foreign Service, and in university faculties. Rank-in-person systems differ from traditional job classification and evaluation (**rank-in-job** systems) because their focus is not on the duties of a particular position, but on the KSAs of the employee. Under a rank-in-job system, all employees are classified by type of occupation and level of responsibility, and these factors are tied to a job analysis, classification, and evaluation system. Under a rank-in-person system, employees qualify for promotion from one rank to another based on skills, knowledge, experience, and education (assuming promotional opportunities are available).

Since the rank attaches to the person rather than to the position, employees can be freely assigned or reassigned within the organization without its affecting pay or status. This has the advantage of reducing the immobility and status concerns generated by traditional job evaluation. It also enables the matching of employees to work based on the specific skills or abilities required. This feature offers organizations that use rank-in-person systems tremendous flexibility, and it is much more effective at utilizing workforce diversity to match employee talents with agency needs. For example, assume the U.S. Public Health Service needs to respond to an increased incidence of hepatitis among hospital workers in Phoenix. Since the USPHS uses a rank-in-person system, it can search its employee data banks to come up with a list of specialists who are experienced in hepatitis-B research and education, bilingual, and living in or able to relocate to Phoenix. Once identified, individuals can quickly be put to work without worrying about whether they are in the "right" grade level or occupational specialty.

Market Models

An even less formal option is also available—abandoning job classification and evaluation altogether, and relying on managerial flexibility, performance appraisals, and the market mechanism to set salaries. Under this **market model,** which is mostly followed in small, entrepreneurial private businesses, **management to budget** is the authority. This means managers can hire as many employees as they need, at whatever salary they choose, in order to accomplish their mission. Employees (and the manager) are hired under short-term performance contracts. Successful managers are those who hire the right employees, pay them appropriate salaries, and utilize them effectively to meet mission requirements. Successful employees are those who can negotiate mission-oriented performance contracts, price themselves realistically in the job market, and sell themselves to a succession of managers and employers. The validity of the system is based on the financial survival of the employer. If you get a paycheck, you are being paid fairly and doing well; if not, you aren't!

There are obviously major disadvantages to both alternatives. Rank-in-person systems still must control total budget allocations for personnel by personnel ceilings and average grade levels. And employees will continue to focus on assignments perceived as developmental or as required for advancement to the next highest rank ("ticket punching"). The agency must develop relatively sophisticated human resource management information systems if it is to effectively match work with employees. A traditional rank-in-job system requires only a match of the occupational code and grade level of the vacant position with a roster of employees who meet the minimum qualifications for that grade level. A rank-in-person system requires cataloging (and confidentiality) of a range of employee data, detailed analysis of the KSAs required by an agency, and rapid matching of skills with needs through a real-time, user-accessible information system.

Market models are often used in the private sector. They are frequently used in conjunction with job evaluation systems to validate them. But they do not allow for the external (executive and legislative) control of inputs that characterizes the public sector. However, both political and contract positions are filled on this basis, in that pay or contract provisions can be set politically through the approval of individual political appointments or the contract approval process. And they raise profound questions of equity, such as those addressed in the following discussion.

Grade Banding

Grade banding has emerged in recent years as a useful compromise to retain the benefits of job evaluation, while at the same time permitting more effective management of people and work.[4] In place of complex systems with dozens of pay grades and hundreds of occupational classifications, grade banding systems arrange jobs into broad occupational classes and a few pay bands (such as "training level," full performance level, and "expert performance level"). Within these broad distinctions, managers have authority to manage human resources effectively, without having to gain approval from personnel for endless reclassification requests. And employees have clearer and less restrictive career mobility ladders.

Grade banding originated in the 1980s in the private sector in the United States, where it was adopted by Citicorp, General Electric, Xerox, and AT&T. It was introduced on an experimental basis in the federal government in 1981, as a research innovation authorized by the Civil Service Reform Act of 1978. Successful examples were developed for the Pacer Share project, Naval Laboratories, and the National Institute of Standards, among others.

In general, broad banding has produced favorable results: fewer requests for reclassifications, less wasted time in job analysis for reclassification purposes, a diminished importance of hierarchical levels inside the organization, improved managerial ability to use salary increases to stimulate productivity, and more flexible employee mobility. At a broader level, grade banding enhances the reputation of personnel managers, who are more likely to be viewed as enablers rather than as part of the problem; and it reestablishes the relationship between job classification and evaluation systems and contemporary objectives of personnel management systems: enhanced employee performance and utilization of employees. But there is one negative outcome—most examples report a tendency for average salaries to "creep" upward toward the top of whatever pay ranges are authorized. So it remains to be seen whether managers can resist this pressure and manage effectively within their budgets.

There have been efforts, primarily spurred by the National Academy of Public Administration, to gain congressional approval for the general adoption of grade banding within the federal government.[5] But these efforts have been thus far unsuccessful.

JOB EVALUATION AND PAY EQUITY

The relationship between job evaluation and pay equity is perhaps the clearest example of the way in which competing values and systems affect pay in public agencies.

Market models are clearly the most efficient method of setting pay rates. They are flexible, mission-oriented, and externally valid. They have traditionally been followed in the private sector (except for collective bargaining). And several public-sector personnel systems (political and contracting out) use them as well.

But market models frequently conflict with two other values: individual rights and social equity. The conflict between individual rights and efficiency is exemplified by collective bargaining, which will be discussed as a partial personnel system in Chapter 13. Under collective bargaining, pay rates are set by bilateral or multilateral negotiations between labor and management. From an employee's viewpoint, collective bargaining is necessary because of the power of large employers to depress wages below the rate considered fair or necessary.

The conflict between efficiency and social equity is epitomized by the civil rights and affirmative action movements. The private sector can legitimately save money by paying lower wages to youth, the elderly, women, minorities, and disabled employees. This is considered good business practice and is justified by the resultant cost savings. But public agencies must treat employees equitably based on merit factors. Clearly, a public agency that is required to provide equal protection to all employees as persons, and that is required to follow due process in setting pay, could not justify paying lower wages to these groups simply because market factors would justify it.

This conflict has given rise to demands for **pay equity** among women and minorities (equal pay for work requiring equivalent skill, effort, and responsibility); and to conflicting demands for acceptance of market economics by private-sector employers.

JOB EVALUATION AND OTHER PERSONNEL ACTIVITIES

Analysis, classification, and evaluation are clearly the heart of personnel management, and the key to an effective match between the individual employee and the organization. They help the employee know whether or not duties are being assigned equitably. And by viewing the hierarchy of job descriptions within a particular occupational cluster, an employee can develop ideas about the direction of possible career advancement and the KSAs necessary for advancement. From the manager's perspective, they connect human resource planning to the budgetary and legislative process. They improve employee relations by clarifying the terms of work in an equitable and flexible manner. And they achieve external political responsiveness through control over inputs and accountability for results.

SUMMARY

Many current controversies in public personnel management center around the appropriateness of a focus on jobs, work, or employees. Traditional job analysis defines the position as the unit of analysis, and develops classification and evaluation systems based on the type of work and its level of responsibility in the organizational hierarchy. More contemporary approaches focus on flexible use of human resources to accomplish the mission of the agency. Examples of the differences in these two approaches are the transition from traditional job descriptions to newer results-oriented descriptions, and the use of rank-in-person systems, market models, or grade banding. There is no doubt that job analysis will continue to be an important personnel activity, because it is required not only for civil services systems but also for alternatives to them. And one of the key points of conflict within public personnel management is the extent to which the system should be driven by market models (which are more efficient), or by broader concerns of social equity and individual rights.

KEY TERMS

employee management
exempt (unclassified) position
grade banding
grade level
job analysis
job classification
job description
job evaluation
job worth factor
level of responsibility
management to budget
market model
organization chart (table of organization)
pay equity
point-factor evaluation
qualifications standard ("qual standard")
quality level
rank-in-job
rank-in-person
results-oriented description (ROD)
staffing table
standards
tasks
work management

DISCUSSION QUESTIONS

1. How does the historical development of analysis and classification relate to the differing objectives of position management, work management, and employee management?
2. Why are traditional job descriptions unsuitable for supporting personnel management as its focus has changed to work management and employee management?
3. How do results-oriented descriptions (RODs) differ from traditional job descriptions? Why are RODs more effective?
4. Why are jobs classified, and how?
5. What is the point-factor method of job evaluation? What steps does it involve?

6. How does traditional job evaluation limit agency effectiveness? What alternatives are there to it? What are the disadvantages of these alternatives?
7. How does job evaluation relate to alternative personnel systems (collective bargaining and affirmative action) and values (individual rights and social equity)?
8. How do analysis, classification, and evaluation relate to other personnel activities?

CASE STUDY *WHO'S MOST QUALIFIED TO BE MINORITY RECRUITMENT DIRECTOR?*

BACKGROUND

You have recently been appointed by the governor of your state as personnel director of the state police. The organization consists of about 1,000 uniformed officers and 200 civilian employees. Its primary mission is to promote highway safety through enforcement of traffic laws and assistance to motorists.

In recent years, the state police organization has come under increasing public criticism. The major complaint is that too much attention is being paid to writing traffic tickets; a more appropriate focus would be on organized crime and drug trafficking. In addition, many community activists believe that the state police routinely discriminates against blacks and Hispanics in both employment and enforcement of traffic laws.

Morale is low among younger officers, who see themselves as victims of societal conflicts. Turnover among recruits, those who have completed a three-month training course, averages 25 percent during the first year. Reasons most often given for leaving the state police are working conditions, lack of immediate promotion opportunities, and the feeling the advancement is based on "who you know, not what you know."

Many observers consider the state police to be a highly political organization because its top administrative positions are appointed by the governor. Some observers believe that, as a result, top management lacks experience in law enforcement or management, and that this reduces the organization's morale and effectiveness.

As director of personnel for the state police, your task is to select an assistant who will be responsible for developing, administering, and evaluating a minority recruitment program for the agency. An outside consulting firm has selected three candidates as being the most qualified of several hundred applicants who responded to nationwide advertising for the position. You and your panel have interviewed each applicant. Now it is time to pick the one most qualified for the position.

PROCESS

Divide into discussion groups with four of five people in each group (groups A, B, C, etc.). Within twenty-five minutes, place all three candidates in rank order, based on their relative qualifications for the position. Before you do so, be prepared to defend your selection by writing a brief results-oriented job description (ROD) for the position:

1. What *job duties* are most important to the position?
2. What *knowledge, skills, and abilities* (KSAs) will successful applicants need to perform these essential job functions?
3. What objective performance *standards* could you use to assess whether the minority recruitment director is doing a good job?
4. What *conditions* make the job particularly easy or hard to perform? How do these affect the performance standards that should be established, or the KSAs required?
5. What minimum *qualifications* will successful applicants need to ensure that they have these KSAs?
6. In what rank order should the three candidates be placed? In your group's column, write a "1," "2," or "3" opposite each candidate's name in Table 4–3.
7. Why is the applicant you chose the most qualified for the job?
8. What selection criterion was most important in making the choice? Place a check beside it in Table 4-4.
9. Which value (political responsiveness, efficiency, or social equity) is most enhanced by your selection decision and criteria?
10. How confident are you that your selection criteria are job related?
11. How would you validate the criteria if asked to do so by a federal court or by an affirmative action compliance agency?
12. What is the appropriate definition of *merit* in this situation?

TABLE 4-3 Rank the Applicants

Candidate	*Group A*	*Group B*	*Group C*	*Group D*	*Group E*
Harold Murphy					
Willie Jones					
Norma Sikorsky					

TABLE 4-4 Pick the Most Important Selection Criterion

Criterion	*Group A*	*Group B*	*Group C*	*Group D*	*Group E*
Education					
Experience					
Degree					
Politics					
Race or Gender					
Other (what?)					

WILLIE JONES
1327 W. ADDISON STREET
MINNEAPOLIS, MN

Job Objective: A responsible professional position in minority recruitment, higher education administration, or personnel management

Employment History:

1993 - Assistant Director of Admissions, Northern Minnesota State College. Responsible for minority recruitment, minority financial aid, and internship programs for a 25,000 student state university system institution. Since 1993, the percentage of minority students has increased from 7 percent to 11 percent, despite cuts in federal loans and other financial aid programs.

1986 - 1993: 1st Lieutenant to Captain, U.S. Army. Responsible for a variety of combat assignments in the U.S. and overseas. Rifle Platoon Leader responsible for the health, morale, welfare, and safety of 43 men (1986-1989). Company executive officer (1989-1991). Battalion Air Operations Officer responsible for scheduling aircraft and helicopters to support personnel and units of the battalion in Operation Desert Storm (1991-1992). Battalion Advisor 11th Airborne Division: one of 20 officers selected to advise in combat 10 Armored Battalions of the Royal Saudi Army in the use of U.S. weapons and tactics.

Awards and Decorations:

1996: "Who's Who" (Outstanding Young Men in America)

1986 - 1993: Silver Star, Bronze Star Medal with "V" Device for Valor (2 Oak Leaf Clusters), Air Medal, Army Commendation Medal with "V" Device for Valor, and Purple Heart (2 Oak Leaf Clusters)

1984-1995: Medgar Evers Memorial Scholarship, Jackson State University

Education:

1986: BA in Psychology, Jackson State University, Mississippi.

Personal Data: 5'11", 180 pounds, married, two children, excellent health, willing to relocate

---

HARODL MURPHY

3732 18TH STREET

ARLINGTON, VA

Job Objective: A responsible professional job as a human resource manager.

Employment History:

1992 - Personnel Director, Northern Virginia Community College. Responsible for management of labor relations, recruitment and selection, training, and affirmative action compliance. Represents NVCC in negotiating session with staff union.

1988 - 1992: Assistant Personnel Director, Manassas Crossroads Bank, Manassas, VA. Responsible for selection, payroll and benefits administration, and staff development.

Education:

1992: M.S. in Government (Personnel Management), the George Washington University, Washington, DC. Master's Thesis: "Minority Recruitment Problems in Virginia State Government."

1988: B.A. in Business Administration, George Mason University. Senior Honors thesis: "Politically Incorrect: Conflicts between Union Seniority Systems and Affirmative Action Compliance."

Honors and Awards:

1988: Phi Beta Kappa, Pi Sigma Alpha, cum laude.

Professional Activities:

"Managing Privatization and Labor Relations Issues in State University Systems," National Association of University Personnel Administrators Conference, New Orleans, 1995.

Personal Information:

married, good health

NORMA SIKORSKY
P.O. BOX 6597
SALEM, OR

Job Objective:	A responsible position in management, media relations, or affirmative action compliance.
Employent History:	
1993-1996:	Assistant to the Chief of Staff of the Governor of Oregon, responsible for the coordination of statewide affirmative action plans for state agencies. Made recommendations on affirmative action programs to state agency affirmative action program directors. Responsible for media relations and legislative relations between the governor's office and affirmative action compliance agencies. Represented the state at numerous state and national affirmative action compliance conferences and news conferences.
1989-1993:	Assistant Coordinator of Title IX Planning. Principal staff assistant to the deputy director of education, State Board of Education. Responsible for advising the deputy director on design and implementation of statewide funding and curriculum changes required for compliance with federal funding guidelines for women's athletic programs under Title IX.
Education:	
1993:	M.A., Education, University of Oregon
1988:	B.A. Education, University of Oregon
Honors and Awards:	
1996:	"Golden Tongue Award," Oregon Media Relations Association
1988:	NCAA Finalist, Track and Field, State of Oregon

References:

The Hon. Mark O. Hatfield U.S. Senate Office Building Washington, DC	William Groves Director, Affirmative Action Program State of Oregon Eugene, OR

NOTES

[1] Plachy, R. (April 1987). The case for effective point-factor job evaluation. *Personnel,* 64, 30-32.

[2] Barrett, G. V., and D. Doverspike (March 1989). Another defense of point-factor job evaluation. *Personnel, 66,* 33-36; Biondi, C., and J. MacMillian (November 1986). Job evaluation: Generate the numbers. *Personnel Journal, 65,* 56-63; and Sahl, R. (March 1989). How to install a job evaluation. *Personnel, 66,* 38-42.

[3] Lawler, E. III. (November 1986). What's wrong with point-factor job evaluation. *Management Review,* 75, 44-48.

[4] Risher, H., and B. Schay (1994). Grade banding: The model for future salary programs. *Public Personnel Management, 23,* 187-199.

[5] National Academy of Public Administration (1991). *Modernizing classification: An opportunity for excellence.* Washington, DC: NAPA.

5

Pay and Benefits

Pay and economic benefits are important to employees because they provide for economic well-being and offer an objective economic measure of an individual's worth. They serve as a measure of comparison for internal equity (compared to other employees in the agency) and external equity (compared with other employers in the job market). Both measures are important, for they affect satisfaction, performance, and turnover. Thus, they affect the well-being of both the employee and the employer.

An employer must invest enough in compensation to attract and retain employees with valued knowledge, skills, abilities, and personal characteristics (KSAP). To be effective, pay and benefits—total compensation—must be competitive, equitable, flexible, and easy to administer. They must meet the needs of both employee and employer.

Benefits are an important aspect of total compensation. Despite the fact that different measuring approaches lead to different conclusions about the percent of payroll devoted to benefits, the number is substantial. For example, in 1992, for public and private employers combined, the cost of employee benefits equaled about 20 percent of total compensation, excluding paid time off.[1] A different survey conducted by the U.S. Chamber of Commerce indicated that benefits totaled 41 percent of payroll costs in 1993.[2] The high cost of employee benefits, the importance and expense of health care, and the need to combine flexibility and ease of administration to meet employer productivity needs and employee equity concerns means that compensation and benefits managers enjoy an increasingly important role in human resource management.

By the end of this chapter, you will be able to:

1. Identify the elements included in a total compensation package.
2. Identify the laws governing compensation policy and practices.
3. Identify the issues involved in pay disparity based on race and gender.
4. Discuss the methods of setting pay under alternative public personnel systems.
5. Identify the conditions necessary for a pay-for-performance system to work.
6. Discuss merit pay and its relationship to seniority and cost-of-living allowances.

7. Describe the concept of "new pay" and its three essential elements.
8. Describe the statutory benefits to which employees are entitled by law (Social Security, workers' compensation, and unemployment compensation).
9. Discuss public employee pension systems and the public policy issues associated with pension fund management.
10. Discuss health insurance plans, and the managerial and public policy issues associated with the cost of health care.
11. Discuss other emergent benefit issues and their relationship to work/family conflicts.
12. Discuss the relationship between pay and benefit systems and the conflict among public personnel systems and values.

THE NEW COMPENSATION AND BENEFITS ENVIRONMENT

Traditionally, civil service compensation systems were designed with the assumption that an individual job was a basic unit of measurement and that the relationship of one job to another could be determined and its value assessed apart from the job incumbent. Seniority and equity were valued as products of a stable working environment. Today, the basic assumption of stability has been replaced by dynamism and change. Even if not fully experiencing the tumultuous changes occurring in the private sector, public employers and employees are not shielded entirely.

Siegel[3] has described the modern-day model of the civil service in the following way and has identified elements 2, 3, and 4 as influencing the future of compensation policy and practices:

1. Publicly held negative image of the civil service
2. Turn away from long-term (seniority) toward shorter-term perspective
3. Performance orientation in compensation
4. Retrenchment in level and types of benefits
5. More emphasis on accountability
6. More adaptable workforce with emphasis on contract management versus service delivery and regulation; increases in managerial discretion
7. Gradual replacement of present workforce with employees adapted to the changes described in 1–6

The impact these elements might have on public-sector compensation policy and practices could be captured with the term *new pay* that is currently being explored in the private sector. This emerging concept is characterized in a model Howard Risher[4] describes with the following:

1. Responsibility for day-to-day salary management shifts from the human resources staff to managers and supervisors
2. Traditional salary grade and range structure is replaced by broad banded classes and wide salary ranges
3. "Paying the job" gives way to "paying the person"

4. More variety in performance appraisal emphasizes wider range of raters, including peers, subordinates, and clients/customers
5. Conventional merit pay for individuals is called into question by team and group incentives
6. An increased willingness is seen to tailor pay plans to specific work situations rather than a "one size fits all" perspective

Each of these changes is predicated upon the changing work environment we have been describing in this book. In the contemporary work world, the concept of stable job content is in jeopardy; and traditional pay plans are based on predictability. Along with this instability is the emphasis on accountability and shaping individual and team performance toward specific organizational goals and objectives. Pay associated with performance is seen as a crucial, if not proven, incentive in this regard.

We will set the stage for a more detailed discussion of new pay with a traditional look at the subject of compensation and benefits.

While we have only included examples, from Figure 5-1 one can see the basic components of a **total compensation package**. Usually, when employees think about their salary, they think of direct and variable compensation. In the

FIGURE 5-1 Total Compensation Package (Adapted with permssion from T1-Total Compensation Management, American Compensation Association (ACA), 14040 N. Northsight Blvd., Scottsdale, AZ 85260; 602-951-9191.)

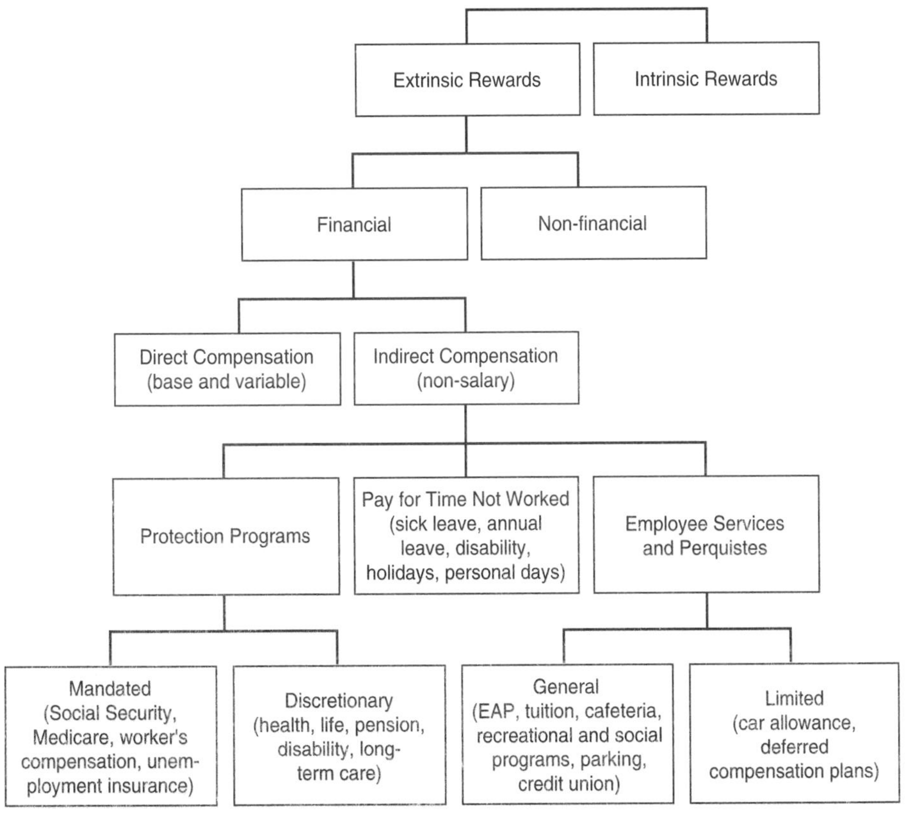

figure, some of the indirect, or non-salary, "benefits" involved in compensating an employee are identified. Furthermore, employees usually never even see a record of some benefits such as the employer's contribution to Social Security, workers' compensation, and unemployment insurance. Thus, most employees are unaware of their total compensation.

THE LEGAL CONTEXT OF COMPENSATION POLICY AND PRACTICE

Pay setting in public agencies is governed by legal constraints, historical practice, and the relative power of stakeholders. Along with various state statutes, four primary federal laws apply: the Fair Labor Standards Act of 1938, the Equal Pay Act of 1963, the 1964 Civil Rights Act (Title VII), and the Age Discrimination in Employment Act of 1967. In this section we discuss the provisions of the laws that apply to public agencies, the outcome of these laws' interaction with historical practice, and the impact of these outcomes on the pay-setting process under alternative personnel systems.

The **Fair Labor Standards Act (FLSA)** was originally passed in 1938 to regulate minimum wages, overtime pay, and record-keeping requirements for private employers. In 1985, the U.S. Supreme Court's decision in ***Garcia v. San Antonio Metropolitan Transit Authority*** made state and local governments subject to its wage, hour, and record keeping requirements. *Garcia* has profoundly affected public personnel practices in state and local government. Employees must be paid the minimum wage ($5.15 per hour). Employees (with the exception of executives, administrative employees, and professionals) must be paid time-and-a-half for overtime, defined as more than forty hours per workweek (or given "comp time" during the same pay period). Employers are required to keep records going back two to three years of *all* employees' wages and hours, and to provide these records to the Department of Labor upon request.

Because it is not always clear whether employees are exempt from or covered by the FLSA, and because covered employees require more complex staffing patterns or considerably higher personnel costs, keeping up with FLSA provisions is critical to state and local governments. Many local government employees (particularly police officers and firefighters) have irregular work schedules that pose particular problems for compensation specialists.[5]

The Equal Pay Act of 1963 requires employers to provide men and women with equal pay for equal work. In order to win relief under this law, the plaintiff must demonstrate that jobs requiring equal skill, effort, and responsibility, and performed under similar working conditions, are paid differentially on the basis of sex. But "equal work" is narrowly defined under the terms of this act—it does not include dissimilar jobs, and it exempts pay differentials resulting from the impact of seniority or merit systems.

The Civil Rights Act of 1964 (Title VII) forbids discrimination with respect to pay and benefits on the basis of non-merit factors. While it does not prohibit any sex-based pay differentials that are legal under the Equal Pay Act of 1963, subsequent court cases have held that it goes beyond the equal pay provisions of the EPA by, in some cases, allowing equal pay for comparable jobs—those not identical, but requiring equivalent skill, effort, and responsibility, and performed under similar working conditions.

The Age Discrimination in Employment Act prohibits employers from paying older workers less than younger ones for equal work. And as the workforce gets grayer, it has another important provision—prohibiting employers from using pension plan provisions to force older employees to take early retirement.

ISSUES INVOLVED IN PAY DISPARITY BASED ON RACE AND GENDER

Judging by its laws related to pay equity, the United States is an egalitarian society —discrimination in pay and benefits on the basis of age, sex, race, or other nonmerit factors is prohibited. But judging by its history of personnel practice with respect to pay equity, ample evidence justifies the conclusion that our society has unfairly discriminated against women and minorities in particular. There are, however, two sides to this question, and one should not reach even tentative conclusions on so important an issue without examining both.[6]

Proponents of labor market mechanisms for pay setting admit that women and minorities earn less than men, and that pay rates for male-dominated jobs are higher than those for female-dominated jobs. But they deny that these differences are based on sex or race discrimination as such. They attribute the difference in men's and women's salaries to traditional labor market explanations: Women have lower seniority than men because they leave the labor market to have children or move from one job to another to accompany their husbands (without commensurate increases in pay or status). Minorities tend to be clustered in low-paying, low-status service jobs.

Proponents of pay equity, on the other hand, charge that women and minorities find themselves concentrated in these occupations and employment situations because of social values and conditions. As justification for this view, they compare salaries for different groups in the public and private sectors. In the private sector, where anti-discrimination laws apply but "employment at will" laws limit the power of women and minorities to protest employment conditions, the disparity between salaries of white males and other groups remains. In the public sector, where similar laws apply but are more enforceable because of merit systems and collective bargaining rights, the pay differential between white males and other groups is almost nil at entry level and only marginally different moving up the pay scale.

At the heart of this controversy is a fundamental dilemma that must be recognized and addressed, but can never be resolved as long as the two values of social equity and efficiency compete across the range of personnel systems and activities. For advocates of government efficiency, it simply makes no sense to pay women and minorities more than one would have to pay them under a market model (unless required to by specific laws such as minimum wage provisions of the FLSA). The fact that women and minorities receive lower wages may be socially and ethically unfortunate, but it is the primary responsibility of the employer to provide services while meeting a payroll at the lowest possible cost, not to be an instrument for solving social problems. Advocates of comparable worth hold exactly the opposite view. For them, balancing the budgets of public agencies by maintaining lower salaries for women and minorities is morally indefensible. It violates Title VII for private employee and denies public employees the rights to equal protection and due process they are guaranteed under the Fourteenth Amendment. At present, the judicial status of comparable worth is unclear, but the decisions of the Supreme Court in the 1990s suggest that this issue is more likely to be dealt with in legislatures and through labor relations than in the courts.

SETTING PAY IN ALTERNATIVE PERSONNEL SYSTEMS

The manner in which pay is set under alternative public personnel systems reflects the conflict among the values of efficiency and equality, and the historical practice within which these values and systems have evolved.

Pay for political appointments is set by the appointing executive, though always within general limits established legislatively. Adjustments to pay are set the same way, based both on statutory limits and external and internal market comparisons. In local governments, frequent trade-offs occur between salaries and benefits, so that it is (some would say this is deliberate) hard to determine the actual rate of pay increase or to compare it meaningfully with pay paid for similar work in other jurisdictions.

Pay for civil service employees usually is established by the chief executive but authorized by the legislature. While civil service pay increases are usually justified or opposed on the basis of market comparisons, market factors are only indirectly used as the basis of setting pay. And the greater job security of civil service employees represents an intangible financial benefit that is difficult to factor into the market equation. This model applies most directly to federal civilian employees, whose pay and benefits are set directly by Congress rather than through collective bargaining.

Under a collective bargaining process (which is described more completely in Chapter 13), pay, benefits, and working conditions are set by direct negotiations between agency management and employee union representatives. But there are critical differences between collective bargaining in the public and private sectors. Public employees are usually prohibited from going on strike to influence the outcome of salary negotiations; and economic issues (such as pay and benefit increases) must be ratified by the appropriate legislative body prior to taking effect. This is because state and local governments are prohibited from deficit financing of operating budgets, and because state legislatures may not legally delegate their appropriations authority to management negotiators in the collective bargaining process.

In practice, this means that collective bargaining systems set wages through a combination of direct negotiations and indirect political influence on the legislature. For example, teachers' and police officers' unions (or their auxiliaries) frequently support local candidates to the school board or city council in exchange for promises of support for pay and benefit increases when negotiated agreements are up for legislative ratification.

In the past decade, the increase in privatization, contracting out, exempt appointments, and the use of temporary workers to reduce full-time equivalent staffing levels have proven powerful alternatives to union political influence over the contract negotiation and ratification process. Union supporters call it a threat. It offers managers and elected officials the option of approving a negotiated contract, or of deciding to provide the same services through privatization or by replacing public employees and hiring contract workers instead. Usually contract employees without sought-after technical knowledge and skills have much lower pay and benefits than their unionized or public counterparts (because these salaries and benefits are set by a market model rather than through legislative deliberations and collective bargaining). To be blunt, elected officials usually regard employees as voters and constituents and as people who can help or hinder their efforts to respond to citizen requests. Finally, they see them as employees with needs.

Affirmative action initially developed because of concerns by minorities over *access* to jobs. But inevitably, as access has increased, minorities and women have altered their focus to the *allocation* of pay and benefits. A prime target of affirmative action proponents has been the impact of seniority systems on minority access to promotions, and the resultant effect on salaries. In most cases, courts have held that seniority systems developed with a race- or sex-neutral intent are legitimate, even if their effect is to give preference to white males. In some cases, however, courts have ordered modification of seniority systems, primarily by establishing dual seniority lists and requiring quota-based promotions until workforce comparability is achieved. This extreme solution is invoked only in cases where historical patterns of racism or sexism exist, where voluntary affirmative action compliance is ineffective, and where the resultant quota system is a temporary expedient that does not entirely bar qualified white males from consideration.

Setting Civil Service Pay through a Wage Survey

Wages and salaries in public agencies are set by a variety of processes (job evaluation, individual negotiations, collective bargaining, and court order), depending on the type of personnel system and the interplay of law and historical practice. For the majority of positions filled through civil service systems, wages are set by salary surveys that establish external equity. These are then used as the basis for proposing and gaining legislative approval of pay structures. Here's how the process works.[7]

Jobs are first analyzed, classified, and evaluated according to the guidelines presented in the previous chapter. A typical classification and evaluation process will place jobs into major categories like professional, administrative, technical, and clerical, and public safety. **Benchmark positions**, those common to many employers, are identified to facilitate wage comparisons. Sometimes a government or agency can participate with other governments in a multi-jurisdiction wage survey to broaden data available and reduce survey cost. Surveys are likely to include positions for which the employer hires many applicants, or those which present recruitment or retention problems. Second, the relevant labor market is defined for different types of positions. It is usually national or regional for professional and administrative occupations, and local for technical and clerical jobs. Third, the employer obtains information about prevailing salaries for previously identified benchmark positions. This information is available from newspaper ads, job descriptions, or wage surveys conducted by professional organizations.

The selection of equivalent positions for wage comparison is important. Usually, this requires a detailed analysis of the job title, qualifications, duties, and wage/salary. This kind of survey permits comparison of midpoint and range of wages or salaries.

After the labor market survey is completed, the employer uses the results to set tentative wage or salary levels. For jobs that have relatively few positions at the same level of responsibility, a single pay grade may suffice. For jobs that have a range of responsibilities and pay levels (such as engineer or manager), it will be necessary to establish a series of pay grades. The compensation specialist faces a dilemma in setting pay grades and rates. On the one hand, it is desirable to have a large number of **pay grades** so that jobs may be adequately defined based on market conditions and the agency's needs. On the other hand, a large number of pay grades within one occupation makes it difficult for managers to reassign employees easily, or for employees to move around based on the relationship of their skills to the agency's needs. One solution that has been proposed to both problems is **pay comparability** (based on market surveys) and **broad banding** (establishing relatively few pay levels within an occupation, and allowing managers considerable discretion in setting individual salaries within these levels). At the heart of this controversy is the argument about whether the purpose of a job classification and evaluation system is external control over wages or internal equity and flexibility.

Once the pay structure is established, it may be necessary to adjust pay rates to fit local labor markets. For example, the federal government recently conducted a wage and salary survey that led to the establishment of higher pay rates (**locality pay**) for general civil service employees in high-cost areas. These adjustments are made as well for positions demanding scarce knowledge, skills, and abilities.

PAY FOR PERFORMANCE

In the 1980s skepticism of the government's ability to solve public problems contributed to government cutbacks and demands that government become more businesslike. Public-sector experiments with performance-based compensation systems grew out of this movement, with the federal government leading the way.

The Civil Service Reform Act of 1978 required Washington to develop job-related and objective performance appraisal systems that could be used for training, promotion, and disciplinary personnel actions. The act also mandated performance-based compensation systems for senior and middle-level federal managers. According to a recent comprehensive review of these efforts, "The reforms have by most measures fallen short of expectations, despite fairly substantial mid course corrections. Yet the belief in merit principles remains strong, as does the expectation that performance appraisal and linking compensation to performance can provide incentives for excellence."[8]

FIGURE 5-2 Pay for Performance Classes (Source: Reprinted with permission from *Pay for Performance*, © 1991 by the National Academy of Sciences. Published by National Academy Press, Washington, DC.)

CONTRIBUTION TO BASE SALARY		LEVEL OF PERFORMANCE: Individual	LEVEL OF PERFORMANCE: Group
	Added to base	(a) Merit plans	(d) Small group incentives
	Not added to base	(b) Piece rates commissions bonuses	(c) Profit sharing gainsharing bonuses

Why have performance-based compensation systems resulted in unrealized expectations? And in the face of these unmet expectations, why do employees, managers, legislators, and the public continue to profess faith in them? Exploring these questions requires an understanding of what is meant by a **pay for performance** system. Figure 5-2 classifies several of these systems without distinguishing between public and private- sectors.

Merit plans add to the individual employee's rate of pay contingent upon an employee's performance during a previous period of time. Increases usually are specified according to a schedule or grid and are tied to the rating an employee receives on a performance appraisal. Since the vast majority of employees receive "satisfactory" or better ratings, merit pay has come to be seen as an expected annual increase in an employee's base pay. Even though marginally effective, merit plans are commonly used to connect pay to performance in the public sector and in large private-sector organizations for managers and professionals. It may be surprising to learn that not much research evaluating the effectiveness of these plans has been conducted.[9]

Piece rates, commissions, and bonuses are also tied to individual performance but are not added to the employee's base rate of pay. Applications of these kinds of incentive plans have proven effective where outcomes are easy to calculate and attribute to individual employees, but research shows that they account for only 9 to 16 percent of the variance in individual performance.[10]

Small-group incentives are similar to merit plans in that money is added to the employee's base rate of pay, but team performance rather than individual accomplishment is rewarded. There are few examples of these plans. More common is profit sharing, gainsharing, and bonuses distributed to groups, often on a company-wide basis but not added to the base rate of pay.

Several benefits are associated with pay-for-performance which accompany the fundamental belief that a person's pay ought to reflect what that individual has contributed to the organization.[11] First, it is argued that pay-for-performance systems affect a person's decision to join or leave an organization, to perform, and even to come to work. Second, pay-for-performance is seen as a way of increasing organizational effectiveness. Another benefit comes from the communication between supervisors and subordinates that occurs regarding performance goals and feedback on performance. And last, performance-based compensation systems are seen as more businesslike in our society, and it is believed that organizations employing them are somehow more legitimate in the eyes of internal and external stakeholders. Again, there is little systematic, empirical research comparing the effectiveness of different pay-for-performance plans in achieving these benefits.

Based on an understanding of equity and expectancy theory (see Chapter 8), it is clear that several elements must be present for a pay-for-performance system to motivate employee performance:

- Employees must know what work performance will be rewarded.
- Employees must have the opportunity—the tools, the time—to perform.
- Employees must believe they have the knowledge, skills, and abilities to accomplish the desired performance.
- Employees must value the monetary reward when they calculate the costs and benefits of performing at the desired level.
- Employees must believe that if they perform well they will be monetarily rewarded.
- Employees must perceive that monetary rewards will be distributed fairly.

In addition to these specific conditions, other factors complicate the effective implementation of performance-based compensation systems. First, not all work lends itself to pay for performance. For example, where goals are difficult to identify or quantify and when discreet individual contributions are hard to distinguish, such plans face severe obstacles. Second, some organizational cultures and structures do not lend themselves to performance-based compensation. For example, organizations that pride themselves on teamwork and cooperation often find the competitive and individualistic norms underlying many pay-for-performance plans contrary to their organizational culture. Third, external factors like the presence of a union or legal constraints or political forces may block successful implementation.

Given these many preconditions, it is not surprising that existing performance-based compensation systems—whether found in public or in private sectors—do not accomplish very well the several goals set out for them.[12] Milkovich and Wigdor found that less than one third of the employees in the various surveys they reviewed rated their performance appraisal plan effective in tying pay to performance or communicating organizational expectations about work.[13] In a recent survey of federal employees, 54 percent responded it was "very" or "somewhat unlikely" that if they performed better they would receive more pay.[14] In a 1988 survey of federal personnel officers, only 27 percent indicated that the present performance-management system that ties pay to performance had "greatly" or "somewhat improved" organizational effectiveness, while some 35 percent indicated that it had "greatly" or "somewhat impeded" organizational effectiveness.[15] And Risher indicates that despite the predominance of merit pay policies in the private sector, there is little confidence that anyone has figured out how to make them work effectively.[16]

At the federal level, where pay-for-performance has been researched thoroughly, it has been found that not enough money is set aside to establish a motivating effect, that performance appraisals are inflated, and that employees suspect the equitable distribution of the monetary rewards. Gabris and Mitchell summarize the pay-for-performance experience by writing: "So much do we want to think that extrinsic incentives will, under proper conditions, motivate employees, that we somehow refuse to accept the overwhelming evidence suggesting that this theory does not work well in an applied and general sense. The theory may be internally elegant and logical, but not practical."[17]

Given the overwhelming evidence suggesting at best only cautious optimism for performance-based compensation systems other than piece-rate incentive plans, why do they continue to attract advocates? Perry suggests that pay-for-performance systems have become ingrained in the institutional order of our society.[18] They are "part of the ritual and myth that help to retain the legitimacy of the governance system." Bureaucracies are established as rational instruments of public policy, and nothing appears more rational than rewarding employees monetarily on the basis of their performance. According to Kellough and Lu, the professed link between performance and pay suggests control by politicians, administrators, and the public over bureaucrats and conveys to the public that government is both responsive and efficient.[19]

In addition, in a typical governmental setting where equity concerns permeate public policy making and service delivery, it should not be surprising that attempting to measure, differentiate, and reward performance would find an unwelcome home. Without the discipline and driving force of a competitive market-oriented environment, internal equity is likely to drive out the underlying rationale for variable pay.

MERIT PAY, SENIORITY, AND COST-OF-LIVING ALLOWANCES

In theory, pay systems maintain a separation between merit pay, pay for seniority and cost-of-living increases. First, **merit pay** is given to reward superior performance on the assumption that once rewarded the performance will be repeated. Second, seniority pay increments (also known as **time-in-grade** increases) are given on the assumption that seniority increases an employee's skills, and hence value to the agency. Third, **cost-of-living allowances (COLA)** or market adjustments are given to employees to maintain external pay equity in the face of a competitive labor market.

But in reality, there is no clearer example of the confusion between intent and effect of pay systems than the practical relationships that exist among these three factors. First, the total amount of payroll budget allocated to merit increases is usually quite small (1 to 2 percent at most) because of budget constraints and uneasiness among elected officials about voter reactions to "paying employees bonuses to do what they ought to be doing anyway," or unwillingness to trust managers to allocate bonuses fairly. This means that personnel managers and supervisors are faced with the unpalatable alternatives of allocating relatively large bonuses to a few employees (thereby heightening conflict over the distribution of a relatively small merit pool), or spreading the merit money in small, symbolic increments among a larger group of employees and thereby diluting its effectiveness as a reward. Second, merit pay is usually permanent, in that it becomes part of the base pay upon which future increments are computed. It never is reduced, thus mitigating its motivating potential. Further, it is usually given for satisfactory performance, which almost every employee attains as a matter of attendance not performance. Third, despite the impact of work groups on organizational performance, merit pay is usually allocated to individuals. Thus, it tends to undermine an organizational culture of teamwork regardless of how it is allocated. Under these circumstances, it is easy to see why many employees, supervisors, and managers consider merit pay not to be worth the trouble. Last, **seniority pay** has also been named as a culprit in discouraging performance, turnover, and risk taking in agencies. Just because employees have done things longer is no guarantee they do them better. Indeed, given the need for innovation in the face of technological change, it is equally likely that experience is an impediment to efficiency.

Taken together, these three types of adjustments have a questionable impact on agency efficiency and employee performance in civil service systems. If pay increases fail to keep pace with inflation or a competitive labor market, managers and personnel directors out of necessity seek to retain competent employees by inappropriately using combinations of COLA, time-in-grade increments, and merit increases. In the end, the distinctions between the purposes of these systems and their effects tend to disappear.

Clearly, one of the problems faced in civil service systems is the tendency to blur the distinction between cost-of-living increases and merit increases. Traditionally, merit increases become part of an employee's base salary from which future increments are calculated. Since the total amount of payroll allocated to merit pay is generally slight (1 to 2 percent), this guarantees that merit awards will be perceived as either insignificant or unrelated to performance. One innovative solution is to (1) make performance awards on an annual (one-time) basis rather than building those awards into the employee's base salary, and (2) lump a range of financial awards together to increase their economic and symbolic value.

Non–civil service personnel systems do not have this problem, though they avoid it by different strategies. Political systems (and contracting out) use a market model: The salaries paid to individuals are set on the basis of personal qualifications and value. While this method is subjective and open to inequities, the individual has one response that always brings results—get a higher job offer elsewhere, show it to the employer, and be prepared to get a pay increase (if the negotiations are successful) or move (if they are not). Under collective bargaining, merit pay for individual employees does not exist. Employees as a group may receive salary increments based on increased productivity (**gainsharing**); negotiated contracts may provide for seniority increments; and the periodic renegotiation of economic issues compensates for changes in the cost of living.

ONE SUPERVISOR'S VIEW

March 1996

TO: John Nalbandian

RE: Reactions to the state's merit pay system:

1. The state never funded it the way it was supposed to be funded when it was first implemented. Employees received ratings of STANDARD, ABOVE STANDARD, and EXCEPTIONAL. If employees received a STANDARD evaluation, they moved up one step on the pay scale. If they received ABOVE STANDARD, they moved up two steps, and three steps for EXCEPTIONAL. Unfortunately, the state could never fund the plan, so as long as an employee received a STANDARD or above rating, they moved only one step. There is no incentive for employees to do anything above STANDARD work. Classified workers say, "Pays the same!"

2. My second complaint is that since the state is not funding it, then they should not be requiring supervisors to justify the ABOVE STANDARD and EXCEPTIONAL ratings. For example, if an employee receives STANDARD, the supervisor is not required to make any comments. If an employee receives ABOVE STANDARD or EXCEPTIONAL, then the supervisor has to write comments under each of the critical elements being evaluated. Many supervisors are not going to take the time to rate employees accurately; it's easier to rate everyone STANDARD. I'm sure you can imagine how that affects morale!

Performance evaluations are important and have a purpose. We need them especially when we have to deal with "problem employees." Paper trails are a must. However, I feel like I can make a much better connection with the employee if I sit down and talk with him/her about the job. So, for myself, I would rather spend more time talking with the employee than jumping through hoops to complete paperwork.

NEW PAY

New pay is a term used to connote a new way of thinking about compensation. It contrasts to traditional pay, especially compensation practices in the public sector where practically speaking pay is determined by seniority and internal equity—the relationship between jobs within an agency or public organization. Internal equity is determined by comparing jobs on common factors like difficulty of the work, level of responsibility, and working conditions. These factors may have little to do with the market value of an individual's knowledge, skills, abilities, and personal characteristics. According to Schuster and Zingheim, "The new pay view provides that organizations effectively use all elements of pay—direct pay (cash compensation) and indirect pay (benefits)—to help form a partnership between the organization and its employees."[20] This view includes two basic elements. First is the belief that all elements of pay should be used to connect individual and group work effort and organizational goals and that pay should reflect the external market rather than internal equity. Second, it supports the notion that compensation policies and practices should be more experimental and flexible and should focus on three elements—base pay, variable pay, and indirect pay or benefits.

Part of the new pay partnership that Schuster and Zingheim discuss includes pay banding.[21] Pay banding collapses several pay grades into a few and provides flexibility in the assignment of work within those broader pay ranges. Thus, there is more emphasis on "rank-in-person" than on "rank-in-job." It is easier to move people around from job to job based on organizational need without worrying about whether employees are being treated unfairly working outside of narrowly defined pay grades or classes.

Broad pay banding also provides flexibility in base pay because the pay bands incorporate larger ranges than traditional classes. Thus, it is easier to bring an entry-level person in at a higher wage if encouraged by a competitive marketplace. One version of broad pay banding, consistent with an external market for establishing pay rates would encourage increases in **base pay** for individual employees contingent upon skill acquisition.[22] Otherwise, base pay is increased as part of a market adjustment in order to keep salaries competitive. These adjustments are made for occupational groupings within an agency, not for the agency as a whole, and they are distinguished from cost-of-living increases which have little attraction in new pay approaches because across-the-board cost-of-living increases fail to recognize the market value of different jobs.

The new pay concept suggests that benefits be tailored to meet employee needs. This requires the involvement of employees in choices about kinds and levels of benefits they receive.[23]

While base pay and indirect pay influence attraction and retention of quality employees, **variable pay** affects an employee's motivation and the channeling of work toward organizational goals and objectives. Essentially, variable pay is a one-time payment to an employee for accomplishment of preset goals or objectives. These rewards can be given individually or to teams of employees, but the critical feature is that they be contingent upon organizationally valued performance and they do not become part of base pay in contrast to traditional merit pay.

The resulting formula is that base pay and benefits are periodically adjusted so the employer knows it is not overpaying or underpaying for an employee's knowledge, skills, abilities, and personal characteristics. The formula features a variable pay component designed to reward organizationally valued employee performance. This payment is reusable by the organization because it is not folded into an employee's base pay.

In order to connect this formula to an organization's broader goals, an objective of new pay advocates, Schuster and Zingheim suggest that an organization adopt a "total compensation strategy statement." Some contrasting examples taken from their work are shown in Table 5-1.

TABLE 5-1 Total Compensation Strategy Statements[24]

NewCorp	*ProCorp*	*UsualCorp*
Cash compensation is the key element of total compensation because it is flexible and can be changed to respond to new goals, priorities, and contingencies. Cash compensation is more important than benefits as a communicator of goals and objectives	Base pay will involve paying for the acquisition of skills that are valued by ProCorp. The acquisition of skills will result in moderately competitive base pay. Employees who participate in skill-based pay can participate in variable pay plans.	UsualCorp will pay base pay and benefits that are equal to or better than the 75th percentile of competitive practice. Competitive practice is defined based on UsualCorp's direct business and labor market competitors. Base pay will be internally equitable and fair. All jobs of equal internal value will be paid similarly.
Variable pay is more important than base pay because it is the most flexible reward NewCorp has and can significantly recognize teamwork and collaboration and achievement of results.	Variable pay in terms of gainsharing, lump-sum awards, and other group or individual incentive plans will be used wherever such plans give ProCorp the chance to outperform its competitors.	A merit system will be used to grant base pay increases based on individual employee performance.
Employee benefits will provide a basic level of protection from unexpected health, life, and disability risks. NewCorp assumes that employees will contribute to their own future security and will share in the cost of employee benefits.	Employee benefits will be moderate and provide the opportunity for cost sharing between employees and ProCorp.	Employee benefits will insure that employees have an attractive retirement after a full career with UsualCorp. UsualCorp. will provide very competitive benefits to ensure that employees are well protected.

From Table 5-1 one can see the difference in these firms with regard to compensation policy. UsualCorp operates in a stable environment where the past is an accurate guide to the future, and this policy could well be that of a traditional public employer. NewCorp operates in a dynamic environment, one where the past cannot be relied upon to predict the future. The various compensation strategies reflect a different organizational environment and culture, and convey to employees an important aspect of the employment relationship.

STATUTORY ENTITLEMENT BENEFITS

Part of a total compensation package includes benefits. Employee benefit programs may be separated for analytical purposes into two categories: entitlement or mandated benefits, and discretionary benefits. **Entitlement benefits a**re those to which employees are entitled by law (Social Security, workers' compensation, and unemployment insurance). **Discretionary benefits** are not mandated by law, but the employer may provide them as part of a benefit package to attract or retain employees. There is considerable range in the discretionary benefits offered to employees, depending not only upon the employer's budget but also upon the type of personnel system.

Social Security

Beginning in 1983, all state and local governments were required to deduct employee contributions to the Social Security system, a federally administered **defined contribution** plan intended to supplement employer-sponsored discretionary retirement systems. Currently (1997), employees pay 7.65 percent of wages up to a maximum of $65,400. Employers are required to match this contribution. The Social Security system also provides disability, death, survivor, and senior citizens' health benefits (Medicare). Federal employees do not belong to the Social Security system; they have their own defined contribution pension system or the optional federal employee retirement system (FERS). In 1992, 50 million individuals, 71 percent of those 55 and older, received some kind of retirement benefit or Social Security.[25]

Workers' Compensation

Workers' compensation is an employer-financed program that provides a percentage of lost wages and some medical and rehabilitation benefits to employees who are unable to work because of a job-related injury or illness. Employers pay a percentage of payroll into a state-operated insurance pool or a jurisdiction self-insures or can buy a private insurance contract. Because the percentage paid is based on the history of claims against the fund, employers seek to avoid payment of benefits for claims they consider fraudulent, and to adopt workforce health and safety policies to reduce the incidence of job-related injuries and accidents.

Unemployment Compensation

In 1976, state and local government employees became eligible for **unemployment compensation.** This benefit provides a portion of regular wages to employees who have been separated without misconduct, and who are actively looking for work and unable to find it. There is wide variation from state to state concerning waiting periods for eligibility, length of time benefits paid, and level of benefits provided. States establish unemployment compensation funds through enabling legislation and the system is funded through a federal tax on employers based on size of payroll.

DISCRETIONARY BENEFITS: PENSIONS

Retirement benefits, usually mandated by law for federal, state, and local government public employees, nevertheless largely remain as an important discretionary element in many other employee benefit systems. In addition, they vary from state to state. Annual pension costs for state and local governments are estimated at some 15 percent of wages and salaries. In 1990, 90 percent of all state and local employees were covered by defined benefit pension plans.[26]

Obviously, the magnitude of public pension funds, and the value of their benefits to the individual employee mean that there are many managerial and policy issues associated with their development and administration. From the viewpoint of the individual employee, some primary issues are vesting, portability, defined benefit versus defined contribution plans, disability retirement, and the relationship between pension plan requirements and age discrimination. From the viewpoint of pension fund management policy, key issues are disclosure requirements, actuarial standards, and strategic investment potential.

Vesting and Portability

Normally, employers require employees to have worked a minimum number of years (usually five) prior to vesting. **Vesting** simply means that an employee is entitled to that portion of accrued retirement benefits contributed by the employer (naturally, any employee contributions can be reclaimed by the employee upon withdrawal from the system when employment is terminated). Vesting discourages turnover. This may be an advantage or a disadvantage to the agency. Employees and some employers favor **portability**, which means that benefits earned in one agency may be transferred to another. Many state systems are already portable, in that employees working in one state agency or local government are eligible to transfer benefits if they work for any other agency that is a member of that state system. True portability involves transferring assets from one plan to another or from one jurisdiction to another (such as the TIAA-CREF system, the International City/County Management Retirement Corporation, or employer-sponsored tax sheltered annuities authorized by the Internal Revenue Service).

Defined Benefit versus Defined Contribution

State and local systems have traditionally been **defined benefit** systems. That is, employees and employers contribute a portion of salary, but the benefits are predictable based on number of years' service and salary level and some multiplier. Social security is like this as well. Private pension funds are more likely to work on a **defined contribution** basis. That is, employees or employers contribute and thereby invest a fixed percentage of tax-deferred salary, and benefits upon retirement or withdrawal from the system will vary depending on the success of investments by the fund. In a defined contribution plan, like a 401(K), individual employees are able to make choices about how their tax-deferred contributions are invested, as opposed to defined benefit systems where these decisions are made for them by financial managers.

Defined contribution plans are gaining popularity because they place more responsibility on employees, are more suited to employees who expect to work for several employers over their work life, are easier to administer, and often cost less because an employer's contribution completely ceases once the employee leaves or retires. But defined contribution plans require more education of employees regarding their retirement needs, investment opportunities, and risk. Many employers offer some combination of a defined benefit plan along with a defined contribution plan that employees may utilize if they wish.

Defined benefit plans rarely are offered to part-time or temporary employees, whereas defined contribution plans may be available. The challenge is that even though a defined contribution plan may be available to these employees, if they make a lower wage they have little incentive or ability to save.

Disability Retirement

At its best, **disability retirement** allows employees who are unable to work because of illness or injury and not normally eligible to retire (in terms of age or years of service) to retire with benefits. At its worst, it is a device used by employees to retire early at the employer's expense, or by employers to induce an unwanted employee to retire early. Personnel directors can fulfill the intent of disability retirement programs and minimize fraud by considering alternatives such as light duty positions or early retirement programs. Long-term disability benefits are provided either by insured or self-insured long-term disability plans or with a disability retirement benefit through the pension plan.

Age Discrimination

One additional issue faced by public pension systems is the relationship between benefit accrual provisions and age discrimination in employment. Traditionally, pension systems interlocked with mandatory retirement policies in that employees were forced to retire by a certain age (65 or 70, earlier for public safety employees) because the employer stopped paying benefits into the pension plan when the employee reached that age. However, recent court decisions have held that such provisions represent disparate treatment of older workers, and thereby violate the Age Discrimination in Employment Act of 1967.[27]

This logic was enacted into law in 1990 by the Older Workers Benefit Protection Act (PL 101-43). This law permits early retirement programs provided that they do not result in age discrimination. Early retirement incentives that provide a flat dollar amount, service-based benefits, a percentage of salary to all employees above a certain age, or give employees who retire credit for additional years of service will be lawful. In addition, many agency managers favor the flexibility that such programs offer, as opposed to involuntary layoffs based on reduction-in-force criteria.

This law was applied to state and local governments beginning in 1992. In those states where state law denies disability retirement to an individual after a certain age, modifications have to be made in the plan.[28]

Standards of Disclosure

In the private sector, pension systems are regulated by **ERISA (Employee Retirement Income Security Act of 1974).** There is no public-sector counterpart to this law. This means that public sector pension plans, like collective bargaining activities, are regulated by a hodgepodge of state laws. There are no uniform standards for informing beneficiaries, taxpayers, or elected officials concerning their financial condition. In some cases, public pension funds have been managed by private investment firms whose speculative investments during the junk bond era of the 1980s have placed them at risk and have given rise to issues of disclosure and accountability for fund management.[29]

Actuarial Standards

Much confusion also exists about the actuarial standards to which public pension systems should conform. These standards are assumptions about the rates of employment, death, inflation, and so on that are used to calculate the relationship between payments into the system and benefits drawn from it. Two types of systems are used—*fully funded* and *pay-as-you-go.* In a fully funded system, contributions of current employees are adjusted to meet the demands on the system by retirees, so that the system always remains solvent. Under a pay-as-you-go plan, employee contributions bear no necessary relation to payments, and funds are appropriated from general revenues to pay retirees' pensions. However, there is no federal requirement that public pension funds be operated in conjunction with generally accepted accounting principles applicable to private pension plans as set forth in ERISA.

Strategic Investment Potential

Perhaps the most neglected aspect of defined benefit public pensions is their strategic investment effect. Traditionally, the administration of state and local pension systems restricted pension fund investments to low-interest, low-risk assets. During the 1980s, some pension fund managers were able to obtain higher rates of return by investing more speculatively (unsecured government bonds, real estate). While the excesses of the 1980s have put a halt to much of this activity, it is still necessary for states to establish some reasonable balance between security and rate of return. This is particularly true given the potential of public pension funds, because of the sheer size of their investment activity, for stimulating and directing economic growth in specified geographic areas or industries. For example, in Minnesota the Minneapolis Employee Retirement Fund (MERF) has formed an investment corporation that lends money to high-tech industries wishing to relocate to the area.

DISCRETIONARY BENEFITS: HEALTH INSURANCE

There is widespread agreement today that serious problems exist with the system of health-care delivery in the United States. According to the Congressional Budget Office, expenditures on health-care were estimated to have reached $898 billion in 1993, up from $752 billion in 1991, a 19.4 percent increase.[30] Despite this high cost, there are tremendous inequities in the distribution of health-care benefits. Many Americans are denied health care because they cannot afford it: In 1984, 34.7 million Americans (17.4 percent) had neither private nor public health insurance coverage.[31] The percent was the same in 1992.[32]

The greater cost of medical technology and increased longevity are primarily responsible for the increase in health costs. Our present system is geared toward the development of high-technology advances that provide a longer life span for the elderly at a high price; it is driven by a third-party reimbursement system that discourages cost control or cost-benefit analysis. As a result, retirees are creating a staggering liability for employers.

In the absence of sweeping public policy reforms needed to overhaul our health system, employers have adopted what for them are reasonable strategies to contain health-care costs. These are (1) providing "permanent" employees (those with job security through civil service or collective bargaining systems) with education, early detection, and treatment programs; (2) using temporary or contract employees to meet fluctuating employment needs; and (3) working vigorously to encourage managed care programs and competitive bidding for health-care-benefit contracts. There is preliminary evidence that this may be working. A recent survey by the U.S. Chamber of Commerce shows that the cost of health-care benefits per worker declined from 1993 to 1994 for the first time in five decades. The decrease was attributed to flattened or falling health insurance premiums.[33]

OTHER EMERGENT EMPLOYEE BENEFIT ISSUES

To all these items must be added some other employee benefit issues which are either continually in ferment or newly emergent. These include sick leave and vacations, parental leave, child care, prepaid legal assistance, and flexible benefit plans.

Sick Leave, Vacations, Holiday Pay, and Discretionary Days

Employers provide sick leave so employees are not forced to work sick, and so they may accrue enough sick leave to last them through a major illness or injury without loss of pay. In this respect, sick leave is an employer investment in employee health. Unused sick days are usually computed for pension purposes as part of time worked when the employee retires, but are not credited to the employee if he or she leaves the organization prior to retirement eligibility.

Vacation days are provided as a traditional benefit. Some jurisdictions provide discretionary days or personal days as well, and all provide some holiday leave for full-time employees. In contrast to sick leave, vacation and discretionary days are perceived to be the property of the employee (since employees are usually compensated for some unused vacation days upon termination of employment). Since the number of days provided usually increases with seniority, they may also provide an incentive against turnover.

Two elements of sick leave and vacation policy are worth examining here because of their implications for employee cost and performance. First, regardless of their differing purposes for the employer, many employees tend to treat sick leave and vacation indistinguishably, taking either type of leave whenever they want to be away from work. Employers can discourage this practice by clarifying the difference between the two types of leave during employee orientation, and by enforcing this distinction through disciplinary action against sick leave abuse. Employers should recognize that changing family roles have resulted in numerous single-parent households. Under these conditions, sick leave policies must reflect parental responsibilities to care not only for themselves but also for children and parents.

Accrued sick leave and vacation time represent an unfunded liability for the agency. It may be accrued at one salary rate and used at another. While this liability is acceptable in the case of sick leave, agencies should prohibit employees from accruing large amounts of annual leave. In addition to the unfunded liability issue, the fact that employees are not choosing to take vacations means that they may become burned out; if supervisors are not allowing them to take vacations because of heavy workload, this indicates more fundamental human resource management problems.

Family-Related Benefits

Family and Medical Leave Act of 1993. The increasing number of single parents and dual-income families has focused attention on work/family conflicts.[34] Situations traditionally taken care of by "mom," like attending sick children or an elderly parent, become challenges for the contemporary family. A call from the school nurse that Heather isn't feeling well goes to the parent's workplace rather than home because no one is home during the workday. Heather's mother or father has to figure out how to take care of her without jeopardizing a job or relationships with co-workers.

The ***Family and Medical Leave Act (FMLA)*** of 1993 recognizes work/family conflict by providing twelve weeks a year of unpaid leave to an employee to cope with a family sickness, elder care, childbirth, or adoption. The leave may be taken all at once but need not be: There are provisions for intermittent leave. The law applies to employers with fifty or more employees and is estimated to cover some 50 million American workers. For some employers the FMLA represents a major departure from past practice, but for others it simply reinforces existing policy.[35]

Recent congressional hearings assessing the impact of the act generally show positive results. According to a survey conducted by the U.S. Bureau of Labor Statistics, 3 million to 6 million workers have taken leave under provisions of the act, and over 90 percent of the businesses surveyed reported little impact on operations.[36] In a three-year study of states which implemented parental leave legislation in the 1980s, the majority of respondents reported no increase in the percentage of women who took unpaid leave after childbirth, and no increase in the length of leave. There was also no increase in the cost of training administration or unemployment insurance as a result of the state laws.[37] Smaller companies have experienced problems with adjusting work schedules, and in replacing workers with specialty skills. However, the thirty-day prior notice (wherever possible) does offer opportunities for replacement planning.

Experts suggest the FMLA be implemented uniformly within an agency, based on coordination with existing absenteeism and leave policies, workers' compensation programs, and annual leave. Employees eligible and ineligible for FMLA should be identified in advance. Specific policies should be developed for requesting leave (including intermittent or reduced leave), along with procedures for medical certification. The personnel department should establish formal procedures for maintaining contact and monitoring the status of leave and scheduled return to work for employees granted FMLA leave. The agency should plan ways to cover the workload of an employee on leave, such as temporary replacement or distribution of workload. Policies and procedures should be clearly communicated to employees through orientation and training.

Implementation and enforcement of the FMLA is the responsibility of the U.S. Department of Labor. According to statistics from the Wage and Hour Division of the Department of Labor, from August 1993 through December 1994, 2,065 complaints had been received under the act and compliance actions had been completed for 1,967 complaints. Sixty-one percent of the complaints adjudicated were valid. Of these, 63 percent involved an employer's refusal to reinstate an employee to the same or equivalent position following FMLA leave. Twenty percent involved refusal to grant FMLA leave; 8 percent involved a refusal to maintain group health benefits for an employee on leave; and 8 percent involved interference or discrimination against an employee using FMLA leave.[38]

Child Care and Elder Care.[39] While the Family and Medical Leave Act provides some relief from intermittent work/family conflicts, the continuing problem of daily care for children and the elderly is not addressed in this law. The decrease in parents staying at home during the workday has led to increases in employer-operated day-care centers, flexible spending accounts for **child care,** child-care referral services, and flexible scheduling for employees. At first, these actions were seen primarily as an employee benefit. But as agencies began to face shortages of qualified employees, child care has been demonstrated to be necessary primarily to recruit or retain qualified female employees or dual-income families. In an era of increased workforce diversity, it is essential to recognize that employees' ability to find satisfactory child-care arrangements will substantially reduce a major work/family conflict.

The issues with employer-subsidized child care include cost, fee setting, and liability risks. But these are technical concerns rather than major impediments to the adoption of child-care policies and programs. And the fundamental value orientation of child care remains unassailable. If employees are a human resource and an asset, then children are the seed corn from which future assets are developed for use by the employer and the society.

As the elderly population increases, care for elderly family members becomes a crucial work/family issue. Elder care involves time off, flextime, or subsidized adult care in an attempt to minimize this conflict. As the elderly population increases, this problem will become a greater challenge. According to a member survey conducted by the International Personnel Management Association, elder-care assistance was offered by 10 percent of agency respondents, including 14 percent from state government and 10 percent from municipalities.[40]

Flexible Time. One way of dealing with work/family conflicts is to give employees more flexibility in scheduling their work.[41] Compressed workweeks, flexible scheduling of the workday, and negotiating the location of work are all possible ways to permit employees to deal with family issues that affect their day at work.

In addition, some employers are using the concepts of buying and selling vacation days and moving to the concept of "paid days off" instead of vacation days, holidays, sick days, and personal days. Trading vacation days actually involves the employee buying time from the employer or selling to the employer. There are tax implications and administrative costs, but it does give employees flexibility over time. Providing "paid days off" gives employees more flexibility as well, and it doesn't require employees to "call in sick" when they have a child-care problem.

Long-Term Care. With a longer life span, workers face the problem of long-term care for themselves and spouses as well as their parents. In a survey the National Council on Aging conducted, 59 percent of respondents indicated they already were involved in some way in providing long-term care for a friend or family member. Twenty-five percent indicated they provide some financial support.[42] Long-term care has become a key part in retirement planning, and some employers provide the opportunity for employees to purchase **long-term care insurance**. A recent International Personnel Management Association survey of agency members showed that 26 percent offer long-term care insurance as a benefit.[43]

Prepaid Legal Assistance[44]

Most people know how a HMO (health maintenance organization) works. Employees (or employers) pay a flat fee in return for access to a network of medical services. The same is possible with legal aid. Most people do not have a lawyer, and most legal questions can be answered quickly, often over the phone. Prepaid legal assistance can come in many forms, but most often it is an optional benefit large employers offer as part of a benefit package; the advantage to employees is similar to that found with group health benefits. More employees purchasing the benefit means lower cost per employee. The average cost is about $120 per year. Coverage can include a family rider and a variety of services depending upon the premium. In 1995, some 18.5 million Americans were enrolled in prepaid legal plans.

Flexible Benefit Programs

Flexible benefit programs are sometimes called cafeteria plans because they offer employees a menu of benefits. A full-fledged plan is developed by costing the employer's contribution to each of a variety of employer-sponsored benefit programs, and allowing employees to select alternative mixes of benefit packages depending on their needs. This has the major advantage, for the employee, of full utilization of benefits without duplication or gaps. This makes the employer's benefit package of greater value to the employee, and is a tool for recruitment and retention.[45]

There are administrative and financial barriers to flexible benefit programs. First, given the wildly fluctuating cost of alternative benefits, it may be difficult for the employer constantly to calculate (and recalculate) the comparative costs of all options. Second, reconfiguring alternative benefit packages on a constant cost basis may be difficult for employees, who are unable to project benefit usage or the relative utility of alternative benefits accurately. Third, full employee utilization of benefits may increase benefit costs for the employer (who may have been able to reduce costs by relying on such overlaps as duplicate health insurance for two employees in a family). Fourth, increased benefit costs tend to force health and life insurance providers toward uniform defined benefit programs to reduce "shopping" from one program to another. In this environment, the advantages of flexible benefit programs may tend to diminish.

Rather than this full-service cafeteria approach, more typically, flexible benefit programs are isolated to a pretax premium plan for group health insurance and various flexible spending accounts. A medical flexible spending account might permit workers to direct a pretax payroll deduction which can be used for medical expenses not covered by health insurance. In another version the worker could authorize a pretax payroll deduction for child care. These medical flexible benefit programs give workers a tax break without great administrative cost.

PAY, BENEFITS, AND CONFLICTS AMONG PERSONNEL SYSTEMS

From this discussion of benefits, a conflict emerges between individual rights (pay and benefits for employees) and agency efficiency (reduced pay and benefit costs). And the outcome of this issue directly affects the conflict among competing personnel systems. For in the short term, at least, the systems that offer the lowest costs are those that provide employees with the lowest pay and least benefits—temporary and contract employment. Furthermore, the attractiveness of temporary and contract employees who are granted few, if any, benefits by the purchasing employer, is the fact that a number of benefits like vacation, holiday pay, and sick leave are pegged to an employee's salary, which usually reflects longevity.

It should be noted that despite their relatively short expected tenure in office, political appointees have frequently been able to include themselves in the benefit provisions offered public employees. The justification for this is that the relatively low salaries paid to political appointees (compared with their private-sector counterparts) necessitates attracting top candidates with a benefit package as well. Cynics would say that because legislators have the authority to approve statutory benefits for public employees, they have often used their authority to approve pay and benefit increases for themselves as well. The traditional orientation toward getting more benefits for members of unions runs headlong into the increasing realization that benefits cost money and many are tied to seniority and base pay.

SUMMARY

Pay and benefits are a fundamental way that employers attract, reward, and retain employees. Pay setting takes place on the basis of job evaluation and market comparisons, through different processes depending on the personnel system involved and the philosophy of the public employer. And depending on the personnel system, employee benefits are regarded as an important motivator of employee retention as well as an increasing cost to employers. At least for civil service systems that define employees as a public resource, the emphasis is on providing a range of flexible benefits that will enhance the performance of an increasingly diverse workforce.

One of the difficulties that the traditional civil service system of human resources management faces is questioning the value of employee retention. In a working environment where new jobs are created and old ones disappear with innovations in technology as well as demands for services, the need to retain existing knowledge, skills, and abilities seems illogical, and pay systems designed with employee retention in mind inadvertently may be working against their own long-term benefit.

The logic behind new pay is attractive even if it conflicts with civil service pay traditions. New pay advocates seek to attract individuals with valued KSAP by paying a competitive market wage and benefits, but their retention strategy is to reward performance through variable pay. This does not reward longevity nor does it add to benefit costs associated with pay rates inflated by merit or time-in-grade increases or cost-of-living adjustments.

KEY TERMS

base pay
benchmark positions
broad banding
child care
cost-of-living-allowance (COLA)
defined benefit
defined contribution
disability retirement
discretionary benefits
elder care
Employee Retirement Income Security Act (ERISA)
entitlement benefits
Fair Labor Standards Act (FLSA)
Family and Medical Leave Act (FMLA)
flexible benefits

gainsharing
Garcia v. San Antonio Metropolitan Transit Authority
locality pay
long-term care insurance
merit pay
new pay
pay comparability
pay-for-performance
pay grade
portability
seniority pay
time-in-grade
total compensation
unemployment compensation
variable pay
vesting
workers' compensation

DISCUSSION QUESTIONS

1. What are the elements of a total compensation package?
2. What laws govern compensation practices in public personnel management?
3. If you were arguing pros and cons of wage discrimination based on race/gender, what kind of arguments would you develop?
4. What are the differences between merit pay, pay based on seniority, and cost-of-living allowances?
5. What is new about "new pay"? How does it reflect a departure from the way pay has traditionally been viewed in civil service systems?
6. Review the strategic statements of pay for NewCorp, ProCorp, and UsualCorp. Which would you rather work for? Why? What kind of public agencies are best suited for each of the three alternatives?
7. What are the statutory benefits to which employees are entitled by law?
8. What are some of the managerial and public policy issues associated with public pension and health benefits? If you were a benefits manager and saw the costs of these benefits rising, what kind of recommendations might you make to account for employer and employee needs and interests?
9. Which benefits do you believe are most attractive to today's and tomorrow's public employees?
10. What is the relationship between pay and benefit systems and the conflict among public personnel systems and values?

EXERCISE NEW PAY

Pick an organization you are familiar with, and write a strategic compensation statement, including a pay-for-performance provision. Design the pay-for-performance element, and specify the reasons you think your system will work, including reasons for/against folding your pay-for-performance into base pay.

CASE STUDY THE COST OF ABSENTEEISM

The municipality of Cityville employes 500 people. Last year, excluding vacation time, which averages two weeks per employee per year, the rate of absenteeism was calculated at 3 percent. This 3 percent loss in scheduled work time is attributed to clerical workers (55 percent), blue-collar workers (30 percent), and professional staff (15 percent). The average hourly wage for clerical workers is \$5.76

with an additional 30 percent in fringe benefits; for blue-collar workers $9.62 with an additional 35 percent fringe benefits; and for professional employees $14.42 with 33 percent fringe benefits.

Twenty-five supervisors, whose average wage and fringe benefits total $12.50 per hour, handle most of the absentee worker problems and estimate they spent about 30 minutes a day rearranging schedules and trying to organize work to compensate for the unscheduled absences. Cityville's finance director indicates that some $30,000 in incidental costs are associated with absenteeism. These include items like overtime, temporary help, and even an educated guess as to the costs attributed to lower quality of work done by the replacement workers. Problem: Using these amounts and the guide in Figure 5-3, estimate the total cost of absenteeism to the taxpayers of Cityville.

FIGURE 5–3 Total Estimated Cost of Employee Absenteeism. (Source: Wayne F. Cascio, *Costing Human Resouces: The Financial Impact of Behavior in Organizations*, 3rd ed. Boston PWS-Kent Publishing Company, 1991, p. 61.)

1. Compute total employee hours lost to absenteeism for the period.

↓

2. Compute weighted average wage or salary/hour/absent employee.

↓

3. Compute cost of employee benefits/hour/employee.

↓

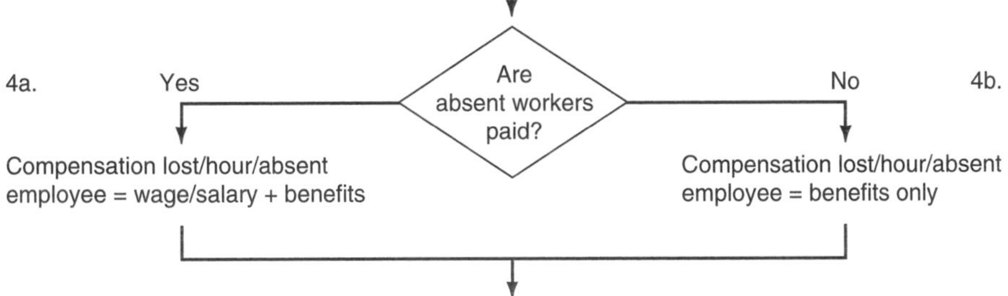

↓

5. Compute total compensation lost to absent employees (1. × 4a. or 4b. as applicable).

↓

6. Estimate total supervisory hours lost to employee absenteeism.

↓

7. Compute average hourly supervisory salary + benefits.

↓

8. Estimate total supervisory salaries lost to managing absenteeism problems (6. × 7.).

↓

9. Estimate all other costs incidental to absenteeism.

↓

10. Estimate total cost of absenteeism (Σ 5., 8., 9.).

↓

11. Estimate total cost of absenteeism/employee (10. ÷ total no. of employees).

ANSWERS TO CASE STUDY QUESTIONS

After several years, we and our students have reached reasonable consensus on the answers to these questions:

1. 30,000 hours
2. $8.22/hour
3. $2.68/hour
4. (a) $10.90/hour
   (b) $2.68/hour
5. $327,000
6. 3,125 hours
7. $12.50/hour
8. $39,062.50
9. $30,000
10. $396,062.50
11. $792.13

NOTES

[1] Employee Benefit Research Institute (June 1994). *EBRI issue brief—Questions and answers on employee benefit issues.* http://www.jobweb.org/cohrma/ebri/ib150.htm.

[2] Reported in "Currents," *Compensation and Benefits Review, 27* (May-June 1995), 15.

[3] Siegel, G. B. (1992). *Public employee compensation and its role in public sector strategic management.* New York: Quorum, p. 161.

[4] Risher, H. (Winter 1994). The emerging model for salary management in the private sector: Is it relevant to government? *Public Personnel Management, 23,* 649-665.

[5] A detailed discussion of the impact of the FLSA on state and local governments is beyond the scope of this text. For more information, see F*air labor standards handbook for states, local governments and schools,* Thompson Publishing Group, 1725 K St. NW, Washington, DC (May 1986), as updated; and Cooper, R. S. (1993). FLSA: *The public employer's guide,* Washington, DC: International City/County Management Association.

[6] Abraham, Y. T., and M. T. Moore (Fall 1995). Comparable worth: Is it a moot issue? *Public Personnel Management,* 24, 291-314.

[7] For more on salary surveys, see various issues of *Compensation and Benefits Review.*

[8] Milkovich, G. T., and A. K. Wigdor, (Eds.). (1991). *Pay for performance: Evaluating performance and merit pay.* Washington, DC: National Academy Press, p. 135.

[9] Ibid., p. 77.

[10] Ibid., p. 82.

[11] Ibid., p. 136.

[12] Kellough, J. E. and H. Lu (Spring 1993). The paradox of merit pay in the public sector. *Review of Public Personnel Administration, 13,* 46; Milkovich and Wigdor. *Pay for performance,* Risher, H. (Winter 1994). The emerging model for salary management in the private sector: Is it relevant to government? *Public Personnel Management,* 23, 651.

[13] Milkovich and Wigdor. *Pay for performance,* p. 106.

[14] United States Merit Systems Protection Board (1990). *Working for America: A federal employee survey.* Washington, DC: U.S. Merit Systems Protection Board, p. 18.

[15] United States Merit Systems Protection Board (1989). *Federal personnel management since civil service reform.* Washington, DC: U.S. Merit Systems Protection Board, p. 11.

[16] Risher. *The emerging model for salary management*, pp. 650-651.

[17] Gabris, G. G., and K. Mitchell (Winter 1988). The impact of merit raise scores on employee attitudes: The Matthew effect of performance appraisal. *Public Personnel Management, 17,* 375.

[18] Perry, J. L. (1991). Linking pay to performance: the controversy continues. In Ban, C., and N. M. Riccucci (Eds.). *Public personnel management: Current concerns—future challenges.* New York: Longman, p. 80.

[19] Kellough and Lu, *The paradox of merit pay,* p. 55.

[20] Schuster, J. R., and P. K. Zingheim (1992). *The new pay.* New York: Lexington Books, p. xi.

[21] Risher, H., and B. W. Schay (1994). Grade banding: The model for future salary programs? *Public Personnel Management, 23,* 487-500.

[22] Shareef, R. (Summer 1994). Skill-based pay in the public sector. *Review of Public Personnel Administration, 14*, 60-74.

[23] Bergmann, T. J., M. A. Bergmann, and J. L. Grahn (Fall 1994). How important are employee benefits to public sector employees? *Public Personnel Management, 23*, 397-406.

[24] Schuster and Zingheim, *The new pay*, pp. 42-45.

[25] Employee Benefit Research Institute, EBRI issue brief.

[26] Cranford, J. (December 1993). Providing cover: A look at public employee benefits. *Governing*, pp. 45-53.

[27] *Equal Employment Opportunity Commission v. Commonwealth of Massachusetts.* November 1, 1990. Docket Nos. 90-10640-H and 90-10150-Z.

[28] Reichenberg, N. (December 1990). President signs ADEA bill. *IPMA News.* Alexandria, VA: International Personnel Management Association, pp. 10-11.

[29] County government sues financial advisors. Out-of-court settlement reached. (April 1991). *PA Times, 14* (4), 1.

[30] Employee Benefit Research Institute, EBRI issue brief.

[31] Chollet, D., and R. Friedland (Summer 1987). Health care costs and public policy toward employee health plans. *Review of Public Personnel Administration, 7*, 68.

[32] Employee Benefit Research Institute, EBRI issue brief.

[33] Benefits costs decline (May-June 1996). *Compensation and Benefits Review, 28*, 11.

[34] Reed, C., and W. M. Bruch (1993). Dual-career couples in the public sector: A survey of personnel policies and practices. *Public Personnel Management, 22*, 187-200.

[35] Allred, S. (1995). An overview of the Family and Medical Leave Act. *Public Personnel Management*, 24, 67-73; Crampton, S. M., and J. M. Mishra. (Fall 1995). Family and medical leave legislation: Organizational policies and structure. *Public Personnel Management, 24*, 271-290.

[36] Reported in Buchanan, C. N. (July 1996). Oversight hearing on the Family and Medical Leave Act. *International Personnel Management Association News*, pp. 7-8.

[37] Taylor, P. (May 23, 1991). Study of firms finds parental leave impact light. *The Washington Post*, p. A-9.

[38] *Daily labor report.* (June 5, 1995). Washington, DC: The Bureau of National Affairs, Inc. (1995 DLR 107 d30).

[39] Kossek, E. E., B. J. DeMarr, K. Backman, and M. Kollar. (1993). Assessing employees' emerging elder care needs and reactions to dependent care. *Public Personnel Management, 22*, 617-638; and Healy, M. (June 17, 1996). *Los Angeles Times*, pp. A-1, 12.

[40] Long-term care: Choices and knowledge. (July 1996). *International Personnel Management Association* News, p. 10.

[41] Ezra, M., and M. Deckman (1996). Balancing work and family responsibilities: Flextime and childcare in the federal government. *Public Administration Review, 56*, 174-179.

[42] Ibid., p. 8.

[43] Long-term care: choices and knowledge. (July 1996). International Personnel Management Association News, p. 10.ø

[44] Flynn, G. (October 1996). Legal assistance offers prepaid peace of mind. *Personnel Journal*, 75, 48-56.

[45] Cafeteria plans, wellness programs gaining in popularity. (July 1990). *Employee Benefit Plan Review*, pp. 90-92.

6

The Saga of Social Equity: Equal Employment Opportunity, Affirmative Action, and Workforce Diversity

> Today, the man or person or corporate entity "offering the job" is, in fact, probably hiring for reasons other than somebody's personal preference or qualifications or demonstrated performance. Like it or not, the present-day employer is operating under orders from the government, and the government's first priority is to maintain the officially approved mix of genders, races, ethnic backgrounds and so on, not to hire the people best equipped to meet the stated goals of the organization.
>
> Jim Wright, *Dallas Morning News*, September 4, 1990

This controversial editorial statement is hardly true, although it reflects the perceptions of a number of Americans, especially those who have not gotten a job they thought they were qualified for. "Orders" from the executive branch of government or the courts are rare, but social equity considerations attract attention and scrutiny and seem to challenge the belief that personnel decisions should be made solely on the basis of knowledge, skills, and abilities. Given that public jobs are scarce resources, and that individual hiring decisions reflect the current relative importance of alternative values such as individual rights and social equity, conflict over affirmative action mirrors the larger societal debate over employment criteria and preferences.

The ambivalent public attitudes toward affirmative action were reflected in media commentary on the recent presidential candidacy of retired General Colin Powell. At the time he was considering running for President, opinion polls showed that a large majority of Americans were opposed to employment quotas or preferential hiring of minorities. Yet at the same time, most thought that affirmative action was a good thing because it had allowed previously excluded minorities, as exemplified by General Powell, to rise to positions of prominence based on merit. Thus, Americans are opposed to preferential employment rules in general (because they are perceived as unfairly limiting opportunity for members of groups excluded from preferential treatment), yet favorably disposed toward them in practice (because they result in improved opportunity for qualified individuals). The apparent contradiction between these two viewpoints does not stop people from believing in both simultaneously!

So, despite its apparent declining political acceptability, affirmative action will continue to have a significant effect on public employment, although probably not the same effect as was initially intended. Its legacy may be found in the judicial influence it has spawned over personnel decisions in all the core personnel functions. The **Uniform Guidelines to Employee Selection Procedures** have asserted that equal employment opportunity provisions extend to all employment decisions involving distribution of organizational resources. Clearly, some progress in the hiring of women and minorities has been recorded over the past three decades. But the critical test of affirmative action is whether the value of social equity has penetrated the core personnel functions and become a routine consideration in public personnel management, even though the political salience of affirmative action itself may have declined.

In addition to this political legacy, workforce diversification programs have an economic impetus. They grow out of the demand for productivity and effective service delivery, and recognition of the changing demographic composition of the labor pool in America may overshadow affirmative action driven by compliance with laws and regulations.

By the end of this chapter you will be able to:

1. Understand why confusion exists between equal employment opportunity and affirmative action, and distinguish between them.
2. Discuss the laws that require affirmative action by public employers, and the agencies responsible for affirmative action compliance.
3. Describe the process of voluntary and involuntary affirmative action compliance.
4. Describe the impact the judicial system has in interpreting and enforcing affirmative action laws.
5. Discuss how increased contracting has shifted the focus of affirmative action compliance from employment preference to minority contractor "set-asides."
6. Discuss how workforce diversity differs from both equal employment opportunity and affirmative action.
7. Describe the impact of workforce diversification programs on organizational mission, culture, policy, practice, and productivity in a culturally diverse community.
8. Discuss how conflicts over the fairness of equal employment opportunity, affirmative action, and workforce diversity have affected the role of the public manager in achieving both productivity and fairness.

EQUAL EMPLOYMENT OPPORTUNITY AND AFFIRMATIVE ACTION: WHAT ARE THEY?

Affirmative action began legislatively as an attempt to reinforce equal employment opportunity by challenging conventional recruitment and selection procedures. It has evolved, largely through judicial interpretations of the law, into a tool to remedy the effects of long-standing discrimination in employment.

Given that EEO and AA are often referred to in the same breath and are almost invariably the enforcement responsibility of the same public agencies, it is understandable that distinguishing them is confusing. The distinction can be clarified by remembering that **equal employment opportunity** is designed to protect individual rights and promote employment opportunities and fairness in employment processes and decisions. **Affirmative action** is oriented more toward the value of social equity. It is more results-oriented and is designed to promote a more diverse and demographically representative workforce. It is often mistakenly associated with quotas.

AFFIRMATIVE ACTION LAW AND COMPLIANCE AGENCIES

The movement from equal employment opportunity to affirmative action can be shown by looking at the laws designed to achieve social equity, and the agencies responsible for enforcing these laws through affirmative action compliance policies and programs.

The first and most important social equity law is legislative: **Title VII of the Civil Rights Act of 1964.**[1] With a few exceptions, it prohibits public or private employers, labor organizations, and employment agencies from making employee or applicant personnel decisions based on race, color, religion, gender, or national origin. Although originally applied to private employers, the concept of EEO was extended to state and local governments by the Equal Employment Opportunity Act of 1972.[2] The EEO Act of 1972 also increased the authority of the designated compliance agency, the **Equal Employment Opportunity Commission (EEOC).**

In contrast with equal employment opportunity, affirmative action not only prohibits discrimination but also *requires* employers, unions, and employment agencies to take positive steps to reduce underrepresentation through the preparation and implementation of **affirmative action plans (AAPs)**. The two most critical governmental acts enforcing the value of social equity, through the achievement of proportional representation, are **Executive Order 11246** and the **Equal Employment Opportunity Act** (1972) (which really concerns AA rather than EEO). Table 6-1 summarizes several EEO/AA laws and compliance agencies.

Executive Order 11246, signed by President Johnson in 1965, prohibited **discrimination** by most employers providing goods or services to the federal government. Furthermore, it required those with fifty or more employees and government contracts of $10,000 or more annually to prepare a written plan identifying any **underutilization** of women and minorities and establishing goals and timetables to correct it. This executive order has had great impact, since all sub-

TABLE 6-1 Federal AA/EEO Laws and Compliance Agencies

Law	Practice Covered	Agencies Covered	Compliance Agency
Age Discrimination in Employment Act of 1967, as amended in 1974 (29.U.S.C Sec. 631 and 630B)	Age discrimination against employees over 39	Virtually all employers	Equal Employment Opportunity Commission
Americans with Disabilities Act of 1990 (P.L. 101-336)	Discrimination against qualified individuals with handicaps	Employers with 15 or more employees	EEOC
Civil Rights Act of 1964 as amended by the Equal Employment Opportunity Act of1972 (40 U.S.C. Sec. 2000e) as amended by the Civil Rights Act of 1991 (P.L. 102-166)	Discrimination based on race, color, religion, gender, or national origin	Employers with 15 or more employees	EEOC
Equal Pay Act of 1963 (29 U.S.C. Sec. 206d)	Discrimination in pay based on gender	Employees covered by the Fair Labor Standards Act	EEOC
Executive Order 11246	Discrimination based on race, color, religion, gender, or national origin	Employers with federal contracts and their subcontractors	U.S. Department of Labor
14th Amendment to the U.S. Constitution	Prohibits application of law unequally	All public employers	Various federal courts
Vietnam Era Veterans' Readjustment Act of 1974 (38 U.S.C. Sec. 2012, 2014)	Promotion of employment opportunity for disabled and other Vietnam-era veterans	Federal government and employers with federal contracts and their subcontractors	U.S. Department of Labor
Vocational Rehabilitation Act of 1973 (29 U.S.C. Sec. 701)	Prohibits discrimination against qualified individuals with handicaps	Federal , agencies grant recipients, and contractors	U.S. Department of Labor

contractors of covered contractors must also comply—regardless of the size of their contracts or number of employees. By 1990, this executive order covered some 27 million workers and over $194 billion in federal contracts.[3] The **Office of Federal Contract Compliance Programs (OFCCP)**, located within the U.S. Department of Labor, prepares regulations and enforces this order. Under the 1972 Equal Employment Opportunity Act, state and local governments were also required to file affirmative action plans and to take the same types of remedial action required of federal contractors. In addition, this act granted the courts broad power to remedy the effects of employer discrimination.

Given the different objectives of EEO and AA, it is easy to see how enforcement strategies might conflict. Under AA, a plan might establish a goal of hiring more minorities or women until the percentage of employees in an organization equaled an appropriate percentage in a relevant labor market. Under EEO, however, concern for the protection of each applicant's or employee's rights would prevent the establishment of a hiring quota ("three of the next ten employees hired must be African-American," for example) unless such a quota were established by a court order or consent decree.

AFFIRMATIVE ACTION COMPLIANCE: VOLUNTARY AND INVOLUNTARY

Voluntary affirmative action compliance occurs when a public employer recognizes a compensatory need to diversify its workforce and complies with affirmative action laws (and pursuant regulations issued by compliance agencies) through the preparation of an affirmative action plan that (1) identifies underutilization of qualified women and minorities compared to their presence in a relevant labor market, (2) establishes full utilization as a goal, (3) develops concrete plans for achieving full utilization, and (4) makes reasonable progress toward full utilization.

Involuntary affirmative action compliance occurs when a private employer or public agency alters its personnel practices as the result of investigation by a compliance agency that ends in a negotiated settlement, when the employer settles out of court with a compliance agency by means of a consent decree or by court order. Understanding these three types of involuntary compliance mechanisms requires some background knowledge of the process by which compliance agencies investigate employers.

An applicant or employee who believes he or she has been discriminated against usually seeks redress through administrative channels within the organization where the alleged discrimination occurred. This may involve an appeal, informal and then formal, to the personnel office, affirmative action officer, or through union channels if available. If dissatisfied, the employee may file a formal complaint with the appropriate compliance agency (that is, with the government agency responsible for execution of the particular law).

Filing a complaint results in a formal investigation in which the investigating officer contacts the employer asking for a written response to the applicant's or employee's charge of discrimination. The investigation may result in the complaint being rejected or the compliance agency filing a formal complaint against the employer. Frequently (in nearly half the EEOC's cases), complaints have been resolved "administratively" (with a finding in favor of neither the applicant nor the agency). This might occur when an applicant moves or changes jobs.

Once a complaint is filed by the compliance agency, the employer may agree to the changes in its employment practices plus whatever specific remedies will "make whole" the injury to the aggrieved employee or applicant. This acknowledgment is called a **conciliation agreement**. It is entered into by the employer primarily to avoid costly litigation and court interference in cases where a court decision would likely go against the employer.

A **consent decree** is a second type of involuntary affirmative action compliance. It results when an employer and a compliance agency negotiate an agreement subject to the approval of a court and judicial oversight. Unlike the conciliation agreement, it is usually entered into by an employer in litigation who "smells" defeat. In such cases, the employer may consider it beneficial not to admit guilt, and to agree to terms which may be more advantageous than those resulting from a guilty verdict, though they may result in the payment of substantial damages.

For an employer, the most damaging form of involuntary compliance is a **court order.** In situations where a compliance agency or individual has taken an employer to court over alleged affirmative action violations, and neither a conciliation agreement nor a consent decree can be agreed upon, a guilty verdict against the employer will result in court-ordered remedies. Cases involving "egregious" and "pervasive" discrimination may result in mandatory hiring quotas, changes in personnel policies, and back pay for the victims of discrimination. Because of the cost and unfavorable publicity associated with lengthy litigation resulting in a guilty verdict, public officials will generally do their best to avoid this outcome.

With declining budgets and increased workloads, it is understandable that compliance agencies such as the OFCCP and the EEOC are under continual pressure to resolve cases administratively rather than resorting to court action. And they are also targeting complaints of multiple abuses by large employers (such as joining the 1996 class action suit filed by female employees against Mitsubishi Motors, alleging sexual harassment at its assembly plant in Illinois).

IMPACT OF THE JUDICIAL SYSTEM ON INTERPRETING AND ENFORCING SOCIAL EQUITY THROUGH AFFIRMATIVE ACTION

Given the confusion and conflict over the best way to achieve social equity, it is to be expected that the federal court system, and particularly the Supreme Court, have played a major role in interpreting and enforcing social equity through case law. Therefore, tracing the history of employment discrimination since passage of the Civil Rights Act of 1964 requires an understanding of how the Supreme Court has interpreted civil rights legislation and the Constitution. The earliest opinions strongly endorsed EEO and traditional merit system values of individual rights and efficiency. But as the Court encountered unexpected cases of systemic and pervasive employment discrimination, it became more sympathetic to the value of social equity, reinforcing affirmative action programs and race-based remedies.

The Court's initial approach in interpreting the Civil Rights Act of 1964 was contained in its unanimous opinion in ***Griggs v. Duke Power Company.***[4] Willie Griggs was a laborer at the Duke Power Company in North Carolina where for years the workforce was segregated, with African-Americans doing manual labor. In the early 1960s Duke Power Company acknowledged that it had discriminated in the past but argued that in good faith it had recently instituted objective testing of applicants for selection and promotion. Griggs sued on the grounds that the tests unfairly discriminated against African-Americans and were unrelated to job performance. In a unanimous opinion written by the Chief Justice, Warren Burger, the court established several points that prevailed until 1989. First, regarding Congress's intent, the Court said: "The objective of Congress in the enactment of Title VII is plain from the language of the statute. It was to achieve equality of employment opportunity and remove barriers that have operated in the past to favor an identifiable group of white employees over other employees."[5] Thus, the act was interpreted to have remedial as well as prospective intent. That is, an employer could not simply say, "We discriminated in the past, but no longer do so." Second, the Court said that if an employer's personnel practices resulted in discrimination, lack of intent to discriminate would not constitute a valid defense. In other words, the consequences of employment practices were more important than their intent. Third, the Court said that once an inference of discrimination could be drawn, the burden of proof shifted to the employer to show that the personnel practices that had the discriminatory effect were in fact job related. In other words, the employer must be able to demonstrate objectively that those applicants who performed better in the selection process would, in fact, do better on the job than those who did not fare as well in the selection process. Each of these findings sent a significant message to employers, and the case is viewed as a landmark employment discrimination decision.

From a values perspective, the Court's opinion emphasizes the traditional merit system values of individual rights and efficiency. The Court would protect *individuals* subject to discrimination and would open doors to allow them to compete on the basis of their knowledge, skills, and abilities (efficiency). It would not sacrifice job qualifications in favor of minority origins. In fact, writing for a unanimous court in 1971, Chief Justice Burger observed:

> Congress has not commanded that the less qualified be preferred over the better qualified simply because of minority origins. Far from disparaging job qualifications as such, Congress has made such qualifications the controlling factor, so that race, religion, nationality, and sex become irrelevant. What Congress has commanded is that any tests used must measure the person for the job and not the person in the abstract.[6]

From 1971 to 1987 the Court confronted challenges which Congress had not anticipated with passage of the Civil Rights Act of 1964 and the Equal Employment Opportunity Act of 1972.

- What should the Court decide if discrimination was systemic rather than isolated to identifiable victims?
- What should the Court decide about cases where employers voluntarily showed racial preference to remediate a discrimination problem that had not been litigated or formally alleged?
- What should the Court decide in the case of seniority systems that in their routine application discriminated against minorities, but that were not originally conceived with that purpose in mind?
- What balance should be drawn between compensation for those discriminated against and the innocent non-minorities who might have to bear some of the cost in delayed promotions or loss of training or advancement opportunities?

Answers to these questions could not be found in the wording of civil rights legislation or the Constitution. Further, the legislative debates leading up to the Civil Rights Act of 1964 and the EEO Act of 1972 were so entangled that *any* answer to these questions could be justified with reference to legislative intent. The Court had to use the letter of the law, its intent as interpreted by the Court, and its own precedents in deliberating and reaching answers to these and other questions. *Griggs* was the last unanimous vote the Court recorded on an affirmative action case.

By 1987 the Court had moved away from its color-blind interpretation in *Griggs* and embraced the value of social equity, struggling to find a balance between social equity, individual rights, and to a lesser extent efficiency. Sixteen years after *Griggs*, the Court confronted two very different cases. Litigation leading to a Supreme Court review in ***United States v. Paradise***[7] began in 1972 when a district court found pervasive, systemic, and obstinate exclusion of African-Americans from employment with the Alabama Department of Public Safety. Continued failure to comply with consent decrees led the district court in 1983 to order the state to promote to the rank of corporal African-American troopers at a 1-1 ratio with Caucasian troopers. This order would be enforced until at least 25 percent of the corporals were African-American or the department could produce a valid promotional examination—that is, one which had no adverse effect on qualified minority candidates. Supporting the state of Alabama, the federal government appealed the ruling to the Supreme Court, claiming it violated the individual rights, protected by the Fourteenth Amendment to the Constitution, of the innocent non-minorities in the Department of Public Safety. The innocent non-minorities were the Anglo troopers who may have benefited from the discrimination, but could not be shown to be party to it.

Also in 1987 the Court reviewed the reverse discrimination case of ***Johnson v. Transportation Agency.***[8] The transportation agency in Santa Clara County, California, noting a substantial imbalance in the number of women working in the agency compared to those available in the county workforce, voluntarily developed an affirmative action plan designed to ameliorate the imbalance by considering gender as one factor in employment decisions. After adopting the plan, the agency promoted Diane Joyce to the position of road dispatcher over Paul Johnson, who had achieved a nominally higher score than Joyce in a promotional interview. Johnson claimed reverse discrimination based on Title VII of the Civil Rights Act, and the case eventually reached the Supreme Court. Joyce's promotion was upheld.

To decide whether the use of race and gender preference were lawful in *Paradise* and *Johnson,* the Court employed a two-pronged analytical framework it had developed since *Griggs* in 1971. First, employing the **strict scrutiny** standard for evaluating the use of affirmative action, the Court asked: "Is there a compelling justification for the employer to take race into consideration in its affirmative action program?" In *Paradise,* all the justices answered this question in the affirmative, agreeing that the "Alabama Department of Public Safety had undertaken a course of action that amounted to 'pervasive, systematic, and obstinate discriminatory conduct.'"[9] Therefore, the use of race to remedy the effect of this conduct was justified.

In *Johnson,* a majority of the Court answered in the affirmative as well. The majority inferred discrimination based on gender from a comparison of the number of women working in several of the transportation agency's job classifications compared to their numbers in the county's total labor pool. Thus, they found justification for the use of gender in the county's affirmative action plan.

In both cases, the Court then turned to the second and usually more important question involved in the strict scrutiny standard: Is the affirmative action plan narrowly tailored to solve the discrimination problem, or does it create additional, unacceptable problems? In asking this question, the Court is concerned with the effect the remedy will have on the lives of the innocent non-minority employees who may have to bear part of the cost of the affirmative action. With this question the Court tries to avoid remedying past discrimination with a solution that in itself discriminates.

In *Paradise,* a majority noted that the order to promote African-American troopers to the rank of corporal at a 1-1 ratio with Caucasian troopers was "narrowly tailored" and minimally intrusive on the innocent non-minority troopers for the following reasons: The promotion quota was in effect only until a valid promotion procedure could be developed or until 25 percent of the corporals were African-American; the requirement could be waived if no qualified African-American troopers were available; it would apply only when the department needed to make promotions; because it was limited in scope and duration, the remedy imposed a *diffuse* burden on the Caucasian troopers, and no individual non-minority employee must bear the entire cost of the remedy.

In *Johnson,* a majority of the Court found the county's plan was narrowly tailored, and it did not "trammel" the rights of male employees. The Court noted that the plan did not set aside any positions for women; it did authorize consideration of gender as one factor in promotion decisions. It found that Johnson had no absolute right to the position; he and Joyce were among several "acceptable" candidates whose names were sent to the person who finally decided who would be promoted. The Court noted that Johnson retained his employment and seniority and would be eligible for a future promotion. Last, the Court found that the county's plan was intended to "attain" a racial balance, not "maintain" one, which would have been illegal.

In both *Paradise* and *Johnson,* the Court showed its willingness to attack the barriers of discrimination with remedies benefiting those who had not been the specific or identifiable victims of discrimination. None of the troopers who might benefit from the court's order in *Paradise* claimed to have been specifically discriminated against; and Diane Joyce did not claim gender discrimination. Nevertheless, they were members of a class who had been discriminated against. This shows the Court's willingness, in contrast to *Griggs*, to endorse the value of social equity. But in both 1987 cases the Court was unwilling to dismiss the value of individual rights, as it considered the effects the affirmative action in both cases would have on the lives of the innocent non-minorities. Further, the Court acknowledged the value of efficiency by requiring that the minority troopers in Alabama be qualified and by noting that Diane Joyce was qualified.

THE SHIFTING FOCUS OF CONTROVERSY: FROM EMPLOYMENT PREFERENCES TO CONTRACT "SET-ASIDES"

As governments increasingly sought to implement programs through contractors for goods and services, affirmative action advocates increasingly recognized that the focus of compliance efforts needed to be shifted from government employment to the personnel policies and practices of government contractors and subcontractors. Initially, efforts to improve the "mix" of contractors were thwarted because contractors were overwhelmingly controlled by white males. This led to the elaboration of procedures making it easier for **minority business enterprises (MBEs)** to qualify as bidders, to post performance bonds, and to respond to **requests for proposals (RFPs)** issued by government agencies seeking contractors to provide a good or service. In some cases, this included formal or informal quotas—minimum percentages of contract funds (or **set-asides**, as they are sometimes called) that had to be awarded to minority contractors or subcontractors by a jurisdiction.

Naturally, adoption of these revised criteria led to abuses, such as the creation of so-called MBEs that showed minorities or females as corporate directors, but were actually covertly created and financed by white-owned firms as a mechanism for winning set-aside contracts. And awarding contracts to MBEs that in some cases were not the lowest or best-qualified bidders provoked opposition among white-owned contractors and advocates of efficiency or cost reduction as the dominant criterion for awarding contracts.

In resolving conflicts between equal opportunity and preferential treatment of contractors, the Supreme Court has faced the same issues underlying similar conflicts for employees. And it has tended to resolve these conflicts based on prevailing political weight of the two opposing values. By 1989, with the inclusion of President Reagan's appointees, the minority in *Paradise* and *Johnson* became a majority on the Supreme Court. As could be expected, the value of individual rights grew and the value of social equity declined. This reversal was seen in ***Richmond v. Croson*** in 1989 and then reinforced in ***Adarand v. Peña*** in 1995.

In *Richmond v. Croson*[10] the Court ruled 6 to 3 against the city of Richmond's voluntary plan that required at least 30 percent of each city contract to be sublet to minority contractors. Faced with the necessity of balancing the competing values of individual corporate rights to compete fairly in the marketplace with the set-aside provisions of municipal programs to encourage MBEs, the Court ruled that minority set-asides unfairly exclude white-owned corporations from participation unless they are narrowly tailored and established for a compelling reason. While recognizing that the city's population was 50 percent African-American and less than 1 percent of the city's prime contracts had gone to minority business enterprises, and despite substantial anecdotal evidence of widespread discrimination against minority contractors, the Court ruled that the city had shown no direct evidence establishing discrimination *by the city* against minority contractors.

Thus, the city of Richmond's plan failed to meet the Court's first test in its two-part analytical framework established by *Paradise* and *Johnson*: It failed to establish a compelling reason for the affirmative action by the city in minority contracting. In addition, it failed to meet the narrowly tailored test because it could not tie the derivation of the 30 percent figure to the actual degree of discrimination that could be attributed to the city's actions.

In *Adarand v. Peña*, a white-owned contractor sued the secretary of transportation over the constitutionality of minority set-asides in federally funded highway projects.[11] In resolving this case, the Court extended its ruling in *Croson* to the federal government. In so doing, it firmly established that the use of race as a preferential category in an employment context would be subject to the strictest judicial scrutiny. In essence, the court reaffirmed and anchored its guidance in *Croson* that whether used for "benign" purposes or not, racial preferences must be justified by a compelling government reason and be narrowly tailored as a solution.

So it seems that the general trend away from social equity and toward individual rights and efficiency that is reflected in legislation and case law concerning affirmative action is paralleled by case law affirming the right of corporations to compete for contracts without minority set-asides. Whether this shift reflects recognition that equality of opportunity has already been achieved for minority contractors, or simply a turning away from social equity as a dominant value because of changes in the political climate, depends upon one's point of view.

FROM AFFIRMATIVE ACTION TO WORKFORCE DIVERSITY

Workforce diversity is a term that describes the range of employee characteristics that are increasingly present in the contemporary workforce of the United States and other developed countries. Although disagreement does exist over the specific definition of diversity, for our purposes it includes differences in employee and applicant characteristics (race, gender, ethnicity, national origin, language, religion, age, education, intelligence, and disabilities) that constitute the range of variation among human beings in the workforce.

Origin and History of Workforce Diversity

The workforce in modern industrialized nations is becoming socially more diverse. In the United States, it is comprised increasingly of immigrants whose primary language is not English, and whose primary norms are not those of "mainstream" American culture. By the year 2000, only 15 percent of new entrants to the workforce will be U.S.-born white males: The others will be people of color, women, and immigrants.[12] Workforce diversity is not an isolated social change. It results from economic globalization, immigration, and increased **cultural diversity** in nations that were formerly considered to be linguistically and culturally homogeneous. In brief, our image of America has changed from a "melting pot" to a salad bowl.

In the private sector, workforce diversity can be attributed to increasing economic pressures for organizations to remain competitive in the new global economy. The general argument that workforce diversity makes good business sense grows out of a fundamental premise—that businesses whose employees "can speak the same language" as their customers/clients will be more successful than those that cannot. The market will sort out the successful from unsuccessful firms in diverse markets, and those that succeed will probably be the ones whose workforce matches the customer base in diversity.

The difficulty comes when a business is under no market pressure to innovate to meet client needs. This would be true of monopolies, businesses operating in parts of the country where there is little diversity (in particular those that cater to a homogeneous clientele), and governments that may be under political pressure but no market pressure to innovate when it comes to diversity.

Thus, for governments achieving workforce diversity probably is motivated less by the need for efficiency than it is in the private sector. Nevertheless, the pressures are significant, but they are political rather than economic. The values of representation and equity are articulated by demands for recruitment and selection of minority group members, especially for administrators in influential public contact positions. For example, over half of the students in the Los Angeles school district are Latinos. In 1996, the announced departure of the first African-American superintendent was met by rallies endorsing the appointment without a search of the second-in-charge, a Latino. In fact, newspaper reports cited threats of a recall election for board members who did not support the Latino candidate.

The process by which diverse minorities have been incorporated into the workforce in the United States varies dependent upon state and local conditions and laws, and overgeneralizations should be avoided. Nonetheless, the relationship among economics, politics, and workforce diversity can be seen by examining the evolution of minority groups through several stages of empowerment and protection.

In the beginning, members of diverse groups were almost automatically excluded from the workforce, except for unskilled positions, because they were outside the "mainstream" culture. This exclusion was based in law as well as custom. Second, as economic development and labor shortages increased (such as in the United States during World War II), these groups were admitted into the labor market (particularly if they possessed job skills in short supply), though they faced continued economic and legal discrimination and were excluded from consideration for desirable professional and technical positions. Third, as economic development and labor shortages continued, and as their political power continued to increase, group members were accepted for a range of positions, and their employment rights were protected by laws guaranteeing equal employment access (equal employment opportunity). In the United States, for example, applicants' equal employment rights have been protected by Title VII of the Civil Rights Act (1964) and by the Americans with Disabilities Act (1990). Fourth, as these groups became increasingly powerful politically, efforts to reduce the considerable informal discrimination that continued in recruitment, promotion, pay, and benefits led to establishment of workplace policies such as salary equality and employment proportionate with their representation in the labor market. Achievement of these goals was encouraged by voluntary affirmative action programs. If voluntary achievement efforts were unsuccessful, conformance was sometimes mandated by affirmative action compliance agencies or court orders. Fifth, continued social and political changes are now leading to the welcoming of diversity as a desirable political and social condition, and continued economic pressures lead to the development of **workforce diversification programs** for organizations that desire to remain economically competitive or politically responsive.

These stages in the evolution of political power and legal protection for diverse groups in the workforce are shown in Table 6-2.

Difference between Workforce Diversity, Equal Employment Opportunity, and Affirmative Action

Because the workforce diversification programs found in the contemporary workplace are the current stage of an evolutionary process defined by increased social participation, political power and legal protection for minorities, it is understandable that some people consider workforce diversification programs to be simply "old wine in new bottles"—a contemporary variant on the equal employment opportunity or **affirmative action programs** that have characterized personnel management in the United States for the past thirty years. However, workforce diversification differs from equal employment opportunity or affirmative action programs in five important respects.

First, their purposes are different. Equal employment opportunity programs are based on organizational efforts to avoid violating employees' or applicants' legal or constitutional rights. Affirmative programs are based on organiza-

TABLE 6-2 Political Power and Legal Protection for Diverse Groups in the Workforce

Stage	*Employment Status*	*Legal Protections*
1	excluded from the workforce	none
2	admitted to the workforce, but excluded from desirable jobs	none
3	accepted into the workforce	EEO laws
4	recruited into the workforce	AA laws and programs
5	welcomed into the workforce	diversification programs

tional efforts to achieve proportional representation of selected groups. But workforce diversification programs originate from managers' objective of increasing productivity and effectiveness.

Second, diversification programs include all employees, not just employees in specified groups. Affirmative action laws protect only the employment rights of designated categories of persons (in the United States, such groups as blacks, Hispanics, native Americans, Asian-Americans, workers over 40, women, and Americans with disabilities). Workforce diversification programs are based on recognition not only of these protected groups but also of the entire spectrum of characteristics (knowledge, skills, and abilities) that managers and personnel directors need to recognize and factor into personnel decisions in order to acquire and develop a productive workforce.

Third, workforce diversification programs affect a broader range of organizational activities. Affirmative action programs emphasize recruitment, selection, and sometimes promotion because those personnel functions are most closely tied to proportional representation of protected groups. However, workforce diversification programs include all personnel functions related to organizational effectiveness (including recruitment, promotion and retention, job design, pay and benefits, education and training, and performance measurement and improvement).

Fourth, workforce diversification programs have a different locus of control. Affirmative action and equal employment opportunity programs are based on managerial responses to outside compliance agencies' requirements. However, workforce diversification programs originate as internal organizational responses to managerial demands for enhanced productivity and effectiveness (although this response is itself a reaction to demographic changes in overall population).

Fifth, because of all of the above factors, the entire effect of diversification programs is different. Affirmative action programs tend to be viewed negatively by managers and employees, because they are based on a negative premise ("What changes must we make in recruitment and selection procedures to demonstrate a 'good faith effort' to achieve a representative workforce, and thereby avoid sanctions by affirmative action compliance agencies or courts?"). In contrast, the most successful workforce diversification programs tend to be viewed as positive by managers and employees, because they are based on a different question ("What changes can we make in our organization's mission, culture, policies, and programs in order to become more effective and more competitive?").[13]

IMPACT OF WORKFORCE DIVERSIFICATION PROGRAMS

Workforce diversification encourages changes in the organization's mission, or purpose. It starts from a recognition among managers and personnel professionals that human resources are increasingly vital to organizational survival and effectiveness;[14] and that diversification programs are the best way to foster the effective use of human resources.[15]

Mission, Organization Culture, and Personnel Policy and Practice

Workforce diversification requires changes in organizational culture—the values, assumptions, and communication patterns that characterize interaction among employees. These patterns are invented, discovered, or developed by members of the organization as responses to problems or sensitivity to client needs; they become part of the culture as they are taught to new members as the correct way to perceive, think, and feel in relation to these problems or needs.[16] Viewed from this perspective, diversification is a change in the way organizations do business, rather than just an adaptation of existing personnel policies and programs to meet the specialized needs of minorities and women. It is is an effort to describe and understand the range of knowledge, skills, and abilities (KSAs) that members of diverse cultures of diverse groups can bring to the work place. Diversification is an effort to consciously utilize these KSAs as a key to making organizations successful and productive.

An organization's decision to use workforce diversity to increase effectiveness causes changes in its human resource management policy and practice. Policies and practices are the rules and procedures that implement organizational objectives, and they are management's strategic plan for accomplishing its mission through workforce diversification. They are a message to employees, managers, and political leaders about the value the agency places on diversity in particular and on human resources in general.[17] In an agency with effective human resource management and effective workforce diversification policies and programs, this message is explicit and positive.

Workforce diversification programs affect five specific areas of human resource management policy and practice: recruitment and retention, job design, education and training, benefits and rewards, and performance measurement and improvement.

Recruitment and retention policies and programs include those strategies already commonplace in affirmative action programs: increasing the applicant pool of underrepresented groups, increasing their selection rate by developing valid alternatives for tests that have a disparate impact, and evaluating performance evaluation and **mentoring** systems so as to encourage retention. Yet they differ because of the ways workforce diversification differs from affirmative action. Their purpose is productivity enhancement through a diverse workforce rather than legal compliance through recruitment or selection quotas; they apply to a broader spectrum of applicant and employee characteristics; they include a broader range of personnel activities; their locus of control is internal rather than external; and their tone is positive rather than negative.

Job design is also affected, in that workforce diversification efforts usually lead managers to consider changes in where and how employees do work.[18] To attract and retain women with child- and elder-care responsibilities into the workforce, options that offer flexibility of work locations and schedules need to be considered. To attract and retain persons with **disabilities,** reasonable accommodation must be offered to make the workplace physically accessible and to make jobs available to persons who are otherwise qualified to perform the primary duties.[19]

Education and training programs are influenced in two ways by diversification programs. First, employer concerns with the educational preparation of future workers have led to greater employer involvement in areas that used to be considered the domain of public school systems. Workforce training programs now include basic skills unrelated to specific job tasks (such as literacy and English as a second language).[20] And there is increasing interest in strengthening federal and state sponsored job training programs, and in sponsoring joint business-government policy initiatives such as tax incentives for costs associated with business training programs.[21] Second, employers now routinely develop and present managerial and supervisory training courses on multicultural awareness and sensitivity.[22]

Pay and benefit policies often become more flexible and innovative as diversification progresses. Because women are the traditional family caregivers, an employer's ability to attract a diverse workforce depends upon providing flexible benefits; benefits for part-time as well as full-time positions; parental leave; child- and eldercare support programs; and phased retirement policies for older workers.

Performance measurement and productivity improvement programs often change focus because of the assumptions underlying workforce diversification programs. Managers and supervisors now need to consider the differing values and motivational perspectives of a diverse workforce.[23] Workforce diversity has also brought about changing definitions of productivity based on the need for variation in managerial styles, and resultant dramatic increases in organizational effectiveness.[24] And as work teams themselves become more diverse, group evaluation techniques that recognize the importance of individual contributions to these teams also need to be encouraged.

The common threads linking these five areas of personnel policy and practice are their common objective of increased organizational effectiveness, and their cumulative impact on organizational culture. Organizations that wish to attract and keep a diversified workforce must change the culture of the organization to create a climate in which persons from diverse groups feel accepted, comfortable, and productive. And this is why the tone of workforce diversification programs differs from their affirmative compliance program predecessors—affirming diversity is different from tolerating or accepting it.

Examples of Workforce Diversity Programs in Practice

There are many examples of successful and unsuccessful workforce diversification programs in a range of private- and public-sector organizations. Examples include:

- Corning Glass Works evaluates managers on their ability to "create a congenial environment" for diverse employees.
- Mobil Corporation created a special committee of executives to identify high-potential female and minority executive job candidates, and to place them in line management positions viewed as critical for advancement through the **glass ceiling**.

- Dr. Robert McCabe, former president of Miami-Dade Community College, won a MacArthur Foundation Award for educational leadership, including a ten-year emphasis on workforce diversity as a key to community involvement and mission achievement.
- AT&T Bell Laboratories focuses its recruitment efforts on acquiring "the best and the brightest, regardless of race, lifestyle or physical challenges." This has resulted in a comprehensive diversification program.
- Dallas, Texas developed a diversification program that involved modifications in the delivery of city services, and the formation of a development corporation for an underdeveloped minority area of the city.
- San Diego, California initiated a diversification program that involved a shift in organizational culture, and consequent changes in policy and practice.

Characteristics of Effective and Ineffective Programs

Experts have proposed a relatively uniform set of criteria for assessing the effectiveness of workforce diversity policies and programs.[25] These include:

1. A broad definition of diversity that includes a range of characteristics, rather than only those used to define "protected classes" under existing affirmative action;
2. A systematic assessment of the existing culture to determine how members at all levels view the present organization;
3. Top-level initiation of, commitment to, and visibility of workforce diversity as an essential organizational policy rather than as a legal compliance issue or staff function;
4. Establishment of specific objectives;
5. Integration into the managerial performance evaluation and reward structure;
6. Coordination with other activities such as employee development, job design, and TQM; and
7. Continual evaluation and improvement.

On the other hand, insufficient top-level commitment or organizational visibility generally renders diversification efforts unsuccessful because the program's long-term impact on organization mission or culture is inadequate.

Workforce Diversification and Other Management Trends

Workforce diversification programs are consistent with other contemporaneous trends such as employee involvement and participation, employee development, total quality management (TQM) and non-adversarial dispute resolution.

Employee involvement and participation are considered essential for maintaining high productivity (at least among employees in key professional and technical positions). Even in the absence of significant financial rewards, employees tend to work happily and effectively when they have the necessary skills, see their work as meaningful, feel personally responsible for productivity, and have first-hand knowledge of the actual results of their labor. These psychological states are most likely to result from work designed to incorporate characteristics such as variety, significance, self-control, and feedback. They are the objective of workplace innovations such as delegation, flexible work locations and schedules, job sharing, **management by objectives (MBO)**, and total quality management (TQM).

Employee development is related to diversification, at least for key professional and technical employees, because it (1) focuses planning and budget analysis on human resources; (2) facilitates cost-benefit analysis of current training and development activities; and (3) facilitates communication and commitment of organizational goals through employee participation and involvement.

Total quality management (TQM) is an organizational change process that involves a combination of top-down and bottom-up activities: assessment of problems, identification of solutions, and designation of responsibilities for resolving them. It focuses on the connection between the quality of the work environment and the quality of individual, team, and organizational performance. It is similar to team building and organizational development. And it is congruent with workforce diversification efforts because, like diversification, it focuses on a transformation of organizational culture, policies, and programs so as to enhance productivity.

Alternative dispute resolution (ADR) is a philosophy and practice that has become more common because the challenge of channeling diversity into productivity is complicated by the breadth of expectations members of diverse cultures bring to their work, both as individuals and as members of those cultures. Without a method of settling disputes that models the organization's commitment to tolerance and respect, differences lead only to divisiveness that consumes organizational resources without positive results. And there is general recognition that traditional adversarial dispute resolution techniques are not particularly effective at resolving organizational conflicts: They build acrimony, harden bargaining positions, and delay the resolution of the original conflict. Therefore, innovative conflict resolution techniques such as "win-win" negotiation and group problem solving have become more popular. These non-adversarial techniques are often more effective and the have the additional advantage of modeling the organization's commitment to respect, tolerance, and dignity.

CONFLICT OVER SOCIAL EQUITY: THE ROLE OF THE PERSONNEL MANAGER IN ACHIEVING PRODUCTIVITY AND FAIRNESS

As could be expected, conflict over the relative importance of social equity and the appropriateness of alternative strategies for achieving it has caused public administrators concern in some specific areas. What has been the actual impact of all these programs on the employment of minorities and women? How can the positive and negative impacts of diversification programs on productivity and fairness be measured and assessed? What changes does diversification force them to make in how they view their jobs and how they do them?

Impact of Affirmative Action on Employment of Minorities and Women

Has civil rights legislation and employment discrimination litigation reduced discrimination and opened doors for minorities and women? The answer appears to be "yes," but it is difficult to marshall convincing statistics to answer the question.[26] It does seem clear that the kinds of discrimination reported in cases that came before the Court in the 1970s have decreased. It is difficult to conceive today of a case of intentional racial discrimination in employment like that reported in *Griggs* (1971) or *Paradise* (1987). Further, it is clear that the value of social equity has challenged merit systems to demonstrate that personnel practices once assumed to be job related are, in fact. In this way, the force of affirmative action has benefited all employees, regardless of race or gender. It has become standard operating procedure to advertise jobs publicly and widely; to tailor interview questions and tests to specific jobs. Performance appraisal instruments have become more job related, and pay systems have become more equitable and sensitive to gender differences even if they have not erased them.

On the other hand, it seems equally clear that acceptance of diversity is not yet a part of the value structure of all Americans. A *USA Today* poll, taken after the O.J. Simpson trial in 1995, shows significant differences in the beliefs of Anglos and African-Americans regarding the prevalence of discrimination.[27] A deeply felt backlash against affirmative action has been developing for thirty years among white males, based on two arguments. First, they state that affirmative action is unfair to blacks because, while it has helped the best-off blacks enhance their jobs status, it has done nothing to alleviate the employment crisis among a black urban underclass increasingly plagued by poor education, drug abuse, and crime. Second, they state that affirmative action is the opening wedge of a comprehensive ideology that threatens the basic American ideology of equality of opportunity under the law. They fear it will lead to the "Balkanization" of American society, the creation of a culture in which all public policy decisions are made on the basis of social equity.[28]

In addition to its specific impact on the public personnel manager, affirmative action has a more general impact on all public managers and supervisors because it affects the rules by which the acquisition function is carried out. Conflicts between social equity and merit, or even among alternative definitions of social equity, result in the application of confusing and contradictory decision rules regulating the acquisition function.

During periods of agency growth, such as the 1960s and 1970s, managers could overcome these conflicts by hiring more people from all groups—as long as the pie was getting larger, everyone could get a bigger piece. But in periods of lower growth rates, such as the 1980s and 1990s, conflicts between social equity and other values, or even among alternative definitions of social equity, result in heightened conflict over acquisition rules.

What can we expect in the future? This same tension among conflicting values is likely to continue. On the one hand, political pressures for representativeness and economic pressures for enhanced productivity will result in increased workforce diversification efforts. On the other hand, reactions against these pressures will result in either administrative formalism in the implementation of diversification programs, or resistance to them by particular groups that perceive them as threatening to their job prospects. To the extent that economic markets can influence personnel policies and practices, the forecast connecting workforce diversity and productivity seems on target. But the strength of the marketplace contains its weakness as well; it is driven by the value of efficiency, not by concerns of equity, fairness, or justice. While the connection between productivity and diversity may increase representation of racial and ethnic minorities in the workplace, history suggests that if it does so fairly, it will be coincidental. It appears safe to observe that in the 1990s, the value of social equity is being carried into the political arena more by demographic reality than by legislation, litigation, and conscience. At least in large urban areas, the composition of the labor force and the increasing political pressure of racial and ethnic groups should open access to public jobs even wider. From a values perspective, we may see increasing alliances of responsiveness/representation, efficiency, and social equity. While the courts will continue to orient themselves to the protection of individual rights, demographic realities will force legislatures and administrative agencies to respond to representation and the broader political concern of workforce diversity. Further, increasing emphasis on customer satisfaction in multigroup communities may very well connect workforce diversity to productivity.[29]

Changing Role Expectations

The conflicts caused by societal disagreement over the relative importance of social equity as an underlying value, and over the appropriateness of alternative strategies for achieving it (EEO, AA, or diversification programs) have generated changed role expectations for all groups in public agencies: elected officials, managers and supervisors, employees, personnel professionals, and affirmative action compliance specialists charged with developing or implementing personnel management policies in public agencies.

For elected officials, it means making difficult choices among policy options that often conflict. While it is possible to influence the personnel practices of contractors through minority business programs and set-asides (contracting quotas), the use of alternative methods of service delivery reduces the ability of the public sector to directly shape agency mission, culture, policies, and procedures so as to achieve workforce diversity.

Managers and supervisors are faced with the need to maintain productive organizations in the face of two contradictory truths: It is usually easier to make decisions and resolve conflicts in a homogeneous organization, at least in the short run; and organizations must be adaptable to heterogeneous and shifting environments in order to survive in the long run. This means that managers will continue to be evaluated along two criteria—short-term productivity and changes in organizational culture which enable the organization to enhance long-term effectiveness.

Employees face the need to communicate, interact, form work teams, resolve conflicts, and make decisions with other employees who may be unlike them in many characteristics. And they will do so in a climate of increased workplace tension due to the transformation of labor markets and increased employment opportunity for skilled and unskilled foreign workers. These changes pit workers against each other, and pit new applicants against current employees.

As always, human resource managers face the need to manage human resources efficiently and effectively. With respect to workforce diversity, this means the need to develop and apply two apparently contradictory human resource strategies: policies for temporary employees designed to control costs, and policies for permanent employees designed to ensure loyalty, participation and asset development as human resources. Yet because cost control and asset development are both valid objectives, this ambivalence will continue. And because effective human resource management depends upon the communication of clear and consistent messages, public personnel managers find it increasingly difficult when they must send different messages to different employees. In general, therefore, workforce diversity is consistent with demands on public officials and administrators for more innovation. Human resource managers who recognize the dynamism and conflict inherent in their roles are more likely to maintain an innovative and appropriate balance between conflicting objectives. But cultivating innovation among public managers requires characteristics usually not present in the culture of contemporary organizations—reward systems that reinforce risk taking and do not penalize failure.

The transition from affirmative action compliance to workforce diversification presents affirmative action compliance specialists with a difficult dilemma. Traditionally, affirmative action specialists have relied upon their authority as interfaces between the organization and external compliance agencies. Given the five critical differences between affirmative action compliance and workforce diversification, these specialists need to redefine their own role and culture in the organization.

SUMMARY

Equal employment opportunity, affirmative action, and workforce diversification programs have had a profound effect on all personnel functions. They are all based on the value of social equity and individual rights, and on the affirmative action system laws and procedures used to implement these values. Despite the current eclipse of social equity due to the renewed emphasis on other values, affirmative action will continue to have a profound impact on public administration because of its control over the acquisition process and the increasing role of the judicial system in regulating employment decisions and ensuring procedural due process.

In the long run, it may be helpful to view affirmative action simply as a political stage America needed to go through on its way to accepting increasing cultural and therefore workforce diversity. Workforce diversification is the fundamental change in the composition of an organization's workforce that is now occurring in the United States and other developed countries as their cultures and populations become increasingly diverse. This demographic diversity is accompanied by economic pressures, as technological change and globalization of the economy increase public and private employers' demands for a highly trained workforce. And political pressures by women, minorities, older workers, immigrants, and persons with disabilities have resulted in legal changes in the employment rights of groups formerly excluded by law or custom from desirable professional and technical jobs.

As a result of these changes, organizations need to design and implement workforce diversification programs. These involve subtle but sweeping changes in how they do business regarding organizational mission, culture, policy, and practice. The cultural fabric of American society is changing even if its fundamental values remain relatively stable; and in the future, the value of social equity may be advanced by demonstrating a connection between the concept of a culturally representative workforce and organizational productivity.

Predictably, conflict over the relative importance of social equity and the best ways of achieving it have led public administrators and officials to reexamine the impact of diversification programs on productivity and fairness, and on how they do their jobs.

KEY TERMS

Adarand v. Peña
affirmative action (AA)
affirmative action plan (AAP)
affirmative action program
alternative dispute resolution (ADR)
Civil Rights Act of 1991
conciliation agreement
consent decree
court order
cultural diversity
disability
discrimination
employment preference
equal employment opportunity (EEO)
Equal Employment Opportunity Commission (EEOC)
Equal Pay Act (EPA)
Executive Order (EO) 11246
glass ceiling
Griggs v. Duke Power Company
Johnson v. Transportation Agency
management by objectives (MBO)
mentoring
minority business enterprise (MBE)
Office of Federal Contract Compliance Programs (OFCCP)
request for proposal (RFP)
Richmond v. Croson
set-aside
strict scrutiny
Title VII (Civil Rights Act of 1964)
total quality management (TQM)
underutilization
Uniform Guidelines on Employee Selection Procedures
United States v. Paradise
workforce diversification program
workforce diversity

DISCUSSION QUESTIONS

1. What are the definitions of equal employment opportunity and affirmative action, and what is the distinction between them?
2. What federal agencies are responsible for affirmative action compliance? Do you think compliance agencies should spend more time assisting employers in meeting their affirmative action obligations or in regulating employer behavior?
3. Describe the different mechanisms involved in voluntary and involuntary compliance with affirmative action law.
4. Describe the different orientations and values the Supreme Court has endorsed from 1971 to 1989 in interpreting EEO/AA law. Do you think future cases will reverse the trend toward individual rights and away from social equity set in 1989 by the Supreme Court?

5. How has the increased reliance of public agencies for delivering public services through purchase of service agreements rather than through public employees changed the focus of affirmative action compliance? What values and procedures are endorsed by set-asides? What do you think will be the outcome of the conflict between set-asides and contractors' rights under the Fourteenth Amendment?
6. How does workforce diversity differ from both equal employment opportunity and affirmative action?
7. What do you believe is the relationship among affirmative action, workforce diversity, and productivity in a culturally diverse community?
8. How do workforce diversification programs affect organizational culture, mission, policies, and programs?
9. What are the characteristics of effective and ineffective workforce diversification programs?
10. What role do you think the public manager should take in advancing affirmative action and workforce diversity in an environment of conflicting values?

CASE STUDY 1 VALUES IN CONFLICT: EQUAL OPPORTUNITY OR AFFIRMATIVE ACTION?

Read the following passages from Supreme Court opinions, and then answer the questions which follow.

> It is plainly true that in our society blacks have suffered discrimination immeasurably greater than any directed at other racial groups. But those who believe that racial preferences can help to "even the score" display, and reinforce, a manner of thinking by race that was the source of the injustice and that will, if it endures within our society, be the source of more injustice still. The relevant proposition is not that it was blacks, or Jews, or Irish who were discriminated against, but that it was individual men and women, "created equal," who were discriminated against. And the relevant resolve is that it should never happen again. Racial preferences appear to "even the score" (in some small degree) only if one embraces the proposition that our society is appropriately viewed as divided into races, making it right that an injustice rendered in the past to a black man should be compensated for by discriminating against a white. Nothing is worth that embrace.
>
> Justice Scalia, *Richmond v. Croson,* 57 LW 4132, 4148 (1989)

> A profound difference separates governmental actions that themselves are racist, and governmental actions that seek to remedy the effects of prior racism or to prevent neutral governmental activity from perpetuating the effects of such racism. . . . Racial classifications "drawn on the presumption that one race is inferior to another or because they put the weight of government behind racial hatred and separatism" warrant the strictest judicial scrutiny because of the very irrelevance of these rationales. . . . By contrast. . . . [b]ecause the consideration of race is relevant to remedying the continuing effects of past racial discrimination, and because governmental programs employing racial classifications for remedial purposes can be crafted to avoid stigmatization, . . . such programs should not be subjected to conventional "scrutiny"— scrutiny that is strict in theory, but fatal in fact.
>
> Justice Marshall, *Richmond v. Croson,* 57 LW 4132, 4155 (1989)

> Congress has not commanded that the less qualified be preferred over the better qualified simply because of minority origins. Far from disparaging job qualifications as such, Congress has made such qualifications the controlling factor, so that race, religion, nationality, and sex become irrelevant.
>
> Chief Justice Burger, *Griggs v. Duke Power Company*, 401 L Ed 2d, 158, 167 (1971)

QUESTIONS

1. Identify the values in each of the passages.
2. Which passages do you agree with most/disagree with most?

CASE STUDY 2 BETWEEN A ROCK AND A HARD PLACE ON AFFIRMATIVE ACTION COMPLIANCE

Read the following scenario and complete the assignment in the last paragraph.

In 1982 a group of Hispanic-Americans sued the city government for discrimination in employment practices in the police and fire departments. The court encouraged the parties to enter a consent decree, which they did. The consent decree called for the city to cease its discrimination, to identify the victims of discrimination, to make the hiring of the qualified victims a priority, and to establish hiring and promotion goals that would bring the percentage of Hispanic-Americans in the public safety departments on par with the number of qualified potential Hispanic-American applicants in the surrounding labor market.

By 1984, although the city had hired a few of the plaintiffs who had not already found other jobs, the city had shown little effort to comply with the consent decree, and the racial imbalances were hardly affected. The Hispanics complained that those who were hired had been kept in lower-paying job classifications longer than their Anglo peers and were subjected to racial jokes; they were paired with each other in the police department and assigned to Hispanic-American high-crime areas. In the fire department they were isolated in the day-to-day informal activities of the department. It was rumored about city hall that the mayor had encouraged the personnel director to "do as little as possible" in complying with the consent decree.

In 1985 the Hispanic advocates went back to the court, requesting judicial intervention. The court summoned the parties, and a revised consent decree was entered. It provided for a court-ordered trustee to monitor the consent decree. In 1986 the city halted all hiring, citing budgetary problems. By 1988, the city began to hire on a case-by-case basis in other departments, but not in public safety, citing the lack of need for additional officers and fire fighters.

The Hispanic plaintiffs returned again to the court, seeking relief. After consulting with the trustee, the judge, citing the court's exasperation and failure to note good faith on the part of the city, was determined to craft a solution that would make a difference. At this point, the mayor announced the hiring of a chief administrative officer and assigned the CAO the responsibility of coming up with a plan to "deal with this mess." The city successfully persuaded the judge to give it six more months to rectify the problems. The judge reluctantly agreed.

You are the CAO. Develop a plan, recognizing that it will have to be approved by a judge who will tolerate no more delays. At the same time, you must understand that the judge is bound to analyze the plan according to the strict scrutiny standard. Thus, you must remedy the effects of the discrimination, but your plan must not place too much of a burden for the remedy on innocent non-minority workers.

CASE STUDY 3 FROM AFFIRMATIVE ACTION COMPLIANCE TO WORKFORCE DIVERSIFICATION PROGRAMS

You are the personnel director of a major metropolitan government. For years, you and other city administrators have emphasized affirmative action compliance by (1) making it a key organizational objective; (2) taking steps to reduce underutilization of protected classes by targeted programs for recruitment, testing, selection, training, and career development; and (3) establishing separate grievance systems to protect against sexual harassment, racial and ethnic discrimination, and other violations of employee rights.

Now, you hear increasing complaints about the adequacy of these affirmative action compliance policies and programs from managers and employees. Managers ask, "Isn't there a way that we can create a climate of ethnic harmony without resorting to slow and costly administrative proceedings?" Employees in protected categories are unhappy: "Why don't you treat us as employees and human beings, rather than focusing only on gender, race, disability, or ethnicity? Aren't our skills and performance more important than these." Other employees also dislike affirmative action: "I can't get ahead in this organization because I'm a white male. We're discriminated against all the time, but we don't have any legal protection because we're not members of a protected class."

You decide that the best way to deal with these unsatisfactory conditions is by developing workforce diversification policies and programs. You prepare a formal presentation to the city manager and other department directors explaining how these policies and programs will help the city run better. They listen to your presentation, and then ask questions. How do you answer them?

QUESTIONS

1. How does workforce diversification differ from EEO or AA? Isn't this just "old wine in new bottles"?
2. Why does this diversification require changes in our mission, culture, or values? It's just a personnel issue, right? Can't we just say we value diversity, and let it go at that?
3. How will workforce diversification programs affect these specific areas of human resource management policy and practice: recruitment and retention, job design, education and training, benefits and rewards, and performance measurement and improvement?

4. Won't this put the affirmative action office out of business? How will you ever sell it to them?
5. Has anyone else done this before? What results did they see?
6. If we're going to do it right, what are the characteristics of a successful diversification program? Of an unsuccessful one?

NOTES

[1] *The Civil Rights Act of 1964.* P.L. 88-352, 78 Stat. 241, 28 USC ss. 1147 [1976].

[2] *The Equal Employment Opportunity Act of 1972.* P.L. 93-380, 88 Stat. 514, 2-0 USC 1228 [1976].

[3] Employment Standards Administration, U.S. Department of Labor, *Office of Federal Contract Compliance Programs: Director's Report Fiscal Year 1989* (Washington, DC, undated).

[4] *Griggs v. Duke Power Company,* 28 L Ed 2d 158 (1971).

[5] Ibid.

[6] Ibid.

[7] *United States v. Paradise,* 94 L Ed 2d 203 (1987).

[8] *Johnson v. Transportation Agency,* 94 L Ed 2d 615 (1987).

[9] *United States v. Paradise.*

[10] *Richmond v. Croson,* 102 L Ed 2d 854 (1989).

[11] *Adarand v. Peña,* 115 S. Ct. 2097 (1995).

[12] Strenski, J. (1994). Stress diversity in employee communications. *Public Relations Journal, 50,* 32-35.

[13] Roosevelt, T. R. (1990). From affirmative action to affirming diversity. *Harvard Business Review, 68,* 107-117.

[14] The Hudson Institute (1988). *Opportunity 2000: Creating affirmative action strategies for a changing workforce.* Indianapolis: The Hudson Institute.

[15] National Performance Review (1993). *Reinventing human resource management.* Washington, DC: National Performance Review, Office of the Vice President.

[16] Schein, E. (1981). *Organizational culture and leadership.* San Francisco: Jossey-Bass.

[17] Jamieson, D., and J. O'Mara (1991). *Managing workforce 2000.* San Francisco: Jossey-Bass.

[18] Morgan, H., and K. Tucker (1991). *Companies that care.* New York: Fireside.

[19] U.S. Equal Employment Opportunity Commission (1991). *Americans with Disabilities Act handbook.* Washington, DC: U.S. Department of Justice, Equal Employment Opportunity Commission.

[20] Solomon, C. (1993). Managing today's immigrants. *Personnel Journal, 72,* 57-65.

[21] Rosow, J., and R. Zager (1988). *Training—the corporate edge.* San Francisco: Jossey-Bass.

[22] Bernhard, H., and C. Ingols (September/October 1988). Six lessons for the corporate classroom. *Harvard Business Review, 88,* 40-48.

[23] Rubaii-Barrett, N., and A. Beck (1993). Minorities in the majority: Implications for managing cultural diversity. *Public Personnel Management, 22,* 503-522.

[24] Loden, M., and J. Rosener (1991). *Workforce America! Managing employee diversity as a vital resource.* Homewood, IL: Business One Irwin.

[25] Denison, D. (1990). *Corporate culture and organizational effectiveness.* New York: John Wiley.

[26] Kellough, J. E. (1989). *Federal equal employment opportunity policy and numerical goals and timetables.* New York: Praeger; Welch, F. (1989). Affirmative action and discrimination. In S. Shulman and W. Darity, Jr. (Eds.). *The question of discrimination.* Middleton, CT: Wesleyan University Press, pp. 153-198.

[27] ________. (February 23, 1995). *USA Today,* p. 8A.

[28] Lemann, N. (June 11, 1995). What happened to the case for affirmative action? *The New York Times Magazine,* pp. 36-43.

[29] Cox, T. H., and S. Blake (1991). Managing cultural diversity: Implications for organizational competitiveness. *Academy of Management Executive, 5,* 3, 45-56; Coleman, T. (October 1990). Managing diversity at work: The new American dilemma. *Public Management, 72,* 2-6.

7

Recruitment, Selection, and Promotion

> The Los Angeles Board of Education on Wednesday shook off public pressure to immediately appoint the district's highest ranking Latino as the next superintendent, deciding instead to spend time considering its options.
>
> The decision not to name Deputy Superintendent Ruben Zacarias touched off angry protests from Latino activists, who vowed to express their displeasure with drastic measures, which they said could include keeping children out of school or trying to recall board member David Tokofsky, who represents a majority Latino district.[1]

In government jurisdictions with strong merit systems, recruitment, selection, and promotion activities are frequently viewed as routine administrative functions. This perspective masks the dynamic conflicts that frequently characterize debate over the appropriate criteria to use in the recruitment and selection of job applicants and the promotion of employees. In addition to describing some of the technical aspects of recruitment and selection, this chapter reviews the value conflicts and the compromises that take place over the criteria used in these acquisition and planning functions. Also, it discusses how contemporary views of work and organizations of the future affect this personnel function.

By the end of this chapter, you will be able to:

1. Define the acquisition function.
2. Describe the influence different values have on the objectives of the acquisition function.
3. Describe briefly the differences in perspective between political appointees and career civil servants.
4. Describe several external factors and contemporary challenges that influence the acquisition function.
5. Describe eight steps in the recruitment and selection process.

6. Discuss the comparative characteristics of centralized, decentralized, and electronic staffing techniques, and outsourcing.
7. Describe the concept of test validation and three validation strategies.
8. Describe the relationship between job analysis, test validation, and performance evaluation/productivity.
9. Describe the main provisions of the Americans with Disabilities Act and how the ADA affects recruitment and selection.

THE ACQUISITION FUNCTION

The second of the four functions every comprehensive personnel system must fulfill involves the acquisition of knowledge, skills, and abilities (KSAs) that will enable the organization to fulfill its purposes. It may seem cold and impersonal to talk about the recruitment and hiring of people in terms of acquisition. But traditionally, the impersonality of merit systems—the most comprehensive and pervasive personnel systems in government—has been a virtue. In merit systems, personnel decisions are supposed to be made on the basis of an applicant's knowledge, skills, and abilities and the performance that results from the employee's application of his or her KSAs to the agency's work, not on the basis of whom an applicant or employee knows. When we talk about the acquisition of labor, we are talking about an employer's acquisition of knowledge, skills, and abilities through the recruitment and selection processes.

It is here that differences in the focus of job analysis (on positions, work, or employees) can cause divergence in the objectives of the **acquisition function.** For example, the emphasis in civil service systems on an individual employee's KSAs often masks the importance to the organization of motivation, ability to get along with others, and effective performance in an organizational context.

VALUE CONFLICTS AND THE ACQUISITION FUNCTION

As he faced a reelection campaign in late summer 1988, former Mayor Tom Bradley of Los Angeles was being pressured to appoint more Latinos to top City Hall vacancies.[2] The growing Latino population had topped 30 percent in Los Angeles, while the number in top city jobs reached only 7 percent. The mayor faced a unique opportunity—to fill five top vacancies at once. Three of the vacancies had occurred because of mismanagement, nepotism, and falsification of a résumé. He could not ignore the knowledge, skills, and abilities of the candidates for these positions. Moreover, as he prepared for a stiff challenge in the upcoming election, he could use the appointments to shore up his traditional base of support among African-Americans. Complicating the situation was a mayoral challenger who claimed strength in the largely Anglo-populated, affluent west side of Los Angeles.

Bradley's recruitment and selection of candidates for these positions reflect a combination of values and the interaction of recruitment, selection, and promotion practices. Bradley was required by law to select from lists of finalists developed by the personnel department in accordance with civil service rules, giving the impression that KSAs would dominate the selection criteria. However, the Latino employee association worked hard to ensure adequate representation of Latinos on a list that, according to the *Los Angeles Times*, was pared down through an examination and interviews by a panel of citizens.

Bradley chose two African-Americans, one Latino, and two Anglos for the positions, with each evidently bringing substantial knowledge, skills, and abilities to his or her new position. Two weeks prior to making the appointments, the mayor announced the promotion of a Latino firefighter to the position of deputy chief, making him the highest-ranking Latino on the force.

From these appointments, one can see the complex set of political factors the mayor and his closest aides weighed before making their choices. Clearly the racial-ethnic mix of the appointees entered the picture; the inclusion of the promotion in the fire department may have given the mayor some flexibility in his other appointments. The scandalous departures of previous appointees also played a role. Driving the entire process was the mayor's concerns about the upcoming election.

It would be erroneous to conclude that most recruitment, selection, and promotion decisions are made within such a highly politicized environment. Yet it would be naive to argue that all are conducted according to routine procedures designed only to reward knowledge, skills, and abilities. Tension occurs when the elected leadership believes it could accomplish more to advance its political platform—legitimized through an election—if it had more influence over top-level classified positions. In these cases, partisan pressures crop up either formally or informally to influence career appointments. Over time, if these attempts are successful, the response is that the knowledge, skills, and abilities necessary for informed public policy formulation and implementation are eroded. If the inroads result in notoriety or scandal involving political appointees, counterpressure is felt to strengthen the merit system.

While this pendulum swings, the values of social equity and individual rights often throw it on another course. Not only does the merit system have to respond to political pressures to accommodate the value of responsiveness, it must also adapt to public policy initiatives and political pressure stemming from the values of social equity and individual rights.[3] In fact, some argue that the tension between equity/representation and efficiency has displaced traditional political challenges to merit systems. The quote opening the chapter provides one example, and Arvey and Sackett write, "Most organizations value productivity; a great many also value cultural diversity. When selection systems known to contribute to the first detract from the second, as in the case of valid selection systems with adverse impact on protected groups, conflict arises. No clear solution has emerged, although what is surfacing is a clear sense that fairness is a ***social issue rather than a scientific one*** [emphasis added]."[4]

The most direct way of realizing social equity is through the establishment of selection quotas—for veterans, women, or racial and ethnic minorities. But the historic strength of merit systems and the ongoing appreciation of the need to bring expert knowledge to bear on public policy formulation and implementation decreases the availability of this solution. In fact, even though quotas are commonly associated with affirmative action, they are rarely part of formal affirmative action programs. It is useful to remind ourselves that where hiring or promotion ratios do exist, they have resulted from a court order that usually follows convincing evidence of egregious and systemic discrimination attributed to a specific employer. Even when hiring ratios are present, they are usually tempered by the phrase "qualified minorities," and they are not enforced if legitimate budgetary constraints place limits on hiring.

While several years ago it may have been legal and appropriate to show a preference to a woman or minority if two applicants had similar scores on an examination and one was Anglo, recent events suggest that kind of affirmative action may fail the judicial test of strict scrutiny.[5] Along the same lines, with initiative from the governor, the regents of the University of California declared that admissions criteria will disregard race as a factor.

It is difficult to talk about issues of diversity in selection processes in part because of its multiple value foundations. For some a diverse workforce is necessary to understand and respond to a diverse clientele's needs (efficiency); for others, it is a matter of fairness for suffering past discrimination (social equity); and for still others, it is a matter of political representation—"we pay taxes, we deserve a piece of the pie." In multiracial communities, the politics of diversity in selection processes are complex. Should a workforce be selected solely on the basis of knowledge, skills and abilities? The quick answer is "yes," and for some, that is the only answer. Frank L. Schmitt, distinguished professor of human resources and former director of a research program in personnel selection at the U.S. Office of Personnel Management, writes, "One key problem hobbling personnel selection is the dilemma created by the conflict between productivity and the need to increase minority representation." He continues, "Will it be politically and legally possible to employ valid selection methods (with or without adjustments or mechanisms to reduce adverse impact) to improve the efficiency and productivity of our economy in our litigious, multicultural society?"[6]

But if politics is about building and maintaining a sense of community, does it make sense to divorce human resource management from political considerations? And if the effectiveness of public agencies in a diverse and unpredictable environment depends upon situational and team-based KSAs rather than abstract individual ones, might this presumed conflict be in fact spurious? Maxwell and Arvey use this logic to argue that the most valid selection method will produce the least adverse impact.[7] Could the most capable and enlightened Anglo police force help build a sense of community in a predominantly African-American community as much as a multiracial force? What if that force was not shown to be as capable in terms of law enforcement knowledge, skills, and abilities as one selected strictly by merit? Obviously, the goal is to select those who are both qualified and represent diversity, hoping that is always possible.

So far, we have talked about issues of political responsiveness, efficiency, and equity in the staffing process. The value of individual rights enters as protection from partisan political influence. Thus, acquisition routines that include open access and selection criteria based on knowledge, skills, and abilities derived from the job to be performed have the effect of protecting the rights of individual job applicants to fair treatment.

The value of individual rights is also expressed significantly in the promotion process, where upward mobility is allocated, or in layoffs, where jobs themselves are allocated through the planning and sanction functions. Collective bargaining systems, seeking to protect the rights and treatment of their members, are particularly oriented toward these kinds of allocational decisions rather than acquisition—recruitment and selection—decisions.

Even though a union may not seek to influence recruitment and selection decisions in non-apprenticeship positions, it will make every effort to convince newly appointed employees to join the union if the job falls within the union's bargaining unit. In Kansas City, Missouri, every newly appointed firefighter joins the union, even though Missouri is a right-to-work state. During the initial training period, peer pressure is applied to accomplish this goal.

One of the ways unions protect their members from management favoritism is by insisting that seniority play a major role in allocational decisions like promotion and layoffs. Similarly, they argue against contracting out of city services if those services are currently performed by unionized city employees. Again, where merit systems exist alongside collective bargaining systems, compromises are commonly reached. For example, it would not be unusual to see promotion scores calculated according to a formula that includes credit for an examination score and for years of service.

A major thesis of this book is that these value conflicts, whether between responsiveness and efficiency, efficiency and equity, or responsiveness and individual rights, cannot be avoided because the values themselves are fundamental to the political culture. As long as public jobs are considered scarce resources, these values will be brought to bear on acquisition and planning or allocation personnel decisions. This results in merit systems under continual pressure from advocates of values other than efficiency (KSA), and public policy compromises that eventually are reflected in personnel routines, techniques, and regulations.

What complicates human resource management tremendously is that advocates of individual rights rely on legislation and judicial tools to constrain managers, while organization theorists and commentators are arguing for flexibility, consideration of contextual factors, and personal attributes in selection decisions. Advocates of these two views rarely have to confront each other. And, in the absence of an authoritative reconciliation of these perspectives, managers dealing daily with personnel issues must find their own solutions.

DIFFERENCES IN PERSPECTIVE: POLITICAL APPOINTEES AND CAREER CIVIL SERVANTS

Staffing is seen as a method of enhancing managerial efficiency through the acquisition of employees with desired knowledge, skills, and abilities and as a tool to advance the aims of social equity advocates. But recruitment takes a different shape when it is aimed at advancing political responsiveness. The public often views government employees who they see issuing statements on television, holding press conferences, and making visible and critical decisions as government bureaucrats. Yet few of these individuals actually are career government employees. Almost all agency heads at the state and federal levels of government, and many at the local level, are political appointees. That is, they are not appointed as a result of a competitive examination, and they serve at the pleasure of the elected officials who appoint them.

At the federal level, political appointments include people like cabinet secretaries, assistant secretaries, and other ranking agency officials; employees who work in the Office of the President; many legislative employees; judges; and ranking officials of independent agencies. Similar positions are available in state government. Depending on the form of local government, the chief administrative officer and department heads may serve at the pleasure of the governing body or perhaps the mayor. If one is unfamiliar with a particular organization or government, the difference between politically appointed versus career officials can usually be determined by asking which positions are part of the civil service system. **Career civil servants** usually occupy "classified" positions covered by policies, rules, regulations, and procedures that constitute a merit system—a comprehensive personnel system where decisions are made primarily on the basis of knowledge, skills, and abilities.

Political appointees view public employment from different perspectives than career civil servants.[8] Political appointees owe primary allegiance *upward*—to the elected official who appointed them—and they get in trouble when they fail to remember that. Merit criteria are subordinate to a political clearance or at the very least, among equally qualified job candidates, political loyalty will be the deciding factor. Incumbents of political positions value loyalty to a political philosophy or elected official or party, and they usually are unfamiliar with the structure and operations of the agency they are being called upon to run, even though they may bring impressive political qualifications and a solid background of experience in the private sector to their posts. Highly visible examples include Walter Mondale as U.S. ambassador to Japan, Clarence Thomas as Supreme Court Justice, and Frederico Pena as secretary of transportation.

Like the elected officials who appoint them, political appointees usually bring a short-term perspective and long-term political loyalty to their work. Frequently they regard career civil servants as politically unresponsive, believing their loyalties are to programs or policies adopted by previous administrations. Hence, politically appointed officials, just like many citizens, may view civil service protections as "red tape" that keeps "unproductive and unresponsive" civil servants in jobs, frustrating the political aims of the elected leadership and the "will of the people." Over time, career civil servants begin to value continuity and stability in public policy making and consistency in policy implementation, and they are less likely to embrace short-term initiatives they see as having little chance of long-term success or to grant exceptions to rules if, in their view, those exceptions frustrate efficient or equitable service delivery.

Because personnel managers work closely with department directors to attract qualified applicants to available positions, the credibility and status of personnel officers derive in large measure from the degree to which they are regarded as helpful. But as the previous discussion indicates, personnel managers must adhere to other standards as well. For example, they attempt to fulfill the acquisition function while keeping recruitment and selection costs low. Further, personnel managers trained in merit systems attempt to develop recruitment and selection processes which instill confidence that applicants are being treated fairly and will be selected according to their KSAs. Obviously, these criteria do not always coalesce harmoniously, and part of the ongoing tension in the professional personnel manager's role is the struggle between facilitating the work of line managers and elected officials, and regulating their decisions to keep them in line with accepted and legal personnel practices.[9]

EXTERNAL INFLUENCES AND CONTEMPORARY CHALLENGES

In addition to the conflict over values in the allocation of public jobs as scarce resources, other factors also influence the acquisition function. The demand and supply of labor for government employers are influenced by demographic factors, and the economic, political, and legal environment of public employment.[10] The demand for labor is determined by the specific knowledge, skills, and abilities needed to fulfill public agency missions and objectives. Fundamentally, competition with private and other public employers, financial resources, authorized positions, and the formulation and content of agency missions influence the demand for labor. Another influence, sometimes unspoken, over the shape of that demand is the degree of political pressure both within the government and within communities, regarding the need for diversity.

One demand that appears to be growing, but for which little data have been gathered historically, centers on contingent (temporary or part-time) workers and the insecurity of the job market. The U.S. Bureau of Labor Statistics issued a report in 1995 on contingent workers. This is the first comprehensive survey seeking information from people who were employed but did not perceive themselves as having an implicit or explicit contract for ongoing employment.[11] While a large share of the contingent workforce is employed part-time, the vast majority of part-time employees have permanent job arrangements and are not included in the survey.

The report concluded that nearly 5 percent of those employed considered themselves contingent workers; this represents some 6 million people who are working but who feel they may not have a job within a year. Workers identified as falling into "service" industries accounted for over 50 percent of the total; workers in the "public administration" category totaled 3.6 percent, or some 220,000 government employees.

The report compares these workers to the non-contingent workforce as follows: They are younger, slightly more likely to be female and black, more likely to be enrolled in school, part-time (although the vast majority of part-time workers do not fall into the contingent worker category), employed in the services industry, less likely to have health insurance, and desirous of permanent employment.

Regarding the supply of labor, several questions are relevant: Who is available in the relevant labor market, and what KSAs do they possess? Where can potential employees be found, and how can they be reached and recruited for public employment? What will it take to retain workers with valued knowledge, skills, and abilities?

Analyzing age demographics, Lane and Wolf[12] suggest that the overall problem affecting recruitment and retention in the near future is too many baby boomers (those born between 1945 and 1965), too few younger workers, and too many older workers leaving the workforce prematurely. The problem associated with the baby boomer generation is too many competent workers competing for limited opportunities for upward mobility. Simultaneously, a shortage of younger workers is anticipated. Finally, as increasing numbers of public employees become eligible for retirement, critical shortages can be anticipated.

Looking at the same data, the U.S. General Accounting Office (GAO) suggests caution in predicting future mismatches between the supply and demand for knowledge, skills, and abilities.[13] There is widespread agreement on certain demographic changes that have occurred and are expected to occur. First, women are constituting a greater and greater portion of the workforce. In 1950 only about one third of the civilian workforce consisted of women. In contrast, by 1990 that figure had jumped to nearly 60 percent, and it is expected to continue to rise. The participation rate of men in 1990 was about 76 percent, and it is expected to drop. Most noticeably, the participation rate for married women with children climbed from 39 percent in 1960 to 75 percent in 1990. While the traditional family is dead—only 4 percent of families fit the traditional model of a husband who works and a wife who stays at home with two children—caregiving family needs have not declined. In fact, as non-family influences on children become more prevalent and as the elderly live longer and require more family care, these needs probably will increase. It is apparent that human resource policies and practices that fail to account for these demands on employees will erode employee loyalty, commitment, and productivity and make recruitment of talented employees more difficult.

The second trend is the increasing percentage of minority representation in the labor force. If current projections hold, some 27 percent of the workforce in the year 2005 will be minority. In 1980 that number was 17 percent. The biggest increases are expected to come among people of Hispanic and Asian ethnic groups. If these numbers hold, dealing with diversity at work will not only be the right thing to do, it will be the only thing to do.

Finally, the workforce is aging in ways we have not seen before. The median age is expected to be 41 in the year 2005, similar to 1962. The difference is the baby boom generation, which will begin turning 55 in the year 2001 and pushing the median age higher. This may result in KSA shortages, but, more assuredly, because there will be relatively more retirees than younger workers, it will take more younger workers to support the retirement of older generations.

In addition to demographic influences on recruitment and retention, political factors play a role as well. Changes in program priorities affect the demand for and supply of labor. For example, increased emphasis on the space program in the 1970s created thousands of jobs for aerospace workers; then financial concerns resulting in cutbacks decreased demand for these same workers. Similarly, as Hispanic and other immigrant populations grow, political pressure on educational systems for bilingual educators and administrators will increase.

The sheer size of government means that agency needs will have a significant impact on the labor market. As the federal government has shed itself of direct service delivery, state and local governments have begun to fill the void, requiring increases in the numbers of state and local employees.

As shown in Figure 7-1, economic conditions influence recruitment and retention of public employees as well. Public jobs are usually seen as being less susceptible to recession, and economic setbacks commonly see increasing numbers of available applicants for public jobs. At the same time, economic recession decreases the number of people resigning from jobs in public agencies. Lower revenue projections will diminish recruitment efforts, since the demand for new employees will be reduced.

The legal environment influences recruitment and retention practices as well. Laws affecting retirement age directly influence retention rates and the supply of existing labor. Judicial interpretations of affirmative action law, recently limiting the ability of employers to show preference to women and minorities, put greater emphasis on outreach in recruitment practices and on research that identifies effective outreach efforts. Also, residency requirements may affect the availability of individuals with critical knowledge, skills, and abilities.

While mission and policy goals and the political values we have been talking about significantly influence the type of KSAs needed, the way work is performed requires rethinking of recruitment and selection functions as well. Most prominently, the increasing reliance on teams and teamwork emphasizes what traditionally are seen as important but non task-related factors connected to productivity in the work environment. Borman and Motowidlo call them **contextual factors** and include:

- Volunteering to carry out task activities that are not formally a part of the job
- Persisting with extra enthusiasm or effort when necessary to complete task activities successfully
- Helping and cooperating with others
- Following organizational rules and procedures even when personally inconvenient
- Endorsing, supporting, and defending organizational objectives[14]

FIGURE 7-1 Economic Conditions and Recruitment

Economic Growth

1. Scarcity of qualified applicants
2. High demand for internal promotions and external recruitment
3. Open and continuous recruitment

Economic Decline

1. Surplus of qualified candidates
2. Low demand for internal promotions and external recruitment
3. Recruitment managed or targeted toward shortage-category occupations

To these factors one might add conflict resolution skills and working within a demographically diverse environment. According to Borman and Motowidlo, these activities "do not support the technical core itself as much as they support the organizational, social, and psychological environment in which the technical core must function."[15] Their research shows that the contextual parts of management jobs are substantial, and they should be considered in recruitment and selection processes. Along this line, Guion's literature review shows that social skills and motivation are as important as knowledge in predicting job performance.[16] The challenge is that these and other contextual factors relate to personality attributes, complicating recruitment and selection processes which in the last few decades have increasingly become more formalized and impersonal in order to avoid the risk of civil rights violations in employment decisions. Guion asks, "What are decision makers to do if the people predicted to perform tasks well are not predicted to do very well contextually—or vice versa?"[17]

It seems reasonable to conclude that some of these contextual factors may be more important in some situations than others. In his discussion of privatization of government services, Mintzberg has identified five models for managing government.[18] Each has implications for recruitment and selection. In the normative-control model, attitudes, values, and beliefs significantly influence task accomplishment, and he argues that they should be considered as part of the recruitment and selection process. This is probably more true with regard to social service delivery than other government work, but traditionally the virtue of public service has been found in the dedication of public servants to the collective good.

In their edited volume, Hesselbein, Goldsmith, and Beckhard describe leadership and organizations of the future. The essence of their message is that traditional hierarchical structures will have limited utility because they are best suited to operating in stable environments. In dynamic environments, more loosely structured organizations, composed of individuals with the capacity and willingness to learn continually, are more effective.[19] Related to this theme, Snow and Snell propose three models to distinguish basic components of the staffing process: staffing as person-job match; staffing as strategy implementation; and staffing as strategy formation.[20] In Table 7-1, we can see how traditional staffing functions in model 1 compare to what Snow and Snell see as future trends.

Relating to our previous discussion of the impact of contextual factors on the acquisition process, we might consider model 1 as typifying the traditional emphasis on job analysis and position management. Model 2 expands the staffing process to include more personal attributes related to situational effectiveness and team performance, but the processes are still limited to existing goals and methods. Model 3 exemplifies what happens to the matching of individuals and jobs in organizations where there is a high degree of environmental uncertainty, and employee self-direction and group performance are essential. Here, the focus of acquisition activities will probably be on those employee KSAs determined to be of greatest importance to effective self-directed employees functioning as team members—in other words, a focus on people and work, rather than on jobs and position management. Model 3 differs significantly from model 1 where it is assumed that the dimensions of a job are known in advance; that the knowledge,

TABLE 7–1 Three Models of the Staffing Process

	Model 1: Staffing as Person–Job Match	*Model 2: Staffing as Strategy Implementation*	*Model 3: Staffing as Strategy Formation*
Characteristics	Staffing based on job analysis Many candidates available per job Tests to measure individual differences Validation studies Closed-system perspective	Staffing based on competitive strategy (part of implementation) Role descriptions Interdepartmental team synergies Open-system perspective	Staffing based on strategy formation Broad skill base Rapid deployment of resources Open-system perspective
Assumptions	Organizations and jobs can be separated into individual components People and jobs are stable Job performance can be measured validly and reliably	Deductive logic Reactive staffing Tight fit between strategy and staffing	Inductive logic Proactive staffing Loose fit between strategy and staffing (slack)
Applications	Organizations with stable, definable jobs	Organizations with clear strategies and known competencies	Organization that need the ability to develop or change strategy quickly

Snow, Charles C., and Snell, Scott A. "Staffing Is Strategy," Table 14-1 (p. 451). In N. Schmitt, W.C. Borman, and Associates *Personnel Selection in Organizations.* Copyright 1993 by Jossey-Bass, Inc., Publishers. Used by permission.

skills, and abilities to perform that job can be identified, measured, and evaluated as performance elements; *and* that they will remain stable.

An interesting example may serve to illustrate the differences in the relationship between job analysis and staffing under different assumptions about the organization and its environment. During World War II, the military began to employ an increasing number of nuclear physicists who were working on the development of the atomic bomb. In typical fashion, personnel specialists were dispatched to analyze, classify, and evaluate the worth of these positions. But they were unable to do so because the factors essential for writing a job description (tasks, performance standards, and minimum qualifications) could not be determined by watching nuclear physicists at work and recording what they did. Had the job description been written in traditional fashion it might have included: "They sit and stare into space, drinking coffee. Every so often one of them gets up and writes an equation on the chalkboard. Most of the time, he looks at it awhile, shakes his head, erases it, and sits down again. Sometimes, he gets excited and calls other physicists to look at it. Most of the time, they say there's a problem with it, erase it, and sit down again. Every once in a while, they all get excited, leave it on the board, and congratulate each other. They then sit down again, stare into space, and drink more coffee." Clearly, the problem here is that personnel specialists were attempting to apply a model suited to staffing as a person-job match, rather than staffing as strategy implementation (where job objectives are known, but methods of achieving them are to be determined by the employee) or strategy formation (where the general organizational mission may be clear, but specific objectives and methods must be determined by the employee in the course of the job)

STEPS IN THE STAFFING PROCESS

Before proceeding with a discussion of recruitment and selection methods, it will be useful to identify various steps and responsibilities in the staffing process, which includes both planning and acquisition functions:

1. Identify human resource needs
2. Seek budgetary approval to create and/or fill the position
3. Develop valid selection criteria
4. Recruit
5. Test or otherwise screen applicants
6. Prepare a list of qualified applicants
7. Interview the most highly qualified applicants
8. Select the most qualified applicant

Different jurisdictions or agencies will carry out these steps in different ways. The important point to be made here is that the line manager—the person the potential hire will actually be working for—is most heavily involved in steps 1, 2, 3, 7, and 8. The personnel department's job is to assist the line manager in finding and hiring the best applicant (a staffing role), and to ensure that the staffing process takes place without the undue influence of politics or favoritism (a regulatory role).

The next step is establishing the minimum qualifications for a position through job analysis. Then, the hiring authority must determine the appropriate method(s) to measure the extent to which applicants or employees possess these qualifications. Nine methods are commonly used: review of biographical data, aptitude tests, ability tests, performance exams, references, performance evaluation (for promotional assessment of current employees only), interviews, assessment centers, and a probationary period.

A review of an applicant's education and experience, through a standardized application form, is fundamental to the selection process.[21] Levine and Flory estimated that in 1976 over *one billion* résumés and job applications were completed and reviewed annually. One can imagine what that number is today! Even if education and experience are not important selection criteria, they do serve other important purposes: They are a tally of the number and the qualifications of applicants for research and record-keeping purposes; they provide a basis for interviewing; and they serve as a component of the personnel record of selected applicants. Research suggests that the data provided through job applications are more valid and reliable than information provided during interviews.[22]

Four types of written tests are commonly used for selection purposes: aptitude, characteristics or traits, ability, and performance. Aptitude tests measure general intelligence or cognitive ability (for example, the federal government's now-discontinued Professional, Administrative Career Entrance (PACE) examination, or the Otis-Lennon). Aptitude tests are both relatively inexpensive to administer and score, and highly reliable. Some commentators are wary of the ease with which responses to psychological tests can be "faked" to match the presumed desired responses to the set of test scores. However, interim reliability checks can reduce the likelihood of this happening. The validity of such tests, however, can range from minimal to moderate, depending on the quality of the job analysis and the resulting construct validation of the aptitude as a predictor.

Several factors contribute to low validity.[23] For one thing, as standardized tests, they are not adaptable to the particular objectives, conditions, or circumstances of different positions having the same title and general range of duties. As a consequence, some experts consider aptitude tests generally reliable for training purposes but less so for selection. Others consider them particularly useful for screening large groups of employees, particularly if they are carefully validated so that they are not inherently biased against minority group members.

A second type of paper-and-pencil test measures personality traits or characteristics. The resulting personality profiles are then compared against profiles of current employees considered successful in the position, or against traits judged as job related through construct validation. Examples are the Edwards Personality Preference Scale (EPPS) and the Minnesota Multiphasic Personality Inventory (MMPI).

Ability tests measure the extent to which applicants possess generalized abilities or skills related to job performance through empirical or construct validation. Examples would be verbal or mathematical ability, such as the Scholastic Aptitude Test (SAT) or the Graduate Record Examination (GRE). The more closely an ability test simulates actual job tasks and context, the more it becomes a performance test. A realistic typing or word processing test would be a good example. A performance test would be position-specific in that it would measure an applicant's ability to type a given kind of material on the specific machine used on the job. Research studies generally confirm that ability tests which result from job analysis are logically related to subsequent job performance.[24]

References are another selection tool. They are usually used to verify educational and employment records or to obtain information about the applicant's skills or personality. Their validity depends upon the opportunity that the writer has had to observe the applicant and upon the relatedness of this relationship to the prospective job. Because recommendation letters are overwhelmingly positive, readers frequently fall into the trap of looking for the smallest of differences as they attempt to distinguish one applicant from another. A better use of reference letters is to stimulate questions that can be asked in an interview.

Reference checks pose challenging legal problems in today's society. If employers fail to reveal damaging yet relevant information about a former employee or if they give out the damaging information but it unfairly harms the employee's chances of obtaining employment, they may become involved in litigation.

Previous performance evaluations are often used to assess potential for reassignment or promotion. They are valid to the extent that the ratings are based on job performance and this performance involves the same skills or abilities required in the prospective job. Their reliability is based on the extent of interrater agreement among previous supervisory evaluations.

Interviews are a popular selection or promotion method.[25] Most organizations will not hire an employee without one because they believe the interview gives them the opportunity to observe an applicant's appearance and interpersonal skills and to ask questions about subjects not adequately covered on the application form. However, interviews are not recommended as a primary selection method. Not only do they take a good deal of the supervisor's time, but they also require interviewing skills on the part of the supervisor or interviewing panel. Since interviews are a prime method of rejecting candidates who look good on paper but might not fit into an organization, they are subject to close scrutiny as potentially invalid selection criteria.

What, then, are some good guidelines to follow concerning interviews? If they are used to screen applicants, they must be validated by the same methods as are other selection devices; that is, justified by job analysis and supported by a content validation strategy. Structured interviews, those using a prepared series of questions relating to the position, previous experience, career objectives, and so on, are preferable to unstructured ones. Panel interviews (those involving more than one interviewer) are more reliable than individual interviews, though they also increase the cost of this already expensive selection method.

Assessment centers attempt to present several applicants with simulated job situations in order to stress performance on job-related tasks. They are used in both the public and the private sectors; in the public sector, their use is most prevalent among law enforcement organizations. If performance criteria are validated, they can be useful in selection, promotion, and career development.

The last selection or promotion method is the probationary appointment. This technique possesses the highest possible validity and reliability factors because it measures actual performance on the job. However, it also carries the highest cost and greatest risk to the organization, since a potentially unqualified employee may occupy a critical position until he or she makes enough serious mistakes to be considered unfit. The use of the probationary period places upon supervisors the responsibility of weeding out unsatisfactory or marginal employees before they attain career status (and hence the right to grievance hearings to protest a discharge after they have attained a "property interest" in their jobs) and upon personnel managers the responsibility of developing valid probationary period evaluation systems.

As might be expected, choosing among these alternative selection and promotion methods is difficult. The methods have differing degrees of validity or job relatedness. They have varying degrees of reliability, or the consistency of scores

TABLE 7-2 Comparison of Selection Methods

Method	*Validity*	*Reliability*	*Cost*
1. Biodata	moderate	high	low
2. References (letters of recommendation)	low	low	low
3. Aptitude tests	moderate	moderate	low
4. Characteristics of trait tests	moderate	moderate	low
5. Ability tests	moderate	moderate	moderate
6. Performance tests	high	moderate	moderate
7. Interviews	low	low	high
8. Assessment centers	moderate	high	high
9. Probationary appointment	very high	very high	very high

for one applicant over time. They range from the inexpensive to the costly. Even beyond the three criteria of validity, reliability, and cost are the values alternative methods can enhance or retard. Those who favor agency efficiency tend to support selection methods that measure quantifiable qualifications cheaply and easily: biodata, tests, and credentials. Those who favor political responsiveness support selection methods that provide information about an applicant's values or personality, or those that maximize flexibility for the hiring officials: references, interviews, and the probationary period. Advocates of social equity favor reliance on the probationary period. They fear that tests and minimum education and experience requirements, while easy to measure and effective at reducing the size of the applicant pool, will reject minority applicants who could perform well if hired ("false negatives").

Because each of these methods differs in value orientation, cost validity, and reliability, organizations must compare them.[26] Table 7-2 summarizes their comparative advantages. Standardized test scores are usually used to screen out persons unable to meet the basic requirements for a position, while interviews, assessment centers, or a probationary period are used to select the most qualified applicant from among all those who are basically qualified.

Research shows that applicants favor selection procedures clearly connected to job content, especially when administered in work samples or simulations rather than paper- and pencil-formats.[27] Furthermore, it appears that in general, applicants accept some controversial selection procedures like drug testing and personality testing.[28]

RECRUITMENT AND SELECTION MODELS

Because both the number of positions agencies need to fill and the conditions under which staffing is conducted may vary, staffing models differ with circumstances. Generally, four types are possible: centralized, decentralized, and electronic models, and outsourcing.

Centralized

If the agency has several thousand employees, and if different departments recruit large numbers of clerical or technical employees for the same types of positions, **centralized recruitment** will frequently be used because it is more efficient. These situations correspond to those classified by Snow and Snell as model 1, where KSAs are standardized and employee qualifications can be measured quantitatively with a high degree of precision.

If recruitment is centralized, the central personnel agency will be responsible for requesting from agency personnel managers periodic estimates of the number and type of new employees needed in the future (the next quarter or fiscal year). The staffing needs of all agencies are entered into a computer, after being classified by occupational code and salary level, and a summary listing of all projected new hiring needs is produced.

In reality, producing an accurate projection of new hiring needs is rarely this simple. To begin with, it is not always possible for agencies to predict their needs a year ahead of time. A political crisis or budget cut can drastically affect recruitment needs, and hence the quality of the estimate. Central personnel agency recruiters also realize that agency personnel managers will tend to overestimate the number of employees they require, just because from their point of view it is better to have too many applicants than too few. Naturally this conflicts with the need of the central personnel agency to reduce selection costs by reducing the number of applicants to the minimum number needed to ensure that all available positions are filled with qualified applicants. In addition, specialized positions require a greater ratio of applicants to projected vacancies, because a higher percentage of applicants is likely to be rejected by the selecting agency as not meeting the specialized requirements of the position.

Based on all these considerations, the central personnel agency will issue a job announcement that formally notifies potential applicants a vacancy exists. To meet affirmative action laws and regulations, each job announcement might include the following information:

1. Job title, classification, and salary range
2. Duty location (geographic and organizational unit)
3. Description of job duties and responsibilities
4. Minimum qualifications
5. Starting date
6. Application procedures
7. Closing date for receipt of applications

If the agency underutilizes women or minorities, it will be interested in targeting recruitment efforts toward individuals from these groups. Community organizations, churches, shopping centers, minority newspapers, state employment services, and minority recruitment centers are all possible avenues for targeted recruitment. Given the hesitancy of many minorities and women to apply for jobs in public agencies in which they have historically had little opportunity for employment, it is to be expected that recruitment will also occur over a longer period of time if it is targeted toward these individuals. One might argue that the best tool for attracting minority applicants is an agency's reputation for fairness in personnel practices.

Decentralized

Decentralized recruitment is traditionally likely to occur in agencies that are relatively small, for which recruitment needs are limited, and where each agency employs different types of workers. Increasingly, it is used in larger units.[29] It is almost always used for professional, scientific, or administrative positions peculiar to a particular agency. For example, smaller municipalities may not have enough vacancies to utilize the services of a central personnel department. Or the department heads may have successfully argued that their particular employees are unique and that it is more appropriate to handle recruitment and selection on a departmental level. Police and fire departments are likely to make this argument at the municipal level. Particularly during a recession, many agencies will find it more effective to utilize decentralized recruitment, because no cost savings can be gained through centralized recruitment when demand for public jobs is great but the number of available openings is small.

Thus, decentralized techniques are likely to be used where considerations of efficiency are less important than the need to match specific employees to an agency, based on their ability to function as members of a work team or in an unstable and unpredictable environment. These situations are likely to correspond to those categorized by Snow and Snell as models 2 and 3.

If recruitment is decentralized, individual public agencies will go through essentially the same steps required for centralized recruitment, except that dealings with the central personnel agency are limited. Agency personnel managers will work directly with the supervisors in their agencies to make periodic estimates of hiring needs. Then agency recruiters will meet with agency affirmative action specialists to determine whether recruitment efforts should be targeted toward specific minority groups. After evaluating both the need for new employees and the diversity goals of the agency, the agency personnel director will determine what recruitment efforts are required. The job announcement process is exactly the same as that of a central personnel agency, except that applicants are requested to send their applications to the specific agency.

While individual agencies are likely to favor decentralized recruitment because it gives them more control over the process, it has the disadvantage of reducing the chief executive's control over expenditures or affirmative action compliance. In a centralized personnel system, for example, the chief executive will be able to stop new hiring simply by forbidding the central personnel agency from recruiting any new applicants and from sending the names of any applicants already on the register (list of eligibles) to individual agencies. In a decentralized system where the chief executive has no direct control over the recruitment process, it is more likely that individual agency directors will insist on their right to recruit people to meet program needs, and to manage their own budgets more autonomously.

In addition, decentralized recruitment is more likely to result in reliance upon word-of-mouth recruitment techniques, particularly in smaller agencies. If underutilization of women or minorities is a problem, word-of-mouth recruitment will probably make it worse; existing employees will be those most likely to discuss the job vacancy with their friends. Group pressure will make it unlikely that they will seek out qualified applicants who might be regarded by their co-workers as "different." In this situation, it is particularly important that formal job announcement and application procedures be scrupulously observed, and that recruitment efforts targeted toward the appropriate groups be carried out.

Some agencies utilize a combination of centralized and decentralized recruitment. For example, a central personnel agency may authorize individual agencies to recruit and test applicants independently, subject to audit by the central personnel agency once they have been hired. This compromise will provide for a greater degree of centralized control than is possible with a decentralized system, while simultaneously providing agencies with timelier and more flexible recruitment available from a central personnel agency.

In response to criticisms that personnel practices are burdensome, time-consuming, and unresponsive to sister agencies, the federal government has increasingly decentralized recruitment and selection over the past decade. Presently, over 80 percent of federal jobs in the executive branch are filled through decentralized agency processes. Furthermore, a recent U.S. Merit Systems Protection Board report concluded that the decentralization has occurred with no corruption linked to "spoils," no decline in the quality of federal employees, and increases in diversity.[30]

Electronic

For twenty-five years, touch-tone dedicated phone lines have allowed agencies to advertise current vacancies, and to refer applicants to agencies with hiring needs. Now, the development of the Internet allows agencies and associations to advertise current vacancies through **job banks**; and applicants to submit résumés and have their qualifications evaluated through the establishment of a "virtual" electronic "hiring hall."[31] Among the available job banks is America's Job Bank (www.ajb.dni.us/), a cooperative effort between the U.S. Department of Labor and some 2,000 state employment service offices. Jobs are listed by category, by state, and in other ways as well. Job Bank includes links to many other web sites, including those of the states. A net search is guaranteed to produce numerous other sites of interest to job seekers and employers.

Outsourcing

The increased use of contracting to achieve economies of scale without sacrificing core organizational competencies has meant that agencies are increasingly choosing to use outsourcing as a recruitment device. In particular, they are likely to use employment services for hiring temporary employees, or executive search firms ("headhunters") for professional and managerial recruitment.

The efficiency in time of outsourcing for temporary workers is evident. The process is shortened noticeably with responsibility for recruitment and selection resting with the temporary employment agency. And while this type of outsourcing seems to make sense, it raises a larger issue: Is it necessary for a government jurisdiction itself to recruit and select for other positions or can these activities be performed just as effectively by private employment agencies under contract? Searches for chief administrative officers and some department heads now are conducted by executive search firms. Why not other positions?

The goal of outsourcing is to save money. But it also allows an organization to concentrate on its mission, that which it can do uniquely. Why not contract with a private employment agency for recruitment and selection with the stipulation that all applicant pools will contain individuals with required knowledge, skills, and abilities and will reflect demographically the appropriate labor market?

In some ways, the real challenge here is first to identify what the agency or government jurisdiction considers its core mission and values. Tom Lewinsohn, former personnel director in Kansas City, Missouri, and past president of the International Personnel Management Association, suggests that recruitment and selection are so integrally connected to the concept of merit, a core governmental value, that outsourcing these activities undermines the concept of the public service.[32]

Seven Recruitment and Selection Models

The availability of centralized, decentralized, electronic recruitment methods, and outsourcing means that the actual staffing process followed by public agencies is complex, and varies with the nature and context of the agency. Table 7-3 depicts seven recruitment and selection routines that take place in Lawrence, Kansas, a council-manager city with a permanent population of some 65,000. By reviewing the information, one can find a number of the steps and methods already discussed as well as the influence of the values of efficiency, social equity, responsiveness, and individual rights. Knowledge, skills, and abilities are weighted very heavily in each of the selection processes. For both the non-public-safety and public-safety entry-level positions, usually the city administers a test of knowledge or skill supplemented by interviews and reference checks. For all positions in the city, a preemployment physical includes a drug screening test. Oral interview boards have replaced interviews with individual supervisors in order to get a broader range of opinion on the suitability of applicants. Interview boards also protect the individual rights of applicants to fair and equal treatment. A review of licenses and certificates is particularly important in screening applicants for technical positions. In the last few years, electronic mail bulletin boards and a dedicated information phone line have expanded recruitment efforts.

No paper-and-pencil testing takes place for department heads or for the city manager. The national recruitment procedure indicates a desire to secure professionally trained talent. In addition, the interview board usually includes a professional in a related field who is not a member of the city staff. For example, selection of a new finance director might include a banker or the city's auditor as a member of the interview board.

Social equity is particularly noticeable in the public-safety positions, where special efforts are made in the recruitment process. Recent *recruitment* efforts for police and firefighters featured a poster advertising the positions and showing minority and female officers and firefighters; special booths at a shopping mall in the metropolitan Kansas City area with concentrations of minority populations; special visits to a junior college with a large minority population; and special outreach in the Topeka, Kansas, area working with the YWCA to identify female candidates. No special efforts were made to show preference to women and minorities in any of the four *selection* processes.

The value of responsiveness is apparent only in the selection for city manager. The manager serves at the pleasure of the governing body, and elected officials are heavily involved in all phases of the selection process, whether they hire an executive search consultant or handle the process through their own personnel department. They employ criteria designed to determine whether the manager will work well with the governing body and will fit in with the political and social culture of the city.

While Table 7-3 shows the value of responsiveness isolated to selection of the city manager, that is not an entirely accurate portrayal. In many jurisdictions, even though the chief administrative officer legally can hire and fire department heads, it often is wise to consult with the governing body or mayor before doing so. For example, hiring and firing a police chief in most communities is fraught with potential political problems; the same often is true of the planning director.

Finally, the table shows that recruitment for temporary and part-time positions is not nearly as time consuming when compared to other categories of employees. Efficiency is the dominant value with little attention paid to individual rights.

TEST VALIDATION AND THE ACQUISITION FUNCTION

A test is any device used to separate qualified from unqualified applicants for selection or promotion. Included are written examinations as well as selection methods not normally thought of as tests, including interviews, medical examinations, drug tests, background investigations, and physical requirements. To be valid, a test must separate qualified from unqualified applicants on the basis of knowledge, skills, or ability related to job performance.

Social equity advocates are often associated with promoting preferential treatment of minorities and women. But their greatest and most lasting contribution to personnel management may prove to be in the area of test validation. For in seeking to remove barriers to equal opportunity based on discriminatory hiring criteria (those based on race, religion, or other non-merit factors), social equity advocates have been responsible for general acceptance of the merit system principle that job applicants are to be chosen on the basis of job-related criteria. In the 1970s, when the Civil Rights Act of 1964 was first being litigated, tests that discriminated against minorities were scrutinized to see if those who scored highest really did turn out to be high performers. In other words, were the tests which purported to assess appropriate knowledge, skills, and abilities truly measuring qualities

TABLE 7-3 Recruitment and Selection Process in Lawrence, Kansas

Entry-Level Positions (Non-Public-Safety)	*Public-Safety Positions*	*Department Director*	*City Manager (Chief Administrative Officer)*	*Temporary Employment Agency*	*Part-Time Positions*	*Technical Positions*
RECRUITMENT						
•Local newspaper •Announcements to 80 local agencies including Jobs Service Center, NAACP, Haskell Indian Nations University •E-Mail Bulletin Boards •Dedicated Information Telephone Line	•Local and regional newspapers •Announcements to 80 local agencies and law enforcement and fire agencies •Special effort to recruit women and minorities •E-Mail Bulletin Boards •Dedicated Information Telephone Line	•Local and regional newspapers •Professional associations (national) •Announcements to 80 local agencies •Dedicated Information Telephone Line •E-Mail Bulletin Boards	•Local and regional newspapers •Professional associations •Announcements- to 80 local agencies •E-Mail Bulletin Boards •Dedicated Information Telephone Line	Bid process on key positions	•Local news-paper- •Announce–ments to 80 local agencies • E-Mail Bulletin Boards •Dedicated Information Telephone Line	•Local and regional newspapers •Professional associations National and/or State/Regional •Announcements to 80 local agencies •E-Mail Bulletin Boards •Dedicated Information Telephone Line
SELECTION						
•Applications screened by personnel office •Reduced applicant pool reviewed by hiring authority	•Written test •Physical fitness evaluation •Interview with board •Interview by Chief •Reference checks	•Applicants screened by personnel/office selection committee/ City Manager •Reduced pool	•Applications screened by consultant/ personnel depart-ment/committee of the governing body/entire	Order position as needed for specified time needed	•Applications screened by Department •Interview by supervisor •Reference checks	•Applicants screened by Personnel Office and Department •Reduce pool reviewed by Division Manager

•Test where appropriate •Interview with board •Reference checks •Post-offer physical, including drug screening •Appointment by Personnel Director	•Post-offer physical, including drug screening and Physiological test for Police Officers •Appointment by Department Director	reviewed by City Manager •Assessment lab •Committee interview •Interview with City Manager •Reference checks •Post-offer physical, including drug screening •Appointment by City Manager	governing body •Reference checks •Interview with governing body (may also include visits with department heads •Post-offer physical including drug screening •Appointment by governing body		•Appointment by Supervisor	•Assessment lab •Interview with Committee •Interview with Department Director •Reference checks •Test on Technical Data •Review of Certificates •Appointment by Supervisor/Department Director
LENGTH OF TOTAL PROCESS						
4–8 weeks	3–4 months	2–3 months	3–5 months	1–5 days	3–5 weeks	2–3 months
TRAINING						
On the job	•Law enforcement academy •Fire Training Program	On the job	On the job	On the job	On the job	•On the job •Technical training as needed to retain certifications

necessary for on-the-job performance? This focus challenged personnel practices at the merit system's core and found that many tests were not job related—like unsubstantiated strength requirements for firefighters. Over time this scrutiny resulted in more impartial and job-related selection tests and other selection devices. Examples include interviews conducted by boards rather than individuals in order to decrease the likelihood that individual bias will enter the selection process. In public-safety positions, in particular, testing has been subject to continual review, and ad hoc height and strength requirements have given way to those empirically derived from an understanding of what kinds of knowledge, skills, and abilities are truly needed to perform police work and firefighting.

Discrimination is legal. Personnel directors are required to distinguish between qualified and unqualified applicants, between those who will do better on the job from those who will not do as well. If a test does this, regardless of its effect on women and minorities, traditionally it is considered a fair test. This kind of discrimination is legally acceptable even if it might be politically unacceptable. Before deciding whether a test or other employment requirement *unfairly* discriminates against minorities and women, we must first know whether it discriminates against them at all. Two methods for determining whether selection devices discriminate against minorities have developed over the years. One method of detecting discrimination or the adverse impact of selection procedures against minorities or women is by comparing the percentage of minority individuals employed by the organization in specific jobs with those qualified minorities present in the relevant labor market. Statistical analysis can determine the likelihood of these ratios occurring by chance.

Another method more clearly aimed at testing itself involves the 80 percent rule. This rule, presented in the 1978 **Uniform Guidelines to Employee Selection Procedures,** states that discrimination has occurred against a particular group if the selection rate for that particular group is less than 80 percent of the selection rate for the group with the highest selection rate. Table 7-4 illustrates the 80 percent rule showing that discrimination has occurred against Anglo and Hispanic males and Hispanic females. The passing standard is established by the Anglo females, and African-American males and females pass at a rate between 80 and

TABLE 7–4 The 80 Percent Rule

Ethinic Group	*No. of Applications*	*No. of Selections*	*Percent Selections*	*Percent Selections Compared to Highest*	*Discrimination?*
W Male	20	5	25%	62.5%	yes
W Female	20	8	40	(highest)	—
B Male	15	5	33	82.5	no
B Female	20	7	35	87.5	no
H Male	15	3	20	50.0	yes
H Female	20	0	0	0	yes

100 percent of the Anglo females. The 80 percent rule applies to all parts of a selection process, not just the overall selection rate.

Test Validation Methods

The impact of affirmative action on selection processes concentrates on what constitutes acceptable qualifications and how job qualifications are determined. This emphasis is seen in the area called **test validation**—the determination of the extent to which a selection device is related to a job. Even though validity is stimulated by a concern for social equity and individual rights, it is theoretically consistent with the value of administrative efficiency.

The Uniform Guidelines established three acceptable validation strategies as acceptable: empirical, construct, and content validation. *Empirical validation,* also known as **criterion validation,** requires that a test score be significantly correlated, in a statistical sense, with important elements of job performance. For example, let's assume that we have developed a written test to examine applicants for the position of personnel director. Over the past several years we have given this test to several hundred applicants, hired them regardless of the results, and later evaluated them on the basis of a performance evaluation test (which actually measures desired work performance). When we compare the written test results with the performance evaluation scores, we get the results shown in Table 7-5.

This test is unquestionably a good predictor of subsequent performance as a personnel manager. If you had to state the relationship between preemployment test scores and subsequent job performance, you would conclude that the test score, divided by 10, was a very close approximation of the subsequent performance evaluation. Of course, this assumes that a satisfactory performance can be established and measured by the organization's performance evaluation system.

The relationship between these test scores and subsequent job performance scores is plotted in Figure 7-2. The matrix is divided into four quadrants separated by a passing grade of 70 on the test and a minimum performance rat-

TABLE 7-5 Empirical Test Validation

Applicant Name	*Test Score*	*Performance Evaluation Score*
Allen	70 (out of 100)	7 (out of 10)
Smith	45	4
Jones	93	9
Hammell	94	10
Wolfe	88	9
Kendall	62	6
Taylor	55	6
Mendoza	82	8

FIGURE 7–2 Test Scores and Job Performance

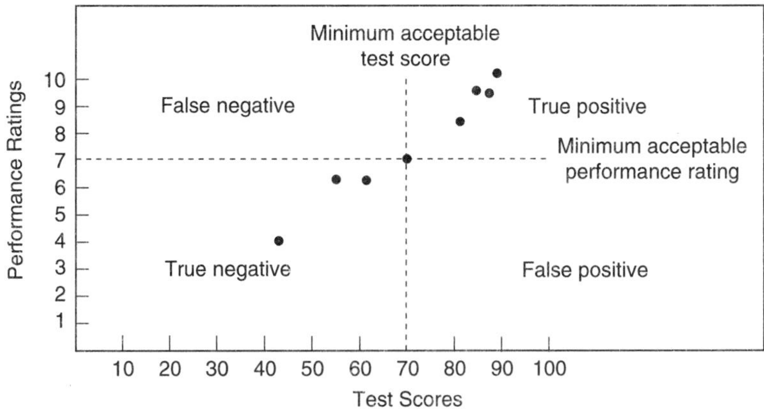

ing of 7. The goal of any selection device is to place most "hires" into the upper-right quadrant. These are the people who score well on the selection device and then also turn out to do well on the job. Another goal of a good test is to place applicants in the lower-left quadrant, so that those who do poorly on the test would also be those who do poorly on the job.

The more scores that fall in these two quadrants, the more valid a test is; in other words, the better job it will do of predicting subsequent performance. Most tests do not have anything near the predictive quality of our example. This means that people who do poorly on the test might end up doing well on the job (the upper-left quadrant), or that other applicants might score high on the test but not perform well on the job (the lower-right quadrant). Table 7-6 summarizes these relationships. The more valid the test, the more **true positives** and **true negatives;** the less valid the test, the greater the occurrence of **false positives** and **false negatives.**

Construct validation involves both identifying psychological traits or aptitudes that relate to successful job performance and devising a test that measures these traits. For example, most insurance companies give psychological tests to applicants for sales positions. These tests purport to measure the applicant's congeniality, outgoing nature, liking for people, and other traits supposedly related to ability to sell. Police departments require a psychological profile on new recruits. In the sales example, tests have been developed by identifying the best

TABLE 7–6 Test Scores and Job Performance

	Test Score	*Job Performance*
1. True positives (higher, do well)	high	high
2. True negatives (not hire, do poorly)	low	low
3. False positives (hire, do poorly)	high	low
4. False negatives (not hire, do well)	low	high

salespeople in the organization, giving them a psychological test measuring a variety of traits, and establishing a personality profile of the "ideal salesperson." Police professionals are trying to eliminate individuals with unacceptable traits—overly aggressive, inflexible—from the applicant pool. Profiles are then used as a yardstick against which the characteristics of applicants are measured. Those who approximate this yardstick move on in the selection process; those who do not are more carefully screened.

Content validation requires that the job be analyzed to determine its duties; the particular conditions that make work easy or difficult; realistic performance standards; the knowledge, skills, and abilities required to perform these tasks up to these standards under these conditions; and the minimum qualifications required to ensure that an applicant would have these KSAs. For example, it is logical to assume that a prison guard, responsible for transporting prisoners by car from one location to another, would need to know how to drive. An example of the application of the relationship between content validation and job analysis is given in the section on results-oriented job descriptions (RODs) in Chapter 4.

Content validation, therefore, links the functions of affirmative action and job analysis. In addition, it connects them with a third function, productivity. This is because the establishment of a logical relationship between duties and qualifications is not only a defense of validity, it is also a justification for discriminating between qualified and unqualified applicants on the basis of their anticipated performance. It would follow from this that a content-valid job description (such as an ROD) could be used to assess the validity of a selection or promotion criterion by measuring the performance of an employee hired on the basis of that criterion.

Although each of these validation methods is equally acceptable to the EEOC (and other federal affirmative action compliance agencies), each is considered appropriate for different circumstances. Empirical validation requires that the organization hire many employees in the same type of work during a short time period, and some authors suggest that a group of several hundred employees is necessary.[33] Under the best of conditions, it would also require that the agency hire people who fail the test. After all, going back to Table 7-6, a valid test will minimize false negatives. In sum, empirical validation takes time and money, and it can be impractical for organizations that hire few people in a job class.

Construct and content validation both require a relatively thorough job analysis to determine, respectively, the psychological traits or skills required for the position. Construct validity can be determined for a variety of jobs in different organizations. But because it requires the services of research psychologists, construct validation is beyond the abilities of most smaller public agencies. Its validity also depends upon the relationship between traits and performance, a link that is sometimes difficult to establish. This leaves content validation as the method of choice for the overwhelming majority of public employers. Its advantages are strengthened when we realize that the development of RODs can result not only in content validation, but also in the enhancement of productivity and clarity of performance expectations between employees and their agencies.

TABLE 7-7 Comparative Advantages of Alternative Validation Procedures

		VALIDATION PROCEDURE		
	Appropriate Context	*Criterion*	*Construct*	*Content*
1.	Meets federal guidelines	yes	yes	yes
2.	Requires job analysis	some	thorough	thorough
3.	Requires large sample	yes	no	no

Even though its central role in establishing valid selection procedures remains unchallenged, skepticism regarding traditional job analyses is increasing. Analyzing a job assumes that the job elements themselves have more influence than the job incumbent on what work will be done. It also assumes the unit of analysis is the individual job and that the contextual factors identified earlier are peripheral to identifying the critical elements in a job.[34] These assumptions stand on the shaky foundations of the large, stable, bureaucratic organization where a lot of people serve in a single job capacity; for example, secretary I or firefighter I. They rest on the notion that the past is a good predictor of the future.

The nature of work is changing and the ways we organize to perform our work is changing as well. Job analysis techniques have not kept pace and find themselves in a transition period trying to accommodate these contextual factors, teamwork, and the personal influence that individual workers have on job definitions. Offerman and Gowing suggest, "Job analytic procedures must be undertaken, but at a higher level of abstraction, such as analyses of occupations or occupational groups. Researchers must use these procedures to search for underlying commonalities in the work and for the personal dimensions or constructs contributing to effective performance across occupations."[35] They add, "It is not sufficient for occupational analysis systems to identify generalized work requirements. They must also capture the situational or organizational factors within which the work is carried out" (p. 391).

Table 7-7 shows the comparative advantages of alternative validation methods.

Test Validation Strategies

Despite the challenges that contemporary work trends pose for traditional recruitment and selection methods and job analytic techniques, it would be rash to assume that these techniques should be discarded. Legislation and judicial opinions protecting individual rights would not permit their dismissal. The Americans with Disabilities Act provides a contemporary example of this legislative force. In order to judge whether or not a disabled applicant can be rejected, the employer must know whether he or she can perform the critical elements of the job if a reasonable accommodation is made. This judgment presumes the employer has analyzed the job in question to know what the critical elements are. The impact of the ADA on selection processes could become as great as the influence that affirmative action has had on test validation.

Even though test validation procedures require a time-consuming and costly process frequently, they are worth the effort. Given the limited resources of many personnel departments—and the unwillingness of personnel directors to devote resources to validation studies unless a selection or promotion system is questioned—how should public personnel managers treat the entire issue of validation? Our previous discussion has indicated that validation is theoretically useful to advance the values of social equity and administrative efficiency. That is, a test that is valid not only will be legally defensible under employment discrimination laws but also will result in the hiring of true positives and the rejection of true negatives.

Yet while it is theoretically sound to validate all criteria for employment, personnel professionals may wish, or be forced by circumstances, to adopt the next best approach, summarized as follows:

1. **Identify the classes of positions with the largest number of employees**. Since most public organizations are pyramidal in nature, these are likely to be entry-level positions or first-level supervisory positions. It is easier to conduct empirical validation studies with large groups of employees, and these positions are likely to be those subject to the greatest pressure for access by different groups.
2. **Identify the positions most likely to be the subject of an affirmative action investigation or lawsuit**. Indications of this might be the rate of internal complaints, the experience of other similar organizations, or the presence of a high percentage of minority group members or women in lower-level positions from which the position in question is considered a promotion or a desirable lateral reassignment.

Given these two factors, personnel managers should prepare a schedule according to which selection procedures for all organizational positions will be periodically reevaluated. In presenting a budget request to upper management, personnel managers should emphasize the comparative costs and consequences of validation procedures versus affirmative action investigations or lawsuits. Remember—it can cost several thousand dollars to validate a test, but a successful lawsuit will cost several times this amount in court costs, attorney's fees, and compensatory damages.

In *Griggs v. Duke Power Company*, the Supreme Court concluded that the use of a professionally developed test (aptitude or ability) does not in and of itself qualify the test as legal under Title VII. Although the Tower Amendment to the Civil Rights Act of 1964 (Section 703[h]) specifically approves the use of "professionally developed ability tests," provided that such tests are not "designed, intended or used to discriminate because of race, color, religion, sex or national origin,"[36] other court decisions have held that the mere fact that a test is professionally developed does not guarantee that its use is proper in all circumstances.[37]

In addition, what would normally be classified as non-merit factors (for example, race, sex, or religion) may be used to exclude members of a particular group from employment consideration if membership in a certain race, religion, or sex is a legitimate job requirement. For example, chaplains may be required to be of a certain religion. However, the exclusion must be based on *business necessity* rather than mere convenience. For instance, the lack of separate bathroom facilities is not sufficient grounds for excluding women from a work site. It may be costly to build additional facilities, but this is not an insurmountable hardship.

AMERICANS WITH DISABILITIES ACT (ADA)[38]

While civil rights legislation and judicial action have had significant impact on recruitment, selection, and test validation, those impacts have now been felt, and public employers have incorporated the legislative intent, judicial rulings, and administrative regulations into human resource policy and routine practices. In other words, it is no big deal anymore when interview questions are connected to a specific job. In fact, the surprise comes when they are not.

The Americans with Disabilities Act may do for the disabled what the Civil Rights Act of 1964 did for racial minorities and women. The Americans with Disabilities Act (ADA) of 1990 prohibits discrimination against the disabled in areas including public and private employment, availability of public services, and access to public accommodations, transportation, and telecommunications. The employment provisions of the act have been applied to employers with more than twenty five employees since July 26, 1992, and to employers with fifteen or more employees after July 26, 1994. They prohibit discrimination against *qualified* individuals with disabilities, defined as an individual with a disability who meets the skill, experience, education, and other job-related requirements of a position held or desired, and who, with or without reasonable accommodation, can perform the essential functions of a job. What constitutes a reasonable accommodation and an undue hardship on an employer obligated to make the accommodation are dealt with in Chapter 12. Here, we will focus on the recruitment and selection issues more directly.

Who Is Protected?

The definition of individuals with a disability is quite broad—some estimates place the number of qualified individuals at 43 million! A person with a disability is someone who (1) has a physical or mental impairment that substantially limits one or more of his or her major life activities; (2) has a record of such an impairment; or (3) is regarded as having such an impairment.

The ADA specifically states that certain individuals are not protected by its provisions. Persons who currently use drugs illegally are not individuals protected under the ADA when an employer takes action because of their continued use of drugs. However, people who have been rehabilitated and do not currently use drugs illegally, or who are in the process of completing a rehabilitation program may be protected by the ADA. The act also states that homosexuality and bisexuality are not impairments and therefore are not disabilities under the ADA.

What Practices Are Prohibited?

Employers cannot discriminate against people with disabilities in regard to any employment practice. This includes application, testing, hiring, assignments, evaluation, disciplinary action, training, promotion, medical examinations, layoff/recall, termination, compensation, leave, or benefits.

Applicants may be asked about their ability to perform specific job functions. But an employer may not ask a job applicant about the existence, nature, or severity of a disability. An employer may not make medical inquiries or conduct a medical examination until after a job offer has been made. A job offer may be conditioned on the results of a medical examination or inquiry, but only if this is required for all entering employees in similar jobs. Medical examinations of employees must be job-related and consistent with the employer's business needs.

It is not a violation of the ADA for employers to use drug tests to find out if applicants or employees are currently using drugs illegally. Tests for illegal use of drugs are not subject to the ADA's restrictions on medical examinations. Employers may hold illegal users of drugs and alcoholics to the same performance and conduct standards as other employees.[39]

Enforcement and Remedies

The U.S. Equal Employment Opportunity Commission (EEOC) has responsibility for enforcing compliance with Title I of the ADA, which prohibits discrimination by private employers. An individual who believes that he or she has been discriminated against in employment can file a charge with the EEOC, using the same procedures as with Title VII of the Civil Rights Act of 1964. Remedies that may be required of an employer who is found to have discriminated against an applicant or employee with a disability include compensatory and punitive damages, back pay, front pay, restored benefits, attorney's fees, reasonable accommodation, reinstatement, and job offers.

Title II of the ADA, enforced by the U.S. Department of Justice, prohibits discrimination in all state and local government programs and activities, including employment. Governments receiving federal financial assistance, as well as federally funded private entities, will continue to be covered by Section 504 of the Rehabilitation Act. In addition, Section 503 of the Rehabilitation Act forbids discrimination against individuals with disabilities by federal contractors and subcontractors. The Rehabilitation Act of 1973 is enforced by the Office of Federal Contract Compliance Programs (OFCCP) in the U.S. Department of Labor. The EEOC, the Department of Labor, and the Department of Justice will coordinate their enforcement efforts under the ADA and the Rehabilitation Act, to assure consistent standards and to eliminate unnecessary duplication.

The ADA's Implications for Public Personnel Managers

Because the employer must demonstrate that a requested accommodation is unreasonable, or that the employee could not in any case perform the essential functions of the job, employers now may have the burden of proof shifted to them to demonstrate a rational basis for employment decisions. At a minimum, the ADA reinforces requirements in existing civil rights laws that personnel policies be rational, and that selection and evaluation criteria be job related. Job analysis criteria and procedures may need to be clarified, so that each position includes information on essential functions, and requisite KSAs. This requirement comes at a time when human resource specialists and academicians are questioning the formality and utility of existing job analysis techniques, which tend to reinforce existing ways of thinking about work and organizations rather than incorporate futuristic thinking. In addition to the job analysis requirement, employment applications and interview techniques should be examined to ensure compliance.

Personnel managers should bear in mind that, unlike most laws affecting the workplace, the ADA did not provide for any enabling regulations to be issued by the compliance agency. This means that the exact meaning of key phrases such as "reasonable accommodation," "undue hardship," and "direct threat to health or safety" will be resolved only by case law. Three recent cases provide some guidance. In *United States v. City of Pontiac*, the District Court for Eastern Michigan ruled that the city violated the ADA by refusing to hire a firefighter with sight in only one eye. Although the individual had a disability in one eye, he was otherwise qualified because he was already working part-time as a firefighter and was ranked seventh on the eligibility list for full-time employment. In *James Champ v. Baltimore County*, the U.S. District Court in Maryland ruled that the disability retirement of a police officer was not a violation of the ADA, since he could not perform essential functions with or without reasonable accommodation. The Court ruled that Champ's "inability to make a forcible arrest, drive a vehicle under emergency circumstances, or qualify with a firearm poses a direct threat to the health and safety of others."[40]

SUMMARY

Because public jobs are regarded as scarce resources, the acquisition function reflects conflict among the competing values of responsiveness, efficiency, individual rights, and social equity as the basis of allocating public jobs. The goal of most public employers is to hire and promote those with the best knowledge, skills, and abilities to perform the job. But other interests—represented by politics, collective bargaining, and diversity—frequently challenge this goal. Ultimately, the differences in value and policy orientations must be transformed into workable recruitment, selection, and promotion procedures that permit routine, cost-effective application and promise fair treatment for applicants.

The changing nature of work and organizations affects recruitment and selection processes as well. As organizations become less hierarchical, more is demanded of employees than traditional knowledge, skills, and abilities connected to a narrowly defined job. As the context within which public agencies operate becomes more heterogeneous and unstable, job analyses become less dependable, recruitment is expanded to include situational skills, and personal traits such as the ability to contribute to a work group. And selection decisions become more tentative as loyalty between employee and employer is weakened by contemporary trends toward downsizing and privatization.

While contemporary trends question traditional approaches to job analysis, recruitment, and selection, legal requirements imposed by the Civil Rights Act of 1964 and the Americans with Disabilities Act are built on traditional assumptions about work and reinforce the status quo of personnel management.

KEY TERMS

acquisition function
career civil servant
centralized recruitment and selection
construct validity
content validity
contextual factors
criterion validity
decentralized recruitment and selection
fairness as a social issue
job bank
political appointees
test validation
true and false positives and negatives
Uniform Guidelines to Employee Selection Procedures

DISCUSSION QUESTIONS

1. How does one's value perspective influence the objectives of the recruitment and selection process?
2. Describe the different basic values and perspectives of political appointees and career civil servants. How do these differences affect their working relationship?
3. Describe several external environmental factors that influence the acquisition of public employees.
4. What kind of flexible personnel policies are needed to accommodate the caregiving needs of the modern family where both mother and father work? Or where the family consists of children with a single parent?
5. What is meant by contextual factors that influence how well a person performs as an organizational member? How easy do you think it is to recruit and select for these factors? Does an emphasis on contextual factors conflict with an emphasis on recruiting for diversity?
6. Compare and contrast centralized and decentralized recruitment techniques.
7. What does it mean to say that fairness is a social judgment rather than a scientific calculation? What are the implications for the tension between efficiency and diversity?
8. Outsourcing or privatization of government services displaces value issues governments deal with in recruitment and selection processes. Which values do you think will be emphasized by private employment agencies?
9. Describe the concept and importance of test validation and three validation strategies. How have affirmative action and advocates of social equity and individual rights advanced the importance of test validation, and therefore the value of efficiency?
10. What is the theoretical relationship between job analysis, test validation, and performance evaluation/productivity?
11. How might the Americans with Disabilities Act become as important as the Civil Rights Act of 1964? How do the legal requirements for job analysis implied in the two acts conflict with modern theories about future organizations?
12. Review the recruitment and selection processes in Table 7-3 and identify the values emphasized in each model. How would you improve these processes?

CASE STUDY MERIT OR POLITICS

The following conversation takes place among three members of a state government: Brenda Simon, secretary of the Department of Corrections; her administrative assistant, Mary Rodriguez; and Larry Gordon, from the governor's office. They are talking about applicants for the recently vacated unclassified position of deputy secretary in the Department of Corrections.

1. Citing specific language in the conversation, identify evidence of different values.
2. Which candidate would you choose for this job and why?
3. What would happen if this kind of conversation took place every time a job opening occurred in a public organization? How do public organizations avoid these kinds of conversations every time a job opening occurs?

BRENDA: Well, I don't know about you two, but in my book this John Simpson seems to have enough experience to handle the job. I need someone who can take over the internal operations of the agency while we get this new program off the ground. But what really impressed me was his commitment to the policy direction we're headed in.

MARY: You know I admire your judgment, Brenda, but does he really have the skill to pull off the job? We know Don Johnson is doing a fine job now as a division director. He already knows the ropes around here, and I think he's ready for a bigger job. Besides, it's about time we got another minority into this sacred secretarial hut!

BRENDA: Hold on, Mary. You know I support our affirmative action program. I gave you a boost some time ago, I remember.

MARY: Now wait a minute! Let's not dredge up the history on that one. You know very well I was qualified for this job. This is now, and Don's qualified.

BRENDA: Mary, Don may be able to do the job; I'm not as convinced as you, but this Simpson is on target when it comes to supporting the philosophy behind the new program. And the more I think about it, the more I need that commitment to make this thing go. There's a lot at stake in making the program a success. Don's pretty hardheaded when it comes to seeing us turn this agency into what he feels is a softhearted bunch of social workers.

LARRY: Look, folks, I hate to complicate things for you, but the governor's been getting pressure to find a spot for Jim Masington.

MARY: Jim who? I've never heard of him.

BRENDA: Well, I have. He worked pretty hard in the governor's last campaign, didn't he?

MARY: Oh, no! I can see it coming.

LARRY: Don't get excited. Just give the guy some consideration. Brenda, you know the governor went out on a limb with the legislature to give you the chance to experiment with this new program, and he may need a favor here.

MARY: I just don't like the politics in all this.

BRENDA: Look, Larry, I want to help, but I need someone who is committed to this program.

MARY: And I think we'd better get someone who can manage the internal operations of this agency.

LARRY: Well, I think that you ought to look at Masington's application. You know that's all the governor is asking.

BRENDA: Thanks, Larry. I want to think about this. Mary, let's get together on this tomorrow afternoon.

MARY: Politics!

NOTES

[1] Pyle, A. (April 25, 1996). Delays on school chief draws fire. *Los Angeles Times,* p. B-1.

[2] Connell, R. (August 12, 1988). Bradley comes under pressure to name Latinos to top city jobs. *Los Angeles Times,* II-1, pp. 8.

[3] Mosher, F. C. (1982). *Democracy and the public service.* (2nd ed.). New York: Oxford University Press.

[4] Arvey, R. D., and P. R. Sackett. (1993). Fairness in selection: Current developments and perspectives. In N. Schmitt, W. C. Borman, and Associates (Eds.). *Personnel selection in organizations.* San Francisco: Jossey-Bass, pp. 199-200.

[5] *Hopwood* v. *State of Texas* (Fifth Circuit Court of Appeals), Docket No. 94-50569, March 18, 1996. 11, 1996.

[6] Schmitt, F. L. (1993). Personnel psychology at the cutting edge. In Schmitt, Borman, and Associates (Eds.). *Personnel selection in organizations.* pp. 497 and 499.

[7] Maxwell, S. E., and R. D. Arvey. (1993). The search for predictors with high validity and low adverse impact: Compatible or incompatible goals? *Journal of Applied Psychology, 78,* 433-437.

[8] Aberbach, J. D., R. D. Putnam, and B. A. Rockman. (1981). *Bureaucrats and politicians in western democracies.* Cambridge, MA: Harvard University Press; Heclo, H. (1977). *A government of strangers: Executive politics in Washington.* Washington, DC: The Brookings Institution.

[9] Nalbandian, J. (1994). Reflections of a "pracademic" on the logic of politics and administration. *Public Administration Review, 54,* 531-536.

[10] Lane, L. M., J. F. Wolf. (1990). *The human resource crisis in the public sector.* New York: Quorum.

[11] Bureau of Labor Statistics, United States Department of Labor. (August 1995). *Contingent and alternative employment arrangements.* Report 900, ftp://stats.bls.gov/pub/news.release/conemp.txt.

[12] Lane, L. M., and J. F. Wolf. *The human resource crisis in the public sector.* New York: Quorum, Chap. 2.

[13] United States General Accounting Office. (July 29, 1992). The changing workforce: Demographic issues facing employers. Testimony before the Subcommittee on Census and Population, Committee on Post Office and Civil Service, United States House of Representatives. GAO/T-GGD-92-61.

[14] Borman, W. C., and S. J. Motowidlo. (1993). Expanding the criterion domain to include elements of contextual performance. In Schmitt, Borman, and Associates (Eds.). *Personnel selection in organizations,* p. 73.

[15] Ibid., p. 73.

[16] Guion, R. M. (1993). The need for change: Six persistent themes. In Schmitt, Borman, and Associates (Eds.). *Personnel selection in organizations.* p. 491.

[17] Ibid., p. 493.

[18] Mintzberg, H. (May-June 1996). Managing government and governing management. *Harvard Business Review, 74,* 75-80.

[19] Hesselbein, F., M. Goldsmith, and R. Beckhard. (1996). *The leader of the future.* San Francisco: Jossey Bass.

[20] Snow, C. C., and S. A. Snell. (1993). Staffing as strategy. In Schmitt, Borman, and Associates (Eds.). *Personnel selection in organizations.* p. 467.

[21] Brown, B. K., and M. A. Campion. (1994). Biodata phenomenology: Recruiters' perceptions and use of biographic information in resume screening. *Journal of Applied Psychology, 79,* 897-908.

[22] Levine, E. L., and A. Flory, III. (1976). Evaluation of job applications—A conceptual framework. *Public Personnel Management, 5,* 378-385.

[23] Hartigan, J. A., and A. K. Wigdor. (1989). *Fairness in employment testing: Validity generalization, minority issues, and the General Aptitude Test Battery.* Washington, DC: National Academy of Sciences Press; Vevea, J. L., N. C. Clements, and L. V. Hedges. (1993). Assessing the effects of selection bias on validity data for the General Aptitude Test Battery. *Journal of Applied Psychology, 78,* 981-987.

[24] Arvey, R. D., and R. H. Faley. (1988). Fairness in selecting employees (2nd ed.). Reading, MA: Addison-Wesley.

[25] Dipboye, R. L., and B. B. Gaugler. (1993). Cognitive and behavioral processes in the selection interview. In Schmitt, Borman, and Associates (Eds.). *Personnel selection in organizations.* pp. 135-170; Whetzel, D. L., F. L. Schmitt, and S. D. Maurer. (1994). The validity of employment interviews: A comprehensive review and meta-analysis. *Journal of Applied Psychology, 79,* 599-616.

[26] Arvey and Faley.

[27] Rynes, S. L. (1993). Who's selecting whom? Effects of selection practices on applicant attitudes and behavior. In Schmitt, Borman, and Associates (Eds.). *Personnel selection in organizations.* p. 245.

[28] Ibid., p. 245.

[29] ________. (1993). Award winning programs—interviews with the winners. *Public Personnel Management, 22,* 1-5.

[30] United States Merit Systems Protection Board. (1994). *Entering professional positions in the federal government.* Washington, DC: U.S. Merit Systems Protection Board, p. xii.

[31] For an up-to-date and excellent source of information on Internet sites related to all aspects of public personnel administration, see the International Personnel Management Association's home page at www.ipma-hr.org.

[32] Personal correspondence with the author, July 5, 1996.

[33] Arvey and Faley.

[34] Bridges, W. (1993). Leading the de-jobbed organization. In Schmitt, Borman, and Associates (Eds.). *Personnel selection in organizations.* pp. 11-18.

[35] Offermann, L. R., and M. K. Gowing. (1993). Personnel selection in the future: The impact of changing demographics and the nature of work. In Schmitt, Borman, and Associates (Eds.). *Personnel selection in organizations.* p. 391.

[36] The Civil Rights Act of 1964. P.L. 88-352, 78 Stat. 241, 28 U.S.C. s. 1447 [1976].

[37] *Albemarle Paper Company* v. *Moody.* 422 U.S. 405 (1975).

[38] For information available electronically about the Americans with Disabilities Act (P.L. 101-336, July 26, 1990), see (janweb.icdi.wvu.edu/kinder).

[39] Segal, J. A. (1992). Drugs, alcohol, and the ADA. *HR Magazine, 37,* 73-76.

[40] *IPMA News.* (April 1995). ADA update, p. 8.

8

Leadership and Employee Performance in Turbulent Times

In the 1990s, the focus of personnel systems has changed from defending abstract merit system principles to a concern for maximizing productivity and measurable outcomes. Personnel systems are under pressure to become increasingly responsive to external pressures for productivity, work measurement, and political accountability. Effective human resource management is defined by how well employees are doing tasks which match the overall objectives of the work unit and the organization. The focus is changing from management of positions, as was the case under traditional civil service systems, to more directly facilitating accomplishment of the agency's mission.

For public personnel specialists working primarily within civil service systems, this has required increased flexibility and experimentation in many areas: with privatization, contracting out, and utilization of part-time and temporary workers; rank-in-person versus rank-in-job personnel systems; work classification and evaluation versus job classification and evaluation; increasing recognition of the impact of the person on the job; individual versus group performance evaluation; and experimentation with variable pay based on performance. For managers and supervisors in the public sector, this means obtaining the highest performance and commitment from employees while remaining cognizant of the need to restructure, reorganize tasks, and even downsize in the face of rapidly changing environmental conditions. This challenge places them squarely in the middle of the clash between traditional values of civil service systems and the market-based values underlying the alternative methods we have been discussing for delivering public service. It challenges personnel specialists and managers to objectively evaluate the comparative advantages of alternative personnel systems and different ways of fulfilling the personnel functions to accomplish agency missions under a variety of conditions.

Elected officials and agency directors are also challenged to confront the ways their perspectives have been bounded by traditional views of personnel management. Elected officials are largely responsible for the creation of position management through their focus on external control of agency resources (for example, through line-item budgets, control over appropriations, and control over number of positions and average grade level). Elected officials are responsible for setting agency missions and objectives and for engaging administrative officials in a partnership to achieve those objectives. Some elected officials come to office with a skeptical view of public employment, limiting the trust they have in appointed officials, and turning their focus away from policy issues and more toward the oversight function. Others attend to the policy issues only in symbolic ways or with decisions that make sense politically but not managerially. In today's environment, flexibility in resource allocation is more important than ever for effective service delivery, and it is crucial to build credibility and trust between elected officials and senior administrative officials in order to experiment with a variety of personnel processes and techniques.

By the end of this chapter, you will be able to:

1. Describe the organizational climate, demographic trends, and market-based values that challenge traditional civil service systems.
2. Describe the consequences of these challenges for leadership and employee performance.
3. Describe the differences between political and administrative viewpoints.
4. Describe the basic components of equity and expectancy theory.
5. Describe the ways that elected officials, managers, and personnel specialists affect an employee's motivation to perform.
6. Describe the ways that elected officials, managers, and personnel specialists affect an employee's ability to perform.
7. Identify three alternative work systems: total quality management, job enrichment, and teamwork.
8. Describe how clear expectations, giving feedback, and communicating appropriate consequences enhance employee performance.
9. Describe the causes of employee anxiety and the supervisor/manager's role in addressing it.

THE CHALLENGES TO TRADITIONAL CIVIL SERVICE SYSTEMS

Civil service systems rest on a foundation of assumptions about work and reality:

- Work can be divided into individual packets of duties and responsibilities called jobs.
- These duties and responsibilities remain stable over time because government work is performed in bureaucratic organizations designed to promote stability and routine.
- Knowledge, skills, and abilities of workers are valued and assessed in relationship to particular jobs, and personnel functions are oriented around positions rather than the people who occupy those positions.
- The analytical focus on individual jobs and the relationship of one job to another provide a rational system for pay, recruitment, and selection, and appraisal of employee performance.

These **assumptions about civil service systems** were essential to their emergence from the era of patronage. And they have provided sound guidance for the design and implementation of civil service systems for years. But today, some argue strenuously that they seem less useful, less able to guide elected officials, managers, and employees through environmental and political turbulence. For these critics, the flawed assumptions underlying civil service systems serve as anchors rather than rudders.

We will summarize the challenges and then look at their consequences and the problems they pose for today's workers, managers, and elected officials. The challenges fall into three categories: *modern organizational climate, demographic trends,* and the *market-based, anti-governmental values* we have been discussing throughout the book.

Organizational Climate

The **modern organizational climate** is characterized by increasing specialization of work and the rapidity of change. While the knowledge needed to address today's problems becomes more specialized, the problems themselves remain broad and require teams of specialists. For example, dealing with gangs involves families, social service agencies, the courts, the police, recreation specialists, teachers and school district personnel, as well as the employment of both volunteers and professional workers. This complexity and specialization requires teams of people working together, often in temporary arrangements, until the particular problem they are dealing with changes shape and a new composition of the team must be formed.

The concept of working in teams is very different from the idea that work can be divided discretely into little packages of duties and responsibilities. Rather than managing individual workers, many of today's managers are responsible for teams of workers, where the focus is on the group as well as the members. In teams, the interpersonal dynamics that used to get in the way of individual work, become the glue that allows work to get done. Good citizenship behaviors, skills, and personal attributes like courtesy, friendliness, conflict resolution, effective listening, persuasiveness, and speaking ability become important assets in teams even if they often are difficult to measure and are absent from traditional job descriptions. Rather than a job description determining what the employee does, increasingly, the person with specialized knowledge, working in concert with others, determines what the duties and responsibilities ought to be.

The rapidity of change largely corresponds to the rate of technological innovation and also to the degree of dynamism in the marketplace. The more competitive the marketplace, the more responsiveness private business expects from government. For example, when developers put all the pieces into place: the land, the tenants, the architects and planners, the financing, and so on, they want a responsive city hall that will process a rezoning application and site plan and issue building permits in a timely fashion; and they want the city's work oriented toward the developers' needs, not vice versa, so the project can be built on schedule and the developer can get on to the next project.

Responsiveness to clients and customers of government services requires a significant degree of organizational flexibility. The notion that an individual has one particular job and that job only, flies in the face of these kinds of demands. While employees become more specialized due to developments in knowledge and technology, they are called upon to become more flexible in order to meet the demands of responsiveness. Personnel systems that permit this kind of flexibility are likely to survive in tomorrow's environment. As an example we introduced earlier the concept of "broad banding" pay, permitting the flexible assignment of workers to different jobs without regard to narrow job descriptions and pay grades.

The pace of change influences the degree to which today's knowledge, skills, and abilities are suitable for tomorrow's work. As we saw in Chapter 7, recruiting on the basis of a standard job description may secure talent for today but will limit the organization's ability to respond tomorrow. A worker's willingness, ability, and aptitude to learn what he or she does not know today may be more important than the knowledge, skills, and abilities that person brings to the present job.

Demographic Trends

The fact that virtually all adults, whether married or not, are working outside the home has made balancing work and family obligations a critical challenge for today's worker, manager, and employer. Today's **demographic trends** show that super pop has joined super mom. Women have grown used to stressful responsibilities for nurturing a family and working outside of the home, and now their husbands are experiencing the same kinds of demands and the stress associated with having to balance family needs, work responsibilities, and personal interests. Working too hard in organizations that are downsizing, perhaps holding a part-time job as well, shuffling kids around day care, soccer matches, and music lessons have to change one's expectations about work and one's perspective on what it means to be an employee today. The call for a return to "family values" at a time when balancing family and work obligations has never been harder creates incredible stress in some individuals and families, stress that is bound to carry over into the workplace through demands for family-oriented benefits, flexible work arrangements, and less commitment to organizations when employees are viewed simply as factors of production rather than assets.

Market-Based Values

The now familiar anti-governmental rhetoric is matched by a resurgence of political support for **market-based values.** If government cannot solve certain problems, then let the marketplace try, advocates argue. Downsizing, privatization, contracting out, and staffing by part-time and temporary workers result from this kind of sentiment stimulated by an environment of fiscal stress. Accompanying these arrangements is a return to the value of individual responsibility and accountability. Every employee becomes a career entrepreneur, responsible for managing one's successes and failures.

CONSEQUENCES OF THESE CHALLENGES FOR LEADERSHIP AND EMPLOYEE PERFORMANCE

This clash of new forces with traditional civil service values and principles creates incredible political and managerial challenges.

First, the traditional employment contract between public employees and the public has been fundamentally affected by market-based values in two critical respects. The most obvious is that government work is less secure than it used to be. This causes changes in the perceived equity of public employment, in that public employees have traditionally been willing to trade lower pay for better benefits and greater job security. Less well understood, but probably more significant in the long run, is that anti-government values also call into question whether government work is a worthwhile vocation. Traditionally, public service was considered desirable because it offered the opportunity to serve the public. But after fifteen years of being told that they are part of the problem rather than part of the solution, public employees are finding it difficult to believe that others understand that their motive is public good rather than private gain. And as a public employee, it is increasingly difficult to embrace that motive when one's job is at stake or when one feels under attack by citizens or elected officials.

Second, the resurgence of market-based values and the accompanying implementation of privatization and contracting out cause most reflective human resource managers at times to question their calling. Are there *any* critical differences between the values, job objectives and KSAs required of personnel managers in business and in public agencies? Is there *anything* about civil service system values or principles that contributes to the unique nature of public work and that cannot be privatized? If most personnel functions are contracted out or decentralized to managers, what impact will this have on delivery of personnel services or the internal debate over the values underlying public employment?

Third, the flexibility demanded by specialization, rapidity of change, and the balancing of family and work, challenges the impersonal, routine, stable, and position-oriented character of civil service systems. A bedrock value of civil service systems is fairness and equity, insured through legal and quasi-legal restrictions on managerial discretion. Managing in an environment that demands flexibility, responsiveness, and efficiency has led to attempts to streamline disciplinary and appeals procedures and has placed traditional personnel techniques—oriented in large measure towards eliminating favoritism—under substantial scrutiny.

And finally, the demands to do more with less have affected elected officials as well. They are called upon to make increasingly more difficult decisions—ones that not only require compromise among the four traditional values but also with the emergent anti-government values that result (for example) in privatization decisions. They may even be tempted to run against "the bureaucracy"—even though these are the people they will later need, if elected, to carry out their campaign promises.

DIFFERENCES BETWEEN POLITICAL AND ADMINISTRATIVE VIEWPOINTS

In this kind of environment the challenges have both political and administrative dimensions, and effectively dealing with them requires a partnership. But sometimes it seems like elected and administrative officials are operating in different worlds. The elected official's world tends to be broader than the administrative official's, and governing body members, administrators, and employees tend to approach their work very differently.[1]

One of the ways to understand the differences between politics and administration is simply to look at them as alternative perspectives, as **political** and **administrative logic,** rather than as behavioral differences. Figure 8-1 attempts to chart those differences in broad terms.[2]

For a politician, the primary value is responsiveness to the will of the people. This means sometimes acting to promote efficiency, social equity, or individual rights; sometimes representing the interests of a few; and sometimes doing what is good for the majority over the long run. The elected official's focus is primarily outside of the organization and into the community or environment of political interests that rally for and against specific policies and solutions to problems. Even when elected officials "meddle" internally, it can be justified in terms of an external role like "oversight," or helping citizens find their way through an administrative agency's labyrinthine procedures.

FIGURE 8–1 Characteristics of Politics and Administration

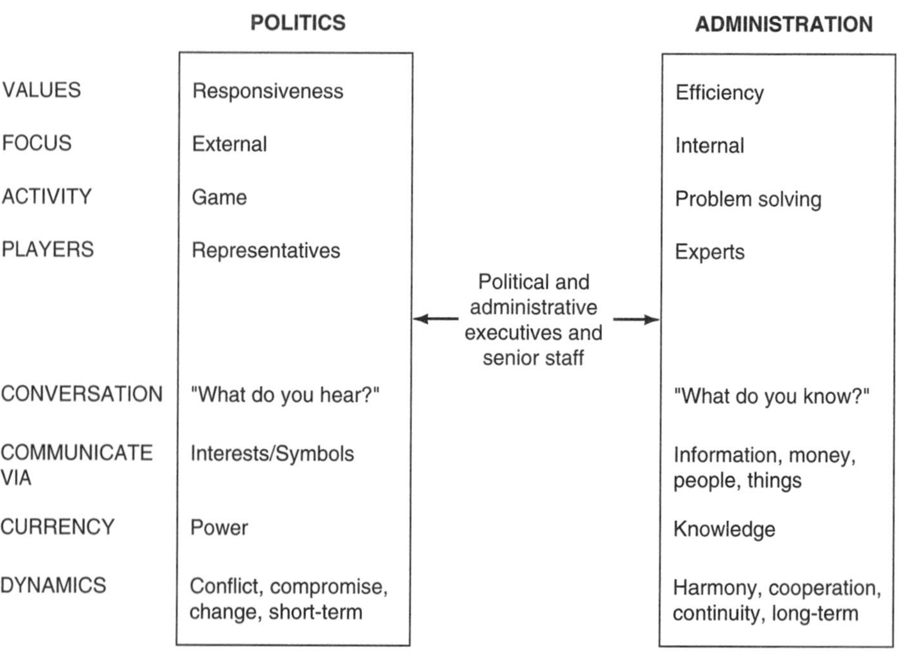

To some extent politics differentiates itself from administration in that part of it can only be understood as a game, with its own rules and strategy and tactics. We even refer to the **game of politics**. Partially, it is a game because the boundaries are so broad and vague. Elected officials must manage their own careers. They cannot count merely on hard work and conscientiousness to keep them in office, and they operate in a world of values where compromise and negotiation are valued more than right answers. They come to their office with no special expertise and often without much relevant experience. They are chosen because they represent something their constituents believe will serve them well.

Because the world of politics is a world of conflicting values, communication is often through symbols that reveal those values. Politicians love to tell stories and, in return, constituents tell them stories—stories about the (in)efficiency of government, about fairness, about the special needs they want represented. The currency is power. The bottom line for an elected official is the ability to influence other elected officials and build community consensus in order to get things done, and there is no formula for success.

Hierarchy removes so much uncertainty from the lives of administrative officials that it is difficult for them to imagine the uncertainty that elected officials work with. It is hard for the outsider to identify how power is acquired and who is powerful, again because in most legislative bodies there is no hierarchy. In addition, in some governing bodies there is no specialization. The elected official's time perspective is shorter than an administrator's because for most elected officials, elected office is not intended to be a career. Even when it is, managing that career requires making short-term, noticeable achievements in an environment of conflicting values.

The administrative world is very different, especially at the level of the personnel specialist, the planner, the engineer, the water plant operator, the scientist at the Environmental Protection Agency, the systems analyst at the Department of Defense, the agronomist at the Department of Agriculture, the budget analyst, and so on. To these people, administration is not a game; it is about the rational, analytical application of knowledge to solve problems. While the problems may have an external origin, the focus is internal; the work is largely internal. The water plant operator may never interact with a citizen unless it's on a tour of the water treatment plant; the same for the budget analyst and the personnel specialist. Their world is bound by their professional/technical knowledge and the hierarchy they work in. They are experts whose knowledge has been acquired over years of education and experience. They were selected for their work on the basis of their knowledge, skills, and abilities, and not because they appealed in some abstract way to a group of voters.

"What do you know?" invites a very different response than "What do you hear?" It suggests a factual exchange where those with the most knowledge are the most valued. Problem solving requires cooperation, and fairness in the implementation of public policy relies on continuity. The administrative specialist thinks in terms of a career, and knowing that he or she is going to be around for the long haul, the vicissitudes of electoral politics are likely to be shunned rather than respected. For every elected official who has bashed a bureaucrat, there are ten public employees who have returned the favor.

The following example illustrates the difference in perception between administrators and elected officials.

August 30, 1996
TO: Journal Entry
FR: John Nalbandian, Mayor
RE: Differences in thinking between professionals and elected officials

Last night I was struck by the continuing differences I notice between the ways that staff and the council think about issues. The city and the county are considering a merger between the city's fire department and the county's emergency ambulance service. They would join to form a new city department. Now, the county provides emergency medical service for city residents as well as for residents of the unincorporated parts of the county. The city fire department provides fire service only within the city's boundaries. Townships and other smaller cities in the county provide their own fire protection.

It is clear that the merger would benefit city residents who have first-class fire service, but second-rate ambulance service because the ambulance stations are not co-located with the fire stations, which are strategically placed within the city. Both fire and ambulance personnel are highly trained, and the new proposal would require all personnel to become cross trained within a designated period of time.

The chiefs of the fire and emergency medical service initiated the idea of the merger. The governing bodies of the city and county encouraged the effort and left it to staff to work up a proposal and work through the details of merging two personnel systems. The sticking point seems to be the differences in rank. In order to retain their pay and seniority, EMS personnel would have to enter the new organization at a higher rank than some of the firefighters. The firefighters have expressed their concern at having to follow direction from EMS personnel who aren't qualified to fight fires. Most of the firefighters have some level of emergency medical skills. When the issue finally came to the city commission, I asked whether the proposal had been formally agreed to by the three smaller incorporated cities in the county. It hadn't been, although the city administrator of one city said his council would favor it because it would increase accessibility to emergency medical service.

But the issue for me is whether residents of the unincorporated parts of the county and of these smaller cities, really will be satisfied with the biggest city in the county deciding about kinds and levels of emergency medical service for their residents without any provision for them to be represented.

The way I approach the rank question is simply to think to myself, "You (staff) get this straightened out or we'll just mandate something because it is clear this is in the best interest of the residents even if it causes problems for employees."

Well, we will get all this worked out because it really is clear that the public interest would be served by this merger, but we sure do come at it from different directions.

The insert describes an incident involving the merging of an ambulance service with a fire department. It shows clearly the different perspective the elected official and staff brought to this problem. One was looking externally at a broader range of values; the other internally. The elected official was concerned about issues of representation and how the agreement would be seen by the smaller cities in the county. The appointed officials were concerned about how to integrate two personnel systems—the furthest thing from the elected official's mind.

As another example in the human resource area, the police department continually operates under pressure from elected officials who want to know yesterday about that incident last night in their district. The elected official is trying to do the best he or she can for the district; to the police department staff, this is just another request that gets in the way of real police work. Also, the police department draws districts and allocates personnel based on a rational analysis of crime statistics. The city council is approached by downtown interests to increase police presence to "manage" the homeless. The mayor, feeling that suburban districts have recently seen an increase in the number of recreation facilities, needs the support of downtown for a major economic development initiative that will require the cooperation of downtown business owners. The mayor urges the council to act on the downtown business owner's request. Again, the perspectives are very different and without adequate interpretation, these worlds grow farther apart as communities become more politically diverse and problems become more technically complex.

These perspectives differ, but successful governance, including the survival of administrative agencies, requires a blend or at least some understanding of the other perspective. It is too much to expect the politician to understand the world of the budget analyst; nor can the wastewater treatment plant operator be expected to know what it is like to see the world from the council chambers. The middle ground is occupied by those who speak both languages, understand both technical and political rationality. This is one of the crucial roles of the chief administrative officer and other senior administrative officials and political executives or their senior staff. In effect, they are called upon to interpret—to translate the world of administration into value questions and to transform value issues into problems subject to administrative expertise. For example, at an orientation of new county commissioners, the purchasing officer was going over purchasing procedures. She said that staff was authorized to accept bids over the phone for purchases of not more than $5,000. Unnoticed by the purchasing director, the commissioners squirmed. After she had finished, the county administrator said, "I would like to clarify something. Staff exercises little discretion in this process. The commission has authorized and scrutinized all of these proposed expenditures during its budget process." In adding this policy clarification, the administrator understood that the new commissioners were very concerned about their oversight role and about government spending. He spoke to their unspoken concern which went unnoticed by the purchasing agent, who was more interested in removing responsibility for "minor" requisitions from the hands of elected officials in the mistaken belief that they would welcome this outcome (or perhaps in enhancing maximizing purchasing department influence over purchasing decisions).

Now that we have established the external environmental conditions, the challenges facing public organizations, and the different perspectives held by political leaders and administrative staff, we can better understand the context within which the employment relationship is managed day-to-day. Much of what we have discussed up to this point in the chapter has addressed environmental and policy issues, now we can introduce concepts and theories to help understand what goes on at the level where an agency's core work is actually performed.

EXPLAINING EMPLOYEE PERFORMANCE: EQUITY AND EXPECTANCY THEORIES

With the decline in resources available to public agencies for productivity improvement through technological innovation, it is even more important to understand the underlying factors which contribute to employee performance and to understand the theories which explain employee motivation. Even in a dynamic environment, this knowledge provides personnel experts and managers with a framework by which to try new methods and innovations to improve that performance and to understand why employees act as they do. The theories explain the link between one's motivation and one's ability to perform as well as the connectedness of performance and job satisfaction. While research has not clearly established the relationship between performance and job satisfaction, it makes intuitive sense, and most people will tell you that such a connection exists in their own motivational pattern.

Equity Theory[3]

Equity theory helps us understand how a worker reaches the conclusion that he or she is being treated fairly or unfairly. It is crucial to an understanding of the "burned-out" worker, the worker who feels mistreated or feels he or she is being asked to do too much, the worker who feels his/her job is threatened but has no alternatives, the employee who is trying to balance family and work and weighing the consequences. Furthermore, equitable treatment of employees is shown to directly affect employee loyalty, expressions of good will, organizational citizenship, and "going the extra mile" (see Chapter 12).

The feeling of being treated equitably is an internal state of mind resulting from a subjective calculation of what one puts into a job and what one gets out of it in comparison to some other relevant person. Inputs can include anything of value the employee brings that he or she thinks deserves special recognition in comparison with others—seniority, expertise, type of work, difficulty of work, level of responsibility and education. Inputs can also include the less formally recognized but still frequently claimed credit for age, sex, race, political influence, and other non-merit factors like ability to get along with others, and demands that family life places on the employee. Outcome credits have an equally wide range: job security, pay, future opportunity, promotion, recognition, organizational climate, work schedule and flexible work arrangements, autonomy, a reserved parking space, a certain size and location of office.

Equity calculations involve two types of subjective comparisons: input to output and comparison with other employees. The comparison is important. You make less than you think your education warrants, but if friends of yours with similar educational backgrounds are out of work, you may be thankful just to have a job. If they are working and make more than you, your reaction will be very different.

The theory can be illustrated with the following formula, where one Person compares what he or she puts into a job with what he or she gets out of that job measured against another person—the Other.

$$\begin{array}{cc} \textbf{Person} & \textbf{Other} \\ \dfrac{\text{Inputs}}{\text{Outcomes}} = & \dfrac{\text{Inputs}}{\text{Outcomes}} \end{array}$$

Equity does not require that all employees receive equal outputs, only that outputs be proportional to inputs, and that employees with comparable inputs receive comparable outputs. For example, managers earn more money (outcomes) than employees, but generally employees find that equitable because of the added responsibility (inputs) managers have.

Let's take a look at how equity theory helps explain one segment in the life of the modern worker. Bill (the Other in the formula above) works very hard and has done work over and above the call of duty (Other's input). One day the nurse at school calls him and says his child is sick and needs to be taken home. He talks to the supervisor who, wanting to be flexible in order to accommodate the family needs of employees, says to him, "You've been working extra hard (supervisor recognizes Other's input), go ahead and take some time off (Other's outcome) and we won't count it against your vacation time." Other says to himself, "I worked extra hard, it's OK if I take the time off without leave." Bill feels that he has balanced inputs and outcomes and feels no discomfort in what he has done. Meanwhile Sally (Person) feels like she works just as hard as Other. Sally is young and single, and whenever she has to run an errand or go to the doctor she is told either to do it during lunch or take leave. She feels like she is being treated unfairly while having done nothing wrong.

Sally now has some choices to make depending on how strongly she feels the perceived injustice. Her goal is to get the ratio back into balance. Now she feels like she is putting more into the job than she is getting out of it, at least compared to Bill, her comparison Other. She can voice her displeasure to the supervisor and hope that the supervisor will change the policy or treat everyone equally (different sometimes from equitably). Or, she can simply acknowledge a difference between her situation and Bill's and say something like, "Bill really does work hard, as hard as I do, and he has a special situation that deserves the special consideration." If Sally comes to this conclusion, from an equity theory standpoint she has given Bill extra input credit to match the outcome, and now the ratio between Sally and Bill, Person and Other, has been restored.

But if Sally does not acknowledge that Bill deserves special consideration, she will still feel mistreated. Her ratio of inputs to outcomes is out of balance when compared to Bill's, so she just might cut back on her own inputs saying, "If they won't reward me for working as hard as Bill, I'm not going to work as hard." This will work for Sally psychologically, as long as she is willing to accept the consequences of not performing at her former level. If she is working in an organization where she feels her job is in some jeopardy, Sally may not say anything to her supervisor about her displeasure, not cut back on her work, and simply internalize the displeasure. She can become a disgruntled employee if the injustice is felt strongly enough. From her view the supervisor acted unfairly; from Bill's point of view the supervisor acted justly; and from the supervisor's view he acted with consideration for Bill's special needs.

Equity issues are confronted in an organization at various levels—in policies regarding human resource management, in supervisory/managerial decisions, and in the supervisor-subordinate relationship. At the policy level (at least within civil service and collective bargaining systems), considerable efforts are made in public organizations to address equity issues. Job classification, performance evaluation, and grievance systems are built around the idea of equal pay for equal work. Political systems and affirmative action programs add complicating factors to the policy level of equity theory. Political systems believe that perceived pay inequities in fact show the personal value of certain individuals to the organization, often reflecting political loyalty and trustworthiness. Affirmative action proponents believe that institutional sexism or racism prevent equity for minorities and women and, therefore, need corrective measures to repair past inequities. These proponents are, in fact, attempting to include certain elements in the equity equation, and the public debate is around whether factors like political loyalty, race or gender are legitimate factors for consideration.

Market-based values complicate the equity implications of policy making. In the privatization case in Chapter 3, the minority sanitation workers may very well feel like they were being treated inequitably. Compared to others, they were having their outcomes reduced even though they did not do anything (inputs) to deserve that treatment. An organization that decides on a compensation policy (Chapter 5) pegged to the external market with less regard toward internal equity, is bound to have equity issues arise. Organizations that employ temporary and part-time workers face equity issues when those employees work side-by-side with permanent staff, doing very similar work but without the equivalent pay or benefits.

Equity issues that arise at a policy-making level inevitably involve a conflict in values. For example, in the privatization case, the council might decide that efficiency argues for privatization at the expense of the sanitation workers. Elected officials are less concerned about internal equity issues than are managers and employees because they do not have to bear the feelings of injustice that may result. They do not have to address the concerns of the temporary worker who is doing a better job than her permanent counterpart but is making less money and has no job security. Furthermore, they have a justification for the decision that they have made, even if the employees affected are not willing to acknowledge it. They may be concerned with the overall financial well-being of the city, and holding the property tax levy down may be more important than the loss of the sanitation workers' jobs or the situation of the part-time employees. If the partnership between elected and appointed officials is working well, the responsible appointed officials will bring the equity consideration to the governing body's attention.

Inevitably, questions of equity will occur at the working level in any organization because inputs and outcomes are not usually discussed explicitly. What Person considers an input worthy of reward, Other may discount, and the supervisor may simply be unaware of. There are several ways to deal with an employee's feeling of being treated unfairly. First, the supervisor must recognize that reaching a conclusion that one has been treated unfairly is the product of someone's unique internal logical processes, driven in many cases by a gnawing sense of injustice. Also impeding simple resolution of equity issues is the tendency to distort input-output ratios to justify feeling ill-treated.

The supervisor may feel that dealing with an employee's perception of unfair treatment is hopeless because the sense of injustice is part of the employee's character rather than a rational response to the situation. Nonetheless, the supervisor should try to find out what the employee perceives his or her rewards and contributions to be and who an appropriate person for purposes of comparison might be, in order to clarify the source of perceived injustice. Finally, the supervisor can attempt to forestall equity claims by making clear what inputs justify organizational rewards, consistently applying rewards and punishments, and specifying the reasons behind the actions. Supervisors who establish expectations and provide timely feedback on performance can also prevent unrealistic assessments of the individual's inputs and outputs.

Expectancy Theory[4]

Expectancy theory attempts to reconstruct the mental processes that lead an employee to expend a certain amount of effort toward meeting a work objective. It also augments equity theory in part by showing how employees' feelings of job satisfaction are translated into performance. It assumes that effort results from three factors:

1. The extent to which an employee believes that he or she can do the job at the expected level
2. The employee's assessment that identifiable rewards or consequences will occur as a result of doing (or not doing) the job at the expected level
3. The value the employee places on these rewards or punishments

In reality, employees do not make these calculations explicitly or formally. Rather, they adjust their level of effort (or change focus from one task to another) based on implicit and intuitive responses to these issues. For example, if an employee is given a task with an indication that a promotion is possible for performing the task well, she will probably do the task well provided that she believes she has the ability and wants a promotion. Given the same circumstances, another employee who wants to spend more time with his family may turn down the promotion because it means more work (an undesirable consequence), even though he believes he could do the job and might get the promotion.

Expectancy theory helps explain employee reactions to many situations at work including burnout, for example. Burnout results when an employee has challenging work (moderate to high confidence in one's ability to perform the work) but few valued outcomes are associated with doing a good job. Performing the job does not lead to rewarding outcomes. In fact, doing a good job just leads to more work or to punishing consequences without offsetting rewards. The consequences usually are a combination of **extrinsic** and **intrinsic** factors. For example, there may be little positive recognition of the work's value (extrinsic) by the lay public or elected officials and high-ranking administrators. Successes are so infrequent that self-satisfaction or a sense of achievement (intrinsic) are hard to come by. At some point, the person becomes burned-out—the effort just doesn't produce rewarding outcomes.

A temporary employee may expend a lot of effort believing that good performance could lead to a permanent job. If there are no positive outcomes associated with performing well, it is doubtful that over time the employee would do so. An employee who is trying to balance work and family may determine that the outcomes associated with expending effort on family life are more rewarding than overtime. Of course, the difficulty comes when this employee wants to be with the family, but the family needs the money the overtime can earn.

Expectancy theory and equity theory help us understand why the satisfied worker may not be productive. People at work can be satisfied for a variety of reasons that may have nothing to do with their performance. For example, an employee may be very satisfied because pay is good, the social environment at work is lively and rewarding, the working conditions are good, and the workload is not unduly taxing. There is nothing in these elements that would lead one necessarily to expect this person to be a productive worker. The worker may lack some knowledge, skills, or ability or maybe enjoys the work environment so much that it detracts from work.

In order for the productive worker to be satisfied, high performance must lead to satisfying outcomes. In addition, the recognition or rewards for high performance must be perceived to be distributed equitably. Furthermore, it is easy for a productive worker not to be satisfied. The worker could be very productive and be paid well, but hate the job, be overworked, see no value in the work, and so on. This is why the relationship between satisfaction and performance is not a direct one—that is, all satisfied workers are not productive and all productive workers are not satisfied.[5]

Using These Theories in Management

The expectancy model provides an excellent diagnostic tool for analyzing an employee's work behavior because it focuses attention on how the organization affects employee effort and performance in several ways. First, the probability that effort will result in task performance is low if the task is difficult and high if the task is easy. But since easy jobs are usually boring, supervisors must delegate responsibility appropriately by striking a balance between setting a performance level so high as to be perceived as unattainable, or so low as to be seen as attainable but boring. Second, the perceived equity and adequacy of performance evaluation and reward systems have a major influence on the employee's perception that performance will lead to rewards (or punishment). Performance appraisal systems that do not distinguish high and low performers, or that do not result in differential rewards (or punishments) for them, will lead to a downward adjustment of inputs to meet outputs by all workers. Finally, consequences must be desirable to result in effort. A detective who is rewarded for solving cases quickly and well by the assignment of more cases and more difficult ones, will soon learn to work more slowly, unless other rewards are available to adjust the balance or the cases turn out to be interesting and intrinsically rewarding to work on.

Equity theory and expectancy theory lead thoughtful supervisors away from more prescriptive, universal theories of human motivation and performance (such as Maslow's hierarchy of needs or Herzberg's motivator-hygiene theory). In reality, employees are individuals with subjective perceptions of their own needs and abilities. No employee is an unmotivated person. Everyone is motivated to certain behaviors. For example, the employee who expends little effort at work may play his/her heart out for the softball team. The failure of an employee to expend desired effort at work can be attributed to factors identified through equity and expectancy theory. These theories provide useful starting points. Effective human resource managers are those who can develop personnel functions which recognize the impact of organizational climate on employee performance, and good supervisors are those who can use these systems to develop relationships based on open communication and trust.

INFLUENCES ON EMPLOYEES' MOTIVATION TO PERFORM

Let's now take each of the primary factors—motivation and ability—which influence performance and explore the factors that affect each. In addition, we will suggest techniques and alternative work systems which would strengthen that factor's ability to enhance performance. Throughout this discussion, it should be evident that we are discussing the shared roles of personnel managers, supervisors, and appointed and elected officials in promoting effective employee performance.

Increasing Employee Motivation

There are an array of organizational and environmental factors which affect employee motivation or effort. Political leaders, agency managers, and human resource directors are responsible for creating and funding personnel programs that provide incentives for superior performance. These include merit pay, bonuses for employee suggestions, and recognition for detection of client fraud and abuse. With regard to pay for performance, will sufficient money be appropriated so that it actually serves as a reward or will the amount merely symbolize an effort to make government more like a business? Politicians and agency executives are so engaged externally, that sound internal human resource practices often fall beyond their attention span even though the decisions they might make can have crucial impact on the ability of managers to manage. David Blumenthal, a highly successful private sector executive, said about his term as secretary of the treasury,

"A Secretary often tends to ignore administrative things because it is not worth his time, it's not where he should put his emphasis. That doesn't mean you neglect administrative matters, but it does mean that you do far less than you might wish."[6]

Political considerations may require compromises on staffing levels, wages, benefit packages, the availability of incentives, privatization, and contracting out. For most politicians, these compromises are ends in themselves. Their primary goal is to get something done amidst conflicting political objectives, and their work is done when the policy compromise is reached. Many of the nitty gritty consequences of these decisions are simply left to managers to deal with. Managers trying to promote progressive and comprehensive changes internally face uphill battles in this environment, and their primary task must be to make elected officials and political executives aware of the consequences of the political compromises on the agency's day-to-day operations.

At the departmental level, linking incentives to desired performance will critically affect the employee's belief that high performance will be rewarded and poor performance dealt with. The creation of challenging jobs will tap the intrinsic desire people have to master their work and avoid boring, fatiguing activities that hold few positive outcomes. Moreover, establishing career paths allows employees to look ahead to a future with their employer. Endorsement of fair but streamlined disciplinary procedures will carry the message to managers as well as employees that unsatisfactory performance will not be overlooked.

Perhaps the greatest influence on employee effort involves the fairness with which employees feel they are being treated. The day-to-day interactions between supervisor and subordinate, the small seemingly inconsequential matters of doing one's job daily, and the cordial relationships between co-workers are the foundation on which employees build trust that they will be treated fairly by those applying the organization's policies and procedures. Thus, the organizational climate in the work unit as guided by the manager will be the main determinant of the perception of fairness for the entire organization. The personnel office, in turn, can influence this climate indirectly by training supervisors on how to motivate employees and how to enhance perceptions of equity in the workplace. They can monitor pay and evaluation processes to ensure no obvious abuses are occurring. They can assist departments in the design of challenging jobs and can work toward developing classification and compensation plans that foster innovative work design and work assignments, and the availability of monetary incentives.

Increasing Employee Commitment[7]

Employee motivation and effort is demonstrated by **employee commitment** to the organization and its goals. If all a manager had to worry about was increasing employee commitment, the task would be fairly simple—provide incentives, challenge, security, and meaningful work. However, conflicting forces in today's public organizations make securing commitment a difficult task. On the one hand, managers are encouraged to promote teamwork and participative decision making to give employees more voice in determining how their work life will proceed. They encourage commitment to the work group and its goals and provide incentives to work together well. On the other hand, employees see the rising trend for privatization of any and all governmental services and the downsizing of the public workforce in the interests of cutting costs. They see full-time jobs being divided into part-time jobs in order to avoid benefit payments. Employees become quite cynical about team building and commitment if they believe their efforts will not stave off the possible loss of their jobs. They may feel the conflict within themselves between loyalty to the work unit and colleagues and the necessity to "look out for yourself" in uncertain times. Nevertheless, managers need to continue to try innovations to build that commitment while being honest with employees about the current status of the organization's plans because external political influences on government continue to demand more for less, and one can never be sure whether this is just rhetoric or a real call to action.

Flexible Work Locations and Schedules[8]

There are several common innovations in working conditions that serve to increase employee commitment. In the past all employees were expected to have identical working hours and a fixed job location, but this is no longer true nor necessary. Changes in technology (primarily telecommunications and computers) have meant that employees can work productively at decentralized workstations, or even at home. The need for broader service delivery to clients and the complex child-care and elder-care arrangements necessitated by two-career families have resulted in the development of part-time and flexible work schedules. And the focus on employees as resources has led to the development of variable models of resource use that have proved effective at achieving improved performance.

Under **flextime**, all employees are expected to work during core hours (such as 9:30 to 3:00). Depending on agency needs and personal preferences, each employee is free to negotiate a fixed work schedule with different start and end times. Some agencies have flextime programs which enable employees to work longer days in order to have fewer workdays in a week or month (such as ten hours per day, four days a week). Research on flextime experiments in both the public and private sectors generally reveals positive results in employee attitudes and in the reduction of absenteeism, tardiness, and, in some cases, increases in productivity.

Job sharing is the splitting of one job between two part-time employees on a regular basis. There are obvious advantages for employees (part-time work rather than having to choose between full-time work or no work at all) and the agency (lower costs, more skill sets for the job). Job sharing requires clear expectations and precise coordination between the employees, with their supervisor, and with clients/customers inside and outside the agency. And the agency must develop policies for contributions to and division of pensions, health care, and other benefits.

Under **flexiplace**, employees may work away from the office provided a suitable outside workstation is available. This works best for professionals who can work independently and yet remain in contact with the agency through a variety of electronic media (such as, e-mail, voice mail, fax). The advantage to the agency is that it may be able to attract competent individuals who value independence and flexibility as well as to save on overcrowded work space. The downside, of course, are predictable things like communication and control, and unpredictable ones like workplace health and safety and workers' compensation claims.

INFLUENCES ON EMPLOYEES' ABILITY TO PERFORM

In addition to motivation, employees must have the necessary knowledge, skills, and abilities in order to perform well. Legislatures and personnel experts have the most significant effect on the ability of the worker through the wage-setting process. The more money allocated to salaries, the more competitive a governmental employer will become in the labor market and the more talent it will attract. For example, some attributed the problems in the yearlong troublesome effort to change a pay system at the University of Kansas to a vendor's failure to attract and hold on to the needed computer programming talent. Similarly, salary level and working conditions affect an employee's intention to stay with an employer. Unfortunately, public agencies often serve as training grounds for the private sector by paying relatively low salaries for experienced employees. For example, social workers hired by a state human service agency are usually paid competitive entry-level salaries, but if they are not given pay increases as they gain experience, they may choose to leave state employment for nonprofit or private-sector jobs. This turnover of experienced employees can reduce productivity by making case tracking more difficult, by hampering management development, and by diminishing organizational memory.

Department managers and personnel directors affect productivity significantly through employee selection. If a market wage will attract talented applicants to the public employer, then the hiring process must be able to select the candidates with the best potential to perform current responsibilities as well as learn new skills and possess personal attributes necessary to work in tomorrow's organizations. Other important departmental influences on the employee's ability to perform include the quality of on-the-job training and coaching and the quality and timeliness of feedback regarding performance.

It is in the area of training (covered in more detail in the next chapter) that the human resource department has significant effect on the ability factor by conducting training needs assessments and by locating or offering training opportunities. In addition, the department can support managers by emphasizing and researching the validity of selection methods, by working with supervisors and employees to develop performance-based appraisal methods, and by increasing supervisory skill in communicating constructive feedback to employees. In some cases, personnel departments will track labor market conditions and gather data on prevailing wage rates for input into legislative decisions regarding allocation or collective bargaining positions.

The Ability to Succeed

Frequently overlooked among the factors connected to productivity is the employee's **opportunity to perform well.** Political leaders, agency managers, and personnel directors have the primary responsibility for ensuring that the opportunity to perform well exists. First and foremost, political leaders can create agencies with clear missions, adequate resources, and internal administrative stability. Or, they can tie public employees' hands by allowing the continuation of organizational factors that hinder performance: conflicting objectives, inadequate budgets, frequent reorganizations, lack of realistic work planning or time frames, and constant pressure on agency managers for partisan political objectives, desire for involvement in administrative detail, and, in general, lack of appreciation and value for government employees.

In addition to opportunity, employees must be given reasonable expectations. This includes both the clarity of goal statements and the feasibility of the goals. For example, measuring police officers' performance by variations in the crime rate discounts the variety of factors not under a police department's control which influence crime in a community. Similarly, the National Education Association and the American Federation of Teachers have hotly criticized what they feel is the simplistic notion that incentive pay for teachers will improve student performance. These professional associations cite a host of factors outside the classroom that can have more effect on student performance than teacher behavior.

From a positive perspective, political leaders and agency managers can provide the technology that enables employees to "work smarter" rather than just demanding that they work harder. The availability of the tools of one's trade, be they reliable snowplows or computers or laboratory equipment, is essential to employee performance.

Another factor related to the opportunity to perform well is attention to safe equipment and working conditions with appropriate safety training. Sick leave and workers' compensation cost public employers a great deal, and unsafe working conditions reduce the employee's opportunity to work productively. Positive working conditions also include such things as adequate space and commonsense procedures and policies.

A final factor has to do with the personnel system itself. If a system is too rigid there may be few opportunities for flexibility in work assignments, career mobility, and implementation of incentive plans. On the other hand, a system with too few controls might encourage favoritism, capricious personnel actions, and too many individual exceptions which undermine morale and confidence in the overall merit concept.

ORGANIZING FOR PRODUCTIVITY: ALTERNATIVE WORK SYSTEMS

Total Quality Management[9]

Total quality management (TQM) is a management philosophy which combines scientific methods for experimentation and continuous improvement of processes with teamwork and participative decision making as the approach for implementing improvement changes. The central theme is the improvement of quality and the gaining of customer satisfaction. Four key ingredients of TQM are customer focus, data-driven decisions, participative decision making, and continuous improvement. The organization is seen as a complex of systems, with each system made up of interrelated processes which deliver services or goods to "customers." Identifying and understanding these processes is often the starting point of developing a TQM approach in an organization. Finding root causes of quality problems and collecting data before and after implementing solutions to track the success of such solutions are often the mundane and difficult aspects of TQM. In addition, defining quality for the organization, clarifying the values and mission of the organization, and identifying who are the customers and their wants are basic activities that TQM organizations engage in to provide direction for their quality efforts. TQM organizations often reorganize themselves into cross-functional teams to better reflect core processes and improve responsiveness to customer needs.

Critics of TQM in public organizations site a number of concerns of the applicability of TQM. Among them, they caution against the view that TQM advocates fail to distinguish between customers and citizens. Second, they claim that ambiguous and conflicting political policy goals make TQM in the public sector unrealistic.

As to the first concern, there is validity in cautioning that citizens are not always customers. Traditionally, customers who are dissatisfied with something they buy simply choose another brand. This is not very often an option in government. Furthermore, customers have no obligations to make their dissatisfaction known (other than switching to another product), nor do they have any obligations to help improve the service. In addition, the private-sector stories of companies going out of the way to satisfy individual customers would be seen as favoritism and inequitable treatment and would be severely criticized in the public sector.

The criticism regarding ambiguous and conflicting goals cannot be disregarded. James Q. Wilson premises his book, *Bureaucracy,* on the idea that public organizations are fundamentally different from private ones because they are prone to have conflicting or ambiguous objectives that are the result of political compromises.[10] TQM works best where objectives can be clarified.

Acknowledging these criticisms, numerous government activities are still suitable to TQM or related philosophies. Issuing driver's licenses, water bills, running a motor pool, and organizing a recruitment and selection procedure that is applicant friendly are just a few examples. The difficulty with implementing TQM in the public sector is not its applicability, but rather the absence of a private market to drive an innovation of this or a related kind. For TQM to work in the public sector, it must be administratively driven by innovative managers with a public-service ethic who believe they have an obligation to provide the most efficient, effective services to citizens. In contrast, in the private sector TQM may offer a competitive economic advantage to one firm over another.

Advocates claim that successful TQM requires a supportive organizational culture. Amidst downsizing, privatization, frozen wages, reduction in benefits, and hiring freezes, the conditions necessary for TQM to work are threatened. TQM draws upon employee commitment, and it presumes a level of trust throughout the organization, conditions more difficult to find in governments under fiscal and political stress.

Job Enrichment

The effort to identify conditions conducive to high performance led in the 1970s and 1980s to research into **job enrichment**. "Enriched jobs" are those where performance of the work itself is rewarding. Figure 8-2 illustrates this approach to designing work which leads to high job satisfaction and effectiveness. High internal work motivation, "growth" satisfaction, general job satisfaction, and work effectiveness result when people experience their work as meaningful, when they feel responsible for the quality and quantity of work produced, and when they have firsthand knowledge of the actual results of their labor. These psychological states are likely to result from work designed to incorporate the characteristics of variety, work with a beginning and identifiable end, work of significance, and work characterized by autonomy and feedback.[11]

Jobs that are high in these characteristics are said to be enriched and to have a high motivating potential. Whether high internal motivation, satisfaction, and productivity actually do come about as outcomes for employees depends on their knowledge and skill, their growth need strength (such as the need for self-esteem or the esteem of others), and their satisfaction with working conditions (such as pay, supervision, and co-workers).

Results of research into this model have been generally supportive. Personnel policy innovations have been adopted first as experiments, and then as

FIGURE 8–2 Job Characteristics Model. (Source: Richard Hackman/Greg Oldham, *Work Design*, © 1980 by Addison-Wesley Publishing Company. Reprinted with permission of the publisher.)

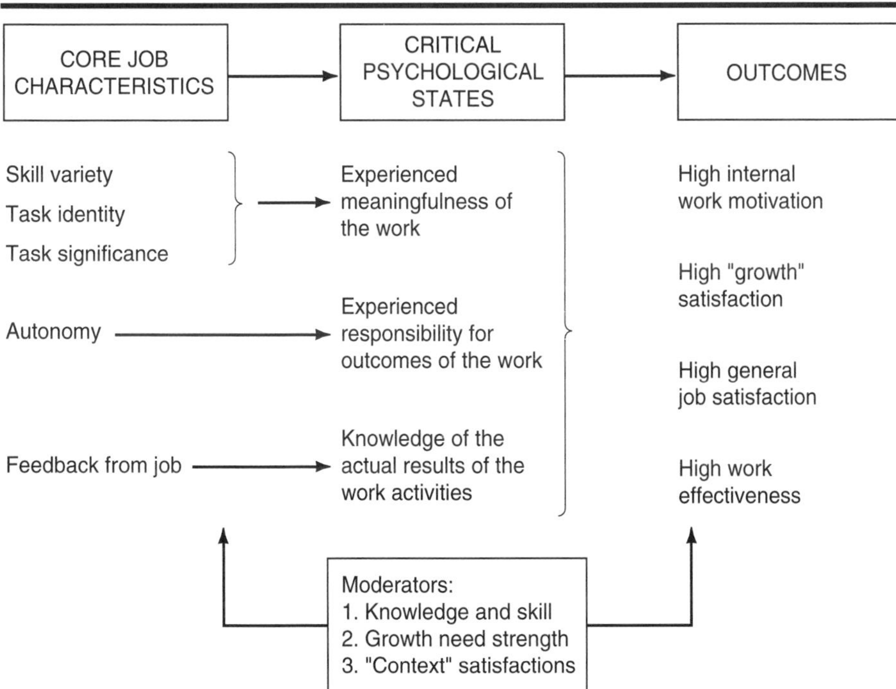

options in the "tool kit" the supervisor and personnel director use to match employees with work and to generate good individual and team performance. The design of jobs to enrich them assumes that employees are long-term assets. Once again, we find a technique employed to promote high performance is challenged by contemporary working conditions in many organizations.

Teamwork

Organizing employees into groups to work together on certain projects or on everyday tasks is increasingly the structure that public and private organizations are choosing.[12] There are several reasons for the popularity of **teamwork** as the preferred approach. Organizational problems and issues are so complex today that no one person can grasp all of the information nor have all the skills to adequately and thoroughly analyze and choose the best solutions. The complexity of problems also requires innovativeness and diversity of viewpoints to see all of the options and consequences involved. Finally, today's most serious problems do not fall neatly into our traditional functional departments. For example, to promote economic development a local government must coordinate financial incentives, zoning and site plan issues, infrastructure issues, and code enforcement. In the usual organizational structure, this would involve several different departments: finance, planning, engineering, and public works.

In terms of employee performance, the team concept addresses both the motivational and ability aspects of performance. Because teamwork usually involves participation by team members in decision making, commitment to work tasks and organizational goals are enhanced. When teams work together well, team members learn from one another, thus increasing each individual member's ability to perform. If the combined efforts of the team are directed well, the results can be innovative solutions, highly motivated employees, and efficient use of resources.

The challenge for managers and supervisors is to be able to direct and guide the team toward these results while allowing time for team cohesion to develop, for conflicts to be faced and resolved, for diverse opinions to be heard, and for learning from mistakes.

Much has been written recently about teams in both academic journals and management books. Several factors appear to be most important for team leaders to understand if they are to succeed in team building:

A Stable Work Force That Values Organizational Goals. For teams to work effectively, their members must be able to get to know and trust one another. Furthermore, the team members must value the team goals as worthy of their collective effort.

Agreement That Teams Are Useful and Needed. Before the team approach can be used, group members must realize that there are some problems and tasks that teams can do better than individuals, that the time invested in building a team is worthwhile, and that priorities have to be negotiated with the understanding that their individual (or departmental) concerns may not always receive the highest priority.

Clear Expectations and Goals. Teams need to spend time, especially in the beginning, clarifying why they are there. Often teams are given broad general goals which they must then understand and accept as well as translate into concrete objectives they want to achieve with recognizable outcomes.

Understanding and Training in Communication and Group Dynamics. Team members need to recognize what is happening interpersonally among them. They must realize that not everyone expresses teamwork and commitment to the team in the same way. They must be comfortable in talking about "process" matters, such as conflicts between different factions on the team, competition for leadership, power struggles, hidden agendas, fight/flight behavior and other symptoms of anxiety and stress experienced by team members. They must be able to talk productively about these matters which require communication skills such as giving and receiving feedback, listening, responding to feelings, and interpreting nonverbal communication. It is unlikely that these skills will develop through on-the-job training without some kind of developmental skill-building program.

Agreed-upon Procedures and Policies. Team members need to agree upon the approach they will use as they work toward goals. Will they use, for example, a systems approach such as TQM? What ground rules for meetings and procedures for reporting will they have? Many times teams will assume that everyone agrees and knows what the approach will be but find that not articulating them up front becomes a stumbling block later on.

Clear Lines of Accountability. Team members need to know and have an opportunity to negotiate with the leader and with each other about how individual members will be held accountable for tasks done well and done poorly. What is the penalty for a missed deadline by an individual which may put the team behind schedule? How should stellar individual performance be rewarded? What will be the team reward as a team for a job well done?

Organizational Rewards. Nothing can stifle teamwork more than failing to recognize it with formal organizational rewards. Teamwork is work. To be successful, it requires efforts of leadership, cooperation, and conflict resolution beyond what is often formally rewarded in individually based merit or variable pay systems. Identification of these types of behaviors and skills as crucial to organizational success has led to the inclusion of "personal characteristics" with the traditional knowledge, skills, and abilities formula of personnel management, especially in the areas of selection and promotion. Some people are more comfortable working in teams than others, and some personalities are better suited to the ambiguity and predisposition to learn from organizational experiences that often accompany teamwork.

Much of what is written in this chapter applies to team performance as it does to individual performance. However, teamwork is complicated by the fact that another goal is to enhance group performance and build synergistic group effort. The leader of the team must balance fair treatment of each individual with flexibility to encourage diversity of contribution by those individual members along with the idea that the team and its goals may have to come first.

TOOLS MANAGERS USE TO ENHANCE EMPLOYEE PERFORMANCE

Throughout the chapter we have outlined the conflicts in values that undermine conditions necessary for high performance. But this is not true of all public organizations, and even where the psychological contract between employee and employer is strained, managers and supervisors are obligated to themselves, the public, and their employees to work toward high performance. Several managerial skills have been mentioned as important in implementing ideas for improving employee performance. These skills are applicable whether the supervisor is working with an individual or with a team. Here are some guidelines on how best to use these skills.

Setting Clear Expectations

Employees may be motivated and have the requisite ability to perform well, but without **clear expectations** they will not know where to focus their efforts. There are several things a supervisor can do to ensure that expectations are clear for the employee and in line with organizational goals.

1. Ask the employee to develop an informal job description which emphasizes the major tasks and some reasonable performance standards (stated objectively in terms of quantity, quality, or timeliness of service).
2. If the position is hopelessly misclassified, request a desk audit from personnel for any position for which the informal job description appears unrelated to the formal position description.
3. Use the informal and formal job description to give the employee a clearer idea of what is expected.
4. Establish a clear understanding with the personnel department over shared responsibilities for new employee orientation. Use your best employees for the unit orientation.

Providing Effective Feedback

Basically, effective **feedback** allows people to see themselves as others see them. In supervision, the objective is to give this feedback in such a way that the employee will be motivated and be capable of making improvements in behavior. In order to increase the probability for this to occur, feedback should be given with respect and encouragement, and it may be useful to include feedback from team members or peers, internal and external customers, and subordinates.

Supervisors can also role model the willingness to receive feedback given in such a manner.

1. Focus on behavior rather than the person. Refer to what a person *does* rather than comment on what the person *is*.
2. Be descriptive and specific, then describe the behavior's impact and consequences. Avoid broad generalizations and the use of absolutes, such as "always" and "never."
3. Be sure it is well-timed. Usually feedback given shortly after the behavior is observed is the most effective. However, consider the person's readiness to hear it (is he too upset to listen right now?) and the availability of a private place to talk.
4. Direct toward behavior that the receiver can do something about. Reminding a person about some shortcoming over which she does not have control leads only to frustration and defensiveness.
5. Check to be sure of clear communication. If the person looks confused, you want to check for an understanding of what was said. There may not be agreement on the accuracy of what was said, but it should be based on accurate understanding.

Communicating Appropriate Consequences

Setting goals and expectations and **communicating the consequences** of success or failure are crucial managerial tools. Managers and supervisors need to apply both positive (rewards) and negative (punishments) consequences equitably and consistently to influence employee behavior.

1. If money is to be an incentive, support the development of a variable pay provision that allocates enough money to make a difference to employees. Seek the right to allocate variable pay based on objective performance relative to previously established performance standards.
2. Separate merit pay from other pay systems based on cost of living or seniority.
3. Use non-economic rewards freely, such as praise, more responsibility, or task variety.
4. Work with the personnel department to clarify personnel regulations regarding employee conduct. These not only aid productivity efforts but also safeguard union contracts and protect against legal liability.
5. Be aware of the doctrine of "vicarious liability," which means that supervisors are responsible for employee behavior that violates the rights of clients and other employees.

MANAGING EMPLOYEE ANXIETY

Life in public organizations today is complicated with rapid change, re-structuring, changing and often conflicting political pronouncements and policies, and concerned and often critical citizenry demanding full accounting of its tax dollars. For public employees this can create an atmosphere of anxiety. Leaders, especially managers and supervisors, must help employees cope with the stress and anxiety of this ever shifting work environment. When stress becomes too high, it leads to counterproductive behaviors by employees that can range from absenteeism, low productivity, and low morale to more destructive behaviors such as alcohol and drug abuse, sabotage, and workplace violence. The consequences for not **managing anxiety** can be very high, as the following illustration of the disadvantages of "re-engineering" show:

April 5, 1996
To: John Nalbandian
Fr: Department Head
Re: Downsizing

As organizations "thin" and the competition for scarce public jobs increase, the process of filling vacancies that are retained in the budget becomes a war within the organization. If the position is actually rebudgeted and advertised, the competition for this public job now creates a large number of applications. Many times, individuals with real qualifications for the position are at a premium due to private-sector competition. Other applicants will cite that local residency, community knowledge, and even friendship with staff or local officials should outweigh required job skills. Thus, often we are confronted with a selection process with many wrong solutions and few win-win outcomes. The end result will often be a political or legal challenge to the selection decision. In addition, many public organizations are losing the "in-house generalists" in the middle management ranks of the organization through the thinning of the organization. These individuals began their careers in very technical areas. But, due to tenure, career advancement, and program needs, they have grown into positions of mid-management and effectively operate the organization day-to-day. These positions are exactly those that are at risk in each and every budget cycle. In an attempt to reduce personnel costs, we quickly rule out department heads, technical staff, and lower-level operating staff from serious consideration for a reduction-in-force. This leaves the middle management supervisors and operational generalists or program operators as the moving targets of the budget process. Each time a person like this is cut, it becomes more difficult for program staff to negotiate needed compromises within the organization.

The result is a decline in staff who share a public-sector philosophy of providing service in an equitable manner for the community. Instead, the hard-core technical staff remain and find themselves unable to communicate with other parts of the agency. The greatest challenge from this conflict is that many of the day-to-day decisions on operations are now made at the highest level of the organization, where they may become politicized. They are brokered on the top floor of city hall or among the department heads of the city. The remaining energy and time of the administrative team after these in-house wars provides little opportunity for creative solutions or ideas leading to better public services.

Managers and supervisors must be alert to the early signs of high stress manifested by their employees and address the issues directly. Information takes on a critical role during times of change. In order to deal with the anxiety of the unknown, employees will seek information wherever they can. If there is a void of legitimate information, it will be filled with rumor, gossip, and exaggerations which can only sabotage good efforts. Participation in discussions and decision making will also help employees feel more in control of their destiny and enable them to comfortably commit to changes. Part of the anxiety employees feel is based on the need to learn new skills and procedures which will affect performance as well as self-confidence. Training is the foundation on which employees can build new performance standards.

Leaders need to be very visible during times of high anxiety. They must be role models of compassion, concern, and control and be willing to share information and knowledge as it becomes available, all while managing their own anxiety. Human resource departments play an important role in providing counseling and coaching, stress management programs, and referrals for employee assistance programs.

SUMMARY

Elected officials, managers, supervisors, and human resource specialists have a significant influence on employee performance. Within the parameters set by legislators and chief executives, human resource systems must be developed that make the fullest use of employee motivation and capabilities. This requires an understanding of what employees need to perform well (such as adequate skills, clear instructions, feedback, and rewards). The external focus of political leaders often deflects their concern for the impact of policy compromises on human resource management within public organizations. Equity theory and expectancy theory provide a useful framework to understand the link between performance and motivation and job satisfaction as well as diagnostic tools for implementing techniques and methods and also for understanding how and why organizational members are responding as they do to higher-level policy and managerial decisions. Those responsible for improving employee effort and performance must be willing to experiment with new approaches and to know how to evaluate their effectiveness in employee performance.

Tomorrow's organization with increased specialization, downsizing, teamwork, and pay for performance all add challenges and anxiety to the work of elected and appointed executives, managers, supervisors, and employees. Organizing work in this type of environment of change highlights the importance of an organization and its members who are capable of dealing with the resultant ambiguity and who are willing and able to learn from their organizational experiences and make personal and organizational changes based on that learning.

KEY TERMS

administrative logic
assumptions about civil service systems
clear expectations
communicating consequences
demographic trends
employee commitment
equity theory
expectancy theory
extrinsic motivation
feedback
flexiplace
flextime
game of politics
intrinsic motivation
job enrichment
job sharing
managing anxiety
market-based values
modern organizational climate
opportunity to perform well
political logic
teamwork
total quality management (TQM)

DISCUSSION QUESTIONS

1. What are the organizational climate, demographic trends, and market-based values that challenge traditional civil service systems as well as the consequences of these challenges.
2. Identify the differences between political and administrative logic and give examples of each. How important do you think these differences are when it comes to understanding the ways that elected and appointed officials act?
3. Describe the basic components of equity and expectancy theory and how they help to explain employee performance. Identify an example from your own life where equity theory or expectancy theory helps you understand why you did what you did.
4. Describe the ways that elected officials, managers, and personnel specialists affect an employee's *motivation* to perform.
5. Describe the ways that elected officials, managers, and personnel specialists affect an employee's *ability* to perform.
6. Describe three alternative work systems: total quality management, job enrichment, and teamwork.
7. Describe how clear expectations, giving feedback, and communicating appropriate consequences enhance employee performance.
8. Describe the causes of employee anxiety and the supervisor/manager's role in addressing it.

CASE STUDY 1 REQUIEM FOR A GOOD SOLDIER

"How about Rachel Fowlkes?" Gordon asked. "She's certainly in line for the job. Rachel has had all the requisite training and experience to become an assistant director."

Harold Nash, manager of the Department of Health and Welfare, rolled a ballpoint pen between his fingers and rocked slowly in his executive desk chair. "I don't know," he said soflty. "I really don't know. Give me another rundown on her experience."

Clifton Gordon opened the manila personnel folder and laid it on Nash's desk. "Six years with this bureau, but she'd been with the old Vocational Rehabilitation Department for almost nine years before the reorganization. She started as a clerk, was in line for assistant director at the time we reorganized."

"We had too many chiefs as a result of that merger," Nash said. "As I recall, a few people were bumped."

Gordon smiled. "I remember that, all right. She was one that was bumped and I was the one who took over as assistant director."

"How did she take it?" Nash asked.

"No problem," Gordon said. "She was a good soldier."

"A good soldier," Nash echoed.

"She was very capable and versatile," Gordon said. "In fact I relied on her heavily for new personnel training. Many of those green young men she trained are now directors and assistant directors." Gordon pointed to the personnel folder. "Rachel was made acting assistant director of the information and public assistance section four years ago and apparently was seriously considered for the positon of assistant director when Tom Walters retired."

Nash shook his head. "Regrettably, I had a difficult choice then as well. I had to choose between a capable career woman and an equally talented young man. Both were on the cert as bests qualified. In the end I felt Manpower Research was not the right place in which to place our first female assistant director."

"Now would be a perfect time," Gordon said, "especially in view of the governor's recent order on the EEO Act and the stress on the utilization of minorieties and women. I think that's what all this talk of affirmative action is all about. Wouldn't promoting Rachel be an affirmative action?"

Nash winced. "Don't remind me. That report to the governor is due shortly! But back to Rachel; promotions must utlimately be based on merit and not on sex or color of skin."

"I agree completely," Gordon replied quickly, "but with all other things being equal, why not select a woman?"

"If that were true, I just might. But all other things are not equal. Not only do I again have several capable candidates along with Rachel on the cert, but there have been problems with Rachel lately."

"I wasn't aware of that. What's happened to Rachel, the good soldier? I can't imagine her causing problems for anybody."

"That's what I'd like to know," Nash said. "For the past six months I've given her several responsibilities and she just hasn't responded the way she used to. Her work output is definitely deteriorating and her attitude is, too."

"What's her complaint?"

"No one seems to be able to put his finger on the problem: I even had her in the office once for a casual chat, but she claimed there was nothing causing her any concern. I mentioned her slipping work performance and she promised to improve."

"And?"

"Oh, she's improved. I guess her work is O.K., but that old spark is gone."

"That's a shame," Gordon said. "Rachel has done so well . . . for a woman." Nash nodded, "Yes, it is a shame. I'm afraid we'll have to look elsewhere to fill that assistant director position."

Source: U.S. Civil Service Commission Bureau of Training, *The Equal Employment Opportunity Act: Implications for Public Employers.* Washington, DC: U.S. Government Printing Office, 1973.

QUESTIONS

1. Using equity theory, analyze how and why Rachel's behavior has changed during the time period of the case.
2. What are the important inputs and outcomes from Rachel's point of view? Who is the focus of her social comparison?
3. What factor(s) has Harold Nash given input credit for that Rachel may have overlooked?
4. Utilizing expectancy theory, analyze how Rachel's behavior has changed during the time period in the case.

5. How has Rachel's estimation of her ability to perform as assistant director changed? Has the value she places on different outcomes associated with being assistant director changed? Has her expectation changed that good performance in her current job will lead to a promotion?
6. How would you define "old spark" in terms of a performance goal or job standard? How would you feel as an employee if someone failed to promote you justifying it, in part, by your loss of the "old spark?"
7. How do you think Rachel feels at this point in her job? How do you think you might feel? How common do you think the case of Rachel is in modern organizations?
8. Who is responsible for the changes in Rachel's behavior in this case? Who is accountable for them? What is the difference?
9. If you were Harold Nash, would you promote Rachel, given the deterioration of her morale and her apparent competent but lackluster performance?

CASE STUDY 2 RECRUITING A WATER PLANT TECHNICIAN

The city of Valdez is recruiting for a water plant technician. Shelly Wong appears to be head and shoulders more qualified than the other candidates. Her knowledge is up to date; she has had enough experience to establish a reliable work record; and she comes with great recommendations as a solid organizational citizen by her present employer. She has outgrown her present job.

Everything seems to be going well with the recruitment and selection process. When Ms. Wong is asked if she has any questions she responds, "This looks like a great place to work, but we take care of an elderly parent in our home, and we have day-care needs for our children." She continues, "I am looking for an employer who can offer a flexible work schedule. Will I need to take leave each time I have to pick up a sick child from day care? And on occasion my mother, who lives with us, needs transportation to the doctor's, and I like to be there when she talks with the doctor because she doesn't speak English very well."

The personnel officer responds, "I'm sorry, we run a pretty tight ship around here, and the water treatment plant technicians are mostly men who don't seem to have these kinds of needs. We'll try to work something out; we really want you to work for us. But I don't want to mislead you, maybe we aren't where we should be in this area."

QUESTIONS

1. Could the personnel director have approached this situation differently?
2. If the city wanted to "get where it should be in this area," what should it do?
3. What possible problems might this organization encounter in "getting where it should be," and how might it overcome them?

CASE STUDY 3 BETWEEN A ROCK AND A HARD PLACE

To: John Nalbandian and Donald Klingner

Fr: Under-Secretary, State Department of Human Resources

Date: April 15, 1996

Subj: Downsizing

The Department of Human Resources administers Workers' Compensation Insurance, Unemployment Insurance and a variety of Employment and Training programs. We do it with 150 fewer employees than we did 16 months ago. Real dollar reductions in federal funding have harshly cut into our ability to support our operations. Unlike most other cabinet-level agencies, the Department of Human Resources is 99 percent federal funded or employer-fee funded. Like most state agencies, personnel salaries and benefits are more than 80 percent of our total cost. When the federal budget takes a bite out of our budget, the only recourse is to reduce staffing. That is a polite euphemism for firing real people. It's a hard thing to do.

In January 1995, the department had 1,079 full-time equivalent positions and about 1,000 people actually on the payroll. The new administration inherited a funding problem that had been building for five years. Shifting personnel and costs between programs and funds had prevented layoffs during that time. The bill came due with the change of administrations. Unemployment insurance funds declined about 10 percent this year. Employment and training funds took a bigger hit. In total, the department received about $6 million less this year than last year. That was a 15 percent decrease. Again, I point out that this was a real dollar decrease, not a typical inside-the-beltway decrease in the increase.

Our programs are on staggered fiscal years, so the budget reality came home in July, and then was reinforced with further funding cuts in October. In July, we instituted a hiring freeze to take the most advantage of attrition. About fifty people left the payroll and were not replaced. By October it was clear that a layoff would occur, and we spent the next three months going through all the hoops and barrels at the division of personnel services in the department of administration. This was a learning experience for us as well. The most senior worker there could not remember when the state had last had a layoff. We were rewriting the book. The "bureaucracy myth" is not always fair, but in this case, it took us until the day of the scheduled layoff announcement before all the process was approved and paperwork cleared. We struggled with holdups, delays, and paper-shuffling to no end. Every time we thought we were good-to-go, another person had to bless everything.

We were in constant communication with employees, talking about budgets, revenues, expenses. Layoffs were discussed at length. Positions for abolishment were identified based on the requirement to get the job done. All local offices were run through a staffing formula and nine were identified as too small to function at the soon-to-be reduced staffing levels. Those offices were announced for closing the same day as the layoff letters were mailed and layoff announcements made.

Despite our efforts to be open and clear, many employees were shocked and in disbelief that layoffs actually occurred and that offices were actually locked and shuttered. The culture of governmental/bureaucratic invincibility that has developed over the last thirty years made it impossible for the employees to believe what they were being told. The paradigm of government growth shifted, and they were blinded by their old ways of thinking about government employment.

We established contact teams to assist laid-off workers with unemployment benefits and job placement. The Secretary and I made special contacts on behalf of many workers to gain placement at other state agencies. We wrote many letters of reference. Some laid-off workers were rehired within our department on a temporary basis due to the unexpected arrival of a special grant. All these efforts helped ease the situation.

However, after all the bumping rights were exercised, the layoff affected more than 300 of the 1,000 employees in the department, either through demotion, reduction in pay, or termination. With one third of our department family dysfunctional, performing even daily operations was difficult. It took excessive and redundant planning to ensure that the public still received services during this time. It is a credit to all our public employees that little disruption occurred.

Due to civil service regulations and policies, seniority still rules in our state government. Among the saddest tasks of management is to tell highly skilled, fresh, gung-ho, young public employees and administrators that they will be laid off while older, less effective workers remain. The questions of equity, individual rights, and efficiency cut in many directions.

Now, with Congress locked-up, government shut-down, block-grant proposals, devolution to the states, and election-year posturing, we are preparing for additional cuts and taking steps to plan for future layoffs. It is naive to assume that our department and others are through with downsizing. I think it is only beginning.

QUESTIONS

1. The author raises a number of concerns about the functioning of the agency. After identifying the problems the author states, try and separate them into those which can be addressed (if at all) by (a) elected and appointed officials, (b) managers and supervisors, (c) the personnel director, (d) employees.
2. What are the solutions to those problems which you identified as resolvable in your response to question 1? For each solution, specify the person or group responsible for implementing it, and how you would recommend they work to overcome any implementation barriers.
3. For those problems which are not resolvable under current conditions, specify the changes that would have to occur for the problem to be solved? How bad would things have to get? How would that make the problem resolvable?
4. If you were a manager in this organization, how would you deal with employee anxiety and the performance issues it can create?

NOTES

[1] Dubnick, M. and B. S. Romzek. (1991). *Public administration: Politics and the management of expectations.* New York: Macmillan, Ch. 12.

[2] Nalbandian, J. (1994). Reflections of a "pracademic" on the logic of politics and administration. *Public Administration Review, 54,* 531-536.

[3] Adams, J. S. (1965). Inequity in social exchange. In L. Berkowitz (Ed.). *Advances in experimental social psychology* (Vol. 2). New York: Academic Press.

[4] Vroom, V. H. (1964). *Work and motivation.* New York: John Wiley.

[5] Iaffaldana, M. T., and P. M. Muchinsky. (1985). Job satisfaction and job performance: A meta-analysis. *Psychological Bulletin, 97,* 251-273.

[6] Blumenthal, D. (January 1979). Candid reflections of a businessman in Washington. *Fortune,* p. 40.

[7] Balfour, D. L., and B. Weschler. (1996). Organizational commitment: Antecedents and outcomes in public organizations. *Public Productivity and Management Review, 19,* 256-277; Romzek, B. S. (1990). Employment investment and commitments: The ties that bind. *Public Administration Review, 50,* 374-382.

[8] Nelton, S. (December 1993). A flexible style of management. *Nation's Business, 81,* 24; Olen, H. (February 1996). Getting a handle on flextime. *Working Woman, 21,* 55.

[9] Deming, W. E. (1982). Out of the crisis. Cambridge, MA: MIT Press; Juran, J. M. (1989). *Juran on Leadership for Quality.* New York: Free Press; Walton, M. (1986). *The Deming management method.* New York: Putman.

[10] Wilson, J. Q. (1989). *Bureaucracy.* New York: Basic Books.

[11] Hackman, J. R. (1986). *Psychology and work.* Washington, DC: American Psychological Association; Hackman, J. R., and G. R. Oldham. (1980). *Work redesign.* Reading, MA: Addison Wesley.

[12] Hesselbein, F., M. Goldsmith, and R. Beckhard. (Eds.). (1994). *The leader of the future.* San Francisco: Jossey-Bass; International City Management Association. (1994). *Building teams and teamwork.* Washington, DC: International City Management Association; Katzenback, J. R., and D. K. Smith. (1993). *The wisdom of teams.* Cambridge, MA: Harvard Business School; Senge, P. M. (1990). *The fifth discipline.* New York: Doubleday.

9

Training, Education, and Staff Development

The need for enhanced investment in the training and development of public employees in the 1990s and beyond is widely recognized. Several factors are responsible for projected shortages in valued knowledge, skills, and abilities and the resultant need for training. Demographic projections of the future workforce coupled with heightened demand for professional and technical skills suggest critical gaps. Rapid technological change suggests that the knowledge, skills, and abilities of workers today will be obsolete tomorrow.

The capability of public organizations to seek continual improvement requires workers who are committed to continuing education. However, recent research data generally paint a dismal picture about our ability to educate ourselves with basic knowledge and skills.[1]

- At a New York telecommunications firm, 60,000 applicants had to be tested for 3,000 openings.
- An advertising company in Minnesota reported that 20 applicants were required to fill each secretarial position and 10 for a supply or mail clerk.
- Sixty percent of the young people applying for jobs in Colorado had insufficient skills to be competitive, according to a research study.
- An Oregon electronics manufacturing firm found that 20 percent of its workers did not have the basic skills needed to make the transition from a traditional assembly line to newer manufacturing methods.
- Kansas employers report deficiencies among current and new employees in basic job performance skills like goal setting, personal motivation, work habits, listening and communication, and problem solving.[2]

Finally, the *acquisition* of new knowledge, skills, and abilities by hiring new employees will be limited by the public's willingness to invest more taxes in more government. If new knowledge, skills, and abilities cannot be hired, they must be developed internally. Yet despite evidence that more needs to be invested in the knowledge, skills, and abilities of workers, fiscal conditions and the political climate make it difficult for many public employers to justify the expenditures.

It appears, then, that training and staff development are like other personnel functions under stress. We know they are needed; yet the conditions for making them effective, and the resources required to do so, often seem not to exist.

By the end of this chapter, you will be able to:

1. Distinguish between training, education, and staff development as part of the development function.
2. Identify five challenges to the contemporary human resources development function.
3. Discuss the organizational responses to the contemporary development challenges.
4. Identify five ongoing issues in human resources development.
5. Identify and briefly describe the three roles of the human resources development specialist.
6. Briefly describe training needs assessment, design, and evaluation.
7. Discuss the way the development function is viewed from the perspectives of alternative personnel systems.

OBJECTIVES OF THE DEVELOPMENT FUNCTION: TRAINING, EDUCATION, AND STAFF DEVELOPMENT

Organizations rely on the knowledge, skills, and abilities of their employees to produce goods and services efficiently, effectively, and responsively. Because missions change, employees change jobs, and knowledge, skills, and abilities (KSAs) become outdated, organizations must continually renew their human resources—their employees.

The most common way of doing this is to hire new employees to acquire the needed knowledge, skills, and abilities. Alternatively, an organization can negotiate with other organizations to purchase or lease required KSAs. As we have seen in other chapters, it is becoming increasingly common for public employers to contract with other employers—private and public—for both service delivery and staff work. In this chapter, we explore a third way of renewing human resources—working with existing employees to develop new knowledge, skills, and abilities.

Every organization must invest time and money developing employees. Different organizations fulfill this function to varying degrees and with varying priority. Most organizations provide new employee orientation, on-the-job training, and mandated training such as training in safety procedures and preventing sexual harassment. Others have a comprehensive human resources development plan which includes formal and informal instruction, internal and external programs, and sophisticated tracking systems for every employee. The **development function** is seen as more important in organizations where employees are considered assets rather than simply a cost of production, and training is viewed as integral to mission accomplishment.

Nadler and Nadler have identified three categories of development activities—training, education, and staff development.[3] Most often the development function is associated with **training** of employees to perform existing jobs more efficiently, effectively, and responsively. But in many organizations the development function includes more than training for short-term improvement. It is not uncommon for organizations to *educate* employees for the longer term, to build the knowledge, skills, and abilities they will need for promotions to specific jobs in the career ladder. For example, some agencies offer supervisory training for non-supervisory employees who might be in line for a promotion to a supervisory position. **Staff development** is designed to open the organization to broader vistas and new ways of thinking. Staff development aims to build the knowledge, skills, and abilities of employees to enhance the general knowledge base of the organization and to prepare a cadre of people to think strategically even if strategic thinking is not required in their present jobs.

The primary distinguishing feature among these three development functions is the time continuum. Training provides learning for current responsibilities and tasks. Much of this learning focuses on skill building but can also include understanding concepts and theories and increasing self-awareness of one's own perceptions, attitudes, thinking, and behaviors. For example, supervisory training often includes performance management as a main topic, which can include skills such as setting goals and performance standards, assessing performance, and giving feedback. It can also include learning theories of motivation and understanding one's own communication style and its impact on others. All of this learning is directed toward improving the supervisor's current responsibilities in the area of performance management of employees.

Education is more future-oriented. It can include skill building but may put more emphasis on learning that can be generalized to different situations and on preparing the individual for new responsibilities and challenges. A supervisor who aspires to a managerial position may be encouraged to continue his or her formal education by obtaining a college degree at the bachelors or masters level. A literacy program offered by an organization has specific benefits currently for the employee, but its benefits are more to enhance the overall functioning of that individual once his or her reading skills are improved.

Staff development is also future-oriented, but the future is less clear and less defined. The focus is to prepare employees for changes that are not specifically anticipated or clearly known. Employees are being asked to prepare themselves to meet unknown problems and to be ready to face a changing, uncertain future. While skill building may still be a component of this type of development, the emphasis is much more on building attitudes and knowledge that are consistent with the organization's values and changing requirements. The emphasis is also on developing the personal qualities and understanding that will enhance the individual's ability to lead. Many leadership programs fall into this category of development in which self-awareness, change management, strategic planning, visioning the future, and becoming a leader who will inspire and build confidence in others are taught.

ENVIRONMENTAL CHALLENGES AND ORGANIZATIONAL RESPONSES

In a study (*Workforce 2000*) funded by the Department of Labor, Johnston and Packer observe: "The income generating assets of a nation are the knowledge and skills of its workers."[4] As business and government come to recognize the growing importance of building the knowledge and skills of America's workforce, they realize the necessity of addressing the shortcomings that characterize much of today's training. But the contemporary political and economic environment, along with long-standing challenges in the development area, make it difficult to address these challenges. In this section, we will identify some of the challenges and some of the organizational responses and adaptations to them.

Limited Resources

As governments adjust to revenue shortfalls and stable tax bases, there are conflicting pressures, on the one hand, to eliminate training as a non-essential function and to make training a responsibility of individual employees, and on the other hand, to fit training into the strategic mission, goals/objectives of the agency or governmental unit. These conflicting responses—minimize the investment in the development function, maximize it through a link to strategic planning—create tension within an organization. Some of the tension is resolved by the nature of the government work. For example, wastewater treatment plant operators must be trained to operate increasingly sophisticated instruments. But sanitation work can be privatized, thus eliminating the responsibility for training. In another example, water plant operators have different levels of certification that permit them to handle different levels of responsibilities, and the public employer must invest in that employee to get the knowledge, skills, and abilities needed to run the water treatment plant. In contrast, either the temporary worker has the necessary knowledge, skills, and abilities or he or she does not. If not, the person is not rehired or the employment agency's contract is not renewed.

Shifting Focus of Organizational Productivity: From Individuals to Work Groups and Strategic Goal Accomplishment

The changing nature of work creates dual objectives for the development function. On the one hand, as the problems governments address become more complex, more specialized knowledge, certification, and licenses are necessary to deal with them. This trend emphasizes additional training and education for individual employees. On the other hand, the increasing use of teams as a way of organizing work creates a need for a group orientation to training. In addition, the desire to link all parts of an organization through strategic planning adds pressure to look at an organization in terms of work groups rather than individuals. Training as strategic planning, planned change, and total quality management broaden the development focus to include groups and the organization as a whole.

Training Part of Strategic Planning. Bernhard and Ingols, a human resources development executive and an academician, have commented that in many organizations the development function produces "pleasant but basically irrelevant" activities resulting from corrective but not strategic goals.[5] According to Rosow and Zager, "Today a new notion has begun to take hold—that the sole objective test of relevance for a training program is whether the corporation's business strategy requires it."[6] A recent U.S. Merit Systems Protection Board report found that, in the federal government, one of the main characteristics was the absence of a connection between training and strategic planning. The study found that training budgets were more likely to be supported when the costs were included as part of the cost of funding a particular program.[7]

Aligning a development strategy with agency goals has several advantages.[8] First, it helps to clarify budget options in the human resources development area. It provides guidance for determining how much money an agency is going to invest in development. Also, alternative investments can be evaluated in terms of how well they advance agency goals. Second, the alignment provides a framework to evaluate whether or not the development activity has actually produced a cost-effective result. Finally, it provides additional resources and mechanisms to advance agency goals. It facilitates communication about agency goals and can advance commitment to agency goals through participative and team-based discussion, design, and implementation of development activities.

Linking training objectives to strategic agency goals presumes consensus among political executives, legislators, senior administrative staff, and union officials regarding agency purposes and objectives. The field of education provides an example where this external environment impacts on the training of schoolteachers. School districts face the political reality of low teacher pay and high demands for increased quality of teaching. Building a training plan to address the strategic goal of upgrading the subject matter knowledge of teachers as well as their teaching skills without acknowledging how the rate of pay affects the quality of the applicant pool is a political reality that undermines the linkage between training goals and agency goals. Similarly, a teachers union's failure to acknowledge skill deficiencies among teachers limits ability to connect training objectives and strategic goals. Both of these issues, essentially involving personnel functions such as acquisition and development, relate closely to broader issues of conflict among values and systems.

Organization Development and Planned Change. Managers and supervisors are responsible not only for training individual employees to improve their work skills, but also for helping to make changes in the work environment so that skills are used most effectively. This process is called **organization development (OD).** It developed in the 1960s as a combination of *sensitivity training,* a focus on the emotional side of interpersonal work relationships, and *action research.* Action research is based on gathering data about practical problems and feeding the data back to employee participants for interpretation and assessment. These phases are followed by an employee-centered problem-solving process. OD is similar to training in that both are change-oriented. However, OD is usually participant-focused rather than trainer-oriented; it seeks to increase productivity by increasing employee identification with the objectives of the organization rather than by increasing employee job skills; it focuses on the process variables that comprise human interaction rather than the work product itself; and it tends to be systems- and group-oriented rather than aimed at building the knowledge and skills of individual employees.[9]

One widely used method of organization development is **team building.** Team building activities are designed to assist members of a work group to increase their productivity as a group. Typically, team building begins when a consultant is called into an organization to diagnose and correct a problem in the relationships within a department or between departments. Rather than define the problem alone, the consultant will invite members of the work group(s) to engage in diagnostic exercises aimed at assessing how well the group is working together and where the problem areas might be. Data are collected through questionnaire or discussion, then summarized and fed back to the participants. Work group members are asked to help the consultant interpret the results. "What do these data tell you about how well you are working as a group?" the consultant might ask. Problems are identified, discussed, given a priority, and then a process for dealing with them is devised by the group with the help of the consultant.

Team building is gaining more notice currently because of the emphasis on team work, as discussed in the previous chapter. It focuses on training individuals to work together in teams, rather than on enhancing the job skills of individual members. Thus, it is closely tied to a number of related trends, such as diversity training, 360-degree evaluation, team-based performance pay, and strategic human resource management.

Training in Total Quality Management (TQM). As discussed in the previous chapter, **total quality management** is a management philosophy for improving employee performance through a focus on quality and satisfying customer needs. The training function is an integral part of the TQM framework. TQM views the organization as a complex of systems, one of which is the learning system. For continuous improvement to occur, the organization and its employees must continually learn and make changes in the various systems. Employees are trained in both problem-solving and teamwork techniques, such as data gathering and analysis, problem identification skills, statistical process control, conflict management, communication skills, and group dynamics. Experiments and pilot studies are conducted as part of the improvement process for which employees must acquire basic research skills. A research study by Zeitz suggests that there is a positive relationship between the amount of training an employee receives and the degree of satisfaction with TQM efforts.[10] This may be because training leads to more involvement in TQM activities and increases the chances for successful results to occur. In addition, training clarifies TQM concepts, methods, and philosophy and thus reduces the uncertainty which accompanies all changes in operations.

As an organization progresses in its TQM efforts, additional education and development efforts are called for. Employees, especially those with managerial responsibilities, must re-think a system for rewarding both team and individual performance, must reexamine their attitudes about performance appraisal and whether there is a need for it, and must review their ideas about whether hierarchy is the best structure for the organization. A recent TQM implementation report by W. V. Rago of the Texas Department of Mental Health and Mental Retardation emphasizes the "personal transformation" required of managers in order to accomplish the organizational transformation.[11] The personal struggle for managers is to change their attitudes and behaviors in the way they think about and approach their work.

Changing Demographics and Alternative Work Systems

The composition of the workforce is changing both demographically and in terms of the number of temporary and part-time workers, and these trends pose several challenges to the human resources development specialist.

Training on Appreciating Diversity. One of the biggest development challenges for public employers in the 1990s and beyond will be accommodating administrative processes and human relations to differences in culture and ethnicity. America's minorities will be entering the workforce at a faster rate than ever before; immigrants will constitute a larger proportion of the workforce than at any time since World War I; and women will make up 60 percent of the new entrants into the workforce.[12] A generalized tolerance for differences and adherence to procedural rules simply cannot be expected to absorb the organizational shocks these demographic changes are bringing.

The nature of bureaucracy itself may mitigate some of the differences. That is, job descriptions, work goals, performance standards, and the general impersonality of bureaucracy can be expected to have a homogenizing effect on the workforce. Nevertheless, the remarks of Bellah and associates provide words of caution. They observe: "Americans, it would seem, feel most comfortable in thinking about politics in terms of a consensual community of autonomous, but essentially similar, individuals. For all the lip service given to respect for cultural differences, Americans seem to lack the resources to think about the relationships between groups that are culturally, socially, or economically quite different."[13]

It seems reasonable to think that investments will be needed in training and educating employees to understand, deal with, and even appreciate diversity. But training and education will not be enough. In some cases, organizations will have to come to grips with prejudice not only among Anglos but also among the minorities. In such cases, organizational expectations will need to be clarified, and rewards and discipline may be required to make the point that, at a minimum, differences are to be tolerated if not valued. Training in team building and in creativity and innovation may serve to reinforce and add to specific diversity training. See for example, the following training program outline:

OUTLINE FOR A ONE-DAY DIVERSITY TRAINING PROGRAM

1. *Appreciating Differences*
   Introductions and overview
   What is diversity? Why is it important?
   Differences that matter in your organization

2. *Identifying Our Uniqueness*
   Influences on our attitudes and behaviors
   Issues around being seen as "different"
   Impact of family background

3. *Understanding Diversity in Others*
   Assumptions and stereotypes
   Cultural and ethnic differences
   Gender differences

4. *Managing Conflict Productively*
   Types of conflict
   Negotiating strategies

5. *Constructing a Professional Work Environment*
   Norms and practices
   Activities and programs
   Developing effective working relationships

6. *Summary*
   Personal plan for improvement
   Evaluation

Training in workforce diversity (see appendix at end of chapter) should include several components:[14]

- Skilled instructors sensitive to multicultural awareness
- Experiential learning, including role playing, exercises, discussions, and group experiences
- Flexibility and latitude for tailoring to specific work group circumstances
- Clearly identified goals that connect to a larger organizational philosophy and effort
- Evaluative instruments to assess effectiveness
- Follow-up programs and other activities because increasing awareness may occur in a half-day training session, but changing attitudes and behavior takes much longer

Training for Temporary and Part-time Employees. With the increased use of temporary and part-time employees, organizations face the practical question of how much training to offer these workers. Since these employees may constitute a significant portion of the workforce, the financial investment could be considerable. Because these employees often are not considered as part of the "regular" workforce, their training needs are forgotten. It is not unusual for someone to be a "temporary" worker for two to three years and not have received any training. If there are too many of these forgotten workers in an agency, productivity will eventually be affected. There will be serious gaps between the competency of full-time personnel and temporary and part-time employees. There will also be a "class" distinction made which can affect teamwork and feelings of commitment and loyalty.

Training for Basic Skill Development

Public employers are no different from private employers in their need for job applicants with increasingly sophisticated basic skills. Estimates are frightening of the number of Americans whose reading, writing, and computing skills limit their employment opportunities. These estimates bear heavily on job opportunities for disadvantaged minorities.

According to the Hudson Institute, while disadvantaged minorities will be entering the workforce in larger numbers, it is not clear whether their economic outlook will improve: "The jobs that will be created between 1987-2000 will be substantially different from those in existence today. A number of jobs in the least-skilled job classes will disappear, while high-skilled professions will grow rapidly. These occupational changes will present a difficult challenge for the disadvantaged, particularly for black men and Hispanics, who are under-represented in the fastest growing professions and over-represented in the shrinking job categories."[15] They continue: "Many workers will need advanced skills simply to give them access to useful job training. For example, assembly-line workers in many manufacturing plants are learning statistical process control, a system that is beyond the reach of those without a solid grounding in mathematics."[16]

The Hudson Institute's report *Workforce 2000* paints a bleak picture, and one that makes basic skills training not only an organizational problem, but more importantly a public policy problem of significant proportions. Just as many have assumed that government employers should take the lead in affirmative action, it may be that public agencies will be seen as primary agents of public policy initiatives emphasizing **basic skill development** in the workplace.

In today's work environment, the knowledge of computer operations, especially of word processing and database management, can be considered a basic skill not unlike those of reading and writing. In this area, it is the younger workers who have been schooled early on in computer technology and are more comfortable with electronic media who will have the advantage over older workers. Unfortunately some older employees are reluctant to admit their limited skill in this area and will not seek the necessary training. Their advantage of work experience will not benefit them in an era of rapidly changing technological conditions. However, it is also amazing how some older workers want to learn new technology that builds on what they already know.

Upgrading Skills of Permanent Employees

Even though the trend toward hiring temporary employees and outsourcing work reduces the need for the in-house training of employees, it would be shortsighted to conclude that upgrading the skills of permanent employees is unimportant.

Integrating On-the-Job Training (OJT) with Other Training. Sometimes **on-the-job training (OJT)** is carried out simply by directing an experienced worker to "teach Sam your job" or "break Jan in." It is often overlooked as an integral part of the development function, especially since it is directed in each unit idiosyncratically. For this reason, there is wide variability in the effectiveness of on-the-job training. It is among the best and poorest of development activities. It is done informally at all levels most often including new employee orientation and training in job tasks, policies, and procedures. Formal programs include apprenticeships and internships. A good example of a formal progression of skill training on the job is found in many police and fire departments.

OJT can be a highly successful and highly motivating form of training because the individual puts into practice right away what he or she has learned. There is immediate feedback on the level of proficiency attained, and it often occurs at the moment that the individual needs and wants to learn a particular skill. For example, a new employee is using the computer and gets stuck because he or she doesn't know how to perform a particular function. The employee may ask a co-worker who then spends a half hour instructing him or her on that particular function.

One problem associated with OJT activities is that it is not planned in any systematic way to provide a progression of skill development at regular intervals. If conducted haphazardly, there is no way of tracking who has received what kind of training. In addition, often OJT is not seen as a part of the responsibilities of supervisors and other employees and, therefore, they are not given credit or training for performing this function. It may be seen more as an imposition by the co-worker selected to "break in" the new employee.

Besides tracking and recognition as part of a systematic approach to OJT, evaluation procedures must be incorporated so that individuals will see their progress. Human resource development (HRD) specialists can provide assistance by developing tracking and evaluation procedures, by identifying skill sets which are appropriate for OJT, and by training staff to be OJT trainers. If certain competencies can be well-defined, if instructional materials are developed, and if individuals can evaluate their progress, OJT can also be a self-paced, individualized activity with minimal supervision.

Commitment to Continuous Learning. Underpinning many innovations in the development area is the overriding precept that organizations increasingly must prepare themselves to adapt to change. They can do this by seeing themselves as learning systems, with employees serving as both learners and teachers. **Continuous learning** requires that the organization teach its employees new skills, new technology, and new knowledge. It assumes that the more employees know about their equipment and work processes, the better prepared they will be to discover problems and ideas for solutions. The commitment to continuous learning also requires that employees use their knowledge and skills to proactively discover administrative and production problems they can then help to solve. It also requires developing the attitudes of the learner—curiosity, creativity, open-mindedness, willingness to take risks, willingness to learn from mistakes, and willingness to teach others.

At first, the concept of continuous learning seems simple. No one consciously would oppose continuous learning, yet many resisting forces exist. Argyris identifies organizational norms like avoiding conflict and "straight talk" that work against questioning an agency's basic assumptions and operating procedures.[17] Managers are more likely to reward workers who solve problems rather than discover them. Further, in a hierarchical system, workers are often reminded that management has the upper hand, and improvements in work methods may threaten job security. In the face of today's external environmental pressures which require organizations to make rapid changes in the least costly way, organizational norms often do not allow for mistakes much less learning from them. Finally, history would suggest that organizations are more likely to make technical work simple and mask its complexity in order to accommodate basic employee skills rather than investing in an upgrade of basic skills so that employees could learn more about their equipment. Rosow and Zager observe, "The amount of training required to profit from a new technology varies directly with the amount of diversity of new knowledge embodied in it."[18] In sum, a commitment to continuous learning takes more than a slogan on the wall or a phrase in a mission statement; it requires a philosophical orientation that challenges many of the ways Americans are used to conducting business and government.

Coaching and Counseling: Whose Job Is It? Coaching and counseling are often overlooked as training activities and yet are done by every manager, supervisor, and HRD specialist at one time or another. Coaching involves a situation or behavior-specific characteristic that has been identified as needing improvement. Coaching is conducted in one-to-one sessions with either an outside consultant, an HRD specialist, or with one's own supervisor. The latter option has the advantage of being conducted by someone who has seen the behavior in context and who can provide immediate feedback and reinforcement for improved progress. However, because of the inherent authority of the supervisor, the individual may resist exploring the causes of the situation and be unwilling to be honest with him or herself and thereby too defensive to make any improvements. The solution may be to have individual confidential sessions with someone outside the reporting hierarchy but enlisting the individual's boss and peers to provide support, reinforcement, and feedback in day-to-day interactions.

A development activity related to coaching is counseling, a more general approach to helping the employee. It may involve correcting a particular behavior or attitude which is more person-centered than situational. It may involve career counseling to help the individual develop a plan for building that worker's career. It may involve helping a person deal with a personal crisis which is adversely affecting his or her work performance. While no one should engage in doing therapy without the clinical training and knowledge, managers and supervisors are often called upon to work with employees on a personal level. There are several points that should be considered.

Managers and HRD specialists should know their own limits and comfort in this area. A manager may refer a person to the human resource department or specialist for counseling without ever personally attempting it because it is a terribly uncomfortable situation. While it is true that referral in this case to HR or an outside referral may be appropriate, the manager will also need to increase his or her comfort level and skill in this area.

Managers and supervisors should know when and how to make referrals for outside professional help. Whether the referral is to an employee assistance program, to an outside consultant, or to another type of professional, it is important that they recognize what is appropriate and how to suggest this alternative in a way that will not increase the employee's resistance.

Department managers and supervisors should understand the human resources policies when providing coaching and counseling assistance. What is available? For which type of matters? Is training for managers and supervisors offered?

Coaching and counseling sessions should be conducted in private and, to the extent possible, confidentially. A climate of support will enable the individual to more honestly and willingly examine the behavior and issues in question.

Development Programs for Executives. This type of staff development activity takes on critical importance if an organization is to build a cadre of effective and responsive leaders who will guide the organization in the uncertain future. Often entire levels of managers are required to participate in a particular seminar or series of seminars and activities as condition of their current position or to be considered for higher level promotion. There are several advantages to this **executive development** approach: (1) Managers develop a common language and foundation by which to communicate with one another; (2) When a critical mass of managers share common experiences, organizational culture changes will more likely occur; (3) when managers attend a seminar together, they can use the time to face difficult team work issues; and (4) when the experience involves some emotional intensity and involvement, a sense of camaraderie can develop among the participants. Typical activities include formal presentations by leadership experts, problem-solving simulations, outdoor experiences or "challenge courses," group interactions facilitated by a consultant, and individual skill and attitude assessments with group feedback.

Several observations can be drawn from a review of these environmental challenges and organizational responses. Those responsible for the development function find themselves facing the same uncertain environment, pressures, and trends as the recruitment or pay specialist. In the development function, that confusion is reflected in conflicts over productivity today versus investments for tomorrow; an unclear focus on training for individuals versus groups; uncertainty regarding training responsibility for contingent workers; unclear boundaries of responsibility for basic skill development for employees; ambiguity regarding responsibility for career development of employees; and pressure to eliminate or reduce in-house development activities and responsibilities in favor of OJT or outsourcing both the agency's core work and the development function itself.

But these issues are not the only ones that affect contemporary human resource development. In addition, the perennial low priority established for the development function as well as shortcomings in the education of those staffing the development function have contributed to several recurring problems we examine next.[19]

ONGOING ISSUES IN HUMAN RESOURCE DEVELOPMENT

First, the human resources development function is usually evaluated in terms of activities and costs and not business results whether the focus is on training, education, or staff development. Furthermore, there is a continual conflict over whether limited training dollars should be spent on minimizing liability for accidents through training, upgrading of present skills, or investing in longer-term staff development.

Second, human resources development staff are usually held accountable for the design and number of programs they deliver, rather than the impact of the programs. This contributes to the willingness to purchase packaged training programs which may or may not be suited to the needs of the purchasing organization or unit.

Third, the dynamics of transferring knowledge, skills, and abilities from the development setting to the job is not well understood in most organizations. Efforts to train individuals and work groups are rarely integrated into their daily work life. Consequently, making the connection between the development function and the strategic goals of the organization or agency frequently is difficult except in abstract terms.

Fourth, the shared development responsibility between the human resources development staff and line management goes largely unexplored. Without focused discussion, little effort is made to deal with deficiencies in the performance of political appointees, temporary workers, or in services delivered through outsourcing.

Fifth, while frequent complaints are heard regarding basic skill deficiencies in workers, individual employers have little incentive to invest in that kind of upgrade knowing that workers are mobile. Similarly, while one reason for outsourcing service delivery is to cut training costs, in many cases services provided at lower cost are delivered by less trained workers—whether public or private employees.

Some public organizations, especially larger federal agencies, states and cities with accomplished development staff, have recognized these problem areas and have worked for years to overcome them. But for most of the some 83,000 governmental units in the United States, the development function still focuses on the individual employee, the short-term, and activities rather than results measured in the successful application of knowledge, skills, and abilities. Also, it is usually staffed by employees with little advanced knowledge related to the development function. In an administrative world where specialized knowledge brings respect and influence, the development function often is given low organizational priority because those who staff it are unable to convincingly add value to the work of other organizational units.

THREE ROLES OF THE HUMAN RESOURCE DEVELOPMENT SPECIALIST

Trends in the development function impact the way the role of the human resource development specialist is envisioned, independent of fluctuations in funding for training, education, and staff development. The trend away from canned training packages to training designs tailored to strategic agency goals places the HRD trainer in a more essential organizational position.

Nadler and Nadler have conceptualized the HRD specialist's role in three ways.[20]

Learning Specialist

- Facilitator of learning
- Designer of learning programs
- Developer of instructional strategies

Manager of HRD

- Supervisor of HRD programs
- Developer of HRD personnel
- Arranger of facilities and finance
- Maintainer of relations

Consultant

- Expert
- Advocate
- Stimulator
- Change agent

Although all roles must be filled if the development function is to operate comprehensively and effectively, they can be merged, and one is not necessarily exclusive of the others. The list roughly approximates the historical evolution of the human resource development function. In addition, it is clear that for development to be tied to the agency's goals and mission, the HRD specialist must be well-versed in strategic planning theories and processes.

In general, human resource development staff must demonstrate several competencies to fulfill these roles: knowledge of the organization, its purposes, and structure; knowledge of adult learning; knowledge of the relationship between an organization's culture and its learning environment; and knowledge of organizational, group, and individual change.

These competencies and the trends in the development function create a career track for the HRD specialist that requires formal management education and a consultant orientation. It is no longer adequate for the HRD specialist oriented to organizational productivity simply to receive vendors and decide which training packages to buy.

TRAINING NEEDS ASSESSMENT, DESIGN, AND EVALUATION

There are a number of practical issues connected to training that HRD specialists face. For example, when is training appropriate? And how does one design and evaluate training development programs? Even though we will concentrate in this section specifically on training programs as opposed to education and development, much of the information will be applicable to all three categories of development interventions.

Assessment Function

When Is Training Appropriate? Training is frequently used as a solution to a performance problem without considering alternatives. Table 9-1 summarizes the causes of performance problems, the preferred organizational responses to them, and the personnel activity involved.

Many organizations ignore performance problems if they are insignificant or if there is no readily apparent solution. The second response to a performance problem involves examining selection criteria to determine if they really reflect the knowledge, skills, and abilities needed to perform the job; and if not, then raising the standards or reexamining the criteria themselves. This involves a trade-off between the higher salaries that must be paid to attract more qualified people and the higher cost of on-the-job training after they are hired, plus the greater risk of losing them to a competitor once they are trained. The third response is deceptively simple, for it involves merely clarifying standards by providing orientation or feedback to employees. This assumes, of course, that performance standards have already been established for the job—a big assumption in many cases. The fourth possible solution is to train employees by giving them the job-related skills needed to meet current performance standards. Finally, supervisors may offer greater rewards to employees who meet performance standards, or initiate disciplinary action against those who do not.

TABLE 9-1 Organizational Responses to Performance Problems

Situation	*Organizational Response*	*Personnel Activity*
1. Problem is insignificant	Ignore it	None
2. Selection criteria are inadequate	Increase attention to selection criteria	Job analysis
3. Employees are unaware of performance standards	Set goals and standards and provide feedback	Orientation, performance evaluation
4. Employees have inadequate skills	Provide training	Training
5. Good performance is not rewarded; poor performance is not punished	Provide rewards or punishments and connect them to performance	Performance evaluation, disciplinary action

Some of these options are more difficult to implement than others. Changing selection criteria or rewards and punishments may be difficult, since these involve changes in job evaluation and flexible compensation plans. Because training is one of the easiest options to implement, the probability is relatively high that it will be used regardless of its appropriateness to the situation and even though it is problematic it will produce the desired results. Employers can train their employees and increase their ability to perform the work, but generally they are in for a disappointment if they think one can *train* people to expend more energy on the job. If the person could perform up to standard if his or her life depended upon it, low performance is not a training problem![21]

Before designing a training program or a series of training programs, the HRD specialist should conduct some kind of assessment. What problems exist? Are they suitable to a training solution? Then the content of the program is designed. Once the program is completed, an evaluation should be conducted to measure the reactions of the trainees and, where appropriate, the objective impact of the training on the original problem area.

Assessing Training Needs. Management may require training for all employees in a job classification without regard for data concerning a particular employee's performance. For example, all newly appointed supervisors may be required to take training in supervisory methods and delegation; or employees whose jobs require extensive public contact may be required to take communications training. This type of **training needs** assessment may be called a *general treatment need.*

A second type of training needs assessment is based on *observable performance discrepancies.* These are indicated by problems such as standards of work performance not being met, accidents, frequent need for equipment repair, several low ratings on employee evaluation reports, high rate of turnover, the use of many methods to do the same job, and deadlines not being met. In this case, management's job is to observe the jobs and workers in question and uncover the difficulties. This may be done through observation, interviews, questionnaires, and performance appraisal, and by requiring employees to keep track of their own work output.

A third type of development assessment is related not to present performance discrepancies but to future human resource needs. Nadler and Nadler would call these educational and staff development needs. For example, an organization contemplating the networking of personal computers with linkage to a central computer will need to account for the training necessary for the employees. This type of needs assessment is based on the anticipation of a future discrepancy caused by technological advances and changes in mission and strategic goals.

Designing and Administering the Training Function

Designing a Training Program. Once a problem area is identified, an intervention can be planned. Often sending someone to training is a naively simple solution. To reiterate, training can only benefit an employee who does not know how to work effectively; it should not be used in cases where employees know how to perform effectively, but for other reasons do not perform up to standard.

If training is an appropriate intervention, the appropriateness of a particular **training design** depends upon the target of the change. The simplest distinction in training objectives is whether or not the change will involve an interpersonal dimension. Traditional training methods, which are more directive, teacher-oriented, and have as their objective transferring knowledge, work best where the trainees are motivated to change, see the value in the change, and where the change can be readily incorporated into the way the employee currently performs the job.[22]

The more significant the change anticipated, the more likely it will involve rejection of something the employee already knows and relies upon. Training techniques appropriate to these situations must be trainee-oriented, with the trainer taking a more facilitative role. If the anticipated change is tangible and involves technical training, the trainer must maintain a delicate balance between getting the material across and recognizing that not all the trainees may be eager to reject what they already know and what may still serve them well.

Supervisory training is probably as difficult as any other because it involves a degree of new knowledge, but knowledge that has to be filtered through an interpersonal and cognitive screen unique to each individual. Further, there is no one best way to be an effective supervisor. Mass production supervisory training falls victim to the charge that it is activity-oriented rather than results-oriented. Results-oriented supervisory training must at some point be tailored to individual supervisors. Regardless of the goal of the intervention, group discussion, case studies, and role play are techniques commonly used to get trainees involved and invested in the learning process. By encouraging the trainee to integrate material presented with his or her own knowledge, and by reinforcing the integration through performance at the training session, the likelihood increases that training will result in the learning of new behaviors.

The steps involved in tailoring a training intervention to a specific agency or work group moves through five phases:[23]

- *Problem perception:* sensing that a problem exists because previous work methods or relationships are no longer effective.
- *Diagnosis:* defining the nature of the problem(s).
- "Unfreezing": reducing reliance on unsuccessful methods and exploring reasons why standard operating procedures are not working.
- *"Movement" or increased experimentation:* committing time and money to testing alternatives and working to reduce the forces resisting change.
- *"Refreezing":* integrating changes into the organization's natural work processes and anchoring them to reward and other administrative systems.

Evaluating Training Program Effectiveness

To be effective, training must be an appropriate solution to an organizational problem; that is, it must be intended to correct a skill deficiency. For optimum learning, the employee must recognize the need and want to acquire new information or skills. Whatever performance standards are set, the employee should not be frustrated by a trainer who requires too much or too little.

Many learning theories revolve around the idea of reinforcement. It is natural for people to repeat behavior that is followed by rewards and to avoid actions they associate with negative outcomes. If employees in a training situation are given no feedback, there is no opportunity to guide the desired learning. It is extremely important that supervisors understand the value of positive reinforcement. Supervisors are in the best position to observe performance problems, show employees the correct work method, provide feedback, and connect subsequent rewards or punishments to performance. Most organizational training is informal and occurs on the job, through precisely this process.

To justify itself, training must demonstrate an impact on the performance of the employee. By determining how well employees have learned, management can make decisions about the training and its effectiveness. The mere existence of a training staff, an array of courses, and trainees does not ensure that learning is taking place. Because development activities consume both time and money, evaluation should be built into any program.

Training can be evaluated at five levels: reaction, learning, behavior, results, and cost effectiveness.

Reaction	How well did the trainees like the training? Do they feel they benefited from the training?
Learning	To what extent did the trainees learn the facts, principles, and approaches that were included in the training?
Behavior	To what extent did the trainee's job behavior change because of the program?
Results	What increases in productivity or decreases in cost were achieved? To what extent were unit or organizational goals advanced?
Cost effectiveness	Assuming the training is effective, is it the least expensive method of solving the problem?

The first two measures of effectiveness can be demonstrated by interviews or questionnaires administered to trainees at the training site. Changes in job-related behavior and productivity results are best measured by comparing employees' responses with data gathered from supervisors concerning employee behavior or productivity. There is little doubt that this criterion of effectiveness is important. George Odiorne has observed:

> The systems approach to evaluation of training starts with a definition of behavior change objectives sought through a conscious development effort. This definition then remains a yardstick for measurement throughout the course and achievement against the stated goals is the measure of success. All other forms of evaluation measure the internal character of the activity itself, not the effectiveness of training.[24]

While training may be an appropriate solution to an organizational performance problem, and while it may be effective in changing employee behavior, it is not cost effective unless the cost of the training program is less than the cost of the problem, and less than the cost of alternative solutions. The cost effectiveness of a training program is determined by subtracting the cost of the program from the cost of the problem.

Cost of the problem are the tangible economic losses an agency suffers as a result of using untrained personnel. These include:

Equipment breakdown	Cost of downtime and repair
Salaries and benefits	Wasted compensation for unproductive employees
Monitoring and quality control	Cost of supervision
Personnel costs	Increased recruitment, selection, or sick leave abuse costs

Cost of the program are the expenses incurred in developing, implementing, and evaluating the training program:

Program development	Salary and fringe benefits for the training specialist's time spent in assessing needs, setting training objectives, and selecting training methods
Program presentation	Costs of room rental, supplies, equipment, marketing, handouts, refreshments, and trainers' salaries
Trainee expenses	Trainees' salaries and fringe benefits during training, travel, lodging, and per diem (if applicable)

Training program proposals should also consider intangible problem costs such as reduced employee morale, client complaints, or loss of legislative support. Although dollar figures cannot realistically be assigned to these costs, they are often influential in the decision about whether to hold a training program. If the training program will cost less than the projected cost of the problem, it is cost efficient.

Several factors inhibit the evaluation of training program effectiveness. The effectiveness of training depends upon how relevant the chosen criteria of effectiveness are to the development purposes of the program. While we have used the term *training* to stand for all development activities, assessing the success of activities with educational and development purposes requires a less stringent attitude toward assessment.

Nadler and Nadler point out that with training activities, it is possible to evaluate what the trainees learned at the training session and how the training affected work performance.[25] After all, training is designed to correct a work-related problem. With educational activities, the challenge is greater because the learning is designed to facilitate the employee's performance in a future job. Development activities suffer most under strict evaluation criterion because they are not specifically job related.

Perhaps the greatest challenge facing those who evaluate training is to recognize that while most development activities are delivered to individual employees, the goal is to get the organization as a whole learning, growing, and pulling together. Modest individual changes directed uniformly toward organizational goals may be highly desired yet difficult to achieve and measure.

DIFFERENT PERSPECTIVES FROM ALTERNATIVE PERSONNEL SYSTEMS

The development function is viewed differently from the perspective of alternative personnel systems. Political executives are selected for their partisan loyalty and partisan policy orientations. Usually, they receive little training prior to or following their appointment, despite the fact that many have little public policymaking experience and few of the skills required to manage complex public organizations. Because training, education, and staff development represent time-consuming investments in the future, political executives who frequently spend a short time in government have little interest in the development function, either for themselves or for those who work for them. The function takes on a special significance, however, if political executives are able to influence the selection of training consultants.

As the permanent bureaucracy, members of the civil service value the development function more than do political executives. In fact, many professionals working for public employers, like those in health-related professions, are required to enroll in a minimum number of continuing education hours annually in order to maintain various certifications or licenses.

By its very nature, the civil service houses an abundance of public-policy-related knowledge as well as the knowledge, skills, and abilities needed to translate public policy goals into service delivery and regulatory actions. The quality of public policy making depends on the knowledge of a government's civil servants. Without the ability to acquire and enhance the valued knowledge, expertise, and experience of government employees, civil service systems lose their credibility and focus as the reservoir of society's knowledge about its own problems. One could argue that as a result of major cost-cutting measures, the knowledge base of civil service systems has been seriously eroding since the late 1970s.

As we have seen during the discussion of training for basic needs, the development function is of vital importance in advancing the goals of affirmative action. The danger in the next decade is that equity gains for minorities will be lost if disadvantaged minorities enter the workforce without advanced competencies in reading, writing, and computing or if they cannot obtain these skills once hired.

The development function meets with mixed reaction in the collective bargaining personnel subsystem. On the one hand, union members value the continuous development of knowledge, skills, and abilities needed to maintain timely competencies and to involve union members in organizational decisions about work processes. For example, the National Treasury Employees Union has given a positive reception to total quality management initiatives that promise to involve union members in decision-making processes previously off limits to them. Further, the development function is connected to a long-standing apprenticeship tradition involving structured experiences designed to transform the apprentice into a skilled craftsperson. As a counterexample, because of perceived threats to job security, union members often have resisted organizational development efforts designed to improve the quality and efficiency of work processes. Training is rarely seen as an organizational priority for temporary workers or when a service is being contracted out. Temporary workers are seen as either sole proprietors, responsible for their own level of knowledge, skills, and abilities and personal attributes, or as referrals from employment agencies that are accountable for their expertise. The competence of employees of private contractors is accounted for through a bidding process where the contract itself specifies expected levels of service.

SUMMARY

Even though training budgets seem the first to be cut in times of fiscal stress, ample evidence suggests that the development function will increase in importance in the 1990s. Demographic trends and changes in technology signify there will be serious gaps in the number of workers prepared to work in tomorrow's workplace. Revenue shortfalls suggest that public employers will have to find ways of enhancing the knowledge, skills, and abilities of their existing workforce rather than simply procuring needed KSAs in the labor market.

Seeking quality requires an employer investment in the KSAs of a workforce that must become intimately acquainted with service delivery systems and committed to a customer orientation. The value of efficiency that is captured in the basic concept of civil service systems provides the foundation for government to face these challenges. However, investments in the development function go beyond traditional training and extend into the areas of education and staff development, where employers indicate their willingness to make long-term investments in their employees. In part, this depends upon whether public employers are able to view their employees as assets rather than costs and whether citizens are willing to do the same.

KEY TERMS

basic skill development
coaching and counseling
continuous learning
development function
education
executive development
on-the-job training (OJT)
organization development (OD)
staff development
team building
total quality management
training
training design
training needs

DISCUSSION QUESTIONS

1. Distinguish between training, education, and staff development as part of the development function.
2. Identify five challenges to the contemporary human resource development function. Which of the five do you think presents the most serious obstacle to the devel-

opment function in an organization you are familiar with. Discuss the organization's responses. Have they been effective?

3. Identify five ongoing issues in human resource development. Which of these do you regard as presenting the most serious obstacles to effective human resource development?
4. Identify and briefly describe the three roles of the human resource development specialist.
5. Briefly describe training needs assessment, design, and evaluation.
6. Discuss the way the development function is viewed from the perspectives of alternative personnel systems.

APPENDIX: A PERSONAL VIEW OF DIVERSITY TRAINING

TO: John Nalbandian
FROM: Carol Nalbandian
RE: Diversity Training

Diversity training is often referred to as cultural sensitivity training. When the emphasis is on teaching the diversity of cultures or ethnic groups, the assumption is that if one knows more about a different culture (for example, the behaviors, values, communication styles, concept of time, individuality versus group identity) one will be better able to interact appropriately with individuals of that particular culture. One will be more sensitive and aware of the differences between one's culture and someone else's, and will hopefully be less inclined to make judgmental and insensitive remarks to that person. I think for the most part this is true. The more a person knows about the differences that exist between cultures, ethnic groups, religions, and so forth, the less likely the person will be to unintentionally offend; and the more a person believes that these differences are just different, not good or bad, the more likely the person will be able to work with a variety of people.

However, the difficulty lies in providing information about cultures and ethnic groups. In training situations with its time constraints, information is necessarily condensed and generalized. What happens is that we are presenting information that is stereotypical — the very thing we are so adamant about not doing. In diversity training, we talk about the damaging effects of stereotyping individuals and of acting on assumptions we make about categories of people. But when we talk about Asians having a high need for preserving family name and honor, aren't we doing the exact same thing?

I have tried to approach this dilemma in two ways. One, I don't refer to cultural traits too often in my training. For example, I have presented a case study in which one person does not make eye contact with another. I say that cultural differences could be one reason, but I do not refer to any specific culture. In fact, I say that there are several cultures in different parts of the world where making eye contact would be considered impolite. Secondly, my approach is to emphasize that each person is an individual and that even individuals within the same culture will behave differently. My main point is that each person wants to be treated as an individual.

The value of diversity training is not so much to increase knowledge of different cultural or ethnic groups, but to increase one's tolerance and, eventually, one's appreciation for diversity in thought, action, and ideas. To me that is the ultimate value to the organization and to the employees. It is not just because diversity is a reality of our workforce, but because organizations need different ways of thinking and a variety of ideas to be efficient and effective. In addition, an appreciation of diversity develops open-mindedness, flexibility, and a wider comfort zone which all employees will need to survive in a rapidly changing environment.

Diversity training is really about changing attitudes more than skill building, so that it might be better considered as a development activity than strictly training. Yet, we all know that attitudes are very difficult to change; we can only hope to succeed in changing behaviors. So diversity training cannot succeed by itself. There really has to be other activities to support and enhance that appreciation of diversity. These can be social activities such as potlucks with ethnic dishes or community service projects; specific mention in team-building activities, performance evaluations, and staff meetings; informative articles in newsletters. All of these can support the attitude of appreciating diversity.

There is one type of skill building that, I believe, should be part of diversity training—conflict management. Whenever there is a diversity of people, opinions, ideas, values, there is bound to be conflict. Employees need to know how to confront issues which may be blocking the effective discussion of solutions to problems. They need to know how to deal with interpersonal issues which may be blocking effective working relationships.

CASE STUDY 1 DEVELOP A DIVERSITY TRAINING PROGRAM

You are the director of the human resource development department of a city with a population of 105,000. Your city provides its citizens with a full array of services, including police, fire, water, sanitation, roads, parks, and recreation. Your city employs some 750 employees, including 150 police officers.

Over the years there has been an influx of recent Asian immigrants and Spanish-speaking people into this city, which used to be predominantly Anglo, with about a 5 percent African-American population. Some of the immigrants are joining the city's workforce and racial/ethnic cliques are developing. Over the years, the African-Americans have complained that the police treat them differently than other citizens, and they are being joined by spokespersons for the other minorities.

The values of tolerance, dignity, and fairness were underlying issues in the most recent election for city council. The new council has requested that the chief administrative officer develop a program of diversity training to heighten awareness of the value of differences in the workforce and the community. The CAO calls you into the office and asks you to work on a proposal.

Develop a proposal that includes a plan for assessing the need, designing the program, and evaluating it. What problems do you anticipate with the training program?

CASE STUDY 2 TRAINING VIGNETES

What factors would you consider to make a decision in the following situations. Identify these factors from the manager or supervisor's perspective as well as from the perspective of the HRD specialist who is called in for assistance.

1. Focus on your present work or work you are familiar with. You have an employee temporarily assigned to your area. What kind of training would you have the person go through if the person is assigned for three months? What if the time frame is uncertain, but you know it will be at least six months?
2. It has come to your attention that an employee who is going through a divorce is having performance problems (lower productivity, absenteeism, and tardiness). What would you do?
3. You suspect an employee may have an alcohol problem. What would you do?
4. You are considering promoting a very capable manager to an upper-level position, but his abrasive style is causing problems in his working relationships with peers and subordinates. What should you do?

NOTES

[1] Gold, P. (1989). A powerful solution meets an overwhelming problem. *Instructional delivery systems.* Reprinted in R. B. Frantzreb (Ed.). (1990). *Training and development yearbook: 1990 edition.* Englewood Cliffs, NJ: Prentice Hall, 7.7.

[2] Krider, C. E., R. Ash, and H. Schwaller, IV. (Fall 1991). Adult basic skills and the Kansas workforce. *Kansas Business Review, 15,* 1-2.

[3] Nadler, L., and Z. Nadler. (1989). *Developing human resources* (3rd. ed.). San Francisco: Jossey-Bass.

[4] Johnston, W. B., and A. E. Packer. (1987). *Workforce 2000.* Indianapolis: The Hudson Institute, p. 116.

[5] Bernhard, H. B., and C. A. Ingols. (September-October 1988). Six lessons for the corporate classroom. *Harvard Business Review, 88,* 40-48.

[6] Rosow, J. M., and R. Zager. (1988). *Training—The competitive edge: Introducing new technology into the workplace.* San Francisco: Jossey-Bass, p. 9.

[7] United States Merit Systems Protection Board. (1995). *Leadership for change: Human resource development in the federal government.* Washington, DC: U.S. Merit Systems Protection Board.

[8] Casner-Lotto, J., and Associates. (1988). *Successful training strategies: Twenty-six innovative corporate models.* San Francisco: Jossey-Bass, pp. 5-6.

[9] Cunningham, J. B. (1995). Strategic considerations in using action research for improving personnel practices. *Public Personnel Management, 24,* 515-530; Gardner, N. (1974). Action training and research: Something old and something new. *Public Administration Review, 34,* 106-115.

[10] Zeitz, G. (1996). Employee attitudes toward total quality management in an EPA regional office. *Administration & Society, 28,* 120-143.

[11] Rago, W. V. (1996). Struggles in transformation: A study in TQM, leadership, and organizational culture in a government agency. *Public Administration Review, 56,* 227-234.

[12] Johnston and Packer. *Workforce 2000,* Chap. 3.

[13] Bellah, R. N., R. Madsen, W. M. Sullivan, A. Swidler, and S. M. Tipton, (1985). *Habits of the heart: Individualism and commitment in American life.* Berkeley: University of California Press, p. 206.

[14] Solomon, C. M. (August 1989). The corporate response to workforce diversity. *Personnel Journal.* Reprinted in Frantzreb (Ed.). *Training and development yearbook: 1990 edition,* 7.59-7.66.

[15] Johnston and Packer. *Workforce 2000,* p. 96.

[16] Ibid., 103.

[17] Argyris, C. (1980). Making the undiscussable and its undiscussability discussable. *Public Administration Review, 40,* 205-213.

[18] Rosow and Zager. *Training—The competitive edge,* p. 4.

[19] Robinson, D. G., and J. C. Robinson. (1989). *Training for impact: How to link training to business needs and measure the results*. San Francisco: Jossey-Bass.

[20] Nadler and Nadler. *Developing human resources.*

[21] Mager. P., and P. Pipe. (1980). *Analyzing performance problems.* Belmont, CA: Wadsworth.

[22] Nalbandian, J. (1985). Human relations and organizational change: Responding to loss. *Review of Public Personnel Administration, 6,* 29-43.

[23] French, W. L., and C. H. Bell, Jr. (1990). *Organizational development* (4th ed.). Englewood Cliffs, NJ: Prentice Hall.

[24] Odiorne, G. S. (1970). *Training by objectives.* New York: Macmillan, p. 181.

[25] Nadler and Nadler. *Developing human resources,* p. 114.

10

Performance Appraisal

Performance appraisal is supposed to play a key role in the development of employees and their productivity. Theoretically, the appraisal of performance provides employees with feedback on their work, leading to greater clarity regarding organizational expectations and to a more effective channeling of employee ability and effort.

When a formal performance appraisal leads to organizational decisions regarding promotion and pay—allocational decisions—the process becomes more complicated; it is accompanied by heightened legal scrutiny for civil rights violations and employee demands for reasons behind the decisions. Where the results of an unsatisfactory appraisal lead to disciplinary action or denial of an organizational reward, due process guarantees are invoked through union contracts, merit system rules, or possibly even through the United States Constitution. Often these legal, accountability, and due process considerations overshadow the feedback purpose of appraisal systems, forcing a formalism better suited to litigation than to management and employee development.

Even though the appraisal function is related to employee productivity and employees' desire to know how well they are doing, rarely are supervisors or employees satisfied with the process. On the one hand, in some organizations it is not taken very seriously and is viewed as a waste of time. In others, it plays a major role in the distribution of organizational rewards and frequently becomes the source of considerable tension in the employee-employer relationship. For example, in 1994 the federal government ended its 16-year experiment with pay for performance for civil service employees, on the grounds that it had contributed to organizational conflict without increasing employee motivation or performance.

In an era that emphasizes productivity improvement, performance evaluation represents the best and the worst personnel management has to offer. In theory, there is a clear conceptual link between feedback, satisfaction, motivation, and productivity. But in reality, other individual and situational variables (such as skill, opportunity, and resources) have a heavy impact on employee performance. In civil service systems, seniority-based layoff systems de-emphasize the link between good performance and keeping one's job. Most contingent workers' performance is not evaluated at all. If their performance is satisfactory, they keep their jobs; if not, they are simply released without counseling or the necessity to show cause for discharge. Finally, traditional evaluation of individual job performance in an organizational hierarchy where positions are clearly defined and the environment is predictable, loses its relevance as organizations become flatter, performance becomes teambased, and environments become more unstable and diverse.

By the end of this chapter, you will be able to:

1. Clarify the goals of performance appraisal.
2. Describe the role of appraisal in different personnel systems.
3. Identify contemporary work trends and their challenges to the appraisal function.
4. Differentiate between performance-based and person-based performance evaluation criteria.
5. Distinguish among seven performance appraisal methods; and discuss the comparative validity, reliability, and cost.
6. Discuss the controversy between traditional supervisory evaluation and alternatives (self, peer, and 360-degree evaluation).
7. Describe the characteristics of an effective rating system.
8. Describe the human dynamics of the appraisal process, including the supervisor's motivation to assess the performance of subordinates.
9. Describe the relationship of performance appraisal to the sanctions function, and particularly its role in creating a sense of fairness in an organization.

WHY EVALUATE PERFORMANCE?

Performance appraisal is directed toward technical and management goals but rarely toward employee aspirations. The technical part focuses on developing an instrument that accurately measures individual performance in order to identify an individual's strengths and weaknesses and to differentiate one employee from another. Because personnel decisions like promotions and merit pay increases are connected to individual performance, the instrument used to evaluate performance must withstand serious scrutiny by employees and managers.

Management hopes to achieve several objectives through the performance appraisal process:

1. Communicate management goals and objectives to employees. It is clear that performance appraisal reinforces managerial expectations. After instructing employees what to do, it is management's responsibility to follow through by providing feedback on how performance matches the stated criteria.
2. Motivate employees to improve their performance. The purpose of providing feedback, or constructive criticism, is to improve performance. Appraisal, then, should encourage employees to maintain or improve job performance.

3. Distribute organizational rewards such as salary increases and promotions equitably. One of the primary criteria of organizational justice and quality of employee work life is whether rewards are distributed fairly.
4. Conduct personnel management research. Logic suggests that if jobs have been analyzed accurately, and if people have been selected for those jobs based on job-related skills, knowledge, and abilities, their subsequent on-the-job performance should be satisfactory or better. If not, one might suspect defects in the job analysis, selection, or promotion criteria—or in the performance appraisal system itself.

From the employee's standpoint, the issue is fairness. Title VII of the 1964 Civil Rights Act, as amended (1972), requires employers to validate any personnel technique that affects an employee's chances for promotion. This includes performance appraisal. For this reason it is strongly suggested that personnel managers adopt one of the performance-oriented techniques discussed later in this chapter. Latham and Wexley[1] cite the Civil Service Reform Act of 1978 as providing the model for a sound, straightforward approach to performance appraisal. The act requires most federal agencies to:

1. Develop an appraisal system that encourages employee participation in establishing performance standards
2. Develop standards based on critical job elements
3. Assess employees against performance standards rather than each other or some statistical guide like a bell curve

It is interesting to note the parallel between these requirements and those applying to techniques for the selection of employees. The common ground is found in the overall mandate that personnel decisions be based on job-related criteria.

PERFORMANCE APPRAISAL AND ALTERNATIVE PERSONNEL SYSTEMS

Much of the discussion in this chapter focuses on civil service systems. Civil service personnel systems often are called merit systems, frequently confusing even government employees. Personnel systems based on merit are those where a variety of personnel decisions are based on knowledge, skills, ability, and performance rather than seniority or politics. **Merit pay** plans are those that attempt to tie compensation to performance. Performance appraisal and civil service systems go hand in hand, and to the extent they can help distinguish and document employee performance, they advance the goals of personnel systems based on merit.

Affirmative action personnel systems also have a significant investment in reliable and valid appraisal systems. This interest parallels a similar interest in the development of selection devices free of inappropriate or irrelevant judgments. This interest has thrust performance appraisal systems into the judicial arena, subjecting them to standards of validity and reliability that they may not be able to meet when preserving the essential subjectivity involved in one person evaluating another's work.

Performance appraisal systems are largely irrelevant to political personnel systems. Political executives rarely remain on the job long enough to benefit from or suffer formal appraisals. Their superiors are other political executives, often elected officials whose subjective criteria for effective job performance make formal assessments like those in civil service systems difficult to implement. Further, the higher up in an organizational hierarchy one travels, the more likely that the substance of an individual's job will be determined by that individual, with only limited guidance by superiors or the previous incumbent's job description.

Collective bargaining personnel systems generally oppose pay for individual performance and appraisal plans developed as a part of performance-based compensation. Unions prefer to negotiate wages for their workers and see individual incentive or merit plans as ways of pitting one union member against another and introducing conditions where managers can favor one employee over another.

Performance evaluation systems have little applicability to the emergent personnel systems (alternative organizations and mechanisms for providing public services, and contingent employment). First, where public services are provided by contractors or other organizations, traditional supervisory practices (setting performance standards, providing feedback, and arranging consequences) are replaced by the contract negotiation, administration, and compliance process. While this process involves many of the same elements as performance appraisal, it has a different basis in law, administrative procedure, and managerial practice.

From the public employer and employee's standpoint, formal performance appraisals for part-time or temporary workers seem much less relevant than for career employees, except for those looking for a permanent, full-time job. In those cases, the employer's interests may differ from the employee's. The employer sees little gain from investing time in performance appraisal. But the employee may see the appraisal as essential to the search for a permanent, full-time position, in that it results in documentation of performance relative to job standards or other employees in similar positions.

There is one exception. In some cases, it may be desirable for supervisors to evaluate volunteers' performance. Sometimes, this is done to "weed out" volunteers who are incompetent, or those whose behavior creates legal or financial risks for the agency.

CONTEMPORARY CHALLENGES TO PERFORMANCE APPRAISAL

Traditionally, performance appraisal has been regarded as a necessary and basic technical personnel function, even though it has never quite lived up to its expectations. It is not difficult to understand why its stature has remained secure among human resource management advocates over the years. It is difficult to imagine behavior changing without feedback. So, it stands to reason that formalizing feedback from supervisor to employee would lead employees to behave in ways their employer valued.

Even though in practice an employee's behavior is influenced by feedback from a variety of sources (most significantly from peers and colleagues), performance appraisal has usually been associated with communication from supervisor to employee. This tradition coincides with the view that organizations are hierarchies of command and control and the premises upon which employees make decisions should be hierarchically determined.

While formal appraisal systems are comfortably nested in routinized administrative procedures and hierarchical structures, several contemporary work trends challenge the utility of the traditional appraisal. These trends are:

- The changing nature of work means less commitment between organization and employee, and therefore less possibility of influencing employee behavior through feedback and rewards.
- Part-time or temporary work makes performance appraisal less important for the employer, but more important for the employee seeking a permanent, full-time job.
- Privatization eliminates the need for appraisal of individual performance, but substitutes the importance of contract compliance monitoring.
- Flatter organizational hierarchies challenge traditional superior-subordinate appraisals.
- Greater spans of control hinder supervisory observation of employee work.
- The shift from individual positions to work teams necessitates multi-rater evaluations, which run counter to many supervisors' notions of control and are technically more difficult to perform.
- Limited organizational rewards and punishments make evaluation ineffective at linking pay or disciplinary action to performance, particularly in personnel systems governed by civil service rules or collective bargaining agreements.

These factors combine to diminish the value of performance evaluation in all but traditional civil service systems, where evaluation systems are legally required to demonstrate the job relatedness of promotion or disciplinary action. Because supervisors must exercise discretion in the allocation of organizational rewards and discipline, the demand for fairness requires organizational focus on the criteria used to make these decisions, the processes used to reach them, and the outcomes or sanctions they produce.[2] In other words, procedural and substantive fairness argue for formalized appraisal systems which encourage rational judgments.

However, even in civil service systems, performance evaluation is widely regarded (in private) as irrelevant by employees and supervisors. The ambivalent status of the performance appraisal function in essence parallels the tension that exists more generally in human resource management between the values of efficiency (the flexibility to manage and control employees) and political responsiveness on the one hand, and individual rights and equity on the other. The future of the appraisal function will evolve out of this tension as well as the way we organize ourselves to work—whether in teams or individually; whether relatively permanently or temporarily; whether publicly or privately.

PERFORMANCE-BASED AND PERSON-BASED EVALUATION CRITERIA

If we assume that the appraisal function will not disappear, if only because organizational justice demands some formalization of the criteria used to allocate rewards and punishments (as it does in the allocation of jobs through the staffing function), the fundamental question is: What factors should be evaluated? There are two basic sets of criteria, *person-based* and *performance-based,* though some appraisal methods employ a mixture of the two types.

In the **person-based rating system**, the rater compares employees against other employees or against some absolute standard. **Performance-based rating** systems measure each employee's behaviors against previously established behaviors and standards. Each criterion has advantages. Person-based systems are, beyond a doubt, the easiest and cheapest to design, administer, and interpret. Many organizations evaluate employees on the extent to which they possess desirable personality traits—initiative, dependability, intelligence, or adaptability. Ratings are easily quantified and compared with past appraisals or ratings of other people or units through computerization so that the appraisal process can be completed by frequently overburdened supervisors in a minimum of time. However, person-oriented appraisal systems share the same drawbacks as trait-oriented job appraisal and classification systems—they have low validity, have low reliability, and are of dubious value in improving performance.

First, such systems are invalid to the extent that personality characteristics are unrelated to job performance. For example, organizational and environmental characteristics heavily influence the nature of a given position and, by implication, the kinds of skills or characteristics needed for successful performance. It is impossible to specify for all positions in an organization, a uniform set of desirable personality characteristics that can be demonstrably related to successful job performance. Second, the reliability of trait ratings are frequently marginal at best; two supervisors may have very different definitions of loyalty, depending on their views of the job or their level of expectation for their employees. Third, comparative trait appraisals are not useful for counseling employees because they neither identify areas of satisfactory or unsatisfactory performance nor suggest areas where improvement is needed. Since an employee's personality characteristics are central to his or her self-concept, it is difficult for supervisors and employees to discuss them without lapsing into amateur psychology and defensiveness. As a result of their low validity and reliability, person-oriented systems are not very useful for personnel management research aimed at validating selection or promotion criteria.

For these reasons, most performance specialists advocate the use of performance-based systems that evaluate job-related behaviors. In fact, person-based systems can rarely stand the test of legal scrutiny that examines their reliability and validity in relation to actual job performance. In contrast to person-based systems, performance criteria communicate managerial objectives clearly, are both relevant to job performance and reasonably reliable, and better fulfill the purposes of reward allocation, performance improvement, and personnel management research. If objective performance standards are established between employees and supervisors through some process of participative goal setting, the employee becomes clearly aware of the specific behavioral expectations attached to his or her position.

The fact that desired behaviors are specified makes the evaluative criteria more valid. That is, the job behaviors themselves are evaluated, rather than personality characteristics *believed* to be related to performance. Performance-based appraisals are more reliable because the use of objective standards enables raters, employees, and observers to determine whether or not predetermined performance standards have been met. As a result, changes in salary levels, promotions, or firings can be amply justified by reference to employee productivity. Reward allocation decisions can be explained to employees by discussing their performance objectively, rather than by arguing about the desirability of changing certain negative personality traits. Areas where performance improvement is needed can be identified for counseling, training, or job assignment purposes. The performance-based system increases job-related communication between employees and supervisors, primarily because performance standards must be altered periodically to meet changes in organizational objectives, resource allocation, or environmental constraints. In short, performance-based appraisal systems are more fair than person-based systems, even though personal qualities of employees are highly valued.

Tziner and colleagues found that performance-based rating systems produced higher levels of goal clarity, goal acceptance, and goal commitment; resulted in greater levels of employee satisfaction with the appraisal process; and were associated with greater improvements in individual performance over time.[3] Taylor and associates found that perceived fairness in appraisal systems results in more loyalty and organizational commitment to and satisfaction with the appraisal process even when employees receive lower evaluations.[4]

However, performance-based systems are considerably harder to develop than person-based systems. Because performance standards will vary (depending on the characteristics of the employee, the objectives of the organization, available resources, and external conditions), separate performance standards must be developed for each employee, or for each class of similar positions. Second, the organization may wish to specify desired methods of task performance as well as objectives. Third, the changing nature of organizations and environments means that employee performance standards may also change, and seldom at regularly scheduled or administratively convenient intervals. As a result, supervisors will need to spend more time working with employees to develop performance standards and subsequent appraisal interviews. Since supervisors are rewarded primarily for improving their work unit's short-term productivity, they may view developmental counseling as an inefficient use of their time.

Fourth, it is difficult to develop objective performance standards for many staff people or for positions that are complex or interrelated in a job series. Job-related, objective measures are more suited to simple jobs with tangible output that can be attributed to employee performance. Attempts to measure performance in complex jobs objectively can focus attention on concrete but trivial factors. Further, an employee's performance is also subject to other influences: the quality of the performance standards-setting process, the relationship with others in the work unit, and environmental factors. An example would be when teachers point out that in addition to teacher performance, student accomplishments are influenced by home environment, peers, level of ability, class size, and other factors that complicate the assessment of teachers based on student performance. Since evaluative standards are individualized, computerized scoring or interpretation of results is difficult.

Last, it is difficult to compare the performance of employees with different standards. If each of three employees has met previously established performance standards, how does a supervisor decide which of them should be recommended for a promotion?

APPRAISAL METHODS

The criterion question concerns whether personality characteristics or behavior will be the object of appraisal and the difficulty of separating the two; the methods question concerns the format or technique by which the criterion will be evaluated. Seven methods are commonly used:

- Graphic rating (or adjectival scaling)
- Ranking
- Forced-choice
- Essay
- Objective
- Critical incident (or work sampling)
- Behaviorally anchored rating scales (BARS)

Some of these techniques, primarily the first three, are more adaptable to person-oriented systems. Others are utilized primarily in performance-based systems.

1. **Graphic-rating scales** are the most easily developed, administered, and scored format. They consist of a listing of desirable or undesirable personality traits in one column and beside each trait a scale (or box) which the rater marks to indicate the extent to which the rated employee demonstrates the trait. An example of a graphic-rating scale appears in Figure 10-1.

2. **Ranking techniques** are similar to graphic-rating scales in that they are also based on traits. However, they require the rater to rank-order each employee on each of the listed traits. While they overcome one fault of graphic-rating scales, the tendency of raters to rate all employees high on all characteristics, it is difficult for raters to rank more than ten employees against one another.

3. **Forced-choice techniques** are the most valid trait-rating method. Based on a previous analysis of the position, job analysts have determined which traits or behaviors are most related to successful job performance. Several positive traits or behaviors are given in the form of a multiple-choice question, and the rater is asked to indicate the one that corresponds most closely with the employee's job performance or personality. Because supervisors are unsure which item is the "best" response according to the person who designed the test, forced-choice techniques reduce supervisory bias. Naturally, they are disliked by supervisors, who want to know how they are rating their employees. An example of the forced-choice format appears in Figure 10-2.

4. The fourth appraisal technique, the **essay format,** is among the oldest and most widely used forms of appraisal. The rater simply makes narrative com-

Figure 10–1 Employee Rating

Date of Rating ____________________

White—Personnel; Canary—Dept./Div.; Pink—Employee

Rating Period: From ____________ To ____________

___ Probationary

___Annual

___Special

___Final

Soc. Sec. No.	Activity	Class	Obj..	Employee Name

INSTRUCTIONS

Evaluate employee's performance and behavior to the degree he or she meets job requirements, taking into consideration all factors in the employee's performance. Individual factors under each trait should be designated, where applicable, as (+) high; (✓) average; (-) low. The overall mark for each trait should be indicated by placing an (x) in the applicable columns labeled Outstanding, Above Average, Average, Below Average, and Unsatisfactory. BEFORE RATING EMPLOYEE, PLEASE REVIEW YOUR RATING MANUAL.

TRAIT			Outsdg.	Above Average	Average	Below Average	Unsat.
Quality of Work	___ Accuracy ___ Completeness ___ Oral expression	___ Written expression ___ Soundness of judgment in decisions ___ Reliability of work results					
Work Output	___ Amount of work performed ___ Completion of work on schedule	___ Physical fitness ___ Learning ability					

TRAIT			Outsdg.	Above Average	Average	Below Average	Unsat.
Work Habits	___ Organization and planning of assignments ___ Job interest ___ Attendance	___ Compliance with work instructions ___ Observance of work hours ___ Conscientious use of work time					
Safety	___ Care of equipment, property, and materials	___ Personal safety habits					
Personal Relations	___ Cooperation with fellow employees ___ Personal appeareance and habits	___ Dealing with the public ___ Ability to get along with others					
Adaptability	___ Performance in emergencies ___ Performance with minimum of instruction	___ Performance under changing conditions ___ Self-reliance, initiative, and problem solving					
	FOR USE IN RATING SUPERVISORS ONLY:						
Supervisory Skills	___ Leadership ___ Acceptance by others ___ Decision making ___ Effectiveness and skill in Planning and laying out work	___ Fairness and impartiality ___ communicating problems to others ___ Training- Safety					

TRAIT		Outsdg.	Above Average	Average	Below Average	Unsat.
General Evaluation	Indicate by an (x) in the appropriate column your own general evaluation of the employee's rating, taking all the above and other pertinent factors into consideration. A written statement must be made on the reverse side of this form if the ratings is OUTSTANDING or UNSATISFACTORY on this item				*	*#

Signature of Rater:____________________________ Signature of Rater's Supervisor:____________________________

Title: ____________________________ Title: ____________________________

*An (x) here indicates loss of annual salary increase
An (x) here indicates employee must be rated again in 90 days.
TO EMPLOYEE: Your signature is required, however, it does not imply that you agree with the rating.

Date________________ Employee Signature____________________________

ments about the employee. Since these may relate to personality or performance, the essay method is suitable for person- or performance-oriented systems. However, it has the disadvantages of being time-consuming, biased in favor of employees with supervisors who can write well, and impossible to standardize. It is frequently used in conjunction with graphic-rating or ranking techniques to clarify extremely low or high ratings. But the burden on supervisors is so great that when essay elaboration is required to justify high or low ratings, supervisors have a tendency to rate employees toward the middle of a normal curve.

5. The **objective method** is a measure of work performance—quality, quantity, or timeliness—against previously established standards. It is used most often in private industry by companies with piece-rate pay plans; however, public-sector organizations are adopting a variant of this approach by measuring workload indicators. For example, employment counselors may be evaluated on the number of jobs they fill or on the percentage of placements who remain on the job after three months.

FIGURE 10–2 Forced-Choice Performance Evaluation Format

Person Evaluated ______________________________

Position ______________________________

Organization Unit ______________________________

Date ______________________________

Instructions: Please place a check on the line to the left of the statement that best describes this employee.

1. This employee

 ___ a. always looks presentable

 ___ b. shows initiative and independence

 ___ c. works well with others in groups

 ___ d. produces work of high quality

2. This employee

 ___ a. completes work promptly and on time

 ___ b. pays much attention to detail

 ___ c. works well under pressure

 ___ d. works well without supervisory guidance

3. This employee

 ___ a. is loyal to his or her supervisor

 ___ b. uses imagination and creativity

 ___ c. is thorough and dependable

 ___ d. accepts responsibility willingly

6. The sixth technique has been termed **critical incident** or **work sampling**. This objective technique records representative examples of good (or bad) performance in relation to agreed-upon employee objectives. It has the same advantages and disadvantages of performance-oriented systems generally. One cautionary note, however: To the extent that the selected incidents are not representative of employee performance over time, the method is open to distortion and bias. Figure 10-3 presents an example of a critical incident appraisal form.

7. The **behaviorally anchored rating scale (BARS)** is a technique that employs objective performance criteria in a standardized appraisal format. The personnel manager who wishes to use BARS develops a range of possible standards for each task and then translates these statements into numerical scores. To be job related, these performance-oriented statements must be validated by job analysis.

BARS are handy because they make use of objective appraisal criteria and are easy to employ. But they are time-consuming to develop, and they have not lived up to expectations because the distinction between behavior and traits is not as salient as once thought.[5] Figure 10-4 presents an example of a behaviorally anchored rating form for student performance in a classroom setting.

FIGURE 10–3 Critical Incident Performance Evaluation Format

Person Evaluated ______________________________

Position ______________________________

Organization Unit ______________________________

Time Period ______________ to ______________

Employee Objectives	*Examples of Successful or Unsuccessful Performance*
1.	a.
	b.
	c.
	d.
2.	a.
	b.
	c.
	d.
3.	a.
	b.
	c.
	d.

FIGURE 10-4 Health Center

HEALTH CENTER

JOB DESCRIPTION

JOB TITLE __Primary Nurse__

Department __Nursing Service__

Date________

Job Code No________

Job Title of Person to Whom Reporting __Head Nurse__

Pay Grade________

Date Revised________

Job Summary: A professional nurse, who has responsibility, authority, and accountability for quality nursing care for an assigned group of patients.

PERFORMANCE EVALUATION

Probationary Review [ ]

Merit Review [ ] Special [ ]

Present Grade________ Step________

Name________

Date of Hire________

Evaluation Due Date________

RESPONSIBILITIES	*PERFORMANCE STANDARDS*	*ATTAINED YES/NO*	*IF NO, HOW CAN SUCH BE ATTAINED*
ASSESSMENT:			
1. Complete the admission procedure to include	Within one hour of patient's admission to the unit, introduces self and identifies the primary nurse's role to the patient and/or the family.		
Orientation	Orients patient/family to the unit.		
Assesses the patient needs	Tentative assessment and nursing judgment, based on the patient's immediate needs at the time of admission to the unit, will be reflected in the initial notation on the nurse's progress notes and/or trhe nursing history summary		

RESPONSIBILITIES	PERFORMANCE STANDARDS	ATTAINED YES/NO	IF NO, HOW CAN SUCH BE ATTAINED
	Performs assessment within 24 hours of admission to the unit. Assessment is based on subjective and objective data which may include records, consultation, and test data. Physical: breath and bowel sounds peripheral pulses level of consciousness general skin condition and color physical abnormalities		
Completes a nursing history	Completes nursing history within 24 hours of admission to the unit and enters notation on Patient Care Guide.		
PLANNING:			
1. Initiates a patient care guide	Assures that a 24 hour patient care guide is completed within 24 hours of patient admission to the unit. This will define patient/family problems and formulate plan of care that attempts to modify or eliminate each nursing problem.		
2. Includes the patient and family in the planning of the patient's care.	Includes the patient and the family in the planning of the patient's care both initially and throughout the hospitalization and reflects this action via documentation on the patient care guide and verbal feedback from the patient and/or family.		
3. Initiates discharge planning	Describe short and long term goals, as identified by the patient and/or family, beginning at time of admission.		

RESPONSIBILITIES	PERFORMANCE STANDARDS	ATTAINED YES/NO	IF NO, HOW CAN SUCH BE ATTAINED
INTERVENTION:			
1. Performs all independent nursing functions and performs dependent nursing functions as ordered by the physician and documents all nursing assessment, plans, and interventions	Within the framework of the health center policies and procedures, and documents accordingly on the patient chart.		
2. Communicates patient's status to other health care and family members.	Communicates daily with patient and/or family regarding events of the day and current status. Provides time for questions. Communicates to personnel on her tour of duty verbal and written assignments with deadlines for completion. Communicates patient data to oncoming shift via organized, pertinent, factual walking report and updates Kardex accordingly. Attends doctors' rounds, and communicates with physicians.		
3. Utilizes social service department and resources in order to promote, restore, and maintain optimal health care for patient/family	Initiates utilization of community health resources with the cooperation of the physicians and communicates these actions.		
4. Utilizes team members appropriately; according to their abilities and position description	Establishes priorities of nursing care based on assessment of patient needs, reflected on the daily primary nursing assignment worksheet.		

RESPONSIBILITIES	PERFORMANCE STANDARDS	ATTAINED YES/NO	IF NO, HOW CAN SUCH BE ATTAINED
	Assures that delegated assignments have been completed before the end of the shift. Schedules break and meal times for team members.		
5. Coordinates patient/family teaching, based upon assessment of patient readiness.	Patient/family teaching will be reflected in the chart at the time of discharge.		

JOB SPECIFICATIONS

Comments on Work Habits:____________________

Supervisor　　Date　　Department Head　　Date

My supervisor has reviewed my Job Description and Performance Evaluation with me. My signature does not necessarily mean that I agree.

Comments____________________

________________ Signature________________ Date__________

TABLE 10–1 Performance Evaluation Systems

Purpose	*Criteria*	*Methods*
Communication of objectives	Performance-oriented	Critical incident (work sampling), objective measures, BARS
Reward allocation	Person- or performance-oriented	Graphic rating, ranking, forced-choice, BARS
Performance improvement	Performance-oriented	Critical incident (work sampling), objective measures, BARS
Personnel research	Performance-oriented	Essay, work sampling (criticial incident), objective measures, BARS

So far our discussion has emphasized that the purpose of an employee appraisal system must be clearly stated and that evaluation methods must be suitable to the evaluative criteria chosen. Table 10-1 summarizes these relationships.

While Table 10-1 points out the uses of each appraisal method, judicial reviews of discrimination cases involving appraisal instruments will be forcing more uniformity in future appraisal systems. Feild and Holley[6] report that on the basis of their research examining employment discrimination court decisions involving appraisal systems, the following characteristics clearly contributed to verdicts for the defending organizations: A job analysis was used to develop the appraisal system; a behavior-oriented versus person-oriented system was used; evaluators were given specific written instructions on how to use the rating instrument; the appraisal results were reviewed with employees; and the defending organizations tended to be nonindustrial in nature. A recent survey of 3,052 firms suggested that successful appraisal systems included written goals, supervisory instructions, senior management training, training in objective setting and providing feedback, and integration with the pay system.[7]

WHO SHOULD EVALUATE EMPLOYEE PERFORMANCE?

An employee's performance may be rated by a number of people. The immediate supervisor most commonly assesses the performance of subordinates, and this is the way most employees prefer it.[8] Supervisory assessments reinforce authority relationships in an organization and are frequently seen as the primary function distinguishing a superior from a subordinate. Because the superior-subordinate relationship itself is affected by so many factors, supervisory ratings are easily biased. Self-ratings can be employed to promote an honest discussion between superior and subordinate about the subordinate's performance. But self-ratings receive mixed support: Some studies find them inflated, others see them deflated in comparison with supervisory ratings.

While alternatives to traditional superior-subordinate appraisals have received much discussion recently, a 1989 study of Fortune 100 companies found only two organizations using self-appraisals, less than 3 percent of the appraisals were conducted by peers, and no subordinate appraisal systems were reported.[9/10] In a federal employee survey, 67 percent surveyed indicated that they should have a "considerable/great" input into their performance rating.[11] In the same group, 84 percent indicated their supervisor should have "considerable/great" input into their performance rating. Peer ratings, while infrequently utilized, have proved acceptable both in terms of reliability and validity. Peer ratings solve several problems associated with traditional superior-subordinate evaluations. They offer multiple raters who have more access to the ratee's (employee's) behavior, including a more comprehensive view of the ratee, and they are able to assess collegiality or teamwork, an increasingly salient behavior in today's work environment.

But peer ratings are difficult to sell to employers and employees. Fifty-six - percent of the federal sample indicated they felt peers should have "little or no" input into their rating. Subordinate ratings are equally rare, and their main function is to provide data to begin discussion of the superior-subordinate relationship in a work group.

One of the challenges these findings on peer and subordinate ratings pose for human resource management is that future trends in the design and philosophy of work point toward the necessity of peer and self-ratings. Working in teams and seeking quality through an organizational philosophy of continuous improvement suggest less emphasis on methods of human resource management that grow out of current assessment techniques. More emphasis on teamwork requires greater emphasis on "getting along with others," and a host of other specific team-related, personal behaviors. Any appraisal system must fit into an organization's larger system of command, control, and coordination. And if an organization retains a hierarchical orientation, anything other than superior-subordinate ratings are going to cause friction. One reconciliation is the possibility of retaining allocational decisions and formal evaluative judgements in the superior, while emphasizing the developmental role of appraisals with peer and subordinate ratings.

Nevertheless, it would appear difficult to reconcile the goals of continuous self-improvement with hierarchical control and authority. This observation, frequently made in normative statements during the human relations movement of the 1960s and 1970s, is becoming more relevant in the 1990s as technological changes and pressures for quality and productivity challenge traditional methods of organizational command and control. Table 10-2 summarizes perhaps the most important factor in credible appraisal systems—access to information about the ratee. Peer ratings stand out as the most useful in this regard.

A significant amount of effort has gone into creating accurate appraisal instruments and in training supervisors to dismiss inappropriate and irrelevant considerations when making formal assessments, and one wonders if technique dominates purpose in this area. The goal is to minimize rater bias without jeopardizing the supervisory discretion necessary in making judgments about employee performance. The difficulty in eliminating rater bias is that people, including supervisors, tend to make global evaluative judgments of others.[12] The

TABLE 10- 2 Access to Information about Task and Interpersonal Behaviors and Results

	SOURCE				
	Sub-ordinates	*Self*	*Peers*	*Next Level (Supervisor)*	*Higher Level (Upper Management)*
TASK					
Behaviors	Rare	Always	Frequent	Occasional	Rare
Results	Occasional	Frequent	Frequent	Frequent	Occasional
INTERPERSONAL					
Behaviors	Frequent	Always	Frequent	Occasional	Rare
Results	Frequent	Frequent	Frequent	Occasional	Rare

Source: Reprinted with permission from *Understanding performance appraisal*, © 1995 by Kevin R. Murphy and Jeannette N. Cleveland. Published by Sage Publications, Thousand Oaks, Ca.

fact is that supervisors come to conclusions about employees without the help of assessment instruments. Raters tend to use the performance appraisal process to *document* rather than *discover* how well an employee is performing. This probably helps account for Milkovich and Wigdor's observation that "There is no compelling evidence that one appraisal format is significantly better than another . . . Global ratings do not appear to produce very different results from job-specific ratings."[13] This leads them to assign marginal value to the expenditure of more time and money developing more accurate assessment instruments.[14]

The inevitable global assessments that supervisors make acknowledge the complexities of work, the multiplicity of factors causing different levels of work performance, the difficulty of actually describing the constituent elements of a job without trivializing it, and the critical role that who a person is influences the kind of work a person does, both its quality and its quantity. In addition, supervisors know that each employee creates an environment for the work of other employees, and to separate out individual performance artificially distorts what happens in an office.

A recent effort to meet several of the traditional criteria of performance appraisal with modern emphasis on teams, clients, and customers is the 360-degree appraisal.[15] With this method the ratee is placed in the middle of a metaphorical circle, and salient members of his or her role set become potential raters, usually with the immediate supervisor either conveying a summary to the ratee or actually gathering the information and evaluating it individually. This kind of appraisal encourages communication of the ratee's goals and understanding of organizational expectations to members of the role set, and it enhances communication with "customers," whether internal or external to the organization. These multiple views give a more accurate picture of the employee's contribution to the organization than a traditional superior-subordinate appraisal would. This approach, however, is time-consuming, may challenge the hierarchical nature of an organization, and may bring issues of trust, confidentiality, and anonymity to the forefront among peers.

CHARACTERISTICS OF AN EFFECTIVE APPRAISAL SYSTEM

Even though different evaluative methods are likely to identify the same employees as high or low performers, we have already seen in Table 10-1 that different appraisal methods are suitable for different evaluative purposes. Several guidelines follow for the effective use of appraisal *systems* by public organizations.[16]

First, it may be wise to utilize separate systems for separate purposes. It seems clear when one looks at the purposes of appraisal systems that two fundamentally different supervisory roles can be detected. If the purpose is allocation of rewards, the supervisor or other rater becomes a judge. If the purpose is to improve employee performance, the supervisor is a counselor, coach, or facilitator. The fact is that supervisors assume both roles in their day-to-day work, but the roles are difficult to integrate successfully. It may well be that different appraisal instruments lend themselves to the different functions, just as different times should be set aside to discuss allocation decisions and developmental issues with employees. Furthermore, it may be that the developmental function can be better fulfilled with ratings by peers, subordinates, and customers than by a superior who does not have as frequent access to the ratee's behavior or, in some cases, is not as credible.

Second, raters should have the opportunity, ability, and desire to rate employees accurately. Since employee understanding and acceptance of evaluative criteria are keys to performance improvement, it follows that employees should participate jointly in the determination of goals. The performance appraisal system must be job related, must allow the opportunity for interaction and understanding between rater and ratee, and must serve the performance improvement needs of both individual and organization.

Third, job analysis and performance appraisal need to be more closely related by developing occupation-specific job descriptions that include performance standards as well as duties, responsibilities, and minimum qualifications. Such job descriptions must specify the conditions under which work is to be performed, including such factors as resources, guidelines, and interrelationships. Necessarily, they will be specific to each occupation and perhaps to each organization as well. If the organization is attempting to structure itself along team lines, traditional, individual-oriented appraisals will become questionable and where present will have to adapt themselves to assessing behaviors that make teams work well.

Fourth, appraisal must be tied to long-range employee objectives such as promotion and career planning and more generally capture the employee's motivation for self-improvement. Performance appraisal is not an end in itself; nor should it be driven solely by short-term consequences like pay for performance. While performance improvement is administratively separate from promotional assessment and organizational human resource planning, both employees and organizations realize that performance appraisal relates to rewards, promotional consideration, and career planning. Further, connecting pay to performance places a significant burden on performance appraisal systems.

THE HUMAN DYNAMICS OF THE APPRAISAL PROCESS

Despite the attention appraisal techniques have received, there is no reason to believe that Lazer and Wikstrom's observation from two decades ago is outdated. They commented that appraisal systems are "still widely regarded as a nuisance at best and a necessary evil at worst."[17] Considering that feedback is essential to goal accomplishment and productivity, why were appraisal systems regarded so lightly prior to judicial scrutiny and the emphasis on pay for performance?

One reason is that not all employees are interested in productivity. When the caseload of an income maintenance worker in a social service agency is increased because of budgetary constraints to the point where the unspoken emphasis is on quantity of cases processed at the expense of quality, the individual worker begins to value his or her welfare, working conditions, and equity of the workload more than productivity. A second reason is that multiple sources of performance feedback exist in an organization, with the formal appraisal system constituting only the most visible and tangible. People in organizations are constantly receiving and interpreting cues about others, and attributing motives to their behavior. A third reason concerns the human dynamics of the appraisal process as opposed to measurement issues surrounding the reliability and validity of the appraisal instrument itself.

Douglas Cederblom has reviewed literature on the appraisal interview—the formal part of the appraisal process where the rater and the person being rated sit down to talk about performance.[18] He found three factors contributing to the success of the appraisal interview. First, goal setting during the interview seemed positively associated with employee satisfaction with both the interview and its utility. Underlying the goal-setting process is the employee's confidence in the rater's technical knowledge about the subordinate's work. Second, the encouragement of subordinate participation in the interview—"welcoming participation," "opportunity to present ideas or feelings," and "boss asked my opinion"—seemed to produce positive subordinate assessments of the interview process. Last, the support of the rater expressed in terms of encouragement, constructive guidance, and sincere, specific praise of the subordinate also results in positive feelings about the interview.

Criticism from superior to subordinate produces mixed results. On the one hand, a certain amount of criticism should lend perceived credibility to the superior's assessment. On the other hand, research rarely shows much lasting change in an employee following a supervisory critique. In part, this is because few raters know how to provide a constructive critique of an employee, and when a trait-rating form is used, employees inevitably interpret criticism in personal rather than behavioral terms. The obvious here warrants mention. Anything in the appraisal interview that produces a defensive employee reaction (regardless of the rater's intent) is likely to detract from the subordinate's satisfaction with the interview and is unlikely to have much success in altering an employee's behavior at work.

Palguta observes that while it may be statistically impossible for all employees to perform better than average, the emotional investment of employees in believing they are better than average is significant.[19] When pay is tied to performance, this investment is magnified because pay tangibly reflects supervisory judgments about employees in ways that employees cannot ignore or easily discount. The goal of feedback on below-average performers is to encourage poor performers to quit or to improve. There is some evidence that poorer performers are more likely to leave the federal government than those who rate higher.[20] But when the results of appraisals are used for allocation decisions like pay, superiors tend to become more lenient in their ratings.[21] While some poorly rated employees may leave, most stay, harboring feelings of inequity and discontent. In the federal government less than one percent of employees receive a rating below "fully successful." In fact, the majority receive a rating of better than fully successful, which is 3 on a 5 point scale. A rating of fully successful puts an employee in the bottom 10 to 20 percent of many occupations in federal agencies.[22] The difficulty with inflated ratings is that the emotional investment of workers in their performance leads them to discount "satisfactory" ratings—which carry few economic rewards—and become disgruntled and then blame their discontent on organizational factors like supervision and managerial policies and practices.[23]

In looking for reasons why appraisal systems seem to have little real effect as a managerial tool despite theoretical promise, Nalbandian has turned to expectancy theory for an explanation.[24] He argues that the appraisal tool an organization uses may increase a supervisor's ability to assess employees, but many factors affecting the willingness of supervisors to evaluate employees seem easily overlooked. From an expectancy theory perspective, raters anticipate few positive outcomes from an honest attempt to rate subordinates. Most supervisors generally know who their effective and ineffective employees are even if they cannot always articulate their reasoning to someone else's satisfaction. From the supervisor's perspective, then, the formal appraisal process duplicates an assessment the supervisor has already made. Thus, when the supervisor conducts an appraisal, it is seen as benefiting someone else. Further, research in the federal government has shown that in 1989, according to supervisory reports, in 43 percent of the cases where employees received a less-than-satisfactory rating no difference resulted in the employee's performance, 34 percent of the supervisors said performance improved, and 20 percent said it made things worse.[25]

In addition, many authors and practitioners have pointed to the emotionally discomforting outcomes, the ones with negative valences, that the rater associates with the appraisal interview. This is where the supervisor's assessment of the employee must be communicated face to face. Behaviorally oriented rating systems are designed to make assessments more objective and thus more acceptable to employees. Unfortunately, bad news is bad news regardless of whether it results from an assessment a supervisor feels is objective. When employees argue; sulk; look distraught, bewildered, or disappointed; or threaten to file a grievance because they disagree with the supervisor's assessment; most supervisors will experience such behavior in negative terms. The supervisor is likely, then, to find ways of behaving in the future that will not stimulate these employee responses. Is it any wonder that supervisors are prone to assess employees similarly, with most employees rated at least satisfactory? In fact, as we have seen already, in many organizations a satisfactory rating is taken by employees as a sign of disapproval, and the majority of ratings exceed satisfactory.

The negative experiences supervisors have when rating subordinates appear unappreciated by others. For example, in a recent survey federal employees were asked if they would prefer to change the existing five-level system to a simple "pass/fail."[26] While only 25 percent favored the change, 42 percent of the second-level supervisors favored it; 35 percent of the first-level supervisors favored it; only 22 percent of nonsupervisory personnel favored it. The more experience supervisors have with performance appraisal, the less complicated they want it to be.

In sum, while a considerable amount of effort goes into the seemingly endless task of producing accurate measurements of performance, the human dynamics of the appraisal process probably remain a greater challenge. Until supervisors experience the appraisal process positively, the underlying motivation to make appraisal systems work will be absent.

PERFORMANCE APPRAISAL, THE SANCTIONS PROCESS, AND FAIRNESS

Discipline is a formal way for an organization to perform the sanctions function by letting employees know they have violated an organizational expectation and by imposing negative consequences. Employees can be disciplined for poor performance or for inappropriate conduct. A performance appraisal is a critical precursor to disciplining an employee for poor performance, unless the discipline involves a performance incident that is a clear policy violation. Usually, if an employee gets into a fight or is drinking on the job or sleeping on the night shift, a performance appraisal is not required prior to discipline.

An employee who has been disciplined has had something taken away—a suspension involving pay, a demotion, or dismissal—or has been set on this path with a formal warning or a letter of reprimand.

With the consequences of disciplinary action as great as they can be, the issue of fairness in exercising discipline is paramount in the employee's mind. If the organization can withhold an employee's pay or take away a job for poor performance, the employee wants to know what is expected. An employee who is performing below supervisory expectations wants an opportunity to respond to these concerns (so that an alleged performance deficiency is demonstrated in fact to be valid before discipline is imposed), and a chance to improve.

A performance appraisal is essential in this process because it formally serves as a warning device, and then as documentary evidence if a third party is called upon to make a judgment about the fairness of the discipline. It is a crucial step in establishing an environment of organizational justice because a valid performance appraisal requires (1) preset expectations, (2) accurate observations of behavior, and (3) a written record that can form the basis for a discussion between employee and employer and a third party or higher up if necessary.

The struggle human resource managers face is this: How far does an organization go in establishing formal procedures, including performance appraisal, to advance fairness and organizational justice when added formality limits managerial flexibility and responsiveness? There is no set answer to this question. It is a values question that is complicated in the case of performance appraisal especially, by contemporary work trends outlined earlier in this chapter: part-time and temporary workers, privatization, organizing into teams, and promoting flatter organizational hierarchies.

SUMMARY

This chapter has identified the purposes and methods of assessing employees as well as the legal framework affecting the appraisal process. The benefits and costs of each method were described, along with the observation that while different methods may be more acceptable to subordinates, they do not seem to produce significantly different ratings of employees.

Does the appraisal process actually fulfill its various functions, or does it represent a triumph of technique over purpose? There is no doubt that the formalism of appraisal systems challenges the essentially subjective nature of one person assessing another's work or even one person assessing his or her own performance. However, as long as the distribution of organizational rewards and punishments is connected to individual performance, the formalism can be expected to remain. The desire for organizational justice and the protection of individual rights require that employees know how and why rewards are distributed and that employees be given an opportunity to appeal these judgments and question the processes. This promotes formal performance appraisal methods and processes. If the technology and design of work and the philosophy of total quality management successfully transfer the appraisal process from the individual to the work group, the formalism associated with individual performance appraisal may diminish even if the employee's demand for fair treatment does not.

Ultimately, in order to produce effective performance appraisal, for those personnel systems for which appraisal serves a useful purpose, some groundwork needs to be laid:

1. Promoting to supervisory positions people who, among their other qualifications, want to supervise and will not look upon the appraisal of employees as a necessary evil
2. An appraisal tool that has been developed with employee participation and that focuses more on performance than traits
3. Training programs directed at supervisory use of the appraisal instrument and understanding of the human dynamics surrounding the appraisal process
4. Rewards for supervisors who competently and seriously approach the appraisal function
5. An open discussion and understanding of the superior-subordinat relationship at work
6. Consequences that mean something for good/poor performance

KEY TERMS

behaviorally anchored rating scale (BARS)
critical incident (work sampling)
employee-ranking scale
essay format
forced-choice techniques
graphic-rating scale
merit pay
objective method
performance-based rating system
person-based rating system
ranking techniques

DISCUSSION QUESTIONS:

1. Describe four operational functions of a performance appraisal system. Do you think all four can be accomplished with one appraisal method? Are the four functions complementary?
2. Why is performance appraisal associated most closely with civil service systems? How has it contributed to public perceptions that civil service systems are inefficient or ineffective, in comparison with those systems based on employment at will?
3. Identify the contemporary challenges to performance appraisal. How is the tension between administrative efficiency and individual rights reflected in the appraisal function?
4. Draw up a list of pros and cons for person-based and performance-based rating systems.
5. Identify the four characteristics of an effective rating system. Why are the four so difficult to implement?
6. Utilize an expectancy theory perspective and analyze the motivation of supervisors to rate the performance of subordinates honestly and accurately.
7. Some research shows that fairness in performance appraisal leads to positive employee behavior, commitment, and satisfaction. But fairness is associated with formality, due process, rules, and procedures. Tomorrow's organizations need to be flexible and adaptable. How can you devise a fair appraisal system that is consistent with the attributes of tomorrow's organization?

CASE STUDY EVALUATING APPRAISAL INSTRUMENTS

Figures 10-1 and 10-4 present the appraisal instruments used in two organizations. Review the figures and respond to the following questions:

1. Which of the two forms is more job-related? Which type would you rather use to evaluate employees? Which type would you rather your supervisor use to evaluate you?
2. Discuss the two forms with regard to the following criteria:
   - Job relatedness
   - Cost in developing
   - Ease of completing
   - Use in counseling and developing employees
   - Use in promotion, pay, or other personnel decisions
   - Rater bias
   - Use in providing specific feedback
   - Accuracy in measuring employee performance

NOTES

[1] Latham, G. P., and K. N. Wexley, K. N. (1981). *Increasing productivity through performance appraisal.* Reading, MA: Addison-Wesley, pp. 28-30.

[2] Freedland, M. (1993). Performance appraisal and disciplinary action: The case for control of abuses. *International Labour Review, 132,* 493.

[3] Tziner, A., R. E. Kopelman, and N. Livneh (1993). Effects of performance appraisal format on perceived goal characteristics, appraisal process satisfaction, and changes in rated job performance: A field experiment. *The Journal of Psychology, 127,* 281-291.

[4] Taylor, S. M., K. B. Tracy, M. K. Renard, J. K. Harrison, and S. J. Carroll (1995). Due process in performance appraisal: A quasi-experiment in procedural justice. *Administrative Science Quarterly, 40,* 495-523.

[5] Milkovich, G. T., and A. K. Wigdor (Eds.). (1991). *Pay for performance: Evaluating performance appraisal and merit pay.* Washington, DC: National Academy Press, p. 143.

[6] Feild, H. S., and W. H. Holley (1982). The relationship of performance appraisal system characteristics to verdicts in selected employment discrimination cases. *Academy of Management Journal, 25,* 397.

[7] The Wyatt Company (Fourth Quarter, 1989). Wyatt communicator: Results of the 1989 Wyatt performance management survey. Chicago: The Wyatt Company, pp. 7-8. Reported in Milkovich and Wigdor (Eds.). *Pay for performance.*

[8] United States Merit Systems Protection Board (June 1990). *Working for America: A federal employee survey.* Washington, DC: U.S. Merit Systems Protection Board, p. 17.

[9] Cited in Latham, G. P., K. N. Wexley (1994). *Increasing productivity through performance appraisal* (2nd ed.). Reading, MA: Addison-Wesley, p. 112.

[10] Ash, A. (1994). Participants' reactions to subordinate appraisal of managers: Results of a pilot. *Public Personnel Management, 23,* 237-256.

[11] United States Merit Systems Protection Board (June 1990). *Working for America,* p. 17.

[12] Milkovich and Wigdor. *Pay for performance,* p. 50.

[13] Ibid., p. 149.

[14] Ibid., p. 3.

[15] Milliman, J. F., R. A. Zawacki, B. Schultz, S. Wiggins, and C. A. Norman (1995). Customer service drives 360-degree goal setting. *Personnel Journal, 74,* 136-142; Milliman, J. F., R. A. Zawacki, C. A. Norman, L. Powell, and J. Kirksey, Jr. (1994). Companies evaluate employees from all perspectives. *Personnel Journal,* 73, 99-103.

[16] Longenecker, C. O., and N. Nykodym (1996). Public sector performance appraisal effectiveness: A case study. *Public Personnel Management, 25,* 151-164.

[17] Lazer, R. I., W. S. Wikstrom (1977). *Appraising managerial performance: Current practices and future directions.* New York: The Conference Board.

[18] Cederblom, D (1982). The performance appraisal interview: A review, implications, and suggestions. *Academy of Management Review, 7,* 219-27.

[19] Palguta, J. (May 6, 1991). Performance management and pay for performance. A presentation before the Pay-for-Performance Labor-Management Committee and the Performance Management and Recognition System Review Committee. Washington, DC: U.S. Merit Systems Protection Board.

[20] United States Merit Systems Protection Board (July 1988). *Toward effective performance management in government.* Washington, DC: U.S. Merit Systems Protection Board, p. 6.

[21] Milkovich and Wigdor. *Pay for performance,* p. 72.

[22] Palguta. Performance management and pay for performance.

[23] Gabris, G. T., and K. Mitchell (1988). The impact of merit raise scores on employee attitudes: The Matthew effect of performance appraisal. *Public Personnel Management, 17,* 369-386.

[24] Nalbandian, J. (1981). Performance appraisal: If only people were not involved. *Public Administration Review, 41,* 392-396.

[25] United States Merit Systems Protection Board. *Working for America,* p. 20.

[26] Ibid., p. 17.

11

Health and Safety

The general topic of employee health and safety includes a variety of issues that at first may seem only tangentially related to each other. The typical public agency personnel manager's job may involve programs in any or all of the following areas: accident prevention, compliance with occupational safety and health regulations, health insurance, health benefits, smoking cessation, stress management, drug testing, AIDS and other life-threatening diseases, workplace violence, and employee assistance programs. These health and safety issues are linked to each other because they are concerned with common core functions and values.

First, health and safety are a *sanction*-related issue. In other words, these issues have become a significant concern of the employee-employer relationship because of legal compliance responsibilities and legal liability risks. The regulations of the **Occupational Safety and Health Act (OSHA),** which protect employees against agency violations of health or safety standards, apply to public agencies as well as private companies. The Family and Medical Leave Act (1992) requires public and private employers to grant employees leave to meet child- or elder-care commitments. And employers who do not have programs to counter workplace violence, or drug and alcohol abuse, risk being held liable in civil lawsuits for the consequences of these problems that result in death or injury to customers or other employees. In one widely reported case, for example, Southern Pacific Railroad was found liable in a multimillion dollar lawsuit arising from a fatal auto accident involving an employee. The employer was liable because a supervisor told an employee who showed up for work drunk to go home, rather than calling a cab and sending the employee home in it. Therefore, because the employee was following a lawful supervisory order, and because the supervisor knew the employee was drunk, the employer was responsible for damages arising out of the accident!

Second, this topic is a *development*-related issue because there is increasing evidence that healthier employees are more productive (and happier) than unhealthy ones. Preventive maintenance is necessary to reduce the cost of unscheduled downtime—not just in lost productivity but also in health care and disability retirement costs. Considering how much money employers may have invested in training skilled technical and professional employees, it makes sense to develop employee assistance programs (EAPs) that help employees manage stress, reduce drug and alcohol abuse, stop smoking, and make other positive **lifestyle choices.**

Third, because of the increasing cost of health care for employers, health and safety are an *allocation* or *planning* issue for the employer. Workplace programs to reduce accidents and injuries are important not only for legal compliance but also to reduce health benefit costs and workers' compensation insurance rates. Because healthy employees use less sick leave and have lower rates of accidents and injuries, employers must be concerned about health and safety even if they are hiring only temporary and part-time employees. Employer-sponsored health programs are not a "frill"—they are a calculated effort to reduce operating costs.

High health-care costs and legal liability risks offer employers a powerful incentive to "weed out" applicants and employees whom they consider unacceptably high risk. These legitimate employer objectives (legal compliance, risk management, and cost control) often conflict with employee rights to privacy and job retention, particularly for civil service employees with a property interest in their jobs. Do employers have the right to deny employment to otherwise qualified applicants based on invasive testing procedures that may indicate potential health problems, even if the employee is currently able to do the job and where there is no direct link of the risk factor to current job performance? Do employers have the right to refuse employment to smokers? To illegal drug users? To HIV positive applicants or to those with unacceptably high blood pressure or to those with a family history of heart disease? At what point do these employer objectives conflict with employee rights under the Americans with Disabilities Act (ADA)?

By the end of this chapter, you will be able to:

1. Discuss occupational safety and health, including the costs borne by employers for job-related accidents and injuries, workers' compensation, legal requirements under the Occupational Safety and Health Act (OSHA), and personnel policies and programs to reduce workplace accidents and injuries.
2. Explain what employers can do to reduce the problem of workplace violence.
3. Assess the impact of tobacco, alcohol, and illegal drugs on the workplace.
4. Discuss the impact of AIDS and other life-threatening diseases on personnel policy.
5. Explain how employee assistance programs (EAPs) are a response to these health and safety issues.
6. Show how drug testing, ADA compliance, and AIDS illustrate the dilemma personnel directors face in balancing employers' concerns for productivity and safety with employees' concerns for job rights, health care, and privacy.

OCCUPATIONAL SAFETY AND HEALTH

Despite the best efforts of government and industry to improve environmental, health, and safety performance, major industrial accidents are just as likely to occur today as they were ten years ago. Yet over the same period, society's expectations for environmental health and safety management have risen.[1] Prevention of work-related accidents is of primary concern to public personnel managers. In addition to the personal pain and suffering caused by these incidents, they are also significant because of associated organizational costs. These include not only the direct cost of reduced productivity but also the hidden costs of sick leave, employer insurance payments (for disability and worker's compensation policies), and the costs of processing or contesting disability retirement and workers' compensation claims. These costs represent billions of dollars annually. Moreover, some government employees (police officers and firefighters) receive occupational injuries and disability retirements at more than three times the rate of employees in other jobs.

Workers' Compensation

Workers' compensation is a system established within each state to compensate employees for job-related injuries and illnesses. These systems were developed early this century because of dissatisfaction with the previous practice of discharging injured employees without any employer responsibility for treatment or rehabilitation, or of relying on the civil litigation system to recompense employees for the costs of accidents or injuries. Workers' compensation is an insurance system with variable payment rates for employers based on the historical risks of accident or injury their employees have suffered. Employers may self-insure, buy private insurance, or seek universal coverage through a publicly chartered insurance agency in each state. The agency pays death benefits, hospitalization expenses, and expenses for a caregiver if an employee is injured or permanently disabled on the job. It reimburses employees on an actual cost basis, based on decisions rendered by an administrative hearing body that decides whether the injury or illness is job related, and what compensation from the fund is to be awarded for it.

While the workers' compensation system has worked fairly well, it does have problems. First, there is ample opportunity for fraud and abuse by employees, attorneys, and doctors. Second, there is increasing pressure on the system from psychological and environmental illnesses (such as depression), or from stress-related illnesses (stroke, heart attack) where it is difficult to separate the effect of job stress from other stressors. Third, increasing workers' compensation costs lead to increased insurance rates paid by employers. In some highly dangerous jobs in the private sector, such as roofing, workers' compensation costs may be as high as wages. These high costs have led employers to hire independent contractors rather than employees, in order to reduce payroll costs. Unlike employees, independent contractors are supposed to provide their own insurance for work-related injuries or illnesses. But in reality, many do not have any coverage. In the public sector, they are a primary reason why employers might wish to contract out fire and rescue services, or law enforcement, to another public agency.

These problems have led to efforts to reform the worker's compensation system in many states. Typical reforms include substitution of light-duty positions for full-time **disability**, on the theory that paying an employee who can work productively in a light-duty position is better than paying temporary or permanent disability benefits to that employee, and hiring another to take his or her place. Or states may seek to tighten the laws by restricting the award of benefits to employees with stress-related or repetitive strain injuries.

The Occupational Safety and Health Act of 1970

The cost of work-related injuries and illnesses, and their social consequences, led the federal government to pass legislation regulating private and public employers. The Occupational Safety and Health Act (OSHA) was passed in 1970 to ensure that working conditions for all Americans meet minimum health and safety standards.[2] Under the provisions of this act, the **Occupational Safety and Health Administration (OSHA)** in the Department of Labor was charged with setting health and safety standards, inspecting public agencies, and levying citations and penalties to enforce compliance.

While most of the OSHA regulations apply to industrial plants and private industry, many regulations apply to government agencies as well. Typical regulations for office buildings include standards for number and size of entrances, lighting, ventilation, fire protection, and first-aid facilities. While public agencies operating under civil service or political personnel systems are generally not subject to fines, they are subject to administrative sanctions like letters of reprimand.

The Occupational Safety and Health Act does not establish standards for state and municipal agencies. Instead, it gives states the option of complying with established federal standards or of establishing and enforcing standards through a designated state agency. Most states have chosen the option of designating a state agency to administer the plan. If this second option is chosen, the state must develop standards at least as effective as those promulgated by the Occupational Health and Safety Administration under federal regulations, must staff the agency with qualified employees, and must submit required reports on agency compliance to the Department of Labor.

Improving Workplace Health and Safety

Correction of unsafe or unhealthy working conditions is a legal requirement. But it is also a desirable policy to protect employees and their continued productivity. Public personnel managers can exert great influence on occupational health and safety, including the following: correction of unsafe facilities and workplace conditions, designing jobs to make them safer, conducting employee orientation and training programs procedures, and providing feedback and incentive systems for employees and supervisors.

Together with facilities managers and safety engineers, personnel directors and risk managers can *correct unsafe facilities or working conditions* reported by employees or supervisors. If other managers object to the cost and inconvenience of safety regulations, the personnel director can provide them with information on the costs of noncompliance in terms of job-related injuries, workers' compensation insurance rates, and grievances.

In many cases, high rates of injury and illness are due to *faulty job design.* A job that is alternately boring and stressful, or a job that requires the use of dangerous equipment, increases the risk to the employee. Perhaps the personnel department can redesign the work procedure to reduce these factors. For example, many nurses are physically unable to lift and move heavy patients, so hospitals have assigned this duty to male nurses' aides or orderlies. Yet hospitals are frequently understaffed, particularly on the night shift, so nurses often end up doing this themselves. The result can be a disabling back injury. This situation could be prevented by greater recognition of the costs of *not* filling nurses' aide positions, or by redesigning the nurse's job to not include lifting heavy patients.

Ergonomics is the design of jobs and tools to fit human physiological and psychological needs. The issue has become an important one because the incidence of so-called "repetitive strain injuries"—work-related illnesses due to repeated motion, vibration or pressure—has increased rapidly over the past ten years, from 50,000 to 300,000 cases annually.[3] The worst jobs are in meatpacking and poultry processing plants, garment manufacturing, and automobile repair. But many injuries are caused by common office equipment such as computers and video display terminals. In response, many companies have started training programs in how to use computers so as to avoid carpal tunnel syndrome or eyestrain. But OSHA's role in measuring and preventing these types of injuries is also disputed by some business interests, who fear that implementation of regulatory standards for repetitive strain injuries would prohibitively increase the cost of doing business.

The growth of *training and orientation programs* as a means of increasing employee health and safety is an outgrowth of risk management. These programs should contain information on work safety, potentially hazardous conditions that may be encountered on the job, emergency evacuation procedures, the location of fire extinguishers and alarms, and procedures for reporting job-related injuries or illnesses. This will reinforce the importance of health and safety for supervisors and employees. It will also minimize the employer's financial and legal liability for workplace injuries and accidents. If employees have read and signed policies for reporting accidents, they will be ineligible for disability benefits based on claims of accidents or injuries that were not reported at the time.

Training programs need to be comprehensive yet specific to the job:[4] It is no coincidence that employees in high-risk occupations such as public safety and health are required to undergo the most training. For example, firefighters who are also qualified as paramedics need technical training in both fields, and training to improve their ability to provide complex services in a multi-ethnic urban environment.[5] And illiterate employees cannot be expected to properly use equipment or supplies, even if they are provided with explicit written instructions for their safe use.[6]

However, training by itself is not as effective as training combined with *feedback and incentive programs* that reward employees and supervisors for safety. Over the past twenty years, repeated results have shown that reward programs for such safety behaviors as use of seat belts and mandatory protective equipment are effective at increasing safe work practices.[7] Since most local governments are self-insured, it makes sense to pass on some of the savings from safety to responsible employees through incentive programs. For example, some cities award savings bonds to employees whose job duties require the use of a city car, and who drive for a year or more without any chargeable accidents (those attributable to traffic violations).

It is important to reward not only employees for safe work habits but also their supervisors for recognizing, evaluating, and controlling occupational health and safety hazards. This means publicizing the agency's record of time lost through work-related accidents or injuries, comparing this with other work units or over time, and using compensation and disability payouts as one measure of the supervisor's performance evaluation. Granted, supervisors cannot control all the unsafe conditions inherent in a job. But they can work with employees on safer ways of handling jobs, and with top management on ways of designing work so that it can be performed with less risk to employees.

WORKPLACE VIOLENCE

Ours is a violent society, and it is not surprising that this violence carries over into the workplace. Most of us are aware of recent mass murders in such diverse workplaces as a fast food restaurant in San Diego, post offices in Michigan and Oklahoma, and a cafeteria in Killeen, Texas. In 1993 the Bureau of Labor Statistics counted 1,063 workplace homicides in the United States: this is 14 percent of all worker deaths, more than those caused by any other factor except vehicular accidents or being struck by falling objects.[8] Of this number, 106 are classified as involving "work associates."[9] Much more common, however, are non-lethal assaults. Some estimates indicate that there are more than 2 million physical assaults in the workplace every year.[10] In 1992 it is estimated that more than 22,000 work-related violent incidents occurred that required the victim to spend one or more days away from work.[11]

Workplace violence is particularly harmful to women. Homicide in the workplace was the greatest cause of death among female workers from 1980 to 1985.[12] A report done by the **National Institute for Occupational Safety and Health (NIOSH)** found that homicides accounted for 12 percent of the workplace deaths among men, and 42 percent of the workplace deaths among women.[13] Some of the workplace violence can be attributed to domestic violence: Husbands and boyfriends commit 13,000 acts of violence against women in the workplace every year. Abusive husbands and lovers harass 74 percent of employed battered women at work—either in person or over the telephone—causing 56 percent of them to be late at least five times a month, 28 percent to leave early at least five days a month, and 54 percent to miss at least three full days of work a month.[14] The cost for **domestic violence** alone in lost productivity, increased health-care costs, absenteeism and workplace violence is estimated to be $3 billion to $5 billion annually.[15]

Beyond these costs, workplace violence has a less measurable impact on employee stress and organizational climate. For example, the recent rash of violent incidents involving disgruntled postal service workers has caused employees and managers to be concerned about organizational effects. Organizations which are already working to establish principles of objectivity and fairness as part of alternative dispute resolution procedures under a workplace diversification program, will find these efforts undermined by workplace violence or the threat of it.

Employers' Legal Liability for Employee Violence

Yet employers are reluctant to get involved with workplace violence because they fear that if they are aware that an employee is being abused and they do nothing they will be sued.[16] The traditional theory under which employers have been held liable is the doctrine of *respondeat superior:* The employer can be held "vicariously" liable for the violent actions of its employees as long as (1) the employee is acting within the scope of his employment, (2) the employee is authorized by the employer, or (3) the employer ratified the employee's actions subsequent to the occurrence.[17] And more recently, courts have held that employers may be liable to victims under the theory of negligent hiring, retention, and referral. Under these theories, courts have established that there is a duty that the employer owes its employees, customers, suppliers, and other individuals who come in contact with its employees. For example, an employer can be held liable for acts of violence committed by current or former employees: for (1) **negligent hiring** if it failed to verify references or employment gaps which could indicate the applicant had spent time in prison; (2) **negligent retention** if it is aware that an employee has dangerous or violent tendencies but takes no action to reclassify or discharge the employee; or (3) **negligent referral** for terminating an employee for violent behavior and then failing to disclose the violent behavior to prospective employers during reference checks, or provides a positive letter of recommendation to the employee. To establish employer liability, a victim generally must show that the employer breached the duty it owed to the victim and the employer's breach of that duty "caused" the victim's injury.[18] The principal means of limiting or expanding employer liability for negligent hiring and retention claims is the requirement of foreseeability. The stronger the connection between the information known or available to the employer and the harm ultimately suffered, the greater the likelihood that the employer will be found liable in negligence.

Employers who attempt to screen job applicants for violent tendencies run the risk of violating applicants' civil rights. For example, Title VII of the 1964 Civil Rights Act prohibits employers from refusing employment or discharging employees based on (1) an arrest record (since an arrest is not a conviction); or (2) a criminal conviction[19] unless the prospective employer can establish that the conviction would indicate that the applicant poses "a substantial and foreseeable threat to the safety of individuals or property."[20]

Liability issues are not limited to the hiring process. Employers who attempt to discharge an employee for violent outbursts, threatening staff, or demonstrating odd and erratic behavior can also be sued under the Americans with Disabilities Act (ADA). Under this law, employees who exhibit these behaviors may have a legally protected disability, for which the employer is expected to make a reasonable accommodation prior to considering termination. And labor lawyers indicate that it can be difficult to distinguish bad behavior from a protected mental disability.[21]

What Precautions Should Employers Take to Prevent Violence?

What are some of the precautions that employers can take to protect themselves and their employees from workplace violence? First, employers should examine hiring policies and procedures to be sure that information about gaps in employment, disciplinary action from former employers, use of illegal drugs, and previous criminal convictions are available to those making a hiring decision. References should be checked with at least two prior employers documenting everything said about the prospective employee in the event they were not disclosing all the relevant facts. A criminal background check may be worthwhile depending on the position.

Second, employers should understand that the most important step is to prevent violence among current employees by working to create an employee culture that makes violence unthinkable. The characteristic profile of the violence-prone employee is a middle-aged white male, with five to fifteen years' seniority, who collects guns and has few social ties.[22] Yet many nonviolent employees also fit this profile. The best response, therefore, is to take verbal and physical violence seriously, and to establish a "zero tolerance" policy, one which establishes consequences for the perpetrator. An employer who moves immediately to stop dangerous behavior at the first instance, cannot be faulted for allowing it to continue past the point at which when a reasonable person might conclude that the violence-prone employee was placing co-workers or clients at risk. Furthermore, it is almost always easier to discipline or separate an employee for misconduct than it is for poor performance.

Personnel directors should be aware of the link between workplace violence and a deteriorating climate. If the management style of the company allows people to communicate freely with each other and with management, threats will be reported more readily and agency values will be transmitted more clearly. Particularly in a paternalistic agency where employees have come to expect that they will be taken care of, workplace violence is often the result of layoffs or downsizing. Yet if employees feel protected, appreciated, and respected, there is less chance that they will become violent. If management meets with each employee, potential violence can be prevented and the downsizing process somewhat humanized if the manager has the opportunity to explain and clarify the company's actions. For example, companies that use layoff criteria that de-emphasize recent performance in favor of long-term performance history will find that they eliminate many rationalized motives for disruptive behavior.[23]

Supervisors should be trained in how to handle verbal violence. The best form of prevention is to remain calm and decide on the best course of action, listening carefully and being interested in what the angry person is saying. The objective is to let the angry person calm down and lead him or her to focus more on facts rather than opinions or personality dynamics.

Employers should consider establishing a "threat management team" comprising legal staff, security personnel, the personnel director, psychological experts, and employee assistance workers to respond to threats of violence or an actual incident.[24] Special care should be taken when it is necessary to terminate an employee for threats or violence: The termination should be conducted in private with at least two supervisors present; security should be immediately available yet unobtrusive; the last paycheck should be provided by mail so that the discharged employee is not required to return to the premises after termination; and an employee should be designated to work with the employee on such post-termination issues as accrued leave benefits and unemployment compensation.[25]

TOBACCO, ALCOHOL, AND ILLEGAL DRUGS

Tobacco, alcohol, and other drugs are widely used in our society. Because workplace policies on drug use involve basic conflicts between individual rights to privacy and employer concerns with productivity and health-care costs, it is important to examine three critical areas of research: effects of drugs in the workplace, legal requirements for employers, and recommended workplace policies and practice.

Effects on Health, Safety, and Productivity

Thirty years ago, smoking was considered a personal habit rather than a workplace policy issue. Today, most public employers ban smoking in the workplace because it is considered a violation of employees' right to a safe and healthy workplace.[26] Research has shown that smoking is linked to increased risk of cancer, heart attacks, and strokes. Smoking costs employers $25.8 billion in productivity each year, including costs for medical care, absenteeism, premature retirement, and early death.[27] According to a 1982 study, excess insurance costs for each smoker average $247 to $347 annually.[28]

The cost of alcohol abuse is high, measured in impaired performance, absenteeism, injuries, and fatalities. The National Institute on Alcohol Abuse and Alcoholism estimates alcohol abuse results in a yearly $117 billion loss in productivity along with $13 billion in employee rehabilitation expenses.[29] The Institute concluded that alcoholism accounts for about 105,000 deaths each year, and an estimated $136 billion in lost employment, reduced productivity, and health-care costs in 1990.[30] Alcohol abuse increases liability risks for employers because of the increased chance of performance impairments that will affect customers, coworkers, or the public. Also, employees do not like to work with alcohol abusers because this tends to reduce their own morale and productivity.

Drug abuse is a serious public health problem, and the workplace is obviously not immune from its effects.[31] The National Clearinghouse for Drug and Alcohol Abuse estimates that drug abuse costs U.S. employers $7.2 billion per year in productivity losses. A large-scale longitudinal study of 5,465 postal employees found higher rates of absenteeism and turnover for employees who tested positive for drugs (59.3 percent and 47 percent, respectively).[32] One Fortune 500 company released profiles of the typical drug abuser indicating that, in comparison with the typical employee, this person functions at about 67 percent of potential, is 3.6 times as likely to be involved in an accident, receives three times the average level of health-care benefits, is five times as likely to file a compensation claim and more likely to file grievances, and misses more that ten times as many workdays.[33] Substance abuse also results in higher health insurance costs for employers—as much as 170 percent in three years for several major plans.[34]

However, because general population drug use estimates are not valid indicators of employee drug use, there is also considerable controversy over the nature and severity of employee drug abuse. Alcohol is the drug of choice at the workplace, followed by marijuana. A large sample of high school graduates indicated that in 1991, 8 percent of women and 5 percent of men have used alcohol on the job. The next most abused drug is marijuana with 5 percent of the men and 1 percent of the women reporting using marijuana while at work. All other drugs (amphetamines, barbiturates, and cocaine) are used by less than 1 percent of the surveyed employees.[35] Men have higher rates of drug and alcohol use than women; and drug use is highest for young adults.

Therefore, there is little support for concluding that drug and alcohol abuse is rampant in the workplace.[36] A large survey conducted the by National Institute of Mental Health found that casual drug use does not normally influence work performance.[37] However, there is likely to be significant underreporting of drug-related accidents as twenty states deny any compensation claim if drug or alcohol use is present.[38]

Legal Requirements for Employers

Tobacco and alcohol are legal drugs. However, most employers ban smoking in the workplace because of the health and liability issues raised by secondhand smoke. Intoxication by alcohol or illegal drugs is illegal for federal agencies or contractors under Executive Order 12564 (Drug Free Federal Work Place).

Enforcement of policies banning alcohol and illegal drugs in public agencies raises legal questions, primarily constitutional rights to privacy and against self-incrimination. In the past, courts have routinely upheld **drug testing** for cause, when there was evidence of impaired performance or misconduct. In deciding whether drug testing of employees without such evidence represents an unreasonable search, courts must balance the degree to which the search is an intrusion upon the individual's privacy rights, and the degree to which the search reflects a legitimate government interest. Several Supreme Court decisions clarify its thinking concerning this balance. In ***National Treasury Employees Union v. von Raab*** (1988), it upheld the government's right to require drug testing for customs agents carrying guns and seizing drugs. In ***Samuel Skinner v. Railway Labor Executives' Association*** (1988), the Court upheld mandatory post-accident testing of railroad workers on grounds that this was a closely regulated industry where the government had a responsibility to protect public safety. In three cases other cases (*Guiney v. Roache* [1989], *Policemen's Benevolent Association v. Washington Township* [1989], and *Clarence E. Paten v. United States* [1990]), the Court upheld random testing of police and corrections officials on grounds of public safety—these are reasonable actions by the employer to substantially protect or benefit society.

The **Omnibus Transportation Employee Testing Act of 1991** requires drug and alcohol testing of employees required to have commercial driver's licenses (including drivers of trash trucks, dump trucks, buses, and street sweepers), among others. Several types of testing are required under guidelines issued by the U.S. Department of Transportation: pre-employment testing of all applicants, post-accident ("critical incident") testing for all employees involved in an accident, random testing of a specified percentage of the workforce annually, and "reasonable suspicion"—testing of employees who appear to be under the influence of alcohol or drugs. It took effect for some public and private employers on January 1, 1995, and for all others a year later.

Workplace Policies and Programs

Sixteen states and more than 340 localities require at least some *smoking restrictions* in private businesses; thirty-two states regulate smoking by public employees in the workplace.[39] In some cases, employers may forbid employees to smoke because of the increased health-care costs and liability risks that smokers impose on co-workers and on their employer. For example, many municipal fire departments are refusing to hire smokers as firefighters because smoking increases the likelihood that firefighters will subsequently be eligible for workers' compensation or disability retirement based on heart or lung disease. In 1994, the city of North Miami (Florida) won a state supreme court case prohibiting any new employee from smoking, on similar grounds of increased health-care costs. Usually, an exploratory survey by the personnel department to assess employee attitudes toward smoking will show that relatively few people smoke, and that many who do are willing to limit their use of tobacco on the job. A 1985 Gallup poll found that 80 percent of smokers, 92 percent of nonsmokers, and 89 percent of former smokers feel company policies should designate specific nonsmoking and smoking areas or ban smoking altogether. Employee cooperation with smoking policies can best be achieved by managerial compliance with the policies, union involvement, the availability of **smoking cessation programs** offered by the employer, and passing some of the savings along to nonsmoking employees in the form of lower health insurance premiums or health benefit costs. In cases where consensus and voluntary compliance are ineffective, it is sometimes necessary for the agency to discipline employees who violate no-smoking policies or to defend its no-smoking policies in court.

Given the lack of consensus on the magnitude of illegal drug and alcohol use as a workplace problem, there is considerable disagreement on the appropriateness of drug testing as a workplace policy response.[40] Critics argue that drug testing is costly, requires elaborate and complex procedures to ensure integrity, violates employee privacy and has not been causally linked to a reduction in drug use.[41] In addition, drugs do not necessarily have an adverse effect on job performance—the only drug for which a correlation between presence and impairment has been conclusively demonstrated is alcohol.[42] Given the privacy and self-incrimination issues raised by random drug testing, it may be useful to consider alternatives that more directly assess employee performance. Written tests are more effective and reliable than urinalysis testing, particularly at revealing information about drug history or employee involvement in drug sales.[43] Computer tests that measure hand-eye coordination are indicators of employee impairment, which is the critical variable in terms of the effects of drugs on job performance. Skills testing is another technique that can detect drug abuse.[44]

The ultimate solution in the eyes of many authorities is education and changing the norms and values of the workplace. The descriptive literature provides information on a variety of drug and alcohol abuse education programs. The elements of an effective program include cultivating a shared responsibility between labor and management for reducing drug and alcohol abuse, a comprehensive drug education and awareness program, supervisor training on identifying drug use, clear employee policies on drug and alcohol abuse, a fully functioning EAP, and a focused and limited drug and alcohol testing program.

AIDS

Acquired Immune Deficiency Syndrome (AIDS) was first reported in the United States in 1981. It is currently estimated that 1.5 million people carry **HIV** (the **human immunodeficiency virus** that causes AIDS). Although there is an increasing rate of heterosexual transmission, HIV has been transmitted primarily by unsafe homosexual practices, needle sharing by intravenous drug addicts, and transfusions of blood from infected donors. AIDS is a progressive disease. Infected individuals fall into four categories: (1) those who have been exposed to the virus but display no physical symptoms beyond testing HIV positive (HIV+); (2) those who experience some AIDS-related symptoms (such as night sweats, weight loss, swollen lymph nodes, or fatigue); (3) those who have developed opportunistic infections but do not require hospitalization and are physically able to work; and (4) those who are weakened by multiple infections (and are thus unable to work and may require hospitalization). Although there are drugs that will slow its advance or prevent those carrying the virus from developing symptoms of the disease itself, the disease is invariably fatal once the victim's immune system has been destroyed.

The health-care costs of AIDS are enormous. Early studies estimated a cost of $61,000 to $94,000 per person from onset to death, but these figures were based on a brief life span from onset to death (one to three years), and extensive use of volunteer patient care providers from within the gay community. As HIV is detected earlier, and patients survive longer, life span estimates have now increased to seven to ten years. And the magnitude of the AIDS epidemic has increased far beyond the abilities of volunteer social service agencies to provide treatment. This means that health-care providers must be increasingly used at a far greater cost.[45]

AIDS is a workplace problem for two distinct groups of employees. The group that runs the greatest risk of contracting HIV are the health-care workers (doctors, dentists, nurses, dental hygienists, laboratory technicians, paramedics) whose jobs involve working with the body fluids of HIV+ patients. There is a *very slight* chance that one of these workers can become infected through an accidental needle stick from a syringe containing blood from an infected person, or by blood from an infected person entering the employee's bloodstream through a cut.

Although patients may have a strong reaction to being treated by an HIV+ health-care worker, there is no evidence that the AIDS virus can be transmitted *if* the employee is following the safety precautions required by hospitals and other agencies to prevent the spread of blood borne diseases. However, there is a possibility that other opportunistic infections to which the AIDS victim is susceptible may be transmitted from employees to patients through workplace contact, especially to patients whose immune systems may be weakened by the conditions for which they are hospitalized.

The second group is composed of those who have HIV+ employees among their co-workers. While these employees are in no danger of contracting HIV from a co-worker under normal working conditions, the fear and denial that AIDS generates among employees and their families can cause the issue to give rise to serious personnel problems.[46] For example, employees (or their union representatives) might demand that HIV+ employees be identified and isolated or discharged so as to prevent them from infecting others, even if there is no chance of the infection being transmitted in the ordinary course of job duties. Employees with the HIV virus might demand confidentiality and the right not to be discriminated against in personnel actions as long as they can continue to do their jobs.

Thus, AIDS generates increased concern among employers about liability risks and employee productivity. But these are relatively simple issues to address, at least in theory. Liability risks for contracting the HIV virus can be minimized or eliminated (for that small group of employees whose jobs require it) by developing protective policies to eliminate the risk of exchanging body fluids. Liability issues for other positions can be dealt with by educating employees about the remote possibility of contracting the HIV virus in the workplace. Concerns for productivity can be met by developing clear policies designed to determine whether an HIV carrier can perform the duties of the position. The desired outcome is a balanced approach reflecting the employer's desire to make reasonable accommodation to the HIV+ employee while this person is still healthy enough to perform the primary duties of the position, and to clarify policies with respect to sick leave, **disability retirement,** and dependent benefits once the person is forced by failing health to leave the workforce.

But tremendous pressure is being exerted on employers by the health insurance industry. Obviously, although this is a clear violation of the ADA, it is in their best interest to identify carriers of the virus that causes AIDS prior to employment, and to have AIDS or AIDS-related diseases excluded from coverage as preexisting conditions. Similarly, it is in the employer's best interest to do this if the agency is self-insured. Some employers who would want to treat AIDS as an exclusionary precondition may also discriminate against homosexuals in hiring on the basis that they are members of a high-risk group. These pressures cause a fundamental conflict between the values of individual rights (for AIDS victims, homosexuals, and their co-workers) and efficiency (defined as reduced health-care costs and employee productivity).[47]

AIDS is important as a workplace issue because of its implications for productivity and liability. Most of all, the potentially huge losses it threatens for health insurance carriers or self-insured employers means that it brings two fundamental values into open conflict. Under penalty of lawsuit for violation of handicap protection laws (such as Section 504 of the Vocational Rehabilitation Act, or the Americans with Disabilities Act), applicants and employees who carry the AIDS virus have the right to a job as long as they can perform its primary duties with **reasonable accommodation** by the employer.[48] But no employer or health insurance carrier would make a voluntary, rational decision to employ an applicant knowing that this person would live only a few more years, and would cost the employer $100,000 to $250,000 in health care from onset until death.

There are other employment-related AIDS issues that have not yet been addressed by the Supreme Court: (1) does mandatory AIDS testing of employees in health-care agencies violate constitutional privacy protection? (2) Is testing prison inmates a civil rights violation? (3) Is it a violation of federal law for a company to reduce the health-care benefits of an employee with AIDS? and (5) Does barring an HIV+ medical assistant from participating in surgery violate the ADA?

And it is worthwhile to remember that AIDS is only one of many life-threatening diseases that employers confront. Hepatitis B and staphloccocus are bloodborne pathogens that afflict health-care workers; and many virulent strains of tuberculosis are an increasing hazard for all employers because they are airborne. In all such cases, it is necessary to balance the rights of several groups—of HIV+ persons to the right to work, of clients and co-workers to a safe and healthy workplace, and of employers to qualified and productive employees.

EMPLOYEE ASSISTANCE PROGRAMS (EAPs)

Employee assistance programs (EAPs) are designed to diagnose, treat, and rehabilitate employees whose personal problems are interfering with work performance. Usually, employers contract with a private group to provide preventive, diagnostic, and treatment programs. In this way, the personnel function in an agency is expanded without directly increasing the size of the personnel department itself. From the employee's viewpoint, the objective is to treat personal problems before they have an irreparable effect on job status. From the employer's viewpoint, the objective is to rehabilitate employees whose personal problems are a threat to productivity, health-care costs, or legal liability; and to lay the groundwork for possible disciplinary action and discharge (if the employee cannot be rehabilitated) before these threats become a reality.

Over time, both the functions of the EAP and the role of the supervisor have changed substantially and rapidly. First, while the traditional EAP was charged almost exclusively with confronting the problem of alcohol abuse, the contemporary EAP also addresses drug abuse, AIDS education, and a range of other personal problems that may affect job performance (family problems, emotional and psychiatric problems, legal counseling, financial counseling).

Because the EAP deals with a range of personal problems that may affect job performance, it is directly concerned with treating employee stress caused by increased economic pressure, increased family responsibilities, and the weakening of the social safety net of institutions.[49] Stress has an important impact on organizational costs and productivity. First, stress itself leads to physical disabilities such as high blood pressure, stroke, and heart disease. It leads to increased alcoholism and drug abuse, because both of these are often used by employees as stress reduction mechanisms.[50] Finally, stress increases the possibility of poor or erratic work performance, causing risks to productivity and risk management.

Personnel managers can use the EAP to help employees recognize and manage stress by developing good health habits (such as substituting meditation, exercise, or work breaks), and providing health counseling. They can also recognize the ways in which the organizational culture causes employee stress: downsizing, inadequate training and feedback, or management pressures for unreasonable productivity increases or mandatory overtime to cope with economic competition. And then they can exert influence within the organization to reduce organizational policies that contribute unreasonably to job stress.

This increase in the range of functions performed by the EAP has meant that responsibility for the diagnosis and treatment of personal problems is no longer a supervisory responsibility, if indeed it ever was. Today the supervisor is expected to observe and record changes in employee behavior and job performance. This is the documentation that can be used to discipline employees and to refer them to the EAP for professional diagnosis and treatment. And it poses a final ethical issue for personnel directors and employees to consider: Have employers endorsed the concept of the EAP for its value in **rehabilitation** and productivity, or as a sort of legal insurance policy against employee grievances and lawsuits arising out of disciplinary action?

BALANCING ORGANIZATIONAL EFFECTIVENESS AND EMPLOYEE RIGHTS

The ability to predict long-term health risks by evaluating employee health profiles was originally developed as a component of employee **wellness programs** to prevent the occurrence of serious health problems among current employees. But "permanent" employees incur higher benefit costs than temporary workers.[51] Whenever possible, given the limits of available technology and the applicability of handicap laws protecting applicant rights, employers have sought to reduce benefit costs by excluding high-risk applicants (including drug abusers and HIV carriers) from permanent employment.[52]

Excluding disabled applicants who are able to perform a job is a violation of the ADA, yet it is a routine practice among many personnel directors, a practice which underscores the conflict between two legitimate and fundamental values—organizational efficiency and employee rights.

With respect to drug testing, the primary practical issue for personnel directors is whether rejecting applicants and disciplining employees who test positive is a useful way of stopping employee drug abuse. The primary legal issue is whether personnel policies or practices should distinguish between legal drugs (alcohol and prescription drugs) and illegal ones. Ethically sensitive personnel directors may also wonder if **substance abuse** has a greater effect on employee job performance than employees' personalities, family problems, debts, mental illness, or other issues. Once managers admit that some employees have a substance abuse problem, the agency is legally and politically bound to do something about it. Agencies that do **substance abuse testing** of current employees do so primarily based upon incidents or reasonable suspicion, as defined by the supervisor. But because the use of drugs is not clearly and directly related to work performance, it does not seem reasonable to expect that supervisors can identify or refer employees suspected of substance abuse skillfully and equitably, particularly in the face of union opposition and due process protections. Instead, in the absence of clear guidelines and rewards, they are more likely to avoid these risks by declining to identify suspected substance abusers or to refer them for testing and treatment.

AIDS is at present less of a workplace problem than is substance abuse. But it is a more frightening issue to employees, and it raises fundamental questions about protecting the rights of victims, while at the same time educating the workforce to prevent panicky reactions. On the risk-management side, it means treating AIDS like any other life-threatening illness, while recognizing that insurance carriers will have a vested interest in excluding AIDS carriers from the workplace. But in reality, the lengthy incubation period for AIDS means that even screening applicants (which is illegal under the ADA) is not an effective technique for preventing them from entering the workforce.

Employers have always used job-related medical criteria (such as a history of back injuries in an applicant for a job requiring heavy lifting) to exclude applicants who cannot perform the essential functions of a job, and for which no reasonable accommodation exists. And such exclusion is legal under the ADA. But employers are under considerable pressure from insurance carriers and risk managers to illegally exclude otherwise qualified applicants by using more generalized health indicators which may indicate that the applicant is a long-term health risk because his or her general health indicators are outside normal limits.[53] Examples are: abnormal weight to height, abnormal electrocardiogram, abnormal blood chemistry (such as cholesterol levels), history of heavy drinking (as determined by liver enzyme activity), history of substance abuse (as determined by urinalysis), or likelihood of developing AIDS (as determined by HIV antibody tests).[54]

The Supreme Court recently (1991) overturned selection standards under which chemical companies refused to employ females of childbearing age in positions in which there was risk of exposure to chemical toxins that could cause birth defects in unborn children. In the first example, courts have held that the risk to the employer outweighs the right of the individual applicant to be considered for jobs for which they are interested and qualified. In the second example, the Supreme Court has ruled that the risk of birth defects and subsequent lawsuits is relatively slight compared to the employment rights of the affected individuals.

SUMMARY

Employee health and safety are important from the viewpoint of maintaining human resources as an asset and reducing the health-care costs and liability risks generated by unsafe or unhealthy workplace conditions. Personnel directors have a critical role to play in providing a positive work environment to appropriately accommodate qualified persons with disabilities, where such practice does not compromise health, productivity, and safety. Personnel directors are also responsible for providing employees with a safe and healthy workplace by addressing such concerns as occupational safety and health, smoking, drug and alcohol abuse, and life-threatening diseases.

Many public personnel directors justifiably view controversial topics such as AIDS education or substance abuse policy as *risks* because these issues confront them with unavoidable conflicts among key human resource management values—responsiveness to elected officials, administrative efficiency, and protection of employee rights. But these issues also present personnel directors with *opportunities* to play a critical role in the resolution of emergent public policy. The professionalism of the public personnel director, and the personnel director's view of himself or herself within the agency, is a key factor in the extent to which innovative employee wellness policies and programs are adopted.

KEY TERMS

Acquired Immune Deficiency Syndrome (AIDS)
disability retirement
domestic violence
drug testing
Employee Assistance Program (EAP)
human immunodeficiency virus (HIV)
HIV positive (HIV+)
health maintenance organization (HMO)
lifestyle choices
medical risk factors
National Institute of Drug Abuse (NIDA)
National Institute of Occupational Safety and Health (NIOSH)
National Treasury Employees Union v. von Raab (1988)
negligent hiring, retention, and referral
Occupational Safety and Health Act (OSHA)
Occupational Safety and Health Administration (OSHA)
Office of Federal Contract Compliance Programs (OFCCP)
Omnibus Transportation Employee Testing Act of 1991
preemployment physical
reasonable accommodation
rehabilitation
Rehabilitation Act of 1973 (Sections 503 and 504)
Samuel Skinner v. Railway Labor Executives' Association (1988)
smoking cessation program
substance abuse
substance abuse testing
wellness program
workers' compensation
workplace violence

DISCUSSION QUESTIONS

1. What is the relationship between employee health and productivity?
2. What is the Occupational Safety and Health Act (OSHA)? What does it require of employers?

3. What can personnel directors do to improve workplace health and safety?
4. How does employee substance abuse affect productivity, liability, and risk management?
5. What policies and programs have employers adopted to combat workplace substance abuse?
6. Why is AIDS a workplace health issue for public agencies? For health-care employers?
7. What are employee assistance programs (EAPs)? What is their role with respect to workplace substance abuse and AIDS?
8. What dilemmas do public personnel directors face in designing selection, development, and disciplinary action policies and procedures that balance agency concerns for productivity with employee concerns for privacy and individual rights? How should they resolve these dilemmas?

CASE STUDY 1 DEVELOPING A WORKPLACE AIDS POLICY

You are the personnel director of a state government agency. Top management and employees have both been putting pressure on you to develop a comprehensive agency policy for AIDS and other life-threatening diseases. Because the agency does not provide health-care services, there is no risk of blood-to-blood contact in the course of employees' job duties.

1. What would be the major components of your policy?
2. How would you "sell" it to employees and management?
3. What would be the role of the employee assistance program? How would you evaluate the effectiveness of its services?

CASE STUDY 2 WORKPLACE VIOLENCE: "IN HINDSIGHT, WE COULD SEE IT COMING"

THE EVENT

In the predawn hours on February 9, 1996, a disgruntled former park and recreation department employee, Clifton McCree, burst into the maintenance trailer where six of his former co-workers were starting their day's work. In five minutes, six people were dead of gunshot wounds: Clifton McCree had killed five of the six co-workers, and then had turned the gun upon himself; one co-worker escaped to tell the story of horror and death.

THE BACKGROUND

After eighteen years of employment, Clifton McCree had been discharged from the city of Ft. Lauderdale in October of 1994 after failing a drug test. After this, he had been unable to find steady work, and he had grown increasingly depressed and angry over what he saw as racial discrimination and retaliation by white employees and supervisors.

Mr. McCree had a history of workplace confrontations with co-workers. In the past, other employees had complained about his occasional threats to kill them. His supervisors had counseled him informally about the need to control his temper. Although he frequently went into rages, and co-workers were afraid of him, his supervisors and other employees had avoided formal complaints and tried to handle the problem internally because they didn't want him to lose his job. Despite his temper, he continued to receive satisfactory performance evaluations for nine years, and there was no formal record of his problems. Finally, in 1993, after a screaming match with a white co-worker, McCree's supervisor counseled him formally.

PERSONNEL POLICIES AND PROCEDURES

Ironically, the problem came to a head just days after the city issued a new policy on workplace violence in 1994. This policy grew out of another tragedy—the murder of two lawyers in a downtown office building earlier that year. The city's policy was designed to raise awareness of what a potentially violent worker might do, and it set up a procedure for handling such incidents.

Immediately after the policy was issued, the supervisor came to the park and recreation department director, who had just come on the job a few weeks before, and told her about Clifton McCree. Within days, she had interviewed other workers, and prepared a chilling memo detailing McCree's threats and racial slurs against his co-workers. The memo indicated that McCree exhibited at least five of the warning signs of potential trouble, including threats, paranoid behavior, and a fascination with workplace violence.

City officials acted quickly, ordering a psychiatric evaluation and a drug test within days. By the end of the month, McCree had been suspended without pay, he flunked the drug test, and his firing was in the works. Until the day of the murders, eighteen months to the day after his discharge, he never returned to his workplace.

THE POSTMORTEM: SHOULD THE CITY HAVE DONE ANYTHING DIFFERENTLY?

In hindsight, it is difficult to find fault with anyone's actions. Most co-workers and supervisors would initially attempt to counsel a troubled employee informally because they were his friends and they knew he needed the job. With no formal counseling taking place, there would be no written record of previous performance incidents upon which to base a negative performance evaluation. When formal counseling finally occurred in 1993, it was only because co-workers had exerted pressure on management to do something. The city developed a clear and responsible policy on workplace violence in 1994. It was this policy that led to a strong and immediate response by the park and recreation department, and it was the department director's memo that led the city to take action. Appropriately, Clifton McCree was removed from work pending psychiatric evaluation and drug testing. He tested positive and was discharged.

Yet six people died. In addition to the human tragedy, the city will undoubtedly face civil charges from the victims' families, alleging that the city knew that Clifton McCree was violent but did not take adequate precautions to protect co-workers against violence.

QUESTIONS

1. In hindsight, what do you think the city could have done differently (if anything)?
2. Under the standard of "foreseeability," do you think the city can be held liable for failure to take more timely action against Clifton McCree?
3. Did the city's prompt and responsible action (to discharge Clifton McCree under its new workplace violence policy) in fact increase the chance of workplace violence?
4. Personnel management often takes place in communities where racial or ethnic unrest are part of the culture, and where disgruntled employees find it easy to get semiautomatic firearms that can kill many people in a short time. Is there anything personnel managers can do to lessen the chances of these factors resulting in workplace tragedies such as this one?

NOTES

[1] Webb, D. A. (1994). The bathtub effect: Why safety programs fail. *Management Review, 83,* 51-54.

[2] Sand, R. H. (1991). Current developments in safety and health. *Employee Relations Law Journal, 17,* 145-148.

[3] Lohr, S. (April 16, 1995). Waving goodbye to ergonomics. *The New York Times,* pp. 3-1, 14.

[4] Bielous, G. A. (March 1995). Promoting safety in the workplace. *Supervisory Management,* p. 6.

[5] Garza, N. (1992). Riots, fires tax L.A. EMS resources. *Journal of Emergency Medical Services, 17,* 6.

[6] Tompkins, N. (April 1995). Overcoming language barriers for effective safety training. *Supervisory Management,* pp. 12-13.

[7] Streff, F. M., M. J. Kalsher, and E. S. Geller (1993). Developing efficient workplace safety programs: Observations of response covariation. *Journal of Organizational Behavior Management, 13* 2, 3-14.

[8] Castelli, J. (1993). NIOSH condemns workplace-murder epidemic . . . miscarriage warnings . . . infant mortality down. *Safety and Health, 147* 3, 77-80.

[9] Barrier, M. (February 1995). The enemy within. *Nation's Business,* p. 18.

[10] Segal, J. A. (1994). When Charles Manson comes to the workplace. *HR Magazine, 39* 6, 33-40.

[11] Schut, J. H. (August 1994). Killers among us. *Institutional Investor,* p. 125.

[12] Castelli, NIOSH condemns workplace-murder epidemic.

[13] Ibid.

[14] Solomon, C. M. (April 1995). Talking frankly about domestic violence. *Personnel Journal,* p. 64.

[15] Ibid.

[16] Pereira, J. (March 2, 1995). Legal beat: Employers confront domestic abuse. *The Wall Street Journal,* p. B-1.

[17] Feliu, A. G. (1994). Workplace violence and the duty of care: The scope of an employer's obligation to protect against the violent employee. *Employee Relations Law Journal, 21,* 381-403.

[18] Martucci, W. C., and D. D. Clemow (1994/1995). Workplace violence: Incidents—and liability—on the rise. *Employment Relations Today,* pp. 463-470.

[19] DiLorenzo, L. P., and D. J. Carroll (March 1995). Screening applicants for a safer workplace. *HR Magazine,* 55-58.

[20] Feliu, Workplace violence, p. 393.

[21] Feisenthal, E. (April 5, 1995). Legal beat: Potentially violent employees present bosses with a Catch-22. *The Wall Street Journal,* pp. B-1, 5.

[22] Barrier, M. (1995). The enemy within. *Nation's Business, 83,* 2, 18-24.

[23] Johnson, D. L., J. G. Kurutz, and J. B. Kiehlbauch (1995). Scenario for supervisors. *HR Magazine,* 40, 2, 63-68.

[24] Ceniceros, R. (January 30, 1995). Preventing workplace violence. *Business Insurance, 3,* 16.

[25] Fox, J. (March 13, 1995). Security: Keeping the homicidal employee at bay. *Forbes, 155,* 24-27.

[26] Rabin, R., and S. D. Sugarman (1993). *Smoking policy: Law, politics and culture.* New York: Oxford University Press.

[27] Teague, S. (January-February 1990). Smoke gets in your eyes: The hazard of second-hand smoke. *Heart Corps,* p. 60.

[28] Kent, D., and L. Cenci (June 1982). Smoking and the workplace. *Journal of Medicine,* p. 470.

[29] Evans, D. (1994). Employers face difficult questions in initiatives against alcohol abuse. *Occupational Health & Safety, 63,* 58-60.

[30] Nazario, S. (April 18, 1990). Alcohol is linked to a gene. *The Wall Street Journal,* p. B-1.

[31] Newcomb, M. D. (1994). Prevalence of alcohol and other drug use on the job: Cause for concern or irrational hysteria? *The Journal of Drug Issues, 24,* 403-416.

[32] Normand, J., S. D. Salyards, and J. J. Mahoney (1990). An evaluation of preemployment drug testing. *Journal of Applied Psychology, 75,* 629-639.

[33] Greenberg, E. (March 1987). To test or not to test: Drugs and the workplace. *Management Review, 12,* 24.

[34] Donkin, R. (April 1989). New hope for diagnosing alcoholism. *Business & Health,* pp. 20-23.

[35] Crow, S. M., M. F. Villere, and S. J. Hartman (1994). Planes, trains, and ships: Drug testing is no substitute for drug supervision: Part II. *Supervision, 55,* 14-16.

[36] Kaestner, R., and M. Grossman (1995). Wages, workers' compensation benefits and drug use: Indirect evidence of the effect of drugs on the workplace. *American Economic Review, 85,* 55-60.

[37] Gillian, F. (1995). Recreational drug use may not be the biggest threat. *Personnel Journal, 74,* 21-23.

[38] Pouzar, E. (1994). Drug and alcohol abuse present RM challenge. *National Underwriter, 98,* 13.

[39] Trenk, B. (April 1989). Clearing the air about smoking policies. *Management Review,* p. 32.

[40] Crow, S. and S. J. Hartman (1992). Drugs in the workplace: Overstating the problems and the cures. *Journal of Drug Issues, 22,* 923-937.

[41] Macdonald, S., S. Wells, and R. Fry (1993). The limitations of drug screening in the workplace. *International Labour Review, 132,* 95-113.

[42] Manley, S. A.. and G. S. Gibson (1990). Drug-induced impairment: Implications for employers. *Psychology of Addictive Behaviors, 4,* 97-99.

[43] Lavan, H., M. Katz, and J. Suttor (1994). Litigation of employer drug testing. *Labor Law Journal,* pp. 346-351.

[44] Comer, D. R. (1994). A case against workplace drug testing. *Organization Science, 5,* 259-267.

[45] Jacobs, S. (December 11, 1995). New AIDS drugs' aim is "buying time." *The Miami Herald,* pp. C-1, 5.

[46] Stodghill, R., R. Mitchell, K. Thurston, and C. Del Valle. (February 1, 1993). Managing AIDS: How one boss struggled to cope. *Business Week,* pp. 48-54.

[47] Burris, S. (1993). *AIDS law today: A new guide for the public.* New Haven, Yale University Press.

[48] *School Board of Nassau County Fla v. Arline,* 107 S. Ct. 1123 (1987); and *Shuttleworth v. Broward County,* 639 F. Supp. (S.D. Fla. 1986).

[49] Wharton, A. S., and R. J. Erickson (1993). Managing emotions on the job and at home: Understanding the consequences of multiple emotional roles. *Academy of Management Review, 18,* 457-486.

[50] Harris, M. M., and L. L. Heft (1992). Alcohol and drug use in the workplace: Issues, controversies, and directions for future research. *Journal of Management, 18,* 239-266.

[51] Holton, R. (September 1988). AIDS in the workplace: Underwriting update. *Best's Review, Property-Casualty Edition,* pp. 96-98; and Solovy, A. (January 20, 1989). Insurers, HMOs and BC-BS plans talk about AIDS. *Hospitals, 63,* 24.

[52] Masi, D. (March 1987). Company response to drug abuse from the AMA's national survey. *Personnel, 63,* 40-46.

[53] Uzych, L. (March 1990). HIV testing: The legal balance between individual and societal rights. *Southern Medical Journal, 83,* 303-307.

[54] Slater, K. (June 7, 1990). Likely Methuselahs get more life-insurance breaks. *The Wall Street Journal,* pp. C-1, 8.

12

Organizational Justice

In 1981, Ardith McPherson was a clerk in the sheriff's office in Harris County, Texas. While at work, she was talking to her boyfriend on the phone about President Reagan's social policies when it was announced over the radio that the president had been shot. Not knowing anyone else was in the room, she was overheard saying to her boyfriend, "If they go for him again, I hope they get him." The sheriff fired her, claiming she was not a suitable law enforcement employee. McPherson claimed her constitutional right to express herself had been violated by the dismissal. The case went all the way to the Supreme Court. In this case, the Supreme Court sided with McPherson, 5-4.[1]

Does McPherson have a constitutional right to speak out in this way? Has she been treated unfairly? If McPherson had been employed by a private security agency and her boss had fired her under the same circumstances, would she have been able to make a claim that her right to free speech had been violated?

By the end of this chapter, you will be able to:

1. Define the sanction function.
2. Identify the ways an organization establishes and maintains the terms of the employment relationship between employee and employer.
3. Describe the rights of employees who have been sexually harassed or who are considered whistle blowers.
4. Define the terms *reasonable accommodation* and *undue hardship* in the Americans with Disabilities Act and show the value conflict implied in these terms.
5. Discuss the balance the Court examines when deciding whether a public employer has violated an employee's constitutional rights to free speech, freedom of association, or privacy rights.
6. Discuss the transition from sovereign immunity to qualified immunity for public employees.

7. Describe the role of property rights and due process in establishing and maintaining the terms of the employment relationship.
8. Define the concept of organizational citizenship and relate it to employee perceptions of fairness.
9. Discuss how discipline and grievance procedures are connected to the sanction function.
10. Diagram a typical disciplinary procedure and describe various steps in a grievance procedure.
11. Describe the ways different personnel systems view the sanction function.

THE SANCTION FUNCTION

Every organization, public or private, must establish and maintain *terms of the relationship between employee and employer.* This is the **sanction function**, the last of the four core functions. These terms in an employment relationship are captured in expectations employees have of their employer and contributions employees are willing to make in order to have their expectations fulfilled. Similarly, employers have expectations of employees and make contributions to employees in order to have those expectations fulfilled. The heart of the sanction function involves the interplay of these various expectations and contributions or obligations.

The terms in an employment relationship commonly include wages and working conditions. These generally are tangible elements that can be established precisely in writing. But the expectations that employees and employers have of one another go beyond what can be quantified. Employees often expect that an employer will provide "interesting work," "opportunities for advancement," and "recognition." Employers often expect "an honest day's work," "loyalty and commitment," "cooperation and harmony."

The concept of a **psychological contract** helps us understand the interplay between employee and employer expectations and obligations—both the tangible and intangible ones—and it focuses our understanding of organizational life on the relationship between employee and employer rather than on one or the other. Employee and employer bring expectations and obligations to their relationship—which are modified with time and experience—and new ones develop as circumstances change.

The "contract" part of the concept of a psychological contract suggests that expectations and obligations are terms that are exchanged in a quid pro quo fashion. The "psychological" part of the contract denotes that not all expectations and obligations are tangible, all are subject to perception, and the exchanges in expectations and obligations may take place cognitively and subjectively—that is, in the employee or employer's mind rather than at a bargaining table.

Let's see how this might work. Employees have expectations of their employer and are willing to accept certain obligations in return for having these expectations fulfilled. For example, employees may expect to be given job security and interesting work, and in return they will accept the obligation to work hard and be loyal to the organization. In contrast, an employer might expect loyalty from employees but find it hard to realize in an environment of downsizing and privatization.[2] The terms of the contract are these expectations and obligations which are continually changing and being renegotiated—established and maintained.[3] Both parties bring different terms to the relationship, and in order for the relationship to work, some kind of negotiation, adjustment, or acceptance needs to take place.

ESTABLISHING AND MAINTAINING EXPECTATIONS

Employee expectations and obligations come from numerous sources, ranging from what is learned in school to conversations with friends or acquaintances in similar jobs. Employer expectations and obligations are similarly diverse coming from organizational needs, comparisons with other organizations, and the character of the workforce. Regardless of where they originate, there are several formal mechanisms by which these tangible terms, and sometimes the intangible ones as well, are established. The first is the personnel manual, which contains the policies, rules, regulations, procedures, and practices that constitute a particular personnel system. For example, there may be a policy giving priority to promoting from within. There may be rules limiting political activity of employees while on the job. There may be a policy about bonuses or pay for performance. These policies and rules constitute some of the terms of the employment relationship.

Second, in some jurisdictions, the **terms of the employment relationship** are established through collective bargaining between employer and union. These terms are contained in working rules mutually agreed upon by employer and union membership. Third, various local, state, and federal laws establish expectations and obligations of employees and employer. For example, local ordinances authorize merit personnel systems and policies; legislatures establish pay rates for public employees; the Fair Labor Standards Act describes required compensation policies; the Civil Rights Act of 1964 proscribes various forms of discrimination in employment; the Hatch Act and its counterparts in state and local governments proscribe political activity by employees. These and other laws contain provisions that affect the expectations and obligations that employees and employers have of one another.

Last, the sanction function in public employment differs fundamentally from private employment because public employees have certain rights conferred upon them by the U.S. Constitution. Citizens are protected from government action by the Bill of Rights, including the Fourteenth Amendment. When citizens become employees of the government, they give up some of those rights, but they still have substantially more protection in speech, association, privacy, and equal treatment than do employees of private employers. We will discuss these protections later in the chapter.

Maintaining Expectations

Various processes maintain and enforce the terms established through these four mechanisms. Commonly, we think of employees suing their employer for violating some employee right. But more realistically, an organization's discipline and grievance procedures maintain the terms of the employment relationship or contract. Most disagreements are handled informally between supervisor and employee, but when informal channels are inadequate, formal discipline and grievance procedures are invoked. Sometimes, if those prove ineffective in resolving differences, the employee complains directly to elected officials or takes judicial action.

An employee is disciplined when the employer believes the employee is not living up to the terms of the employment contract. Usually, this means that the employee is not contributing to the organization in the way the employer expects. On the other hand, when the employee believes the employer has violated its obligations, the employee "grieves" the employer's action, setting in motion some review. In large measure, the quality of the grievance processes due an employee subject to discipline determines whether employees believe they, and their co-workers, have been treated equitably and with dignity. (We will discuss discipline and grievance procedures in more detail later in the chapter.)

The notion that organizational justice is derived from balancing values suggests that the processes which establish and maintain expectations and obligations are as important as what those expectations and obligations actually are—their substance. In the next sections we will discuss both the substantive and procedural rights of public employees and how those rights are balanced by the values of organizational efficiency and political responsiveness.

PROTECTING EMPLOYEE RIGHTS

In the following sections we are going to describe some of the major rights that public employees have based on federal statutes and constitutional protections. The discussion includes rights regarding sexual harassment, whistle-blowing, disabilities, speech, belief or patronage, and privacy. These are not the only areas of public employee rights. In addition, employee rights are enumerated in state and local statutes and in the organization's personnel manual and working rules.

While laws and constitutional rights exist independent of any public organization, their effectiveness in helping to promote good organizational citizenship hinges partly on the extent to which a public organization incorporates them into the workplace. For example, while sexual harassment violates Title VII of the Civil Rights Act, unless a public employer acknowledges an obligation to protect employees from sexual harassment, the guarantee in law is distant from the employee's working life.

Protection against Sexual Harassment

What is **sexual harassment**? The United States Equal Employment Opportunity Commission, responsible for enforcing the Civil Rights Act of 1964, as amended, and various other employment discrimination laws, has issued the following guidelines:

> Unwelcomed sexual advances, requests for sexual favors, and other verbal or physical conduct of a sexual nature constitute sexual harassment when (1) submission to such conduct is made either explicitly or implicitly a term or condition of an individual's employment, (2) submission to or rejection of such conduct by an individual is used

> as the basis for employment decisions affecting such individual, or (3) such conduct has the purpose or effect of unreasonably interfering with an individual's work performance or creating an intimidating, hostile, or offensive working environment.[4]

In simple terms, sexual harassment is not romance. It is the coercive and hostile behavior of one person toward another based on gender. Evidently, it occurs quite frequently at work. Dresang and Stuiber's literature[5] review cites a Bureau of National Affairs study showing 40 percent of the female respondents having experienced sexual harassment; the United States Merit Systems Review Board studies in 1981 and 1987 of federal employees showed 42 percent of the female and some 15 percent of the male respondents reporting sexual harassment. In the Merit Systems Protection Board follow-up in its 1995 report, the numbers were similar, 44 and 19 percent.[6] In their literature review, Robinson, Kirk, and Powell cite a Cornell study showing 92 percent of the 155 respondents believing sexual harassment was a serious problem and 70 percent who had experienced it themselves.[7] Their own research shows that 71 percent of the business and professional women they surveyed reported being sexual harassed, with only 33 percent actually reporting the harassment. The Merit Systems Protection Board report shows that the majority of harassers were co-workers, not supervisors. In 1993, based on an extensive literature review, the Governor's Task Force on Sexual Harassment in New York concluded, "Sexual harassment is a widespread and continuing problem in workplaces and schools. It transcends occupational and professional categories, age groups, educational backgrounds, racial and ethnic groups, and income levels and affects us all."[8]

Most of the sexual harassment reported in the Merit Systems Protection Board's report included "sexual remarks, jokes, teasing, sexual looks, gestures, deliberate touching and cornering." Less frequently reported were "pressure for dates, suggestive letters, calls, materials, and stalking." Two percent of the male and 7 percent of the female victims of sexual harassment reported "pressure for sexual favors." Sexual harassment is most likely to occur in an occupation or workplace dominated by one gender.

It is clear that men and women see sexual behavior differently, sometimes markedly so. Table 12-1 from the Merit Systems Protection Board report shows some of these differences. Independent analysis of the same survey data led Thacker and Gohmann to conclude that females are more likely than males to define as harassing behaviors that could lead to a hostile work environment, and they are more likely to report the need for emotional or medical counseling as a result of sexual harassment.[9]

The consequences of sexual discrimination appear to be significant both to victims and to the organization. Most women deal with sexual harassment privately, in many cases by simply leaving the organization. The psychological effects of sexual harassment may be traumatic. According to Dresang and Stuiber, "In addition to shame and guilt, women frequently experience feelings of helplessness, of being trapped, and of undirected fear. One of the most prevalent phenomena reported is a loss of self-esteem."[10] Costs to employers are significant as well: the cost of replacing employees; paying sick leave benefits to victims seeking

TABLE 12–1 Is It Sexual Harassment

	PERCENTAGE OF WOMEN WHO CONSIDER IT HARASSMENT		
Type of Uninvited Behavior By a Supervisor	*1980*	*1987*	*1994*
Pressure for sexual favors	91	99	99
Deliberate touching, cornering	91	95	98
Suggestive letters, calls, materials	93	90	94
Pressure for dates	77	87	91
Suggestive looks, gestures	72	81	91
Sexual teasing, jokes, remarks	62	72	83
	PERCENTAGE OF MEN WHO CONSIDER IT HARASSMENT		
	1980	*1987*	*1994*
Pressure for sexual favors	84	95	97
Deliberate touching, cornering	83	89	93
Suggestive letters, calls, materials	87	76	87
Pressure for dates	76	81	86
Suggestive looks, gestures	59	68	76
Sexual teasing, jokes, remarks	53	58	73
	PERCENTAGE OF WOMEN WHO CONSIDER IT HARASSMENT		
Type of Uninvited Behavior By a Co-Worker	*1980*	*1987*	*1994*
Pressure for sexual favors	81	98	98
Deliberate touching, cornering	84	92	96
Suggestive letters, calls, materials	87	84	92
Pressure for dates	65	76	85
Suggestive looks, gestures	64	76	88
Sexual teasing, jokes, remarks	54	64	77
	PERCENTAGE OF MEN WHO CONSIDER IT HARASSMENT		
	1980	*1987*	*1994*
Pressure for sexual favors	65	90	93
Deliberate touching, cornering	69	82	89
Suggestive letters, calls, materials	76	67	81
Pressure for dates	59	66	76
Suggestive letters, calls, materials	47	60	70
Sexual teasing, jokes, remarks	42	47	64

*Based on the percentage of respondents who indicated that they "definitely" or "probably" would consider the identified behavior harassment.

to avoid sexual harassment; paying medical insurance claims for psychological help in dealing with harassment; and reduced worker productivity. In the Merit Systems Protection Board report 21 percent of those who experienced sexual harassment suffered a decline in productivity. Thus, sexual discrimination and productivity incorporates health concerns among its dimensions.

While sexual harassment ultimately must be dealt with in the workplace, conflicts involving claims of harassment frequently find their way into the court system as interested parties seek justice through the law.[11] In ***Meritor Savings Bank v. Vinson*** (1986),[12] the Supreme Court established several significant legal guidelines in its interpretation of the Civil Rights Act of 1964, as amended. Mechelle Vinson, who was employed by the bank in 1974, rose through the ranks to assistant branch manager on her merits when in 1978 she was discharged for excessive use of sick leave. Ms. Vinson claimed that during her four years with the bank she had been constantly subjected to sexual harassment. She estimated that over the four-year period she had sexual intercourse with Sidney Taylor, the branch manager, some forty or fifty times. "In addition, [she] testified that Taylor fondled her in front of other employees, followed her into the women's restroom when she went there alone, exposed himself to her, and even forcibly raped her on several occasions" (p. 55). Vinson testified that she was afraid to report the harassment to Taylor's superiors. Taylor denied her charges completely, contending that they resulted from a business dispute.

Even though the conflicting testimony was never resolved, the Supreme Court made several significant legal points in its 9-0 judgment. First, it concluded that an adverse personnel action need not be taken in order to prove that sexual harassment has occurred. It affirmed lower court findings and the EEOC's guidelines that "Title VII affords employees the right to work in an environment free from discriminatory intimidation, ridicule and insult" (p. 59). Further, it affirmed that "a plaintiff may establish a violation of Title VII by proving that discrimination based on sex has created a hostile or abusive work environment" (p. 59). However, it tempered its stance somewhat by saying that in order for a legal violation to occur, the sexual harassment must be "sufficiently severe or pervasive 'to alter the conditions of the [victim's] employment and create an abusive working environment'" (p. 60) [internal cite omitted].

Second, the Court found that when trying to determine the nature of the relationship, "The correct inquiry is whether respondent by her conduct indicated that the alleged sexual advances were *unwelcome,* not whether her actual participation in sexual intercourse was *voluntary*" (p. 60) [emphasis added]. However, the Court added that evidence regarding sexually provocative speech or dress is not necessarily irrelevant in determining whether the advances are unwelcomed.

Last, contrary to its findings in race discrimination cases, the Court found that an employer is not automatically accountable for sexual harassment by one of its supervisors. At the same time, the presence of a sexual harassment policy does not automatically protect an employer from liability. The Court does suggest that an employer's defense would be strengthened with evidence of a procedure that encourages victims of harassment to come forward.

In 1993 the Supreme Court revisited the issue of sexual harassment in ***Harris v. Forklift.***[13] Teresa Harris worked as a manager at Forklift Systems equipment rental company. At issue was whether Harris would have to show that she had suffered psychological injury in order to prevail in her claim that she was working in a sexually abusive and hostile environment. A unanimous Supreme Court found in Harris' favor, indicating that "Title VII comes into play before the harassing conduct leads to a nervous breakdown." A hostile environment exists where a "reasonable person" objectively comes to that conclusion and when a victim subjectively perceives it as such. The Court acknowledged the lack of a cookie cutter formula for establishing when a hostile environment exists, but it did outline several factors that should be considered: frequency of the conduct, its severity, whether it is physically threatening or humiliating, or a mere offensive utterance, and whether it interferes with an employee's work.

As a footnote, in *Harris* the Court rejected a lower court standard that used the "reasonable woman" to determine whether or not a hostile environment exits. The Court stayed with its frequently relied upon hypothetical "reasonable person." The Merit Systems Protection Board report shows that men and women see these things differently. But the Court is reluctant to acknowledge that justice should be gender specific.

Despite *Vinson* and *Harris*, Dresang and Stuiber observe that sexual harassment is not easy to eliminate or even to minimize: "In part, the difficulties of taking corrective action relate to organizational power and societal sex-role stereotypes, forces beyond the easy reach of reformers."[14]

But the problem of sexual harassment involves more than issues of power, stereotypes, and litigation. It would be naive to claim that productivity in organizations is disconnected from personal attraction and cooperation. Productivity is often enhanced by close, affectionate working relationships that develop with an organizational culture that encourages respect, dignity, and tolerance. But the proper relationship between sexuality, productivity, and fair treatment is difficult to realize in any organizational context because of divergent and unspoken expectations and perceptions. The relationship between sexuality, productivity, and equity promises to become more complicated in the 1990s with increasing ethnic diversity and accompanying expectations in the workplace.

Protection of "Whistle-Blowing"

The tendency of public organizations and administrators to withhold self-incriminating information from the public is counterbalanced theoretically by **whistle-blowing**. This form of dissent focuses public attention on behavior the whistle-blower considers illegal or unethical. It is this moral imperative, accompanied by the whistle-blower's knowledge that his or her charges will be scrutinized and possibly met with reprisal, that distinguishes the whistle-blower's actions from a simple act of insubordination for private purposes.

Whistle-blowing is a well-publicized phenomenon because it plays upon the public's desire to expose corruption and increase responsiveness or efficiency in government agencies. The Civil Service Reform Act of 1978, which applies to federal employees, includes as a merit principle: "Employees should be protected against reprisal for the lawful disclosure of information which the employees reasonably believe evidences: (a) a violation of any law, rule, or regulation, or (b) mismanagement, a gross waste of funds, an abuse of authority, or a substantial and specific danger to public health or safety." Several additional federal laws passed since 1978 contain protections for whistle-blowers who disclose specific types of information.

Despite these protections and similar ones in several state and local governments, employees usually blow the whistle on their employer only as a last resort, when the conflict between their ethical standards and their perception of their agency's behavior is so great as to leave them no choice. In other terms, whistle-blowing results from a perceived gross breach in the employment contract—in this case, the expectations an employee has of his or her employer or co-workers. Often times, this expectation runs counter to the employer's expectation and desire for employee loyalty. Whistle-blowers often exhaust organizational channels for dissent before they "go public" with charges and information.

The U.S. Merit Systems Protection Board surveyed federal personnel specialists in 1980 and again in 1988 regarding the occurrence of prohibited personnel practices. In the 1988 survey, 19 percent of the respondents said they had observed at least one instance of retaliation for whistle-blowing during the previous twelve months. Only half of those surveyed in 1988 believed that protections for persons attempting to expose prohibited personnel practices were adequate—down slightly from 1980.[15]

Comparing the results of a 1992 survey of federal employees with one conducted in 1983, the Merit Systems Protection Board found a similar 20 percent of those surveyed reported having direct knowledge of a wasteful or illegal activity. According to the 1992 survey, half of those with knowledge reported the activity compared to 30 percent in 1983. In 1992, one third of the employees who reported a wasteful or illegal activity said they had experienced or been threatened with reprisal; up from some 25 percent in 1983. Finally, perceived reprisals included poor performance evaluations, social pressure by co-workers or managers, and verbal harassment or intimidation.[16]

How should whistle-blowing be evaluated?[17] On the one hand, it divides the agency and undercuts its management, and causes serious organizational harm—sometimes for the self-serving purposes of a disgruntled employee. On the other hand, it may prevent managers from hiding information harmful to the agency or its managers, using specious reasons such as security and efficiency. Whistle-blowing represents a classic conflict between individual rights, possibly under the rubric of the First Amendment, and the desire of managers to control the flow of information out of the agency in order to preserve individual careers, administrative efficiency, or political support.

THE AMERICANS WITH DISABILITIES ACT: BALANCING ORGANIZATIONAL EFFICIENCY AND THE RIGHTS OF EMPLOYEES AND APPLICANTS

The Americans with Disabilities Act of 1990[18] is probably the most significant piece of civil rights legislation since Congress passed the Civil Rights Act of 1964. Its purpose is to eliminate discrimination against individuals with disabilities or against those perceived to have a disability. Individuals recovering from drug or alcohol abuse are considered disabled, and those who are HIV infected are covered as well. The act parallels the Rehabilitation Act of 1973, but the scope is broader, extending coverage to all employers with fifteen or more full-time employees.

According to the act, some 43 million Americans suffer from a physical or mental disability. The act states: "Individuals with disabilities are a discrete and insular minority who have been faced with restrictions and limitations, subjected to a history of purposeful unequal treatment, and relegated to a position of political powerlessness in our society, based on characteristics that are beyond the control of such individuals and resulting from stereotypic assumptions not truly indicative of the individual ability of such individuals to participate in, and contribute to, society."[19]

The act, which covers both private and public employers, prohibits discrimination in employment against otherwise qualified applicants and employees, and requires that reasonable accommodations in employment conditions and facilities be made for otherwise qualified disabled applicants and employees. Some examples of reasonable accommodation include (1) making existing facilities used by employees readily accessible to and usable by an individual with a disability; (2) job restructuring; (3) modifying work schedules; (4) reassignment to a vacant position; (5) acquiring or modifying equipment or devices; (6) adjusting or modifying examinations; training materials or policies; (7) providing qualified readers or interpreters.

The requirement that employers make *reasonable accommodations* for the disabled may be mitigated if the employer can show an *undue hardship*—usually financial—would be incurred. Undue hardship is defined by the ADA as an action that is "excessively costly, extensive, substantial, or disruptive, or that would fundamentally alter the nature or operation of the business." In determining undue hardship, factors to be considered include the nature and cost of the accommodation in relation to the size, the financial resources, the nature and structure of the employer's operation, as well as the impact the accommodation would have on the specific facility itself.

The terms *reasonable accommodation* and *undue hardship* represent Congress' attempt to balance employee and employer expectations and obligations, and the values of individual rights and efficiency. An employee may expect and an employer is obligated to make a reasonable accommodation for an employee who is disabled but otherwise qualified. But efficiency tempers this expectation/obligation; an employer is not obligated to make the accommodation if it forces an undue economic hardship or hardship in service delivery. These terms represent a political compromise over conflicting values and expectations/obligations, and they provide general guidance. But the particulars of implementation will require administrative interpretation and action, and what is reasonable and undue hardship will eventually be defined administratively and judicially representing a maturation of the law.[20]

The act also requires public entities to make reasonable modifications to government facilities and programs to make them accessible to the disabled. The act is far-reaching as well in the areas of transportation and telecommunications, and in its requirement to make public accommodations like supermarkets, retail establishments, movie houses, restaurants, and day-care centers accessible to the disabled except where an undue financial hardship can be demonstrated by the owner. Under the Civil Rights Act of 1991, those discriminated against may sue successfully if the discrimination is shown to be intentional.

FREEDOM OF SPEECH, ASSOCIATION, AND PRIVACY

Citizens who work for a government are covered by various amendments to the Constitution. The Bill of Rights protects citizens from arbitrary action against them by the government, and when citizens become employees of a government, they are similarly protected although their rights as employees are balanced against their employer's necessity for administrative efficiency. The balance among values we discussed earlier is particularly relevant here, because as an employer the government cannot simply dismiss the values of administrative efficiency in favor of employee rights. Thus, as we see in the following sections, various government employers argue that the constitutional protections public employees claim often disadvantage the government's ability to operate efficiently and responsively. In this section we try to share some of the discussion the Supreme Court engages in to give some sense of how the balance is discussed and how solutions are reached.

Freedom of Speech

The First Amendment to the constitution states that "Congress shall make no law respecting an establishment of religion, or prohibiting the free exercise thereof; or abridging the freedom of speech, or of the press; or the right of the people peaceably to assemble, and to petition the Government for a redress of grievances." This amendment protects citizens from government's intrusions on the free exercise of religion, speech, political beliefs, and political association. Citing passages from many of the Court's precedents, Justice Brennan in ***New York Times v. Sullivan*** (1964)[21] indicates the importance of the First Amendment in our form of government. The constitutional safeguard "was fashioned to assure unfettered interchange of ideas for the bringing about of political and social changes desired by the people." The First Amendment "presupposes that right conclusions are more likely to be gathered out of a multitude of tongues, than through any kind of authoritative selection. To many this is, and always will be folly; but we have staked upon it our all." Justice Brennan himself writes: "We consider this case against the background of a profound national commitment to the principle that debate on public issues should be uninhibited, robust, and wide-open, and that it may well include vehement, caustic, and sometimes unpleasantly sharp attacks on government and public officials" (p. 701).

Commonly, we think that the purpose of the First Amendment is to protect a speaker's right to expression—as an end in itself. Actually, as Cooper observes from his review of judicial opinions, the free flow of information is vital to the *listener's* ability to come to conclusions about government affairs, and this is what justifies the "untrammeled communication of ideas."[22]

While citizens often endorse the First Amendment uncritically, the Court faces a difficult task when applying it to public employment situations. The First Amendment provides the vehicle for classic confrontations between advocates of administrative efficiency and the rights of public employees. On the one hand, government has a duty to conduct its business efficiently, which means requiring respect for hierarchy and organizational loyalty. On the other hand, no one knows better how taxes are being spent than civil servants; and if they feel their jobs will be jeopardized if they speak out, is the public being deprived of information vital to its understanding of government?

The way the Court decides free speech cases regarding public employees is first to ask whether the employee has expressed himself or herself on a *matter of public concern.* If the answer is "yes," the Court looks to see how much the administrative efficiency of the agency has been or is reasonably anticipated to become disrupted. It then tries to balance the two considerations, asking if the disruption is sufficient enough to outweigh the individual's right to free speech.[23] The more clearly the matter addresses a significant public concern, the more difficult the employer's defense becomes.

In many ways, the balance the Court tries to draw among the values of administrative efficiency and individual rights depends on the extent to which the justices believe that public employees should give up the constitutional rights they have as citizens when they go to work for a public employer; on the extent to which they feel that what goes on *inside* a public agency is a matter of public concern; and on the extent to which they feel the judiciary should be involved in public personnel management at all.

The contemporary Supreme Court, compared to its recent predecessors, appears to tip the balance in favor of administrative efficiency over individual rights. For example, in ***Rust v. Sullivan*** (1991), the Court upheld administrative regulations prohibiting the discussion of abortion by Title X grant recipients of the Public Health Service Act against a First Amendment challenge. Those recipients argued that the regulations precluded health-care workers from disseminating a full range of information to patients on a matter of public concern—one of "'the most divisive and contentious issues that our Nation has faced in years.'" Writing for a 5-4 Court, Chief Justice Rehnquist argued in part: "The employees' freedom of expression is limited during the time that they actually work for the project; but this limitation is a consequence of their decision to accept employment in a project, the scope of which is permissibly restricted by the funding authority."[24] In his dissent, Justice Blackmun counters: "It is beyond question 'that a government may not require an individual to relinquish rights guaranteed him by the First Amendment as a condition of public employment'" (p. 268; internal citations omitted).

In ***Connick v. Myers*** (1983)[25] a 5-4 Court decided that Sheila Myers was appropriately discharged for insubordination when she refused a transfer and then distributed a questionnaire to colleagues regarding the way Harry Connick, the elected district attorney in New Orleans, ran his office. The Court's deference to administrative efficiency is seen in two ways in this case. First, the Court tempered its decision on whether Ms. Myers was speaking out on a matter of public concern by noting that she was a disgruntled employee. In other words, her aims and motives were considered, as well as the content of the information she was providing with the questionnaire results. Further, the majority dismissed the importance of most of the information itself, suggesting that matters of internal agency operations are not a matter of public importance in judging the performance of the district attorney.

Because the Court acknowledged that a few of Myers' questions addressed matters of public concern, they turned to the government's argument on why she should be dismissed. The Court concluded: "The limited First Amendment interest involved here does not require that Connick tolerate action which he reasonably believed would disrupt the office, undermine his authority, and destroy close working relationships" (p. 724). Here the Court retreated from previous judgments where *evidence* of disruption would have been required before the employer could have justly considered terminating the employee.

Connick v. Myers points out the difficulty in assessing the whistle-blower's claim. Was Myers a potential whistle-blower who was shut up? Was she simply a disgruntled employee? Does it really matter whether a whistle-blower is a disgruntled employee?

While *Connick v. Myers* involved a public employee's First Amendment rights, in 1996 in the case of ***Wabaunsee County v. Umbehr***[26] the court held that a private business holding a contract with a public employer has similar rights. Umbehr hauled trash for the county and was a frequent critic of the county commissioners. When the county failed to renew his contract, he successfully alleged that they were retaliating for his criticism and thereby violating his First Amendment right to free speech.

Freedom of Association: Patronage versus Civil Service

Governments have struggled since the early 1800s to draw a balance between a responsive and an efficient government. Advocates of responsiveness have generally favored more political control over public bureaucracies; advocates of administrative efficiency have fought to keep politics out of administration. Political personnel systems fight for the allocation of public jobs on the basis of political loyalty as a reward for service to a political party and as a way of ensuring that newly elected officials can appoint people committed to their goals.

For years, limitations on the political activity of employees as well as constraints on political influence over them have been dealt with in legislatures and executive branches of government.

The courts stepped into this battle in the mid-1970s by limiting the patronage practice of discharging public employees on the basis of political affiliation. The Court argued that patronage dismissals violated a public employee's First Amendment right to freedom of belief and association—to belong to a political party of choice and maintain one's own political beliefs. In ***Rutan v. Republican Party of Illinois*** (1990), a 5-4 Court extended its ruling to hiring, promotion, transfer, and recall decisions.[27/28]

In 1980 Governor James Thompson, Republican of Illinois, declared a hiring freeze for every agency under the governor's control. Only the governor's office could grant exceptions, of which there were some 5,000 a year. Evidently, agencies were screening applicants under the state's civil service procedures and then forwarding eligible names to the governor's Office of Personnel for approval or disapproval. The governor's office determined whether the candidate had voted in Republican primaries and had supported the Republican party. Cynthia Rutan, who had been a state employee since 1974, claimed that since 1981 she had been "repeatedly denied promotions to supervisory positions for which she was qualified because she had not worked for or supported the Republican Party" (p. 61).

The Court said the government must show a vital governmental interest before it could condition personnel actions on political belief and association. The majority claimed that preservation of democratic processes was not advantaged by patronage enough to outweigh a public employee's First Amendment rights.

In an earlier case, ***Branti v. Finkel*** (1980), the Court decided 6-3 that in trying to determine what positions were exempt from restrictions on patronage dismissals, "The ultimate inquiry is not whether the label 'policymaker' or 'confidential' fits a particular position; rather, the question is whether the hiring authority can demonstrate that party affiliation is an appropriate requirement for the effective performance of the public office involved."[29] In light of *Rutan,* this restriction on patronage dismissals would seem to apply to hiring as well.

Advocates of civil service systems and administrative efficiency may take heart in *Rutan*. But Justice Scalia's dissent, joined by three other conservative justices, may anticipate a reversal of *Rutan* and restrictions on the constitutional rights of public employees more generally. In his dissent, he argues like the majority in *Rust v. Sullivan* that the government's relationship with its employees is different from its relationship in private matters with citizens. In other words, the government should be able to regulate the lives of its employees more easily than it may regulate the lives of private citizens. The government may treat those who work for it as employees first and citizens second. This issue, of course, is at the heart of determining the extent to which public employee rights in the future will be protected through the Constitution or through legislation, civil service regulations, and collective bargaining agreements.

The Court always has shown some reluctance to enter personnel management in public agencies, but Justice Scalia's dissent in *Rutan* may anticipate increasing deference to legislative and administrative discretion in place of judicial venues.[30] In dissent, Justice Scalia wrote: "The whole point of my dissent is that the desirability of patronage is a policy question to be decided by the people's representatives" (p. 85). The Court's 5-4 majority in *Connick v. Myers* expressed similar reluctance to enter the realm of public personnel management when Justice White wrote: "When employee expression cannot be fairly considered as relating to any matter of political, social, or other concern to the community, government officials should enjoy wide latitude in managing their offices without intrusive oversight by the judiciary in the name of the First Amendment. Perhaps the government employer's dismissal of the worker may not be fair, but ordinary dismissals from government service which violate no fixed tenure or applicable statute or regulation are not subject to judicial review even if the reasons for the dismissal are alleged to be mistaken or unreasonable."[31]

To summarize this discussion of the public employee's rights under the First Amendment: It appears that recent Court decisions suggest a balance shifting toward the value of administrative efficiency and away from the protection of constitutionally guaranteed individual rights. There are some indications that citizens may have to relinquish some constitutional rights when they become public employees; that the standard a public employer must meet in order to discipline an employee claiming a First Amendment interest has diminished; that what constitutes a "matter of public concern" has become more restrictive; and that the Court may be showing more of a predilection than its recent predecessors to distance the judiciary from public personnel management.

Privacy, Drug Testing, and the Fourth Amendment

We have seen that citizens who are public employees often are protected less by the Bill of Rights than ordinary citizens are. The Fourth Amendment to the Constitution protects citizens from unreasonable search and seizure and is a crucial foundation for privacy. It does this in law enforcement cases by requiring the searching authority to obtain a search warrant prior to the search. The search warrant is issued by a neutral party, a judge, who must be convinced that the searching authority has probable cause to believe that the suspected individual has broken the law.

The Fourth Amendment to the Constitution states: "The right of the people to be secure in their persons, houses, papers, and effects, against unreasonable searches and seizures, shall not be violated, and no Warrants shall issue, but upon probable cause, supported by Oath or affirmation, and particularly describing the place to be searched, and the persons or things to be seized."

But in some non-criminal cases, the government is able to conduct a search without a warrant. These are cases like border searches and searches of employee desks and lockers, and searches of individuals themselves—as in drug testing. In these kinds of situations, no probable cause is required. A balance test is performed weighing the government's interest or special need with the individual's expectation of privacy.

For example, working in a state hospital, Magno Ortega was a psychiatrist who was suspected of several improprieties including his acquisition of a computer and charges of sexual harassment as well as taking inappropriate disciplinary action against a resident. While on administrative leave pending an investigation, hospital officials searched his office and seized his property, which it turns out included personal items. Ortega sued, claiming that hospital officials had violated his Fourth Amendment rights. In ***O'Conner v. Ortega*** (1987), the court ruled that the government's interest in maintaining an efficient, effective workplace outweighed Dr. Ortega's privacy interest.[32] This special needs doctrine and balancing test guided the court's subsequent adjudication of drug testing cases. In these cases, the public employee's individual right to privacy is balanced against the government's necessity to insure public safety.[33]

In 1985 the Federal Railroad Administration promulgated rules to curb alcohol and drug abuse by railway employees. Among other provisions, the rules called for drug and alcohol testing for certain railway employees following a major train accident. The Railway Labor Executives' Association, acting on behalf of several unions, charged that the regulations violated the employees' Fourth Amendment rights against unreasonable search and seizure. They claimed a violation because the rules called for the testing of all employees covered by the regulations, regardless of any evidence leading to suspicion that they had broken the law.

In ***Skinner v. Railway Labor Executives' Association*** (1989),[34] the Supreme Court ruled 7-2 that where "special needs" go beyond normal law enforcement and make impractical the securing of a warrant and establishing probable cause, the Court must balance the government's interest against the privacy interests of the individual in order to determine if the Fourth Amendment has been violated. According to the Court in *Skinner*, regulating the conduct of railroad employees to ensure safe transportation constitutes a compelling government interest, especially because the railroad industry had a history of alcohol and drug abuse by its employees. Further, the Court ruled that the drug testing constituted a minimal intrusion into the privacy of the railroad workers since they knew in advance who would be tested, and when and under what conditions the testing would take place.

The Court's reasoning in its drug testing cases has implications generally for the relationship between the courts and public employers. In ***National Treasury Employees Union v. Von Raab*** (1989), the Court said that the intrusion of privacy by United States Customs Service drug testing procedures was minimized by the administrative regulations themselves: "These procedures significantly minimize the program's intrusion on privacy interests."[35] In other words, the Customs Service developed a set of procedures on drug testing that successfully anticipated a constitutional challenge. Those procedures were aimed not only at promoting political responsiveness and administrative efficiency but also at recognizing the individual rights of the employees. In other words, the impact of the Court on public personnel administration is evident in these drug testing cases not only in the specific decisions it has rendered, but in the Court's power to encourage administrative agencies to think like a judge and anticipate judicial challenge as they develop administrative rules and procedures.[36]

LIABILITY OF PUBLIC EMPLOYEES

In the 1970s the Court enlarged the scope of its constitutional inquiry, granting more rights to public employees, clients or beneficiaries of the government, prisoners, and citizens who otherwise might come in contact with government officials. It is one thing for the courts to grant new rights; it is another to enforce recognition of and respect for them. One mechanism to advance these ends is the threat that a public official might be held personally liable for violating a citizen's constitutional rights. Traditionally, administrators came to share the same immunity from civil suits arising out of actions connected with their official functions as had formerly belonged only to legislators and judges and other special classes of public employees. But in order to balance the need to protect the rights of citizens with the need to protect public officials who are required to exercise discretion that affects citizens, the doctrine of **sovereign immunity** gave way to a more limited form of immunity for administrative officials. The revised doctrine, captured clearly now in ***Harlow v. Fitzgerald*** (1982), states that "government officials performing discretionary functions generally are shielded from liability for civil damages insofar as their conduct does not violate clearly established statutory or Constitutional rights of which a reasonable person would have known."[37]

The concept of **qualified immunity** outlined in *Harlow* suggests that in order to perform their job effectively and with only minor fear of being sued, public officials must become aware of the constitutional law that impinges upon their work and the work of their agency. Moreover, the threat of liability for a public official is directly related to the scope of constitutional rights the Court is willing to grant public employees and citizens. The broader the rights, the greater the threat of liability; the narrower the interpretation of rights, the less the threat, because it takes a strong case for a plaintiff to substantiate a claim that a right has been violated. A more liberal Court might have found that Harry Connick violated the First Amendment rights of Sheila Myers. If it had, the threat of liability would have hung more threateningly over the heads of future public officials contemplating adverse personnel actions against public employees who speak out against them and disrupt the workplace. But it did not, and the threat to public officials in the 1990s seems less ominous. Whether or not the public benefits is less clear.

A recent development is the potential liability that public employers have for criminal acts of their employees. "Typically, these lawsuits claim a failure by the employer to exercise proper care in the hiring, supervision and/or training of an employee" (p. 491).[38] Thus, in contrast to common practice, the public employer may be responsible for the private actions of an employee. For example, a housing authority unwittingly hires as a housing inspector an individual with a history of theft. The inspector is subsequently found guilty of theft and assault of one of the tenants. The tenant sues the housing authority claiming a negligence in hiring. The authority put the tenants at risk, and it should have known about the inspector's criminal history. Some state statutes limit the liability of public employers in this regard. But in cases of gross negligence and where constitutional rights have been violated, a victim may sue under Title 42 U.S. Code 1983, which imposes liability on public employees for "deprivation of any rights, privileges, or immunities secured by the Constitution."

Interestingly, this negligent employee process liability can cause confusion for the human resource manager who also is under notice not to reveal information about discharged employees that might harm their ability to secure another job. Employees have liberty interests guaranteed by the Constitution's Fifth Amendment. The government cannot abridge a person's liberty without due process. The freedom to work is considered a liberty, and if a public employer stigmatizes an employee in the context of discharging or failing to rehire, it may have violated the employee's Fifth Amendment right if due process has not been observed.[39] Sometimes, due process is a simple matter of giving the employee an opportunity to respond in writing to adverse information that may be filed in an employee's personnel records. In other cases, it may require a pre- or post-termination hearing that would allow the employee to respond to any adverse information connected with the discharge.

PROPERTY RIGHTS AND DUE PROCESS

Earlier, we suggested that the sanction function is concerned with both the substance of employee and employer expectations and obligations, and the processes by which these expectations and obligations are established and maintained. Now, we will look at procedural rights and how they are balanced by the value of organizational efficiency.

The process side of this concern is found in two concepts—**property rights** and **due process**. It has become popular to assert that civil service rules "hamstring" management by making it impossible to discipline or discharge employees protected by civil service systems. In one respect, this statement is correct. Public employees have rights to their jobs that exceed those of their private-sector counterparts. Yet this statement is also incorrect, for these rights ultimately are derived from the constitutional requirement of due process, rather than civil service regulations. Constitutional protections accorded *public* employees are an extension of the government's responsibility to guarantee certain freedoms to its citizens. The key here is that the *government* is bound by the Constitution, whether in its dealings with citizens simply as individuals or citizens as employees.

The Fifth and Fourteenth Amendments to the Constitution require that a government may deprive an individual of life, liberty, or property only after due process of law. Over the years, the courts have come to conclude that public employees have a property interest in their jobs, if they have been led to expect that they will hold their jobs permanently as long as they perform satisfactorily. Courts have found these expectations implied in personnel policies and manuals that specify an employee will be discharged for good cause only, or where specific grounds for dismissal are identified, or where progressive discipline is endorsed and steps identified.[40] In other words, a job can be considered a public employee's property, and once that is established, the government—the public employer—can take the property/job only after due process.

One of the efficiency arguments for contracting out for service delivery or hiring temporary workers is that their expectations of due process are less than that of permanent civil service employees. With fewer rights, managerial discretion increases and flexibility in handling human resources is enhanced. On the one hand, private-sector employees who handle the contract work have no constitutional rights as employees, and in the case of temporary workers, even if hired by a public employer, there are no expectations of job security.

What is due process? Minimal due process requires that an employer notify an employee of the employee's violation and give the employee a chance to state his or her side of the story. Due process comes in degrees, where the amount depends on the scope of the discipline contemplated. The critical step in linking due process with fairness comes when the person or board hearing the employee appeal or grievance is not in the employee's normal chain of command. This conveys the message that the employee will be heard impartially—by an investigator, board, or arbitrator.

A simple written reprimand might appropriately call for minimal due process, but a contemplated firing that would deprive a public employee of the economic means of supporting himself or herself and possibly create difficulty for the employee when seeking another job (infringe on the employee's liberty to seek employment), would require a pre-termination hearing.[41] Once again, we see personnel policies and practices growing out of an attempt to balance an employee's expectations of fair treatment (individual rights) with the employer's necessity to manage the public workforce efficiently.

ORGANIZATIONAL CITIZENSHIP AND EMPLOYEE PERCEPTIONS OF FAIRNESS

Organizational effectiveness hinges on intangible elements of the psychological contract like the willingness to cooperate, courtesy, sportsmanship, loyalty and commitment. These characteristics can be included within the concept of **organizational citizenship.** The concept of the employee as a citizen of the organization leads us to the frequently overlooked fact that work in complex organizations is a social enterprise, and a healthy organizational climate in part depends upon the quality of that citizenship. Even though we still hold individuals accountable for their performance, rarely are they solely responsible for it because one employee's work is usually so intertwined with the work of others. The willingness of an employee to be a "good" citizen in part depends on personality predispositions. But, in addition, it is influenced by job satisfaction and the degree to which the employee experiences fair treatment.[42]

Thus, striving to treat employees fairly is not simply the right thing to do; it is smart as well. Fairly treated employees are more likely to cooperate, be courteous, show good sportsmanship with colleagues—in short, to be good organizational citizens—than those who feel they have been treated unfairly.[43] This makes sense considering that a person who feels an expectation has been violated may "get even" more easily by being uncooperative, discourteous, and disloyal than by shirking essential work duties. Similarly, an employee who feels the organization has exceeded its obligations may find it easier to "pay back" the organization with cooperative behavior rather than producing more or better work—which may be beyond the employee's control.

Calculations of fairness are both substantive—assessing the fairness of specific decisions regarding organizational rewards and punishments—and procedural—how these decisions are made and carried out. The importance of procedural justice should not be underestimated in promoting organizational citizenship. According to Neihoff and Moorman, "Procedural justice is instrumental in promoting group concerns because fair procedures communicate the message that the group values each member."[44]

Moorman has found that procedural justice consists of both the policies and methods to make organizational decisions regarding the distribution of rewards and punishments as well as an interpersonal aspect—the way supervisors and managers implement the policies and methods. His literature review confirms that employee perceptions of substantive justice are influenced by how those decisions are arrived at and carried out.[45] Perhaps most important, his research shows that perceptions of fairness emanating from how supervisors treat employees is a cornerstone of organizational justice and thus, organizational citizenship. This is one reason why how downsizing decisions are made and how they are implemented are so crucial in influencing the behavior and commitment of employees who stay.

While downsizing is an obvious challenge to maintaining perceptions of fairness, there are many others. The context of public employment today creates a two-tiered world of permanent employees with stable expectations of job security and others who fear their jobs are threatened by privatization, contracting out, or replacement by temporary or part-time workers. The manager and supervisor's job is incredibly difficult in this situation. How does a supervisor convey genuine concern for employees when privatization may be just around the corner of the next election? The psychological contract is fluid and comprised of expectations and obligations stemming not only from each worker's own experiences but also on what the employees see and hear about the treatment of others. Bad news is always bad news to the person receiving it no matter how it is delivered. But the way a person arrives at a decision containing bad news and communicates it will become known throughout an organization. While the goal of due process is to treat individual employees fairly, the consequence is the climate that is set and the larger picture that is drawn for all employees regardless of whether they ever utilize grievance or other due process channels or are the recipients of bad organizational news.

DISCIPLINE AND COUNSELING OF THE UNPRODUCTIVE EMPLOYEE

The employee's sense of fairness is significantly affected by how disciplinary and grievance procedures are carried out, and this puts a premium on the supervisor's role. Disciplinary action is the last step—never the first—in dealing with an employee whose performance is substandard. It assumes that the supervisor of a poorly performing employee has asked a number of questions regarding job design, selection, orientation, performance appraisal, training, and compensation:

Job design	Are the tasks, conditions, and performance standards of the position reasonable and equitable?
Selection	Does the employee meet the minimum qualifications established for the position?
Orientation	Were organizational rules and regulations, and position requirements clearly communicated to the new employee?
Performance appraisal	Was the employee's performance adequately documented, and was the employee provided informal and formal feedback on the quality of his or her performance?
Training	Does the employee have adequate skills to perform the required tasks at the expected level of competence?
Compensation	Is good performance rewarded, or are there factors in the work environment that make it impossible or punishing to perform well?

Theoretically, therefore, discipline represents the last step in supervising employees because it symbolizes a failure to adjust the expectations/obligations of the employment relationship by less intrusive means. It is primarily a supervisory responsibility, since most performance problems are handled informally within the work unit with minimal involvement by the personnel department.

If the performance problem cannot be resolved informally by the supervisor and other employees within the unit, the supervisor may request that formal disciplinary action be taken by the personnel department. If this occurs, it is the personnel manager's responsibility to ensure that all other causes of the performance problem have been considered. Figure 12-1 shows the sequence of personnel activities that occur prior to disciplinary action. It is the primary responsibility of the employee's immediate supervisor to ensure that each of these steps is followed. Together, they represent the counseling and disciplinary action process.

The personnel manager has three important responsibilities with respect to disciplinary action. Initially, the personnel department is responsible for establishing the process. Once it has been established as part of the agency's personnel rules and regulations, the personnel director is frequently responsible for counseling unproductive employees and for assisting the supervisor in implementing evaluation and training procedures to improve performance or institute disciplinary action. Last, the personnel director is responsible for making sure the system

Figure 12-1 Disciplinary Action and Other Personnel Activites

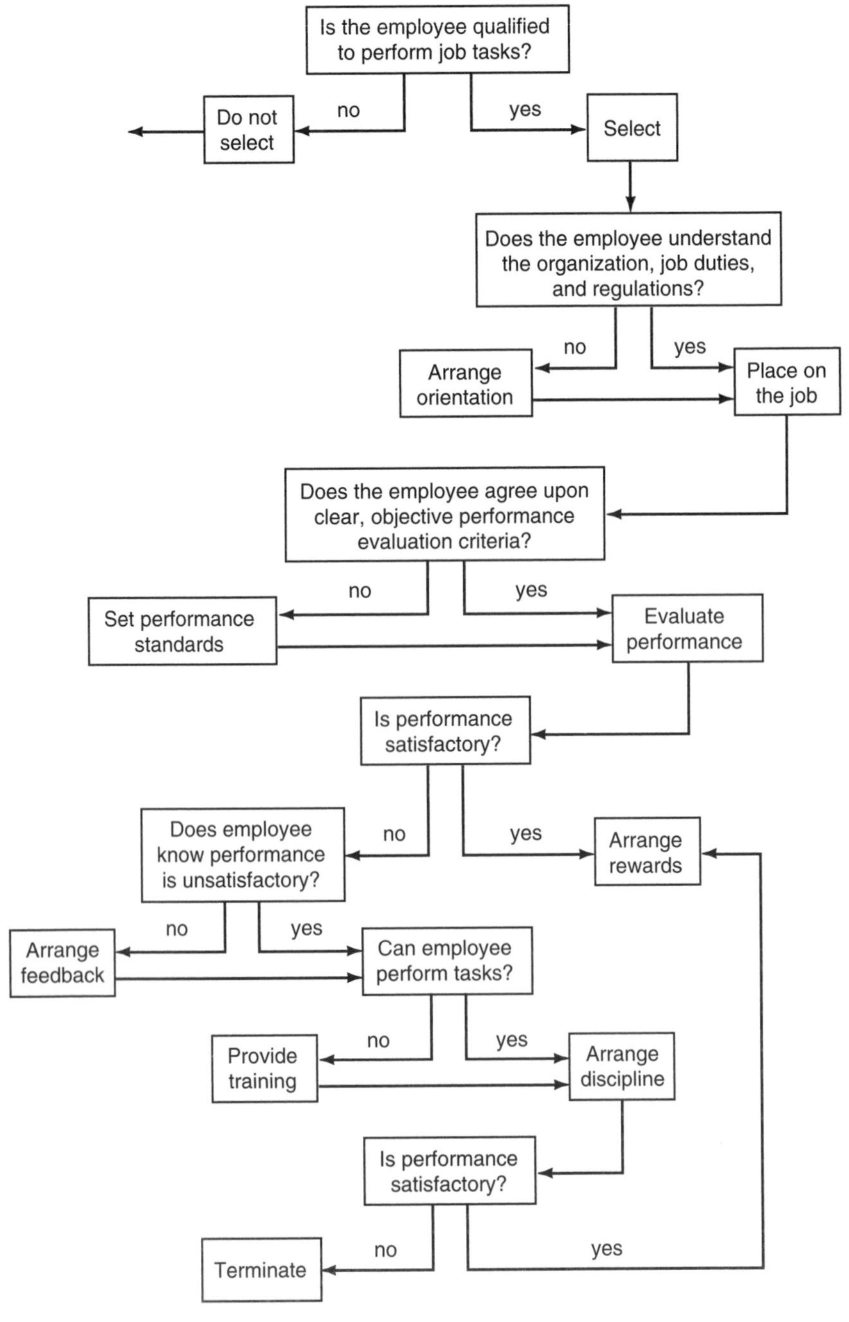

is applied equitably. The following memorandum from the personnel director in Kansas City, Missouri, to department heads, shows that the personnel director has both a facilitating and a policing role in the disciplinary process.

To: All Department Heads

From: Tom F. Lewinsohn, Director of Personnel

Subject: Employee Rights and Obligations

In today's world of work we hear much about employee rights but seldom hear about employee obligations. With our departmental budgets becoming tighter those employee obligations deserve even more critical attention. For their paychecks, which is only one of their rights, employees can be expected to fulfill obligations such as showing up for work regularly and punctually, taking directions from supervisors, doing their jobs correctly, and following rules.

Too often supervisors do not act soon enough in trying to correct employees not living up to their job obligations. Employees failing to show up for work regularly and/or punctually may be accommodated by giving them status as part-time employees which more accurately reflects their availability for work. Some employees not living up to their job obligations are tolerated until their supervisors can no longer bear it. Then, by taking disciplinary action, the supervisors may have overreacted to one offense with no back-up data to support their action. Supervisors must be able to justify their disciplinary actions which may be more often justified and upheld when they acted after having considered the following:

1. Did the employee know that his or her behavior could result in disciplinary action?
2. Was the rule being enforced fairly, and was it applied consistently?
3. Was there an objective investigation of the offense?
4. Does the severity of the discipline reflect the seriousness of the offense and, when possible, take into consideration the employee's service record?

Most of the employees' rights and obligations, listed in the Personnel Rules and Regulations, are sometimes expanded upon by departmental regulations. However, departmental regulations must not conflict with the Personnel Rules and Regulations. Even though departments may become legally bound by their departmental regulations, in cases of appeal of disciplinary action, the departments may lose their enforcement of that disciplinary action if the disciplining supervisor failed to follow departmental regulations.

Employee rights and obligations will become, if they have not already become, a crucial part of managing better with less in the coming austere budget year. It is perhaps the time to rejuvenate the work ethic, "a fair day's pay for a fair day's work," which includes fair and equitable treatment. Also, it may be time for a reminder that no one has a right to a job, only a right to compete for a job and to retain a job with its rights as a result of fulfilling job obligations.

TFL:njc

It is often necessary to confront an unproductive employee in order to bring the person's poor job performance out into the open. This is done through a counseling session. The personnel manager should prepare for this session by reviewing its objectives, namely, behavioral change in the direction of increased productivity. Its purpose is not to attack the employee's personality, habits, or attitudes; nor is it intended to intimidate the employee or drive him or her out of the organization.

If an employee has violated agency regulations or has not responded to previous counseling or performance deficiencies, an interview informing the employee of disciplinary action would be in order. However, where a performance problem has not been previously discussed with the employee or where the employee shows evidence of a gradual deterioration in productivity or work habits, a nondirective interview may be in order. During the nondirective interview it is the supervisor's responsibility to advise the employee of the supervisor's concern and to try to determine what factors are influencing the employee's behavior and if the supervisor is in a position to be of assistance. If, after ensuring that the employee knows not only what the problem is but what the supervisor considers desirable employee performance, after a reasonable period of time discipline may be in order.

The supervisor and the personnel department play mutually supporting roles for the disciplinary system to work effectively. The personnel manager must help establish a clear and equitable system; the supervisor must provide adequate supervision of employees and enforce work rules fairly. If discipline is required, it is a good idea for it to be handed out by the personnel department on the basis of information provided by the supervisor. This will provide equitable treatment for employees throughout the organization.

STEPS IN THE GRIEVANCE PROCESS

Every day, in thousands of instances, employees—public and private—claim they have been treated unjustly. In a very provocative statement, David Ewing, a well-known authority on employee rights, recently observed: "It appears that very few [nonunion] companies in this country — possibly as few as thirty to fifty — have had effective grievance procedures in place for several years or more."[46] This will come as a surprise to most public employees and their employers, who have had **grievance procedures** for years as an integral part of merit systems.

It is important that discipline and grievance systems and procedures provide for protection of the employee's substantive and procedural rights. An employee's appeal of a disciplinary action will usually follow the same channels as a grievance initiated by an employee. In the case of discipline, documentation showing that an employee's performance is contrary to expectations the employer holds of all employees must be provided. The employee must be given ample opportunity to respond to these charges. Figure 12-2 provides a diagram of typical disciplinary action and grievance procedures. Note that if the employee is a member of a minority group, the affirmative action officer may be involved in the process.

FIGURE 12–2 Disciplinary Action Procedures

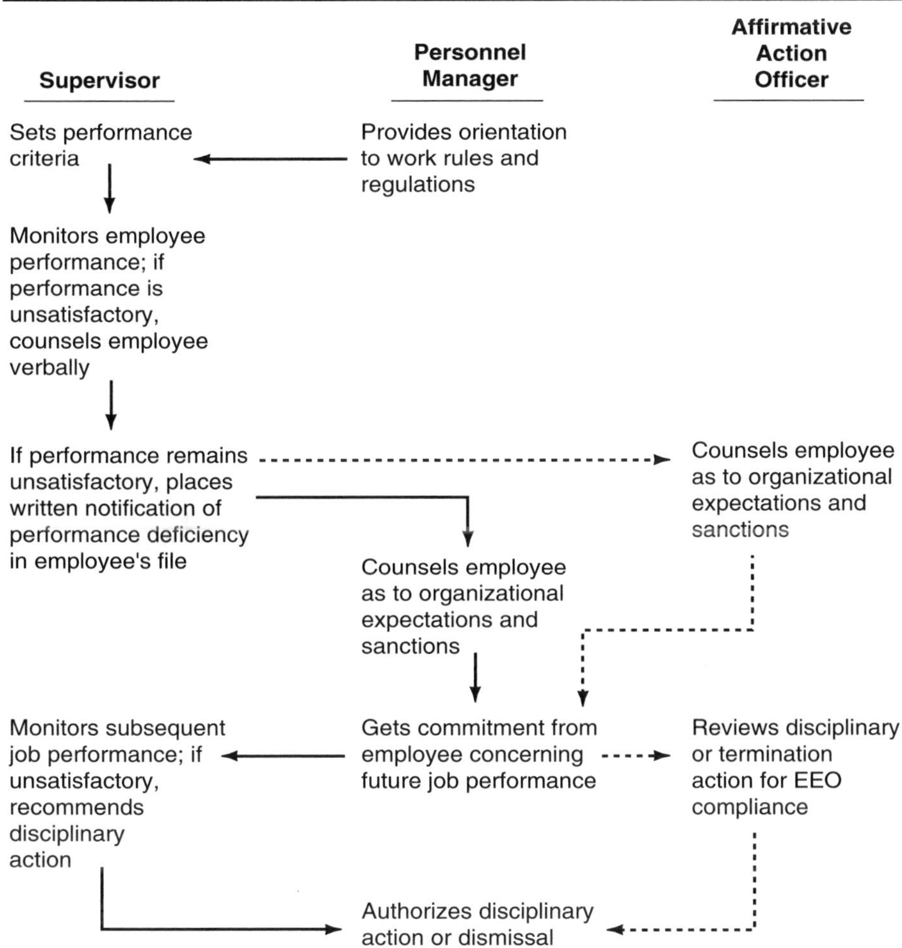

Management should establish with employees grievance procedures that clearly establish the employee's right to file written complaints concerning alleged unfair management practices, and procedures for hearing these complaints in the agency. The specific items that might arise and be subject to a grievance complaint could be defined in personnel rules and regulations. If a collective bargaining agreement exists, the grievance procedure will be defined in the contract. Usually, grievances will be limited to topics in the working rules that an employee believes management has violated. Topics such as the following will probably be included as issues contained in a negotiated contract or in personnel rules enforced by a civil service board. Under each possible area of grievance we have given an example drawn from the exit interview files of a state agency in Kansas.

Work assignments Employees may feel that work assignments are made subjectively.

I don't know how other sections are, but in our section conditions were very bad. There is too much favoritism by the supervisors. Not all employees are treated equal; some are picked on. Blacks are favored only because they are afraid of them, and that they will yell "discrimination" when whites are really the ones discriminated against. There is also a lot of unfairness as to who does what work.

Promotion	An employee may feel that the promotional criteria established for a position were not valid or not utilized, or that promotional procedures were improper.

The chances for advancement, unless you knew the correct people, were very poor. There were some cases I knew for sure that people who were most qualified for the job were passed over in favor of a friend, relative, or friend of a friend. There was one case in particular I remember. A person started out at a Clerk I position, took the test for Clerk-Typist I, failed the test, but still secured a Clerk-Typist II position elsewhere in the department.

Poor supervision	Employees may feel that supervision is inadequate, and that supervisors are biased or incompetent.

The people I worked beside were nice, for the most part. There was a supervisor in the position above me who was only 19 years old and lacked the knowledge of how to handle the situation. I brought this up to her supervisor and was told that it could be made very hard for me if I "caused waves," so I gave up my job.

Political interference	Conflict arises between elected and appointed officials, or among supervisors.

Also, the department should back up its own policies. I found several cases during my five years of employment when I received a memo dictating what my actions should be in certain circumstances, which I followed to the letter. However, if someone complained to the department heads stationed in the capital, they changed the rules on the spot and left me looking like I didn't know my own job. In general, I feel that the state should quit playing politics with civil service employment. Then they could get a little efficiency back into the system.

Sexual discrimination	Gender inequities and sexual harassment often lead to employee perceptions of unfair treatment.

It is a little unfortunate that the chiefs are allowed to carry on, then customers make comments to the effect: "Are he and missy still playing doctor or hanky panky in the halls or in the observation booth?" The same chief allows some of his girls to do whatever they want and only a few have to toe the line anytime the others crack the whip. It's also a shame the same man is capable of destroying your future.

In any of these instances, it is important that the agency have an established informal and formal grievance procedure that would allow employees to bring their charges to the notice of higher ups and get a fair hearing. The following steps might constitute a typical grievance process:

1. *Informal counseling.* The aggrieved employee should meet and discuss the situation with his or her supervisor or the next higher up if the complaint is about the employee's immediate supervisor. The success of this step depends on an organizational environment that encourages employees to speak openly about their concerns.
2. *Formal grievance.* If informal counseling is unsuccessful, the aggrieved employee should have the opportunity to file a formal grievance in writing stating the problem and what the employee thinks ought to be done to correct the situation. If asked by the employee, the personnel department can help the employee prepare the necessary document.
3. *Consultation between supervisor and personnel director.* After the grievance is filed, the personnel department should consult with the employee to verify the situation and then work with the parties to see if an agreement can be reached.
4. *Investigation/adjudication/arbitration.* A number of steps can follow the attempt by the personnel department to work out a solution between the parties. These might include assigning an impartial person—often from the personnel department—to investigate and make a decision; convening a panel to hear the complaint and make a decision; and securing an outside arbitrator to hear the complaint and render a decision.

Employees can seek redress of grievances by following agency procedures. The more due process afforded the employee internally, the less likely it is that an employee will seek an external channel to air a grievance.[47] In fact, some legal proceedings will require that internal grievance procedures be followed before undertaking judicial avenues. In other cases, the external investigating agency or court will incorporate the proceedings of an internal process as part of its own review.

THE SANCTION FUNCTION IN ALTERNATE PERSONNEL SYSTEMS

We have talked in general about organizational justice, the mechanisms for establishing the terms of the employment relationship, and various processes for maintaining or enforcing those terms. But there truly are significant differences in the sanction function, depending upon which personnel system the employee is part of. This is because with the sanction function, the rules of the personnel game are established and maintained. This is where the expectations and obligations of employee and employer are determined and enforced. Every so often, one group or another will test its power to influence the rules. This is what inevitably happens with a strike. Regardless of the outcomes on wages, a strike gives the adversaries the opportunity to see where they stand with regard to setting expectations and obligations of employee and employer. Taking a case to court or arbitration can serve the same purpose. Battles between the legislature and executive branches of government are often fought over who has the discretion to set the personnel rules.

The reason why unions were so successful in early years of this century was because they held out the promise of organizational justice for employees. One of the first objectives of a union is to negotiate a grievance procedure that includes a third-party decision-making process—one that takes the employee's grievance outside the managerial chain of command. Civil service systems similarly value individual rights as a way of protecting employees from partisan political pressure. The first objective of civil service reform in the late nineteenth century was to legislate the elimination of politics from administration through the creation of systems in which employees could be dismissed only for performance deficiencies, not because they belonged to the wrong party or failed to pay voluntary dues. With regard to the sanction function, however, civil service systems differ from collective bargaining, because civil service systems are founded on dual values—individual rights and efficiency. Thus, even though we often see elaborate due process protections for public employees, we also hear complaints from managers, themselves covered by the same civil service protections, about the red tape and due process that hardly makes it worth the effort, in their eyes, to discipline employees.

Affirmative action personnel systems are driven by the value of social equity and, depending upon the context, individual rights. The expectation in affirmative action systems is that each person will be treated on his or her own merits and performance. But the benign use of racial classifications benefiting minorities at the expense of the individual rights of non-minorities are rarely rejected by affirmative action advocates. Affirmative action personnel systems strongly advocate due process as a way of ensuring fair treatment in organizational systems suspected of bias.

When it comes to political personnel systems and also to contracting out, the value of individual rights diminishes in favor of responsiveness and efficiency, respectively. Due process may not be highly valued. Political executives who serve at the pleasure of elected leaders enjoy virtually no employee rights. Their positions do not fall under merit system provisions, and they are hired, moved, and dismissed largely based on a calculation of the political value they bring to an administration. Consequently, they may be less respectful of the rights of others, and see them as impediments to political and administrative action.

Contracting out is often seen as a way of circumventing personnel systems where individual rights have become entrenched at the expense of efficiency and responsiveness. Once a service is contracted out to a private employer, employees will find themselves operating under a new personnel system, usually with fewer employee rights. The constitutional protections that employees enjoy under a public personnel system no longer apply, and the due process public employees generally enjoy may be sacrificed to the goal of administrative efficiency and profit.

ORGANIZATIONAL JUSTICE, PRODUCTIVITY, AND WORKFORCE DIVERSITY

It seems clear that over the years the expectations employees have of their employers have risen. Employees expect job security, a decent wage, health benefits, a sound retirement system, safe working conditions, an environment free of unfair discrimination, participation in decisions that affect them, and in some cases, child care and parental leave. At the same time, demands on public employers for productivity have resulted in layoffs, declining health benefits, and reduced rights, privatization, and part-time work. These contrasting forces place considerable strain on the sanction function and complicate perceptions of organizational justice and organizational citizenship.

Furthermore, there is substantial sentiment among public managers as well as the public at large that the relationship between the rights of public employees and managerial flexibility has tilted towards the side of employees at the expense of government efficiency and responsiveness.

Recent statements by the U.S. Merit Systems Protection Board, created by the Civil Service Reform Act of 1978 to hear federal employee appeals, are significant in this regard.[48] In 1994, the Merit Systems Protection Board conducted a survey of federal managers asking them about their actions in dealing with poorly performing employees. According to the report, "Our findings demonstrate the need to correct the imbalance between forces discouraging supervisors from firing poor performers and the near total absence of forces encouraging them to act."[49]

The report indicates that the "problems in dealing with poor performers are so pronounced" that several steps should be contemplated including consolidating the paths available to discipline employees; consolidating the opportunities for employees to appeal disciplinary actions; and, finally, permitting poor performance to be considered in reduction-in-force procedures.

But the sanction function is driven by more than demands for individual rights versus productivity or administrative efficiency. Added to this contentious set of factors is the demographic trend toward increasing ethnic diversity in the workforce. Ethnic diversity will complicate employee expectations and what employers can expect from employees. This heterogeneity in expectations and obligations can be expected to place additional strain on the organizational processes aimed at matching them.

It appears that one of the issues that will dominate human resource management is how organizations can effectively manage the relationship between workforce diversity, organizational justice, and productivity. The relationship between any two of these factors might be predictable, but inserting the third adds a dimension of significant uncertainty.

SUMMARY

In some ways, the sanction function is the most important of the four core functions. Activities designed to fulfill this function aim to establish and maintain the terms of the relationship between employee and employer. These terms consist of expectations and obligations employee and employer have of each other, and they constitute the rules of the game. Expectations and obligations arise from a number of sources. Of these, only public employees enjoy rights stemming from the Constitution. However, practically, these rights are balanced against the duty a public employer has to operate efficiently. In this balance we can see the inevitable conflict between administrative efficiency and individual rights and resultant perceptions about organizational justice.

Recent rulings suggest that the contemporary Supreme Court has tipped the balance in favor of administrative efficiency over individual rights. With the judicial avenue narrowing, the rights of employees are likely to result from new legislation and administrative policy, rules and regulations rather than appeals to constitutional protections.

Internal disciplinary and grievance procedures are mechanisms to enforce the terms of the employment relationship. Increasing diversity of the workforce will bring a broader array of employee expectations and obligations to the workplace. Relatively objective disciplinary guidelines and impartial grievance procedures might be expected to ameliorate the negative impact of these differences and provide a foundation of respect necessary to channel the differences into creativity and productivity. The challenge is to accomplish this in a political environment where public employees are seen as entrenched and as obstacles to government efficiency and responsiveness.

KEY TERMS

discipline
due process
grievance procedure
organizational citizenship
property rights
psychological contract
reasonable accommodation
sanction function
sexual harassment
sovereign versus qualified immunity
terms of the employment relationship
undue hardship
whistle-blowing
Branti v. Finkel (1980)
Connick v. Myers (1983)
Harlow v. Fitzgerald (1982)
Harris v. Forklift (1993)
Meritor Savings Bank v. Vinson (1986)
National Treasury Employees Union v. Von Raab (1989)
New York Times v. Sullivan (1964)
O'Conner v. Ortega (1987)
Rust v. Sullivan (1991)
Rutan v. Republican Party of Illinois (1990)
Skinner v. Railway Labor Executives' Association (1989)
Wabaunsee County v. Umbehr (1996)

DISCUSSION QUESTIONS

1. Define the sanction function, and identify the ways an organization establishes and maintains the terms of the employment relationship between employee and employer.
2. Public employees are granted more rights generally than private-sector employees. Why is this so? Do you think public employees should give up their rights as citizens in their capacity as employees? Do you think public-sector employees should have fewer rights? Do you think that private-sector employees should have more rights?
3. Describe the rights of employees who have been sexually harassed or who are considered whistle-blowers.
4. Discuss the balance the Supreme Court examines when deciding whether a public employer has violated an employee's First Amendment right to free speech.

5. Do you agree with the provisions of the Fourth Amendment? Do you agree that public employers ought to be able to conduct drug screens of their employees? If you answer "yes" to both questions, how do you reconcile the tension between your positions? How does the Court reconcile the tension?
6. Why do you think the Supreme Court considers a person's job as property? Describe the role of property rights and due process in establishing and maintaining the terms of the employment relationship.
7. Is it useful to consider employees as organizational citizens? If so, what expectations might they hold of their employer? And what expectations might the employer have of them in return? Today, it is frequently asserted that in society at large people seem more concerned with their rights than their community or citizenship obligations. Do you think this is true of organizational citizens as well? How do you think the contemporary employment environment affects organizational citizenship?
8. Discuss how discipline and grievance procedures are connected to the sanction function.
9. Diagram a typical disciplinary procedure.
10. Are the interests of employee and employer the same in establishing a grievance procedure? Construct a model grievance procedure from the employee's standpoint. Construct it now from the employer's standpoint. Do you have any differences? As an employer, which process would you use to construct a grievance procedure?
11. How does the sanction function differ in alternate personnel systems?
12. What relationship do you see between organizational justice, productivity, and workforce diversity?
13. Use the various court cases described in the chapter to show how the courts reach a balance among the four values.
14. When discussing politics, sometimes we refer to "inalienable rights." What does this mean? Do you think that public employees should have any inalienable rights?
15. Some have argued that democratic values must be practiced in order to be learned. If democratic values were practiced in organizations, how would the relationship between employee and employer change? What would be the benefits and the costs?

CASE STUDY JUAN HERNANDEZ V. THE COUNTY

INTRODUCTION

Metropolitan County is the largest local government in the state. County-government is divided into about 50 operating departments and employs about 20,000 people. Among the departments is the Office of Data Processing Center (DPC).

Juan Hernandez, a Hispanic male, was employed by the DPC on July 15, 1982, as a data processing trainee. On May 10, 1983, he was promoted to the position of Computer Operator I and attained permanent status in that position six months later. He remained in that position until his termination on March 9, 1992.

This case study will examine the circumstances leading to his dismissal, his role as a union steward for Local 121 of the American Federation of State, County and Municipal Employees (AFSCME), and the various steps involved in his termination. It will reach conclusions relating to the disciplinary action and grievance process in public agencies in general.

EMPLOYMENT HISTORY

From his initial employment until April 1987, Juan Hernandez's record reflected satisfactory and dependable service. On April 25, 1987, however, he received a written reprimand for failing to satisfactorily back up numerous documents that were lost in a power outage.

Mr. Hernandez reacted to the reprimand by a letter of rebuttal which indicated that he disagreed sharply with management's allegations of his lack of general competence.

In October 1987, he received an evaluation summarizing his performance as "in need of attention." His schedule merit increase was deferred for three months. Although the overall tone of the evaluation was encouraging, it implied an incompetence in his ability to grasp the concepts of a larger computer system. Mr. Hernandez appealed the evaluation, but withdrew the appeal when he received a satisfactory evaluation along with his merit increase three months later.

In January 1988 the Director of operations for the DPC brought about a reorganization that resulted in Mr. Hernandez being switched from the day to night shift. Despite his objections to this change, Mr. Hernandez's employment continued satisfactorily for the next 18 months, until he suffered a severe on-the-job injury on July 26, 1989. A portion of the raised computer floor collapsed while he was on it carrying a box of computer paper. His resultant knee and leg injuries caused Mr. Hernandez to be absent from work for 425 hours.

Upon his return to work on October 27, 1988, he was presented with a formal record of counseling dated July 29, 1989, just three days after his injury had occurred. This record, which was prepared by his supervisor as a summary of the informal counseling that had occurred with him, cited a number of infractions, having to do with failure to make up time for a long lunch; failure to produce a leave slip for his absence; and for improperly printing various forms needed by other departments.

On June 29, 1991, Mr. Hernandez was given a formal record of counseling citing his involvement in a technical failure that occurred in the computer room at the main console. The essence of the incident concerned Mr. Hernandez' evident unfamiliarity with the software that both he and the operators under his supervision were utilizing.

SHOP STEWARD

On July 27, 1991, Mr. Hernandez was elected to the position of shop steward representing the DPC employees with AFSCME Local 121. During his term as shop steward, he aided several employees who were contemplating filing grievances against the DPC on the grounds that the agency was illegally testing computer operators prior to giving them permanent appointments.

TERMINATION

On January 9, 1992, Juan Hernandez was himself given an "unsatisfactory" performance evaluation based on his failure to complete certain training courses, designed to insure his knowledge of the hardware and software both he and his subordinates were utilizing. He refused to sign this evaluation.

On January 23, 1992, he was charged one day without pay for calling in sick the day before the start of his scheduled one-week vacation. Upon returning to work, he submitted a doctor's statement excusing him for the absence. This doctor's statement, coupled with other evidence, would later prove the grounds for his termination.

Mr. Robert Hess, an administrative officer for the DPC, began to compile evidence that Mr. Hernandez had falsified doctors' statements that excused several of his absences. He had observed that the handwriting of doctors' excuses dated June 15, 1991, and January 23, 1992, did not match the handwriting of other excuses obtained from the same doctor for the injuries suffered in his 1989 accident. In addition, the excuses in question were written on Pacific Hospital forms, while the others were not.

Interviews were conducted with the physician, Dr. Herman Wilbanks, and with Mr. Vincent Pico, administrative resident at Pacific Hospital. Dr. Wilbanks denied writing the excuses; and Mr. Pico confirmed that Mr. Hernandez had not been a patient at the hospital on the dates in question.

Mr. Hernandez then altered his story by stating that the excuse that he had submitted for the January 23 absence was a copy of the original. He claimed that his daughter, a pre-med student at Long Beach State University, had copied the original one "as practice for her classes," and he had mistakenly submitted the copy. However, the Los Angeles County Crime Laboratory Bureau confirmed that the handwriting was the same on both forms.

On March 10, 1992, Mr. Hernandez attended a scheduled disciplinary action meeting in the office of the deputy director of the DPC. He was represented by the union. At this meeting, he was given a termination letter and a disciplinary action report effecting his dismissal. He signed the form at the union representative's advice.

APPEAL HEARING

An appeal hearing was held on May 10, 1992. Mr. Hernandez was represented by AFSCME Local 121; the County was represented by the County Attorney's Office.

The impartial hearing examiner concluded that violations 1 through 4 were not substantiated, but that the charge of a false claim of leave was substantiated. Mr. Hernandez's termination was sustained (Exhibit A).

CONCLUSION

Both collective bargaining agreements and disciplinary action procedures provide for progressive discipline of employees for poor performance, and they protect employees against unfair harassment or unsubstantiated allegations.

In the case of Juan Hernandez, the pattern and timing of management's disciplinary action against him are both suspect. A casual review of his record of disciplinary action indicates that it followed on-the-job injuries and his election as shop steward.

On the other hand, it is also clear that Mr. Hernandez's work performance was frequently careless or incompetent. Moreover, his falsification of medical excuses was flagrantly dishonest. Management's efforts to substantiate this required the spending of much time, money, and effort. It was also aided by the fact that the DPC, as a computer-oriented agency, was able to establish objective performance standards (in terms of quantity, quality, and timeliness of production). By monitoring these incidents, it was able to document irregular performance incidents.

Yet despite management's advantages, the only incident of willful misconduct that was upheld was the falsification of medical statements, an infraction relating to personnel rules rather than productivity. The lesson to be learned from this is that management, in the final analysis, when attempting to terminate an employee who is backed by union and legal representation in front of an impartial examiner, must have documentation that unquestionably proves guilt on the part of the employee charged with the violation of a concise, tangible regulation.

QUESTIONS

After finishing the case study and studying the exhibit carefully, be prepared to discuss the following questions in a small group, and to defend your answers in subsequent class discussion.

1. Did the employer (the Data Processing Center) provide Mr. Hernandez with clear performance standards from the time of his employment to the time of his termination?
2. Did the DPC provide Mr. Hernandez with adequate informal counseling concerning his performance discrepancies prior to initiating formal counseling and disciplinary action?
3. Did the employer adequately document Mr. Hernandez's alleged violation of clear performance standards?
4. Who, if anyone, benefited from the outcome of this case study?
5. What functions and values are present in this case?
6. How important is an impartial hearing examiner in developing a sense of organization justice?

EXHIBIT A Hearing Examiner's Report

MONK, MURPHY, TANNENBAUM AND ENDICOTT
ATTORNEYS AT LAW
HEARING EXAMINER'S REPORT

Date: June 20, 1992

To: The Honorable Samuel Shapiro
County Attorney
County

The Honorable Jeremy Irving
Attorney at Law
AFSCME Local 121

On May 10, 1992, the Hearing Examiner heard testimony and considered evidence relative to the termination of Mr. Juan Hernandez from the County, Data Processing Center.

The following charges were advanced to support termination:

1. Alleged violation of time and leave regulations, as described in the formal record of counseling that Mr. Hernandez received on July 29, 1989.
2. Alleged willful negligence in the performance of Mr. Hernandez's job duties in the improper printing of forms, as described in the formal record of counseling which he received on July 29,1989.
3. Alleged willful negligence in the performance of Mr. Hernandez' job duties in the failure to properly load programs CICS (S337) so as to prevent damage to the System 3000 Data Base on June 9, 1991, as described in the formal record of counseling which he received on June 29, 1991.
4. Alleged failure to complete required training courses (MVS, Payroll system, OMICROM OMEGAMON, and OPS-JES2) by January 23, 1992, as required by his performance evaluation of January 9, 1992.
5. Alleged falsification of physician's excuses for sick leave for June 15, 1991, and January 23, 1992, as described in the Laboratory Analysis Report dated March 5, 1992, LACPSD Case #101374).

Having evaluated all evidence and testimony presented relative to these charges, the Hearing Examiner finds that insufficient evidence exists to document discharge on grounds 1,2, 3, or 4. However, under the terms of the collective bargaining agreement between AFSCME Local 121 and the Board of Supervisors of the County, dated October 27, 1991, sufficient evidence has been presented to document discharge on ground 5.

Discharge is hereby affirmed.

NOTES

[1] *Rankin v. McPherson,* 97 L Ed 2d 315 (1987).

[2] Uchitelle, L., and N. R. Kleinfield (March 3, 1996). On the battlefields of business, millions of casualties. *The New York Times,* pp. A-1, 14.

[3] Rousseau, D. M. (1996). Changing the deal while keeping the people. *Academy of Management Executive, 10,* 50-58.

[4] United States Equal Employment Opportunity Commission. (November 10). Final amendments to guidelines on discrimination because of sex. *Federal Register, 45,* 219.

[5] Dresang, D. L., and P. J. Stuiber (1991). *Sexual harassment: Challenges for the future.* In C. Ban and N. Riccucci. (Eds.). Public personnel management: Current concerns—future challenges. New York: Longman.

[6] United States Merit Systems Protection Board (1995). *Sexual harassment in the federal workplace: Trends, progress, continuing challenges.* Washington, DC: U.S. Merit Systems Protection Board.

[7] Robinson, R. K., D. J. Kirk, and J. D. Powell (1988). Sexual harassment: New approaches for a changed environment. In John Matzer, Jr. (Ed.). *Personnel practices for the '90s.* Washington, DC: International City Management Association, pp. 202-208.

[8] The Governor's Task Force on Sexual Harassment (December 1993). *Sexual harassment: Building a consensus for change.* Albany, NY: New York State Division for Women, Chap. 4, p. 9.

[9] Thacker, R. A., and S. F. Gohmann (Fall 1993). Male/female differences in perceptions and effects of hostile environment sexual harassment: "Reasonable" assumptions? *Public Personnel Management, 22,* 461-472.

[10] Dresang and Stuiber. *Sexual harassment,* p. 115.

[11] Robinson, R. K., B. M. Allen, G. M. Franklin, and D. L. Duhon (1992). Sexual harassment in the workplace: A review of the legal rights and responsibilities of all parties. *Public Personnel Management,* 22, 123-136; Strickland, R. A. (1995). Sexual harassment: A legal perspective for public administrators. *Public Personnel Management, 24,* 493-513.

[12] *Meritor Savings Bank v. Vinson,* 91 L Ed 2d 49 (1986).

[13] *Harris v. Forklift,* 126 L Ed 2d 300 (1993).

[14] Dresang and Stuiber. *Sexual harassment,* p. 123.

[15] United States Merit Systems Protection Board (1989). *Federal personnel management since civil service reform.* Washington, DC: U.S. Merit Systems Protection Board, pp. 3-8.

[16] United States Merit Systems Protection Board (1993). *Whistle-blowing in the federal government: An update.* Washington, DC: U.S. Merit Systems Protection Board.

[17] Near, J. P., and M. P. Miceli (1995). Effective whistle-blowing. *Academy of Management Review, 20,* 679-708.

[18] Americans with Disabilities Act of 1990, Public Law 101-336, July 26, 1990; Kohl, J. P., and P. S. Greenlaw. (1996). Title I of the Americans with Disabilities Act: The anatomy of a law. *Public Personnel Management,* 25, 323-332; Greenlaw, P.S., and J. P. Kohl. (1993). AIDS: Administrative decisions and constitutional rights. *Public Personnel Management, 22,* 445-460.

[19] Americans with Disabilities Act, Sec. 2, Para. 7.

[20] Greenlaw, P. S., and J. P. Kohl (1992). The ADA: Public personnel management, reasonable accommodation and undue hardship. *Public Personnel Management, 21,* 411-427.

[21] *New York Times v. Sullivan,* 11 L Ed 2d 686 (1964) at p. 700.

[22] Cooper, Phillip J. (November-December 1986) The Supreme Court, the first amendment, and freedom of information. *Public Administration Review, 46,* 622-628.

[23] *Pickering v. Board of Education of Township High School,* 20 L Ed 2d 811 (1968) at p. 817.

[24] *Rust v. Sullivan,* 114 L Ed 2d 233 (1991) at p. 259.

[25] *Connick v. Myers,* 75 L Ed 2d 708 (1983).

[26] *Wabounsee County v. Umbehr,* 116 S. Ct. 2342 (1996)

[27] *Rutan v. Republican Party of Illinois,* 111 L Ed 2d 52 (1990).

[28] Roback, T. H., and J. C. Vinzant (1994). The constitution and the patronage-merit debate: Implications for personnel managers. *Public Personnel Management*, 23, 501-512.

[29] *Branti v. Finkel,* 445 U.S. 507 (1980) at p. 518.

[30] *Rutan v. Republican Party of Illinois.*

[31] *Connick v. Myers,* pp. 719-720.

[32] *O'Connor v. Ortega.* 480 U.S. 709 (1987).

[33] Richman, R. (1994). Balancing government necessity and public employee privacy. *Administration and Society, 26,* 99-124.

[34] *Skinner v. Railway Labor Executives' Association,* 103 L Ed 2d 639 (1989).

[35] *National Treasury Employees' Union v. Von Raab,* 103 L Ed 2d 685 (1989) at fn 2.

[36] Daly, J. (1993). Substance abuse policy adaptation in Florida municipal government. *Public Personnel Management, 22,* 201-214.

[37] *Harlow v. Fitzgerald,* 73 L Ed 2d 396 (1982) at p. 410.

[38] Walter, R. J. (September-October 1992). Public employers' potential liability from negligence in employment decisions. *Public Administration Review, 52,* 491-496.

[39] Shearer, R. A. (Winter 1992). Due process liability in personnel records management: Preserving employee liberty interests. *Public Personnel Management,* 21, 523-532.

[40] Markowitz, D. L. (Spring 1995). The demise of at-will employment and the public employee conundrum. *The Urban Lawyer, 27,* 321.

[41] *Cleveland v. Loudermill,* 470 U.S. 532 (1985).

[42] Moorman, R. H. (1991). Relationship between organizational justice and organizational citizenship behaviors: Do fairness perceptions influence employee citizenship? *Journal of Applied Psychology,* 76, 845-855.

[43] Organ, D. W. (1990). The motivational basis of organizational citizenship behavior. *Research in Organizational Behavior, 12,* 43-72.

[44] Niehoff, B. P., and R. H. Moorman (1993). Justice as a mediator of the relationship between methods of monitoring and organizational citizenship behavior. *Academy of Management Journal, 36,* p. 535.

[45] Moorman. Relationship between organizational justice and organizational citizenship behaviors.

[46] Ewing, D. E. (1989) *Justice on the job: Resolving grievances in the nonunion workplace.* Boston: Harvard Business School, p. vii.

[47] Ibid.

[48] United States Merit Systems Protection Board (September 1995). *Removing poor performers in the federal service.* Washington, D.C.: U.S. Merit Systems Protection Board.

[49] Ibid., p. 10.

13

Collective Bargaining

Collective bargaining is the process by which agency managers negotiate terms and conditions of employment with the recognized representative of public employees. It is an alternative personnel system which is based on the primacy of the value of individual employee rights achieved through the collective voice and power of employees. Collective bargaining is primarily focused on the sanction function, in that through collective bargaining the conditions and terms of the employment relationship between employee and employer are determined and maintained. The context for bargaining and resolution of disputes is determined by law and state and federal compliance agencies. Collective bargaining is a set of techniques under which employees are represented in the negotiation and administration of the terms and conditions of their employment. Because collective bargaining can conflict with other personnel systems (primarily civil service, privatization, and affirmative action), it is also an arena which focuses conflict over a number of public policy issues. These include job security with no privatization, employment quotas versus seniority, drug testing versus employee rights, adversarial dispute resolution versus alternative dispute resolution techniques, and win-lose bargaining versus TQM (total quality management).

The past fifteen years offer contradictory answers to questions about the future of public-sector bargaining. While the number of public employees covered by collective bargaining agreements has continued to increase, actual union influence over personnel practice has been besieged by political pressure on collective bargaining systems, economic pressure for job competitiveness, and changes in organizational culture. And even conflicts over such issues as privatization and seniority rights are merely the most visible sign of underlying conflict among personnel systems and values amidst changing conditions. Therefore, it is important to first look at the conflict over the future of collective bargaining within a broader context of competing public personnel management systems.

Next, it is helpful to examine underlying political, social, and economic realities that shape public collective bargaining today. While there are many such pressures, analytic clarity permits clustering them in three general groups which will be discussed and evaluated in turn. First, there is continued *economic* pressure on collective bargaining *outcomes.* Second, there is continued *organizational* pressure on collective bargaining *processes.* Third, there is continued *political* pressure on collective bargaining systems.

In the final analysis, the strength of collective bargaining as a public personnel system will be affected by unions' ability to persuade the public and legislators that strong unions are tied to vital public policy concerns that go beyond the more narrow economic concerns of their current members. Some such concerns which may prove persuasive are: (1) employment access by minorities, women, and persons with disabilities; (2) organizational justice in the allocation of employee benefits, training, and involvement; (3) organizational productivity; (4) economic necessity for employer-financed retirement and health-care systems.

By the end of this chapter, you will be able to:

1. Discuss the history of collective bargaining in the public and private sectors.
2. Explain why collective bargaining has a unique role in the public sector because of the close connection between the legal obligation of public agencies to protect employees' constitutional rights, and the focus of unions on the value of the individual rights of their members as employees.
3. Describe the primary practices involved in collective bargaining: unit determination, recognition and certification, contract negotiation, and contract administration.
4. Discuss the changing context of public-sector collective bargaining in terms of continued economic pressure on collective bargaining outcomes, organizational pressure on collective bargaining processes, and political pressure on collective bargaining systems.
5. Identify some key "crossover issues" that unions might focus on in order to survive.

THE HISTORY OF COLLECTIVE BARGAINING

The Private Sector

In the private sector, collective bargaining began in the late 1800s with the rise of industrial unions (The Congress of Industrial Organization) and craft unions (The American Federation of Labor). In the face of bitter opposition by management, aided in many cases by the federal court system, these unions gained political power and legal protection. The New Deal brought about the passage in 1935 of the **Wagner Act** (or the **National Labor Relations Act**) which union leaders hailed as the "Magna Carta of organized labor." This law recognized the right of all private employees to join unions for the purpose of collective bargaining, and it required management to recognize and bargain collectively with these unions. It prohibited management from many previously common practices: blacklisting union members, signing "sweetheart contracts" with company unions, and so on. It established a federal agency—the **National Labor Relations Board (NLRB)**—with the responsibility of certifying unions as appropriate bargaining representatives, supervising negotiations to ensure "good faith" bargaining, and adjudicating deadlocks (impasses) that might arise during contract negotiations. This law was counterbalanced (from management's point of view, at least), by the **Taft-Hartley Act** (1947), which prohibited labor unions from engaging in **unfair labor practices** and which allowed states to pass "right to work" laws (statutes forbidding unions from requiring that employees be union members in order to apply for employment).

With the change in economic focus from manufacturing to service that began during the 1960s, the percentage of employees operating under collective bargaining agreements has declined steadily from a high point of about 35 percent in 1957, to a low of about 12 percent today. And with current economic trends (including **outsourcing**, job export, automation, **two-tiered wage and benefit systems**, and continued growth of service jobs in the secondary labor market), it can be expected that labor unions will decline still further. In many cases, their focus on win-lose bargaining over economic issues, and the adversarial approach taken by many negotiators, has made them seem an outmoded method of insuring equitable treatment of employees in an economy where the demand for union-protected jobs has declined substantially.[1]

The Public Sector—Federal

The history of collective bargaining in the public sector has been different. With the exception of a minor provision of the Taft-Hartley Act prohibiting strikes by public employees, and the **Postal Service Reorganization Act** (1970), which provides for supervision of the U.S. Postal Service collective bargaining by the NLRB, neither the Wagner Act, the Taft-Hartley Act, nor the NLRB is involved at all in public-sector collective bargaining. Rather, collective bargaining in the public sector is regulated by a complex of laws that apply differentially to federal, state, and local governments.

Collective bargaining developed differently in the public sector for two fundamental philosophical reasons. First, in the private sector, the unitary nature of company management makes it possible for a single union to negotiate bilaterally with a single employer. In the public sector, agency managers are accountable to the chief executive, to the legislature, and ultimately to the taxpayers. Thus, it is impossible to negotiate binding contracts at the negotiating table (especially on economic issues) without their being subject to further negotiation and ultimate ratification elsewhere within the political arena. Second, the strike, as an ultimate weapon for exercising collective employee power by withholding services, is more difficult to justify and apply in the public sector because its direct impact is on the public (possibly involving essential services like police, fire, and sanitation) rather than simply affecting corporate directors or stockholders.

Within the federal government, the development of collective bargaining lagged behind the private sector because the types of jobs were different, treatment of employees by employers was better, and federal agencies were relatively small compared to the large industrial firms organized during the 1930s in the private sector. Civil service employees were largely incorporated into the merit system that arose between 1923 and 1945. At the same time, politicians began to lose interest in protecting civil service employees because their jobs were no longer subject to favoritism. Between 1961 and 1975, a number of executive orders were issued which gradually granted federal employees the right to join unions and to bargain collectively. Public employees' unions were recognized as legitimate bargaining agents in 1961. Binding grievance arbitration with management was permitted (though not required) in 1969, and the scope of bargaining was broadened in 1975.

In 1978, Congress passed the **Civil Service Reform Act, Title VII** of which incorporated these executive orders into legislation, and it created a **labor relations regulatory agency** (the **Federal Labor Relations Authority**) formally authorized to mediate disputes between federal unions and agency managers. Though this law has clarified such issues as unit determination, scope of bargaining and impasse resolution procedures, federal agency employees still may not strike or bargain collectively over wages and benefits, both of which Congress sets. The most significant variation from this practice is the U.S. Postal Service. Collective bargaining for this agency, an independent government corporation, is supervised by the NLRB rather than the FLRA.

The Public Sector—State and Local

It is more difficult to comprehend and summarize the status of collective bargaining in state and local governments. This is primarily due to federalism, which means that the authorization and regulation of collective bargaining for state and local governments is a state responsibility. Many federal laws (such as affirmative action requirements and the wage and hour provisions of the Fair Labor Standards Act) regulate personnel practices in state and local government. But without violating federal law, each state is responsible for developing and administering its own laws to regulate collective bargaining by state agencies, and for local governments within the state.

State governments have often gone beyond the federal government in enacting laws to clarify collective bargaining for their employees and for employees of local governments within their jurisdiction. Forty-three states presently have enacted laws affording at least some public employees the right to "meet and confer" or negotiate on wages and working conditions. Public employees in six states are not covered by any labor relations laws, with the possible exception of no-strike provisions applicable to public employees.

In our federal system of government, both national and state governments have sovereign powers. Local governments are created and regulated by state governments, so they have no sovereignty. With respect to collective bargaining, this has meant that they cannot enter into collective bargaining agreements with employee organizations unless the state has passed legislation authorizing them to do so. Home rule powers make it possible in some cases for local governments to opt out of the state law if state law makes it optional, or to create its own "meet and confer" ordinances. Typically, this has meant that pressure for public sector bargaining first arose among teachers, police, or firefighters in big cities and spread to other areas of a state once the state statutes or constitutional revisions authorized it. In the 43 states allowing some form of collective bargaining, over 14,000 governments were conferring or negotiating with over 33,000 bargaining units by 1980. In 1985, 62 percent of all federal employees (1,266,000) were **unionized**, compared with 40 percent (1,163,000) of state employees and 52 percent (3,868,000) of local government employees.[2] The most heavily unionized groups are mail carriers (90 percent), school teachers (64 percent), and fire fighters (67 percent).[3]

The conditions imposed on public-sector collective bargaining make the extent of unionization and the growth of collective bargaining understandable. First, the inability of employees to negotiate bilaterally with management has meant that public-sector unions have developed primarily as interest groups whose objective is to influence the decisions of the legislatures (Congress, state legislatures, city councils, and school boards) that will have the ultimate authority to ratify or reject negotiated agreements, or to set pay and benefits if these are outside the scope of bargaining. This has meant the focus of union organizing activity has been on gaining certification by the state collective bargaining regulatory agency as the designated employee representative and on persuading as many employees within the bargaining unit to become members as soon as possible so that their dues are contributed to the union. Because the Taft-Hartley Act forbids states from enacting "closed shop" provisions applicable to public agencies, public employees are not required to join a union as a condition of employment in a public agency, even though these employees will be covered by the provisions of the collective bargaining agreement negotiated between the union and agency management. These "free riders" benefit from the gains won by the union for its members, but are able to avoid paying dues if they so choose by declining to join the union.

COLLECTIVE BARGAINING, INDIVIDUAL RIGHTS, AND THE CONSTITUTION

Collective bargaining is one method by which terms and conditions of employment are determined. But while collective bargaining contracts demonstrate employee influence on some personnel functions (primarily pay, benefits, promotion, and disciplinary action), it is not a complete personnel system. That is, it has no impact on selection (applicants are not eligible for union membership until they are hired and pass their probationary period) and no formal control over other personnel systems (like affirmative action). Both agency managers and unions are required to comply with affirmative action laws. In this sense, affirmative action has influenced both unions and management much more than collective bargaining has influenced the selection and promotion process. Although *bona fide seniority systems* are protected under affirmative action law, systems developed after 1964 that discriminate against particular groups are illegal.

Redress may require that particular applicants or employees be given "fictional seniority" to enable them to compete fairly for promotions or reassignments.

The compensation and benefits granted to public employees have been particularly affected by collective bargaining. Control over these activities has passed from management to the legislature, which now has three roles in the process: to pass enabling legislation governing contract negotiations, to pass appropriations bills funding negotiated collective bargaining agreements, and to pass substantive legislation incorporating non-economic issues into the jurisdiction's personnel laws and relations.

Collective bargaining plays a unique role in the public sector because of its close and interactive relationship with the constitutional rights afforded public employees within civil service systems, and because of the union's role in protecting the individual rights of public employees as a dominant value.

In the private sector, only two dominant values are competing in the context of collective bargaining—administrative efficiency and employee rights. And management's only legitimate interest is the "bottom line"—protecting profits by keeping production costs (including wages and benefits) low. In the absence of collective bargaining or employment contracts, most employees are hired and fired "at will" (meaning they may be discharged for any reason or for no reason at all). Similarly, pay and benefits are often negotiated on an individual basis, without general awareness by other employees in the company. Employees are more mobile, often moving from company to company in a quest for higher salaries and benefits. At the same time, companies seek to lower production costs by eliminating jobs, and by moving jobs to regions (or countries) where labor costs are lower (or where environmental health and workplace safety laws are less onerous for employers).

In the public sector, government agencies are required to protect the individual rights of employees. This goal originates in the desire of civil service reformers at the turn of the century to protect public employees from partisan political pressure and to promote efficiency rather than favoritism in public service delivery by eliminating favoritism. In the last few decades, federal courts have recognized that agencies which are constitutionally required to protect the rights of citizens in general cannot violate the constitutional rights of citizens as public employees. But the cumbersome nature of civil service laws regulating disciplinary action, and the need of public managers to maintain efficiency along with other values, has meant that elected officials and public managers continue to exert pressures challenging the individual rights of employees. These include contracting out, privatization, political appointments, and affirmative action (where the rigidities of civil service or collective bargaining systems based on seniority have had an adverse impact on minorities).

In responding to these pressures, public-sector unions have three advantages over their private-sector counterparts. First, public agencies are required to provide services to residents of a particular geographic area. This means that with some exceptions (primarily contracting out or outsourcing), the employer is required to remain in a fixed geographic area. Second, union members are not just employees, they are voters as well. Given the key role of legislative action in ratifying negotiated collective bargaining agreements in the public sector, the strength of union members as political action arms and voting blocks is important in understanding their political strength. Third, unions in the public sector have been able to obtain court opinions enforcing the value of individual rights as it is defined and protected by seniority systems. This means that not everyone's individual rights are equally protected, only those of union members (which frequently conflict with the rights of protected groups under affirmative action, or of applicants for employment).

Thus, understanding the unique role of collective bargaining in public agencies means understanding the relationship among union power and individual rights, constitutional protection, and political action.

COLLECTIVE BARGAINING PRACTICES

In accordance with the enabling legislation and administrative regulations that federal and state governments enact, collective bargaining has evolved into a formal and technical process. It is an administrative ritual that involves a number of prescribed concepts: unit determination, recognition and certification, scope of bargaining, contract negotiation, impasse resolution, ratification, contract administration, and unfair labor practices. In this section we discuss their meaning and general application to public-sector collective bargaining.

Unit Determination

Before collective bargaining can occur, a primary responsibility of the federal or state collective bargaining agency is to determine appropriate criteria for the formation of unions.[4] The two most commonly used criteria are to divide employees by agency or by occupation. Agency bargaining units establish each state or local government agency as a separate bargaining unit. While this offers the advantages of working within an existing management structure, it can cause a proliferation of bargaining units and inequities among agency contracts.

An alternative is to group employees into general occupational classes, usually on the basis of the state or local government's job classification system. This will result in the establishment of bargaining units such as health, public safety, teachers, general civil service employees, state university system employees, and so on. This method has the advantage of limiting the number of bargaining units and automatically including employees of new agencies in preestablished units. It also clarifies, on a system-wide basis, which employees are excluded from participation in bargaining units because their jobs are managerial or of a policy-making nature. Its disadvantage is that it lumps workers with different interests and needs into one large bargaining unit, for example, all health care workers.

Both agency-based and occupation-based methods of **unit determination** require the creation of coordinating mechanisms to ensure that negotiated contracts treat employees in different agencies or occupations equitably. Some public organizations—New York City, for example—have opted to establish a multilevel system of bargaining. Agency-based units bargain over salaries and benefits, while department- and occupation-based units bargain over work rules and grievance procedures.

Both management and labor tend to prefer a relatively small number of bargaining units. From management's viewpoint, it avoids the administrative work created by bargaining with multiple unions and avoids the risk of being "whipsawed" (each union demanding that any changes in pay, benefits, or working conditions recently negotiated for one union apply to all other unions with which management is negotiating). Established unions also prefer fewer bargaining units because they reduce the pressure on union leaders, and increase the economic and political power of large unions. Small and growing unions are more likely to favor proliferation, either because the members consider themselves poorly represented by larger units or because the leaders wish to gain "a piece of the action" for themselves.

Recognition and Certification

Once appropriate bargaining units have been established by the federal or state labor relations agency, unions are free to organize employees for the purpose of bargaining collectively. While no uniformity among state laws exists, **recognition** and **certification** procedures are generally similar in all states, because New York State's Taylor Law was used as a model by many of them.

An employer may voluntarily recognize a union as the exclusive bargaining agent for employees in that bargaining unit without a recognition election *if* the union can demonstrate that a majority of the employees in the bargaining unit want to be represented by that union.

If voluntary recognition does not occur, the union can win recognition through a representation election. Here, employees are offered the option of approving any union that has been able to show support (through signed authorization cards) from 10 percent of the eligible employees, or declining union representation. Depending upon state law, winning the representation election requires that the union win a majority of the votes cast, or a majority of votes from eligible members of the bargaining unit, regardless of the actual number of votes cast.

Once a union has been voluntarily recognized or has won a representation election, it is formally certified by the labor relations agency as the exclusive agent for that bargaining unit. Certification requires that management recognize this union as the legitimate representative of employees, and that it engage in collective bargaining over all items required or permitted by applicable law.

Scope of Bargaining

The **scope of bargaining** is simply the range of issues which applicable law requires or permits be negotiated during collective bargaining. If the laws specify which issues are included or excluded, the scope of bargaining is considered *closed*. If no restrictions are placed upon **bargainable** issues, the scope of bargaining is termed *open*.

Nonetheless, certain issues are usually excluded from the scope of bargaining because they are management prerogatives. Among these are agency structure, agency mission, and work methods or processes. The Civil Service Reform Act (Title VII) prohibits covered federal employees from bargaining over wages and other economic issues such as retirement and health benefits, which are established by Congress. Most state collective bargaining laws allow or require bargaining over wages, benefits, and working conditions. Yet the distinction between issues included in bargaining—or excluded from it—is not always clear. Issues that management considers excluded, such as adding drug testing to selection or promotion criteria, are frequently considered bargainable by unions because they affect member rights or important public policy issues. In such cases, their bargainability must be clarified by the state labor relations agency.

Contract Negotiation and Preparations for Negotiation

Contract negotiation usually begins immediately following recognition and certification, or (if the union has previously been certified) in anticipation of the expiration of an existing contract. Local union officials may represent their own membership, or a professional negotiator who has negotiated similar contracts with other state or local governments may be employed. Management is represented by an experienced negotiator supported by a team of experts that will include the personnel manager, the budget officer, a lawyer, and some line managers who understand the impact of contract provisions on agency operations.

In most cases, negotiation occurs "in the sunshine." That is, negotiations are conducted in public because states have an open meetings law that prohibits government officials from determining public policy through back-room deals. Prior to the negotiations, it is important that management's negotiator reach a clear understanding with elected officials concerning their preferred contract provisions and their minimally acceptable contract provisions (particularly with respect to economic issues). And it is important that the management team prepare adequately for negotiations by collecting comparative data on other agencies and contract agreements, by preparing spread-sheet analyses of the cost of alternative settlements on economic issues, and by estimating projected revenues available to pay the price tag on economic items. Good negotiation is impossible without good research.

Negotiation itself is concerned with both task-oriented and process-oriented issues. Both sides see it as the opportunity to shape organizational human resource policy and practice. As in any strategic contest, each side attempts to discover the other's strengths and priorities, while keeping its own hidden until the opposition appears most willing to concede on an issue. Good negotiations depend on the negotiators' ability to marshal facts, sense the opposition's strengths and weaknesses, and judge the influence of outside events (such as job actions or media coverage) on the negotiations. Good faith bargaining requires negotiators to work for the best deal their side can get, while still remaining receptive to the needs of the other party. Symbolically, negotiations also represent the opportunity for both labor and management to assert their influence over the human resource management policy process within the agency.

Impasse Resolution during Contract Negotiations. There are two types of collective bargaining impasses. The first are disagreements that occur during the negotiations over the *substance* of negotiations (such factors as pay or benefits). The second are disagreements over the interpretation of contract provisions that have previously been negotiated and approved. The first of these will be discussed below, and the second in the section on contract administration.

If management and union are unable to resolve differences through two-party contract negotiations, there remain three procedures involving intervention by a third party: mediation, fact-finding, and arbitration. The order in which these are employed, and whether they are used at all, will depend on the provisions of the state's collective bargaining law (or federal law, if the negotiation involves a federal agency).

Mediation is the intervention of a neutral third party in an attempt to persuade the bargaining parties to reach an agreement. This may be an independent individual, or one from a group designated by an agency such as the **American Arbitration Association** or the **Federal Mediation and Conciliation Service (FMCS)**. It is in the interest of both parties to make a good faith effort to reach a voluntary mediated settlement, since this is the last stage at which they will have full control over contract provisions.

If mediation is not successful, negotiations may progress to the second step—**fact-finding.** A fact-finder appointed by the federal or state collective bargaining agency will conduct a hearing at which both sides present data in support of their positions. After these hearings, the fact-finder releases a report to both parties, and to the public, that outlines what he or she considers a reasonable settlement. Although this advisory opinion is not binding, the threat of unfavorable publicity may make either side more willing to reach a negotiated settlement.

If fact-finding is unsuccessful, the final stage may be **arbitration**. Essentially the same procedures are followed as in fact-finding. However, the arbitrator's formal report contains contract provisions that both parties have agreed in advance will be binding. In an effort to avoid having to "split the difference" between extreme positions, the arbitrator may decide in advance to take the "last, best final offer" presented by either side, on the basis of either the entire contract or on an issue-by-issue basis. Arbitration of substantive items at impasse during contract negotiation is termed **interest arbitration**, to distinguish it from subsequent arbitration over the meaning of previously ratified contract provisions (**grievance arbitration**) during the contract administration process.

The cost of third-party interest dispute resolution during negotiations is usually borne equally by both parties.

Contract Ratification

Once a contract has been negotiated by representatives of labor and management, it must be ratified by both the appropriate legislative body and the union's membership before becoming law. For the union, **ratification** requires support of the negotiated contract by a majority of those voting. For management, it requires that the legislature (state, county, school district) appropriate the funds required to finance the economic provisions of the contract. Because all states have laws or constitutional provisions prohibiting deficit financing of operating expenses, revenue estimates impose an absolute ceiling on the pay and benefits that may be negotiated through collective bargaining. Nor is it considered bad faith bargaining for a legislature to refuse to ratify a negotiated contract on the grounds that projected revenues will not meet projected expenses. This is why connecting contract negotiations to the budgeting process is so important to effective fiscal management in government.

The requirement that a negotiated contract be ratified by the legislature is a key difference between private- and public-sector negotiations. It is also a sore point for union advocates because it limits the application of binding interest arbitration to public-sector contract negotiations, because courts have uniformly held that the legislature cannot delegate its responsibility for keeping expenditures within revenues. Although union advocates frequently (and justifiably) protest that the legislature is biased toward management, state laws require that the state or local legislature take all interests into account—including those of the union and its members—in deciding whether to ratify a negotiated contract.

Contract Administration

Once a contract has been negotiated and ratified, both union and management are responsible for administering its provisions. Key actors in implementation include the union steward, a union member who will interpret the contract for the employees and serve as their advocate and representative to management; supervisors, who will be implementing contract provisions relating to everyday employee-employer relations; and the personnel manager, who is management's expert on how the contract affects human resource policy and practice.

Conflicts are bound to arise during **contract administration** because reaching compromises during negotiations often requires agreement on what will later turn out to be ambiguous contract language. For example, labor and management may agree during contract negotiations that the shop steward "may spend a reasonable amount of time not to exceed two hours per week on union activities." Subsequently, differences may arise over such issues as whether the steward is in fact spending a "reasonable" amount of time on union business, or whether management has the right to approve when this time can be taken. Negotiations will then be needed to determine whether the shop steward's or the supervisor's actions constitute a violation of the contract's provisions.

Part of the contract will therefore outline the process for resolving grievances that occur during contract implementation. The process may begin very informally with discussion between union and management representatives. If the issue is not satisfactorily resolved informally, it is written up as a formal grievance and appealed through channels up to a neutral third party outside the agency. Binding grievance arbitration is the norm (in contrast to the lack of binding *interest* arbitration over contract negotiation impasses).

Management should view the **grievance** process as one more potentially beneficial effort by employees to make the organization more effective by calling attention to inefficient or inequitable supervisory practices. It can serve as an internal evaluation device, a means of instituting planned change, and a method of redressing inequitable organizational practices. It is recommended that supervisors and public personnel managers know the contract, maintain open lines of communication with employees, meet and deal informally with union representatives over potential grievances, exhibit uniform and adequate documentation for all personnel actions, and keep the record open to unions and employees.

One method of keeping both parties honest in handling grievances is requiring the losing party to pay for the services of a third party arbitrator. This discourages unions from pursuing frivolous grievances just to satisfy a disgruntled member; and it encourages management to handle grievances fairly rather than simply opposing the union on every issue.

Unfair Labor Practices

Federal and state collective bargaining laws all include lists of personnel practices forbidden to labor and management. In this regard, it is most important that management remember that employees have an *absolute* right to organize and bargain collectively in federal agencies, and in those states where enabling collective bargaining legislation exists. Management has no corresponding right to prevent employees from doing so. This means that management cannot seek to influence the outcome of a representation election by coercing, threatening, or intimidating employees. It can present information on the comparative advantages and disadvantages of union membership; and it can restrict union organizing to public locations (lunchrooms, bulletin boards) that do not interfere with the work of the agency and do not occur on company time.

During negotiations, each party is bound to bargain in good faith. This means that each party will listen to the other side and will negotiate. A failure to show up for scheduled negotiations, or a "take it or leave it" approach to the negotiations themselves, will likely lead to a formal charge of unfair labor practices being filed with the labor relations regulatory agency. Findings against the agency can result in fines, administrative sanctions, or the invalidation of negotiated settlements or representation elections.

Whether or not public employees should have the right to strike is a hotly contested issue in public agencies because it pits fundamental rights against each other. On the one hand, public employees are guaranteed constitutional protection of association and expression. In addition, there is strong justification for extending to employees the same right to withhold their services as a bargaining weapon that private employees enjoy. On the other hand, the importance of public services to the public, and the monopolistic nature of most public agencies, strengthens the argument that public-sector strikes are less tolerable or politically acceptable than those in the private sector.

In practice, the outcome of strikes by public employees seems to depend on a variety of fairly predictable factors, among them applicable laws, historical practice, and the relative control of the union over the job market. In the federal government and most states, all strikes by public employees are illegal. In some cases (such as the ill-fated strike of the 10,000 member **Professional Air Traffic Controllers Organization** [**PATCO**] in 1981), employees who strike are fired, the union is decertified, and union officers are fined and jailed. Yet in fields where strikes are the norm (such as education), and where there are no available qualified substitutes for union members (such as law enforcement) strikes often occur with impunity. Or they occur under a different guise, such as "sickouts," "job actions," and "blue flu" (where employees are absent or unproductive in concert, without a strike formally being called).

In reality, increasing economic pressures have both increased and diminished the likelihood of strikes by public employees. Most employees have lost real purchasing power over the past two decades and see themselves as making sacrifices in order to maintain a high level of public service without tax increases, under conditions of inflation. However, the willingness of management to use alternative instruments (such as contracting out or privatization) to provide public services frequently reminds public employees (or threatens them, depending on your perspective) that they are likely to have better job security, pay, and benefits within civil service systems and collective bargaining than they would ever get under contracting out or privatization.[5]

PRESSURES ON PUBLIC-SECTOR COLLECTIVE BARGAINING

Given that collective bargaining is but one alternative public personnel management system, and that the history of public personnel management and collective bargaining can be viewed as a history of conflict and compromise among alternative values and systems over the allocation of public jobs, it seems reasonable to examine the influence of societal realities on the collective bargaining. For purposes of analysis, these trends and events will be grouped into three clusters: *economic* pressures on collective bargaining *outcomes, organizational* pressures on collective bargaining *processes*, and *political* pressures on collective bargaining *systems*.

Economic Pressures on Collective Bargaining Outcomes

The percentage of unionized employees in the United States dropped from one out of three in 1950, to one out of six in 1990.[6] This is due to a number of factors: the erosion of manufacturing industries (which formed the backbone of industrial unionism) in favor of nonunionized service and white-collar employment, the gradual shift of jobs away from the Northeast to the Southeast and Southwest (parts of the country without a strong tradition of industrial unions), and the increased effectiveness of union avoidance strategies.

While the relationship between collective bargaining and economic outcomes for organized employees is by no means clear or direct, the historical purpose of collective bargaining has been to increase employees' share of profits as pay or benefits. Thus, much current debate about the effectiveness of unions in the new global economy is influenced by beliefs that unions themselves hinder economic competitiveness,[7] employment growth,[8] and investment activity by unionized firms.[9] Salaries and benefits are the main reason employees unionize, and there is some evidence that employees who bargain collectively enjoy higher pay and benefits (about 7 percent higher) than their nonunionized counterparts. Yet other factors like urbanization, population, the local economic climate, and the relative demand for employees in the field are more significant determinants of salary. Any continued pressure to reduce the cost of government has lessened the impact of collective bargaining on public employee salaries.[10]

But in any event, unions are viewed as a structural constraint that increases employer costs. And collective bargaining outcomes, among other costs, increase competitive pressure on employers. Among such other pressures are (1) rising health-care costs, (2) rising pension system concerns, and (3) development of segmented labor markets to reduce personnel costs.

Rising health-care costs (and related workers' compensation, sick leave, and disability retirement expenses) constitute a large share of personnel costs.[11] Total employer liabilities for health-care coverage for current employees are $85 billion for those Americans who are covered by employer-financed plans.[12] Nationally, medical costs have climbed from $248 million to $600 billion in 1990, growing at twice the rate of inflation even when adjusted for population increases.[13] And despite this high cost, there are tremendous inequities in the distribution of health-care benefits.

Like health-care systems, troubled public and private pension systems are rapidly becoming a political issue. First, the increase in corporate indebtedness and economic restructuring that characterized the 1980s have increased tendencies to borrow against employee pension plans, or to eliminate them altogether to avoid compliance with the **Employee Retirement Income Security Act (ERISA)**. Second, while the Social Security trust fund is currently solvent, demands on the system can be expected to increase as concern over the federal government budget deficit intensifies pressure to cut entitlement programs, and as the post-World War II "baby boom" generation enters retirement age.

Dual labor markets are both an economic reality based on the need to reduce personnel costs, and some economists' explanation for the inadequacy of traditional explanations of unemployment and underemployment.[14] It differentiates between a primary labor market comprising applicants for skilled managerial, professional, and technical positions characterized by high pay, high status, and job security; and a secondary labor market comprising applicants for less skilled laborer and service positions filled on a temporary or part-time basis. Secondary labor market mechanisms are attractive because they enable personnel administrators to reduce benefit costs and to circumvent personnel ceilings and civil service rules. The threat of privatization or contracting out is also a powerful tool for breaking unions or gaining **givebacks** during contract renegotiation. The labor market is segmented in that the markets remain separate. Jobs filled (coincidentally mainly by white males) through the primary labor market have relatively high qualifications, and a "glass ceiling" hinders development or promotion from jobs filled through the secondary market. And while employers will increasingly utilize minorities and women because of changing workforce demographics, most new jobs will be created in the service sector and filled through the secondary labor market.[15]

Divergent views of employees as assets or costs are one organizational implication of dual labor market theory. Skilled managerial, professional, and technical employees hired through primary labor market mechanisms into career positions are considered human resource *assets* who bring human capital to the labor market.[16] This assumption underlies human resource asset accounting models in private industry[17] and public civil service systems.[18] The relatively high job security, pay, training, and benefits of these positions are considered essential for asset maintenance and development. On the other hand, employees hired through the secondary labor market are more likely to be considered personnel costs. Employers utilize personnel practices predicated on cost reduction through elimination of benefits and advancement opportunities.[19] And employers also reduce legal liability risks because temporary employees have fewer rights.

Organizational Pressures on Collective Bargaining Processes

While there is continued emphasis on legal liability for public employees and officials, this trend is counterbalanced by a societal trend toward **alternative dispute resolution (ADR)** techniques in a number of areas: family law, torts, and workplace grievances. The steady growth of these techniques is due to realization that adversarial techniques build acrimony, harden bargaining positions, and delay the resolution of the original conflict.

And within organizations, there has been a similar transition from adversarial bargaining over wages and conditions of employment, to non-adversarial dispute resolution processes such as quality circles and TQM (total quality management). In an era when policy and program initiatives are predicated on "budget neutrality," managers and supervisors have come to conclude that budgets are a fixed resource. Budget directors respond to budget cuts by telling the agency to do the same with a lower budget, or more with the same budget. In contrast, good personnel managers recognize that employees are a variable resource. That is, even in the absence of significant financial rewards, employees tend to work happily and effectively when they have the necessary skills, see their work as meaningful, feel personally responsible for productivity, and have first-hand knowledge of the actual results of their labor.

Managers, supervisors, and personnel directors have responded to this realization by creating work systems that enhance involvement and participation. The common thread among these systems is their emphasis on the connection between the quality of the work environment and the quality of individual, team, and organizational performance. Training can also enhance involvement and participation because they include not only individual job skills but also improvement in employees' work relationships. Examples are team building and organizational development,[20] total quality management (TQM),[21] and training for diversity.[22] In the private sector, employers' team-building and TQM efforts are somewhat hindered by provisions in the Taft-Hartley Act that prohibit employer-sponsored employee associations. This is because, in the "bad old days" of industrial collective bargaining, managers sometimes attempted to subvert collective bargaining by creating a union led by management sympathizers, recognizing it as the official bargaining agent, and signing collective bargaining agreements favorable to management rather than the employees. No such prohibition exists in the public sector (because this Taft-Hartley provision does not apply to public agencies), so competition often exists between employee unions and employer-sponsored quality circles or TQM groups.

Traditional collective bargaining processes also run counter to the current transition from affirmative action compliance to workforce diversity. Workforce diversity has brought about changing definitions of productivity based on the need for variation in managerial styles, and resultant increases in organizational effectiveness.[23] The challenge of channeling diversity into productivity is complicated by the breadth of expectations members of diverse cultures bring to their work, both as individuals and as members of those cultures. Without an organizational commitment of respect, tolerance, and dignity, differences lead only to divisiveness that consumes organizational resources without positive results.[24] Personnel administrators will be increasingly responsible for protection of justice and fair play through organizational processes designed to negotiate and resolve differences in expectations and obligations.

Pressures for public agency accountability and performance have meant increased emphasis on situational definitions of merit related to effectiveness of agency performance. Specifically, it has meant increased flexibility in job matching for individual employees (based on competency-based job matching, rank-in-person personnel systems, and individualized development plans); and on competency-based job matching systems (such as results-oriented job descriptions, delegation, and management by objectives) to "manage to mission." Seen in this light, traditional criteria for determining merit (seniority and "blanket" qualifications standards for a range of positions) are simply not considered valid enough to be used as the sole basis of selection, promotion, layoff decisions, or even work arrangements. What many observers see as the politicization of personnel actions is in fact the application of more flexible definitions of merit based on situational competencies required of an employee on the job, and a reasonable managerial effort to end the overrationalization of personnel procedures.

Political Pressures on Collective Bargaining Systems

Economic and organizational pressures, if they are generalized and persistent, soon make themselves visible as political pressures on the validity of collective bargaining as a personnel system. Within the public sector, the perceived anachronism of traditional industries and traditional industrial relations has interacted with demands for "reinventing government." This slogan epitomizes the continued pressure on public agencies to measure outputs, increase efficiency, and enhance political accountability.[25] In public agencies, it has meant the relative ascendancy of political responsiveness and efficiency as values; and the need for personnel administrators to work with other systems (besides traditional civil service and collective bargaining) to enable agencies to reach objectives and control costs. Critics have argued that the private sector can often provide services more cheaply and efficiently by eliminating unnecessary personnel costs and employee protection. And desires for both political payoffs and political accountability make provision of public services through the private sector more attractive. For example, there is a movement in local government toward charter schools (privately managed schools that function under the control of a school board without being bound by collective bargaining agreements for school teachers and administrators) and private security agencies (which provide protective services without the pay and benefits paid to unionized police officers).

Consequently, much government growth has been through a secondary labor market of part-time, temporary, and seasonal employees which at least give the appearance of controlling the size of the public "bureaucracy,"[26] and through alternative instrumentalities which share responsibility: purchase of service contracting, franchise agreements, subsidy arrangements, vouchers, volunteers, self-help, regulatory and tax incentives.[27]

The political attack on the validity of collective bargaining systems began with a watershed event which focused public concern on changing political realities: the failed PATCO strike of 1981. In this strike, proponents of collective bargaining learned painfully that a relatively small union, without significant public support for its members' demands, and without a monopoly on the supply of air traffic controllers, would lose in a political confrontation with an incoming President with an ideological and pragmatic preference for alternative instrumentalities for delivery of public services. As a result of this miscalculated confrontation, PATCO was broken, its leaders faced criminal charges, and its members were barred from future federal employment.

THE FUTURE OF COLLECTIVE BARGAINING: FROM PRIVATE PRIVILEGE TO PUBLIC INTEREST

The ability of unions to make collective bargaining a continuing alternative public personnel system is at heart a political issue. What advocates of collective bargaining systems must do, most simply, is to build a constituency that focuses broad public concern on "crossover" issues. These are the issues that political leaders may consider seriously because they invoke genuine public interests, rather than representing merely the attempts of union members to maintain what opponents consider the private privilege of jobs, benefits, and due process protection.

Some such concerns which may prove persuasive are (1) employment access by minorities, women, and persons with disabilities; (2) organizational justice in the allocation of employee benefits, training and involvement; (3) organizational productivity; and (4) economic necessity for employer-financed retirement and health care systems.

Employment Access by Minorities, Women and Persons with Disabilities

Traditionally, unions have been perceived as more concerned with protecting the pay, benefits, and due process rights of current members than ensuring equality of job opportunity for minorities, women, and persons with disabilities. Indeed, public employee unions have historically opposed promotional opportunities for women and minorities, and have been parties to many lawsuits establishing the relative priority accorded individual rights based on seniority, and social equity based on affirmative action (see, for example, in chapter 6, *Johnson v. Transportation Agency* [1987] and *United States v. Paradise* [1987]).

This perceived or actual lack of support for social equity may be a function of discrimination within union leadership. A recent study indicates that although women are proportionally represented in leadership positions within Massachusetts AFL-CIO locals, they are overrepresented as secretaries and seriously underrepresented as presidents, or the chairs of key grievance or negotiations committees.[28] This in turn may be due to sex-role stereotypes (for example, the belief that confrontational dispute resolution requires a male personality) which are at variance with the research findings of workforce diversity advocates who have studied the impact of alternative leadership styles on organizational effectiveness.[29]

But whatever the cause, unions must enlarge their base of support by focusing on employment access issues critical to blacks,[30] Hispanics, women,[31] and Americans with disabilities. Unions must sensitize themselves to workforce diversity, to pay equity, and to those employee services that help employees meet family obligations. Because women are the traditional family caregivers, an employer's ability to attract a diverse workforce depends upon the provision of these same services and benefits: flexible benefits,[32] parental leave,[33] child- and elder-care support programs,[34] alternative work locations and schedules, and employee-centered supervision. Organizations which wish to attract and keep asset employees by supporting "family values" need to select and train supervisors who are sensitive to these issues.

However, given the political strength of "right to work" laws and the inability of public unions to gain closed shop status, it is still possible that enhancing the diversity of union membership and leadership will not result in increased political power for public unions, unless gains in representation are translated into proportionate gains in dues-paying membership and political clout. This in turn will depend upon two things: The ability of unions to settle the free-rider issue depends upon the success of litigation to require free riders to pay their fair share of benefits;[35] and the ability of unions to organize workers around political action as well as internal bargaining issues.[36]

Organizational Justice in the Allocation of Employee Benefits, Training, and Involvement Opportunities

From a societal human resource perspective, the United States currently is suffering from the absence of concerted public policy that ties together educational development, national human resource development, industrial policy, and economic growth.[37] Public and private employers uniformly express alarm at the ineffectiveness of our educational system in producing the skilled workers needed by high-technology industries. Lack of high-tech job training or retraining capacity is a major obstacle to retention of manufacturing jobs, which have fallen to their lowest level in twenty years. But the organizational implication of economic pressures for increased productivity and lower personnel costs are clear: a "shake-out" between core employees and contingent workers.

Increasingly, employers reduce costs by hiring **contingent workers** through secondary labor market mechanisms into low wage and non-benefited jobs. Skill requirement of these jobs are reduced by job redesign or work simplification (which ironically contributes to the perpetuation of segmented labor markets and the glass ceiling by reducing developmental opportunities for employees "stuck" in secondary labor market jobs). Where commitment *and* high skills are required on a temporary basis, employers may seek to save money or maintain flexibility by using contract or leased employees.

Core employees continue to receive comparatively liberal health benefits, at least compared to other employees, to help ensure retention and loyalty. But health insurance carriers (and self-insured employers) have responded to rising health-care costs by increasing premiums, reducing benefits, lengthening the waiting period for exclusion of preexisting conditions, or adopting sub-benefit limitations on coverage for health problems that may be considered "lifestyle choices."[38] Benefit managers for self-insured agencies are responding, on a case-by-case basis, to advance questions from health-care providers about whether reimbursement for specific treatments will be authorized.

This trend troubles personnel managers. Though the logic of simultaneously applying these divergent views is apparent to personnel administrators and supervisors, it is often hard to explain to contingent workers who find themselves working side-by-side with core employees. And it is admittedly not easy for them to strike a good balance between asset maintenance and cost accountability, or between primary or secondary labor market mechanisms. While the secondary market offers the advantage of lower short-term pay and benefit costs, many examples support the conclusion that viewing employees as assets results in long-term benefits, not just for employees but also for the employer.[39]

But this trend threatens employees who lose their jobs or who lose a "career job" as a core employee and are forced into a succession of low-paying, dead-end contingent jobs because nothing else is available. This economic necessity translates into a psychic tragedy—the loss of dignity, of hope for the future. This is a powerful, explosive issue that political leaders can use to capitalize on racial and ethnic divisiveness, or a national agenda for education, economic reform, and job creation.

Union members, and adherents of collective bargaining systems, may be able to take advantage of public support for fair and decent wages by supporting pay equity for women, minorities, and the disadvantaged—groups that have been traditionally discriminated against in the private sector because market-based pay plans allow employers to pay them less than the wages offered their white male counterparts. Pay equity may be a particularly fruitful issue in state and local government, where employment of women and minorities in service jobs is disproportionately high.[40] But again, this requires a prior transformation by unions against traditional seniority systems in favor of wider employment access by women, minorities, and the disabled.

Organizational Productivity

Unions build a broader constituency to the extent that they can demonstrate that union strength is critical to employee involvement,[41] and that employee involvement is critical to enhanced workplace productivity.[42] For example, one recent study investigates the effectiveness of employee participation in achieving product quality improvement in union versus nonunion settings and in programs unilaterally administered by management versus programs with joint union-management administration. Findings suggest that among unionized firms, those with jointly administered programs achieved significantly greater improvements in product quality than did those with more traditional adversarial collective bargaining relationships (that is, with no participation programs), but those with programs administered solely by management fared no better than those with no programs. The gains associated with jointly administered programs in unionized firms were at least equal to the gains associated with participation programs in nonunion firms.[43]

And a related case study indicates that enhanced industrial productivity may be possible by combining the advantages of company-based employee involvement programs with those of independent local unions, especially in a high-tech industry which has moved away from adversarial management employee relations.[44] But obviously, more research and experimentation are needed into the impact of workers councils, quality management teams, and independent local unions (ILUs) on organizational productivity in the United States.[45] And continued conflict over the allocation of revenue generated by productivity increases certainly complicates implementation of the "new pay" discussed in Chapter 6.

Employer-Financed Employee Retirement and Health Care Systems

Union strength will increase to the extent that the public perceives problems with private pension and health benefit systems to be major public issues. Examples might be the impact of collapsing private pension systems on Social Security, or the impact of bankruptcy on public health system.[46]

SUMMARY

Collective bargaining is law, process, and ritual. As law, it provides the constitutional and statutory foundation that enables employees collectively to negotiate the terms and conditions of employment with managers (and indirectly, with legislators and the public). Second, it is the standardized procedures by which this collective negotiation takes place. And third, it is a ritual through which employees demonstrate their relative power (through the sanctions process) over employment policy and practice. As such, it is an alternative personnel system based on the primacy of individual employee rights.

Collective bargaining conflicts with other public personnel systems, and with alternative instrumentalities, over policy outcomes of job allocation and service delivery. A number of factors now influence the outcome of this conflict: economic pressures on collective bargaining outcomes, organizational pressures on collective bargaining processes, and political pressures on collective bargaining systems. And the response of public-sector unions to these pressures will determine, in hindsight, whether the glass called collective bargaining is half full, half empty, or broken.

In the final analysis, the strength of collective bargaining as a public personnel system will be affected by unions' ability to persuade the public, and its leaders, that strong unions are tied to vital public policy concerns that go beyond the more narrow economic concerns of their current members. Some such concerns which may prove persuasive are (1) employment access by minorities, women, and persons with disabilities; (2) organizational justice in the allocation of employee benefits, training, and involvement; (3) organizational productivity; and (4) economic necessity for employer-financed retirement and health care systems.

KEY TERMS

American Arbitration Association
arbitration
bargainable
certification
Civil Service Reform Act (Title VII)
contingent worker
contract administration
contract negotiation
core employee
dual labor market
Employee Retirement Income Security Act (ERISA)
fact-finding
Federal Labor Relations Authority (FLRA)
Federal Mediation and Conciliation Service (FMCS)
givebacks
grievance
grievance arbitration
interest arbitration
labor relations regulatory agency
mediation
National Labor Relations Act (Wagner Act)
National Labor Relations Board (NLRB)
outsourcing
Professional Air Traffic Controllers' Organization (PATCO)
Postal Service Reorganization Act
ratification
recognition
scope of bargaining
Taft-Hartley Act
two-tiered wage and benefit systems
unfair labor practice
unionized
unit determination

DISCUSSION QUESTIONS

1. Why is the history of collective bargaining in the public sector different from that in the private sector?
2. Why is the legal structure of collective bargaining more complex and confusing in the public sector than in the private sector?
3. What are the reasons for the current crisis among public-sector unions?
4. What are some crossover issues that unions might focus on to change the public perception that their primary objective is economic benefits for their members, rather than public policy issues affecting a broader segment of society?
5. Should management's strategy toward collective bargaining be (a) opposition to unions and avoidance of collective bargaining, or (b) acceptance of unions' legitimacy and participation in collective bargaining? What factors will influence which option management chooses to pursue?

CASE STUDY GOOD MANAGEMENT OR BARGAINING IN BAD FAITH?

Read the following case study, and then use the information provided to answer the questions that follow.

BACKGROUND INFORMATION

You are the new city manager for Sunbelt City. It is small (50,000 population), but growing at about 10 percent annually as retirees and business owners move south seeking warmer winters and lower taxes. The city currently employs about 100 sworn police officers. The city charter classifies police officers as within the civil service system. Because public-sector collective bargaining is authorized for local governments in this state, those officers in non-supervisory positions are also represented by the PBA (Police Benevolent Association).

Sunbelt is governed by a five-member elected city council. Last November, three incumbent council members were defeated by newcomers who ran on a platform of keeping taxes down by making government more effective and efficient. The two remaining council members also favor this objective.

Your family is happy in Sunbelt. For the first time in ten years, it looks as though you will stay in a city for at least five years. You have based your success on keeping the council happy by keeping political wrangling to a minimum, and always counting votes before taking a policy position on anything. You want to keep it that way, and so does the council.

The council has enthusiastically supported your strategy of reducing the city budget by bargaining hard with unions over salary and fringe benefits. By using the veiled threat of privatization or outsourcing as a "hammer," you have successfully renegotiated contracts for the city's solid waste and public works employees. Under the new contracts, trash collectors now work a full eight-hour day instead of being allowed to go home when their routes are finished. And the public works department is now operating under a two-tiered contract that protects salaries and benefits for current employees, but requires new employees to enter at lower salaries and to pay a higher proportion of their health benefit costs.

Now you face a challenging situation. One of the new council members has suggested that you use the same strategy in renegotiating the contract with the PBA, up for renewal this year. You immediately sense trouble ahead as other council members have indicated a similar interest. Threatening solid waste and public works employees with privatization is one thing—it's been done all over the country, and many private trash haulers and maintenance companies do a thriving business. But what are the alternatives to police officers hired through a civil service system? And will any alternative satisfy voters and the rest of the council, given that Sunbelt residents want lower taxes and high-quality police protection?

THE CHOICES

Your first move is to hire a collective bargaining consultant and labor negotiator to provide you with expert advice in the matter. The consultant recommends that you consider three options: (1) hard bargaining with the PBA, (2) contracting out for police services with the county sheriff's office, or (3) contracting out with a private security firm.

Hard bargaining would mean taking a number of bargaining positions designed to reduce pay and benefit costs. Options might be (a) proposing a tiered contract offering lower pay and benefits to new officers than current ones; (b) routinely challenging police officer requests for disability retirement and workers compensation for injuries suspected of being caused by outside employment; (c) hiring civilian employees to do office work and putting all sworn police officers on the street; and (d) proposing early retirement provisions to reduce lower personnel costs by reducing the number of senior officers. This is politically the least risky of the three options, but it will work well only if citizens are convinced the quality of law enforcement will not suffer, and if PBA negotiators fear that one of the other two options will be imposed if they do not agree to contract provisions providing for reduced pay and benefit costs.

Contracting out with the county sheriff's office would mean changing the city charter by abolishing the police department, and contracting with the county sheriff's office for police services. The contract would need to be carefully negotiated. It would have to include (a) reimbursement to Sunbelt for any capital equipment (such as police buildings or vehicles) sold to the county; (b) qualitative and quantitative measures of service (such as number of officers, response time, and responsiveness to the council; and (c) provisions for city police officers to join the county sheriff's department (this would involve complex negotiations over seniority, pay, and benefit packages for both organizations). This option offers the probability of dramatic short-term cost savings. But the down side is less control over quality of service, no assurance that costs for contracting out will remain lower than the cost of the Sunbelt police department, and a large one-time lump-sum payment of accrued annual leave to those Sunbelt police officers who elect to retire rather than join the county sheriff's department.

Contracting out with a private security firm offers the greatest potential benefits and risks. Private security corporations already provide security at many condominiums and public facilities, operate county and state correctional facilities, and are starting to move into municipal law enforcement. Informal negotiations with officials in private security firms lead you to believe that they will offer to provide sworn law enforcement officers at less than half the cost of the current police department's budget, largely because of lower pay and benefit costs. Not only will payroll costs be lower, but administrative expenses are capped by the contract, and legal liability risks are covered by the contractor's bond. The risks are also great. Public opinion will probably be against hiring "rent-a-cops" to replace municipal police officers, and the PBA will use this opposition to build a firestorm of political opposition to the proposal. Certainly the quality of service will be in doubt, and the training and fitness for duty of sworn officers may be questionable if, as rumored, the security company hires retired police or corrections officers because they have already been certified (sworn) by the state as law enforcement officers.

THE OUTCOME

You decide on the first option (hard bargaining), backed up by credible statements that if hard bargaining is unsuccessful you intend to pursue council approval for either of the other two options. The PBA fights back hard, stirring up public opinion against you, directly lobbying the council against your proposal, and filing an unfair labor practice charge with the state collective bargaining regulatory agency, alleging that your purported threat to contract out for law enforcement services is in fact a refusal to bargain in good faith. Several weeks later, the hearing officer decides that you have not violated the requirement for good faith bargaining. But in the meantime, PBA and public pressure have forced two council members to publicly come out against contracting out. And the county sheriff's department becomes the subject of investigation by the State Attorney General's office and the State Department of Law Enforcement, when it is alleged that sheriff's deputies are guilty of widespread bribery and extortion efforts to protect drug dealers and gambling interests in the county. The PBA agrees to a contract that is essentially the same as the previous one, with a cost-of-living increase in pay and no changes in benefits. As a condition of ratification, the PBA insists privately to council members that you be fired. The council fires you at the same time it approves the collective bargaining agreement with the PBA.

QUESTIONS

1. What does this case study show about the current strengths and weaknesses of public-sector collective bargaining as a public personnel system?
2. Looking back at the situation, are there any options that would have been better for you to select than the three you were offered by the consultant?
3. What arguments could you have presented to make a stronger case for hard bargaining or contracting out?
4. Is there anything else you could have done to handle this situation better, or were you simply a victim of bad timing and corruption in the county sheriff's department?

NOTES

[1] Kochan, T., and H. Katz (1988). *Collective bargaining and industrial relations.* Homewood, IL: Business One Irwin.

[2] Union Recognition in Government. (January 18, 1988). *Government Employee Relations Report, 71,* 208.

[3] U.S. Department of Commerce, Bureau of the Census. (1985). *Labor Relations in State and Local Government, 3,* 3.

[4] A good general reference for public-sector unit determination is: Gershenfeld, W. (1985). Public employee unionization: An overview. In Association of Labor Relations Agencies. (1985). *The evolving process: Collective negotiations in public employment.* Ft. Washington, PA: Labor Relations Press.

[5] Naff, K. (January-February 1991). Labor-management relations and privatization: A federal perspective. *Public Administration Review, 51,* 23-30.

[6] Coleman, C. (1990). *Managing employee relations in the public sector.* San Francisco: Jossey-Bass.

[7] Mishel, L., and P. Voos (1992). *Unions and economic competitiveness.* Armonk, NY: M. E. Sharpe.

[8] Leonard, J. (Winter 1992). Unions and employment growth. *Industrial Relations, 31,* 80-94.

[9] Hirsch, B. (Winter 1992). Firm investment behavior and collective bargaining strategy. *Industrial Relations, 31,* 95-121.

[10] Derber, M. (1987). Management organization for collective bargaining in the public sector. In B. Aaron, J. Najita, and J. Stern (Eds.). *Public sector bargaining* (2nd ed.). Washington, DC: BNA.

[11] Blostin, A., T. Burke, and L. Lovejoy (December 1988). Disability and insurance plans in the public and private sector. *Monthly Labor Review,* pp. 9-17.

[12] Allan, I. (1988). Financing and managing public employee benefit plans in the 1990s. *Government Finance Review, 4,* 32.

[13] Luthans, F., and E. David (1990). The health-care cost crisis: Causes and containment. *Personnel, 67,* 24.

[14] Doeringer, P. and M. Piore (1975). Unemployment and the "dual labor market." *The Public Interest, 38,* 67-79.

[15] The Hudson Institute (1988). *Opportunity 2000: Creating affirmative action strategies for a changing workforce.* Indianapolis: The Hudson Institute.

[16] Johnston, W., and A. Packer (1987). *Workforce 2000: Work and workers for the twenty-first century.* Indianapolis: The Hudson Institute.

[17] Flamholtz, E. (1974). *Human resource accounting.* Encino, CA: Dickenson.

[18] Advisory Committee on Federal Workforce Quality. (August 1992). *Federal workforce quality measurement and improvement.* Washington, DC: Advisory Committee on Federal Workforce Quality.

[19] O'Rand, A. (1986). The hidden payroll: Employee benefits and the structure of workplace inequality. *Sociological Forum, 1,* 657-683.

[20] French, W., and C. Bell (1990). *Organizational development* (4th ed.). Englewood Cliffs, NJ: Prentice Hall.

[21] Deming, W. (1988). *Out of the crisis.* Cambridge, MA: MIT Center for Advanced Engineering Study.

[22] Solomon, J. (February 10, 1989). Firms address workers' cultural variety: The differences are celebrated, not suppressed. *The Wall Street Journal,* p. B-1.

[23] Loden, M., and J. Rosener (1991). *Workforce America! Managing employee diversity as a vital resource.* Homewood, IL: Business One Irwin.

[24] Thomas, R. (1990). From affirmative action to affirming diversity. *Harvard Business Review, 68,* 107-117.

[25] Osborne, D., and T. Gaebler (1992). *Reinventing Government.* Reading, MA: Addison-Wesley.

[26] Chandler, T., and P. Feuille (June 1991). Municipal unions and privatization. *Public Administration Review, 51,* 15-22.

[27] International City Management Association (1989). *Service delivery in the 90s: Alternative approaches for local governments.* Washington, DC: ICMA.

[28] Melcher, D., J. Eichstedt, S. Eriksen, and D. Clawson (1992). Women's participation in local union leadership: The Massachusetts experience. *Industrial and Labor Relations Review, 45,* 267-273.

[29] Rosener, J. (November-December 1990). Ways women lead. *Harvard Business Review, 68,* 119-126.

[30] Mladenka, K. (June 1991). Public employee unions, reformism, and black employment in 1,200 cities. *Urban Affairs Quarterly, 26,* 532-548.

[31] Riccucci, N. (1990). *Women, minorities and unions in the public sector.* Westport, CT: Greenwood.

[32] ________. (July 1990). Cafeteria plans, wellness programs gaining in popularity. *Employee Benefit Plan Review,* pp. 90-92.

[33] Taylor, P. (May 23, 1991). Study of firms finds parental leave impact light. *The Washington Post,* p. A9.

[34] ________. (March 1987). Child care and recruitment boost flexible plans. *Employee Benefit Plan Review,* pp. 32-33.

[35] Voltz, W., and D. Costa (March 1989). A public employee's "fair share" of union dues. *Labor Law Journal, 40,* 131-7.

[36] Masters, M., and R. Atkin (1990). Public policy, bargaining structure, and free-riding in the federal sector. *Journal of Collective Negotiations in the Public Sector, 19,* 97-112.

[37] Dunlop, J. (Winter 1992). The challenge of human resources development. *Industrial Relations, 31,* 1, 50-79.

[38] Faden, R. and N. Kass (1988). Health insurance and AIDS: The issue of state regulatory activity. *The American Journal of Public Health, 78,* 437-38.

[39] Morgan, H., and K. Tucker (1991). *Companies that care.* New York: Fireside.

[40] Orazem, P., P. Mattila, and S. Weikum (Winter 1992). Comparable worth and factor point pay analysis in state government. *Industrial Relations, 31,* 1, 195-215.

[41] Herrick, N. (1990). *Joint management and employee participation: Labor and management at the crossroads.* San Francisco: Jossey-Bass.

[42] American Productivity Center (1987). *Participative approaches to white-collar productivity.* Washington, DC: U.S. Department of Labor, Bureau of Labor-Management Relations and Cooperative Progress.

[43] Cooke, W. (1992). Product quality improvement through employee participation: The effects of unionization and joint union-management administration. *Industrial and Labor Relations Review, 46,* 1, 119-127.

[44] Jacoby, S., and A. Verma (Winter 1992). Enterprise unions in the United States. *Industrial Relations, 31,* 1, 137-158.

[45] U.S. Department of Labor (1989). *An orientation to joint labor-management initiatives.* Washington, DC: U.S. Department of Labor, Bureau of Labor-Management Relations and Cooperative Programs.

[46] U.S. Congress, House, Select Committee on Aging, Subcommittee on Human Services (March 9, 1992). *Left at the gate: The impact of bankruptcy on employee and retiree benefits.*

14

Developing a Strategic Human Resource Capability

INTRODUCTION

Strategic human resource management is the purposeful resolution of human resource administration and policy issues so as to enhance a public agency's ability to accomplish its mission. It requires an *understanding* of how organizational human resource management functions relate to one another and to their environmental context, a *vision* of the strategic importance of human resources, and a *commitment* on the part of elected officials, personnel managers, supervisors, and employees to work for change.

By the end of this chapter, you will be able to:

1. Describe the concept of strategic human resource management.
2. Discuss some examples of how public and private employers have successfully implemented the components of strategic human resource management as the emergent model of personnel administration.

STRATEGIC HUMAN RESOURCE MANAGEMENT

Strategic human resource management has emerged as a concept and an organizational capability stimulated by the dynamic environment of public agencies. Conceptually, it consists of the elements that follow.

Recognition That Human Resource Management Is a Critical Organizational Function

Public personnel management consists of the techniques and policy choices related to agency human resource management. Taken together, these techniques and choices send messages to employees, managers, and external stakeholders about the value the agency places on human resources. In an organization with an effective human resource management capability, these messages are clear and positive. For managers and employees within the agency, this is the message: "We need you to achieve our mission." For elected officials outside the agency, the message is: "Employees are a cost and an asset. Through progressive personnel management, agencies reduce costs and maintain assets."

And for the personnel director, the message is: "You are the lead member of the management team in developing, implementing, and evaluating human resource policies and programs so as to develop assets and cut costs."

Shift from Position Management to Work Management and Employee Management

Traditionally, legislators and chief executives have sought to maintain bureaucratic compliance, efficiency, and accountability through budgetary controls and **position management** (limiting the number and type of personnel an agency can employ). Frequently, position and budgetary controls are combined through the imposition of average grade level restrictions.

Within agencies, public personnel directors have sought to achieve the efficient allocation of work and equitable allocation of rewards through **work management**—the development and maintenance of classification and pay systems. This also decreases the opportunity for political favoritism by insuring that pay is based on a realistic assessment of duties and qualifications, rather than as a reward for political responsiveness.

Employees have a third perspective—**employee managemen**t. They want their individual skills and abilities to be fully utilized in ways that contribute to a productive agency and to their own personal career development. They want to be managed as individuals, through a continual process of supervision, feedback, and reward. Most supervisors share this view. They want to be able to match employees with work needs, flexibly and creatively, so that they can get their jobs done. They want to be able to use and reward employees based on their contributions to a work unit. At heart, they see job descriptions and job classification systems as "administrivia," needed to justify budget requests and to keep the folks in personnel happy, but not related to agency mission or day-to-day supervision.

Due to a variety of political and economic pressures, the focus of public personnel management changed from management of positions, as was the case under traditional civil service systems, to accomplishment of agency mission through work management and employee management.[1] For public personnel managers accustomed to working primarily within civil service systems, this has meant recognizing the need for increased flexibility and experimentation in many areas such as rank-in-person personnel systems, broad pay banding, and group performance evaluation and reward systems. Outside civil service systems, it includes contracts, leased employees, and other secondary labor market mechanisms.

Clear Differentiation between Core and Contingent Jobs Based on Divergent Concerns for Assent Accountability and Cost Control

In the absence of coherent national strategies for public pension system reform, health-care cost control, or human capital investment, public personnel directors have had to adopt reasonable organizational-level policies for asset accountability and cost control.

First, employers continue to hire managerial, professional, scientific, and technical employees through civil service systems into core positions. The relatively high job status, security, pay, and benefits that go with these positions are considered essential for long-term employee retention and productivity. This includes preventive education through employee wellness programs, and treatment through employee health plans. However, health insurance carriers (and self-insured employers) have also responded to the cost of medical care by increasing premium costs, reducing benefits, lengthening the period within which health care benefit claims may be excluded as preexisting conditions, or adopting sub-benefit limitations on coverage for health problems that may be considered preventable because they are lifestyle choices (for example, smoking, alcohol or drug abuse, or AIDS). Benefit managers for self-insured agencies are even responding, on a case-by-case basis, to advance questions from health-care providers about whether reimbursement for specific treatments will be authorized.

Second, employers have tried to "cap" benefit costs and liability risks by greater use of secondary labor market mechanisms (such as contract or contingent employment) to meet fluctuating workloads. While the phenomenon of contingent workers is recognized as a characteristic of the contemporary workforce, the exact number of contingent workers is the subject of some controversy among personnel managers and economists. Estimates range from 2 percent to 16 percent of the workforce; the upper estimate is more likely to be valid because it includes contingent workers, independent contractors, and self-employed individuals.

Third, whenever possible given the limits of available technology and the applicability of laws protecting the employment rights of persons with disabilities, employers have sought to reduce benefit costs by excluding high-risk applicants from "career" employment through civil service systems. The ability to predict long-term health risks by evaluating employee health profiles was originally developed as a component of employee wellness programs to prevent serious health problems among current employees. But because core employees incur high benefit costs, and because these costs correlate with health indicators, medical health indicators are also being used as selection criteria. Use of such indicators is illegal under the ADA (since there is no impact on current job performance), yet some personnel directors—especially those from self-insured governments—attempt to obtain this information in an effort to reduce potential future health-care costs. Or they may simply elect to fill core jobs through performance contracts which offer high pay, but no job security.

For Core Jobs, a Clear Focus on Employee Training and Development

The Workforce 2000 study concludes, "The income generating assets of a nation are the knowledge and skills of its workers."[2] Judged by this standard, the United States currently is suffering from the absence of concerted public policy that ties together educational development, national human resource development, industrial policy, and economic growth. Public and private employers uniformly express alarm at the ineffectiveness of our educational system in producing the skilled workers needed by high-technology industries. Lack of high-tech job training or retraining is a major obstacle to retention of manufacturing jobs, which have fallen to their lowest level in twenty years.

Consequently, two contradictory trends follow from the "shake-out" occurring in the economy between core jobs and contingent jobs. First, employers reduce the requisite KSAs of most contingent jobs by job-redesign or work simplification techniques. For example, cash registers at many fast-food restaurants show pictures of food items on the keys rather than numbers, so cashiers without arithmetic skills can still perform adequately. Ironically, by increasing the monotony and diminishing the learning opportunities in contingent jobs, these personnel practices contribute to the perpetuation of segmented labor markets and the glass ceiling.

Second, employers accept the human resource asset assumptions underlying core jobs filled through primary labor market mechanisms. That is, employees in *these jobs* are human capital whose retention and utilization depend on appropriate placement and continued development. A close relationship between employee development and corporate human resource policy helps the organization in three respects: (1) It focuses planning and budget analysis on human resources; (2) it facilitates cost-benefit analysis of current training and development activities; and (3) it facilitates communication and commitment of organizational goals through employee participation and involvement.[3]

Organizational productivity improvements focus both on individual performance and work group effectiveness. Therefore, training and development include not only individual job skills but also improvement in employees' work relationships. Examples are team building and organizational development, total quality management (TQM), and diversity training.

For Core Jobs, a Clear Focus on Involvement and Participation

Performance management is the management of resources to agency mission. This includes not only financial resources, but human resources as well. It is here that human resource managers have an advantage over their financial counterparts. Financial resources are finite and fixed. In an era where policy and program initiatives are predicated on "budget neutrality," managers and supervisors have come to conclude that financial managers respond to problems by telling the organization to do the same with less, or more with the same amount of money. Human resource managers recognize that employees are a variable resource. That is, even in the absence of significant financial rewards, employee performance will continue to improve if the characteristics of work and the climate of the organization are appropriate.

The assumption underlying all new ways of designing work is that high internal work motivation, "growth" satisfaction, general job satisfaction, and work effectiveness result when people experience their work as meaningful, when they feel responsible for the quality and quantity of work produced, and when they have firsthand knowledge of the actual results of their labor. These psychological states are likely to result from work designed to incorporate the following characteristics: variety, work with a beginning and identifiable end, work of significance, and work characterized by autonomy and feedback. Jobs that are high in these qualities are said to be "enriched" and to have a high motivating potential. Whether high internal motivation, satisfaction, and productivity actually do result for holders of these kinds of jobs depends on differences in the workers' knowledge and skill, their growth need strength (such as the need for self-esteem or the esteem of others), and by context satisfaction (including such aspects of work as pay, supervision, and working conditions). Obviously, these psychological states and work characteristics are most likely to accompany career positions filled by core employees.

Results of research into this model have been generally supportive. For example, federal agency workforce quality objectives emphasize the connection between the quality of the work environment and the quality of individual, team, and organizational performance.[4] At an operating level, they have resulted in the adoption of personnel policy innovations first as experiments, and then as options the supervisor and personnel director use to match employees with work, and to generate good individual and team performance. These include employee empowerment, flexible work locations and schedules, job sharing, MBO, and TQM.

These examples of managing for performance have a common thread—working with employees as unique human resources rather than as uniform inputs to a production process. For example, delegation and MBO are not only management techniques; they also imply assumptions and values related to the human resource development and employee involvement in accomplishing the mission of the agency. **Alternative work locations and schedules** are not just troublesome exceptions to normal working hours and duty stations; they are innovative ways of using people's talents which are possible because of new work technologies.[5]

Not only that, they are necessary because of changing role expectations and cultural norms. Those who promote workforce diversity as a new approach to productivity (rather than just a new name for affirmative action) believe that different races, ethnicities, and genders bring diversity to the workplace, and that this diversity introduces variations on white male management styles that can make organizations more effective. For example, some researchers conclude that women have a more interactive and nurturing management style that makes organizations more flexible and effective stewards of human resources.[6]

Human resource managers and supervisors have a unique and irreplaceable role in the agency. Within the parameters set by legislators and chief executives, they must develop and implement corporate human resource systems for maintaining and improving the performance of individual employees and work groups. This requires an understanding of what employees need to perform well (adequate skills, clear instructions, feedback, and rewards); and insight into the impact of equity theory and expectancy theory on employee effort and performance. Most important, it requires understanding of the critical role played by human resource specialists in managing a variable, strategic resource (employees) so as to achieve agency objectives.

Public personnel managers share responsibility with managers and political leaders for developing and implementing personnel systems—the rules and procedures by which personnel functions occur. These choices involve the implicit or explicit selection of alternative personnel systems, each reflecting different dominant values. And it is not surprising that the selection of alternative systems sends a different message to employees.

For example, placement of a job within civil service systems or within a collective bargaining unit implies that the dominant value will be protection of employee rights, along with a message to employees: "You are a human resource asset: We need your knowledge, skills, and ability to attain productive and responsive agency performance." On the other hand, placement of a job within another instrumentality (an outside contract, or a payment for services agreement) implies that the dominant value will be short-term productivity and sends the following message to employees: "You perform a needed service, but you are not a core (asset) employee. Rather, you are a replaceable or expendable production unit whose service can be controlled by contract compliance procedures or the sanction process, and who can be hired and fired to match fluctuations in workload."

Because these messages are quite different, and because personnel activities are interrelated, public personnel managers have had to be much more explicit with employees about which messages are sent to which groups of employees. And they have had to be aware that employee productivity is affected by these messages, and by the dissonance between them—not only for contingent employees, but for core employees as well. And concern for social equity values has meant that public personnel managers are responsible for making sure that access to core employment is equitably distributed among protected classes. Otherwise, public employment loses the representativeness that is required for maintenance of both democratic values and effective public service.

And the lengthy and cumbersome selection process characteristic of core positions actually serves many purposes for managers, political leaders, personnel directors, and applicants. Managers accept the costly and tedious screening of large numbers of applicants as necessary to compensate for the generally uneven quality of job applicants. Political leaders under pressure to fill vacancies with friends or campaign contributors can refer people to the personnel department, and then blame the personnel director or the selection process if a particular applicant is not hired. Personnel directors dislike being criticized by political leaders, managers, and applicants for the cumbersome selection process, but they also find that a ritualized selection process, which includes procedures and criteria favored by adherents of alternative personnel systems, also tends to regulate the conflict among systems over each selection. And applicants, like players in any lottery, may get symbolic satisfaction from the opportunity to apply for high-status jobs, regardless of the slight chance that they will actually be accepted. The equality of opportunity to apply for core positions fosters the belief among most applicants that the number of core positions is large, and that it is relatively easy to advance from a contingent job to a core position.

For Core Jobs, a Shift in Focus from EEO/AA Compliance to Workforce Diversity

Workforce diversity is not just a variant on civil rights or affirmative action. While the two concepts are related, they differ in three important respects. Workforce diversity is broader and more individualized; it focuses on accomplishment of agency mission rather than compliance with sanctions; and, as a result, its locus of control is internal rather than external.

The objective of affirmative action is the full representation of protected classes of employees within the agency workforce, proportionate to their share of the appropriate labor market. Personnel directors who focus on affirmative action compliance therefore tend to regard employees as members of classes, and use these categories to drive or influence personnel decisions. The focus of affirmative action is therefore on inputs (number and percentage of positions filled by members of particular groups). And the locus of control is external, in that it is based on review of personnel practices by affirmative action compliance agencies.

The concept of workforce diversity implies a broader and more individualized perspective on diversity—not just affirmative action categories, but a range of knowledge, skills, and abilities which managers must recognize and factor into personnel decisions. The importance of this change is accentuated by agency managers' changing focus on work management rather than position management. Once agency managers and personnel directors have changed their focus from position management to work management, they are forced to alter their focus on employees from categorical to individual. Good managers have always done this, of course. They have recognized that the secret of assigning the right employee to the right job means (1) determining the important tasks of the position, (2) specifying the combination of KSAs needed to accomplish these tasks, and (3) picking the employee who has the best combination of requisite KSAs.[7]

To see what this shift in focus means, personnel managers might look at the development of **individual development plans (IDPs)** for employees. These require a matching, and a conscious assessment of the adequacy of this match, of employee characteristics with mission objectives not just for the present, but as a continual process that takes into account changes in employee KSAs and agency mission. As a second example, personnel directors might look at the individualized matching of jobs and employees with disabilities. It has often been difficult for employers to comply with federal laws—such as the Americans with Disabilities Act—requiring accommodation of what used to be called "handicapped" employees because making "reasonable accommodation" requires flexible, individualized, and insightful matching of employee characteristics and work requirements.

Second, workforce diversity differs from affirmative action in that it focuses on outputs—what combination or balance of KSAs is needed to get the work done—rather than inputs—what is the racial and ethnic composition of the workforce? Workforce diversity is therefore linked to a number of other recent trends such as performance management, MBO, delegation, and results-oriented job descriptions (RODs). All of these focus on work and on mission accomplishment, rather than on position management or process conformity.

Third, workforce diversity differs from affirmative action in that its locus of control is internal rather than external. Agency managers must ask, "Is the agency allocating resources appropriately so as to accomplish its mission?" rather than, "Is our workforce sufficiently representative to avoid externally imposed sanctions by affirmative action compliance agencies?" or "Are our personnel policies and procedures adequate to avoid externally imposed sanctions by affirmative action compliance agencies?" Thus, acceptance of workforce diversity goes hand in hand with increased accountability of agency managers for mission accomplishment, and increased focus on employees as resources rather than as positions to be controlled.[8]

For Core Jobs, Productivity-Based Pay Systems

The shift from position management to management of work and employees has meant a shift toward development of compensation systems designed to reward high performance by key employees, not just to pay positions equitably based on job worth or position management guidelines. Several trends are part of this emphasis. First, the increasing movement toward exempt positions means that highly skilled professional, technical, and managerial employees can be paid on a performance basis. This rewards performance in two respects that are beyond the capability of traditional civil service systems. On the one hand, employees can receive higher rates of pay than might otherwise be allowed if the position were classified; on the other hand, short-term contracts mean that poor performance can be grounds for non-renewal without having to resort to time-consuming civil service discipline or discharge procedures.

Second, the shift toward team-based evaluation and reward systems emphasizes the shift from individuals to work groups as the key to productivity. Leaders are in effect being paid based on their ability to manage diverse work teams productively; team members are rewarded on the basis of their ability to function productively as a team.

For Core Jobs, Emphasis on Family-Centered Leave and Benefit Programs

Family-centered leave and benefit programs are integrally related to employee involvement and participation, and to workforce diversity. First, the productivity of core employees is directly related to their involvement and participation, which is in turn related to the extent to which the employer provides services and benefits which help employees meet family obligations. Second, because women are the traditional caregivers in our society, the effectiveness of an employer in attracting a diverse workforce depends upon the provision of these same services and benefits. Major components of a family-centered corporate human resource policy for core employees are (1) flexible benefits, (2) family leave, (3) child-care support programs, (4) alternative work locations and schedules, and (5) employee-centered supervision.

Flexible benefits. The high cost of benefit programs means that employers will seek to maximize their attractiveness to employees by offering benefit flexibility. **Flexible benefit** programs are sometimes called cafeteria plans because they offer employees a menu of benefits. They are developed by costing the employer's contribution to each of a variety of employer-sponsored benefit programs, and allowing employees to select alternative mixes of benefit packages depending on their needs. This has the major advantage, for the employee, of full utilization of benefits without duplication or gaps. This makes the employer's benefit package of greater value to the employee, and is a tool for recruitment and retention.

There are administrative and financial barriers to flexible benefit programs. First, given the wildly fluctuating cost of alternative benefits, it may be difficult for the employer constantly to calculate (and recalculate) the comparative costs of all options. Second, reconfiguring alternative benefit packages on a constant cost basis may be difficult for employees, who are unable to project benefit usage or the relative utility of alternative benefits accurately. Third, full employee utilization of benefits may increase benefit costs for the employer (who may have been able to reduce costs by relying on such overlaps as duplicate health insurance for two employees in a family). Fourth, increased benefit costs tend to force health and life insurance providers toward uniform defined benefit programs to reduce "shopping" from one program to another. In this environment, the advantages of flexible benefit programs may tend to diminish.

Family Leave. Changing family roles have resulted in numerous single-parent households. Under these conditions, sick leave policies must reflect parental responsibilities to care not only for themselves but also for children and parents. And because medical emergencies and day-care crises are seldom predictable, policies and supervisory practices must be flexible in this regard. For employees facing childbirth, adoption, or terminal care for a parent, the long-term negative consequences of a forced choice between remaining on the job or giving up employment rights is not socially justifiable.

Therefore, this type of **family leave** has essentially been granted to employees of most major employers through the Family and Medical Leave Act. While there have been no studies of its implementation cost, a recent three-year study conducted in four states that passed parental leave laws during the 1980s found that 91 percent of respondent personnel directors reported no difficulty with implementation of the laws; 67 percent said they relied on other employees to do the work (rather than hiring replacement employees); and the percentage of working women who took leave and the length of leave were virtually unchanged by the legislation.[9]

Child-Care Support Programs. The increased number of single parents (and two-parent families where both parents work) has led to increases in employer-operated child care facilities. At first, this was seen primarily as an employee benefit. But as agencies began to face shortages of qualified employees, child care has been demonstrated to be necessary to recruit or retain qualified female employees (such as in hospitals or on military bases). In an era of increased workforce diversity, it is simply essential to recognize that employees' ability to find satisfactory child care arrangements will reduce job stress, turnover, sick leave abuse, and other causes of low productivity.

There are some issues with employer-subsidized child care. These include cost, fee setting, and liability risks. But these are technical concerns rather than major impediments to the adoption of **child-care programs** and policies. And the fundamental value orientation of child care remains unassailable.

One innovative proposal allows closer cooperation between employers, parents, and the local school board by allowing parents to place their children in schools close to the job rather than close to home. This reduces the length of time school-age children go without supervision, and makes it easier for parents to leave work for child-care emergencies without so much use of leave or disruption of employer productivity.

Alternative Work Locations and Schedules. In the past, all employees were expected to have identical working hours and a fixed job location, but this is no longer true. First, changes in technology (primarily communications and computers) have meant that employees can work productively at decentralized workstations, or even at home. Second, the need for more flexible service delivery, and the complex child-care and elder-care arrangements necessitated by two-career families, have resulted in the development of part-time and flexible work schedules. Last, the focus on employees as resources has led to the development of variable models of resource use that have proved effective at achieving performance.

Under flextime, all employees are expected to work during core hours (such as 9:00 to 3:00). Depending on agency needs and personal preferences, each employee is free to negotiate a fixed work schedule with different start or end times. Research on flextime experiments in both the public and private sectors generally reveals positive results in employee attitudes and in the reduction of absenteeism, tardiness, and in some cases even increases in productivity.

Job sharing is the splitting of one job between two part-time employees on a regular basis. There are obvious advantages for employees (flexible part-time work rather than a choice between full-time work or no work at all) and the agency (mentoring, light duty work). But the employees must coordinate their activities with each other, with their supervisor, and with clients/customers inside and outside the agency. And the agency must develop policies for contributions and division of pensions, health care, and other benefits.

Employees may work away from the office, provided a suitable outside workstation is available. This works best for professionals who can work independently, and yet remain in contact with the agency through phone systems, a computer, and a modem. The advantage to the agency is that it may be able to get work done just as well, and to attract individuals who value independence and flexibility. The downside, of course, is predictable things like communication and control, and unpredictable ones like workplace health and safety, and workers' compensation claims.

Sensitive Supervision. As with all aspects of public personnel management, the quality of the relationship between the supervisor and the employee is of much more importance in determining the climate of the organization than is the mere existence of family-centered leave policies, child-care and elder-care support programs, and alternative work settings and schedules. Organizations wishing to attract and keep core employees by supporting family values need to select and train supervisors who are sensitive to these issues.

Enhanced Human Resource Management Information and Evaluation Systems

The collection and use of information for program planning, control, and evaluation purposes are essential to public management. Yet this collection and use need not be systematic. That is, data can be collected and used on an ad hoc and piecemeal basis, rather than through a management information system whose pieces are related to one another and to the objectives of the agency. For example, a manager can be concerned about a particular problem, such as equipment downtime and low employee productivity. In the absence of a management information system, a manager will probably collect data on this problem by conferring with supervisors and examining existing records (such as equipment repair costs) to determine the extent of the problem. This will result in the development of a solution that seems correct on an intuitive or judgmental basis. For instance, the manager might propose a training program to increase employees' ability to use equipment correctly, or develop an incentive system to increase their desire to do so.

Yet it is also possible to design a management information system that routinely collects information on various factors related to organizational effectiveness, and to present this information to managers in the form of reports they can use to make necessary changes in policies or procedures. A department might routinely produce information on equipment costs, personnel costs, overtime, and productivity. If the method of collecting and compiling information into reports is systematically designed to answer the needs of planners, managers, and other evaluators, it is called a **management information system (MIS)**; those elements of the system that concern management of employees are called the **human resource management information system (HRMIS)**.

Let's look at a typical city and see how its HRMIS might relate to the four personnel functions introduced in Chapter 1. The relationship between the HRMIS and planning occurs during the budget preparation and approval process. Revenue estimates are matched against program proposals. The cost of proposed programs depends upon such factors as the number and type of employees, their pay and benefits, and the training they will need. All these data are collected and stored as part of the budget and payroll system. Affirmative action is the personnel activity that dominates acquisition of human resources. The extent to which social equity considerations will influence selection is determined by the extent to which particular groups are underutilized, and the validity of the selection criteria. Both utilization analysis and empirical validation techniques are dependent upon computerized applicant data such as race, sex, age, test scores, and performance evaluations. Employee **development** involves the comparison of performance and productivity data against organizational objectives. Performance appraisal systems and organizational productivity data are routinely computerized. Training needs assessment can be based on a comparison of computerized skill inventories against jobs' required KSAs. The *sanction* function involves outside organizations such as unions in organizational personnel management. The success of a municipal negotiator, for example, will depend on how well documented the city's wage position is. An outside arbitrator will accept the position as reasonable only if comparative wage data show that the salaries and benefits proposed by the city are comparable with those of employees in similar jobs in similar communities; or that the existing tax structure will not support increased personnel costs. Both require access to an HRMIS, one compatible with the systems in neighboring communities.

Despite widespread recognition that an HRMIS is important, some confusion exists concerning both the criteria that should be used to select such a system and the problems associated with its use. First, public personnel managers need to specify the **data elements** they need to provide the information required to answer questions such as those raised above. Data are the facts on employees and positions needed to assess organizational programs. For example, **position data** might include the salary range, occupational code, and organizational location of each position. **Employee data** might include each employee's age, sex, classification, duty location, seniority, pay, benefits, skill inventory, and affirmative action status.

These data elements are summarized to form **reports.** This function is most often associated with an HRMIS. Report generation requires that personnel managers ask: "What reports do we need, and how often do we need them, in order to monitor agency inputs, activities, or outputs." In this context, employee skills and tax revenues might be considered inputs; programs are activities; and program results are outputs. Here are some typical reports produced periodically by personnel departments:

1. *Payroll:* total personnel expenditures, by employee, during a pay period
2. *Human resource planning:* number and classification of all filled or vacant organizational positions; turnover rate for selected departments or occupations
3. *Affirmative action compliance:* race and sex of applicants and selections, by organizational unit or type of position
4. *Collective bargaining:* total pay and benefit costs for employees covered by a collective bargaining agreement

Last, program planners use current reports as a means of predicting the future. For example, if health-care costs for civil service employees have increased 12 percent annually over the past five years, it is reasonable to assume (barring a reduction in benefits or increased employee contributions) that they will increase 12 percent next year as well. This forecasting combines the use of current or past data with **modeling** (the development of assumptions about the future to help predict the probable outcomes of alternative policy decisions).

To sum up, an HRMIS is used to collect and store data, to produce reports used to control and evaluate current programs, and to develop simulations to support policy decisions. Therefore, a good HRMIS provides the kind of information needed to the people who need it when they need it. The personnel director must decide what the system needs to do before computer specialists decide how to do it; the HRMIS must be designed to be compatible with the larger organizational management information system (MIS); and computerization should be recognized as a change in work technology that also involves such issues as employee acceptance, job redesign, and training. Because the costs of some applications are high, HRMIS systems designers need to balance them against user expectations and capabilities.

An HRMIS can also provide essential assistance to political leaders and stakeholders who wish an agency's programs to remain responsive to policy pressures originating outside the agency. In these cases, data supportive or critical of an agency's performance are compiled into reports that "drive" the agency's planning, control, and evaluation activities. Elected officials, agency managers, or interest groups use these reports to induce changes in organizational policies or procedures (or to compel those changes, if legal sanctions were involved). For example:

1. Interest groups or compliance agencies supporting the value of social equity would use utilization data to reinforce their contention that the organization should increase affirmative action efforts.
2. Legislators seeking to control or direct the activities of an agency would use resource allocation data (size of budgets, number of positions) to do so. For example, a city commission seeking to restrict the power of an independent police department would do so by limiting the size of its payroll budget, or by refusing to authorize new positions in that agency.
3. Managers seeking to increase administrative efficiency would use productivity-related data to recommend changes in work methods. For instance, a city manager concerned about personnel costs in a solid waste department might restrict the use of overtime, investigate possible abuse of sick leave or fraudulent workers' compensation claims, or study the comparative cost effectiveness of privatizing this activity.
4. Unions seeking to stop a privatization proposal might compare wages, benefits, and productivity data for a public solid waste agency with similar figures for its private competitors.

A more extensive list of these HRMIS applications is shown in Table 14-1.

Public Personnel Managers as Entrepreneurs

Public personnel management may be viewed as static or dynamic. Traditional personnel managers view the field as narrow and static. They picture it as a collection of administrative techniques applied within a structure of rules, policies, and laws that clearly define the limits of acceptable professional behavior. They see themselves as continually acting within a consensus on one system and its underlying values. They tend to define themselves, and to be defined by others, as technical specialists working within a staff agency.

More contemporary public personnel managers view the field as emergent and dynamic. They tend to define themselves, and to be defined by others, as interpreters or mediators among competing systems, stakeholders, and values. They see themselves as professionals whose role involves a blend of technical skills and ethical decision making, and as key players in developing corporate human resource management strategy. The essence of this emergent professional public personnel management role is **synergy**, the exploitation of pressure

Table 14–1 HRMIS Applications to Program Evaluation

Activity	*HRMIS Applications*
PLANNING	
Human resource planning	Compile inventory of current employees' skills; determine whether these meet forecast future needs
Job analysis and classification	How many employees are in different occupatons?
Compensation	Determine current pay and benefit costs for all employees; project the cost of alternative proposed pay and benefit packages
ACQUISITION	
Affirmative action	Compare actual utilization of particular groups with their representation in the labor market; assess organizational affirmative action plan compliance
Recruitment	Compile new hire estimates based on anticipated staffing needs; are current recruitment efforts sufficient to meet them?
Selection	Do an applicant's qualifications meet minimum standards for a given position? Do selected applicants meet performance standards for their positions?
DEVELOPMENT	
Productivity	Record performance of organizational units; compare to other units or previous time periods
Performance appraisal	Record employee performance; compare to other employees, performance standards, or previous time periods
Training and development	Summarize training activities and costs; assess training needs by comparing skills; assess OD needs by mearsuring organizational climate
Employee motivation and job design	Measure employee productivity, turnover, absenteeism, and internal motivation; assess effect of changes in job design on productivity and motivation
Safety	Record injuries, accidents, and illnesses; use these data to change safety regulations, selection critiera, or employee orientation
SANCTION	
Labor–management relations	Collect and compare salary and benefit data against that of other positions or jurisdictions; compute the cost of proposed changes in pay and benefits
Discipline and grievances	Compile reports on the number and type of grievances and disciplinary actions; use these data to recommend changes in work rules, employee orientation, or supervisory training.
Constitutional rights of employees	Record cases of sexual harassment or civil rights violations; use these to improve affirmative action compliance, employee orientation, or supervisory training
CONTROL AND ADAPTATION	
Evaluation	Collect data through HRMIS to evaluate all public personnel management activities

points where conflicting systems compete and converge, and the reconciliation of conflicting values, changing conditions, competing stakeholders, and a diverse workforce into a coherent and dynamic whole.

Over the past ten years much research has been conducted concerning organizational innovation. Most of the research, however, has been about technical innovation, not administrative innovation. Yet the strategic design of human resource management systems and structures for the purpose of making agencies more effective is an administrative innovation. This leads to the issue of what causes or enhances administrative innovation in public agencies.

After controlling for external and organizational variables, research studies conclude that the professional role, and the self-perception of that role, is a major factor that leads key agency players to undertake and successfully complete administrative innovations. Those who see themselves as professionals, who recognize the dynamism and conflict inherent in their roles, are more likely to innovate. Both the extent to which they represent a departure from traditional organization policy and practice and the scope of their application (the number of employees they affect) are likely to be greater.[10]

Innovation carries the risk of failure, for it represents experimentation with the unknown. Therefore, those organizations interested (for their own survival's sake) in encouraging innovation must select human resource managers (and other managers) who are experienced and positive risk takers. Fortunately, the same systems, structures, and rewards the organization uses to exploit dynamism and conflict also create the situations to which public personnel directors must respond.[11] By creating these situations, and by encouraging managers to respond creatively and take some risks, the agency can use dynamism not only to force change and augment human resources but also to develop personnel managers who have leadership ability as well as technical skills.

STRATEGIC HUMAN RESOURCE MANAGEMENT IN ACTION

The above analysis has shown that strategic human resource management is best seen as a set of characteristics—an "ideal type" that is more useful as an analytical model of where public personnel management is headed than as an actual description of personnel policies and practices in any one organization.

The following examples show strategic human resource management in action in a variety of organizational settings. Like all examples of emergent trends, they are often fragmentary and hesitant. But taken together, they show how far-sighted personnel managers have continued to respond to environmental change.

Recognizing human resource management as a critical organizational function

- The U.S. Office of Personnel Management has developed a *Strategic Plan for Human Resources Management* that is based on the vision of effective human resource management throughout the federal government, which enables agencies to recruit, develop, and retain a quality and representative workforce.[12]

Shift in focus from position management to work management and employee management

- The federal government sponsored a seventeen-agency review of the position classification system originally created in 1949 under Title V. The review concluded that agencies could make significant changes (such as broad banding) within existing law. The feasibility of these changes has been demonstrated by a decade of experimentation through the demonstration projects operated by a number of federal agencies and authorized by the Office of Systems Innovation and Simplification, U.S. Office of Personnel Management.[13]
- In its most dramatic restructuring in the past twenty five years, the U.S. Postal Service announced plans to eliminate 25 percent of its 120,000 managerial jobs and overhaul its military style hierarchy.[14]
- Among other things, the highly publicized Gore Report recommended the abolishment of the entire national government's personnel manual (the Federal Personnel Manual, or FPM).

Clear differentiation between core and contingent workers based on divergent concerns for asset accountability and cost control

- The Advisory Commission on Federal Workforce Quality recently (August 1992) concluded that, "despite widespread . . . anecdotal evidence, the quality of employees [in the engineering, scientific and computer fields] is not generally deficient and has remained fairly constant over time."[15]
- The University of California developed an early retirement program for faculty which reduced short-term pay and benefit costs by offering selected faculty (those who almost meet minimum age and seniority criteria for retirement) a limited "window of opportunity" during which they would retire at close to full benefits. The university maintained productivity by using adjunct or non-tenured faculty to teach classes. The asset loss represented by professors who retired early was considered a less significant factor, based on a conscious comparison of short-term operating costs with long-term human resource asset values.

For core jobs, a clear focus on employee training and development

- At Aetna Life & Casualty (Hartford, CT), over 1,000 workers have been hired through a cooperative education effort with local organizations that focuses on reading and written communication skills.[16]
- IBM has adopted a high-skill employee empowerment approach as part of its full-employment, no layoffs policy. When managers at its Austin (Texas) plant estimated they could save $60 million by buying circuit boards elsewhere rather than manufacturing them, IBM management had other ideas. They cut costs by upgrading worker skills, organized workers into teams, and gave teams responsibility for quality control, repairs, and materials ordering. Skill requirements for manufacturing jobs were increased, and education and training costs increased to 5 percent of payroll. The bottom line was that productivity increased over 200 percent, quality was up 500 percent, and inventory was cut 40 percent. The plant employs more people than ever before.[17]

For core jobs, a clear focus on involvement and participation

- Madison, Wisconsin, is home to model TQM programs in both state and local governments. For example, the motor equipment division of the city's department of public works used managerial tools and participative decision making to better understand customer needs and to identify basic underlying causes for excessive vehicle downtime. The time invested in these efforts led to improved customer satisfaction and procedures throughout all departments to reduce repair downtime. At a time when staff was reduced by 17 percent, vehicles serviced increased by 25 percent.
- Florida Power and Light (FPL) won the coveted Deming Award in 1991 for successful efforts by work teams to increase customer satisfaction and reduce costs. These

efforts equipped the public utility to perform successfully when Hurricane Andrew devastated Miami's southern suburbs a year later.

For core jobs, a shift in focus from EEO/AA compliance to work force diversity

- Corning Glass Works evaluates managers on their ability to "create a congenial environment" for diverse employees.[18]
- Mobil Corporation created a special committee of executives to identify high-potential female and minority executive job candidates, and to place them in line management positions viewed as critical for advancement through the glass ceiling.
- Dr. Robert McCabe, recently retired president of Miami-Dade Community College, won a MacArthur Foundation Award for educational leadership, including a ten-year emphasis on workforce diversity as a key to community involvement and mission achievement.

For core jobs, an emphasis on performance-based compensation systems

- A recent focus group reveals that South Florida public personnel directors are experimenting widely with the use of exempt employees and short-term performance contracts as a means of more effectively linking pay to performance.
- The U.S. Public Health Service has implemented an alternative personnel system to enhance effectiveness in the recruitment and utilization of medical personnel.[19]

For core jobs, an emphasis on family-centered leave and benefit programs

- A number of commentators and researchers have reported on employers' increased family-centered benefit programs.[20] These include:
- IBM: yearlong maternity leave with supervisory job retention rights
- Stride-Rite (Cambridge, MA): on-site child care and daytime elder-care
- Merck & Co. (Rahway, NJ): parent-run child-care centers
- Joy Cone (Hermitage, PA): split shifts and flexible shift assignments at its factories
- Arthur Anderson & Co.: part-time benefited professional positions, child care
- United States Hosiery Corporation (Lincolnton, NC): child care, sick room for mildly ill children
- Lotus Development Corp. (Cambridge, MA): one-month paid parenting leave to mothers, fathers, and adoptive parents
- Johnson & Johnson corporate philosophy includes the following statement: "We must be mindful of ways to help our employees fulfill their family obligations."
- *Working Mother* magazine identified ten companies as extremely progressive for family/career issues and career opportunities for women: Aetna Life & Casualty (CT), Beth Israel Hospital (MA), Corning (NY), Fel-Pro (IL), IBM (NY), Johnson & Johnson (NJ), Merck & Co. (NJ), Morrison & Foerster (CA), The St. Paul Cos. (MN), and SAS Institute (NC).

Enhanced human resource management information systems

- The U.S. Public Health Service has developed a KSA-based management information system that aids in placing professional, technical, and scientific personnel through a person-based personnel system.[21]
- A consortium of federal agencies, led by the General Accounting Office, the U.S. Department of Labor, and the Social Security Administration, has successfully implemented a management information system tied to a range of personnel functions, and to the human resource planning and evaluation process.[22]

Increased entrepreneurial behavior among public personnel managers

- A top official at the U.S. General Accounting Office recently noted:

  As one looks to the future, it becomes clear that human resource management skills will become simultaneously more essential and more difficult to apply. . . . Supervisors will increasingly face the challenge of relating to staff from diverse backgrounds. People from differing backgrounds often communicate, behave and respond differently. As managers and supervisors, we must be able to accept differences in style, focusing instead on the results achieved.[23]

- The Federal Quality Institute notes that managers' and directors' personal development requires that they train themselves to thrive in a contingent environment where objectives are diverse and means-end relationships are uncertain—and that they train and reward subordinates for taking similar risks, and for learning from them.

SUMMARY

Strategic human resource management is the purposeful resolution of human resource program and policy issues so as to enhance a public agency's ability to accomplish its mission. It will continue to develop because of underlying changes which continue to shape public personnel management as an emergent profession. For personnel directors, it requires the skills and abilities needed to achieve contradictory objectives (asset development and cost control) in a turbulent political environment characterized by conflict and compromise among pro-government and anti-government values.

KEY TERMS

alternative work locations and schedules
child-care programs and elder-care programs
data elements
employee data
family leave
flexible benefits
human resource management information systems (HRMIS)
individual development plan (IDP)
management information system (MIS)
modeling
position data
reports
synergy

DISCUSSION QUESTIONS

1. What is the relationship between professionalism in public personnel managers and dynamism and conflict among public personnel systems, values, and stakeholders?
2. Is it possible to design bureaucratic organizations so that operating divisions, budget officers, and human resource managers can develop and carry out mission-focused resource allocation and program evaluation? If so, how?
3. What is the relationship between the role of the public personnel manager and the future of public service?
4. Do you think the job of the public personnel manager is harder now than in the past? Why or why not?

5. Do you think this course in public personnel management is adequate preparation for a job as a public personnel manager? If not, what additional skills or knowledge do you need, and how could you get them?

CASE STUDY PERSONNEL MANAGEMENT: PART OF THE PROBLEM OR PART OF THE SOLUTION?

The article summarized below appeared recently in a national management magazine.[24] After reading it, answer the following questions:

1. Why does the author think we should get rid of human resource departments?
2. What evidence does he offer to support his assertions?
3. What alternative does he propose?
4. Are the author's suggestions consistent or inconsistent with the recommendations offered in this textbook? Defend your answer, citing specific functions and recommendations.
5. Based on what you have learned in this course, do you agree or disagree with his assessment of the problem? With the solution he proposes? Defend your answers.
6. How does the message in this article compare with Tom Lewinsohn's message on pages 46-47 in Chapter 2.

WHY NOT ABOLISH THE HUMAN RESOURCES DEPARTMENT?

People need people—but do they need personnel? Your company's human resources (HR) department employees spend 80 percent of their time on routine administrative tasks. Chances are its leaders are unable to describe their contribution to value added except in trendy, unquantifiable terms. Yet the department frequently dispenses to others advice on how to eliminate work that does not add value.

Nearly every major HR function now done in-house can be done better and cheaper by private contractors—benefits design and administration, payroll, information systems and record keeping, OSHA compliance, and EAPs. None have much potential to produce competitive advantage for a company that does them in-house; all offer economies of scale to outside suppliers; and some reduce risk by offloading exposure to liability or regulatory claims.

HR still has a useful compliance role in monitoring diversification and EEO/AA compliance, but recruitment and selection are best left to line managers because they know most about the job.

Few companies have the skill to develop and implement complex performance and reward systems that reconcile such elements as encouraging cooperation in work teams, yet rewarding individual performance in hierarchies. It is far better to buy high-quality systems from outside, and leave line managers and supervisors responsible for discipline and rewards.

Most "canned" training programs are also irrelevant and wasteful. The best training is OJT, which is done on-site when needed.

HR directors say that human resources are of great strategic importance to the company. This may be true, but it is all the more reason to turn HR functions over to line managers. They, after all, are the ones who are most concerned with productivity improvement.

So there are two possible futures for HR. One is to become a highly automated employee services operation that functions primarily as a conduit for outsourced personnel functions. The other is to become proactive custodians of strategic human capital, holders to the keys to core competencies and competitive advantages in the global marketplace. And companies clearly need to demand that their HR departments focus on their own future, not that of other units.

NOTES

[1] U.S. Office of Personnel Management (1989). *Manage to budget programs.* Washington, DC: Office of Systems Innovation and Simplification, Personnel Systems and Oversight Group, PSOG-203.

[2] Johnson, W., and A. Packer (1987). *Workforce 2000: Work and workers for the twenty-first century.* Indianapolis: The Hudson Institute.

[3] Bernhard, H. and C. Ingols (September-October 1988). Six lessons for the corporate classroom. *Harvard Business Review, 88,* 40-48; and Rosow, J., and R. Zager (1988). *Training—the corporate edge.* San Francisco: Jossey-Bass.

[4] Advisory Committee on Federal Workforce Quality (August 1992). *Federal workforce quality measurement and improvement.* Washington, DC: Advisory Committee on Federal Workforce Quality, p. 20.

[5] Sashkin, M. (Spring 1984). Participative management is an ethical imperative. *Organizational Dynamics, 12,* 5-22.

[6] Rosener, J. (November-December 1990). Ways women lead. *Harvard Business Review, 68,* 119-25.

[7] Loden, M., and J. Rosener, (1991). *Workforce America! Managing employee diversity as a vital resource.* Homewood, IL: Business One Irwin.

[8] Haight, G. (March 1990). Managing diversity. *Across the board, 27,* 22-30; and Solomon, C. (March 1989). The corporate response to work force diversity. *Personnel Journal,* pp. 43-53.

[9] Taylor, P. (May 23, 1991). Study of firms finds parental leave impact light. *The Washington Post,* p. A-9.

[10] Sabet, M. and D. Klingner (1993). Exploring the impact of professionalism and on administrative innovation. *Journal of Public Administration Research and Theory, 3,* 252-266.

[11] Klingner, D., N. O'Neill, and M. Sabet (1990). Drug testing in public agencies: Are personnel directors doing things right? *Public Personnel Management, 19,* 391-97.

[12] U.S. Office of Personnel Management (1990). *Manage to budget programs.*

[13] National Academy of Public Administration (1991). *Modernizing federal classification: An opportunity for excellence.* Washington, DC: NAPA.

[14] ___________. (September 1, 1992). Postal service restructures. *Public Administration Times, 15,* 3.

[15] Advisory Committee on Federal Workforce Quality, *Federal workforce,* p. x.

[16] Bennett, A. (May 8, 1989). As pool of skilled help tightens, firms move to broaden their role. *The Wall Street Journal,* p. 1.

[17] Karr, A. (June 19, 1990). Workplace panel is urging changes in schools, on job. *The Wall Street Journal,* p. C-15.

[18] Schmidt, P. (October 16, 1988). Women and minorities: Is industry ready? *The New York Times,* p. 25.

[19] Merit Systems Protection Board (April 1991). *The Title 38 personnel systems in the department of veterans affairs: An alternative approach.* Washington, DC: U.S. Merit Systems Protection Board.

[20] Morgan, H., and K. Tucker (1991). *Companies that care.* New York: Fireside, pp. 11-14.

[21] Personal interview with R. Sherwood (May 12, 1991). Washington, DC: U.S. Department of Health and Human Services, U.S. Public Health Service.

[22] Personal interview with S. Marshall (October 10, 1992). Washington, DC: U.S. Office of Personnel Management, Office of Systems Innovation and Simplification.

[23] Goldstein, I. (1989). Managing for performance in the public sector. *The General Accounting Office Journal, 7,* 51.

[24] Stevens, T. (January 15, 1996). Taking on the last bureaucracy. *Fortune, 133,* 105-108.

Index